City in the Sky

• • •

CITY IN THE SKY

...

The Rise and Fall of the World Trade Center

JAMES GLANZ AND ERIC LIPTON

TIMES BOOKS

HENRY HOLT AND COMPANY

NEW YORK

Times Books
Henry Holt and Company, LLC
Publishers since 1866
115 West 18th Street
New York, New York 10011

Library of Congress Cataloging-in-Publication Data
Glanz, James.
     City in the sky : the rise and fall of the World Trade Center/James Glanz and Eric
Lipton—1st ed.
        p. cm.
     ISBN 0-8050-7428-7
     1. World Trade Center (New York, N.Y.) 2. Skyscrapers—New York (State)—New
York. 3. City planning—New York (State)—New York—History—20th century. 4. New
York (N.Y.)—Buildings, structures, etc. I. Lipton, Eric. II. Title.
NA6233.N5W6742 2003
720'.483'097471—dc22   2003061081

First Edition 2003

Designed by Carla Bolte
Charts edited by Steve Duenes

Printed in the United States of America
10 9 8 7 6 5 4 3 2 1

To those who died

and those who lived for them

■ ■ ■

CONTENTS

. . .

List of Illustrations xi

Prologue 1

1 David's Turn 7

2 Gambit 38

3 Street Fighters 62

4 Surprise, Serenity, Delight . . 88

5 Steel Balloons 118

6 Endgame 145

7 Pyramids on the Hudson . . 176

8 City in the Sky 205

9 9/11: The Collapse 236

10 Ruins 273

Epilogue 319

SOURCES AND NOTES 339
BIBLIOGRAPHY AND INTERVIEWS . 398
ACKNOWLEDGMENTS 410
INDEX 413

ILLUSTRATIONS

■ ■ ■

Graphics edited by Steve Duenes

World Trade Center in Maps 36

The Streets of Radio Row 65

Yamasaki's Struggle 112

Structures of the Twin Towers 122

Wind Turbulence and the Twin Towers 158

Shock Absorbers for the Twin Towers 165

Battery Park City 171

World Trade Center Foundation: The Bathtub,
   or "Slurry Wall" 178

North Tower: The Impact 244

The Stairwells in the North Tower 249

South Tower: The Impact 256

The Stairwells in the South Tower 259

A Structure from the Past: 90 West Street 283

The Cranes at Ground Zero 289

Mapping the World Trade Center's
Damaged Basement 294–295

Two Theories of Collapse 328

City in the Sky

. . .

· · ·

Prologue

The gray mass of the wall loomed over Matthew Quesada. The structure was scarred and battered and mighty in its scale, like an unearthed castle that belonged to some forgotten age of giants. Quesada stood in a steel basket painted blue, which was connected by a long telescoping arm to a heavy platform and an engine resting on four rubber tires. As he prepared the equipment that he would need to heal some of the wall's fissures and wounds, he could see long ragged streaks of black and yellow and dull red staining the concrete face of the wall like grimy tears. A crosshatch of rusted reinforcing bars showed through where its surface had been blasted or gouged away. Quesada had descended seventy feet beneath the streets and sidewalks of lower Manhattan to repair the wall, which was three feet thick and more than three thousand feet long. It surrounded what had once been eight city blocks of thriving restaurants and saloons and storefront businesses. But they had vanished decades ago. Until close to two years before this cloudless day in June 2003, the underground wall encircled a pair of newer and immeasurably grander structures. It had been the foundation wall for the twin towers of the World Trade Center.

Quesada, who wore a scuffed black hard hat over a red-and-blue headscarf, stepped into a disposable plastic jumpsuit to protect him as he worked, zipped it up in front, and slipped a safety harness over his shoulders and through his legs. He clipped the harness to a rail on the blue basket. Then he hit the leftmost of the three levers on the basket and it began rising into the perfect morning sky. At his feet, the tinny *putt putt putt putt* of a little mechanical pump that he would use for his work managed

· I ·

to pierce the stop-and-start rattle of jackhammers and the groan of heavy equipment from across the entire floor of the excavation. The noisy crescendos rose from a frenzy of construction. The recovery and cleanup here were over. In fact, aside from the wall itself, there was almost nothing left of the World Trade Center except the gnawed-off remnants of five or six basement levels that stood like pueblo dwellings across the northern part of the excavation. As he ascended near the northwest corner, Quesada could look inside them, where the concrete floors and ceilings were still charred black from the fires of September 11 and isolated safety lights glowed in the darkness. On one level you could still see the pale blue paint on the columns, put there to help drivers remember where their cars were parked. Soon the basement floors would be gone, too.

The rest of the site was covered with things that were needed to build new structures, not tear down damaged ones: whirling cement trucks, row after row of gray-and-white construction trailers, one with an American flag on its roof, huge crates of black piping, mounds of gravel, pickups with big tool racks in the back, ambling men in hard hats and orange reflecting vests. A lunch van marked L'ITALIANO CATERING—SINCE 1969 sat right where the northernmost of the twin towers, the one with the soaring antenna, had once rested on the bedrock of Manhattan Island. But none of the material and machines and bustle did much to fill the immense cavity that the wall surrounded. The steel skeleton of an entire train station, being built to replace one that was smashed in the collapse of the towers on September 11, was tucked against the eastern wall, opposite the spot where Quesada was working. The colossal size of the cavity made the station look like a shiny new toy, too small to hold real people—and certainly not trains.

There was an emptiness here. It hovered between the fragments of the old trade center and the birth of the new, a measureless space filled only with memories and vaporous question marks. The mind could not help tracing out against the blank sky the monumental structures that had risen from this cavity, filling in the people who had worked here, following the invisible and fateful paths of those who had fled, those who had rescued, those who had died, those who with upturned faces had witnessed the debacle and wept. This empty place was haunted by images that would not fade, by history that refused to recede into the distance, by silent voices that echoed back and forth across the canyon formed by the wall, always repeating last words of hope and fear and confusion and love and comfort and resignation. And it was haunted by questions. How did all of this come to be? What forces, what people, what fusion of fate and chance pushed the World Trade Center into the sky? How did it rise? Why did it fall? What caused such mighty structures to collapse in the flames of September 11, like the Ionic columns of some sacked Roman city? What happened here?

Quesada hit the lever again. The boom rotated counterclockwise, swinging him toward the wall. It was studded with row after row of rusty steel snouts pointing upward at a forty-five-degree angle. They held the ends of cables that traveled down to anchor sockets in the bedrock outside the wall to keep it from falling inward. The rows of the stubby snouts were noticeably wavy, reflecting great irregularities in the wall. It had been constructed as the foundation wall in 1967 and 1968, the first part of the World Trade Center to be built, using what was then a fancy new method that involved squirting concrete into a deep trench with no wooden planks inside to smooth up the sides. When the concrete hardened and the soil was scoured away from what would be the trade center's base-ment, the huge wall looked as if it had been born ancient. The soil and stones of Lower Manhattan clung to it, and had left it with an imprint of the island's subsurface textures, a crude version of casting bronze with wax. Some of the bumps were as big as a kitchen table. Men with jack-hammers had to stand on them and chip them away. Most of the tex-tures remained, and they didn't matter much: the wall's main function was to seal the basement against the terrific pressure of soil soaked with groundwater fed by the Hudson River. And if the wall was not especially pretty, it would soon be covered up with more elegant structures and never seen.

But here it was exposed to the light again. As Quesada, a member of the local dock builders union—this was, after all, a kind of subterranean dike—glided closer and closer to its surface, thirty feet above the floor of the excavation, he could see that time and disaster had tacked tortured eons onto the wall's apparent age. The vertical reinforcing bars, as thick as a child's wrist, were dented and surrounded by red shadows made of rust-colored stains that had seeped into the concrete around them. The mot-tled concrete face looked more like a weathered cliff, with jagged little outcroppings coated by floury dust and dark, cool, spongy concavities that seemed to be filled with some kind of sealant that was decaying away. Someone had covered the wall with a screen of rusting chickenwire to keep any sizable chunks of concrete from adding to a talus pile that had already accumulated below. The wall smelled dank. If the wind kicked up and blew the floury dust into your teeth, it tasted flat, alkaline, weary of the sun and rain.

The basket stopped with a little bounce. Then Quesada engaged in a curious operation. He had chosen a spot where dozens of little sleeves or fittings had been inserted into the wall, protruding like taps in a wine barrel. He put one end of a black hose into a container of clear syrupy liquid, fitted the other end over one of the taps, and used the chugging pump to force the liquid deep into the wall. The container held a kind of urethane that expanded into a foam when it encountered moisture. When the foam set, it would help the wounded wall seal out the groundwater. It was a critical procedure, because the wall had been the first structure built for the trade center, and would also be the only one to endure, being asked once more to serve as a stout foundation for whatever new buildings were put here. But through some mystery of internal circulation, the urethane did not just disappear quietly in the wall. One of the other taps suddenly began spitting and popping, attempting to expel some of the pressure that Quesada was exerting. Another tap started spurting brown sandy water, then what looked like runny black river mud, and finally the urethane— but now it had turned bright yellow, having already begun its metamorphosis to foam. The colors streaked the rocklike face anew, the running mascara of the grief that would never abandon this place. Quesada went on to another tap.

■ ■ ■

Of the 232 floors that, altogether, made up the twin towers, just 12 had managed to fit within the boundary of the immense wall that Matthew Quesada was so meticulously repairing. The rest of the towers surged upward, above the rooftops of the world's greatest buildings, to create a city in the sky the likes of which the planet had never seen.

It is hard, now, to grasp how big—how incomparably big—the World Trade Center was when it was built in the 1960s and '70s. The trade center would ultimately contain 12 million square feet of prime, rentable office space. The construction of the trade center was such an epic undertaking that it became a national effort, with more than 200,000 pieces of steel alone being fabricated at plants in Virginia, Pennsylvania, California, Washington, Missouri, Texas, and New York. Even before those pieces converged on Lower Manhattan, the overwhelming scale of the project provoked an outcry from many quarters of a city that, at the time, did not want the gargantuan towers; from the hundreds of bitter shopkeepers whose businesses were razed to make way for construction; from private real estate developers who did not believe they should have to compete with a giant, government-owned citadel crammed with office space; and from architecture critics who vilified the twin towers' esthetic qualities, or lack of them.

Then the pieces came together, and the twin towers went up. From that moment on—gradually, imperceptibly, but assuredly—they shouldered their way into the affections of ordinary New Yorkers, tourists marveling at the Manhattan skyline, and anyone else with the slightest weak spot for the unbridled chutzpah that the towers came to symbolize. Their destruction on September 11, first and most tragically, took nearly twenty-seven hundred lives in the towers and 147 people on board the two hijacked airplanes. But even as the nation began mourning those lives, it became clear that something else was being mourned: the towers themselves. There is no longer a souvenir stand in the city without a painting or a photograph of the departed towers, put back in their place on the Hudson River waterfront. One reason they took root in New York's heart may be that while the towers were completely out of scale to everything around them when seen up close, they rose over the city with the inevitability of geologic formations if given the right perspective. They were the biggest and brashest icons that New York ever produced—physically magnificent, intimately familiar structures.

And they existed because their builders were possessed of a determination that often crossed the line into hubris: they refused to admit defeat before any problem that natural forces, economics, politics, civic hostility, or legal challenges could throw in their way. Nothing was going to stop them from building the world's tallest skyscrapers, and nothing did.

The talisman that the builders brandished, again and again, to counter their opponents was the technological optimism of the early space age. With the gravity-defying confidence of early NASA scientists, the trade center's architects and engineers used brand-new and, in some cases, untested technologies to raise this unprecedented amount of real estate into the sky. They created a pair of lightweight, almost willowy structures that, they said, would nonetheless be able to withstand hurricane-force winds and other natural cataclysms. The builders gave the same assurances when, in warnings that would be forgotten for decades and rediscovered after September 11, opponents of the project claimed that an airplane collision or a huge fire in the towers could cause their unusual and innovative structures to give way and collapse.

Brushing those concerns aside, the builders of the trade center made dozens of decisions, small and large, many now forgotten or half-forgotten, that suddenly became matters of life and death on September 11. When they determined the enormous size of the complex, when they shaped it into a focus of international financial prowess, and, most important, when they drew the blueprints for its construction, they had unwittingly done much to write the script for its eventual destruction. Why did the towers initially withstand the impacts but then collapse roughly an hour later? Why did most of the people below the impact zones escape and live, while nearly all those above were trapped and died? How were so many doomed people able to communicate with loved ones by phone and e-mail, telling the terrible story of their last moments in the towers?

What happened here? The answers lie buried in the trade center's contentious history.

1

. . .

David's Turn

Today, the world stands on the brink of a boom in international trade. . . . To realize its role in the new era dawning for overseas trade and finance, this country must marshal its resources. One primary step in this direction would be to establish a single center, planned and equipped to serve that vital purpose.

—A Proposal for the Port of New York,
by the Downtown–Lower Manhattan Association, January 1960

The phone rang at 7 A.M. in the four-story, red-brick town house on East Sixty-fifth Street where David Rockefeller was just finishing up his breakfast before his commute to work. Rockefeller, the youngest grandson of America's first billionaire, liked to ride the Lexington Avenue subway downtown to his office at Chase National Bank, one hand clutching the dangling strap, the other a newspaper folded lengthwise so that he could read it in the morning crush. As he swayed with the unsteady rhythms of the city's populist heart, he could have been any other executive on his way to work in Lower Manhattan. But the unexpected phone call on this day in February 1955 meant that Rockefeller would make his commute in the back of a gray Cadillac limousine that carried two telephones, enough room for seven passengers, and license plates that read, very simply, wz. Those were the initials of William Zeckendorf, the unpredictable, inventive, and stupendously energetic real estate promoter—and an old Rockefeller family friend—who had called to say he had an idea that couldn't wait.

Rockefeller was used to last-minute brainstorms from Zeckendorf, an enormous, moon-faced man who had been called the P. T. Barnum of real estate. Zeckendorf never thought small, and he could seldom be accused of understatement. He ruled his real estate empire from within a huge architectural turret atop a skyscraper at 383 Madison Avenue. His lofty chamber, designed by I. M. Pei, featured an igloo-shaped, teakwood-enveloped office on the first level and a circular, glass-enclosed dining room on top. While visitors to his office struggled to get a few words in, Zeckendorf often fielded thirty-five calls an hour, furiously doodling tri-angles as he spoke, at times getting haircuts in his office chair, negotiating deal after deal—for properties that in some cases he had never seen. (His secretaries would carefully file the doodles, because they often contained notes about deals among the geometric shapes.) This was the real estate magician who had proposed turning the land under an East River slaughterhouse into the first home of the United Nations, a deal that the Rockefeller family had swung by putting up $8.5 million to buy the prop-erty. Not coincidentally, that maneuver also adroitly removed from pri-vate hands the only Midtown plot big enough to rival the Rockefeller family's own real estate venture, Rockefeller Center. Zeckendorf had bought and sold interests in the Chrysler Building, the Singer Building, 40 Wall Street, and dozens of other city landmarks. For Zeckendorf, doing the deal was the important thing.

Zeckendorf had crisply summed up his philosophy in a saying that became famous in real estate circles: "I would rather be alive at 18 percent than dead at the prime rate." Since the prime lending rate was in the low single digits, the declaration meant that Zeckendorf was willing to pay a tremendous premium for the sake of consummating a deal. That habit would ultimately lead him to a spectacular bankruptcy.

But for now Zeckendorf, with all of his ebullient showmanship, was advising David Rockefeller—an immensely powerful man who was seri-ous, almost to the point of piety, about his city, his family, and his family's money—and Zeckendorf had come up with a sure-fire plan for building a giant new headquarters for Chase. He wanted to pitch it to Rockefeller during the limousine ride downtown.

This was going to be one hell of a deal.

Zeckendorf knew that Rockefeller had just been named executive vice president for planning and development at Chase. The bank had been looking for a place to consolidate its sprawling operations for years now, and as one of his first big assignments, Rockefeller had been asked by

Chase's chairman, John J. McCloy, to help figure out where to build a new headquarters. In the last few decades, Chase had sopped up the assets of more than fifty smaller banks, collecting in the process an awkward little menagerie of nine downtown buildings. None of those buildings had enough space—or stature—for what, through a merger with the Bank of the Manhattan Company, was soon to be the city's largest and the world's second-largest bank, with some nine thousand downtown employees. It would have been all but impossible to find any suitable buildings downtown, in the historic heart of the financial district, because no one had broken ground there on a big new skyscraper since the early 1930s. Instead, the corporate epicenter was moving north, to Midtown—a place so far away, in commercial terms, that it might as well have been a separate city. The new corporate showplaces in Midtown— with their enormous windows, wide-open floor spaces, and, perhaps most glorious, central air conditioning—left the downtown towers look- ing like quaint but shopworn antiques.

So it must have seemed a sure bet that Chase would join corporate brethren like Lever Brothers, Colgate-Palmolive, and Seagram's to Park Avenue or the other glittering streets near Grand Central Terminal. But that would not have meshed with the deal that Zeckendorf had in mind, a deal so complicated that he would later refer to it in the style of a chess champion as his "Wall Street Maneuver."

Zeckendorf's deal would turn out to be the first move in a much larger game. That game, and the shrewd masters of politics, finance, real estate, public relations, urban planning, architecture, engineering, and con- struction who played it, would produce a pair of towers that rose above every other skyscraper in Manhattan and the world. Those towers and the handful of lesser buildings clustered around them downtown, in the part of the city traditionalists still insisted on calling Lower Manhattan, would become known as the World Trade Center.

Decades after his limousine ride with David Rockefeller, Zeckendorf's role in creating the trade center would be so obscured by later history that it would be all but forgotten. "What's his name, the name of the real estate promoter who did a lot of that?" McCloy, the bank's chairman, would say after the trade center had been open for almost a decade and Zeckendorf had died with his empire in ruins. "You know, the big fellow. I never thought I'd forget his name." But it is unlikely that anyone who knew Zeckendorf ever forgot another of his signature lines: "I make grapefruit out of lemons." That is what it would take to keep Chase from moving uptown.

As Rockefeller started looking into the question, McCloy could not help thinking about his downtown neighbor National City Bank and its chairman, Howard Sheperd, who was also looking for a new building. "Howard, what are you going to do?" McCloy had asked Sheperd at about that time. "Well, I want to stay downtown," Sheperd replied. But soon enough Sheperd came back to McCloy: "Jack, I've got a lot of young Turks over at my place who don't agree with the older hands. They think they ought to move uptown." And they did.

But Zeckendorf could scribble another important bit of information among the triangles on his notepad. Rockefeller and McCloy were bankers with an iron focus on the bottom line—"Sentiment should never be the basis for a business decision involving many thousands of people and hundreds of millions of dollars," David Rockefeller would write in what, for him, counted as fiery language—but they also had enough of a sense of history that they wanted to buck the trend. Their cramped headquarters, just north of Wall Street, overlooked the spot where the Dutch had first settled New York. Just across the street was the site of Federal Hall, where the Bill of Rights had been adopted and where George Washington took the oath as the nation's first president. And around the corner once stood a buttonwood tree, under which twenty-four brokers had gathered in 1792 to form a marketplace that ultimately would be named the New York Stock Exchange. Still, the Chase board was stocked with some of the same industrialists who were leading the move uptown, and in that February of 1955, stockholders were far more interested in the bank's $7.5 billion in assets than the view from the windows of its headquarters.

Here is where Zeckendorf came in. He had a little inside information. Within hours, he told Rockefeller on the limousine ride downtown, an old limestone office tower, right next door to Chase headquarters on Pine Street, was due to be sold. At fifteen stories, the 1884 building had been occupied by the Mutual Life Insurance Company of New York before it, too, left for Midtown. The building had been an architectural wonder in its day: arched windows, two-story porticos flanked by polished Quincy granite columns, and an entrance hall with Algerian onyx pillars and a marble frieze. But Zeckendorf had little interest in those flourishes. Stop the sale of the building, Zeckendorf told Rockefeller, and then make the following moves:

Buy the Mutual Life Insurance Building yourself.

Acquire the other buildings that Chase did not already own in this immediate two-block area. Sell off many of Chase's other downtown properties and find a new tenant for its current headquarters at 18 Pine Street.

Persuade the city to close off Cedar Street, which split the area containing the existing Chase holdings and the Mutual Life Building into two blocks.

Demolish much of those two blocks.

Use those two blocks as the base for a new skyscraper that would serve as headquarters for Chase.

Checkmate.

In truth, the Wall Street Maneuver was not nearly that simple, since it required a dazzling set of side moves—which Zeckendorf dubbed "musical chairs"—that shuffled major companies around at some of the locations. But if you believed in the man's ability to pull off the maneuver, the outcome would be a spanking new downtown headquarters.

It would never really be clear how easy it was to amaze the determinedly mild, doggedly unemotive Rockefeller, whose lifelong hobby was collecting beetles. Whatever the threshold, the Wall Street Maneuver made the grade. The audacity of Zeckendorf's proposal astonished him.

But the Zeckendorf magic also persuaded him. They got out of the limousine and hurried to see McCloy in his fourth-floor office at 18 Pine Street.

"The Mutual Life site is under negotiation for sale and you have no time," Zeckendorf declared. "You have to bid for it today."

After Zeckendorf outlined the plan, McCloy became a believer too. He phoned the owner of the company that was making the sale and got him to delay it for a day. Less than twenty-four hours later, Chase had purchased the Mutual Life Insurance Building for $4.4 million.

McCloy and Rockefeller knew that, as with any deal that passed through Zeckendorf's restless hands, there were some imponderables, some Zeckendorfian risks that the bank would have to accept. The most obvious ones revolved around Cedar Street. Even after it purchased the land, the bank would need to go to Robert Moses, the city's powerful redevelopment czar, for the special permits needed to erase Cedar Street and create such a large plot. The famously dictatorial Moses would have to agree to the plan.

In fact, Moses would do more than that.

He would make the next move in the much greater game that Zeckendorf had set in motion.

■ ■ ■

From his bedroom window on the fifth floor of his boyhood home at 10 West Fifty-fourth Street in Midtown Manhattan, David Rockefeller had a lovely view south over the city. Although he could see the tops of some low, aging buildings in the foreground, the near distance was commanded by the spires of St. Patrick's Cathedral, just around the corner from his house, on Fifth Avenue. Farther away were the Empire State Building and the gleaming Chrysler Building, both recently completed—he was fifteen when the ribbon was cut on the Empire State Building on a hazy but cloudless May Day, 1931—and ruling with absolute authority over the Midtown skyline. And if he looked past the muscular western shoulder of the Empire State Building, he could see open, unbroken sky for miles along the Hudson River shoreline toward Lower Manhattan.

Soon the low buildings would be replaced by Rockefeller Center. His father, John D. Rockefeller Jr., pushed ahead with the project through the Depression despite the obvious financial challenges and the withdrawal of the prime tenant, the Metropolitan Opera Company. With that perseverance, Mr. Junior (as he was called) would create one of New York's most storied architectural sites and the single place most associated with the family name. But the family didn't stop there in its remaking of the city. During this same period, David's mother, Abby Aldrich Rockefeller, became one of the founders of the Museum of Modern Art, which in the late 1930s would move to a complex built on the block that was partially occupied by the family home at 10 West Fifty-fourth Street—which would be razed to make way for the project. On an Upper West Side hill overlooking the Hudson River, David's father had also helped finance the construction of the neo-Gothic giant known as Riverside Church. In short, a simple tour of the city gave David Rockefeller a view of his family's adopted role as New York's benevolent parent.

It was a fraught relationship, to say the least. It depended not just on the family's energy and wealth and good intentions but on the city's willingness to accept paternalistic advice from these self-appointed wise men and women. The United States, after all, is supposed to be a democracy, where each individual is born equal to the next. With the power of money, big money, factored in, that theoretical equality was more than a little suspect. But preserving the *pretense* of equality—that, too, was an important American precept. Missteps by David's grandfather had made all too clear what kind of backlash the family could expect if it ended up on the wrong side of public opinion. John D. Rockefeller Sr. had turned a $2,000 investment in 1859 into a corporation that by the 1890s marketed 85 percent of the petroleum products sold in the United States. He righteously defended his high-volume, low-cost operation at Standard Oil by pronouncing that "we must ever remember we are refining oil for the poor man and he must have it cheap and good." But his ambitions and smarts drove him to create such a powerful and profitable enterprise that for much of his life it evoked more fear and hatred than respect and awe. "Our barbarians come from above," Henry Demarest Lloyd had written about John D. Rockefeller Sr. in 1894, in one of the most damaging of the tirades against a man some considered a monster and a thief. "Our great money makers have sprung up in one generation into seats of power kings do not know."

Power mattered. Money mattered supremely. But if not used wisely, they could elicit a venom and a fury that would leave even the richest man lonely and depressed, his true power reduced by forces beyond the ambit of capitalism. Power had to be wielded with a careful eye to every possible ricochet and riposte. And the ultimate source of that power, money, had to be nurtured and respected, its laws—economic laws, as hard-edged as laws of nature—understood and manipulated with consummate skill.

Stewardship. Again and again, that was the word that surfaced when talking about the five Rockefeller brothers, who had absorbed those lessons in the marrow of their bones. No one in the Rockefeller family would ever match the capacity of John D. Rockefeller Sr. to produce great geysers of wealth. But from the moment of their birth, David Rockefeller and his four brothers would live a life defined by both the privilege, and the burden, associated with properly handling and taking advantage of the family's fortune. By the time David was a young man, the Rockefellers, more than any other family in the United States, had assumed a role as royalty. Yes, the Morgan and the Vanderbilt clans stood out among a few other fabulously wealthy industrialists. But no other family with such great wealth had produced a string of such strong-willed descendants who were intent upon not only perpetuating their affluence, but in leveraging it to remake the community, and perhaps even the nation, where they lived. Before David Rockefeller and his brothers retired, they would attempt to extend that mandate to the world.

As the youngest of six children, David would not emerge from academics until his four brothers were already well along with careers that seemed worthy of the family name. John D. Rockefeller III, David's oldest brother, had taken control of the family philanthropic affairs and would later build Lincoln Center. In 1940, President Franklin D. Roosevelt named Nelson A. Rockefeller chairman of the Office of Inter-American Affairs, a bureau that promoted closer ties with Latin America. Laurance S. Rockefeller was busy trying to help start up Eastern Air Lines. Winthrop Rockefeller tried his own hand at the oil business. David, meanwhile, was a chubby young boy, known for wandering around the 3,500-acre family estate in Westchester in search of new beetle specimens he could add to his carefully classified and maintained collection.

A precise and studious young man who seemed to have been born with the outward blandness that would become, curiously, his most remarked-upon personality trait, David Rockefeller always projected a certain self-consciousness about his family name. He had an unexceptional academic career at Harvard, but went on to earn a doctorate in economics at the University of Chicago, and when asked much later why a Rockefeller would bother with graduate school, he replied, "A Ph.D. wasn't something that I was going to buy." He trimmed down somewhat as an adult, and his face was dominated by a nose that was variously described as vulpine, needlelike, evocative of a jester, and simply very long. "In broad outline it is the kind of face a child might construct from an orange and a toothpick," E. J. Kahn Jr. wrote in *The New Yorker*. Behind this odd assemblage of traits, Rockefeller seemed to have decided early in life that there was only one thing upon which he would declare relentless, all-out war: idleness. Downtime had little meaning and no attraction for David Rockefeller. His social and professional calendars were full, and they would stay that way his entire life. In his Ph.D. dissertation, titled "Unused Resources and Economic Waste," he had written that of all forms of waste, idleness was the most abhorrent. "There is a moral stigma attached to unnecessary and involuntary idleness which is deeply imbedded in our conscience," he explained. And he lived by those words.

His first job after completing his studies was an unpaid internship in the administration of Mayor Fiorello H. La Guardia, serving as the Little Flower's personal aide. But Chase seemed to be an inevitable destination for Rockefeller. With his family's significant holdings there, many called it, only partly in jest, the Rockefeller family bank. Two of David's brothers, Nelson and Winthrop, had already taken jobs there briefly. And David's uncle Winthrop W. Aldrich just happened to be the bank's chairman. Aldrich visited David in Paris as World War II was drawing to a close in the summer of 1945. David, who then was a captain in the army, was on his last assignment, gathering intelligence about U.S. allies and possible future economic rivals in Europe and northern Africa. David was consumed at the time with studying the growing tension in Algiers between the Arabs and Berbers and their colonial ruler. Aldrich now had a more practical question for his nephew. Would he like to join the bank? Rockefeller started in 1946 in Chase's foreign department as a $3,500-a-year assistant manager, the lowest of the junior executive slots at the 18 Pine Street headquarters. He would remain at the bank for his entire career. He would boast, in his understated way, that he was the first member of the family since his grandfather to keep a steady job in the world of business.

But with his deep distaste for idleness and inactivity, and his family's dedication to remaking the messy, dirty, complicated city of New York along more elegant lines, that is hardly the only job David Rockefeller immersed himself in.

■ ■ ■

SAVE OUR HOMES, the leaflet screamed in October 1951.

David Rockefeller had been trying the roles of builder, city planner, and social engineer on for size, as perhaps only a Rockefeller could do. The leaflet went around in the northern Manhattan community of Morningside Heights, where a project he had unleashed was aiming to bulldoze ten run-down but densely packed acres of the city just north of Columbia University and replace them with a cluster of high-rise cooperative apartments. "We are told that our neighborhood is a 'slum' and must be 'improved,' " the leaflet said. "Obviously, more than half of us are OUT if the cooperative plan goes through. We believe in neighborhood improvement—for US! We ask—WHO IS THIS COOPERATIVE BEING BUILT FOR????? It seems that our homes are to be torn down to make way for wealthy people who have no housing shortage. WE CAN STOP IT! . . . We CAN win!"

Perhaps.

Morningside Heights rose up from the Hudson River like the side of a butte. Much of the topography was determined by an upward bulge in the fabulously solid bedrock, called Manhattan schist, that lay beneath the island—the same bedrock that made Manhattan such a congenial place for those who would build skyscrapers. Morningside Heights was home to Columbia University, Barnard College, Union Theological Seminary, the Jewish Theological Seminary, Riverside Church, the International House, and the Lincoln School of Teachers College at Columbia, the progressive, even experimental first-through-twelfth-grade school at Amsterdam and 123rd Street that all of the Rockefeller brothers but John had attended. The combination of the hill and the elite cultural institutions—every one of which had received major financial support from the Rockefeller family—had proved irresistible, and the neighborhood had earned the nickname of "the Acropolis of America."

David Rockefeller had no particular standing in the neighborhood; he served in no public office and had been appointed to no local government board. But he decided to immerse himself in what would become a nearly decade-long effort to reshape the cityscape around his childhood school yard—and especially just north of it, where the bedrock dipped down into a little valley that the locals called Manhattanville, before rising again toward Harlem. Manhattanville had been taken over in some areas by prostitutes and gangs. To get things started, Rockefeller, like the amateur naturalist that he was, hired a University of Chicago sociologist to conduct a neighborhood survey and pinpoint why Morningside Heights had gone into a nosedive. Then he enlisted fourteen major educational, religious, and medical institutions in the area to join together in a group they called Morningside Heights Inc. Before the Men's Class at Riverside Church, in

October 1948, David Rockefeller explained that these extraordinary institutions had first started to set up shop in the neighborhood at the close of the nineteenth century because "they evidently felt they were choosing a community which was, and would continue to be, favorable to their growth." But something seems to have gone terribly wrong, he told his friends. "The processes of unguided urban evolution are resulting in a community whose living conditions are unacceptable to the very people who operate and patronize these institutions, and are rapidly becoming more so," Rockefeller declared.

Coded terms like "unguided urban evolution" would have spoken eloquently to the Rockefeller friends at the church meeting, but sometimes it was necessary to be a little more explicit. True to his reticent, unflamboyant character, David Rockefeller, then thirty-two years old, was not exactly comfortable delivering a blunter message. He left it to his associates to explain in far greater detail that he was talking about the arrival in the neighborhood of so many Puerto Ricans and blacks, while middle-class whites were moving out in large numbers. Lawrence M. Orton, a member of the City Planning Commission who had been brought in as executive director of Morningside Heights Inc. to create a humane program for relocating existing tenants at the site, was as compassionate as anyone could be about their plight. But he was also plainspoken about the demographic shifts at the heart of the Morningside Heights initiative.

According to census records, Orton wrote in a memo titled "The Present Crisis" and addressed to David Rockefeller, "the white population decreased 12 percent, while the non-white population increased 71 percent" between 1940 and 1950 in the area between 106th and 135th streets that bounded the neighborhood. "Again, let me repeat," Orton continued, "if these minority groups come into the Heights in the usual way, it will benefit them little, if any, for the usual course of events will bring with it the same disastrous change in conditions which have resulted elsewhere; but the effects on the institutions will be catastrophic. All of these have appealed to me as reasons why the institutions and the City should combine to take the steps necessary to guide local change along constructive lines."

Rockefeller and his allies would rely on one tool far more than any other to, as Orton delicately put it, "guide local change": the bulldozer. The plan was to level ten acres of homes where the schist dipped down into Manhattanville just north of the Columbia University campus. The area that contained what Morningside Heights Inc. called "71 deteriorating tenement apartment buildings, 4 rooming houses and 68 commercial tenants, mostly retail stores" was to be bulldozed and replaced by the six-building high-rise complex dubbed Morningside Gardens. The new housing would be restricted to middle-income families. Once the plan had been drawn out on the Morningside Heights Inc. maps, it was hard not to conclude that its central strategy was to create a barricade, conveniently shielding the Acropolis of America from Harlem.

Whatever the underlying goals—and many of them were clearly well-intentioned, focused purely on making a storied sector of the city a better place to live—it all made perfect sense to the members of the Morningside Heights Inc. board, which included folks like Henry P. Van Dusen, president of Union Theological Seminary in New York, and Grayson L. Kirk, the international relations scholar and president of Columbia University. But the board realized that it couldn't get very far without the power of eminent domain—the legal ability to condemn whole tracts of housing, move the occupants out expeditiously, bulldoze freely, and rebuild according to the plan. So Rockefeller, as he would soon after for the Chase bank project, turned to the city's most powerful unelected bureaucrat, Robert Moses. Moses had spent much of his career erecting miles' worth of highways and bridges across the New York City region, as well as a wonderful collection of new parks. But with the Federal Housing Act of 1949—and its Title I provisions that allowed the government to condemn whole swaths of cities for the purpose of "slum clearance" and redevelopment—suddenly there was a new field for Moses to expand his power base. Moses added the chairmanship of the city's commission for slum clearance to his list of official positions. And once Rockefeller contacted him about Morningside Gardens, Moses said he would back it. The project was on its way.

There was just one outstanding detail. Moses, Rockefeller, and his group neglected to ask the people who actually lived there what they thought about the plan. The day after the slum clearance plan was announced in October 1951, protests erupted right in the street. Between five hundred and six hundred people showed up at a local church, interrogating a priest who was on Rockefeller's board as to why he would ever back a plan that would lead to the eviction of so many members of his own parish. At another protest meeting later that month, a woman named Elizabeth Barker—of 435 West 123rd Street, next door to the proposed demolition site—stood up and gave a fiery speech pleading with area residents to stand up to what she called the "dreadful thing," the clearance plan that would require the relocation of 1,626 families by Morningside Heights Inc.'s count. "If we accept the co-op we are all done," Barker said. "There is no place for the poor now, so they make less places for poor people," she said, mocking the "middle-income" apartment blocks. "Where would we go?" asked one of the mimeographed pamphlets drawn up by the group she formed, Save Our Homes.

Barker, described as a feisty Irish mother of three—who happened to have a university degree—also ridiculed what Rockefeller had called his "scientific community survey," which Rockefeller and Morningside Heights Inc. had cited as proof that the project must go forward. She questioned the labeling of her neighborhood as a slum and asked how it was possible that Rockefeller might think that Morningside residents might be able to "live a fuller and richer life" if they suddenly found themselves evicted from their homes. She held bake sales, raffles, and rallies to support the protests—even dances, one of them featuring what her handbill called *"the famous, one and only MACHITO and his Afro-Cubans and ELMO GARCIA and his Mambo Orchestra."* Thousands of signatures were gathered on petitions; busloads of protesters were delivered to the steps of City Hall. It was more than enough of a ruckus to persuade the city to at least temporarily set the matter aside.

Rockefeller seemed baffled. Didn't they understand the benefits? Without delay, Morningside Heights Inc. organized a counterattack. The group asked an aide, Bernard Weinberg, to find out if Save Our Homes was "Communist inspired." He reported that it wasn't, but through whatever source—and it was clear that the accusations predated Weinberg's attendance at the meetings—the group was eventually smeared as Communist-backed in the press. The sideshow didn't matter much. The Morningside Heights project had more than its fair share of important citywide backers, including the Urban League of Greater New York, Citizens Union of the City of New York, and the *New York Times*. Perhaps most critical, almost every member of the city Board of Estimate, which had the power to approve or kill the project, turned out to be on Rockefeller's side. Rockefeller himself never wavered, and the naysayers were absent that rainy winter's morning in 1954 when Millicent Carey McIntosh, the president of Barnard College, lifted up a crowbar and ripped a red sandstone balustrade off the stoop of a LaSalle Street tenement to start the demolition.

Most of the families that were forced to relocate went to Harlem or the Bronx. Barker, her voice silenced, left as well. In fact, she left the city altogether, moving with her family to New England. The truth was that she and her community protests had scarcely slowed down Rockefeller and his trial run as a builder and planner on an impressive scale. At the ceremony where McIntosh wielded her crowbar, Rockefeller and Moses huddled underneath a single umbrella in matching overcoats and hats, seemingly overflowing with bonhomie.

So it must have been with great optimism that—after the impromptu limousine ride with Zeckendorf that took place only a year later, in February 1955—Rockefeller approached Moses with another request to deploy his great powers in the city. Rockefeller needed a slew of city permits before the cornerstone for a grand new headquarters for Chase downtown could be laid. Of paramount importance was obtaining permission to close off Cedar Street and connect the two blocks Zeckendorf had snared with his Wall Street Maneuver. Only then would the builders and planners have two and a half acres on which to set their new building. "As you realize from your experiences at Morningside, there is a lot of red tape to be unwound before this plan can become a reality," Moses warned Rockefeller on September 27, 1955. But it seemed clear that after a bit of horsetrading, Moses, who hardly ever saw a big construction project he didn't like, would get behind the plan. Among other things, he wanted to be sure that Rockefeller supported the Lower Manhattan Expressway, the Moses pet project that—if built—would lay blacktop across a broad swath of Chinatown and other historic districts in order to connect the Holland Tunnel on the West Side to a pair of East Side bridges. Rockefeller's camp thought the highway, which would cut Manhattan in two, would bring about higher wages and better living conditions. They were in favor of it.

There was just one more condition that Moses said he was going to impose. He wanted Rockefeller to create an elite and powerful group that would champion major downtown redevelopment projects, including his own.

Zeckendorf, with his skilled promoter's eye, had already warned Rockefeller that the new Chase project would ultimately be a failure, and the

Wall Street Maneuver ruined, if the bank did not think bigger and find a way to stabilize the financial district against the defections to Midtown and elsewhere. At a lunchtime meeting in the executive dining room at 18 Pine Street on October 31, Moses amplified that warning to a degree that perhaps only he, on the strength of his immense power in the city, could accomplish. At that meeting, Moses told Rockefeller that unless the bank "got others to see there was a future in Lower Manhattan, they would move out before we finished the building. It could be a disaster. You may find yourselves left all alone down there."

Moses made it quite clear to Rockefeller that he was not talking about some low-key community group like the ones that already churned out their jejune little position papers and sponsored polite gatherings. "The other existing organizations can help," he wrote to Rockefeller after the luncheon meeting, before adding with a putdown in the true Moses style that "they are simply letterhead, annual dinner associations which live to issue statements, eat beef and apple pie à la mode and award scrolls to dubious heroes."

Far from feeling that he had been pushed around, Rockefeller saw some possibilities here. At Morningside Heights, he had tried out the role of a city builder in the great Rockefeller family mold, and he had warmed to it. Lower Manhattan offered much, much bigger challenges, and he had the vastly larger vision for change, for renewal, that he would need to take them on. Following the charge by Moses and his own experience at Morningside Heights, Rockefeller would couch his recommendations behind the facade of a prestigious institution. In this case, the group would be called the Downtown–Lower Manhattan Association, with a membership list that included the chairmen, presidents, or other top officers of Chemical Bank; Morgan Stanley & Co.; American Express; First National City Bank; Cities Services Co.; American Telephone and Telegraph; the New York Stock Exchange; and the American Stock Exchange. But from the start, there was no mistaking it. This was Rockefeller's baby.

The Downtown–Lower Manhattan Association: the name was inelegant, metrically unscannable, no matter how many times it tripped off the tongue. Yet it represented the next step toward the creation of something that sounded undeniably thrilling, the World Trade Center.

The first item on Rockefeller's cluttered agenda, however, was to get the bank building project moving.

The orders from Chase chairman John McCloy were clear: "Spectacular, in the sense that it had to be striking, somewhat unconventional." The bank hired Skidmore, Owings & Merrill, the up-and-coming Chicago-based firm. SOM turned to the functional, gargoyle-and-gable-free architectural style that it had helped to define. Inspired by Mies van der Rohe and Le Corbusier, the style sought beauty not through ornamental flourishes but in the clean lines of a draftsman's table. Rockefeller loved the look, and SOM gave it to him: the tower's exterior would be a flat surface consisting of nothing but glass and steel. Deep beneath the main banking floor and a huge sunlit plaza, the foundation would be sunk 90 feet into the ground, the place where Chase would locate what it called the world's largest bank vault. And at sixty-four stories, stretching 813 feet above the ground, the new Chase headquarters would be the tallest structure built in New York—or the United States for that matter—since 1933.

It was nowhere close to the great downtown structures that Rockefeller and his clunky-sounding association were about to spawn. But for a man who fancied himself as a builder, it was a most impressive start.

• • •

A well-dressed man with a full, black beard rose higher and higher above the gawking crowd. Six feet tall, he stood there looking unperturbed, in a showmanlike sort of way, as a rope hoisted the platform he was standing upon. As the platform rose, it remained steady and level by sliding along vertical tracks or guides on two sides. It was 1854 at the Crystal Palace Exhibition, an elaborate fair in Midtown Manhattan managed by P. T. Barnum, who must have appreciated the crowds that the exhibit involving the platform was drawing. The man with the beard rose to a height of thirty or forty feet. The crowd gasped as he slashed the rope holding up the platform and began to drop.

And stopped.

His name was Elisha Graves Otis, and he had invented the first safety brake for elevators—an innovation that would clear the path for dreamers and promoters and engineers who wanted to build to the sky and multiply the amount of usable space that could be wrung from a modest plot of ground. And that vastly multiplied space meant similarly increased profits. With a little daring, and a little capital, businesses could also erect something much more than a location for office space. Like David Rockefeller and Chase a century later, ambitious merchants could build unmistakable symbols of their companies' wealth and influence and prominence. It all had to do with height, with persuading people that there was sanity in the notion of living and working far, far up in the sky. Otis's brake, no more complicated than a wagon spring and a set of metal teeth, meant that elevators would not plunge to the ground if their cables broke. "All safe," Otis exclaimed, doffing his hat.

"This was a very effective method of advertising," Otis's son would write years later. But for the race to begin, someone not only had to notice the innovation but also recognize how Otis had turned the world of real estate on its head. Before the elevator, anything above the fourth or fifth floor was wasted space, because no one would trudge up that high. Now, easy access to panoramic views above the noise of the street would turn the top floors into the choicest real estate. Among the first to see the possibilities was Henry Baldwin Hyde, founder of the Equitable Life Assurance Society, which he started up with borrowed furniture, a box of cigars on the office mantelpiece, and, aside from Hyde and four other top officers, only a single office boy, paid $1.50 a week. Hyde's first two offices were a few doors away from Trinity Church, whose spire reached 284 feet into the air, a peak visible to any ship out in the harbor or pedestrian strolling downtown. But by the late 1860s, when Equitable's fortunes had grown so tremendously that it was in dire need of new space, Hyde decided it had come time to challenge his ecclesiastic neighbor.

At the time Hyde was preparing to erect a new building for Equitable, elevators had already been tested at the Fifth Avenue Hotel and the Haughwout Store downtown. Why not install two of these devices at the new Equitable headquarters? Hyde asked. It would be a thrilling addition to the tall building he intended to build at the southeast corner of Broadway and Cedar Street. Besides, he was facing deep skepticism over the question of whether anyone would want to rent the upper floors of what would be a building of eight floors. One of his agents would later recall Hyde claiming "that for lawyers and others similarly situated, the upper floors, if made easily accessible, would be more comfortable and appropriate than those near the level of the street."

Hyde, it turned out, was right. When the new Equitable Life Building, 142 feet high including its clunky mansard roof, opened in May 1870, the structure was not only the tallest office building in the nation; it was a phenomenon unlike anything New York had ever seen. Thousands of people rode the elevators just to see the view from the top, and some marveled that the stairway had been rendered almost pointless.

Like some oversized contraption of a flying machine thirty years before Kitty Hawk, real estate in New York City had taken its first jouncing, thrilling ride into the sky. It would never come down.

But the marvel of the elevator would have to be married with another innovation—a system of structural support that relied completely on iron, and later steel—before the skyscraper could achieve its full promise and become worthy of its name.

Before the iron and steel skeleton arrived, buildings were generally heavy masonry structures whose thick and often heavily ornamented outer walls did double duty—important architecturally and esthetically, they were also crucial structural members, holding up a large fraction of the building's weight. Gradually in the early and mid-nineteenth century, builders started to use cast-iron and wrought-iron beams and columns inside the building to save space—iron was stronger than stone, and therefore the support members could be thinner—and make the overall building lighter.

Curiously, the high-quality iron and the technology for assembling the members into a metal frame had long been available when an engineer named William Le Baron Jenney built the ten-story Home Insurance Building in Chicago in 1885. It was, in a sense, a final psychological barrier he smashed through when he embedded vertical iron structural members in his masonry walls and created the first truly modern skyscraper. A race to abandon the vestiges of the load-bearing masonry design ensued, and the external walls soon became known as "curtain walls"—just there to shield the occupants, hold windows, and look nice. The old limits on the height of a building were shattered: while masonry supports had to be made thicker and thicker to hold up ever-taller buildings, eating up huge amounts of usable space, slender iron and steel supports could rise almost forever.

In New York, steel construction drove the promoters and developers and money men to new heights of ambition. And money was almost always the prime mover. After a businessman named John Noble Stearns purchased a twenty-one-and-a-half-foot-wide piece of land at 50 Broadway, he discovered that he would not be able to buy an adjacent lot, as he had hoped. So he asked an architect named Bradford Lee Gilbert to figure out a way to erect a very tall office building at the ridiculously narrow spot. "Is there some way of putting a tall building, a very tall building, on that lot?" Stearns asked the architect in the spring of 1887. "If not I will have to dispose of it at a sacrifice of $100,000." The solution, Gilbert realized, was to erect a metal-reinforced structure whose thin walls would not take up too much of the rentable space. The structure Gilbert would complete in 1889, the eleven-story Tower Building, was New York's first modern skyscraper.

Gilbert did more than bring the steel skeleton frame to New York. He discovered, as Otis had, that a little bit of showmanship helps in getting people comfortable with the idea of working high above the ground. After people began wondering if the Tower Building would topple in a high wind, he clambered up a scaffold strapped to its side on a violently windy Sunday the year the building opened. He would later recall that a crowd below screamed and called him a fool as he crawled along the scaffold—he said the wind had been too strong to stand upright—and smiled from his Olympian height. "There was not the slightest vibration," Gilbert would gleefully write. "The building stood steady as a rock in the sea." The doubts went away, but Gilbert's promotional instincts would not let him stop there. He allowed a plaque to be mounted in the lobby that called the building "the earliest example of the skeleton construction in which the entire weight of the walls and floors is borne and transmitted to the foundation by a framework of metallic posts and beams."

The Tower Building did not merit the claim—most experts would give the distinction to the fourteen-story Tacoma Building in Chicago—but it didn't really matter. The claim got Gilbert some press, and probably Stearns a few tenants. The Tower Building, with its odd dimensions, would be demolished only twenty-five years after it was built.

The starting gun had been sounded. With metal now accepted as the fundamental structural element in buildings of more than a few stories, the construction of skyscrapers took off. In 1891, there were twenty-five tall buildings in New York City. Just five years later, there were ninety-six, most of them clustered around City Hall and along Wall Street. With the start of the new century, the building blitz became what could only be characterized as a stampede. In 1902 alone, sixty-six skyscrapers were under construction, including the Flatiron Building, the trim, elegant, and hugely popular tower at the edge of Madison Square. The new form of construction had already started to move uptown. Freed from the constraints of the old-fashioned masonry design, the new towers in New York were jumping to previously inconceivable heights. Every corporation of any stature had to have one. The Singer Building opened in 1908 at the corner of Broadway and Liberty, a 612-foot-tall needle sticking so far above everything else that it seemed like a staircase to the moon. "THE HIGHEST OFFICE BUILDING IN THE WORLD. IT WILL BE READY FOR OCCUPANCY MAY 1, 1908," screamed an advertisement in the *New York Times*, which included a sketch comparing the still-rising tower to the pyramids in Egypt, the Washington Monument, Philadelphia City Hall, the cathedral in Rouen, France, even the Pantheon in Rome—all of which, of course, were shorter.

The capstone of this early race for the sky was the Woolworth Building, the fifty-five-story, 790-foot tower on Broadway whose neo-Gothic architecture seemed to capture perfectly the soaring verticality of the structure. Because the building rested, financially, on Frank W. Woolworth's empire of five-and-ten-cent stores, it was nicknamed the Cathedral of Commerce. Woolworth chose the architect, Cass Gilbert, on the strength of his earlier office towers, including the twenty-four-story granite, limestone, and terra-cotta gem at 90 West Street, on the Hudson shoreline. After it opened in 1907, 90 West Street boasted a penthouse restaurant that was advertised as the highest in the city. With its own Gothic arches and intensely vertical facade, it had a certain magic to it, even though it was nowhere near the tallest structure in the city at the time. It had all the monumental features Woolworth wanted. He just wanted something taller and that much more extravagant.

When his new building was completed in 1913, Woolworth got that and more. The monumentalism went beyond what Broadway passersby could see. As with most of the skyscrapers of the day, Cass Gilbert's steel frames were much heavier and more powerful than they needed to be just to hold up the building and its masonry facade. Part of the reason was practical: engineers had a hard time calculating exactly how much steel was enough, so they put in plenty of extra. And because the frames were so powerful, they not only held the building up against the force of gravity; with the help of the masonry facades and interior walls, which remained bulky by the later standards of sleek steel-and-glass architecture, the frames handily supported the buildings against gale-force winds, too.

The same year the Woolworth Building opened, the city's center began to shift to Midtown: the new Grand Central Terminal received one thousand trains a day and carried up to 250,000 people in and out of one of the greatest commercial emporiums ever constructed. It was only a matter of months before the old residences and warehouses along Madison Avenue and other streets in the shadow of Grand Central started to come down. In their place, over the coming two decades, giant new towers began to rise.

By 1929, construction was already under way on Walter Chrysler's tower at Forty-second Street and Lexington Avenue, with a planned height that would overtop the Woolworth Building. Developers of another downtown structure at 40 Wall Street briefly tried to keep the prize in Lower Manhattan by making plans to build their tower just a few feet higher than Chrysler's. What they did not know was that Walter Chrysler had been planning a little trick: a 185-foot metallic spire that was secretly being assembled inside the fire shaft of his new building. Only once the new Bank of Manhattan tower had been topped out did Chrysler have it hoisted into place, giving the building a height of 1,048 feet when it opened in May 1930.

Even that record did not last long. On Saint Patrick's Day in that spring of 1930, former governor Alfred E. Smith declared the formal start of construction for a new skyscraper, to be called the Empire State Building, at the corner of Fifth Avenue and Thirty-fourth Street in Midtown. At 102 stories, the building would contain fifty-seven thousand tons of structural steel, more than 10 million bricks, and 200,000 cubic feet of Indiana limestone and granite for the facade. Each floor was outfitted with a miniature railway system from central elevator shafts to where the work was being done. At the height of the job, thirty-four hundred construction workers labored on the building. The first structural steel that spring went in that spring, and the steel had been "topped out," or taken to its highest point, six months later. After Al Smith led the ribbon cutting on May 1, 1931, he invited guests to a gathering on the eighty-sixth floor.

"There's Central Park, no bigger than a football gridiron," one of the guests exclaimed.

Governor Franklin Delano Roosevelt, who attended the ceremonies, was also impressed. He allowed that he might be tempted to rent an office here once his governorship ended.

"About that office," Smith said without missing a beat. "The next day you are in town, I will have you down to the rental department."

It was the Depression, after all.

．．．

Eight years almost to the day after the Empire State Building opened for business, there was an idealistic little ceremony in New York that, by every measure of its immediate impact and significance, should have been swept away in the gusts of history and forgotten.

It happened at the 1939 World's Fair, in Flushing Meadows, Queens. Just north of the Court of Peace in a fair best known for much more stirring sights like the 610-foot-high needle Trylon and its companion, the 200-foot-wide globe Perisphere, a handful of third-tier government officials dutifully raised a flag at the dedication of a rather unpretentious pavilion. Originally built for exhibits to be supplied by China, the pavilion was donated to the International Chamber of Commerce when China abandoned its plans to participate. The Chamber of Commerce lent the space to an entirely new exhibit dedicated to "world peace through trade" and called the World Trade Center. On May 21, the flag was raised, an assistant secretary of state said a few words, none of which were especially quotable, and the pavilion disappeared into the hum of the fair.

That probably would have been the end of the story, had not one of the members of the World Trade Center's organizing committee been Winthrop W. Aldrich, the uncle of David Rockefeller, who was one of the nation's leading promoters of international trade.

Aldrich was an intriguing figure in himself, a man with pale blue eyes and an austere and somewhat imperious manner that made even his nephew uncomfortable. The Aldrich family traced its lineage back to such important colonial figures as Roger Williams, the founder of Rhode Island, and Major General Nathanael Greene, the confidant of George Washington. At the turn of the century, Winthrop's father, Nelson W. Aldrich, was a U.S. senator from Rhode Island, whose power was so great that he was known to the press and public as "General Manager of the Nation." One of Winthrop Aldrich's seven siblings—Abby Greene Aldrich—married John D. Rockefeller Jr. in 1901, and this was the power couple that would produce one daughter and then the five Rockefeller brothers.

Aldrich, a shrewd young lawyer, sensed, as World War I came to a close, an unparalleled opportunity for the United States to expand its interest across the globe. For centuries now, nations had traded goods, moved them by ground or ship, and built empires based in large part on their capacity to corner these profitable trade routes and establish colonies in lands that were rich in either raw materials or cheap labor. To flourish, a city needed to be either a center of goods production or a place where goods were imported or exported, if not both. In part because of the natural advantages its great deep-water port conferred, New York had used that strategy to become an old-style center of world trade beginning with the first Dutch settlers. Aldrich saw early on that the balance of power was about to change, that financial control of international trade—wherever the actual raw materials, manufacturing, and shipping centers were— would begin sustaining great cities like New York. It was an enormous shift, and he saw its early stirrings when he landed a job with a downtown law firm whose primary client was Equitable Trust Co., a bank with substantial Rockefeller holdings. From the start, he found himself immersed in complicated international financial matters, like working out bad loans Equitable had given to sugar mill owners in Cuba or trying to salvage deals involving foreign currency that were now teetering near default because of postwar inflation in Europe.

When the 1929 crash threatened the stability of Equitable, John D. Rockefeller Jr. decided to tap his brother-in-law to take over as the top executive at Equitable. Then, within six months, Equitable and Chase National Bank merged. In a flash, Aldrich led what at the time was the world's largest bank. With a small but growing network of branches in Latin America, Europe, and Asia, Chase's global presence, and his ties to the Rockefeller family, Aldrich now had an international profile greater than that of almost any other banker in American history. As he began to travel the globe—airplanes were just allowing such trips by American corporate executives—Aldrich would be greeted almost like royalty, first in 1947, as he moved through Latin America, including stops in Cuba, Brazil, Argentina, Uruguay, Chile, and the Panama Canal zone, and then in 1950, by flying to Greece, Saudi Arabia, Turkey, Lebanon, and most of the major capitals in Europe. "Dahtong Yinhang" is what Chase's branch was called in Shanghai, translated roughly as "Silver Bank Doing Business All Over the World."

The delicate part of the job for Aldrich—and the same would later be true of Rockefeller—was to figure out a way to push Chase's cause in a way that seemed simultaneously to promote the bank's *and* the nation's interests. And what did all his globetrotting mean, in the end, for New York City? For Chase, with its branches and affiliates now spread across the globe, it mattered very little if a typewriter plant was in Manhattan or abroad. It could finance the construction of the plant, the purchase of the raw materials, the hiring of the labor, and the shipment of the goods, be they in New York, Ohio, or Shanghai. Chase could still profit. What Chase and the other international banks needed—or what Aldrich was about to suggest they needed—was a centralized place where all these goods it was financing could be displayed, where buyers and sellers could meet, and where all the paperwork could be assembled. And it was based on this noble belief that the first World Trade Center, at the 1939 World's Fair, was born.

An organization founded on "world peace through trade" was not likely to survive World War II, and this one didn't. In fact, it was scarcely heard from after the flag raising. But the idea came back to life in 1946— when Aldrich was named by Governor Thomas E. Dewey to a new state agency named the World Trade Corporation. A war had come and gone, but the mission of a revived trade center remained the same. "Expanding international trade, conducted on a basis of mutual confidence and for mutual profit, looms as one of the great hopes for permanent peace," Governor Dewey said. The assignment now was to build a permanent World Trade Center in New York, he said.

For all the speechifying, this time the effort collapsed so fast—"PLANS ARE TABLED FOR TRADE CENTER," the *New York Times* headline declared in November 1946, a scant four months after the board was named—that the proposed shape of the complex was announced only after the idea was dead. It would have cost $150 million, covered ten blocks in Manhattan, with twenty-one buildings and plenty of underground parking, and would have been loosely modeled on the seven-hundred-year-old Leipzig Fair in Germany. Critics on the waterfront and in the business community had sprung up like soldiers from the mythical dragon's teeth, asserting that the setup would be clumsy and impractical for twentieth-century commerce and would never attract the thousands of businesses it would need to turn a profit. The planners themselves determined that an astonishing 80 percent of the country's six thousand largest companies would have to become tenants to give the trade center a chance at financial survival. That quickly, it was over.

Now it would be David's turn.

From the beginning of his career at Chase in 1946, David Rockefeller had shown he was intent upon seeing through his uncle's agenda. He retraced Aldrich's journey through Latin America in 1948, checking in on the bank's sugar cane investments in Cuba and its shipping toll financing network at the Panama Canal. Later, as Rockefeller moved up the ranks at Chase, he would make repeated trips to Europe, Asia, and the Middle East, as the bank opened dozens of new branches or affiliated offices in places like Thailand, Brazil, Malaysia, Honduras, Korea, Greece, and even the tiny but oil-rich Caribbean islands of Trinidad and Tobago. Rockefeller considered these trips an opportunity to follow up smart moves or slip-ups by Aldrich, like reopening the bank branch in Hong Kong that he felt Aldrich had wrongly closed after China went Communist or expanding the network of branches Aldrich had wisely opened at the close of World War II when Japan was still occupied by U.S. troops.

Throughout Rockefeller's meteoric rise at Chase (he would become president by the age of forty-five), he continued to collect international experience and influence, eventually reaching the point that accepting any of the political offers that came his way would doubtless have felt like a demotion. A chance to run for mayor? A nomination to serve as secretary of the Treasury or chairman of the Federal Reserve? It all must have sounded rather parochial. His international reach grew so wide that he was sometimes forced to defend another habit he shared with his uncle, of getting acquainted with some of the world's most notorious dictators. Aldrich had paved the way for this practice, dining with Juan and Evita Peron in Argentina in 1947 and even holding a private meeting with Hitler in 1933, at his heavily guarded summer retreat at Berchtesgaden. Rockefeller's list was even more impressive, including private tête-à-têtes with Pinochet of Chile, Saddam Hussein of Iraq, Jaruzelski of Poland, Botha of South Africa, and even Zhou Enlai of China and Khrushchev of the Soviet Union, among others. "I met them all," Rockefeller declared. The practice only gave more fodder to Rockefeller's critics, who had claimed since his days up at Morningside Heights that he was little more than an ultraprivileged aristocrat whose central goal was getting his way by any means necessary.

Rockefeller was offended by any suggestion that he had imperial tendencies. What he was trying to accomplish, he said, was a boost in the overall standard of living. That applied to his endeavors abroad and at home. Chase, he would argue repeatedly, could use its global deployment to benefit both its shareholders and society at large. He would not be subtle about his assertion. Opening a Chase branch in an isolated western province of Panama, where the bank could give loans to ranchers, Rockefeller celebrated the move by branding the local collateral— cattle—with a Chase logo. Rockefeller would never give much credit to his uncle, or the others who back in the 1940s had served on the World Trade Corporation board. But as with the other projects he picked up from his uncle, he would pursue this one with an extraordinary zeal.

He would do it with the Downtown–Lower Manhattan Association, the group with the unmellifluous moniker but plenty of clout. The first official report released by Rockefeller's committee, in October 1958, proposed knocking down and wiping away whole swaths of old markets, rotting piers, and aged buildings in Lower Manhattan. "Obsolescence, deterioration, traffic congestion and slow economic strangulation have spread over such sections," the report warned, invoking all the shades of urban doom. The residents who had once lived there had moved uptown, leaving behind the old produce markets and streets that grew so silent at night within the granite canyons. Just what would go on all this downtown land that would be cleared was not a subject Rockefeller and his group were ready to discuss. Nor were they ready to suggest who should actually lead the charge. That would take more study. But the general plan was clear: "business centers including offices, banks, telephone and telegraph buildings" should be constructed, as well as parks, a heliport, and perhaps more space for truck depots, parking, and automotive repair centers. Of course, Moses's Lower Manhattan Expressway was in the package. The estimated budget for these investments was a whopping $1 billion.

These sketchy details alone were enough to get people quite excited, or at least the people who mattered, including the editorial board at the *New York Times*. "Downtown Manhattan has, in effect, decided to shape its destiny, and a great future it is bound to be," the paper rhapsodized.

The outlines of that future were soon taking shape in the files of the Downtown–Lower Manhattan Association. The first written mention of what Rockefeller's team initially called the World Trade and Finance Center appears in the Downtown–Lower Manhattan Association records on May 25, 1959, nearly two decades since the concept had made its debut at the New York World's Fair. Uncle Winthrop at this point had already left Chase, having accepted an appointment as the U.S. ambassador to Britain. But the objectives from the start sounded quite familiar. The complex would serve as a place "where the United States and foreign business and financial interests can meet to do business; where representatives of the United States and foreign governments are available for consultation and aid; and where facilities are available to expedite business transactions. Such a center might accelerate the development of international business and act as a symbol of this country's growing world leadership in the international business community," according to the initial proposal.

As the momentum built behind the scenes, Rockefeller turned to his Morningside Heights playbook and decided to commission one of those good old scientific studies—presumably detailing, in this instance, why a World Trade Center in Lower Manhattan was the rational choice. He hired McKinsey & Co., the New York consulting firm, in June 1959. But the firm quickly came up with some startling news. The World Trade Center, McKinsey & Co. had determined, could be a serious financial bust. Almost nothing about the concept—its mission or its target client base—was assured. Major corporations had already started exploiting international trade and would gain little real advantage from a World Trade Center, the firm's report said. All the necessary services were available already. There was no need to put them in one place. Perhaps most embarrassing of all to Rockefeller, the consultants reported that what made the plan an even more likely failure was the decision to build the trade center downtown. Everyone knew that the important business had relocated to Midtown. Why would anyone suffer the "personal inconvenience" of moving downtown, the report asked?

McKinsey's consultants did have a few suggestions. If the World Trade Center was going to work, it "would have to be unusual in nature and spectacular in proportions to act as an irresistible magnet to such lukewarm prospective tenants," the report said. But even then, "promotion and consummation of a project of this type would undoubtedly be a long hard pull. And there is no clear assurance at this time of complete success."

Here, at last, was a true Rockefeller moment. Uncle Winthrop may have tried to build a World Trade Center and failed, but New York City was filled with monuments to the Rockefeller ability to put steel and mortar into the ground. As Rockefeller saw it, there was only one choice. The project would go on. Rockefeller's two chief aides at the Downtown–Lower Manhattan Association—Warren T. Lindquist and William Zucker—tracked down the McKinsey consultants even before they were able to make their presentation to the executive committee, scheduled for August 11, 1959. "You better stand there and say there foursquare, we are for this, we think this is a good idea," Zucker told Gilbert H. Clee, a onetime loan officer at the World Bank who was now the partner in charge of McKinsey & Co.'s international practice and the chief author of the World Trade Center report. "There is going to be no concern. This is good. This is for the benefit of New York. And for the benefit of the economy of the area. That is what you are going to say."

In other words, Zucker would recall decades later, "we stuck a steel rod up his fanny."

The meeting went on as scheduled. McKinsey, Clee announced, would be backing out of the effort. "We have checked out the idea," Clee's final report said. "Our sample is rather small. But the unanimity of opinion is such that, in the interest of saving further time and money, we believe we should discontinue further study."

McKinsey's report would be filed in the Downtown–Lower Manhattan Association records, but never released to the public. The company would be paid $5,000, instead of the original $30,000 contract. And within two weeks, Skidmore, Owings & Merrill, the firm that had just designed Chase's new headquarters and helped draft the first phase of the Lower Manhattan plan, would be given a new contract. This time they would quickly throw together a design for a riverside complex called the World Trade Center, a sketch merely good enough to include in a brochure. This would not be anything on the scale of the World Trade Center the nation and the rest of the world would later come to know—it was, in effect, a placeholder, just another move in the game that Zeckendorf had started. It would take a government organization with vast financial resources and immense power to take the next step. Rockefeller already knew that the government organization would almost certainly be the Port of New York Authority, an entity that carried the powers of two states—New York and New Jersey—and controlled the almost limitless income from many of the area's bridges and tunnels. Rockefeller aides and Port Authority officials were soon discussing the matter in private, months before any announcements had been made. For now, the Port Authority bided its time.

With McKinsey out of the way, Lindquist, Rockefeller's personal aide, would now handle the drafting of any text. And the plan, of course, would move ahead. "Our association's program must be pushed forward as rapidly as possible," Rockefeller said during a speech before the DLMA board at its annual meeting at the Bankers Club on October 8, 1959. "I firmly believe that the next few years will witness a truly remarkable series of accomplishments in the redevelopment of this historic section of New York City."

The call went out to New York City's newspapers toward the end of January. Reporters were invited for a small get-together with David Rockefeller on January 25, 1960, at the headquarters of Seamen's Bank for Savings, run by Rockefeller's strongest downtown ally, John D. Butt. When Butt and Rockefeller entered the room, it was the much younger banker from Chase who sat down at the head of the big wooden boardroom table. In a dark suit, with a handkerchief perfectly folded in his pocket, David Rockefeller at first tried to explain the plan while seated. But his excitement got the better of him. Rockefeller rose from the leather-backed chair, throwing his hands out in front, first with clenched fists, then with open palms. The reporters scarcely looked up, they were so busy scribbling every word he said.

Although the plan would look modest in retrospect, it was no mean item for the day's news cycle, either. The proposal was for a $250 million World Trade Center complex, on 13.5 acres of land, near the site of the Fulton Fish Market on the East River. The centerpiece would be a single office tower of perhaps seventy stories, with a hotel. But there would also be a six-story international trade mart, an exhibition hall, and a securities exchange building, which Rockefeller hoped would someday house the New York Stock Exchange. All of this would be built on a three-story

World Trade Center In Maps

UNITED STATES

Area enlarged

MAINE

VERMONT

NEW HAMPSHIRE

Atlantic Ocean

NEW YORK

MASSACHUSETTS

• Boston

CONNECTICUT

RHODE ISLAND

PENNSYLVANIA

New York City
(Detail below)

NEW JERSEY

NEW YORK

0 Miles 3

BRONX

NEW JERSEY

Central Park

La Guardia Airport

MANHATTAN

(Detail below) **Lower Manhattan**

QUEENS

Kennedy International Airport

New York Harbor

BROOKLYN

STATEN ISLAND

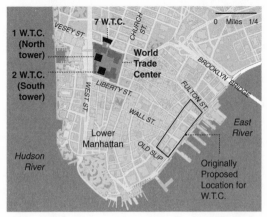

VESEY ST.

7 W.T.C.

CHURCH ST.

0 Miles 1/4

1 W.T.C.
(North tower)

World Trade Center

BROOKLYN BRIDGE

2 W.T.C.
(South tower)

LIBERTY ST.

FULTON ST.

WEST ST.

WALL ST.

East River

Lower Manhattan

OLD SLIP

Hudson River

Originally Proposed Location for W.T.C.

Source: Port Authority

The New York Times

platform that would lift the complex off the ground, giving it nice views of the river. And a theater, restaurants, and shops would line the streets.

"Today, the world stands on the brink of a boom in international trade," read the polished report that Rockefeller's staff had written, excising any hint of pessimism that McKinsey had earlier offered. "In a jet age that shrinks the globe, the exchange of new goods—much of it the product of postwar technology—promises to help raise the standard of living of the people of many nations. The challenge—and the opportunities—are immense. To realize its role in the new era dawning for overseas trade and finance, this country must marshal its resources. One primary step in this direction would be to establish a single center, planned and equipped to serve that vital purpose."

"A WORLD CENTER OF TRADE MAPPED OFF WALL STREET," proclaimed the front-page headline in the *New York Times*. The bubbly text drafted by Rockefeller's staff was printed in full. And perhaps most important, there were hints that key government powers were already on board.

Just as David had planned.

2

· · ·

Gambit

The States of New York and New Jersey, by concurrent legislation, have granted to the Port of New York Authority extraordinary powers to assist in an extraordinary task— nothing less than maintenance of the hegemony of the Port of New York in the western hemisphere.

—Justice Charles D. Breitel, Supreme Court of New York,
dissenting opinion in *Courtesy Sandwich Shop v. Port of New York Authority*

The Port Authority headquarters at 111 Eighth Avenue was built more like a fortress than an office tower. Stepped back like a ziggurat as it rose, it covered an entire city block from Eighth to Ninth Avenue and Fifteenth to Sixteenth Street. The agency had originally built its oversized floors, each fifteen feet high, not for offices but as an enormous freight terminal. The concrete of each floor was eight inches thick and reinforced with steel bars. Outside, letters four feet high proclaimed PORT OF NEW YORK AUTHORITY. The brick-faced upper floors of the building, with their setbacks and parapets, were all but invisible from that perspective, but there was no mistaking their presence: helicopters could be seen shuttling to and from a helipad, somewhere at the very top.

Two floors beneath the helipad, Austin J. Tobin, a man who held exactly the kind of power that his building radiated, gathered with his top advisers in the early months of 1960.

It was not hard to tell when Tobin, the Port Authority's executive director, was serious about a big new construction project. He would call in not only his senior managers, engineers, and lawyers but also his handpicked cadre of young lieutenants to the fifteenth floor of the head-quarters building. Today, Tobin had summoned them to talk about the World Trade Center. Although Rockefeller's proposal had generated the big headlines, it hadn't caught Tobin unawares. During extensive behind-the-scenes negotiations, he had already agreed to undertake a conceptual study of the trade center if Rockefeller's group publicly asked for one. And one of those headlines read, "Downtown Unit Led by David Rocke-feller Asks for Port Authority Study of Plan." (For obvious reasons, the full name of the Downtown–Lower Manhattan Association seldom made it into a headline.) In an indication of how far things had already progressed, one young Port Authority staffer, Richard Sullivan, over cof-fee with his boss, had learned well before Rockefeller's press conference that something big was in the works. "How would you like to head up a study on a World Trade Center?" Sullivan was asked by his boss, Roger Gilman, the director of port development. "What's a World Trade Cen-ter?" a puzzled Sullivan said. "Exactly," came the reply.

Now it was time for Tobin to let his staff know where he stood on the project. At first glance, the possibility seemed bizarre. Tobin's agency had been created in 1921 to run the regional port. So the Port Authority had built wharves and tunnels and bridges. In its role as a builder of trans-portation links throughout the port, it also controlled the airports and a big Midtown bus terminal. But office buildings? Even with the exhibition hall and trade mart and the rest, the United Nations–style complex Rockefeller had proposed would contain some 5 million square feet of space—and much of it would have to be rented to firms that merely wanted office space with a nice view of the East River. Why would the Port of New York Authority get involved in that kind of business?

The easy answer was that without the Port Authority—without its power to condemn land and secure financing with the lucrative tolls from its tunnels and bridges—there would be no World Trade Center, at least not one that cost hundreds of millions of dollars and required the bulldozing of more than thirteen acres in Lower Manhattan. Neither City Hall nor the state legislature had a shadow of a chance of raising that kind of money, and Robert Moses, with his pipeline to federal dol-lars, could never justify this as anything approaching a Title I housing project. Tobin, of course, could not give the easy answer. If he wanted to build the trade center, then he had to explain—first to his agency and then to the outside world—what gave the Port Authority the legal right to put up a huge office complex.

Tobin had figured out how to do that.

He was going to sell the World Trade Center as a port without water, a place to bring together all the people and firms who were now directing international trade and functioning as an ersatz "port" for goods and money that could be moving anywhere on the globe. And in a bow to the traditional, maritime port itself, the trade center would, as its name suggested, centralize the administration of the New York port and all the businesses involved in it, from customs agents to freight forwarders. Rockefeller and his group might have ginned up the plan to revive Lower Manhattan, foster foreign trade, and protect his bank's investment in the new headquarters building. Only Tobin had begun to conceptualize how the threads of history, politics, law, and money could be woven together to create a World Trade Center.

"The Port Authority mission always included promotion of the port," Tobin said, broaching his idea to a mostly silent group.

The World Trade Center would be located on the waterfront, and if that part of the city became an efficient place to conduct the business of world trade, Tobin added, then the port itself could not help but be promoted and protected. Then, as his people had told Rockefeller's that he would, Tobin proposed that his top staff take on a major study—the one Sullivan, of course, had already agreed to lead—so that the agency could formally determine whether the project could be done.

Patrick Falvey, a young legal aide, was among those who broke the respectful silence around the conference table. Tobin's argument struck him as dubious and hard to explain. The agency would need legislation in both states and possibly even Congress to succeed, Falvey said. Somebody was going to have to help him explain, Falvey continued, exactly how such a thing fit into the Port Authority's mandate, and how it would benefit the economy and the port.

Tobin accepted the point. He suggested adding a survey to the study to gauge interest among the business leaders who would have to accept the idea for it to have an economic impact in New York and New Jersey.

Throughout the entire meeting, Tobin had not issued a single direct order. But no one in the room could fail to appreciate several things. The Port Authority had just finished building the second deck of the George

Washington Bridge and the third tube of the Lincoln Tunnel, and was heavily involved in constructing the Verrazano-Narrows Bridge, which would be the longest suspension span in the world when it opened four years later. Tobin and his agency had outmaneuvered both Robert Moses and the city of New York for control of the three regional airports, and had already begun an acrimonious campaign to build a sprawling fourth airport, which he liked to call a jetport, in the swamplands of northern New Jersey.

Tobin had left no doubt that he considered the trade center at least as important as those battles. The World Trade Center—an idea whose journey had begun at a pavilion near the Court of Peace at the 1939 World's Fair—had landed at the Port of New York Authority, an obscure, sprawling, and complicated government agency that defied simple description.

That meant it was in the hands of Austin Tobin.

■ ■ ■

Tobin, a lawyer who had started his career by fighting, and winning, real estate cases for the Port Authority in the 1920s and '30s, regularly issued edicts that changed the shape of New York from his office in Suite 1503, its perpetually shaded windows overlooking the harbor that cradles Manhattan's southern tip like an egg-holder.

Tobin had some legitimate roots in that harbor. His grandfather William Mortimer Tobin had immigrated from County Tipperary, Ireland, and died at the age of thirty in an accident on the Brooklyn docks involving a donkey engine, one of the old steam-powered contrivances that drove winches for lifting cargo. Clarence J. Tobin, Austin's father, grew up in poverty and probably never finished grammar school, but he caught on with the man who became Brooklyn's Democratic boss, John H. McCooey, and eventually found a solid job as a stenographer at the Brooklyn Supreme Court. Clarence always said his life's greatest thrill came as the official stenographer at the 1916 Democratic National Convention in St. Louis, where Woodrow Wilson was nominated for a second term. Clarence married Katherine Moran, and Austin Joseph Tobin, the first of four boys, was born on May 25, 1903, into a well-appointed, middle-class home.

Politics was an enthusiasm that Clarence Tobin did not pass on to Austin, who had no affection for the cigar-chomping hacks at the local

Democratic clubhouses and who would strive to make his agency as free of overt patronage and financial shenanigans as possible.

But the harbor seemed to leave its mark. In the somewhat windy diction that his formal pronouncements would never quite shake, his 1925 salutatory address at Holy Cross had a historical and nautical theme, beginning with a recollection of "the startling rumor that a mad navigator, an Italian, named Columbus" had discovered the New World. His senior yearbook entry captured what would remain his two most prominent personality traits: "No half-way measures for him; do it well, or don't do it at all—with a vengeance. In fact, we would be inclined to smile at his earnestness, if he had not a wealth of genuine talent to justify his actions."

Like the two sides of a seesaw, those traits—an almost amusing earnestness backed up by blazing talent—would rise and fall and rise throughout his entire working life.

The same year, after exchanging a series of rather high-minded love letters, he married Geraldine Farley, who had also attended a Catholic high school in Brooklyn before going on to college. She became a high school English teacher and the Tobins had two children, Austin Jr. and Stacy. They lived in a house in Flatbush with a screened-in back porch where, if the weather was nice enough, Tobin would repair after dinner with the great sheaves of paper he always brought from work, even after twelve-hour days at the office. He joined the Port Authority as a law clerk in 1927, and partly on the strength of his relentless work habits, by 1935 he had risen to assistant general counsel. On July 1, 1942, he was named executive director.

Blue-eyed, compact, and icily self-confident, with a face often described as pugnacious, Tobin as an adult was said to bear some physical resemblance to Mickey Walker, the "Toy Bulldog" who had followed his career as a welterweight and middleweight prizefighting champion with stints as a bartender and nightclub singer. Tobin could be ferociously combative—a bulldog with brains—when shielding the Port Authority and its great projects from anyone who tried to stop them. But flashy he was not. He dressed with businesslike sobriety, had a plodding oratorical style, and struck his opponents as a cold autocrat when he swept into state or municipal hearings flanked by obedient aides. He never became as widely recognized as other master builders like the Rockefellers or Robert

Moses, who were far more comfortable holding forth in a room full of cameras and reporters.

Tobin's brilliance, however, emerged in what lawyers call "the cross." In his line of work, that meant dealing with the often hostile questioning by lawmakers after his latest canned promotional speech. Rather than dismiss even the most negative line of attack, Tobin would consider the substance point by point, arguing each on the merits with a steady, Jesuitical precision that seldom failed to impress—and, usually, win over—his listeners. Among his own people at the Port Authority, he was considered deeply persuasive and charming, even charismatic. And in a more polite time, when manners counted, Tobin's were so exquisite that business acquaintances would remember them decades later.

When Austin Tobin joined the Port Authority, the agency was only six years old, with a few hundred employees, no terminals or transportation links and little resemblance to the behemoth it was to become. It had been created as a quasi-independent government entity in a sort of treaty between New York and New Jersey. The arrangement was supposed to calm what Tobin would later call "ruinous competition and rivalry between the two states." The idea was to keep the entire region functioning cooperatively. The agency's charter, called the Port Compact, required that any of its major initiatives have the approval of both state legislatures. The agency quickly showed its mettle: it finessed a takeover of the Holland Tunnel in April 1930, completed its construction of the George Washington Bridge eighteen months later, and for a while seemed to be cutting a ribbon on another new tunnel or bridge every month.

Those triumphs were celebrated in a city that hungered for new transportation links across the waters that separated it from the rest of the country. The early breakthroughs were followed by years of relative stagnation, but the agency saw a volcanic revival during Tobin's reign at the top. Airports, bridges, tunnels, bus terminals—he would take them all on, just like the old days.

Then something changed. Gradually but unmistakably, New York City and the Port Authority went from partners to rivals. Increasingly, the Port Authority relied on a spectacular source of power: the ability to issue bonds. It was the same source Moses had learned to tap at his Triborough Bridge and Tunnel Authority, and one that would draw both agencies into bitter conflict with the city and the state.

Those bonds, secured by the nearly endless flood of tolls the port agency collected from its own bridges and tunnels, could finance huge new capital projects, whose revenues could support another round of bonds and further expansion of the Port Authority empire. The assurance that those tolls would continue as long as humankind scurried across the earth in automobiles made the bonds lucrative for giant investors like banks and independent financiers. Public authority bonds were the safest of all investments for those big institutional spenders—which included, of course, the Chase bank.

"Above all else," Tobin said, sounding very much like a governmental version of David Rockefeller, "the people expect their officials to give them prudent and conservative management of public funds."

To guarantee success, of course, the new projects also had to be profitable once they opened. Otherwise, the Port Authority feared, the strength of its bonds in the market could sink, imperiling the whole strategy. So, to the irritation of numerous public officials and advocates for public transportation, the agency generally shunned operations like rail mass transit that were sure to run bottomless deficits. There was surely nothing in such enterprises that a banker could call "prudent and conservative."

That stance generated widespread anger, and nowhere was the resentment deeper than in the city, the same city that had so fervently applauded the agency for its transportation successes in the early days. Because Tobin's fiscal policies were immovable, he had little choice but to stop listening to the city's complaints on the issue.

The surging amounts of power he wielded did not help the relationship. By 1960, he ran an agency with five thousand employees and more than $1 billion in freight and transportation structures. The Tobin who the public knew, or thought it knew, took an increasingly unflattering shape. Cartoonists showed him as a freebooter hacking away with his sword at ragged enemies named "N.J. transit" and "cities." Columnists ridiculed his public inaccessibility and the breadth of his powers as an unelected official, and he never quite came up with the breezy rejoinders that Moses could summon. It did not boost Tobin's public image that no one could find a public official outside the president of the United States whose annual pay topped his $60,000 salary.

And he seldom helped his cause when he stepped outside the public relations scrim so carefully maintained by his staff. When a new $30 million arrivals terminal at Idlewild (later Kennedy International) Airport opened a couple of years before anyone had heard of the trade center, onlookers found that Tobin had had it inscribed with four of the five lines from the Emma Lazarus poem immortalized on the Statue of Liberty:

Give me your tired, your poor,
Your huddled masses yearning to breathe free,
The wretched refuse of your teeming shore,
Send these, the homeless, tempest-tost to me,
I lift my lamp beside the golden door!

He had ordered that the "wretched refuse" line be expunged, presumably because he thought it sounded gauche at a modern airport terminal. "That line had meaning during the mass migrations of the nineteenth century," Tobin said when the criticism inevitably burst in his face, "but it has no meaning now. It might be offensive to the fine people of Europe—they might not regard themselves as 'wretched refuse.' " What really incensed Tobin, however, was the allegation that his omission had harmed the metrical pattern of the poem.

"I didn't think I'd be criticized for *that*," he snapped.

▪ ▪ ▪

As his yacht plied the Potomac River on November 12, 1927, President Calvin Coolidge used a golden telegraph key to trigger an electrical current two hundred miles away in New York City. Huge American flags drew aside from the entrances, in New Jersey and in Lower Manhattan, of the Holland Vehicular Tunnel. Over the first hour of its life, twenty thousand curious people walked through the 8,500-foot tunnel and 52,285 cars streamed back and forth in its first full day of regular operation. By the end of its first year, 3.5 million vehicles had passed through its twin tubes. It was a technological accomplishment that certainly merited such a grand celebration. But as it turned out, Coolidge's golden telegraph key was also sending a message—still unheard—that the days of preeminence for the storied Lower Manhattan waterfront were numbered.

From the early Dutch settlers in the seventeenth century to the first ships running freight and passengers on preset schedules between this waterfront and the great European cities in the early nineteenth century, the maritime port of New York had far outstripped its competitors in places like Boston and Philadelphia. As a result, in the three hundred years since its founding, New York had established itself as the dominant port in the United States, with an increasingly dense web of routes by rail, water, and road connecting the region to the rest of the nation.

In an era that focused so energetically on physical symbols of progress, it might seem that the growth and diversification of the regional transportation network could only be a positive development. But now, as the cars and trucks poured through this new tunnel in 1927, the only clear message was that people would find it less and less necessary to make a passage over the water to reach Manhattan. The ferry companies would suffer. And that was not all.

The ease with which vehicles could now reach Manhattan highlighted the one vital piece of the New York City transportation network that was missing. There was almost no direct way to get freight coming by rail from across the United States into or out of Manhattan. The rivers that enveloped Manhattan had turned this city into the greatest commercial emporium in the world. Suddenly, the rivers were turning the nation's largest port into a strangely isolated animal. A dozen different railroad lines had been built in the nineteenth century linking the region to the rest of the nation. The problem was that all but one of the freight lines stopped on the New Jersey shore of the Hudson. Without a tunnel dedicated to freight-carrying railroads between New York and New Jersey, an armada of barges and tugboats was required to carry the produce, merchandise, and all the other goods destined for Manhattan across the river to the Hudson River piers from the railheads in Weehawken, Hoboken, or Jersey City. On a single Monday in 1923, for example, Erie Railroad, which handled most of the fruit that came from California and other western spots, unloaded 352 rail cars sent by barge to Manhattan. Erie Railroad alone had seven hundred men involved in the lighterage operation, as it was called. It made for an electrifying sight on the river, so crowded with boats moving to and fro, their white wakes trailing behind. But it was extraordinarily expensive and laborious compared to unloading the fruit directly at a railroad spur.

With the Holland Tunnel now available to carry food by truck into New York, why couldn't that regional produce market, and the entire port for that matter, be set up in New Jersey, where the rail lines terminated, instead of Lower Manhattan? New York buyers could come across the river to get their goods, and shipping eggs and apples and milk to the other markets in the region would be far simpler if the starting point was New Jersey. Manhattan's port would shrivel, but wouldn't it be better business? Even while the Holland Tunnel was under construction, the threat had been obvious. "If you think the railroads are going to carry the tremendous cost that has been inflicted upon them in trying to deliver produce to Manhattan Island, you are going to be seriously disappointed," H. C. Snyder, general freight and passenger agent for Erie Railroad, announced in 1923 to a West Thirty-ninth Street hall filled with city port officials. "You may not like it, but the commodities are going to be delivered to you in New Jersey and not here."

City merchants were not impressed. "Some of our friends want us to go to the wilds of Jersey and dig up our commodities from the Hackensack Meadows," said a leader of the city's Fruit and Produce Association. "But we say right now that the merchant in New York is not going to relieve the railroad of bringing goods to New York. We have nothing against the railroads, but we don't propose to be the goats." For now, the Interstate Commerce Commission was on the city's side, requiring that the railroads not only continue the lighterage barge service across the Hudson, but to do it for free. As long as the lighterage came gratis, there was no economic penalty to having the regional port in Manhattan.

The challenge to Manhattan's waterfront could not be postponed forever, of course. So why not build that freight tunnel? That, as it happened, was one of the main reasons the Port of New York Authority was created in 1921. But common sense does not always prevail in New York. New York City mayor John F. Hylan advocated a route through Staten Island instead of the loop through New Jersey, Manhattan, and Brooklyn that the Port Authority backed. The railroads, despite the ruinous cost of the lighterage system, feared that a consolidated track system would wipe out any special marketing advantages they offered through their private but redundant barge systems. The merchants who controlled the loading and unloading of goods along the Manhattan piers were no big fans of the idea either. It would mean less money to be made handling and rehandling goods. The Port Authority's leaders, stymied by this intransigence, focused their attention on bridges and tunnels—which came, of course, with those lucrative tolls and the bonds that rested on them like skyscrapers upon bedrock.

Whatever the swirling mix of causes behind the failure to follow through on the reason the Port Authority was created, it was clear that the implications for the regional port—and especially Manhattan's waterfront—were potentially disastrous.

An ominous sign of change came on November 15, 1948, when a new "unloading charge" took effect, to be added to prices for produce at all the major produce piers along the Hudson in Lower Manhattan. After decades of providing free transport by barge, the railroads, facing giant financial losses, had won permission from the federal government to bill the New York wholesalers for lighterage service—transportation of the goods from where the train tracks stopped in New Jersey to the piers in New York. A box of fruit purchased in New York City at the wholesale market now would cost 23 cents more than the same box in New Jersey.

Even the most simpleminded of the fruit buyers on the pier that morning could explain the implications of this pricing change. A store owner from outside New York City would be unlikely to come across the Hudson River to buy his fruit rather than buying it more cheaply at a spot closer to his store. It was enough to provoke fruit buyers at the piers to call for an immediate strike.

"The consignee's address is given as New York City," barked William J. McCormack, the barrel-chested owner of Penn Stevedore, an outfit that employed hundreds of men who unloaded 500,000 tons a year of eggs, carrots, grapes, and other produce at the sprawling Pennsylvania Railroad piers. The freight rates, he said, were paid to that point.

A 23-cent charge might not sound like much of a threat to the world's greatest port. But it was only the latest in a string of troubles that was threatening the very existence of the city's port. Longshoremen at the close of the war had staged a series of debilitating wildcat strikes, repeatedly shutting down almost all waterborne commerce in the city. The city already boasted the highest docking and handling fees of all the major Atlantic ports. And half of the two dozen wooden finger piers in use below Canal Street in the 1950s dated to the nineteenth century. Several still featured hand-painted signs with instructions like TEAM ENTRANCE for horse-drawn wagons. The conditions at the Washington Market, the warehouselike spot at the corner of Vesey and West Streets where thousands of tons of produce were sold each week, were not much better.

"Horse and buggy facilities for the biggest perishable food market in the world," said Representative George M. Grant, an Alabama Democrat and the chairman of a House panel that was inspecting markets nationwide, in 1949. Of all the markets he had visited in the United States, Grant said, this is "probably the most antiquated, crowded and inefficient."

To waterfront bosses like McCormack, whose big fists, ready smarts, and political power had earned him the waterfront nickname of Mr. Big, the new off-loading fee threatened to edge this whole backward system toward collapse. "Drastic action or finis," McCormack wrote, in a long memo to the mayor. "The port threatens to become a relic of a bygone civilization." For the moment, the gross volume of goods moving through the city's piers was still rising, in part because of the surge of shipments to Europe after World War II. But mingling with the sweet smell of fruits and vegetables along the waterfront now was a whiff of fear that the pre-eminence of Manhattan's port could be challenged, could even come to an end if something was not done.

McCormack certainly had the credentials to offer some insight. By the age of twenty-five, McCormack had shrewdly traded up from a one-horse wagon he had run along the waterfront to a small empire of fifteen wagons and thirty horses that loaded millions of pounds worth of beef, lamb, and pork, including most of the meat being sent during World War I to the American Expeditionary Force in Europe. Now McCormack, whose large jagged scar over his left eye was about the only sign of his tough upbringing, lived in an eleven-room duplex penthouse at 1115 Fifth Avenue, not far from David Rockefeller's home. He would tour the waterfront on his fifty-one-foot harbor cruiser called *The Duke*.

McCormack saw the dangers that the port—and his power there—were facing. United Fruit had already built a giant new waterfront terminal across the Hudson River in Weehawken, New Jersey, big enough to handle its entire distribution of bananas and other goods for the region. The Erie Railroad was moving its operations from its dilapidated Hudson River pier at Manhattan's southern tip to a new location upriver. And those moves were just a small part of the story. In 1935, the regional New York port handled half of all imports and exports that passed through the seven largest Atlantic and Gulf of Mexico ports in the United States. But by 1951, that total had dropped to a third. Perhaps for the first time since Dutch traders began plying the waters around Manhattan, the Port of

New York was plummeting in importance rather than rising or at least holding its own.

McCormack was ready to offer the city a solution. It had almost a Rockefeller ring to it. The city must immediately create what McCormack called "the Supreme Court of the Port," in essence a blue-ribbon panel to come up with a detailed, point-by-point plan to reassert the port's greatness. It sounded good, but some of the other profound problems on the waterfront were about to explode into public view, and McCormack would not emerge unscathed. The New York State Crime Commission, which had been investigating waterfront corruption, listed him among those who would be called to testify at hearings early in 1953.

McCormack, his slicked-black hair now gray at the temples, flashed a smile as he strode confidently into the hearing room dressed in a dark suit. At the hearing, records submitted as evidence showed that two of McCormack's outfits employed two hundred or more men with criminal records, many of whom had been hired while they were still in prison awaiting parole. Other records showed that meat and produce slated for wholesalers instead ended up at McCormack's home. And McCormack could not explain what had happened to more than $984,908 in company funds, money the investigators implied might have been used to pay union bosses' bribes. McCormack was also pressed about gifts he had given to the International Longshoremen's Association president, who maintained a slush fund that investigators said he used to pay taxes, the burial costs for a sister-in-law, a short trip to Guatemala, and even his greens fees at a golf club.

"You have been on the waterfront for half a century now," said Theodore Kiendl, special counsel to the crime commission.

"Pretty near to it," McCormack replied.

"Were you . . . informed of the existence of extensive corruption and rampant extortion on the piers of the City of New York in connection with operations of some officials of some International Longshoremen's Association locals?" Kiendl asked.

"No sir," McCormack replied.

"Were you aware that . . . the dues paid by the longshoremen were in some instances put in the pockets of the union officials?"

"No sir."

"Did you read about that in the papers recently?"

"No sir."

"You mean you deliberately avoid reading the papers about this investigation?"

"Yes sir."

"You've been exceedingly fortunate to come from a rather humble start to the position you now occupy."

"That's right, and I always believe that I'm humble too."

"As a matter of fact, on the waterfront . . . you are Mr. Big, aren't you?"

"No sir, I am not."

McCormack, his reputation in ruins, would not be directly implicated in a crime. But the commission would determine that a string of piers from Chelsea to the Battery in Lower Manhattan, including those where McCormack's crews worked, were ruled by looters, loan sharks, and ex-cons who seemed to spend more time taking bribes and arranging no-show jobs than they did loading goods.

The spectacle was not lost on Austin Tobin, who bared his lifelong disgust with political corruption by labeling the Port of New York a "savage jungle" that could be reformed only with radical changes in the laws and regulations governing it.

"After the present shouting is over, a dozen corrupt barons of the port's business, together with some of their organized assassins, will go to jail, but will promptly be succeeded by another dozen who will wind up in the same place ten years from now," Tobin declared as the waterfront commission did its job in 1953. "This process gets us nowhere."

But there was one overwhelming irony in Tobin's attack on the decaying waterfront and the city politics that insulated it from change.

The birth of the Port of New York Authority in 1921 had coincided almost exactly with the start of an era when city waterfronts gradually slid from being unrivaled commercial powerhouses to rotting eyesores whose timbers would sometimes simply float away, posing hazards for shipping elsewhere in the harbor. Whether because of a bizarre historical juxtaposition that no one could have predicted, his agency's own priorities, or both, the Port Authority became identified with the waterfront's slide into oblivion. Even Tobin could not pass off all the problems as the fault of the city. They were also, he conceded, "a mark of the failure of the Port Authority to convince the city that it needs a modern port to keep its position as a leader in commerce."

The Port Authority did eventually build giant new marine terminals at Elizabeth and Port Newark in New Jersey, where it said the wide-open marshlands and lack of urban congestion were better suited to the new shipping technology—which relied on boxcar-size containers of goods rather than small parcels that had to be moved around the docks individually. Later, the agency would lengthen its full name to the Port Authority of New York and New Jersey to reflect its insistence on efficiently developing the regional port, whatever the particular fate of the city's.

Beyond the klatches of high-concept city planners, real estate interests, and New York banking powerhouses like the Rockefellers, those changes were greeted with bitterness—bitterness of the indelible, ineradicable, irredentist kind that few places in the democratic world outside populist New York can generate.

Like a couple whose marriage has deteriorated so far that every conversation ends in argument, the relationship between the Port Authority and the city lapsed into a silence punctuated by disputes. But in this relationship, the Port Authority had the upper hand—the state legislatures, not the city, approved its projects. And the state legislatures, not the city, gave it the power to issue bonds and condemn land in order to carry out those projects.

No matter what the city thought, the bustling, labor-intensive, history-rich port in Lower Manhattan and the businesses that relied upon it were finished as far as Tobin was concerned. It is unlikely that even Tobin could have foreseen the intensity, the emotion, and the scale of the battle he was about to unleash with a simple assertion that the three-hundred-year history of the port would have to find its future in a complex of office buildings called the World Trade Center.

■ ■ ■

When Sullivan's report on the feasibility of the World Trade Center came back, the project could not have sounded more promising. Released on March 10, 1961, the report seemed to assume it was a sure thing, being titled simply, "A World Trade Center in the Port of New York." The cover displayed a silhouette map of the world in an elegant pale olive, with little blue ships and airplanes converging on a city smack in the middle—New York. The report noted that while the volume of ocean-borne cargo passing through New York was on an upward trend, climbing to 13.1 million tons in 1959, the city's share of that cargo in the United States had fallen to a record low of 24.7 percent from 33 percent only seven years earlier. "It is thus of overwhelming importance to the metropolitan area of northern New Jersey and New York," the report asserted, "to do everything possible to maintain the preeminence of the Port of New York, to insure that increasing amounts of cargo in foreign trade continue to move through the Port."

The principal advantages of a World Trade Center, the report said, would be these:

1. Simplify and expedite the processing of administrative and procedural matters involved in arranging for the movement of export and import cargo through the Port, resulting in savings in time and money as well as improved service.

2. Centralize and improve the trade information services now located in scattered areas of the Port.

3. Provide a marketplace for United States products available for export through the Port, which would attract foreign buyers from around the world.

4. Provide an international marketplace for import products for United States buyers.

5. Establish a central location for agencies of the United States and foreign governments concerned with the Port's commerce, thereby making it possible for them to serve the world trade community more effectively.

Sullivan's report would remain a kind of founding document for the project, and its strongest, most clearly stated, and, for decades, constantly repeated rationale. All that and more, even though the trade center that would finally sprout in Manhattan bore little relation to most of those five goals.

On the physical shape of the project, Sullivan and his colleagues basically accepted Rockefeller's notion of a modest, undistinguished jumble of office buildings à la United Nations. It would include places called the "World Trade Mart," with lots of exhibition space, a "World Commerce Exchange," a "Multi-Lingual Steno Pool," a "World Trade Information Service," a hotel, and a concourse atop what appeared to be the biggest parking garage in the history of Western civilization. (Given Tobin's well-known fondness for helicopters, it was probably inevitable that one of the plan's few deviations from Rockefeller's original vision involved a heliport to be constructed on a platform over the East River.) In one of the study's most strongly worded findings, it found that Rockefeller's proposed thirteen-and-a-half-acre site on the east side, a slum-ridden stretch from Old Slip on its south boundary to Fulton Street on the north, was the ideal, almost Edenic spot for the trade center. "Various sites were found which possessed a single outstanding quality such as low cost of land or immediate access to mass transportation facilities," the report concluded. "None of these locations, however, is as well qualified in general as the proposed site. No other single site was considered to be appropriate when all of the requirements were evaluated."

If the study team uncovered any major trouble spots, they didn't find their way into the report. Somehow, the conclusions were very different from those in the secret McKinsey report, which had cast doubt on nearly every assumption that the project's planners had made. But in the new assessment by the Port Authority, mixed results from the survey of interest in the business community spurred by Falvey's skeptical questions were buried under the subheading "Survey Shows Mart Concept Feasible." Although there were sections on the geological conditions of the site and a floor-by-floor breakout of a proposed United States Custom House, there was not a word on any possible local opposition to the condemnation of a vast swath of Lower Manhattan—or indeed on potential objections by anyone at all. The trade center and its "Multi-Lingual Steno Pool" would be built in a quiet Manhattan—a planners' Manhattan. The main finding of the report could not have been clearer: "The establishment of a World Trade Center in this Port would benefit the people of the entire Port area."

The estimated cost of the World Trade Center had risen to $355 million.

Drawing the thinnest of veils over the agency's intentions, the report did not directly propose that the Port Authority build the trade center, saying only that the costs "make it probable that the project could be undertaken successfully only by a public agency."

Tobin, though, who had been flogging the project in speeches since at least the previous spring, removed even that mote of doubt. When Tobin could not speak directly without appearing to compromise the objectivity of Sullivan's study, he let his allies get the word out. During a talk at the Bankers Club in October of that year, David Rockefeller disclosed that the Port Authority had assigned twenty-eight staff members to work full-time on the study, leading reporters to unnamed Port Authority officials who said the study had already determined that the World Trade Center could be operated and financed successfully. Rockefeller made sure he mentioned the heliport in his Bankers Club talk.

One other star of political power seemed to be aligning in the trade center's favor. David's brother Nelson Rockefeller had taken over the governorship of New York in 1959. Family insiders knew that his extramarital dalliances had created severe strains in his relationship with David, and it was obvious to just about everyone that there had been powerful friction between Austin Tobin and Nelson Rockefeller almost since the moment they met. Nelson, though, would stay true to his family's tradition as builders. He decided to support the World Trade Center.

But that was not enough to push it through that other state legislature—the one Nelson Rockefeller didn't control.

■ ■ ■

The Port Authority was a creation of two states, New York and New Jersey. Both of them had to agree when it came to letting the Port Authority take on major new projects. New Jersey abruptly balked on the entire World Trade Center plan, and it appeared to die nearly as fast as Winthrop Aldrich's project had.

There was more than one reason. First, New Jersey governor Robert Meyner made the plain observation that a pile of office buildings, parking lots, and exhibition space on the east side of Manhattan did not seem to have a hell of a lot to do with New Jersey. Second, the state had just spent years coming up with an expensive plan to rescue its increasingly ineffective transit system. At the center of the plan was the rehabilitation of what was now a decrepit Hudson & Manhattan Railroad, the commuter line that ran through a pair of tubes under the Hudson River from New Jersey. Although the tubes still carried 30 million passengers a year, the line had been operating under a bankruptcy agreement since 1954 and suffered from constant service outages and a tumbledown, rat-infested physical plant. If the Port Authority was going to spend millions of dollars on new infrastructure, Meyner wanted the money to go toward saving the H&M.

Under such political pressure, the Port Authority was forced into doing another study, completely separate from the trade center discussions, on the H&M proposal. Port Authority lawyers came up with a legal formula to protect the strength of their bonds, but that did little to change the political reality that New Jersey—and only New Jersey—favored the H&M takeover, and New York—and only New York—favored the trade center. No one seemed to be able to see a way through the impasse that ensued.

Then, shortly after Sullivan's report appeared in March 1961, Nelson Rockefeller made a move that seemed certain to sink both initiatives for good.

Over objections by Tobin and the New Jersey lawmakers, Rockefeller peremptorily introduced new legislation that bundled the east side World Trade Center project and the west side H&M takeover in a single bill. Rockefeller never fully explained the reasons for his move, though the political import was more than obvious. He said the combined projects "reflect a recognition that the self-interest of each state will be advanced in a common effort in support of the great port, which is the prized asset of both states."

The echo of Tobin's reconceptualization of the port could hardly have been stronger, but that victory had little impact at the 111 Eighth Avenue headquarters. Tobin could scarcely contain himself over what he saw as the intrusion of the one thing he could not abide at his beloved Port Authority: pure politics, in the style of the Brooklyn clubhouses he had so despised as a young man. This was something that might be worthy of New York City and its waterfront, not the Port Authority. At the same time, the New Jerseyans, openly bitter over the high-handed treatment by Rockefeller, warned darkly that the region's transportation problems would only sink deeper into crisis if the H&M deal collapsed.

Months of stalemate had passed when Sullivan, remaining on a skeleton World Trade Center staff after issuing his study, got a call late in 1961 from a colleague named Sidney Schachter, who had just gotten a report on the handsome but shopworn H&M terminal buildings, twenty-two-story twin high-rises at 30 and 50 Church Street that had been the nation's largest office buildings at the turn of the century. The structures had been built in a day when there was no need to provide rest rooms for separate sexes. The elevators were out of date and the facades could have used a good cleaning. In an era long before the preservationist movement had developed traction, when an expensive gut-renovation would have seemed all but loony, Schachter said the buildings would probably have to be torn down and the terminal rebuilt from scratch if the H&M project ever went through. Fine, Sullivan said, and hung up.

The information sat idle in his thoughts for a few hours. Then a connection was made somewhere in the circuit diagram of his mind. If they would have to tear down the H&M terminal buildings anyway, Sullivan thought, why not save themselves a lot of trouble and put the World Trade Center right on top of a new train terminal? Moving the trade center from the east side to the west would mean that not only the H&M buildings but acres of the surrounding cityscape would also have to be razed. Then Sullivan remembered a neighborhood of old and what were, to him, obsolete buildings. He phoned Schachter back and asked him to scout the site.

Schachter walked through the neighborhood. He saw the old buildings that Sullivan had remembered, few of them taller than five or six stories, with a lot of discount radio and TV shops and clothes retailers and delis and luncheonettes and liquor stores and florists occupying street-level storefronts, many of the upper floors being used as storage space for inventory. Those structures filled the streets around the H&M terminal, and a few long city blocks to the west were the busy but aging ferry docks, the old wharves, the passenger piers among rutted streets and tumble-down warehouses on the Hudson River shoreline. Just to the north were the mostly abandoned remnants of the ancient Washington Produce Market. Unlike the East River site, the concentration of electronics shops, known as Radio Row, was not a slum by any definition. Nevertheless, to Schachter's eyes, here were the makings of something as large as, and maybe larger than, the east side site: no major structures would have to be demolished except the H&M terminal buildings themselves. "Yeah, I think we can do this," he said when he phoned Sullivan back.

Sullivan took the idea to his boss, Gilman, who called Tobin. "I'm sitting here with Dick Sullivan," Gilman said, "and we have something we think we ought to talk to you about." Sullivan and Schachter presented the idea to Tobin on December 8, 1961. Setting aside his carping on politics, Tobin said the west side plan had possibilities. He asked that it be investigated, but—following the usual Port Authority fashion of doing business—nothing about the possible change would be spoken to anyone outside the agency until he gave the word.

That wall of secrecy remained intact when Richard Hughes, who had succeeded Meyner in the New Jersey gubernatorial elections in November, came up to the fifteenth floor of 111 Eighth Avenue for a daylong briefing on all of the Port Authority's major projects. At the very end of the day, Tobin took him down to the Ninth Avenue side of the floor, where the offices of the staff members working on the World Trade Center were located. Sullivan presented the results of his March 1961 study and showed off a huge model of the complex that his report had sketched out as a potential architectural plan. "It's really just wonderful," Hughes said, before stating the political facts that everyone in the room knew.

"It's too bad we can't do anything with this," he said.

Tobin, of course, was ready. On his word, Sullivan took the wraps off the plan to combine the World Trade Center and H&M projects on the west side of Manhattan. Hughes listened through to the end of the presentation.

"Austin," Hughes said when Sullivan had finished, "I think I can sell that plan."

That is exactly what he did. A few days later he was already in the newspapers with his pitch for the west side site. His words were perhaps the clearest public indication anyone would give that politics, in a kind of portage across Manhattan, had managed to move the trade center.

"The World Trade Center would not face away from New Jersey," Hughes said. "It would face toward New Jersey."

As Hughes worked on the New Jersey legislature, David Rockefeller was the first to say publicly that the switch from his original site was fine with him and his businessmen's organization. "To me personally the new plan seems to offer a number of attractive advantages," Rockefeller said on December 22, 1961, the day the Port Authority suddenly made the switch public. His endorsement helped the authority wash down the crow it had to eat after zeroing in on the east side site as the one, the only perfect spot for the trade center. (Today it is the site of the South Street Seaport.) The Port Authority and its public relations specialist, Lee Jaffe, again chose to echo Rockefeller almost exactly, sending a January 29 memo to the New Jersey lawmakers on the switch that said, "The proposal for the combined project has a number of distinct advantages over the earlier separate proposals."

To emphasize what he hoped would be a complete makeover in the image of the other component of the deal on the west side, the H&M

railroad, Tobin assigned a staff member to find a new name for it. The staffer first worked up an acronym with what he hoped were nurturing overtones: MOTHER, for Manhattan Operating Trans-Hudson Electric Railway. Somehow, that didn't seem right, even for a project this big— the estimated cost of the combined project had now risen to $450 million—and the name that stuck was PATH, for Port Authority Trans-Hudson railway.

Hughes called the H&M railroad "a desperate case" and used its condition as part of his ammunition in pushing the package deal through. "You might liken it to an artery in your body," he said. "You have to keep it going and it has to have immediate medicine."

Then there was New York mayor Robert F. Wagner to deal with. He found out about the west side relocation only by reading the *Newark Evening News*. Afterward he phoned Tobin to express his "very strong displeasure." A few months later, he was hardly even consulted when Tobin, Hughes, Nelson Rockefeller, and the state legislatures worked out the plan on tax abatements, condemnations, street changes, and traffic control to be included in the bill for the west side project.

"It is astounding to me," Wagner said angrily, "that New York City, which is the major unit of government involved and affected by this legislation—fiscally, economically and socially—should not have been at the center of negotiations and deliberations and its interests given paramount consideration."

The city had been treated "as an outsider rather than a central figure" in the negotiations, the mayor said.

It was a fine civics lesson, but it didn't matter very much to anyone at the Port Authority. Tobin told his commissioners that it was "a rather foolish and petulant statement" and was basically a lie. "The statement was foolish because it was not founded on fact and the true facts were well known not only to Governor Rockefeller's office but also to the press," Tobin said.

Tobin had the last laugh on Wagner, who would leave office in 1965, after Tobin negotiated a deal on payments to the city, "in lieu of taxes," that was soon derided as a steal. Because the Port Authority did not have to pay taxes, the only way the city could recoup its lost revenue was by working out the side deal. And because the city did not control the condemnations, its only real leverage consisted of the streets that passed through the trade center site. The city owned those streets, and they would have to be rubbed out and absorbed into the big complex of buildings, whose layout ignored the street grid. Although it was a modest card in the city's hand, it was one whose value Wagner either did not fully understand or did not have the stomach to lay on the table.

• • •

Then, secretly, the World Trade Center got bigger.

Tobin would never publicly explain just when he decided to sweep beyond the already huge proposal by David Rockefeller and his Downtown–Lower Manhattan Association for a trade center with 5 to 6 million square feet of floor space. The Pentagon was the world's largest building in terms of office space, with about 6 million square feet devoted to that purpose alone. By the time Sullivan's report came out, the World Trade Center was conceived as being at least as large as the Pentagon, but—as the relatively modest buildings in the architectural plan made obvious—that figure was somewhat deceptive. If the multistory pedestal containing parking and concourses and retail zones and other spaces were built over a sixteen-acre site, it could account for a large proportion of the space by itself. There were areas elsewhere in the complex for nonoffice uses like exhibition space, a securities exchange, another hotel.

It was only after Tobin's staff had studied the site in detail that he decided the first phase of the project alone would contain 10 million square feet. Fearing criticism, the Port Authority kept its decision largely to itself. The secret was so closely held that the city's powerful real estate barons, whose holdings would surely be affected by the sudden creation of that much new space, said little or nothing publicly about their stance on the project.

The city that Tobin had chosen as the Cape Canaveral of his NASA-like project was oblivious to its magnitude.

The secrecy amounted to no more than what had become the Port Authority's standard operating procedure with the city. But that still left the mystery of why Tobin decided to push the project to such a gigantic scale in the first place. What justifications were powerful enough for Tobin to accept the new risks—in a dozen different political, fiscal, legal, technical, and cultural dimensions—that would surely come with a venture into unprecedented enormousness?

His central motive was straightforward: Port Authority revenues were skyrocketing toward $200 million and its mounting surpluses totaled $37 million in 1956, $65 million in 1958, and $79 million in 1960. The pressure to spend that money on mass transit was rising terrifically, to the point where it could quickly become a chaotic and disruptive force if not tamed. As the Port Authority's surpluses continued to rise, there was not much chance that calls to spend the money on mass transit would do anything but become more intense. A giant World Trade Center would let Tobin invest those surpluses in something other than the mass transit that he saw as a dangerous fiscal sinkhole.

For the first time in its existence, the agency had actually been forced to take on a deficit-heavy rail transit operation. That had been the price of getting a trade center in the first place. But the anticipation of those perpetual losses had the effect of ratcheting even higher the Port Authority's need to make money elsewhere. A big, profitable World Trade Center, with as much rentable space as Tobin could squeeze in, would ensure that his agency got the most out of its side of the almost Faustian bargain it had been persuaded to strike.

▪ ▪ ▪

When the legislative politics had finally been worked out and the H&M–World Trade Center bill had passed in both states, Tobin and his staff, starting at the terminal in Manhattan, took a midnight ride through the H&M tubes to inspect the state of the equipment, what they called a searchlight tour. The cars were unbearably hot. They stank. They rocked and wobbled and screeched as if hordes of dead commuters had swarmed from the bowels of the earth to keen over the lifetimes they had wasted on train delays between New York and New Jersey.

And when the doors opened in Jersey City and Tobin stepped onto the platform, there was a scrofulous old drunk sleeping on a bench in front of him. He rolled over, waved at Tobin, and went back to sleep.

For Tobin, it seemed to confirm all his doubts about the railroad he had just agreed to take over. He might also have taken it as an omen that the troubles his World Trade Center had given him were about to get worse.

3

. . .

Street Fighters

Shaping up in New York City is a legal battle of overriding importance. Its outcome will conceivably affect us all. If the considerable power of the Port Authority is allowed to dispossess the merchants of Radio Row, then, it is our conviction, no home or business is safe from the caprice of government.

—Sam Slate, WCBS Radio, October 4, 1962

Oscar Nadel was in Florida when he got the phone call from the owner of a tiny luncheonette on Cortlandt Street in the first weeks of 1962. The only time Nadel, who owned Oscar's Radio Shop at 63 Cortlandt and Oscar's Radio & TV around the corner at 176 Greenwich, could get away for a vacation was just after the Christmas shopping season. When the neighbors on his tidy street in Queens started disappearing on summer getaways, his shops on the west side of Lower Manhattan were busy with customers who wanted portable radios for their trips to the beach, marine radios for their boats, and nice TV consoles for their living room spruce-ups. Ham radio operators would drive in from all over the Northeast to pick up obscure items like goniometers and rheostats. Sometimes European travelers would walk over from the west side piers, where the summer cruise ships docked, clutching a piece of paper with Oscar Nadel's name scrawled across it. That usually meant a friend had visited Radio Row and met the smiling, bantering, sharply dressed man who brimmed over with such confidence that he could sell anything with a price tag dangling from it. Every now and then, tourists and the sailors from their ships would show up at Radio Row in huge groups and jam one electronics store after another. When that happened,

Nadel's wife, Rae, and his oldest daughter, Leatrice, would come over to help the clerks with the registers.

So Nadel would wait until after the holiday sales and go to Florida with Rae, always by train, always arranging to meet up with the same four or five couples they vacationed with every year. But the owner of the lunch-eonette who had found him down there was not just urgent—he was beside himself. Not many merchants had taken notice when the Port Authority announced on December 22, 1961, the Friday before a Christmas weekend, that it was thinking about moving the World Trade Center to the west side. The stories came out on a Saturday, the biggest business day on Radio Row. Besides, once word got around, no one was too worried—politicians could argue over things like that for years. But the Port Author-ity was talking about condemning land right away. It was on front pages and all the news programs. Engineers had been showing up on Radio Row with tools to test the ground. George Kallimanis, who owned a grocery two blocks north of Oscar's Radio & TV, asked one of the engineers what was going on. As George told the story, the engineer said, "Buster, once the leg-islation is passed, you're going to be out of here in six months." Nadel, fifty-six, was president of the Downtown West Businessmen's Association. He had opened his first Oscar's Radio a block west of Greenwich Street in 1925, a year before TV was invented. Could he do something?

Oscar and Rae Nadel caught the *Silver Meteor* back to New York, phon-ing ahead to ask Leatrice to pick them up at Penn Station. She drove from Queens in his big Buick and asked what was wrong.

"There's problems with the store," Oscar said.

"Can I go down to help?"

"No."

When they got home, Leatrice heard her parents in some sort of intense discussion, and then Oscar began phoning some of the men who owned businesses near his. Oscar and his family lived in Laurelton, Queens, just west of the Nassau County border on Long Island, in a com-fortable, two-story Spanish-style stucco that did not particularly stand out from the dozens of other comfortable, two-story Spanish-style stuccos in Laurelton. Theirs had a cozy finished basement, a big apple tree in the backyard, and a detached garage with a grape arbor built along one side. It was a tranquil suburban landscape—even if things did get a little hectic in August and September, when everyone was borrowing grapes from the arbor to make jam and jelly. But now a fissure had opened up in that placid landscape. Oscar finished his phone calls, slammed the door on his Buick, and drove to Lower Manhattan.

Soon the handbills went up around Radio Row.

"RALLY—ALL WELCOME!!! GET THE ANSWERS TO YOUR QUESTIONS—PAGE ONE RESTAURANT, 112 GREENWICH STREET . . . *FOOD WILL BE SERVED*—DOWNTOWN WEST SMALL BUSINESS SURVIVAL COMMITTEE."

As humble as those handbills were, they were harbingers of a series of new fights that, no less than the political wrestling match with New Jersey, would challenge the World Trade Center's existence and change its form forever. A new era of protest, and a budding new understanding of what truly made cities vibrant, healthy, and profitable, it turned out, was about to catch the once all-powerful Port Authority completely off guard.

The Radio Row protests would do more, serving as a catalyst that helped draw some of the city's most powerful real estate interests into the fight against the trade center. Even the city's political leaders, usually so overmatched by the Port Authority, would eventually freeze the project in its tracks and set in motion a new series of events that would resonate through city history.

On Radio Row, now that the scale and breakneck schedule of the Port Authority's plans had become clear, the handbills drew packed meetings.

The scale of the condemnations the agency was planning took awhile to sink in. The Port Authority had at first insisted that beyond the twin Hudson terminal buildings, which filled up parts of two city blocks, it would have to condemn only seven more blocks—and one of those was just an acre of parking lots where the Washington Market had once been. Although that was a vast expanse in a densely built city, it did spare the southern fringe of Radio Row. By the end of January 1961, Lee Jaffe, the powerful and mercurial public relations chief at the Port Authority, was circulating a map with a boundary that engulfed another block to the north and parts of three more blocks just south of Cortlandt. Clearly, the mysterious expansion of the World Trade Center was already taking place somewhere behind the scenes. With no formal announcement, the boundary crept southward again and the rest of those three partly covered blocks had been corralled into the plan. It became a full thirteen blocks,

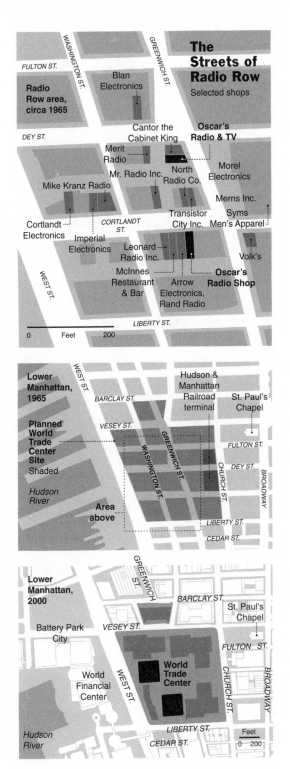

The Streets of Radio Row

Selected shops

Radio Row area, circa 1965

FULTON ST.

WASHINGTON ST.

GREENWICH ST.

Blan Electronics

Radio Row area, circa 1965

DEY ST.

Cantor the Cabinet King

Oscar's Radio & TV

Merit Radio

Mr. Radio Inc.

North Radio Co.

Morel Electronics

Mike Kranz Radio

Merns Inc.

Cortlandt Electronics

CORTLANDT ST.

Transistor City Inc.

Syms Men's Apparel

Imperial Electronics

Leonard Radio Inc.

WEST ST.

McInnes Restaurant & Bar

Arrow Electronics, Rand Radio

Oscar's Radio Shop

Volk's

LIBERTY ST.

0   Feet   200

Lower Manhattan, 1965

WEST ST.

BARCLAY ST.

Hudson & Manhattan Railroad terminal

St. Paul's Chapel

Planned World Trade Center Site
Shaded

VESEY ST.

GREENWICH ST.

WASHINGTON ST.

FULTON ST.

DEY ST.

CHURCH ST.

BROADWAY

Hudson River

Area above

LIBERTY ST.

CEDAR ST.

Lower Manhattan, 2000

GREENWICH ST.

BARCLAY ST.

St. Paul's Chapel

Battery Park City

VESEY ST.

FULTON ST.

World Financial Center

WEST ST.

World Trade Center

CHURCH ST.

BROADWAY

Hudson River

LIBERTY ST.

CEDAR ST.

Feet
0   200

Sources: Frontier News; World-Telegram & Sun   The New York Times

or sixteen acres, amounting to a 50 percent growth in what architects blandly called the "footprint."

After the first expansion, and just after Governors Rockefeller and Hughes signed the bill authorizing the World Trade Center on March 27, 1962, the Port Authority unveiled a detailed architectural model of the west side site. No one was wowed by the proposed structures themselves. The east side concept—the one that Richard Sullivan had shown Governor Hughes that day at 111 Eighth Avenue—had essentially been moved over and dropped on the west side. There was still the epic concourse/parking-garage hybrid that functioned as a pedestal for a UN–style complex; the tallest building, around seventy stories high, still dominated a series of stubbier boxes and cylinders. But the agency cautioned that these were still preliminary designs and that architectural changes could be made in the project, whose estimated cost now stood at $470 million.

No one quite put the site expansion together with the warnings on possible changes in the architecture, but the Port Authority, after operating within its usual cloak of secrecy, would eventually connect the dots in a way no one would miss. In any case, what was apparent from the Port Authority maps was that the "footprint" on the west side of Lower Manhattan would now run from Church Street on the east all the way to the Hudson River and be bounded by Vesey Street on the north and Liberty Street on the south, with a corklike extension on the northern edge reaching all the way to Barclay Street.

The block-wide cork, fashioned out of a boundary drawn to miss the twenty-nine-story New York Telephone Company building to its west and the fifteen-story Federal Building to its east, was the only blemish in the otherwise perfect trapezoid the Port Authority planners had marked out for their pièce de résistance. The streets that would be severed and partly erased by the final version of the site were Washington, West Broadway, Fulton, Dey, Cortlandt, and Greenwich—an urban web that the Port Authority intended to raze along with all the buildings. Out of his Downtown West Businessmen's Association, Nadel carved a "survival committee" that reflected the human and mercantile diversity of those sixteen acres. Early on, he heard Jane Jacobs, whose *Death and Life of Great American Cities* had just been published, speak against the trade center; her vision of a healthy metropolis as a multitude of small-scale interactions meshed perfectly with what Nadel was trying to defend. Working almost in another solar system from the big-think city planners, Jacobs could write a chapter on "the uses of sidewalks: contact" and explain how sidewalk merchants and "well-recognized roving public characters" can help to anchor a neighborhood. "Lowly, unpurposeful and random as they may appear, sidewalk contacts are the small change from which a city's wealth of public life may grow," Jacobs wrote.

Those were the sidewalks to be lost under the record-setting parking garage and the unremarkable buildings scattered atop it like giant freight containers on a pier, and Nadel gave every sign that he picked his committee at least partly with an eye toward ramming home those very principles. There was Kallimanis, a train enthusiast whose shop depended on night business from the Wall Street back offices and the post office in the Federal Building, who could be seen patrolling the streets during the day in his grocer's whites, drumming up contributions door-to-door for the expected legal fight while obsessively scanning for bargains on scale-model locomotives. There were the brothers Sy Syms and George Merns, both of whom owned small clothing stores less than a block apart. Syms—who had gone so far as to change his name so that his shop would not have the same name as his brother's—would stand outside his shop on Cortlandt Street shouting protest slogans through a bullhorn. There was Sam Osman, a former Lower East Side pushcart vendor whose Job Lot Trading emporium did a staggering amount of business at 41 Vesey Street.

Lowly, unpurposeful, and random indeed.

Nadel and his committee estimated that 30,000 people worked in more than a thousand lofts and offices and four hundred street-level stores and generated $300 million of business in the area the Port Authority wanted to raze. The City Planning Commission, at a time when it supported the World Trade Center project, would estimate the total at 17,200 people employed on the site in 1958, a number that did not fully account for the offices in the immense terminal buildings and probably left out others whose livelihoods depended on the area as well. (There were more than 100 people who lived on the site, mainly in apartments on the southeast edge.) Unprepared for the assault, the Port Authority could only vaguely dispute Nadel's numbers, saying they were far too high, and it made a fumbling attempt to contain the damage by claiming, three weeks after the model had been unveiled, that the area to be condemned would probably stop at Cortlandt Street after all. In fact, Tobin's expansion would cover the full thirteen blocks and sixteen acres.

Whatever the correct population figures, most of the private businesses were leasing their space, and the Port Authority angered them further by setting an upper limit of $3,000 on the compensation they might receive for leaving. The limit was to hold no matter how long a business had been there, no matter how lucrative its franchise on Radio Row—the elusive quality that business people call "goodwill"—and no matter how large its outstanding loans. Even Kallimanis, whose father owned the land that his store sat on, said that the condemnation money would do little more than pay off the mortgage—a calamity in the days before 401(k)s, when people counted on income from modest real estate investments for their retirement.

Oscar Nadel, with his makeshift handbills and local rallies, had fired his first volley against the Port Authority, and he had hit home. The newspapers and radio and TV stations, usually handled so smoothly by Lee Jaffe from 111 Eighth Avenue, smelled a big story.

"We intend to fight," Nadel told the *New York Times* in April 1962. "This is not some foreign country where the government can come in and just take a man's business. This is a worldwide center for electronics for the home, and now they are going to destroy it so that the real estate interests can take over."

He also turned to the media he understood in his bones: radio and TV.

"The Port Authority has a Compact, has the right to build what they were supposed to build," Nadel said on the *Casper Citron* program, a popular talk show that ran on WRFM in New York. "Let them stay out of private enterprise and let private enterprise take care of itself."

Each of those statements comprised an uncomplicated series of ideas, a simple chain of sentences, but they revealed why Austin Tobin and the Port Authority were about to encounter a force that was capable of stopping the World Trade Center project. First, Tobin just didn't come across in the media the way Nadel did. Nadel, who had left school at fourteen to work as a bicycle repairman and short-order cook so that he could save enough to open his first radio shop, did not have anything approaching the Holy Cross grad's polish. Now and then, especially at the fund-raisers he was eventually forced to lead, Nadel got so worked up that he sounded like Ralph Kramden yelling at Ed Norton. But he could stand in front of any crowd and toss off fiery, rapid, amusing, and occasionally insulting phrases for hours. Despite Tobin's college-educated suavity, and despite all the coaching Jaffe and his administrative staff gave him, the fact was that Tobin would seldom utter three consecutive, off-the-cuff sentences that a newspaper could quote or a talk-show host would want to put on the air. In a battle that would be fought largely in the public realm, Tobin's inability to adapt his counterpunching, cross-examining style to the media would burn the Port Authority.

And if Nadel's taunting choice of the term *worldwide center* for Radio Row was justified, and something like World Trade Centers could emerge through raw, unguided private enterprise anywhere in New York, then why did the Port Authority need to wipe them out and create an artificial version of the same thing? It might not prime the international trading markets, but Nadel himself was already selling Sonys and Blaupunkts alongside his RCA Victors and Sylvanias; places like World Happiness and American Machine Tool Export, inside the north terminal building, were moving products around the world; and Walter Nussbaum, one of the original merchants on Radio Row, was selling cut-rate German wine at $1.09 a bottle. ("When Low in Spirits" was the slogan at Nussbaum's.)

With obvious exasperation, Nadel wrote a typewritten manifesto, yet another medium he used to get the word out, that "the whole of New York City is a World Trade Center. . . . The idea of 'centralization' of the mainstream of Port commerce is ridiculous and impossible because practically every business conducted in New York City is in one way or another connected with world trade."

Nadel wrote in the same wounded tones that while government had the right to condemn land and everything upon it for legitimate public use, "to appropriate a man's home or business for a public purpose is not something to be lightly undertaken." The west side project did not meet that test, he said, because it existed "to enable the Port Authority to support the Hudson and Manhattan Railroad through the revenue to be derived by the Port Authority from the massive real estate complex. . . . For the sake of legitimizing the 'deal,' it has dubbed its project a 'World Trade Center.'"

Public purpose. Those were the arrowhead-sharp words that had the potential to tear apart the legal wall between the World Trade Center and H&M projects and bring both of them down at once. The Port Authority could wield the states' overwhelming powers of eminent domain to condemn land for the George Washington Bridge or the big container facility in Port Elizabeth. But to create millions of square feet of office space? Tobin had devised a brilliant formulation of the trade center as an ersatz port, but in view of the way that international commerce was changing around him at light speed, would it have practical meaning if challenged in court? If it did not, the trade center was not a public purpose in any traditional sense, and the project could be declared unconstitutional.

And if the trade center were declared unconstitutional, the entire bill would become invalid, because of a provision inserted to make sure that only a unified project—with the obvious benefits on both sides of the Hudson—could be carried out. Disprove "public purpose" and it would all fall down.

Up on the fifteenth floor of 111 Eighth Avenue, aides saw the first real flicker of concern on Austin Tobin's face when he learned that Oscar Nadel had gone out and hired Morris Ernst, the civil liberties lawyer at Greenbaum, Wolff & Ernst who was famous for having represented Margaret Sanger in her efforts to legalize birth control and for having won the case in 1933 that opened the door for James Joyce's *Ulysses* to be published in the United States. He was also a prolific author, and in his book *Too Big*, he had recounted, twenty years before the trade center fight, how the writings of United States Supreme Court justice Louis D. Brandeis had made him aware that in business and government, "oversize carried within itself the seeds of its own destruction." While great size was not inherently evil, Ernst wrote, "it nonetheless carries within itself great forces for evil."

The two fighters, Ernst and Nadel, operating on entirely different intellectual planes, shared what was basically a small-scale, retail view of the human cosmos. Nadel could hardly stop talking about his luck in landing Ernst as a lawyer for the cause.

True to his reputation as a firebrand, Ernst rallied his new clients on a Thursday night in the spring of 1962, when about three hundred businessmen, employees, and property owners on Radio Row showed up for a meeting in Academy Hall, near Union Square. ("Transportation will be provided from Greenwich & Fulton Streets," the handbills announcing the meeting said prosaically.) Ernst told the chanting, shouting crowd that he had been "laughed out" of Austin Tobin's office when he suggested an informal conference to discuss the merits of the World Trade Center. Ernst said the trade center constituted "the first wholesale attack on free enterprise in the history of this country."

Whatever the actual scene in Tobin's office—as usual, Tobin made no public response, although he wrote, with his stiffest bureaucratic disdain, that Ernst had sympathetically used the words *little shnooks* to describe the merchants—Ernst had no intention of wasting the public relations victories that Nadel and the merchants had been scoring. He swiftly filed a complaint against the project in the New York State courts and asked for a temporary injunction to block the condemnations from proceeding until the court case had been decided. The main grounds for the complaints were that the project would wipe out the merchants' livelihoods and that the legislation was unconstitutional because the prime motivation of the World Trade Center was to profit from its millions of square feet of real estate. "The project is primarily for a private purpose and not a public purpose," said the press release on the action sent out by Mortimer Matz Associates, the firm that Nadel, who deeply despised the Port Authority public relations machine but also understood its power, had hired as a kind of anti-Jaffe. "Eminent domain is being used to displace one group of businessmen by others," the Matz release asserted.

The case, played up big in the papers, couldn't have had a better designation when it came to garnering further sympathy for the plaintiffs' cause: it was called *Courtesy Sandwich Shop v. Port of New York Authority*, after a small business in the Hudson terminal buildings, just one among the haberdasheries, luncheonettes, bar and grills, and electronics, flower, and coffee shops that were taking on the governmental giant.

In the Port Authority's initial response to the attacks on its project, Sidney Goldstein, the agency's general counsel, struck a dismissive, almost arrogant note in the brief he filed against the motion for an injunction. After both governors had signed the legislation and an architectural model, ten feet long, sat in a room near Tobin's office, Goldstein argued that the World Trade Center "is so far from realization and contingent upon so many events which may or may not occur that it cannot truly be said that this is an imminent threat."

After all, Goldstein argued, why should the merchants worry when "they concede that they have been assured continued occupancy until the fall of 1963"?

That was not the most diplomatic possible note to strike at the outset of what, it was already obvious, would be at least an emotional campaign to move the tenants out of the area.

But in practical terms, did it really matter? This fight was like so many others that Tobin, the legal department, and the entire agency with its allies had been in. Look at the Verrazano-Narrows Bridge. Eight hundred buildings would be destroyed in Bay Ridge, Brooklyn, and seven thousand people would have to move. In 1959, when the project was announced, it seemed as if every one of them protested, screamed to the press, filed lawsuits, posted handbills, joined the "Save Bay Ridge" committee. That fight was already over—they had been either cowed or convinced by Robert Moses and the Port Authority, and the bridge was on schedule to be finished by 1964. Almost four hundred families had refused to abandon their apartments back in 1948 when the Port Authority wanted to build a vast new bus terminal in Midtown Manhattan. The construction crews started knocking down buildings around the holdouts, the Port Authority offered a choice of cash payments or vacant apartments elsewhere, and everyone was gone by 1949. Moses had leveled the houses and businesses in the way of the Cross-Bronx Expressway, his parkways on Long Island, his "slum clearance" projects all over the city.

Consider Morningside Heights. The committee there had been called Save Our Homes. The same sorts of handbills, legal challenges, and protests were thrown in the path of David Rockefeller and Robert Moses. But Rockefeller and Moses had announced their plan in 1951, and three noisy years later they were watching the president of Barnard College swing a crowbar to start the demolition. The tradition of getting unhappy citizens out of the path of huge progressive projects went all the way back to Baron Haussmann, who smashed the great boulevards through the densely packed streets of old Paris in the nineteenth century. What reason was there to think that Oscar Nadel and his band could be any different?

In reality, there were good reasons to think that this fight could be different, even if few people recognized them. Hints were already appearing for any who were disposed to see them. Jane Jacobs and her allies were fighting a battle to stop a $100 million highway, called the Lower Manhattan Expressway, from hacking through the neighborhood. Jacobs and her allies would, after almost a decade of struggle, kill the expressway, even though it was backed by Moses, Tobin, and David Rockefeller (and of course the Automobile Club of New York). The details were to be found in the specific form of the protests and the legal maneuvering, but the ultimate reason for their victory was that cities were about to change. They would become open to the ideas in Jacobs's book. Call the people of the tiny neighborhoods and small-scale streetscapes "little shnooks," call them "well-recognized roving public characters"—cities would begin weighing the fiscal advantages of huge public projects against all those less grandiose people and things to be cleared out. And many of those projects would collapse, in David-and-Goliath struggles.

If someone could have looked down from the sky on Lower Manhattan as if viewing the most complicated board game ever devised, this observer might have come up with one very simple question: Was the World Trade Center fight taking place in the centuries-old urban world that was about to end, or in the one that was just now being born?

In fact, it would fall into a bottomless chasm between them.

▪ ▪ ▪

"The Receptrad Radio cannot fail you," the stylish ad declared in the *New York Times* in 1925. "**Using No Batteries** the Receptrad Multiflex has behind it the certainty and tremendous power of the central station. **Directly Connected to Lamp Socket or Base Plug** it operates on direct current at a cost of less than a quarter of a cent per hour." Price: $125. In small type at the bottom of the ad, within a list of businesses that carried the product, the following words appeared:

"Oscar's Radio Shop, 172 Washington St."

If Austin Tobin was the toy bulldog that fought for the Port Authority and defined what it stood for during almost its entire history, forging a relationship so close that their identities were nearly inseparable, Oscar Nadel was a bantam rooster that strutted along Cortlandt Street and had the same relationship to Radio Row. Nadel was just two years younger than Tobin and, at five-seven or five-eight and no more than 150 pounds soaking wet, probably the trimmer of the two, tennis being his main passion outside his work in Manhattan and his favorite charity, the Laurelton Jewish Center. And now these two indomitable, supremely self-confident men were on a collision course along with everything they represented.

Nadel's parents, Eastern European Jews, immigrated to the United

States when Oscar was a toddler and moved to the Lower East Side. As Oscar always told the story—and no one was ever quite sure if he was joking or not—he was working on a cheap crystal radio set at home one day when it crackled to life and picked up a station somewhere. "Black magic, black magic," his father said, shaking his head. Oscar knew he had found his profession.

He left school and saved the money he made from repairing bikes, rigging outdoor antennas, and even selling peanuts on the street. Within a year he had saved $1,500, and he was soon operating his first shop out of a tiny storefront. In February 1925, as Tobin was preparing to graduate from Holy Cross, the ad for the fancy new Receptrad Radio appeared with the address of Nadel's tiny storefront at 172 Washington Street, a block east of the Hudson piers. The radio was, the ad said, not only "simply controlled" and "sharply selective" but also "superb in tone." Within a couple of years he had moved to a larger space at 176 Greenwich Street.

Oscar Nadel was in business.

For reasons no one could quite explain, shops that specialized in the mysterious new technology of radio had begun collecting on the west side of Lower Manhattan along Cortlandt, Dey, Greenwich, Fulton, and Church Streets around 1920, when Nadel started knocking about in the area. A 1924 photo shows a poised Harry L. Schneck, a partner in one of the original shops, standing on a Cortlandt Street sidewalk in a gray suit. Schneck commands the attention of at least two dozen curious men as he adjusts a dial on a five-foot-high, wood-paneled—and very, very sweet—RCA Radiola Super VIII. By 1930, the immediate area, already known as Radio Row, was virtually solid with radio shops between Greenwich Street and the river, with more of them radiating out to the north and east.

And what an area it was, especially in its sounds. A walk down the streets presented a constantly shifting cacophony, as most of the shop owners had mounted big cone-shaped vibrating speakers over their doorways, blasting out everything from the teariest opera to big-band orchestral music to step-right-up sales pitches that ran over and over. Piercing through all that noise was the *a-ooga* of car horns on the street, the whistle of the ferries that docked in the slips right at the foot of Cortlandt Street, and the much deeper bellow from the tugboats plying the river. There was the occasional clop of horses—in the late 1920s there were still a few horse-drawn drays moving small loads of cargo or scrapwood, and they could be seen negotiating the widest of U-turns at the Cortlandt intersections. Of course, the TEAM ENTRANCE signs on the docks told them where to go.

In one of those chance juxtapositions that looked almost like a metropolis trying to be witty—and succeeding—Radio Row, with its futuristic wares, clustered in the blocks around Cortlandt and Greenwich Streets, had taken shape just east of the old Hudson River cargo piers. The radio merchants were just the latest wave of entrepreneurs to call this site home. Since the mid-nineteenth century, the neighborhood had been a beehive of commerce, where all kinds of luxury goods, novelties, consumer products, and even a mix of industrial goods were sold. A hundred years earlier, just along the four blocks of Cortlandt Street could be found more than 130 different stores, nine hotels, and at least three barbers.

The popularity of the spot for shopping was no accident, and the source of Radio Row's prosperity lay in its mass transit links. Over the decades, the area had become a tight nexus of transportation links by rail and water, and—if the height of an elevated train is dramatized with a dash of artistic license—by air.

By the mid-1800s the area was already so popular as a stop for the Hudson ferries—the slips sat right at the foot of Cortlandt Street—that when the world's first elevated railway opened in Manhattan, it ran from the southern tip of the island to the corner of Cortlandt and Greenwich. "The car ran evenly from the Battery to Cortlandt Street," the *New York Times* reported on July 4, 1868, after a trial run, "starting at the rate of five miles an hour, and increasing to a speed of ten miles." As technology improved and the speeds increased, the "El" was extended along Ninth Avenue all the way to 155th Street. The El station at the Cortlandt Street stop, with its pitched roofs and filigrees of painted steel, stood like a little Bavarian ski lodge above the street and helped give the place the feel of an enclosed bazaar.

In 1909, the marvel of the Hudson Tubes—the commuter rail tunnels from New Jersey that would one day be renamed PATH—began spilling people onto the streets from the big terminal buildings a block east of Greenwich Street. "Three minutes from Broadway," the signs all over Jersey City boasted like lunatic ravings. Sure enough, after the first train left the station on July 19, 1909, the only dispute among the passengers was whether the trip had taken two minutes, forty seconds, or two minutes, forty-five seconds. The Hudson Tubes traversed the river under the ferry route; once they reached the island, the inbound tube burrowed directly beneath Cortlandt Street, and the outbound one beneath Fulton Street; they met, of course, under the twin Hudson terminal buildings. The dense transit nexus was completed in 1918 with the Seventh Avenue subway, which ran beneath Greenwich Street and had its own Cortlandt Street stop.

The commercial implications of all those commuters were not hard to fathom: in 1930, 39 million pedestrians used the Hudson River ferries; 110 million people rode through the Hudson Tubes; 2.1 billion people used the city's subways and elevated trains overall.

Whatever the reasons, as skyscrapers shot up in all directions around this cauldron of commercial activity, the roofline in Radio Row remained rather low and humble by comparison. But in the shadow of those sequoia-like buildings, Oscar Nadel and Radio Row did a pretty good business. As the commuters and radio buffs and bargain hunters streamed into his store, he did all right even during the Depression. Always dressed in a natty suit and tie, he would stand behind a little counter to the left of the entrance and greet the customers as they came in. "Hi, I'm Oscar, this is Oscar's Radio, how can I help ya?" Once he found out, he would call one of the clerks over and ask him to take it from there. Oscar was careful to add, if the customer needed information or was unhappy for any reason, "Stop by on the way out and see me."

When business exploded again after the war, he opened the second Oscar's Radio, at 63 Cortlandt, and began taking over the leadership of the local businessmen's organizations on Radio Row. Still, in the midst of that same postwar boom, danger signs for Radio Row started turning up. They involved the same knot of mass transit that had given the area commercial life.

First, the Hudson Tubes started making the ferryboats look like an awfully poky way to get across the river. The trans-Hudson ferry traffic, which had already fallen from a high of 51 million pedestrians in 1920 to 39 million in 1930, dropped to 22 million in 1940.

Then, in 1949, the 137-year-old ferry line started by Robert Fulton stopped depositing people at the foot of Cortlandt Street, and overall ferry ridership plummeted and never recovered. Moreover, the availability of the bridges and tunnels, along with the generally decaying condition of the Hudson Tubes, helped create a slide in the number of people using the H&M commuter railroad that ran through them, from the high of 110 million in 1930 to 56 million in 1950 to 30 million in 1960.

Within the city, the subways appeared to be a quicker and less cumbersome way to go than the elevated lines, and the Ninth Avenue El, with its Cortlandt Street stop, made its last run in 1940. That might not have made much difference in the total amount of foot traffic in the area except that overall ridership on the city rapid-transit system fell 34 percent from 1930 to 1960, with some of the greatest losses downtown. And of course the produce and fruit markets and the Hudson piers disintegrated to the west, south, and north.

These things made it easier for a big developer to paint that entire section of the city as falling apart.

But with Radio Row still hopping on Saturdays, and the millions of people still passing through the Hudson terminal every month, often with a few minutes to kill before their train arrived, Nadel told anyone who would listen that his Downtown West Businessmen's Association was making plans to do its own fixing up of the area to help keep their businesses profitable.

Nadel claimed that Cortlandt Street, like Wall Street, Madison Avenue, and Broadway, had become the symbol of something larger than itself because of the special kind of business that dominated the area.

The comparison may have been over the top, but that was part of the point. Like Austin Tobin, who had fought so many times for the agency that was all but inseparable from his being, Oscar Nadel would do what it took to save his world.

■ ■ ■

Morris Ernst, then a wily old man of seventy-three, quickly started coaching the merchants in the art of goading powerful bureaucracies toward anger and, he hoped, damaging mistakes. Nadel followed his advice, leading the Port Authority through a series of hoops as if he were a lion-tamer at a circus. On Wednesday, May 9, 1962, Nadel wrote to Tobin, asking for a public hearing on the World Trade Center. That same day, one of Tobin's top lieutenants called Nadel, and they worked out a deal to meet in about a week. A few days later, Nadel canceled.

There were good strategic reasons. Sidney Goldstein, the Port Authority general counsel and author of the undiplomatic brief in *Courtesy Sandwich Shop v. Port of New York Authority*, had tipped his agency's hand. Goldstein had written to Ernst, refusing to recognize him as the bargaining agent for the merchants represented by the survival committee of Nadel's Downtown West Businessmen's Association. "It is clear that your efforts are directed to stopping the World Trade Center project," Goldstein wrote. "These are individual problems which, we are confident, can and will be solved by individual consideration." He particularly objected to Nadel's insistence that Tobin and the other Port Authority officials attend mass meetings where the merchants would have a chance to air their gripes in person. It was onesy-twosy or not at all, Goldstein in effect said.

Nadel knew that if he let them meet with the merchants one at a time, his whole effort would crumble. Just as it had with the Midtown bus terminal, the Port Authority would start tearing down a vacant building here, a vacant building there, people would get scared, and there would be an exodus. So, thanks to Goldstein's letter, the meeting was off. Tobin and his staff did try to lure the merchants in individually, but they learned that on Radio Row, you had to go through Oscar. Their only recorded success was a meeting with a man the Port Authority memos call "Mr. Buff"—his first name has been lost to history—of Buff & Buff Manufacturing at 69 Dey Street. "Overall discussion of the World Trade Center project," reads the only known description of that meeting.

Sometime in the next month, the Port Authority contacted Nadel and asked him what he was after. Nadel said he wanted a meeting with Austin Tobin himself. The agency's officials who were in charge of the World Trade Center project had to be there, too. And Nadel wouldn't come alone—he wanted to bring a lawyer from Ernst's firm as well as half a dozen of his own top lieutenants.

So they gave him the meeting. The only known, face-to-face encounter between Tobin and Nadel, it took place on June 14, 1962, in the Port Authority headquarters at 111 Eighth Avenue. Among other people, Tobin brought Guy Tozzoli, the man he had chosen to lead the trade center project. Nadel brought five people including Leonard Levy of Leonard's Radio and a lawyer named Leo Rosen from Ernst's firm. Once they got there, Nadel did not let anyone else talk very much. He laid out his case, appealed to what he saw as the unfairness of the merchants' plight, and told them all that he intended to stop the project. He wanted the Port Authority to call it off right now.

One thought kept revolving in Tozzoli's mind: I like this guy. He stands up and tells you when he thinks you're full of beans.

Tobin apparently never said exactly what he thought of the man who, in a different world, was so much like himself. But he made Nadel an offer he hoped would change the equation on Radio Row.

Tobin offered Oscar Nadel a spot for his radio shop in the World Trade Center. There might be room for other shops who wanted it, too, Tobin said.

Nadel turned him down on the spot.

The offer, after all, was not really as good as it sounded. Tozzoli knew that, and Tobin must have, too. Taking the offer meant spending five years or more in commercial limbo while you waited for the trade center to be built. There weren't many businesses that could wait that long.

The meeting ended, and of course everyone down in the neighborhood heard about how Nadel had refused to be taken in. It was a good story for the fund-raisers, but in the end, neither Tobin nor Nadel had changed his goals one iota. Each was absolutely convinced that he was going to win.

The case went to court.

In the summer of 1962, the first two court decisions in *Courtesy Sandwich Shop v. Port of New York Authority* revealed clear signs of trouble for the agency and Tobin's vision of a reinvented port. Technically, the decisions—both on initial skirmishes, really, in the lower state courts—went Tobin's way. But along the way, the courts refused to give their stamp to the two central premises of his argument: that the World Trade Center fit the description of a constitutional "public purpose" and that the project had, so far, brought no harm to the merchants at the site.

The reactions downtown on the west side and at Port Authority head-quarters were so drastically different that it was as if, for a moment, the whole affair really was taking place on some fantasy board game and not the city's streets. There was unrestrained glee on Radio Row. And yet, for his part, Tobin could not help gloating over the two consecutive victories in the lower courts. Tobin went so far as to declare publicly, in apparent defiance of the judges' written opinions, that the constitutional issue had somehow been settled by the lower courts. And then he discovered that the rules were going to be different in this fight. Justice Peter A. Quinn of the

State Supreme Court was moved to issue a remarkable public statement chastising Tobin for the "extramural misrepresentation" of his ruling. In the Appellate Division of the New York State Supreme Court, where Nadel, Ernst, and the Radio Row businessmen were taking the case on appeal, the World Trade Center "might be declared invalid," Quinn said.

The *Times* article on the imbroglio noted briefly that "a spokesman for the Port Authority declined yesterday to comment on Justice Quinn's statement." Nadel was so tickled that Tobin, the omnipotent Tobin, had been reprimanded in the *New York Times* that he called an emergency meeting of the businessmen's association just to read everyone the article aloud and beg them to stick together in the fight.

The association generally liked to have its biggest and most raucous meetings at a place called the Commuters Café, at 32 Cortlandt Street, owned by three Austrian brothers named Tretter and tucked into the side of one of the Hudson terminal buildings a few doors from Sy Syms's clothing store. The Commuters Café had just about the most congenial bar in the whole area and there was plenty of room. Nadel read the entire article into a mike, lingering over the no-comment from someone on the Port Authority PR staff, probably his archenemy Jaffe.

"I need not tell you that the Port Authority has the most efficient and expensive public relations and press staff of any agency in the country," Nadel said. "The staff has been built up over many years with the expenditures of millions of dollars. They are masters of the art of half-truths and misleading innuendoes.

"Where was this vaunted Port Authority public relations counsel last Monday?" Nadel said with evident relish. "I'll tell ya. They were busy telling the press, No comment! The Port Authority half-truths, misinterpretations and misinformation have caught up with them!"

■ ■ ■

Mortimer Matz, the publicity man, and an associate he worked with on the Radio Row work named Max Rosey both loved to use props. Matz and Rosey promoted everything from the Palisades Amusement Park to local radio stations to Nathan's Famous on Coney Island, where they would always claim, with what sounded like typical braggadocio, that they were the ones who picked up a local tradition and organized the first formal hotdog-eating contest. In that hard-fought summer of 1962, it was

Rosey who came up with the idea of a protest that would burst from just about every news outlet in the city and starkly illustrate the dread that the merchants had now begun to feel about the fate that the Port Authority wanted to deal them. First, Rosey had big placard-size signs painted with slogans that would turn some heads: PORT AUTHORITY WANTS TO BUILD A KREMLIN. PORT AUTHORITY HAS NO RIGHT TO CONFISCATE PRIVATE PROPERTY— IT'S UNCONSTITUTIONAL. CONDEMNATION WITHOUT COMPENSATION. Then he had a wooden coffin built with one end of the lid cut away, so that if someone lay inside, only his head and shoulders would be visible. The placard he attached to the coffin itself drove home in a way no one was going to miss:

HERE LIES
MR. SMALL BUSINESSMAN
DON'T LET THE P.A.
BURY HIM

Oscar Nadel got inside, and on a hot, sunny Friday the 13th in July 1962, about a dozen clerks that Kallimanis and Barry Ray sent over, some still in white grocer's aprons, carried him over the sidewalks and subway grates of the area and waved the placards. A loudspeaker blared a protest speech over and over as they walked. When Nadel got out to talk to the mass of reporters and photographers from the city newspapers, the Associated Press, UPI, CBS, and Fox Movietone News, the clerks put a life-size mannequin inside. They paraded about with that for a while and set the coffin down in front of Oscar's Radio at 176 Greenwich Street for more pictures.

There was a dark humor to it all, of course, but Nadel, who had started complaining of fatigue and sleepless nights and the falloff in business since the Port Authority had announced the west side site for the trade center, clearly thought there was a grain of literal truth as well. Matz dubbed the coffin protest "Black Friday" in his regular newsletter and gave it his usual treatment, an arresting style that might have been described as breathlessly mordant:

"BLACK FRIDAY" RESULTS : Chairman Oscar Nadel looked "good" in the coffin as he was interviewed by the press and TV on Friday, July 13th.

Less than a month later, Tobin offered new concessions, promising to pay all moving costs and to hire a relocation firm that would try to find a spot in Manhattan for a new retail electronics center. And he promised not to demolish the H&M terminal buildings until 1964. The merchants still thought the maximum cash payment of $3,000 sounded ludicrous, but there was little doubt that the run of terrible press had now gotten under Tobin's skin. He exploded just after "Black Friday" when the *New York Post* ran a story saying that real estate speculators had been given inside information on the move to the west side. Although Nadel was quoted, Morris Ernst had fed them the story. Tobin was so angry that he got the Rackets Bureau at the District Attorney's Office to depose Nadel under oath.

Nadel denied making the statement, but the *Post* reporter—who apparently thought he had detected a warming trend after Tobin's concessions—gave no satisfaction. As Tobin told it, the reporter "suggested that the matter was academic anyway, since, in his words, 'the Port Authority and Mr. Nadel's group are now palsy-walsy.'"

It did not look palsy-walsy in court.

The arguments for the constitutionality case in the Appellate Division started around Thanksgiving 1962, a few months after the Port Authority made a low-key announcement that a new architect, a relative unknown named Minoru Yamasaki, had been hired to take another look at the design of the trade center. That development was all but lost in the welter of news on the court fight. The Port Authority lawyers were still optimistic, but they gradually realized that they were not receiving the reception they had expected in the courtroom. Tobin fretted that the judges just did not understand the complexities of the case. He used every method at his disposal to make it appear that the outcome was a foregone conclusion, pushing ahead with the takeover of the H&M railroad, especially the visible details.

"By Saturday, Sept. 2, the H&M designations on all of the line's 'black' passenger cars had been covered over with distinctive blue and white PATH decals," a pleased Tobin wrote.

Nadel, who would sometimes sit through an entire day's arguments in court so that he could report back to his association, thought he saw confusion creeping into the great phalanxes of lawyers that the Port Authority would dispatch for the courtroom work. The way he saw it, things seemed to be going his, and Radio Row's, way.

In late November 1962, Nadel persuaded Ernst to come to the Commuters Café and speak to them about the case. "Now it's a privilege to introduce to you Mr. Morris L. Ernst," Nadel said that night in late November after he had warmed up the crowd, his satisfaction evident in every word.

The great civil rights lawyer apologized that because he had a sore throat, his voice was a little scratchy. Even so, Ernst did not just show up and deliver a few off-the-cuff remarks. He gave a powerful and in some ways jarring speech on where he thought the World Trade Center struggle fit into the civil rights battles he had fought during his entire career.

"I've looked around the room, and no doubt about it—I'm the oldest person in this room. So I can afford to be honest," Ernst said.

"Nothing in your lives will leave a greater impress on our community than this battle, because you are the first group that Tobin has been unable to break up by division. You're the first group in forty years that the Port Authority hasn't been able to push around and scare," Ernst said.

"In a way it's a miracle if you win," Ernst said. "If you win it's your victory and if we lose it's our defeat. I honestly feel that way. It's a miracle and I'll tell you why. . . . He had no reason to suspect that guys like Oscar and others, and it's a long list, would be so devoted as to keep all of you together.

"Nobody knows what happens in these cases. I believe with Churchill that it's dishonorable for lawyers or leaders to ever tell less than the truth. I think you're far from home plate. I don't think Tobin crumbles easily."

Then he gave his summation in a kind of guttural snarl.

"What's much more important than any of you is that no Tobin of the future can push your kids around as he tried to push you."

After wishing Morris Ernst "Godspeed," Nadel then started one of his interminable fund-raisers.

The constitutionality decision in the Appellate Division—the case revolving around whether the trade center was a "public purpose," as the Port Authority's charter required it to be—arrived at 111 Eighth Avenue a couple of months later, on February 19, 1963. In the legal offices on the north side of the fifteenth floor, the envelope went directly to the general counsel, Sidney Goldstein. Patrick Falvey, Rosaleen Skehan, and the other lawyers waited as he tore open the envelope.

"Jesus Christ!" Goldstein moaned in his Brooklyn accent.

In a 3–2 decision, the Appellate Court had found that the World Trade Center did not constitute a valid public purpose, and that therefore the legislation authorizing it was unconstitutional.

"Sydney, we'll get a stay from the Court of Appeals," Falvey said. A stay would keep all activities on the project from stopping now, immediately. Fine, Goldstein said.

"Well," Goldstein said then, "we'd better tell Austin."

After about thirty seconds of general silence, Skehan, the crisis manager, turned to her secretary.

"Get me Mr. Tobin's office," Skehan said. "Tell him we need to see him."

They gathered some of the others who were working on the trade center project, and Skehan led them en masse into Tobin's office. "Unaccountably," Skehan began—and she delivered the bad news.

Unhappiness took possession of Tobin's pugnacious face. But overall, he dealt with the news calmly. They all talked for a while about legal strategy during the next level of appeals, Tobin told them he was sure they were going to do a good job, and they left.

"The Giant Killers," was the page 1 headline in the *Newark Sunday News*, above a lengthy story and a two-column picture of Nadel, shown archly grinning, gunslinger-confident, and wearing a sharp tie. The *New York Times* went with the more restrained "Port's Acquisition of Railroad Voided" over a two-hundred-word story on page 13.

Whatever the reception in the press, the only thing worse for the Port Authority than having the World Trade Center be declared unconstitutional was the reasoning of the court's majority. "No one doubts that the operation of the Hudson Tubes would constitute a public purpose," wrote Justice Samuel Rabin for the majority. But the legislation forced the railroad to be considered inseparable from the trade center. And the language of the bill gave too much power to the Port Authority—allowing it to condemn land for anything it chose to define as a World Trade Center, he wrote. "Under this grant of power there is no structure of any kind that may not be built in the 13-block area, provided such structure produces revenues to support the project. . . . In effect, as written, the statute contemplates the building of structures that will provide the fuel to run the railroad."

Then Rabin drove the dagger in, sounding as if he were one of the "little shnooks" himself. The bill was so broad, he wrote, that it would be hard to see what business could not move into the World Trade Center. "Every retailer who has foreign goods for sale; every shipper who handles imported merchandise; every trucker who transports foreign goods or goods destined for the foreign market; every manufacturer of goods for export, and countless others would appear to be eligible for space in the trade center. There are very few, if any, commercial buildings within the City of New York that do not house enterprises of the nature contemplated," Rabin wrote.

The ray of light for the Port Authority was that just as the majority seemed to have accepted Nadel's basic philosophy, the minority had figured out how Tobin had redefined the port to fit his vision of the trade center. The state legislatures had given the port agency "extraordinary powers to assist in an extraordinary task—nothing less than the maintenance of the hegemony of the Port of New York in the western hemisphere," wrote Justice Charles D. Breitel for the minority.

Breitel concluded that "such a center is not a private purpose, but a public purpose, so long as it is reasonably considered essential to the life of the port. It is no more a 'real estate project,' as appellants would characterize it, than is a state fair or a municipal public market."

The two worldviews, Nadel's and Tobin's, had finally met in the cosmic boxing ring of a courtroom, and Nadel had won a split decision.

The rematch came quickly.

In the New York State system, the last recourse is the Court of Appeals in Albany. After that, the only place left to go is the United States Supreme Court. The Port Authority argued that the urgency of the case was extreme because the legal basis it was using to run its railroad, PATH, had just evaporated. As a result, the court heard oral arguments in Albany on Thursday afternoon, February 28, 1963, just nine days after the Appellate Division had decided its case. And the Court of Appeals allowed the Port Authority to reverse the ordinary procedure and file its voluminous brief after the oral arguments, rather than before. Between the oral arguments on Thursday and the filing of its brief the following Tuesday, the Port Authority lawyers worked around the clock, pushing themselves to exhaustion.

The arguments the Port Authority made were the familiar ones: the World Trade Center was a public purpose because it would ensure that the city remained a leader in international trade and would help create a new era of greatness for the Port of New York. But this time the magnitude of the issues at stake seemed to inspire a masterly performance by the Port Authority's resident legal genius, Daniel B. Goldberg, who had won some of the agency's most important cases over the decades.

On April 4, 1963, the decision came down. The court had not only given the Port Authority an overwhelming victory, deciding 6–1 in its favor, but the majority opinion, written by Judge Adrian P. Burke, was devastating for the merchants in its sweeping acceptance of the idea that the port would inevitably be enhanced by buildings dedicated to international trade—and therefore those buildings could constitute a valid public purpose. "It is the gathering together of all business relating to world trade that is supposed to be the great convenience held out to those who use American ports and which is supposed to attract trade with a resultant stimulus to the economic well-being of the Port of New York," Judge Burke wrote. "This benefit is not too remote or speculative as to render the means chosen to achieve it patently unreasonable; nor is the benefit sought itself an improper concern of government. The history of western civilization demonstrates the cause and effect relationship between a great port and a great city."

Then, in an observation that went to the crux of the entire project from its inception, Judge Burke struck a final blow for the Port Authority, for David Rockefeller, for Robert Moses, and for anyone else who was a proponent of building big for the public good: "More recently the indirect benefits deriving from slum clearance and from a 'plan to turn a predominantly vacant, poorly developed and organized area into a site for new industrial buildings' have justified condemnation. To retreat from the public importance of piers, markets and slum clearance, even esthetic improvements have been held to be a public purpose justifying condemnation."

This was the purest possible vision of the old ram-it-through New York, the pre–Jane Jacobs New York in which the power of eminent domain trumped all, once a great project got moving. And it was the vision that triumphed on appeal.

The very next day, Tobin had "To Our Passengers" flyers distributed in the PATH stations. "We are pleased that New York State's highest court, the Court of Appeals, in a 6-to-1 decision, yesterday reversed the lower

Court," Tobin wrote. "For PATH and its passengers this is an important victory," he wrote, adding that it could allow the port agency to "get moving again with the program for the construction of PATH's new fleet of 250 modern, air-conditioned cars." That, however, depended on whether opponents of the project decided to go to the United States Supreme Court, he noted.

"Thank you for your patience, understanding and cooperation. We shall continue to keep you informed of all major developments in this matter," he concluded.

For Nadel, whose voluminous public statements became still more emotional, more committed than before, the next step was obvious. "SAVE YOUR BUSINESS," his handbill shouted, declaring that Ernst was taking them to the United States Supreme Court—"THE LAST STOP ON OUR WAY TO VICTORY," as Nadel put it, calling for a "mass meeting" at the Commuters Café. "IT IS URGENT YOU ATTEND! KEEP ALERT— KEEP INFORMED . . . **FIGHT FOR YOUR CONSTITUTIONAL RIGHTS**."

Nadel hammered away. The United States, he said, had not given the Port Authority the right "to go into the real estate business on somebody else's blood, sweat and tears as it is trying to do with its proposed World Trade Center."

It took most of the year for the Supreme Court to consider the challenge that Ernst mounted to the State Court of Appeals decision. In November 1963, though, the court summarily dismissed the appeal "for want of a substantial federal question."

It was the outcome that Nadel, the bantam rooster, had never really believed possible.

4

...

Surprise, Serenity, Delight

If a building is too strong or brutal, it tends to overpower man. In it he feels insecure and uncomfortable.

—Minoru Yamasaki

ord Motor Company offered the Triangle of the Future, a mock rocket ship set up in a geodesic dome that featured a fifteen-minute flight to Mars and back. The American Gas Association exhibit marked each hour with a giant belch of natural gas–fueled flame. General Electric wowed the crowds at its futuristic model home where the picture-perfect parents, Gerry and Ellen, demonstrated a push-button electric sink. The most thrilling attraction of all was the saucer-topped column that stretched 605 feet into the sky: the Space Needle, the new symbol of Seattle and its 1962 World's Fair, where all these wonders were on display. But something else caught Guy Tozzoli's eye as he strolled among the dazzled crowds, something that didn't look as if it belonged in the Space Age at all.

He was near the northern edge of the fairgrounds. He walked up a short flight of stairs and found himself on a compact, squarish platform. Before him was a zigzagging pathway that led to an overlook with a view of courtyards, pools, fountains, and flowers, none of which had been visible from the fairgrounds. Five low-lying all-white windowless buildings were arranged in a large enveloping U around this serene space. Above his head rose a collection of slender, stalklike structures that resembled the Gothic arches at the entrance to the cathedral at Chartres. But these delicate forms, covered in white quartz, held up nothing. They were just suspended there at the entrance to an exhibit called the Federal Science Pavilion. They seemed to be dancing in the air.

Tozzoli was an edgy, gravel-voiced technocrat and World War II veteran who grew up in northern New Jersey, an executive who seemed to oscillate between sweetness and arrogance in his dealings with subordinates, a builder who considered Robert Moses his greatest mentor. He was here on an espionage mission of sorts. The Port of New York Authority, Tozzoli's employer, had lent him to Moses to help in the preparations for the 1964 World's Fair in New York. In one of his last tasks as Moses's deputy before moving on to new responsibilities, Tozzoli had been sent to the rival fair out west to survey the spreads by the various corporate sponsors, searching out any Pacific Coast ideas that might be appropriated. It was a Moses way of doing things: smart, cynical, and effective.

So Tozzoli scouted the territory. As he walked up to the Federal Science Pavilion, he was expecting yet another Disney-like set piece on one brain-teasing theme or another. Instead, something froze him in place. In an instant, he had stepped into some kind of oasis. Here amid an orgy of noise was a marvelously cool and inviting palace, a constructed space with the serenity of a natural sanctuary, but where the aura almost recalled the majesty of the Alhambra or the Taj Mahal.

Guy Tozzoli felt peaceful. He would never quite figure out how to put his feelings about the shapes surrounding him into words, except that he thought they were beautiful. This spot was beautiful.

He found out the name of the architect who had brought him to a stop: Minoru Yamasaki. Tozzoli had never heard the name before. But he would come to know Yamasaki in a way he had never quite known anyone. Yamasaki was a Japanese-American who grew up in a slum only two miles from the Seattle fairgrounds and who now had his own architecture firm in Detroit; Tozzoli, from an Italian family with a home-building business in Jersey, had spent most of his adult life managing major government construction projects. That moment in Yamasaki's sanctuary would bring the two of them together, and they would eventually lead the conception, design, and construction of the largest office complex in the world. Over the next fifteen years, these two oddly matched men would become friends and bitter rivals, confidants and enemies, colleagues and competitors, in a saga that would fundamentally change the look of New York City and the lives of the people who saw and visited and worked in the structures that Tozzoli and Yamasaki would create.

It would be a complicated and difficult and contested journey. But in the end, it was merely a search for the fragile sense of peace that Yamasaki had created and Tozzoli had discovered in the little sanctuary at the World's Fair.

There was only one condition. The buildings that were going to incorporate those delicate emotions had to be big. They had to be enormous, on a scale like nothing of the kind that had ever been welded and bolted and hammered together before. There would be no compromising on the size of the project, not after everything the Port Authority had done to make it possible.

Tozzoli would see to that.

■ ■ ■

A sixteen-year-old Minoru Yamasaki lay atop a thin straw mattress waiting for dawn, when work would begin again at the salmon-canning factory in this coastal town in Alaska. Yamasaki had soaked the mattress in kerosene in a desperate attempt to kill the swarming mass of bedbugs. It was the summer of 1929 and Yamasaki had come here to try to earn college tuition. Anger burned inside him.

Yamasaki had grown up in Yesler Hill, the Seattle neighborhood that gave birth to the term *skid row*, originally a nickname for the log slides that once carried timber down to the waterfront and later, of course, an insulting slang term for a slum—like the neighborhood. The spot offered extraordinary views of the nearby mountains, which seemed to rise out of Puget Sound straight up into the sky. It seemed an appropriate spot given the family name: *Yama* means mountain in Japanese. That was about where its attractions ended. Minoru's parents—his father was a stockroom manager at a Seattle shoe store and his mother was a piano teacher—had arrived separately in Seattle from Japan around 1908, and then been introduced through a go-between, as was the Japanese custom. In his early years, Minoru, who was born in 1912, lived with his family in a small house that had no hot water or indoor bathroom. The house listed so severely to one side that Yamasaki wondered if, at any moment, it might collapse and slide straight down the hill, as the logs once did.

Early on, there were more than a few hints that Yamasaki would escape from this slum. He was an outstanding student with a natural aptitude for math and science. When his uncle, an architect who was on a visit from out of town, unfurled a set of drawings, Minoru's eyes lit up as if they were on fire. Here was a way of applying the abstract sciences of math and physics to create places of beauty you could see and touch. First, though, he had to pay his own way.

So he worked for five summers at the canning factory. He hated it. A day of labor there would routinely run eighteen hours, with Yamasaki holding up a fire hose and long stick as he pushed mucky piles of fish from giant unloading bins into the mechanical butchering machine that was so insatiable it was nicknamed—with supreme ethnic insensitivity— "the Iron Chink." One Sunday evening, after a day of work that had Yamasaki so fatigued he was nearly in tears, a factory boss walked up and yelled at him to work harder. "You must keep up with the Iron Chink," he screamed. For all of his life, Yamasaki would be described as a manifestly rational man, a soul so gentle that he would often simply smile if insulted, even if it made him burn up inside. But at this one time Yamasaki went momentarily berserk. With no warning, his steel-tipped stick swung wildly up into the air and toward the impatient foreman, who desperately twisted to get away. Yamasaki missed. But the foreman lost his balance and toppled into the bloody fish-filled bin.

It was an act of desperation—even if, in the rough-hewn world surrounding the Alaska fisheries, it didn't cost him his job. Yet it was a moment that would color almost everything he did in his adult life. Again and again he would tell this story—Guy Tozzoli and Austin Tobin would hear it—as an explanation of why he felt so compelled throughout his career as an architect to build serene spaces like the Federal Science Pavilion. For even at the cannery, amid the nightmare of endless labor, Yamasaki had found a source of that serenity. One afternoon he wandered outside, along the Alaskan shoreline. All at once, the beauty of the landscape—maidenhead fern and white lilies formed a silky carpet, a gentle stream turned into a waterfall that fell into a rock-filled pool— overwhelmed his bitterness. In the midst of a place that had brought him so much misery, he had experienced an oasis of peace. For Yamasaki, the question would become how to conjure that feeling with something designed and built by human hands.

"Surprise. Serenity. Delight." That would become Yamasaki's esthetic mantra, a trinity that, he said, informed everything he designed and built.

He would escape the canning factory but not all traces of the ethnic tension he had confronted next to the fish-butchering machine. A few years later he had realized part of his dream: at twenty-five, he was employed as an architect by the big New York firm of Shreve, Lamb, and Harmon. Two days before Pearl Harbor, Yamasaki, a thin, round-faced young man, had married a talented young pianist, Teruko Hirashiki, in a ceremony so rushed that she had no time to buy a wedding gown. She wore a nice red dress instead. Now they were together in upstate New York, where Yamasaki had landed a fascinating assignment: transform a bean-shaped plot alongside Lake Seneca into a training base for thirty thousand navy men, with ten distinct buildings ranging from mess hall to chapel. Yet that Sunday at a local park, they faced cold stares. An air-raid drill had sent everyone into the closest shelter. One woman could not take her eyes off the couple. A police officer confronted Yamasaki as the air-raid siren finally went silent. "That woman insists that I find out whether or not you're spies," the police officer asked Yamasaki and his wife. The old anger burned inside.

As so many other things would be in Yamasaki's cluttered life, the way he balanced his Japanese heritage and his American identity would be complicated, very complicated. On one level, he chose defiance. He told the people who glared at him that day in New York that he was an American citizen. He moved his parents into his New York apartment rather than see them placed in an internment camp. But the questions about his loyalty also prompted an intense drive to assimilate. After the war, he moved his family to a 135-year-old farmhouse in a town outside of Detroit. He bought himself a big gray Pontiac Grand Am, which soon enough would be used to ferry around his three suburban-bred children. He even built a backyard pool and a big carport that doubled as a beach house in the summer. His wife, known as Teri, bragged that she had never been to Japan and had never made a silkscreen scroll, even telling one newspaper reporter in the 1950s that among their wide circle of friends, none she could think of was Japanese.

"We don't really know any of them," Teri Yamasaki said.

Although Yamasaki showed an early affinity for a few of the grace notes that made Japanese architecture so distinctive—things like raised floors and pools of running water—he basically hewed to the fashionable, modernist predilection for flat, unadorned surfaces of steel and concrete and glass in the mainstream homes and commercial buildings he designed. One architecture journal, playing a bit with his name, titled an article about his work simply "American Architect Yamasaki." But his self-consciousness remained. Once, when Yamasaki and a colleague named George Nelson were scheduled to meet with a client, Yamasaki tried to beg off. He thought this particular client might be less than pleased to meet with an architect of Asian descent. "Yama, if he is, we don't take the job," Nelson had to say to get him to come along.

■ ■ ■

A big crowd stood around in a muddy lot in October 1956 next to an intersection at the edge of downtown Detroit. The speeches went on forever. The governor was there, the mayor, a United States senator, the city council president, even Walter P. Reuther, the United Auto Workers leader. The draw was the long-awaited groundbreaking for Lafayette Park, a seventy-eight-acre housing project, the first urban renewal effort in the city's history. A set of chrome-plated shovels was flown in by helicopter from the city airport. The mayor's wife broke a bottle of champagne on a giant bulldozer. A sixth grader named Joann Brown planted the first tree. And the speeches went on and on and on.

Minoru Yamasaki's name was not listed among the honorees or speakers. Yet this would be one of the most thrilling days in his architecture career. The special guest today was Ludwig Mies van der Rohe, the German-born architect who five years earlier had finished a set of sleek steel-and-glass apartment houses in Chicago that, in a single act, had changed the face of American architecture. Suddenly, the steel frame, in its simple elegance, had jumped beyond its role as an indispensable—but largely hidden—structural element. Mies had brought it to the forefront as a central element in the visible architectural design of a skyscraper. Now he was bringing his vision to Detroit as the designer of Lafayette Park's first apartment buildings.

During the ceremony, Yamasaki somehow gathered enough gumption to sidle up to Mies and invite him to join Yamasaki at his house that evening for a few drinks and some food, an invitation that generated a frantic call by him to his wife when it was accepted. It would be a night Yamasaki would never forget, a night saturated in soaring talk of art and architecture—and in martinis. Yamasaki himself was quite a big drinker, getting so drunk at one party that he yelled to everyone in the room to join him in throwing the glasses into the fireplace. But Mies, normally circumspect in his German way, would dominate on all fronts. He drank martini after martini and launched into a rambling speech about a pavilion he had designed nearly three decades earlier for the World's Fair in Barcelona. No one else in the room could get a word in as Mies talked into the night.

No one minded listening, of course. To Yamasaki, Mies was quite simply the world's greatest living architect. So enamored was Yamasaki of his structures that in the early 1950s he had driven way out to Plano, Illinois, to see a Mies house there. With its all-white concrete floor and roof slabs—separated only by uninterrupted panes of glass and held up by a steel frame—Mies's Farnsworth House looked as if it were floating in the prairie. It was pure glass, pure steel, pure space. Carrying a camera, Yamasaki climbed the fence set up to keep Mies disciples at bay. "Are you an architecture student?" asked another admirer, who also had snuck down to the house for a peak. Yamasaki hesitantly replied: "Well, I'm an architect." And with that, Yamasaki turned and crawled underneath the suspended rectangular floor of Mies's creation.

Mies's Lake Shore Drive Apartments in Chicago, completed in 1951, were an even greater revelation for Yamasaki. Twin towers, set up on an angle that echoed the curve of the Lake Michigan shore, these skyscrapers were at the same time muscular and elegant. He let the structure speak for itself. Each face of the towers consisted of countless window-sized rectangles, framed simply by black steel, what some described as a Mondrian painting on a superhuman scale. And the buildings were positioned not so that they looked right into each other but at an angle like two parts of a lakeside sculpture.

Yamasaki's first bid for greatness came when he tried to merge the lessons he had learned from Mies with those of another European giant, Le Corbusier, who understood the way that the newer materials like certain types of concrete could be molded and sculpted into exotic curves. Le Corbusier was also the leading proponent of the idea that skyscrapers could be virtual, self-contained cities, with everything people needed to work and live pleasant lives—from gardens down below to stunning views of the surroundings from the windows high above. Conceptually, merging Le Corbusier and Mies had a curious appeal, but Yamasaki's first try at putting them together in real buildings almost ended his career.

In the early 1950s, he designed a collection of thirty-three nearly identical eleven-story buildings in a St. Louis public housing project called Pruitt-Igoe. Yamasaki described the project in glowing terms, calling it a "vertical neighborhood," complete with a "river" of open green space winding amid the buildings, and large screened-in common areas on different floors that were supposed to create a kind of utopia. Within two years, the complex had disintegrated into a collection of shattered windows, graffiti, and laundry rooms that smelled like urine. Seventeen years after it was completed, Pruitt-Igoe was destroyed—by dynamite. "One of the sorriest mistakes I ever made in this business," Yamasaki would say of this architectural debacle.

But it would not be the last time Yamasaki took on a project so large that it would stretch his delicate esthetic sense past its elastic limit.

For now, Yamasaki kept searching. In 1954, he spent four months traveling around the world—visiting Kyoto, Paris, Milan, Venice, Rome, New Delhi, Chandigarh, Agra, Bangkok, and Hong Kong. The trip had been inspired by an order from his doctor after a nearly fatal attack of bleeding ulcers that left Yamasaki in the hospital for two months in late 1953. In Paris, Milan, and Rome, he stood, awestruck, before the great cathedrals and squares. In Venice, the rhythmic Gothic arches at Doges Palace at Piazza San Marco left him speechless. In Agra, he was entranced by the way the sun reflected off the surface of the Taj Mahal. Japan was a particular revelation. At Ryoanji, a fifteenth-century temple near Kyoto, he found a slanting white-gravel arena, decorated simply with fifteen carefully placed rocks. At the nearby Katsura Palace, bamboo fences, hedges, and some low wooden structures surrounded one of the most sublime man-made spaces Yamasaki had ever seen.

It was in Japan that it hit him. True, he could barely speak Japanese, and he had spent as much time running from his Asian heritage as accepting it. But for the first time in his life, he knew that he was truly both Japanese and American, and that it was only by combining these crosscurrents that he would find his own voice.

"Something was missing and I had to keep running after it," Yamasaki would write. "But look: everyone has a complex. It took the ulcer to show me what mine was—that I was Japanese."

Somehow Yamasaki shook everything he had seen together and came up with a style that was all his own. He kept the raw, exposed structures of Mies van der Rohe. He held on to Le Corbusier's idea of buildings as self-contained entities, set apart from their surroundings. Yamasaki would add to that the Japanese tradition of setting buildings back, off the street, with contemplative pools and gardens and plazas that evoked the serenity he was trying to achieve. Then, within these gardens and on the surfaces of his buildings, he would apply a touch of the wondrous shapes he found across Europe, the decorative, lacy elements that had so grabbed his eye. This merging of influences would lead Yamasaki into a style that defied any simple characterization. Many would say it was trite and confused. Others would marvel over its effect without thinking much about where all the pieces came from.

One thing was certain. Like his big Grand Am when the pedal was pressed to the floor, Yamasaki's career would roar forward with abandon now that he had found out who he was. He was ready to change the world, the way his hero, Mies, had.

• • •

Guy Tozzoli sauntered down the stairway leading into one of his favorite Italian restaurants, a hole-in-the-wall on East Fourteenth Street. He had just been to a cocktail party at the United Nations. Now, his wife on his arm, his work and official socializing wrapped up on this day in 1961, Tozzoli was looking forward to a quiet dinner.

Just as he and his wife sat down at a small table in the nearly empty restaurant, the waiter approached and whispered to Tozzoli: "Mr. Tobin would like to see you," pointing toward a corner table where a man sat alone. "He wants you to join him for dinner."

Austin Tobin wanted some company.

Tozzoli had worked for the Port Authority—and, hence, for Tobin— since coming home from World War II. Tobin seemed to like his special assortment of abilities. Tozzoli had an undergraduate degree in mathematics and a master's degree in physics, both from Fordham University in the Bronx, and the navy had sent him off to study radar at the Massachusetts Institute of Technology and Princeton for eight months before he went overseas. Since August 1946, when Tozzoli returned from the USS *Texas*, where he put his radar skills to use during the invasion of Okinawa, Tozzoli had held down a series of increasingly important jobs at the Port Authority. In the late 1940s, he had helped build airplane hangars at Idlewild Airport; in the mid-1950s, he oversaw the planning for the Newark containership port.

For the past year, Tozzoli had been assigned to help Robert Moses with the World's Fair. In hindsight, it would almost look as if Tobin was conducting a character test by sending him to the dictatorial and sometimes vicious Robert Moses. Tobin had called his protégé in from a vacation in the summer of 1960 to talk about it.

"Guy," Tobin had said in breaking the news, "I have a new job for you."

"Okay," Tozzoli said. "What do you want me to do?"

"Report to Moses. You know him?"

"I never met him in my life."

"Would you be afraid to work for him?"

"No," Tozzoli said. And he explained his lack of concern as perhaps only he could: "The guy has arms, legs, and a head."

In fact, although Tozzoli deeply admired Moses's ruthless ability to get things done, his relationship with the construction coordinator had been anything but easy. Moses from the start had doubted that Tozzoli was up to the job, mocking him for the big write-up Tozzoli had landed in the *New York Times* just for being appointed to the World's Fair staff. "You get more goddamn press for being one of my vice presidents than I get for being president of this thing," Moses barked.

But Tozzoli had done more than survive. He had helped Moses drum up crucial corporate sponsors—big, important names like General Motors and Ford—for the fair, and now Tobin was already thinking about what his talented lieutenant's next assignment might be. So, at the hole-in-the-wall restaurant on East Fourteenth, Tobin summoned Cynthia and Guy Tozzoli to his table and, over dinner, started talking about the World Trade Center.

Tozzoli, of course, had heard about the project. At the moment it was still an east side affair, and of course the architecture looked a lot like a confused version of the United Nations. Tozzoli had seen the architectural model on display at the Port Authority's 111 Eighth Avenue headquarters. For the design, the agency was relying upon a group it called its "genius committee," a trio of the nation's top architects: Edward Durrell Stone, who was about to design the Kennedy Center in Washington; Wallace

Harrison, who had led the design of the United Nations and Rockefeller Center; and Gordon Bunshaft, who had created the Chase Bank's new downtown headquarters. It sounded like a Rockefeller dream team. Over dinner, Tobin said he was impressed at just how ambitious a project the Port Authority was preparing to undertake, with so much talent at its disposal. Then came the natural question for Tozzoli: "So what do you think?"

"Jesus Christ," Tozzoli replied, relieved, finally, for the chance to spill. And spill he did. "You have got to do something about that one. You want to build the world's greatest project and you have a goddamn building with a parking lot up to about the tenth floor. It looks worse than the bus terminal. Terrible! Just imagine. Parking! You'd have parking in this great building! I have nothing to do with this project. But I have to tell you what I think about it. It's for the birds." And Tozzoli was not finished. "I just don't think three architects can do it. It is just impossible."

They all finished dinner. Tobin knew what he was getting with Tozzoli: someone who was incapable of not speaking what was on his mind. What was going through Tobin's mind on the World Trade Center, as it moved to the west side but kept its basically jumbled and uninviting shape, may have been revealed by his next move. "You've been doing a great job for Bob," Tobin told him on February 12, 1962, Tozzoli's fortieth birthday, just as Governor Nelson Rockefeller was signing legislation authorizing the construction of the World Trade Center on the Hudson River site. "I'm going to create the largest department the Port Authority has ever had, the World Trade Department. And I'm going to put you in charge of it.

"You are going to build the trade center."

■ ■ ■

Yamasaki knew there had been an unfortunate mistake. For one thing, the letter arrived without any advance notice. Sent from 111 Eighth Avenue in Manhattan to 1025 East Maple Road in Birmingham, Michigan, it reached Yamasaki's hands one day late in the spring of 1962 and immediately caused a stir around the office. For all of Yamasaki's success, his firm was only eight years old and had never handled an assignment in New York City. It was just now finishing up work on its first real high-rise, the thirty-story Michigan Consolidated Gas tower in Detroit. And now some agency called the Port of New York Authority wanted to know if Yamasaki was interested in serving as chief architect for what the letter said was a $280,000,000 project called the World Trade Center.

Someone had, carelessly and ludicrously, added an extra zero, Yamasaki said, passing the letter around.

"Here is an example of why we must all be careful when we write business correspondences," he told his colleagues in a staff meeting. "Even a single error, like an extra digit, can be a cause of great embarrassment." Everyone had a look at the letter. It provoked a few smirks and nods of approval; his warning was well taken. But there were at least a few who wondered. "It has your name on it," one of the associates said. "You have to call and find out." Richard Sullivan, Tozzoli's newly appointed deputy at the Port Authority, had sent the letter to Yamasaki. So Sullivan fielded the return call.

"We've been sitting here talking about this," Yamasaki explained, trying to address the question politely.

"No, the letter is correct," Sullivan said.

"It is too big for us," Yamasaki replied.

"No, it isn't," was Sullivan's response.

Whether Yamasaki thought he could take on the job or not, it was certainly true that the size of his operation had surged along with his reputation. Just five years before, his practice had consisted of a rented loft above a sporting goods store; now he had a much larger and pleasanter location with about sixty employees, including forty architects. And notable work it was. He had first sprung his "serenity, surprise, delight" esthetic in 1958 with the McGregor Memorial Community Conference Center at Wayne State University in Detroit, which was set on a pedestal with touches that included an accordion-like glass and aluminum skylight and a reflecting, L-shaped garden pool. He followed this up with a composition he called his "jewel on stilts"—a three-story structure, with a lacelike, gold-colored screen on its top two floors, constructed for Reynolds Metals Company as a showcase for its primary product: aluminum. The Federal Science Pavilion for the Seattle World's Fair, like the Reynolds and McGregor buildings, maintained the theme, since all three designs put a great emphasis on the elaborate decorative touches and their reflecting pools.

The Michigan Consolidated Gas tower, which was still being built as the search for a World Trade Center architect got under way in 1962, only enhanced Yamasaki's standing. It was just thirty stories tall, but its forty-eight hundred floor-to-ceiling, hexagon-shaped windows, narrowly arranged between concrete exterior columns, created a sense of intense verticality, an effect Yamasaki desired, since he was looking to pull the eye of the passing pedestrian right into the sky. "The pointed tops and bottoms of these windows will also emphasize the flow of upward movement in the building," Yamasaki said as he was designing it. "We hope that this feeling of beautiful upward movement, if we can achieve it, will give the man on the street an experience of aspiration like the towers of the great Gothic cathedrals did in medieval days."

Words like those gave a grand interpretation to the buildings Yamasaki was designing, but even as Yamasaki was winning commissions, the East Coast architectural establishment dismissed his work as populist rubbish. Vincent J. Scully Jr., the Yale architectural historian and critic, called the McGregor building a "twittering aviary." John M. Jacobus, a Dartmouth College art historian, suggested that his work was "prissy." Fellow architects were even harsher. Gordon Bunshaft, who had been considered for the World Trade Center job, said: "Yamasaki's as much an architect as I am Napoleon. He was an architect, but now he's nothing but a decorator." I. M. Pei dismissed the Federal Science Pavilion in Seattle that had so impressed Tozzoli as "mere artistic caprice."

But he did pretty well in the press. Articles in *Time*, *Newsweek*, even the *New York Times*, left the impression that his structures, despite their modest size, were a welcome alternative to the dehumanizing harshness of the modernist glass box that had been championed by his hero, Mies. Yamasaki stoked that impression as best he could, giving speeches and writing articles explaining how he had found a way back to beauty. It was a pitch that had brought him more than just a whole new list of clients. Yamasaki decided he deserved a new lifestyle. Teri, his wife of two decades, he now deemed not his "intellectual equal." Yamasaki and Teri were divorced in June 1961; a month later he married Peggy Watty, a tall young blond from California. Teri ever so kindly put it this way: "A celebrated man must be superhuman to withstand the tremendous adulation." Yamasaki's longtime photographer and neighbor, Balthazar Korab, put it somewhat more bluntly: "Now Yama is big enough that he could get everything he could not get before."

Tozzoli cared nothing about Yamasaki's love life. He gave no specific

orders to short-list Yamasaki, but Tozzoli did dump the "genius committee" of Rockefeller-preferred architects and told his staff to find a creative
mind who was not so old that he would be dead before the huge project
was completed and not so famous that he would be pompous, inaccessible, or obstinate. But when the evaluations began, Yamasaki impressed the
Port Authority from the start, hitting all the right notes in his June 1962
application for the job: the World Trade Center would be big and unmistakable, yet intimate and humane.

"The basic problem, beyond solving the functional relationships of
space, is to find a beautiful solution of form and silhouette which fits well
into Lower Manhattan and gives the World Trade Center the symbolic
importance which it deserves and must have," Yamasaki wrote in his application letter. "The great scope of your project demands finding a way to
scale it to the human being so that, rather than be an overpowering group
of buildings, it will be inviting, friendly and humane. . . . To be symbolic of
its great purpose, of working together in trade of the nations of the world,
it should have a sense of dignity and pride, and still stand for the humanity
and democratic purposes in which we in the United States believe."

The prose was excellent, but what about the work itself? The Port
Authority inspection team, led by Herman M. Roberts, an architect, went
to Detroit in July 1962 to look over his buildings—and they were
impressed with what they saw. "Warmth and human scale so rarely
found in modern architecture are experienced by those who view or
enter his buildings," they reported. Yamasaki did have one major weakness, a serious one. He had never built a real skyscraper. Pruitt-Igoe certainly did not count. And the thirty-story Michigan Consolidated Gas
Building—his first office high-rise—would have been lost in the shadows
in New York. Yamasaki himself acknowledged the problem in his application. But he had a possible solution. His people could do the creative concept and design work. Then someone else, someone who knew the ins
and outs of New York building codes and union rules, could be hired to
do the drafting of the thousands of pages of detailed construction documents. "We would be pleased to associate with a large New York or other
office acceptable to you," he wrote.

Tozzoli, Tobin, Sullivan, and Malcolm P. Levy, the engineer Tozzoli
had named as one of his top deputies, were all sold. Still, Tozzoli knew
that Yamasaki needed a partner if this was going to work. He decided to

team Yamasaki up with Emery Roth & Sons, the New York firm that, besides many elegant structures, had designed dozens of glass boxes. These may have been some of the ugliest buildings ever constructed in Manhattan—critics mockingly called them Rothscapes—but they were loved by developers because the Roths were unrivaled at maximizing the available rentable space.

Yamasaki still had to confront a familiar question: one Port Authority board member asked how the agency could hire a Japanese architect. The answer: Yamasaki was in fact an American. That hurdle cleared, Yamasaki was going to get his shot at immortality. Even Mies van der Rohe had never attempted anything like this.

■ ■ ■

MIDWEST 6-8400. That was the telephone number the Port Authority would call to check on the status of the plan to rebuild a chunk of Lower Manhattan. Surrounded by golf courses and streets with names like Big Beaver Road and Beachwood Avenue, Yamasaki's office was, at least psychologically, about as far as you could get from the grimy, crooked streets of Lower Manhattan. In September 1962, when Yamasaki was officially awarded the commission to design the World Trade Center, the view from his office windows at 1025 East Maple Road was of the blacktop on the employee parking lot and, off to one side, the trees and neatly mown yards of the suburban houses next door. Yamasaki's entire practice was contained on the upper floor of this brick, green-paneled, two-story office building. A dozen of the youngest members of Yamasaki's staff assigned to the project at the start—most of them recent graduates of architecture school—were assembled in a classroom-sized space not far from Yamasaki's office. None of them had ever played a central role on what a New Yorker would consider a skyscraper worthy of the name.

So, before they even started, Yamasaki took a walk around the neighborhood his creation was meant to erase. Business was still brisk on Radio Row, and Oscar Nadel was already pushing himself to exhaustion in leading his protests and legal challenges against the trade center. But Yamasaki's eyes ran over the old brick walkups, the warehouses, and the two-story storefronts that had accommodated generation after generation of merchants. He saw the decay around the edges of the area—the rotting and boarded-up finger piers, the empty lots where the produce markets had once bustled. Was there really any doubt about the impression it would all have on a suburbanite whose mission was to remake the area after it was flattened? "It was a quite blighted section, with radio and electronic shops in old structures, clothing stores, bars and many other businesses that could be relocated without much anguish," he wrote. The twin Hudson terminal buildings, he wrote, were "dilapidated and no architectural gems." Tobin, naturally, let him fly over the area in a Port Authority helicopter. Not especially fond of heights under any circumstances, Yamasaki was petrified at the size of the job that, from this perch, he could see spread out beneath him.

He nosed around the rest of Manhattan for a little inspiration. He headed east, past the majestic Woolworth tower, and the Singer building, across Broadway, and down a few blocks to Wall Street. At lunchtime the sidewalks were jammed: he decided he needed a lot more space around the bottom of his structures, which would be inhabited by fifty thousand people, and take in and spit out another eighty thousand or so visitors and commuters each day. The feeling that he needed something set off from the crowded, hurried, jostling sidewalk traffic grew stronger when he wandered around the Empire State Building in Midtown. The scale of the building was just so enormous. But perhaps the most striking part of all was that as Yamasaki walked along Thirty-fourth Street or Fifth Avenue, at its base, he noticed that the tower essentially disappeared. He had to stop and lean his head way back to appreciate the monument. And if he had not paused, he might not even have realized he was passing one of the greatest structures ever built. That is not what Yamasaki wanted for his project. Not at all.

He started thinking about a big, thirteen-block plaza—a refuge from all the turmoil on the streets that would be enormous but also, somehow, pleasant and serene in a way that was inviting to individual passersby. The plaza, bigger than any ever seen in Manhattan, would also set the still-unknown arrangement of buildings off by themselves. People on the streets could pause and admire the play of light and shadow along the facade Yamasaki would now have to figure out how to sculpt. That was the effect he would aim for. Now he had at least the germ of an idea to take back to Detroit.

Before getting started, though, he had to meet the bevy of architects; mechanical, civil, and electrical engineers; accountants; and auditors on

Tozzoli's staff who would be guiding and filling out and criticizing Yamasaki's work. Tozzoli invited Yamasaki and his project director on the trade center job, a young architect named Aaron Schreier, to meet them all: Mal Levy, an obnoxious but brilliant engineer; Carl K. Panero and Herbert A. Tessler, obsessively punctilious architects; John B. McAvey and John R. Dragonette, the contract examiners and money men; and Richard Sullivan, now the World Trade Department's top deputy. Also in the room were the key consultants hired to design the electrical system, the elevators, the heating and ventilation networks. Levy, not Tozzoli, was going to lead the technical effort. Levy had prepared a banner and put it up on one of the walls of the conference room. In big black letters it simply said 22. The World Trade Center, he announced, was not to cost more than $22 a square foot to build, a little more than the nearly completed Pan Am building. "We can't afford a corporate status symbol," Levy told the men collected in the room. "This is not a trophy we are building. It is a speculative office building."

Tozzoli also weighed in. The trade center, he said, was going to be beautiful. That was why Yamasaki had been hired. But this was not going to be some esoteric architectural exercise. The commanding force here— besides the bottom line—was going to be "the Program," the nonnegotiable set of specifications for the job. It totaled 10 million square feet of net rentable space. The message was eminently clear. This was not going to be a project in which Yamasaki came up with a design and then presented the results to an awed client. He was facing the prospect of endless interrogation and negotiating and bickering with the Port Authority. His plans would be criticized at every step and changed if they did not meet the test of practicality as defined by Tozzoli and Levy and the others. And it would soon be especially obvious there was no escaping Levy, a man who could be so nasty he could, and often would, make Yamasaki quiver silently with humiliation or anger. Levy was going to be Tozzoli's whip hand on the trade center. The cursing, tantrum-prone Levy was going to make sure that the little group of architects in the Detroit suburbs designed the kind of buildings that the Port Authority damn well wanted.

MIDWEST 6-8400. Yamasaki's drafting room at 1025 East Maple Road had the feel of a kindergarten classroom, at least at the beginning of the effort in September and October 1962. A row of young men, in a uniform that consisted of starched white oxford shirts and thin dark ties, sat on metal and wooden stools in front of big rectangular tables equipped with generous supplies of paper, pencils, scissors, cardboard, and glue. The team included Grant Hildebrand, a twenty-eight-year-old graduate student at the University of Michigan architecture school; Jim Herman, twenty-six, a recent Cornell grad; and Jerry Karn, a twenty-five-year-old architect from Maryland. Schreier, at thirty-one the team leader, had been working on a six-story insurance company building before being pulled away for his new assignment. Karn arrived in Yamasaki's office two days after a wild party where the staff celebrated the World Trade Center commission. He was amused that everyone from Yamasaki on down still seemed to have a nasty hangover.

The first agenda item was a critical one. Just how would they translate the Program into reality? How many buildings? What basic shape and height? And how should they be arranged around the site? To help answer those questions, they had borrowed a sprawling model of Lower Manhattan from the Port Authority. The model showed off everything from the Woolworth Building to City Hall, Battery Park, even the Hudson River piers, and a fleet of ships and tugboats plying the harbor. Hundreds of downtown buildings were there, painted battleship gray. In the spot where the World Trade Center was supposed to go, there was a big empty hole.

Yamasaki's instructions to the group were simple.

"I know it is enormous," he said of the Program. "Find a way to translate it into forms that will be sympathetic to the city, that will respect the man on the street, and inspire him."

Schreier positioned himself at the head of the class and watched as they began this grandest of architectural assignments, at first by simply gluing together pieces of poster board that would stand in as buildings of different sizes and shapes. Then the architects dropped their little productions into the hole that represented the World Trade Center site. There was a triplet of slim towers slightly staggered, reaching just above the height of the nearby Woolworth Building. The team tried a cluster of four identical towers erected face-to-face in a tight square, like the legs of a stool. Then two long, thick, slablike buildings, running parallel to the shoreline and enclosing, like hedgerows, a modest-size duo of towers. There was even a single, monstrous, bulky tower on a huge raised pedestal that may have represented the ultimate parking garage.

Yamasaki, his hands on his hips, or kneeling down, would quietly pass through the drafting room looking over the compositions his crew had offered up. "Too much like a housing project," Yamasaki said of the four-tower option, remembering the failure of Pruitt-Igoe. "That is ugly," Yamasaki said of the single giant tower, evoking laughter among his crew. "That slab just won't work," he said of another option, which—if it was going to meet the Program—would have walled off a huge parcel of Lower Manhattan from view for anyone in the direction of the Hudson River.

Yamasaki was patient. He intended to let the composition emerge organically from this collaborative process. It was Mal Levy who promptly popped the collegial balloon. "I am not sure what you are thinking here," he said to Yamasaki after flying in to look over the first models. Levy, as was his habit, spoke in such a loud voice that there was no doubt that everyone in the drafting room could hear him. "The Port Authority has put together the largest program of buildings ever in history. We do not want just to create another office building development in Manhattan. Nothing here looks distinctive. Nothing here matches the approach that the Port Authority wants to take." Then, without hesitating, he added, "The Port Authority wants this to be the most dramatic project in the world. It must be a symbol of New York. And we want the tallest building in the world." Yamasaki was enraged. But he stood there silently. There was really nowhere for him to turn—Tozzoli would have the same reaction, and he had probably ordered his deputy to visit Yamasaki and straighten him out.

"A whole bunch of little buildings," Tozzoli would say. "Bullshit. That'll never get anywhere."

Now here was an interesting predicament for an architect whose reputation had been built on jewel box–size buildings that celebrated the human scale. No one had previously mentioned that Yamasaki was supposed to design the world's tallest building. With his plaza and the project's overall grandeur of scale, he did have hopes of producing a monument to his artistic vision, something that would stand out from the high-rise forest of Lower Manhattan. But he wanted his buildings to stand on their architectural merit, not their status in the *Guinness Book of World Records*. "If a building is too strong or brutal, it tends to overpower man," Yamasaki had said in one of the speeches he had used to burnish his reputation as a humanist. "In it he feels insecure and uncomfortable. A monument to the ego of a particular owner or architect is contradictory to the principle that each man who uses the building should be able, through his environment, to have the sense of dignity and individual strength to carry on his hopes and aspirations."

Yamasaki never had any intention of proposing the spectacle of the tallest buildings in the city and the world. Levy, though, was not making some vague motivational suggestion for the architect to ponder. He was delivering an order.

Karn watched as Yamasaki's gray Pontiac Grand Am pulled into the parking lot on the Monday morning after Levy's fit. "Now what?" Karn wondered. Yamasaki calmly came into the drafting room and asked everyone to gather. "I've been thinking about what happened on Friday," Yamasaki said. "This is an opportunity that will come along to very few architects in history. I mean, the opportunity to do something like this, on such a grand scale. We're going to do this building. It's going to be the tallest in the world. It's going to be the grandest project ever." The designers in the room looked at each other, shocked. They all knew Yamasaki was as stubborn as an ox. How could he have done such an about-face? "The grandest project ever," they repeated, mocking Yamasaki after the meeting broke up.

The new work started right away. The model shop constructed mockups of the Empire State Building, the Chrysler Building, and the city's other tallest towers, so whatever Yamasaki and his team now came up with, it could be compared directly to what Tozzoli and Levy had made clear was the competition.

As upset as he had been, Yamasaki already had a possible solution percolating through his creative mind. That wonderful set of twins Mies van der Rohe had built along Lake Michigan had stuck with him, particularly the simple but powerful way Mies had arranged the footprints of his twins so that they played off each other—set up in an L-shape instead of just staring straight across at each other. Yamasaki drew a sketch on a piece of onionskin paper that had the twins arranged at a similar angle: instead of putting them in a straight north-south line, he nudged the south tower a bit to the west, the north to the east.

Yamasaki produced models showing twin towers in at least two different compositions, one that had two 80-story towers and another with two 110-story towers. Only the 110-story twins would break the world record. But Yamasaki still was not ready to sign off on building the world's tallest. First of all, he argued, any record would stand for just a short time before someone else built skyscrapers that were taller. What would be the point? Besides, he said, the dimensions of 110-story twins—both their width and height—would be so enormous that he was deeply worried about their visual impact. "They are going to say it looks like a fat lady and she's too tall," Yamasaki had told Kip Serota, an architect in his office who would eventually take over as the World Trade Center project manager.

There was another problem. At 110 stories, the towers would need so many elevators to lift all these tenants into the sky that the shafts would eat up a huge slice of the rentable floor space and make the whole plan unworkable. And Yamasaki was not the only one expressing doubts. Sullivan questioned the wisdom of building the 110-story towers, but for different reasons. It would be easier financially, he suggested, to follow the lead of Rockefeller Center and slowly build a series of smaller towers, filling them up one at a time as the market demanded the space. "Think about the cash flow," Sullivan argued. Julian Roth, one of the lead partners at Emery Roth & Sons, also sided with Yamasaki, arguing that the cost of building so high would break the budget that Levy had draped on the wall. "You guys are crazy," Roth repeatedly told Levy and his staff. "You can't go that high. It is just not feasible."

Neither Tozzoli nor Levy was impressed by the objections. The global attention—call it free advertising—that would be showered on the world's tallest towers was worth the extra cost. "Do they meet the Program?" Tozzoli demanded, when presented with Yamasaki's eighty-story or even ninety-story twin tower plan. "No, they do not," Yamasaki replied. "They are about 2 million square feet short." That was just the segue Tozzoli was looking for. "I like the twin towers scheme," Tozzoli said, pausing for a moment to add some gravitas to his next remark. "Yama, I have something to tell you. President Kennedy is going to put a man on the moon. You're going to figure out a way to build me the tallest buildings in the world."

■ ■ ■

Four men from the model shop, carrying what looked something like two extra-long aluminum caskets, struggled to turn the tight corners in the hallway just outside Yamasaki's drafting room. The Port Authority had gotten what it wanted. These were the models for the 110-story towers, built on a scale of one-sixteenth inch to the foot. Because the towers would be about 1,350 feet high, the models were about 7 feet long. The young architects in the drafting room stood up as the nearly featureless boxes were carried in, gathering around as if eyeing some kind of natural wonder that had turned up in the parking lot. "No way," said Jerry Karn. "That thing is big. I mean *big*." The amazement quickly turned to a riot of laughter as the model crew began to turn the aluminum frames upright. A plywood frame base had been set up on a low table as a base for the models. "Those damn things aren't going to fit," said Jim Herman.

No one had even contemplated this possibility: a model so tall it could not stand upright in the drafting room. Jerry Karn tried to lower the plywood base. That didn't work. The architects started looking up at the tiles of the drop ceiling. Herman grabbed a small ladder and, struggling to control his laughter, he punched out two of the tiles. Karn moved the base so that the twins did not bump into the metal braces that had held the tiles. Then the behemoths were finally moved into place.

"It fits," Herman announced, to a rousing round of applause.

The size had been decided, but that was all. Now, what would the towers look like? What would the architects put on their bare aluminum boxes?

Yamasaki had a special affection for the row after row of narrow windows that had been the most central design element at the Michigan Consolidated Gas Building. Lined up across the building's facade, it pulled eyes skyward. Somehow, Yamasaki also thought that the small module would also make the building more human in scale. Yamasaki was determined to capture that feeling in his new design for the World Trade Center. There was another reason behind his attraction to narrow windows. Oddly enough, for an architect who was designing the world's tallest buildings, he was afraid of heights. Narrow windows meant Yamasaki, and the office workers in the towers, could approach a window and have the security of being able to rest arms against two vertical barriers. "The narrow windows, they give me none, if any, sense of acrophobia," Yamasaki said in explaining his choice. He also thought, for whatever reason, that the pattern had a certain intimacy.

The result of these compulsions was a facade of extraordinary monotony.

One. One. One. One. One. One. One. One. One. One. One. One. One. One. One. One. One. One. One. One. One. Again and again, it was repeated as the eye went across each floor, and then again as the eye went up and down the tower. Horizontally, the composition was made up of a twenty-inch-wide window, two inches of window sash, and then half of the columns on each side of the window, which cumulatively totaled only forty inches. Harold Tsuchiya, who at age forty-two was one of the more senior members of the staff, saw an immediate problem. He prepared a full-size cutout of several columns and windows and set it up near the drafting room. "If you stand at even a bit of an angle," he told Yamasaki, "you will not be able to see out of the windows." Yamasaki was not pleased with Tsuchiya's stunt. "Get rid of it," he told Serota. "The last thing I need is for the Port Authority to see that."

Yamasaki was adamant about at least one other feature of the twin towers. Perhaps the most famous and distinguishing feature about New York City's landmark skyscrapers has been their most visible spot: their tops. The decorative turrets atop the Woolworth Building; the floodlit stainless steel spire that caps the Chrysler Building—this is where the architect really articulated his vision. But Yamasaki wanted a flat, square top to his flat, square tower. Without asking Yamasaki, Jerry Karn prepared a dressing for the aluminum frame that would top the box with a distinctive flare, the steel or aluminum columns continuing outward, almost like a curl of hair. Yamasaki immediately put a stop to the idea. Flat and square. That was the way it was going to be.

And as the design work went ahead, step by step, the architects in the office watched a new Yamasaki emerge. Every great architect struggles to refine his work, to push for perfection in form. But something more fundamental and disturbing was happening. Slowly but surely, Yamasaki was backing away from the style that had earned him fame. It was not evident in the course of a week or two. But as the different model molds were compared, it became obvious. Early models featured a series of elaborately intertwined arches at the base—the steel swerved intricately back and forth, creating a shape that looked almost like a lotus flower. The towers' corners also had a decorative pattern embossed on them that echoed this flowery design. Gradually, the decorative tracery was being stripped and the machine-made look was coming to predominate. Part of the simplification was being driven by the simple physics of the job. The

Program demanded buildings that were so tall, so enormous in scale, that some of his esoteric decorative elements—with their swirling, thin steel designs—were just too delicate to support these mammoth towers. But Karn and Serota, in particular, could see there was much more than that. Yamasaki was fighting with himself. Maybe, Yamasaki was now wondering, the East Coast architecture establishment had been right in criticizing his earlier work. "I wasn't discriminating enough about structure. The bones, the basic structure of a building must be evident and they must be beautiful," he said in January 1963, just as the World Trade Center job reached its peak. "You shouldn't put veils over buildings or barrels around them."

Serota was flabbergasted as he watched Yamasaki strip one decorative element after another from the models. To him, this change could only be explained in one way: Yamasaki, by eliminating tracery and other details that someone might call frilly, was trying to prove to his critics that he was a more serious artist. "That is something we should celebrate," Serota said, describing Yamasaki's more decorative, earlier style. But Yamasaki was unmoved. He told others he considered this new approach a more mature esthetic, since the architect now believed he should only apply elements to a building's facade that were integral to the structural design itself. The denouement came on a day when Yamasaki's oldest child, Carol, who was in college at the time, visited Yamasaki's office and stopped to look at the model in the drafting room. As her eyes ran up along the fine lines of the exterior columns, she suddenly encountered a sort of decorative belt that, for the moment, was still included in the design for several floors—the ones that would hold mechanical and electrical equipment rather than offices. When Yamasaki came into the room to greet his daughter, she announced, before the drafting room crew: "Daddy, you aren't really going to do this, are you?" She then added: "They look like garters." That same day, the garters simply disappeared. "My own kid is criticizing the decoration," Yama said.

With this final simplification, an extraordinary thing had happened. Thousands of hours had been invested. Hundreds of molds featuring different decorative options had been applied to the aluminum models. The tops of the twins would be chamfered, the corners angled, distinguishing these edges a bit if the buildings were viewed up close. But the design Yamasaki was bringing to the Port Authority as his final product had

Yamasaki's Struggle

As Minoru Yamasaki designed the World Trade Center, he prepared dozens of drafts of the plans of the lower arches and corners of the towers. The designs gradually became simpler as Yamasaki, defensive about criticism by some that his earlier buildings were too decorative, decided that the lines of the arches should be as clean as possible.

Earlier, more decorative design

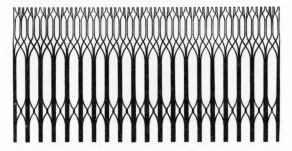

Final, cleaner plan, reflecting the design as built

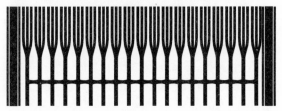

Source: (Early design) Jim Herman,
architect at Minoru Yamasaki &
Associates from 1960 to 1963   The New York Times

about as much tactile delight and textural richness as the plain aluminum boxes that the men from his model shop had delivered.

▪ ▪ ▪

Levy and Tozzoli were content to leave the artsy details to Yamasaki and his crew. Their focus was on a single objective: delivering the Program in the tallest buildings in the world. To ensure such a structure could be built, the Port Authority realized it had to answer one major objection that Yamasaki had raised, when he advocated towers of no more than 80 or 90 floors. The elevator system required for a 110-story tower would be so elaborate, it would eat up large swaths in the buildings' cores. Solving this dilemma was handed over to Calvin Kort, a young engineer with

Jaros Baum & Bolles, a consulting company the Port Authority hired. Kort, who had started his career by working for Otis Elevator, had been enamored of Frank Lloyd Wright's plan for Mile High Illinois, a skyscraper that would never be built. To shuttle people through Wright's 1956 dream tower, the plan stated that "elevator transit is by atomic power; especially designed elevators, each five stories high, serving in series the five divisions of 100-floor heights." Kort would not pitch atomic power. But it was while thinking about the Mile High plans that he came up with a revolutionary alternative for the twin towers. Why not create banks of express elevators that would speed nonstop to different sectors of the tower, where tenants would then take a local to their floor, sort of like the express and local subway system in New York City? Tozzoli declared the idea ingenious—although, typically, he credited his own staff for it.

There was no hint of the bitter disputes over the shape of the towers when Yamasaki's architectural model was unveiled to the public at the New York Hilton Hotel on January 18, 1964. Finally, the city could see what it was getting, and the headline writers never had it easier. "BIGGEST BUILDINGS IN WORLD TO RISE AT TRADE CENTER; Twin 1,350-Foot Towers to Be Surrounded by Plaza With Small Structures." "Trade Center to Be Colossus." "*New Trade Center Towers to Be Taller Than Empire State.*" "BIGGEST BUILDINGS HERALD NEW ERA." "Going Up—World's Two Tallest Buildings." "*THE TALLEST. THE NEWEST. THE MOST.*" For one day, at least, opponents of the project were either overwhelmed or silent in the press. That went for critics like Oscar Nadel, who were already active, and for a new and very powerful group of people—the city's real estate moguls—who were shocked by the unprecedented scale of the towers and the competition they would represent.

Yamasaki's statement to the press did not deviate from the themes he had been propounding since he found himself as an architect. The World Trade Center, he said, should "become a living representation of man's belief in humanity" and should "reflect the qualities of life which he so passionately seeks of truth and serenity, of hope and joy for all men, qualities integral to the kind of democracy for which he aspires." For the trade center's architect, his creation may have been gargantuan, but it was still a spiritual sanctuary.

The Port Authority press packet for the day, put together by Lee Jaffe, left no rhetorical note unsounded: "gleaming metal," "the tallest buildings in the world," "will soar 110 stories," "a great open Plaza," "will be recognized throughout the world," "a focal point for the convenient and efficient administration of all phases of international trade."

There were lots of pictures, some questions from the press, and everyone went home. And the war between Yamasaki and the Port Authority started all over again.

The model that had been unveiled showed a plaza surrounded by a series of linked smaller office buildings. The plan called for a glassed-in walkway around the edges of the plaza. Inside the walkway would be a series of stores and cafés. It had been inspired by Piazza San Marco with its covered arcade around the square. Tozzoli's team axed the plan, insisting that the restaurants and shops be concentrated in an underground shopping mall and transit center. Levy then intensified the dispute by ridiculing Yamasaki's design for the layout of the underground mall. One afternoon, with plans for the shopping concourse spread out on the floor, Levy stood up on Yamasaki's Hans Wegner office armchair, jumped into the air, and then pounced atop Yamasaki's design. "I don't like it. I just don't like it," Levy yelled. Yamasaki was startled at the outrageous performance.

Then Tozzoli decided that the windows planned at the very top of the towers just had to be wider. His reasons were about the same as the ones voiced by Harold Tsuchiya, who had prepared the cutouts of the tightly spaced columns in Yamasaki's office: if you stood back from the window, there were no views at all. And at the very top, Tozzoli intended to open a restaurant that would be called Windows on the World. How could you have the highest restaurant in the world with no view? "I want windows at least one and a half times the size," Tozzoli told Levy to instruct Yamasaki. What Tozzoli did not realize was that he was challenging Yamasaki's obsession with a perfect, never-disrupted module of forty inches for each window and column unit. One day Tobin called Tozzoli up to his office on the fifteenth floor of 111 Eighth Avenue with some bad news for the director of the World Trade Center project.

"Yama has threatened to quit," Tobin told Tozzoli.

Tozzoli held his ground, saying he would not be responsible for the disastrous failure of the restaurant. Besides, he reminded Tobin, Yamasaki had gotten a tremendous amount of good press for the trade center. "There's no way the son of a bitch will quit," Tozzoli said.

Mal Levy was sent to the Plaza Hotel, where Yamasaki, having just announced his intention to quit, was hastily throwing his clothing into his bags to prepare for the trip back to Detroit.

"Let's go to Italy together," Levy said to the architect, trying to figure out a way to calm him down. "We can go look at the marble."

"Don't give me candy," Yamasaki snapped back.

Yamasaki would fly home, burning with an anger that recalled the day he had swung at his boss at the salmon-canning factory. But Tozzoli had Yamasaki figured out. The architect would not quit. And the Port Authority would get its wider windows at the top.

There were, to be sure, areas where Yamasaki and the Port Authority were in agreement. Both the architect and Tozzoli believed the lobbies of the twin towers had to serve as showcases. To Tozzoli, the lobby was central to his sales pitch. It was the first thing potential clients saw inside the building. "I want beautiful lobbies. You've got extra money for lobbies," Tozzoli told him. For Yamasaki, here finally was an opportunity for him to recall that almost supernaturally beautiful place he had encountered outside the Alaskan canning factory. To achieve this effect, Yamasaki sent Harold Tsuchiya on a trip across northern Italy to find an almost pure white marble. "When you look at the wall, I don't want anyone to be distracted by a marking on an individual piece," Yamasaki told Tsuchiya. Furthermore, the stainless steel doors to the elevators would be so finely polished they would almost resemble mirrors. The ceilings would be seventy feet high and, with the towers' arches opening up as they reached the ground, there would be enormous windows that flooded the cathedral-like lobbies with natural light. The idea was obvious: create a serene space at just the spot where the biggest crowds gathered.

But the contest of wills that seemed to predominate in this job put a strain on Yamasaki. Life outside of the office only compounded the anxiety. Yamasaki's second marriage, to Peggy Watty, quickly disintegrated. Within two years of their wedding, they were divorced. Yamasaki, on a trip to Japan, then had met and quickly married a Japanese woman, but they broke up not long afterward. His reaction to this rejection was to continue to push himself, to do whatever was necessary to prove his own worth. He was sleeping very little and ignoring signs that his body was about to revolt. Yamasaki would ask Schreier and three or four others to join him for lunch, and they would then spend hours eating and drinking until Yamasaki was drunk. "Why are we spending so much time doing this?" Schreier wondered. At one point, while out of town on his way home from a business trip, Yamasaki went into seizures and was rushed to a hospital. Teri and the children rushed to see him after he was transferred to Detroit, convinced that he was near death. Desperate to try to regain a piece of his former life, Yamasaki told Teri he had changed his will, "so that the house and everything will be yours."

He survived, but his health remained fragile. And his personal life got only stranger. By the time he left the hospital, he had fallen in love with one of his nurses. He ended up living with her, but soon enough that relationship crumbled as well. The work did somehow continue, with Yamasaki's staff on occasion shuttling plans to his sick bed. Once Yamasaki regained his strength, he came back to the office, revising much of what the team had done in his absence.

■ ■ ■

There never really would be a final World Trade Center design. Part of the reason was just the enormous scope of what Yamasaki was being asked to create. But much of it had to do with Yamasaki's determination to get it right, even if he was not exactly sure what *right* meant. Even as the towers were being built, he would be making revisions, struggling to refine what should have been his masterpiece.

Yet now that he had sided with his harshest critics—turning his back on the delicate forms he had once celebrated—the critics only became harsher. Yamasaki was no longer merely a superficial decorator, as he had been labeled in the past. Now he was thrusting upon New York City a monstrosity, two aluminum-clad steel tubes, so plain in their design that, as the joke went, they could have been the shipping boxes for the Chrysler and Empire State Buildings. "Manhattan's Tower of Babel," *The Nation* said. "Gargantua-by-the-Sea," pronounced *Architectural Forum*. "The World's Tallest Fiasco," wrote *Harper's*. "Homage to Giantism," said Lewis Mumford. "The ultimate Disneyland fairytale blockbuster," said Ada Louise Huxtable. "It is General Motors Gothic."

The harshness of these reviews, as justified as they were in purely architectural terms, did miss something essential about Yamasaki's composition. There was an exquisite if abstract beauty to the gently broken symmetry of the twins, facing each other along the riverside in the architectural models. The towers might well take hold of the eye and lift it forever upward once they were built, just as Yamasaki had intended. And the metallic skin that the Port Authority had made so much of—it seemed perfectly designed to catch the mood of the sky, looking morose as storm clouds pulled in, luminous in the glistening light at sunrise and sunset, gritty in the city haze, and riotously busy with random windows ablaze throughout the night. Of course, the towers would have to be built before the ordinary citizens of the city could decide whether those pleasing qualities offset what the towers most assuredly lacked: anything at all that was human in scale. They were just the kind of overpowering giants that Yamasaki would have condemned not so long before. The seething conflicts in Yamasaki's artistic soul had been written into his towers.

Yamasaki remained successful, but his career, which had been on overdrive, slowed down considerably. His bid for a seat in the pantheon of great modern architects was over. He did reconcile with Teri, his first wife. In 1969, with the World Trade Center design work finally nearing its end, the two decided to remarry, after Yamasaki, on the spur of the moment, had invited her to join him on a trip to Puerto Rico. "I will try to be a more Japanese wife," Teri said. "I'm just going to be nicer to her," Yamasaki replied. Yamasaki, weakened physically and emotionally by the trade center fight, had at least mellowed a bit. Levy and Tozzoli helped celebrate the remarriage. They all went on a trip to Europe as part of the search for chandelier glass for the trade center lobbies. Tozzoli hosted the big honeymoon dinner party, at which Yamasaki, as usual, had too much to drink. Tozzoli had to step in and calm Teri, who grew angry as the night wore on. Her husband, even on their second honeymoon, seemed to be headed off on a tangent, searching for something else. "You know very well he is a great, eccentric artist," Tozzoli said reassuringly to Teri. "He's an architect after all."

5

···

Steel Balloons

Regardless of any regulations that may exist or be enacted, it can be anticipated that similar occurrences are possible as long as planes are in the air, due to the vagaries of weather, mechanical devices and carelessness in operation.

—Report on the Collision of U.S. Army Air Force Bomber with the Empire State Building at 78th and 79th Floors and Ensuing Fire, New York Board of Fire Underwriters, July 28, 1945

John Skilling stood before an easel and a flip chart at the Port Authority's headquarters in the summer of 1962 and drew a series of diagrams showing steel structures, as if he were a strange sort of street artist. There were no glossy brochures, no color graphics. He worked quickly, using only felt-tip markers to create drawings that were both vivid and precisely illustrative of some design principle. The whole presentation was so disarmingly uncomplicated that Skilling, a forty-year-old engineer from Seattle, might have been discussing the expansion of a high school gym. In fact, he was proposing a radically new kind of structure for great skyscrapers—a structure completely unlike that of the Empire State Building or any other traditional high-rise, including the building he was standing in.

Skilling, blue-eyed, with a roundish face and black horn-rimmed glasses, was at the headquarters interviewing for a job: the job of designing the World Trade Center's structure. One reason for the deceptive simplicity of his presentation—which had actually been developed in weeks of intensive work by him and other engineers at his company—was that he knew it would be hopeless to compete with the big New York firms and their limitless public relations resources. The other reason was that

Skilling was at his most brilliant, and convincing, when he had nothing but a pencil, a pad of paper, or just a napkin, and an hour of a prospective client's time. He struck spectators as a cross between a computer and an Irish bartender.

A group of Port Authority engineers, including Mal Levy, assembled in a third-floor conference room and gave Skilling forty-five minutes, with fifteen more set aside for questions. Half a dozen New York engineering firms had already run through their own presentations, assembly line–style, that same day. Skilling's was the last on the schedule. He stood at the easel sketching in solitary fashion with his handful of felt tips. He had come from Seattle alone, bringing no one to help with the pitch. Skilling kept sketching through his forty-five-minute allotment and through the question period. Two hours after he had gotten started, Levy and the other Port Authority engineers were still asking questions, still interested to see the wizard at the easel do one more drawing.

Skilling's job interview was a smashing success, and he won the commission. The Port Authority executed its contract with his firm and with Yamasaki's on the same day: September 12, 1962. Yamasaki would specify the size of the towers, the look of their facades, the ornamental design of the lobbies. Only a structural engineer like Skilling could figure out how to make the towers stand up against the tremendous forces of gravity and wind. There had to be a skeleton inside Yamasaki's creations.

There was a good reason this structural pied piper had gotten his tryout with the Port Authority. Skilling was the structural engineer Yamasaki trusted most, the one he had relied on more than any other to help the traceries and curlicues and pinstripes of his imagination, and his little wooden models, become reality. It had begun with the slender concrete arches above the entranceway at the Federal Science Pavilion—the peaceful structure that Tozzoli would discover at the Seattle World's Fair. Someone at the local architectural firm that was Yamasaki's partner on the project said he knew a structural engineer who would not be intimidated by the assignment. "It's all right with me if he can do what we want," said Yamasaki, clearly skeptical that a local engineering firm could achieve the delicateness of his design, especially the arches' skinny, stilt-like legs. "You'll have to do them that size or we'll find somebody who can," Yamasaki said bluntly.

About a week later, John Skilling came back with his firm's calculations and this answer: "You don't need to make them that big." In this case, the detailed design had been performed by Jack Christiansen, the firm's resident master of thin concrete structures. Wherever the ideas had originated, there was no better way to grab the attention of an architect who had a deep appreciation of engineering, but who had come to despise the way earthbound forces and stresses—or at least the people who calculated them—were constantly limiting his esthetic. "That's the first time an engineer did me one better," said Yamasaki when he was given the news.

Yamasaki had found the engineer who would almost never say no. Indeed, Skilling would not only disdain placing limits on a soaring architectural imagination; he would constantly egg Yamasaki on to even more fanciful ideas. And many architects would come to adore the way that the artful Skilling did not talk in the grease-monkey style of a 1950s engineer. He knew how to melt their creative hearts and design a great building at the same time. "We had worked with some other well-known engineers. We hated them," Yamasaki said. "Skilling has more of an architect's imagination."

And soon after the twin towers began to take shape in Yamasaki's drafting room, the essence of Skilling's structural vision became clear. What he and the other engineers at his firm, Worthington, Skilling, Helle & Jackson, had in mind was a high-rise structure that did not have a matrix of vertical columns piercing each floor every fifteen or twenty feet in order to provide support, as traditional skyscrapers did. Instead, a tight series of steel columns would run vertically along each of the twin towers' facades, like a picket fence around an empty lot. The key idea was to make Yamasaki's pinstripes into structural, load-bearing elements rather than merely decorative motifs. The pinstripes, spaced just a few feet apart, would not be there just for the architecture—they would double as the structure itself. But behind the facade—inside the picket fence, so to speak—the floors would be gloriously free of any columns for as much as sixty feet. The floors would be supported at one end by the perimeter columns and at the other by a cluster of columns in the building's core, where the elevator and stair shafts would be.

This structure would have still another set of innovations around its perimeter. Like the horizontal lengths of wood that connect the staves, or vertical pieces, of a picket fence, deep steel plates called spandrels would run from one perimeter column to the next to give the building stiffness and let it resist the lateral force of the wind. Traditional buildings relied on the combined strength of their perimeter columns as well as everything inside them to resist the wind—from stiff masonry stair shafts, to the zigzagging steel cross-bracing and riveted connections of structural skeletons, to the great mass of the stone facades. There was a certain inefficiency here: using the relatively narrow interior of the building for stiffness was something like trying to resist a sideways push with one's feet bound together. Using the wider perimeter was like resisting the same push with feet spread. Much more efficient. In a building, less steel would be required for the same stiffness if the perimeter became the main element, rather than sharing the duty with the interior.

Such buildings would be akin to stiff tubes, filled with anything the owner wanted to put inside. Even after all the masonry and cross-bracing was stripped away, calculations at the Skilling firm showed, the structure would be stiffer than a traditional structure anyway, more than ten times stiffer.

As a bonus, this kind of skyscraper could be assembled out of huge prefabricated pieces, three columns at a time, in sections almost forty feet long, which would be lifted into place with cranes and bolted together so quickly that the buildings would fly out of the ground. Each piece would have a distinctive number, stenciled right onto the side, and would be delivered just when it was needed. The chaos that a steel job of this magnitude could cause in Lower Manhattan would be all but eliminated. Efficiency: you would have it in the construction phase as well.

It was a measure of Skilling's brashness that his firm's office building was the tallest he or anyone else at the firm had ever designed: the twenty-one-story, 293-foot Washington Building at Fourth and Union Streets in downtown Seattle. The firm had moved into the eighteenth floor of the building, with its fine views of Puget Sound, after construction was finished in 1960. But no one found it hard to believe that this magician was ready to design the world's tallest buildings. "JOHN SKILLING: ARCHITECT'S ENGINEER PLANS THE BIGGEST" was the headline above Skilling's face on the cover of *Engineering News-Record* in April 1964, three months after Yamasaki's model of the twin towers was unveiled to the public. Effusive praise for Skilling's talents spilled across the pages. Skilling had the ability "to think with a soft pencil," said one architect.

By now, the press releases emanating from Lee Jaffe's public relations

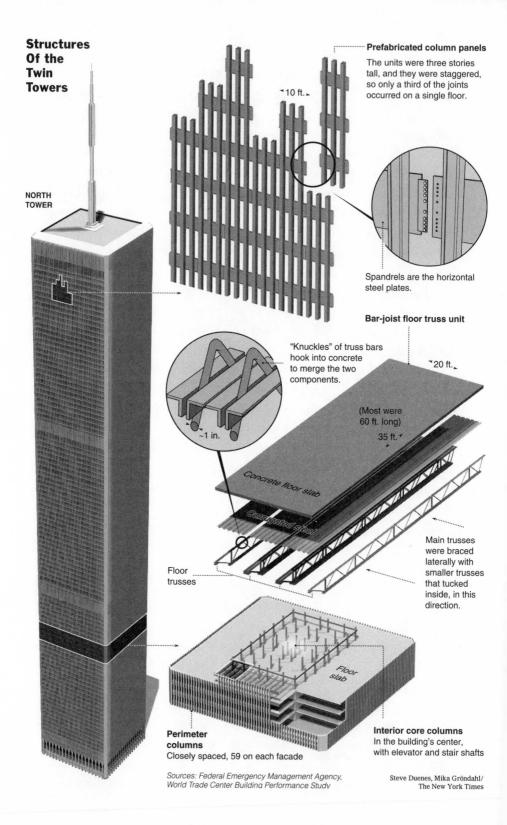

Structures Of the Twin Towers

NORTH TOWER

Prefabricated column panels
The units were three stories tall, and they were staggered, so only a third of the joints occurred on a single floor.

◄10 ft.►

Spandrels are the horizontal steel plates.

Bar-joist floor truss unit

"Knuckles" of truss bars hook into concrete to merge the two components.

◄20 ft.►

(Most were 60 ft. long)

35 ft. ◄

Concrete floor slab

Corrugated steel

~1 in.

Main trusses were braced laterally with smaller trusses that tucked inside, in this direction.

Floor trusses

Floor slab

Perimeter columns
Closely spaced, 59 on each facade

Interior core columns
In the building's center, with elevator and stair shafts

Sources: Federal Emergency Management Agency, *World Trade Center Building Performance Study*

Steve Duenes, Mika Gröndahl/
The New York Times

department at the Port Authority had begun depicting the structural design in almost messianic terms. The agency proclaimed that Walt Whitman's phrase "high growth of iron, slender, strong, light, splendidly uprising toward clear skies," written in praise of the younger Manhattan's skyline, "captured with succinct eloquence the structural characteristics and spirit of the twin 110-story towers." The Skilling tube design would reduce by an incredible 40 percent the amount of steel that would be needed to hold the buildings up, the literature explained. Stripping away the heavy masonry walls and facades of traditional high-rises in favor of glass and steel would make the twin towers the lightest, airiest skyscrapers ever built. Calling into play an array of high-strength steel would give the towers tremendous reserve strength, and even with all the reductions and savings, the towers' ability to withstand wind forces was "far in excess of the design load of any other New York City office building," the literature rhapsodized. The World Trade Center, the agency said, "required engineering ingenuity from foundation to roof."

The truth was a little more prosaic. As outlandish as his design sounded to the Eastern engineering establishment, including the Port Authority's own hardheaded engineering department—which was deeply offended by Mal Levy's decision to have an outside firm do the work— every facet of the design was almost a photographic expansion of something that Skilling and his staff had used on earlier jobs. As far back as 1957, Skilling and Nathaniel Curtis, the New Orleans architect, designed a thirteen-story office tower in Pittsburgh that was among the first modern high-rises whose exterior walls would be built to resist all the lateral forces caused by wind—a system close to the "tube" concept of the World Trade Center. This design let Skilling and his engineers build fifty-seven-foot "clear spans," or floor spaces unencumbered by columns, just like the trade center. The design also used newly available high-strength steel, as the trade center would.

Even the conversion of Yamasaki's pinstripes into structural elements had already been done in the IBM Building in Seattle, a twenty-story, 272-foot high-rise completed in 1963. The steel pinstripes, separated by less than 3 feet, were encased in prefabricated concrete covers, like the prefabricated steel panels of the trade center.

Perhaps the most striking parallel, though, was embedded deep inside the Washington Building in Seattle. Ordinarily, the steel girders and beams supporting the floors get in the way of the ductwork, plumbing, and electrical wiring that must thread their way through the space between the ceiling of one story of the building and the floor of the next. From other engineers, Skilling borrowed the idea of using torches to cut a zigzagging pattern along the length of the support beams, sliding one of the halves a few inches horizontally and welding the pieces back together again. This "castellated beam" method left gaps for the ductwork to fit through, and it let Skilling reduce the total height of each story in the Washington Building by nearly a foot. He and his staff took the idea a step further in their design for the World Trade Center: they proposed replacing the beams entirely with airy, weblike networks of thin steel bars and angle irons called bar-joist trusses. Corrugated decking would be placed atop these floor trusses so that concrete could be poured on it to create the floors.

The ductwork could run without obstruction, and the diaphanous floor trusses would complete a design for the World Trade Center without precedent in its feathery, ethereal lightness. Skilling engineers calculated that for every cubic foot of space inside the Empire State Building, that skyscraper weighed 17 pounds; the World Trade Center would weigh just 10.5 pounds a cubic foot, lighter by an amazing 38 percent.

As with all of the Skilling innovations, the trusses came with several twists. First of all, the trusses that actually went into the building would be stouter than any similar support system ever devised, with cross-bracing and a redundant design unknown in the ordinary bar-joist trusses that are common in warehouse construction. Second, the trusses would be built in such a way that the concrete of the floors would also add to the structural integrity of the system. Still, Skilling and his engineers had, once again, gone into a structural realm where no one else had been.

The trade center design seemed to solve all the old structural problems at once. The solution seemed so technically advanced and so creative that no engineer in the nineteenth or early-twentieth century could have dreamed it up. "Some people think our structures are far out," said Skilling, as unruffled as ever when he was questioned about the World Trade Center's design in Seattle one day. "Actually, we're more conservative than most engineers, but we're conservative in total concept, rather than in the individual structural members. If the total concept is sufficiently sound, it is possible to be conservative without destroying the economics or the esthetics of the structure."

Whatever reference points there might have been in Skilling's earlier work, of course, the twin towers were exponentially larger than anything he had attempted before. And his structural contortions, so unfamiliar to great builders like the Rockefellers or the conservative Port Authority engineers, raised immediate questions, even among supporters of the project. Nelson Rockefeller talked with William Ronan, his chief of staff, about the oddity of floors with no columns and a facade that was meant to keep an entire skyscraper standing. Rockefeller ultimately assumed that the Port Authority, with its reputation as a designer of lasting structures, must know what it was doing, and that was that.

There were also disturbing questions raised much closer to the heart of the project. Rosaleen Skehan, Austin Tobin's crisis manager and urban affairs expert, may have been a lawyer, but her father had been a New York cop and she was close to many officials in the Fire Department. Skehan had, in fact, been appalled when the model of the twin towers was unveiled, and she knew in a heartbeat the battles that the proposal to build such immense structures would spark in the city. As plainspoken as she was, Skehan kept those thoughts largely to herself. But with an unerring talent for discovering a weakness within the most impenetrable bluster, she challenged Mal Levy on a point that would, decades later, become the most important of all.

"In this great project of yours, how do you propose to fight a fire on the high floors?" Skehan said to Levy during a meeting in one of the boardrooms at the Port Authority headquarters. In other words, Skehan said so that there was no mistaking her question, "If there were a fire on the high floors, how would my friend"—she named a New York fire chief—"fight the fire?"

Levy not only refused to be cowed by Skehan; he decided that he would try to make her question look stupid.

"If your chief was really good," Levy sneered, "he would simply drive up the steps into the plaza and put the ladders up there."

After the meeting, one of his aides, John Dragonette, tried to tell Levy that the retort was shocking even by his standards. "Malcolm, you know, you're going to pay for this," Dragonette said. "You cannot talk to Rosaleen like that."

"When I'm right, I'm right," Levy said.

But Skehan was doing no more than giving expression to the historical memory of her friends in the Fire Department, where disasters in tall buildings formed the core of the scare stories told every night in fire houses. That memory went back at least as far as Henry Baldwin Hyde's Equitable Life Building at Broadway and Cedar Street, the building that had so impressed the city with its elevators and the newfound convenience of working on the upper floors. At about 5 A.M. on January 9, 1912, a fire started in the Equitable Building, quickly spread through a shaft to all floors, and caused some of the building's early cast-iron columns and steel and wrought-iron I-beams to buckle. As fierce winter winds whipped up the fire, the building collapsed, leaving only the outer walls standing. The next day, crowds gathered to see a statue of Henry Hyde in the building's rotunda, which had survived, looking at a surreal ice castle where the city's first tall building once stood—now complemented with a frozen hook and ladder.

Of course, buildings did not have to collapse to cause catastrophe—and become etched in the institutional lore of the Fire Department. When a fire started in a ten-story building at 22 Washington Place on March 25, 1911, many of the workers at the Triangle Shirtwaist Company on the top three floors found the fire doors locked shut. The Fire Department ladder could reach no higher than the sixth floor—the terrifying discovery that Skehan's question to Levy would echo—and the water streaming from their hoses no higher than the seventh. With the flames burning behind them, the women workers started to jump in unison. In all, 141 workers would die, 125 of them women. On just one sidewalk, forty bodies came to rest.

Many in the Fire Department still went to work with thoughts not so different from those of Alfred Ludwig, the chief buildings inspector in Manhattan who issued a warning the year after the Triangle Shirtwaist fire. Some of the new high-rise structures, Ludwig said, were too big, with too few fire exits, to evacuate safely in a major fire, whatever the structural merits of the buildings. "The Titanic was unsinkable—yet she went down; our skyscrapers are unburnable—yet we shall have a skyscraper disaster which will stagger humanity," Ludwig declared.

In 1945, that prediction almost came true.

■ ■ ■

The plane, its engines bellowing, shot across Park Avenue, banking wildly to miss the thirty-story office tower behind Grand Central Terminal.

Within moments the plane was soaring south down Fifth Avenue, ducking in and out of a low bank of clouds about a thousand feet off the ground on this rainy, foggy Saturday morning in July 1945. The clouds were just low enough to envelop the top two or three hundred feet of the Empire State Building, at the corner of Fifth Avenue and Thirty-fourth Street. And the plane, a twin-engined B-25 army bomber carrying a pilot, copilot, one passenger, and eight hundred gallons of high-octane aviation fuel in its tanks, was heading directly toward that building, to the stupefaction of thousands of people on the street below. Stanley Lomax, a radio sports announcer who was driving to work in his car, instinctively shouted at the plane to climb after it dipped below the clouds around Forty-second Street. A few seconds later, Lieutenant Allen Aiman, a pilot himself, who happened to be on the Empire State Building's 102nd-floor observation deck, saw the plane sweep out of a cloud bank directly beneath him. In that instant, Aiman could see the plane banking and climbing at full throttle, its pilot desperately trying to avoid the building. Instead, the B-25 blasted into the north face of the 78th and 79th floors at 250 miles an hour. Aiman and his wife, Betty, were thrown to the floor as the Empire State Building swayed back and forth like a whipsaw.

People on the streets heard two rumbling booms—probably the plane's impact and then its fuel tank exploding. A brilliant orange mushroom of flame rushed up the side of the building at least as far as the lower observation deck on the eighty-sixth floor. An engine and part of the landing gear hurtled across the floor and through the south wall of the building, plunging through the skylight of a twelve-story building across the street. Either soaring plane parts or heat from the fire weakened an elevator cable, which snapped, the car plummeting seventy-five floors into a subcellar. Two women inside the elevator car miraculously survived. On the seventy-ninth floor, there were seventeen people at work that morning, all of them employees of the Catholic War Relief Services. Ten of them were killed almost immediately by the fuel-fed blaze that raced across the floor. One man was either blown out of a window or jumped to escape the inferno, and he died when he landed on a terrace seven floors below.

But after being spun around in her chair by the concussion, Therese Fortier, a secretary, somehow managed to avoid a mass of orange flames spewing from the floor's central reception area. So did Kay O'Connor, another secretary, who sat next to her about ninety feet southwest of where the collision had occurred. She had been standing, holding a handful of letters, and now she, too, felt the building sway, and sway again, as if in a great earthquake. Moments later, Fortier and O'Connor saw a horrible sight within the maelstrom of flames in the reception area. A dark shape emerged, walking with dreamlike slowness, a man with his hair burned off, his head swollen to grotesque proportions: their colleague Joe Fountain.

"Oh, Joe!" O'Connor screamed amid the carnage. "Oh, Christ in heaven! Look at what's happened to Joe!"

They rushed to him, but the moment someone touched him, he went ramrod stiff. "Please . . . please don't touch me," Fountain said.

Somehow, he had the presence of mind to direct everyone—five secretaries in all had gathered—to a back office, where they waited in terror as the flames closed in on them. Horribly injured and in agony, Joe Fountain asked them to say the Act of Contrition with him. "Oh my God, I am heartily sorry for having offended Thee," they murmured in words barely audible because of the flames roaring near the closed office door. One of the women began to sob. Therese Fortier, certain that her life was over, threw a ruby ring out a window to keep it from being destroyed in the fire. But within minutes they heard firefighters tromping outside the office, their hoses blasting water. The firefighters escorted the six of them down an escape stairwell to about the sixty-fifth floor, where they caught an elevator to the ground. They all survived except for Joe Fountain, who would drift into a coma and die a few days later.

The next day, the ragged hole that the plane had torn in the world's tallest building drew crowds on Fifth Avenue. Among them was Private First Class Alvin Silverman, who stood near Fifth Avenue and Forty-second Street looking south. Silverman displayed three battle stars above the breast pocket of his khaki uniform—one each for battles in France, Germany, and Austria—and he was on furlough, staying at home in Brooklyn as he waited to be shipped out for the expected invasion of Japan. But on that day, he was just as shocked as some of the other people who had gathered on the street to gape at the punctured north face of the Empire State Building.

All Silverman could see from where he stood was the charred hole with the mangled remnants of the plane's tail sticking out, but he knew from the papers that the plane, piloted by Lieutenant Colonel William F. Smith Jr., a twenty-eight-year-old decorated veteran of bombing raids in Europe, had gotten lost in the fog after ignoring warnings from an air controller at La Guardia Airport. The only other time Silverman, a combat artilleryman in the 44th Infantry Division, had seen B-25s was when they had flown over his head on bombing runs in Europe. Now, he couldn't quite accept what his eyes were telling him. He thought of the plane's crew, the people who had been killed inside the building, and the horrible scar on one of the world's great structures. And he wondered how the building had managed to withstand such a tremendous blow. Not much else was known, except that the Fire Department had somehow managed to put out the fire on the seventy-ninth floor—at 913 feet above the street, the highest blaze the world had seen—within forty minutes of its arrival.

There did not seem to be much prospect that Private Silverman would ever know more than that—particularly with the invasion of Japan looming in his immediate future. But the war ended a month later, he got a Harvard law degree, and in early 1953 he took a job with Lawrence A. Wien, a commanding figure in New York real estate circles. Wien had invented the field of real estate syndication, a system that allowed investors of modest means to band together and invest in the nation's greatest, and often most profitable, buildings. He was, in fact, planning to use this strategy to buy the Empire State Building. It took Wien eight more years, and when the $65 million deal finally went through, it was called the most complex transaction in real estate history. But like any prospective buyer, Wien first checked the property over and looked into its records, the ritual that lawyers call "due diligence." That was when Silverman, as chief counsel on the purchase, came across the Fire Department's detailed report on how the building survived the July 1945 crash whose aftermath he had witnessed on Fifth Avenue.

The report explained how the building had withstood the impact so easily, how the firefighters had been able to arrive so soon, and why the fire could be put out so quickly. The massive steel columns in the exterior walls were surrounded by eight inches of brick and eight more of limestone, so when the plane—weighing twelve tons and measuring sixty-seven feet, six inches from wingtip to wingtip—struck the facade, it punched a hole barely eighteen by twenty feet in size. Just three steel beams in the wall were even damaged: a ten-inch-wide beam was torn from its rivets, a sixteen-inch beam was twisted, and another large beam suffered a ⅜-inch dent. The fire did no structural damage to the steel skeleton, because columns in the wall were protected by from four to eight inches of stout masonry fireproofing—brick or terra-cotta—and interior columns were sheathed in two solid inches of masonry. The maze of thick walls running among the forest of interior support columns also helped block the spread of the fire. Escape stairways were enclosed in at least six inches of masonry, which helped keep them intact and allowed not only the 79th-floor survivors but also people from the observation decks on the 86th and 102nd floors, to descend and escape the building through the impact and fire zones, the report said.

One standpipe riser, or water supply pipe, had been severed by debris from the airplane, but an excellent backup system let the firefighters keep pumping water into the blaze. They were able to take working elevators to the sixty-fifth floor and trudge, albeit slowly and laboriously, carrying hoses and equipment, more than a dozen floors higher. There were some unexpected and frightening problems, like burning gasoline that spilled down an elevator shaft and set fires as far down as the basement level, the report said. All in all, though, the report concluded, tenants in the Empire State Building should feel deeply reassured about its stoutness: "It seems, to some extent, fortunate that if the crash did have to occur, that it was so squarely into such a well-constructed building. It is difficult to fully visualize what the result would have been if the plane had crashed into a less sturdy building."

Silverman took the report to Wien and went through the findings with him. Wien liked the implications for structural integrity, for the ability to fight fires in the building he'd had his eye on for so long. He was ready to close the deal.

The sale, which took place around a thirty-seven-foot mahogany table on December 27, 1961, at the Newark headquarters of the Prudential Insurance Company, required the services of nearly a hundred lawyers, accountants, and realty specialists. The transaction created a complex web of ownership, brokers' fees, leases, and subleases involving Prudential, Harry Helmsley, Wien and his syndication group, and others. Gabe Pressman, a reporter for WNBC-TV, brought in cameras for network television; the *New York Times* reported that just signing all the documents took more than two hours. But for all the complications, Wien, speaking for himself and the group he led, could accurately summarize the deal for the Empire State Building in three short words: "We own it."

Wien embarked on a wide-ranging renovation plan as soon as the building was in his hands, cleaning the entire limestone facade, upgrading the electrical systems and the lighting, and refurbishing the observation decks. And on June 18, 1963, Wien flipped the switch on new lights illuminating a set of elaborate marble panels in the lobby that he called "The Eight Wonders of the World." The first seven were the usual ones: the hanging gardens of Babylon, the Colossus of Rhodes, and so on. The eighth, of course, was the Empire State Building itself.

▪ ▪ ▪

"Salient points with regard to the structural design of The World Trade Center towers" was the low-key title on the white paper in the Port Authority's files. Below the title were eleven numbered points on the structure, beginning with: "1. The structural analysis carried out by the firm of Worthington, Skilling, Helle & Jackson is the most complete and detailed of any ever made for any building structure. The preliminary calculations alone cover 1,200 pages and involve over 100 detailed drawings." At the end of the three-page document was the notation "MPL:fg" above the date "2-3-64"—meaning that the white paper had been typed for Malcolm P. Levy by his secretary, Florence Grainger, on February 3, 1964.

Some of the numbered points gave routine summaries of the expected characteristics of the twin towers' engineering design. But halfway down the first page, the paper contained this astonishing statement:

> 3. The buildings have been investigated and found to be safe in an assumed collision with a large jet airliner (Boeing 707—DC 8) travelling at 600 miles per hour. Analysis indicates that such collision would result in only local damage which could not cause collapse or substantial damage to the building and would not endanger the lives and safety of occupants not in the immediate area of impact.

Whatever the origin of the white paper, it suggests clearly that the Skilling firm—whether with or without the assistance of Port Authority engineers is not specified—looked at what would happen if a Boeing 707 or a McDonnell Douglas DC-8 rammed the World Trade Center.

What those engineers discovered—and failed to discover—would become fateful nearly forty years later. The engineers found, in essence, that the Skilling firm's "total concept" would not just give the twin towers a huge margin of reserve strength to help them survive the initial impact: the peculiarities of their design would let them act almost like a living being to resist overall failure and collapse even when grievously damaged by the plane. But those same engineers, all of them either working for the Port Authority or, like Skilling, under contract to it, did not think through the doubts that Rosaleen Skehan and her Fire Department friends were already starting to raise. That could hardly be a surprise, considering that Levy was seemingly orchestrating the entire operation. Levy had made his views on fire safety painfully clear to Skehan.

Exactly how the notion of studying a plane impact originally came about remains uncertain. Except for the three-page white paper, there is no known description of the study that might reveal the detailed calculations that the engineers carried out and the assumptions that they made. But over the years, Skilling and others said enough about the calculations that a little mathematical sleuthing easily fills in at least some of the gaps.

There were probably two basic phases to the study. The first looked at the force that the impact of a Boeing 707, the largest commercial plane flying at the time, would exert on the structure and compared it to the force produced by the kind of windstorm that the towers were engineered to withstand. (Damage inflicted by the smaller DC-8 would most likely be less severe than what the 707 could deliver.) The second phase took into account the hole the plane would cut and tried to figure out whether the tower would collapse because of that breach.

The first part of the calculation would have been quite simple. The towers had been designed to withstand the forces of windstorms with gusts of at least 120 miles an hour. Specifically, they were supposed to hold up against at least forty-five pounds of lateral force on every square foot without shearing off and toppling. Each tower would be about 1,350 feet tall and 209 feet across on each face: 282,150 square feet. So if a wind sufficient to exert forty-five pounds per square foot of force was blowing directly against one of the faces, that would be about 13 million pounds, all told. And the tower should stand, with a standard safety margin of perhaps 30 to 40 percent to spare.

To figure out if the plane had a chance of tipping the tower over, Mal

Levy's engineers needed to estimate how much force the collision might produce. A Boeing 707 made a B-25 look like an insect by comparison. With a tip-to-tip wingspan of 131 feet and a fuel capacity of more than twenty thousand gallons, a fully loaded 707 can weigh 300,000 pounds on takeoff, and its cruising speed is about 600 miles per hour. The engineers knew that parts of the little B-25 flew all the way through the limestone-encased Empire State Building and out the other side. So it might have been reasonable to assume that the bigger, faster 707, after plowing into the much more compliant facade of a World Trade Center tower, would not come to a complete stop before it reached the opposite side of the floor, 209 feet away. It is a complicated problem to figure out precisely how hard the plane might push on the tower during a collision, but given the plane's known weight, initial speed, and stopping distance, any freshman engineering student could come up with a rough estimate. The number turns out to be 17 million pounds, probably within the safety margin.

Levy's engineers had discovered that not even a speeding 707 would shear off one of the towers.

But would the hole punched out by the plane cause the tower to collapse? If the hole ran from wingtip to wingtip, then more than half the columns on one entire facade could be cut—more than thirty crucial structural supports—potentially endangering the stability of the structure.

The engineers found that the tower would have an even more remarkable kind of resiliency to protect it against a total collapse because of those lost supports. The tightly spaced columns above the damage, each connected to the next by the spandrel plates, would spontaneously form an arch over the hole. The technical term is a *Vierendeel truss*—the same type of archlike structure that supports many pedestrian bridges or other light bridges.

The Vierendeel trusses would be so effective, according to the engineers' calculations, that all the columns on one side of a tower could be cut, as well as the two corners and several columns on the adjacent sides, *and the tower would still be strong enough to withstand 100-mile-per-hour winds.*

The basic study had been completed by February 3, 1964, the day Levy's white paper was typed. Later that same month, Lawrence Wien called reporters to his office high above Forty-second Street, where the elegant silhouette of his most prized possession—the Empire State Building—was framed perfectly in his picture window. By now, the newspapers had taken to calling him "King Wien" because of the breadth of his real estate holdings, and especially because he owned the world's tallest and most famous building, the one King Kong had been known to climb. Wien had something to say about the towers that would surpass it if the Port Authority had its way. Whatever the architectural merits of Yamasaki's vision—and Wien thought there were few—his own building would always have something that the twin towers were certainly not going to have, Wien told reporters. The Empire State Building was structurally sound. The twin towers, he claimed, would be dangerously unstable and prone to catastrophe, especially in a large fire or an explosion, when they could collapse.

There was clearly a hefty dose of self-interest in the claim that became more apparent when Wien and Harry Helmsley, the managing agent of the Empire State Building, were joined in their campaign by a group of men who together owned a fifth of the 157 million square feet of office space in New York. These barons of real estate had decided, first of all, that they did not like the idea of 10 million square feet of tax-free, government-sponsored real estate competing with their holdings. None of them believed Tobin's assurances that he would be able to restrict his tenant list to import-export firms, customs brokers, and so on; this much office space, they thought, would simply glut a market that was already showing signs of weakening. In the weeks since Yamasaki had unveiled the twin towers design, Wien formed them into a group he called the Committee for a Reasonable World Trade Center and began attacking the project.

The Port Authority charged that Wien simply did not like the idea of buildings taller than his own. A lawyer by training, Wien was undoubtedly looking for anything he could find to stop a project he so disdained—preparing a brief, so to speak. Much more to the point, though, Wien was familiar with the Fire Department's way of thinking about structures and fires, just as Skehan was. Because of the Fire Department report that Silverman had dug up for him, Wien knew just how a twelve-ton airplane with a wingspan of sixty-seven feet, six inches—the B-25—could punch a hole in the facade barely a third that size and do little structural damage beyond popping a few rivets and denting three of the building's heavy steel beams. The twin towers, Wien understood, would not have that kind of protection. Their facades would be covered with aluminum cladding, not sixteen inches of brick and limestone. Behind the aluminum, wind and gravity loads would be shared by sixty-one of Yamasaki's delicate pinstripe columns, rather than the smaller number of massive columns in the Empire State Building. The plane could punch straight through, and once it was inside, with the perimeter columns sliced to pieces, there were no more columns to take up the extra loads that would have to be supported.

At least that was how Wien saw it. And that was why Wien, Helmsley, and their real estate allies made the allegation that the twin towers were "unsafe in an explosion or if hit by an airplane."

The notion that an airplane could hit the twin towers was clearly not some fevered product of Wien's imagination. Not only had the B-25 bomber rammed the Empire State Building, but in 1946 a plane had crashed into 40 Wall Street, the tallest building downtown. His warnings would one day come to seem almost impossible to believe in their eerie prescience.

What the real estate people did not know was that Levy already had his script prepared. Nor could they have known how far the Port Authority was willing to go to protect its project. On February 14, the day after Wien made his allegations, Lee Jaffe summoned reporters for a briefing at Port Authority headquarters. She distributed a three-page telegram sent that day from Richard Roth, one of the partners at Emery Roth & Sons, the New York architectural firm that had been assigned to work with Yamasaki on the trade center. Under the prestigious imprimatur of his firm, Roth had sent in an urgent rebuttal of Wien's claims. The telegram "authoritatively refutes the false allegations of 'real estate figures' published in THE NEW YORK TIMES today," Jaffe snarled in the memo she gave to one of those reporters. The telegram was impressive and detailed—pointing out, for example, that for the World Trade Center design,

> THE STRUCTURAL ANALYSIS CARRIED OUT BY THE FIRM OF WORTHINGTON, SKILLING, HELLE & JACKSON IS THE MOST COMPLETE AND DETAILED OF ANY EVER MADE FOR ANY BUILDING STRUCTURE. THE PRELIMINARY CALCULATIONS ALONE COVER 1,200 PAGES AND INVOLVE OVER 100 DETAILED DRAWINGS.

Point number three on the list of design features was this:

> 3. THE BUILDINGS HAVE BEEN INVESTIGATED AND FOUND TO BE SAFE IN AN ASSUMED COLLISION WITH A LARGE JET AIRLINER TRAVELING AT 600 MILES PER HOUR. ANALYSIS INDICATES

THAT SUCH COLLISION WOULD RESULT IN ONLY LOCAL DAM-
AGE WHICH COULD NOT CAUSE COLLAPSE OR SUBSTANTIAL
DAMAGE TO THE BUILDING AND WOULD NOT ENDANGER THE
LIVES AND SAFETY OF OCCUPANTS NOT IN THE IMMEDIATE
AREA OF IMPACT.

To anyone who had not seen Mal Levy's white paper and thought through its implications, such an endorsement from Roth must have closed the case: the twin towers would be safe in the most extreme circumstances conceivable. But to anyone who had read the white paper, something else was clear: Roth had been given Mal Levy's script to transmit as an urgent and authoritative telegram from an expert outside the Port Authority. Point by point, it was the same, almost word for word, as the white paper. Roth was simply parroting Levy, not offering an external judgment. The sudden appearance of these powerful and persuasive details from outside the agency must have obliterated any doubts in the minds of the reporters about who was right in this controversy:

4. BECAUSE OF ITS CONFIGURATION, WHICH IS ESSENTIALLY THAT OF A BEAM 209′ DEEP, THE TOWERS ARE ACTUALLY FAR LESS DARING STRUCTURALLY THAN A CONVENTIONAL BUILDING SUCH AS THE EMPIRE STATE BUILDING WHERE THE SPINE OR BRACED AREA OF THE BUILDING IS FAR SMALLER IN RELATION TO THE HEIGHT.

5. THE BUILDING AS DESIGNED IS SIXTEEN TIMES STIFFER THAN A CONVENTIONAL STRUCTURE. THE DESIGN CONCEPT IS SO SOUND THAT THE STRUCTURAL ENGINEER HAS BEEN ABLE TO BE ULTRA-CONSERVATIVE IN HIS DESIGN WITHOUT ADVERSELY AFFECTING THE ECONOMICS OF THE STRUCTURE. THIS IS NOT THE CASE WITH CONVENTIONAL BUILDINGS WHERE A MORE RADICAL APPROACH MUST BE USED IF THE BUILDING IS TO BE CONSTRUCTED AT REASONABLE COST.

6. THE STRUCTURAL CONCEPT IS NEW BUT THE DESIGN PRINCI-PLES, THE STRESS ANALYSIS AND THE THEORIES OF MECHANICS UPON WHICH THE DESIGN IS BASED ARE WELL KNOWN AND ARE IN ACCORDANCE WITH GOOD ENGINEERING PRACTICE. . . .

There was no elaboration on that assurance, but after a lengthy list of endorsements supposedly given by other outside architects and engineers, the telegram ended on this note:

11. THE TOWERS MAY BE SAID TO BE THE FIRST BUILDINGS OF THE 21ST CENTURY AND THE DESIGN CONCEPTS WHICH THEY EMBODY WILL BE INCORPORATED IN SOME MEASURE IN EVERY FUTURE HIGH RISE BUILDING EVER BUILT.

> RICHARD ROTH
> EMERY ROTH & SONS

For three days, the New York newspapers were merciless in the way they depicted Wien and the others who had been so badly blindsided by engineers who had already thought through the question of an airplane impact. "Empire State Building Jealous? Trade Center Says 'Yes,'" bellowed the *Sunday Journal-American*. The *World-Telegram & Sun* wrote that the Port Authority "charged today that the efforts of realtors to block its $350 million World Trade Center were prompted by fears that it would cause the Empire State Building to lose prestige," and quoted at length from the telegram. The *Times*, whose coverage had sparked the row, ran a prominent story on the Port Authority's rebuttal.

An angry Wien, sounding more like beleaguered little Oscar Nadel than the owner of the Empire State Building, called the Port Authority "an unconquerable Frankenstein," pointing out bitterly that "no one has successfully opposed it in the past." He vowed to carry on his fight. Still, the attention given to his safety claims was over—for now.

Mal Levy, Lee Jaffe, and the Port Authority's engineers had bested the great Lawrence Wien.

In reality, though, there were three serious flaws in the Port Authority's reasoning, at least as it was presented in the urgent telegram and the agency's other public pronouncements on the engineering of the twin towers.

The first flaw was one of candor. Skilling, for one, knew very well what would happen to the thousands of gallons of high-octane jet fuel once the 707 struck the tower. The fuel would ignite, just as the B-25's had in 1945. So, while he probably did believe that the impact would not endanger the lives of people not in the "immediate area" of impact, Lee Jaffe and the Port

Authority conveniently avoided telling all that Skilling knew about how large that area might be or how horrific the scene there could become.

"Our analysis indicated the biggest problem would be the fact that all the fuel would dump into the building," Skilling would recall much later, in 1993, while describing the plane study. "There would be a horrendous fire. A lot of people would be killed."

Even so, Skilling said, "the building structure would still be there."

In fact, the second flaw was that the Port Authority and its engineers did not think very hard about how their structure would behave in a fire, especially an intense, violent fire.

Their calculations indicated that the trade center's myriad lightweight columns and trusses would perform just as well as the Empire State Building's heavier elements under ordinary circumstances, when there was no fire. But simple physics dictated that during an intense fire—the situation not considered in the Port Authority calculations—heavy girders and beams would be much safer. Thin steel elements heat up, soften, and weaken much faster than thick ones in a fire, for the same reason that an ice cube melts faster on a summer day if it is chopped into pieces before being dropped into a drink: many smaller pieces have more surface area, allowing heat to flow in faster. The steel in the World Trade Center probably had much more surface area than a conventional structure would have had. And the trade center steel, unlike the Empire State Building's structure, would not be sheathed in four to eight inches of heavy masonry fireproofing, which would have been far too heavy for the Port Authority's taste. Instead, the trade center steel would be sprayed with a lightweight, foamy product that would dry in place, forming a fluffy coating that would be hard-pressed even to stay in place—let alone give any fire protection—during a blast or impact or violent conflagration.

All of the conclusions reached by the engineers on the resilience of the towers could be proved wrong if the huge fires set by the jet fuel softened that steel to the point at which it buckled. But no one at the firm or the Port Authority seriously investigated that possibility. Neither, apparently, did anyone at either of the architectural firms—Yamasaki's office and Emery Roth & Sons—even though architects traditionally have the responsibility for choosing an effective fire-protection system.

There would be another airplane study performed later, by Leslie E. Robertson, a young and talented engineer who would soon set up an office for the Skilling firm in New York. Although no official report on this study, which was presumably commissioned by the Port Authority, has ever surfaced publicly, individual details have emerged. What is known is that the calculations again focused on a Boeing 707, "the largest jet aircraft in the air at the time," as Robertson would describe it, crashing into one of the towers. The study assumed that the weight of the plane was 263,000 pounds and that its speed was 180 miles an hour. Robertson calculated that under those highly specific circumstances, the tower would stand. Once, again, the unavoidable fires were not taken into account. All of these carefully hedged conclusions would etch themselves in the minds of those outside the design effort in a simple way: as an assurance that the towers would stand if they were hit by a plane.

The Port Authority was about to discover the third flaw in the confident story line it had ginned up on the structure of the World Trade Center, the story line it was using to maintain support for the project in New York.

■ ■ ■

A woman entered the tidy little optometrist's office across the street from the courthouse in downtown Eugene, Oregon. She was seven months pregnant and happened to be wearing heels that day. The sign outside the building said OREGON RESEARCH INSTITUTE VISION RESEARCH CENTER. It was August 1965, and she had answered an ad in the local paper offering free eye checkups at the new research center. The office, where she was greeted by a receptionist, was tastefully decorated in light green carpeting and wood paneling with a Philippine mahogany veneer. The woman signed in and walked up three steps to the examination room, passing a whimsical travel poster that promoted WONDERFUL COPENHAGEN and showed a policeman stopping traffic for a mother duck waddling across a street with seven baby ducks in tow.

The optometrist, Paul R. Eskildsen, a serious-looking thirty-eight-year-old with a cleft chin, glasses, and a rapidly receding hairline, greeted her and closed the door behind them. The room was arranged with two chairs and a table, some charts and optical instruments, and an intercom on the wall.

"Would you please come over here and toe this mark on the floor?" Eskildsen asked her. "I am going to project some triangles on the wall, and I would like you to estimate the height of them."

She complied. But a short time into the test, something seemed to go wrong. Her eyes began darting from side to side.

"How do you feel?" Eskildsen asked.

"Goofy," she said. "I was kind of reeling around."

Maybe it was because she was pregnant, Eskildsen said.

"I never felt this way before," she insisted. "It's a feeling of not being able to control my standing." She staggered to the wall in her heels and leaned against it for support. "Are you hypnotizing me?" she said, completely disoriented now. "Because that's kind of sneaky."

"Okay, Jim, our subject has popped," Eskildsen said into the intercom on the wall when he had seen enough, using researcher's slang to tell a technician that the experiment should be stopped.

Then Eskildsen politely explained to the disoriented woman that a giant set of hydraulics had been heaving the room back and forth, very slightly at first and then with wider and wider excursions, as if it were a giant salt shaker. But the device was so finely engineered, so free of vibration, that virtually no one suspected anything was amiss before detecting the smooth lateral motion itself.

It was another day of bad news for the World Trade Center project. As Eskildsen explained to his pregnant patient—who called later to say that she'd had to leave work, feeling sick after her visit to the "vision research center"—a government agency was planning to build the two tallest buildings in the world in New York, and they would sway at the top. No one had ever measured how much an entire room could be oscillated from side to side before humans were able to detect the motion. There would have been no point. The experiment in Eugene, under the ruse of a free eye exam, had been designed to measure that threshold, and it was hinting at how much it took to make people dizzy, sick, or disoriented. So far, the results were that humans were extraordinarily sensitive to the motion, much more than anyone had realized. A few inches of sway over five or ten seconds set off psychophysical alarm bells.

The fact was that the lightweight steel skeletons that the Port Authority was designing would not only put people unnaturally high in the air, as all skyscrapers do. They would let the buildings sway back and forth in the wind like the biggest, leafiest trees ever planted. Heavy, masonry-clad buildings like the Empire State Building—even if the engineers' calculations showed that, theoretically, they were not as stiff as the twin towers would be—barely moved in the wind. The mass of the stone and brick and thick steel was just too much for the wind to push around. Even in an 80-mile-per-hour gale, the very top of the Empire State Building swayed less than four inches. The flexible, lightweight design of the twin towers would allow them to sway several feet at the top, and possibly much more, the engineers had calculated.

What's more, the Port Authority was beginning to discover that its engineers' original calculations, the ones they had used to rout Lawrence Wien and garner public support for the project, did not sufficiently account for some crucial effects. The perception tests, among other disturbing new technical findings, showed how far they were from a structure that could even be occupied. Pregnant women were not the only people who were sensitive to slight motions. One man reported feeling groggy and rubbery legged. "I feel that I'm not stable. I feel like I'm on a boat," he said, before adding with no prompting: "Back in Pennsylvania we had to take drunk driving tests by walking on a line." Another woman said it felt as if she were visiting a place called the House of Mystery at a local amusement park. "I think you're taking away my gravity or something," she said.

The results were a surprise, but it was the total lack of scientific data on the effect that had induced the Port Authority's engineers to commission the tests. Skilling and Robertson showed up together in the offices of Paul Hoffman, an Air Force navigator in World War II who had served in the South Pacific and who had earned a Ph.D. in experimental psychology after returning home. In 1960 he had given up a faculty position at the University of Oregon to set up an independent institute to study things like human decision making, judgment, and perception. Hoffman mortgaged his house to buy a former Unitarian Church at Eleventh and Ferry in Eugene for his offices, and the Oregon Research Institute was in business.

When Skilling and Robertson met Hoffman at the former church, they first insisted on total secrecy. The Port Authority had settled on a research institute in Oregon partly to be as far away as possible from the prying New York press, where just the existence of such a study would, if discovered, cause a sensation. Hoffman was not to discuss the research with anyone outside the project; he could not publish the results. Confidentiality agreements were hardly unknown in the world of private research institutes, of course, and Hoffman had a separate interest in keeping the work quiet, at least temporarily: he could not recruit what psychologists called "naive" subjects, meaning people who do not know what they are going to be tested on, if word spread too quickly around Eugene. So he agreed, and his institute's report on the investigation would remain secret for nearly forty years.

Hoffman soon found a scientist with the perfect qualifications to carry out the experiment. He hired Paul Eskildsen, an assistant professor of psychology at a nearby university who also happened to be a practicing optometrist. They settled on the eye exams; Eskildsen would send each of the seventy-two subjects a legitimate report on their vision after the experiments were over. As to the location, Hoffman had just purchased a low office building with storefront windows at 800 Pearl Street, across from the courthouse. It had housed an auto parts store and a billboard painting franchise, among other concerns; it had lots of space and—above all—concrete floors.

A Eugene engineering firm mounted the room on wheels that would let it roll around in any pattern, over distances of anywhere from an inch to twelve feet, and hooked the whole thing up to a hydraulic system that had been developed to push logs through a sawmill. The compressors that powered the hydraulics clattered so much that they had to be packed in soundproofing. To operate the device, a hidden technician listened for a code word over the intercom and gradually turned up the motion as he watched the jumping pen on a strip-chart recorder and the glowing trace on an oscilloscope. The experiment was not without mishaps. During a shakedown phase, one of the local engineers forgot to secure the room properly before throwing a hydraulics switch, and another engineer inside was thrown about when the room rolled out of control and smashed into a docking device—earning him the name "Lurch" after the Frankenstein-like character in a '60s TV show, *The Addams Family*. A similar malfunction during one of the eye exams made the room suddenly rumble and jerk so hard that both Eskildsen and the subject lunged toward a wall. "The subject looked at me, startled," Eskildsen carefully recorded in his notepad, "and I realized that I had best call the experiment."

Perhaps most remarkable of all was that when the engineers had it all working properly, the room shifted back and forth with extraordinary gracefulness, almost as if it really were swaying in a breeze off the Atlantic

Ocean. Even when the room was working right, however, the reactions were striking.

"I'm getting dizzy. This is ridiculous. I just seem a little rocky."

"This is beginning to make me sick."

"It feels like the bottom of your feet are rounded."

"Whoa boy! The room is wobbling."

"It's unpleasant. You probably have me on an X ray or something. Maybe I'm on *Candid Camera*."

"That wasn't very nice."

"I feel as though I am tipping forward."

"I suppose you've got the room mounted on hinges."

"I don't think I've ever fainted before, but I think this is the way I would feel if I would."

The testing took two weeks in August. Each eight-hour day, Eskildsen would gradually become seasick. He would recover at home, come in the next morning, and get sick again.

And then Eskildsen had to submit to the grilling of his life when he was visited by Yamasaki and the Port Authority engineers, including Mal Levy, and still more engineers from Skilling's office. The odd experiment had uncovered a remarkable human sensitivity that no one had known before, but, not surprisingly, the engineers were most interested in the implications for their building. Eskildsen told them that the point at which 50 percent of the subjects noticed motion was in the range of five to seven "milligee," where one milligee corresponded to a sideways acceleration that would be caused by one-thousandth the force of gravity. Because the room swayed back and forth within a period of about ten seconds, just as the twin towers were expected to, one milligee of acceleration translated to about one inch of motion in either direction. In some ways, the results were even worse than that, Eskildsen explained. Five to 10 percent of the subjects could sense motion as slight as two to four milligee.

The flummoxed engineers got inside the room and had the technician shake it back and forth so they could check for themselves. At one point, Yamasaki, Helge Helle from Skilling's office, and Eskildsen went inside and shut the door, and someone asked the technician to shake the room the full twelve feet—presumably because that was the amount of sway the engineers had hoped people would be able to tolerate in their workplace. After a minute or so, Eskildsen threw open the door and a Port Authority photographer snapped a picture. It showed Eskildsen braced against the door jamb, a concerned-looking Helle clutching the corner of the table, and Yamasaki gesturing from one of the chairs, where he had been obliged to take a seat in order to avoid falling down.

The Port Authority was still not ready to accept the results. Its officials decided to check the experiment, this time by swinging a huge packing crate, once again made up to look like an office inside, from cables inside one of the Lincoln Tunnel's ventilation towers. There was no attempt at subterfuge this time, of course, but Eskildsen still had to come to New York with his clipboard and run the tests. About forty Port Authority officials rode in the contraption as two men stood outside and pushed the crate, measuring the distance of each swing with a yardstick.

The results were the same.

6

...

Endgame

Who's afraid of the big, bad buildings? Everyone, because there are so many things about gigantism that we just don't know. The gamble of triumph or tragedy at this scale—and ultimately it is a gamble—demands an extraordinary payoff. The trade center towers could be the start of a new skyscraper age or the biggest tombstones in the world.

—Ada Louise Huxtable, *New York Times*, May 29, 1966

John V. Lindsay, who took office as the city's new mayor on January 1, 1966, always listened to Robert Price. An abrasive, hard-nosed Bronx native with a laugh as raspy as a buzz saw, Price was a political operator who seemed to have a picture of every storefront and street corner in New York somewhere in his inexhaustible memory, and who could not have seemed more out of place next to the easygoing Yale-educated Lindsay and his photogenic good looks. But it was Price who had overcome Lindsay's doubts about entering the mayoral race as a Republican in a Democratic city, Price who had run the improbable campaign, and Price who, as deputy mayor, had begun schooling Lindsay in the trench warfare that is New York City politics. Now, after a campaign in which the idealistic Lindsay had promised to go after unelected "power brokers" like Robert Moses and Austin Tobin, Price and his aides looked for anything that Lawrence Wien and the other opponents of the World Trade Center might have missed, any weapon that would give the city a chance against the overwhelming power of the Port Authority.

Price discovered that what he needed had been in plain sight all along. In the final analysis, he learned, only the city had legal control over the narrow, precious strip of land between one curb and its parallel on the opposite side of the asphalt: the city owned the streets.

He knew, of course, that the state legislatures had passed the World Trade Center bill, upheld by the Supreme Court, which allowed the Port Authority to condemn the land under the shops, warehouses, parking lots, and office buildings on Radio Row and the blocks around it. So the Port Authority could start demolishing the shops and constructing the giant complex—except for that one ludicrously minor detail. Not an ounce of concrete could be poured or a stick of steel laid in place unless the city issued permits that allowed the Port Authority to work on the grubby thoroughfares ringing the trade center site, and the others that would have to be erased to make way for Yamasaki's gleaming towers and the plaza beneath them.

Price stepped to the private door between his office and Lindsay's. "We can stop this thing," Price said.

Price reminded Lindsay that the previous administration, led by Mayor Wagner, had let the Port Authority ram through a deal in which it was now paying the city just $1.7 million a year in lieu of taxes, with little prospect that the payments would ever come close to the $25 million the city calculated that a private developer would pay in taxes. Then Price gave his boss another piece of inside information: the Wagner administration had never formalized its agreement with the Port Authority. It amounted to little more than a handshake, with no legal standing.

The mayor's response was immediate. Neither he nor Price thought Lower Manhattan needed the monstrous twin towers, and Lindsay decided that he was going to stop the project in its tracks and review it from top to bottom. In late January, two weeks after settling a transit strike that crippled the early days of his administration, Lindsay met with opponents of the trade center and then asked the Port Authority to halt its preparations for demolition, which had just begun to have some success in inducing people to leave their shops. Although a shaken Oscar Nadel remained, along with nearly all the other electronics merchants, twenty-one stores of various kinds had closed, twenty-two residents had moved out, and a few other enterprises like warehouses had shut down since December 1 of the previous year.

Lindsay had not yet tipped his hand. But the mayor's plea, which included a request for a five-day moratorium on activity at the site, seemed to be reasonably well received at Port Authority headquarters. "Mr. Tobin assured the Mayor that no such action had been contemplated during that period," a spokesman from Jaffe's office told the press.

Then came the sucker punch, when a wave of eviction notices written with threatening and consummately graceless language was abruptly served on Radio Row tenants:

Prompt possession of the property which you now occupy for World Trade Center purposes is imperative in order to commence construction of this vital public improvement. . . . Unless you remove from the premises on or before the termination date of March 11, 1966, appropriate proceedings will be taken by the Port of New York Authority to obtain possession of such premises.

Rosaleen Skehan, as always, had to do the dirty work of mollifying angry city officials, arguing that the Port Authority had complied with the letter of Lindsay's request. But the mayor's swift reaction showed how badly Tobin had again misjudged the city that kept getting in the way of his project. Within a few days, Lindsay's allies in the City Council announced their plans for public hearings at City Hall, the first of their kind on any aspect of the World Trade Center project. Then Lindsay took off the gloves and created a special committee to carry out a full assessment of the city's relationship with the Port Authority on the trade center project.

To lead the committee, Lindsay went back to the closest thing he had to a consigliere; Price would always remember that, for some reason, Lindsay came in to see him that day through the regular visitors' entrance instead of using the door between their offices.

"You're going to be chairman of this World Trade Center committee," Lindsay said.

"What? Oh God, why do I have to fight with Tobin?" Price said.

"Because they want you," Lindsay said, referring to the other members of the Board of Estimate, the body that wielded real power in budgetary and planning matters.

The usually self-confident Price quickly found out that his concerns were justified. In a preliminary meeting, he managed to insult Tobin, who had never had much time for city officials, let alone a thirty-three-year-old deputy mayor who did not know how to summon proper respect for the executive director of the Port Authority. Nor was Tobin much impressed when Price told him what he knew about the street permits; the handshake deal with Wagner should and would stand, Tobin believed.

Then Price had the driver of his city-owned Buick, a former detective, take him down to see the territory he was about to defend. They came in the worst possible direction, along Washington Street from the north, where the remains of the old market had left a decaying gash in the urban fabric. "I know the city damn well," Price said to his driver, "but I never paid attention to Washington Street because there were no votes there. It's all slums." When they arrived, Price saw huge rats gamboling across the street in broad daylight. On the northern fringes of Radio Row, the site of the once-bustling Washington Market at the corner of Vesey and West Streets was by now nothing but a defunct parking lot with cracked, crumbling pavement, surrounded by a chain fence. A watchman's shack, still sporting a beat-up sign that said NO ATTENDANT ON DUTY AFTER 6 P.M., had been tipped over on its side. It was true that in spite of the Port Authority's efforts to portray the rotting docks across West Street and this moribund streetscape as the face of the district it wanted to demolish, many of the shops to the south were still thriving. But if Price drove further on, he would see that the threat of condemnation and the trauma of the first abandoned buildings were taking an undeniable toll there, too, as they would on any neighborhood.

The signs in the windows of the fleeing businesses were the first things to jump out of the landscape. FORCED TO SELL. GOING OUT OF BUSINESS. LAST DAY. DRASTIC REDUCTIONS. MUST VACATE! FIXTURES FOR SALE. NO REASONABLE OFFER REFUSED. FABULOUS BARGAINS. Then there were the empty windows of the shops that had already closed, with uncollected junk often spilling onto the sidewalks in front of them. With the constant threat of eviction, no one had sunk money into repairs or renovations; the old buildings looked much older and dingier than they had only a few years before. And the truly broken-down structures, like the residential loft at 131 Liberty Street, didn't look so out of place anymore. "The building is very old, dirty, decrepit," one reporter wrote. "Push the elevator button. A whirring of cables, a grinding of old machinery. A girl looks out suspiciously. She is a writer, her roommate a dancer. . . . No names, thank you."

Price had no illusions at all about the position he was in. Aside from the

weakening front of the merchants, there was always the chance that the
state legislatures could try to find a way to circumvent the street permits if
Price overplayed his hand. Once again, though, he showed what he was
made of. First he called citizens groups and watchdog committees and
worked up a voluminous list of grievances, criticisms, conditions,
demands, and questions involving every aspect of the Port Authority's
relationship with the city. Then he put it all into a lengthy set of talking
points for a meeting with Tobin on April 14 in the Blue Room at City
Hall—the first negotiating session between the Port Authority and what
became known as the Price Committee. And in an effort to establish a bargaining position, Price launched it at Tobin in an all-out barrage.

What he wanted, Price said, was a complete overhaul of the relationship between the Port Authority and the city. Only when those issues had
been resolved could they discuss the trade center. Price wanted to rene-
gotiate the Port Authority's lease of the city-owned land under the
regional airports, even though a new lease had just been signed under the
Wagner administration. He wanted the agency to spend an immediate
$250 million for improvements to the city's waterfront. He wanted a bet-
ter deal on payments in lieu of taxes to the city for the Midtown bus terminal, the Washington Heights bus station, and other Port Authority
transportation facilities. He wondered why the agency was exempt from
regular taxes at all.

As appalled as he was by the demands—which both sides agreed
would remain secret as the talks proceeded—Tobin took the assault
evenly, according to detailed notes taken by Skehan. Tobin said that he
had only one immediate request. There were some old vaults under West
Street containing outdated telephone switching equipment that would
have to be replaced to accommodate anything like the number of offices
envisioned for the World Trade Center. While the negotiations went
ahead, would the city grant a permit for that work? In exchange, the Port
Authority would issue an elaborate statement saying that the permit was
"not intended and shall not be construed to indicate consent by the City
to the use by the Port Authority of City streets or other property for
World Trade Center purposes"—other than for the vaults. That way,
Tobin said, the preliminary construction could get going. And he would
agree to keep negotiating.

Price agreed to think over the request, Skehan wrote, "and to give

Mr. Tobin an answer when he comes to City Hall tomorrow morning." But Price had no intention of issuing the permit.

As it turned out, Tobin's demeanor had changed completely when he returned to City Hall the next morning. One of his assistants had noticed that during the meeting in the Blue Room, committee member Donald Shaughnessy, an assistant to the mayor, was consulting sheaves of material printed by the Committee for a Reasonable World Trade Center, Lawrence Wien's anti–trade center group. Wien's criticisms of the project had by now made him an intense focus of Tobin's contempt. Threatened with just the kind of scene he had dreaded when the job was handed to him, Price tried to assure Tobin that Wien carried little real influence with the committee. Tobin blew up anyway. "Since when have we come to the point where one selfish individual can tie up and block a public project?" he snapped.

Price, on the defensive, told a suspicious Tobin that he was in favor of issuing the permits, but his committee had voted 6 to 1 against it. Tobin's suspicions, as it turned out, were well founded: in the best tradition of city politics, Price had made up the vote to give himself some breathing room in a confrontation that even he was finding uncomfortable. Tobin immediately complained to Lindsay, who probably knew about the phony vote and who insisted that he couldn't reverse the committee's decision. But Tobin hammered at him, citing public responsibility, the costs of a delay, and what he thought was his poor treatment at the hands of Price. After eight to ten minutes of this telephone fusillade, Lindsay came up with his own masterly bit of understatement. "You feel very strongly about this, don't you?" he said to the Port Authority executive director.

"Unrelenting" would have been more accurate. Tobin, in a fine turn of the screw, decided to take at face value Price's claim that he favored granting the permit. At their next meeting in City Hall, he pressed Price to take another committee vote.

"As I told you, they voted six to one against it the last time, but I didn't vote," said the deputy mayor, who must have felt ridiculous as Lindsay looked on.

"Let me see . . ." Price said, as if considering the whip count. "I'll have to try to swing three votes around my way, and then maybe we can do it."

With the bone-rattling technique that had won him so many fights, Tobin and his allies were finally making headway, if only because no one wanted to face the next negotiating session with him. "Why the hell did I make you chairman of this committee if these guys keep calling me?" an exasperated Lindsay asked Price. They decided that their best option was to engage in a game of brinkmanship that would make the price for the trade center as exorbitant as possible. If Tobin caved in—no sure thing, of course—it meant the project could go forward. But the city could at least insist that relocation payments for the merchants be raised. They might even look for a new district where the electronics shops could go en masse. There were other pressing arguments. Lindsay was already seeing omens of the problem that would plague his administration above all else: a lack of money for improving the city's infrastructure as he struggled to pay for routine, day-to-day operations like snow removal and garbage collection. If they could squeeze the fabulously prosperous Port Authority on the World Trade Center, who knew what they could get for the cash-starved city?

But by opening the project to public scrutiny, Lindsay and Price unleashed a new set of forces that they could not control, any more than Tobin could issue himself the street permits. The citizens and politicians of the city, finally given a chance to go on record, came up with an overwhelming number of reasons to kill the World Trade Center.

There were two critical meetings—before the City Council on May 2 and the Board of Estimate on May 12 and 13, 1966. The first began promisingly enough. About two hundred "hard hats," or members of the construction unions, were picketing in support of the project outside the City Hall hearing room. Inside, Peter J. Brennan, president of the Building Trades Council, waited for his turn to speak in favor of the project along with another group of hard hats in the gallery. Tobin, by now white-haired and somewhat stocky, swept into the heavily paneled room with Skehan, his legal assistant Patrick Falvey, and a cluster of his staff members behind him. Tobin went to the wooden lectern facing a dais where some of the council members were seated and slipped on a pair of black reading glasses.

He then plodded through a deadening, forty-four-page speech extolling the World Trade Center. In the first line, he referred to himself using the royal "we" before setting out his overarching theme in no uncertain terms. "Others have provided you misleading and distorted information," Tobin declared. "Here are the facts." Among many other things, he assailed enemies of the project and defended the sudden eviction notices sent out in February, saying they had gone only to twenty-four tenants on the westernmost part of the site. Tobin, who did not mention the dispute over the street permits, asserted that construction would be staged so that merchants east of Greenwich Street could stay through the end of the year. He uttered the surreal line: "The merchants in that area of the site can therefore look forward to another Christmas shopping season," read a four-page summation and took questions.

Soon Tobin, shaking a clenched fist, was forced to deny charges hurled at him from the gallery that the Port Authority was a "supergovernment" unaccountable to the city and state. He was assailed by everyone from Jane Jacobs to a young Democratic leader named Edward I. Koch, who called the trade center "a conspiracy by people who think they know what is best for New York City." And that was tame compared to the seismic upheaval at the Board of Estimate hearings, which lasted through two solid days of vituperation and were frequently so raucous that the chairman—the beleaguered Price—lost control. An argument broke out when he tried to cut short the remarks of Barry Ray, a voluble deli owner who was a decorated World War II and Korean War vet who seemed to spend all his free time writing long screeds that excoriated the Port Authority, using many capitalized phrases like "THAT WHICH IS UNREASONABLE OR ARBITRARY CANNOT BE JUST."

"I'm appalled at the thought that merchants come here, who are going to have their lives ruined," thundered Stanley Geller, the merchants' lawyer, "and you quibble with them about fifteen minutes or half an hour. I think that's disgraceful." Price, who didn't seem to know which way to turn, backed down.

After Ray used his extra time to lash out at Tobin, state assemblyman Louis DeSalvio of Manhattan added a dash of high farce by declaring that the way he saw it, there was only one government agency that might find a benefit in the twin towers: NASA. "That agency could stretch a rubber band across the towers of the two 110-story buildings and use it like a slingshot to shoot a man to the moon. Beyond that usage, I cannot think of another need for two such buildings at this time," DeSalvio said. Others told wrenching stories of lives uprooted, businesses lost. But it was

Lawrence Wien's voice that would leave the most haunting traces in the historical record. "I don't know whether it's going to be all right," Wien said with his characteristically lilting, stop-and-go diction.

> I do know that from my standpoint, it seems that without any super-vision, without being accountable to anybody in the city of New York, to build the largest buildings in the world with a method of construction which has not been tested and tried and proved appropriate, subjects the city of New York to the possibility of a major physical disaster.
>
> It may never happen; it probably will never happen. But that there should be such—the remotest possibility of such a thing is, in my opin-ion, ridiculous. And the city should insist that there be no such risk.

Wien, a businessman whose main expertise was obviously in real estate and tax law, and who knew firsthand how the tiniest loophole could open the way to vast new enterprises, also expressed outrage over the prospect of a tax-exempt agency owning 10 million square feet of office space. But it was Wien's reprise of his structural criticisms, now even more pointed and poignant than when Mal Levy and Lee Jaffe had seemingly put them to rest, that galled Tobin most of all. Wien's attack, Tobin wrote in his weekly report to the Port Authority commissioners, "was a particularly shabby one which demonstrates his desperation. . . . This type of building has never been tried on this scale before, and there is a chance, he alluded, that it might fall or collapse.

"Yes," Tobin reported to the commissioners, "he really said that."

His ridicule did not have much effect. The pent-up bile had been spilled. WCBS Radio editorialized that "the city unfortunately has never attempted to evaluate the need for the trade center scheme" and called for it to be killed, not renegotiated. Ada Louise Huxtable, the *New York Times* architecture critic, wrote about the "big, bad buildings," and the *Daily Bond Buyer* predicted that the Port Authority had committed a "fatal slip" by arrogantly proceeding with its giant project on the basis of a handshake with Mayor Wagner. "The final lesson to be learned from the Trade Center controversy," the *Daily Bond Buyer* wrote, was "just another replay of the old saw: 'Grasp all, lose all.' "

Price decided it was a good time to raise the stakes. He turned his attention to a confidential, seventeen-page letter that contained the astonishing list of demands the city was privately making to Tobin in exchange for the possibility of granting the street permits for the trade center. It was all there: pumped-up payments to the city, reserved space for city workers in the trade center offices, a fancy new underpass near the site, more than $250 million in waterfront investments, including a new passenger ship terminal and containership facilities, generous relocation allowances for the merchants, a completely renegotiated airport lease. Price assigned poor Shaughnessy, who had been caught reading the Wien literature, to leak the letter. That way, Price could blame Shaughnessy and attempt to get the negotiations started again.

But his whole maneuver backfired, driving Tobin into a frenzy of combative public statements. So a couple of days after the story appeared, Price called Tobin with apologies that a committee member had given the letter to a *New York Times* reporter, who had turned it into a big story. "Shaughnessy shouldn't have leaked," Price said. "I don't blame you for blowing your stack."

A reprimand had been given to Shaughnessy, Price assured Tobin, who replied that what he really wanted was for the city to issue the permits that would let him start working on the telephone vaults under West Street.

Price said he was sure his committee wouldn't allow that. Not until the Port Authority agreed to the city's conditions.

That same day, the *Daily News* ran a cartoon that showed a smirking, double-chinned Price holding a gun to Tobin's back. Tobin's hands were high in the air, hoisting a pouch labeled WORLD TRADE CENTER. The caption gave Price's two-word demand: "Cough up!"

■ ■ ■

When the sun hovered above the humped foothills on the western fringe of Fort Collins, Colorado, in the late afternoon, they looked like nothing more than silvery cutouts in the harsh slanting light. As the sun dropped, more and more colors appeared in the hills. Weathered gray boulders of colossal size. Dark-green scrub pines clinging to impossible slopes. Yellow-green sward, almost tundralike in the smoothness of its contours. Olives. Tans. Ochres. Browns. Folds in the terrain with shadowy gradations so subtle they appeared and vanished within a few minutes in the dregs of the sunset. In the morning, the sun first touched the distant Rocky Mountain peaks; then brilliant light struck the foothills, and dry morning breezes swept across their slopes. The cycle began all over again.

At the extreme western end of the town, where a road called LaPorte Avenue ran flush up to one of those foothills, the breezes wafted past a DEAD END sign and a long, tan-painted, three-story building with a ten-foot-by-ten-foot opening that was blocked, on the inside, by something that looked for all the world like a giant car radiator.

The structure made little sense unless you walked inside the building, past a sign that said FLUID DYNAMICS & DIFFUSION LABORATORY, entered a vaulted room jammed with piping and electronics equipment, and took the bolts off a narrow hatch on the side of a cavernous wooden chamber, one hundred feet long and raised off the concrete floor on a series of stilts.

Inside the chamber, as dim and creaky as a sarcophagus, one end appeared to be capped by another of the giant radiators—actually a maze of metallic coils and wind baffles nearly twenty by twenty feet in size. At the other end of the chamber, looking enormous and forbidding in the darkness, was a four-blade propeller from a World War II–vintage, P-38 fighter plane, mounted on immovable steel braces like a captured monster, ready to cough and roar and suck air through the chamber with the force of a hurricane. The chamber formed one section of a wind tunnel.

In the summer of 1964, Jack Cermak, the engineer and native Coloradan who had built the highly innovative tunnel to study the dispersion of air pollutants and how winds affect evaporation from lakes and reservoirs that supply water to cities, walked into a small room near the propeller, where a hulking dumbbell-shaped generator in a cast-iron shroud sat on wooden blocks, and pressed a red button. Then he went to a control room studded with dial gauges and bulbous knobs and steering wheel–like pressure valves in the middle of the long rectangle formed by the wind tunnel. He pressed another button, this one on a black metal box at the end of a thick electrical cable. As if eager to perform a circus reenactment of its war exploits, the P-38 prop roared to life in its chamber.

The wind blasted northward for a hundred feet, rushed through the wall of coils and baffles that were designed to keep the air at the proper temperature, shot around two corners, and then blew southward down another long segment of the tunnel, this one gradually narrowing to a cross-section of just six feet by six feet. One side of the tunnel in this segment was made of Plexiglas. Just outside the Plexiglas window, the serious, bespectacled Cermak stood looking in, the metal box with the button he had just pressed lying in front of him on a tabletop.

The floor of this part of the wind tunnel told the story of the experiment that was under way.

As it blew down the tunnel, the wind encountered a section of the floor that was covered with coarse sandpaper, its half-millimeter grains facing up. In the artificially shrunken world of the experiment, those grains represented the bumpy, irregular waves beneath a powerful gale blowing in from the Atlantic Ocean toward shore. Cermak knew from his research on evaporation that those waves kicked up little turbulent gusts and created a kind of friction that slowed the speed of the wind near the water's surface. The sandpaper produced a miniature version of those effects in his wind tunnel.

If Cermak had been a man prone to joking, which he was not, he might have found something amusing to say about the material that covered the next stretch of the wind tunnel's floor. It was ¾-inch gravel—a good enough aerodynamic representation of the tightly packed shops and houses of gritty old Brooklyn—creating still more turbulence and drag before the wind in the tunnel plowed into something whose meaning could not have been mistaken. It was a wooden model, painted gray, of Lower Manhattan. The East River piers, great skyscrapers like the Chase Manhattan Bank, the Woolworth Building, and 40 Wall Street, lesser towers like the New York Telephone Company Building, the serried structures along Broadway—to make the experiment work, every significant building below Thirty-fifth Street had to be there. And along the miniature Hudson River shoreline were two structures, painted white, that did not yet exist on the real island: balsa wood facsimiles of the twin towers, each two feet, eight inches high, looming over everything else in the model like two impossibly high sand castles on a beach.

Cermak—and the World Trade Center's structural engineers, when they were in town—watched the towers. Hidden beneath each was a set of four aluminum springs that allowed the structures to shake back and forth in the complex, turbulent wind stream flowing through the tunnel just as the real towers were expected to do when a gale blew in from the Atlantic Ocean. (Balsa wood was one of the few substances light enough to mimic the structures on a small scale.) Instruments mounted above the towers gauged and recorded the motion electronically, but Cermak had no trouble seeing what was happening with his naked eye. As if they formed the prongs of an immense tuning fork, both towers jittered back and forth. They would move in unison for a while, then get out of step, and, after a time, somehow synchronize themselves again. At irregular intervals, the pattern would repeat.

His instruments would give him the exact numbers, but he could easily tell that in their largest wobbles, the tops of the towers were moving back and forth by perhaps half an inch to an inch. The models had been built to a scale of 500 to 1; an inch in the experiment translated to 500 inches in the real world. That meant the tops of the real towers would be moving a maximum distance of somewhere between 250 and 500 inches, or in more understandable units, between about twenty and forty feet.

No matter how many times he did the experiment, turning the model this way and that, fiddling with the gravel and the sandpaper and the speed of the wind, the results kept coming out the same way. Gigantic vortices, like invisible tornadoes, would form on either side of the towers when a strong wind blew past them. The vortices would alternately tear away and re-form themselves, whipping the structures back and forth in ever-larger excursions, an effect that wind engineers refer to in dry technical language as "negative damping" or "aerodynamic instability." But even though this was the first time his wind tunnel had been used for this type of experiment, Cermak and the structural engineers knew very well what the sinister implications of that effect were. On November 7, 1940, a graceful steel structure twenty-eight hundred feet long called the Tacoma Narrows Bridge—which, not coincidentally, was extraordinarily light and flexible, even for a suspension bridge—had fallen prey to negative damping in a wind of just 42 miles per hour. The bridge began bucking and twisting, moving up and down by as much as twenty-eight feet while the vortices sucked and pulled at its steel sinews. Then the central span of the bridge tore away and plummeted into Puget Sound—the same scenic body of water that was visible from John Skilling's offices. Negative damping was potential trouble, serious trouble. At least one of Cermak's early models had ripped itself from its moorings and come to rest at a crazy angle, prevented from toppling completely only by a metal post that was part of the experimental apparatus. Although that miniature catastrophe was probably related more to the way the models were built than to the likely behavior of the actual towers, the event could not be seen as a good omen.

The research on how wind would affect the twin towers would continue, in one way or another, for at least two years. The findings of that

Wind Turbulence and
The Twin Towers

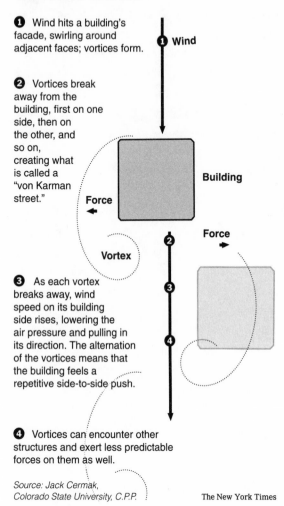

❶ Wind hits a building's facade, swirling around adjacent faces; vortices form.

❶ Wind

❷ Vortices break away from the building, first on one side, then on the other, and so on, creating what is called a "von Karman street."

Building

Force

❸ As each vortex breaks away, wind speed on its building side rises, lowering the air pressure and pulling in its direction. The alternation of the vortices means that the building feels a repetitive side-to-side push.

Vortex

Force

❹ Vortices can encounter other structures and exert less predictable forces on them as well.

*Source: Jack Cermak,
Colorado State University, C.P.P.*

The New York Times

research would be forcing changes in the towers' structural design as late as 1968, a few months before steel was scheduled to be placed into the ground in Lower Manhattan. If the angry New Yorkers who had been omitted from the little wooden streets of the model had gotten the slightest hint of what the experiments had turned up in this placid Colorado town, the most likely result would have been a quick demise for the Port Authority's World Trade Center project. Sways that large could do more than damage internal structures like stairwell enclosures, office partitions, and water pipes; they were a warning that in a very large windstorm, there was a risk that the towers could actually become unstable and tear themselves apart, just as the Tacoma Narrows Bridge had. And after the secret experiments in Eugene, Oregon, in 1965 showed how sensitive people were to the motion of a room, the Port Authority's engineers knew that towers as flexible as these were, with side-to-side motions this great, could never be used as office buildings anyway. How would all of that information have played in the City Council?

When Leslie Robertson, the rising young engineer with Skilling's firm, learned of the early experimental results, he went to Yamasaki with a simple message: "We have a problem." Robertson had a curious relationship to the project. Although he was increasingly central to the design effort, and he set up the Skilling firm's New York office by August 1964, he was still in his thirties. Few of the splashy articles on the innovative design of the twin towers ever mentioned Robertson. Behind the scenes, though, he was an intense presence, even criticizing Skilling for what Robertson said was a preoccupation with outside interests like real estate and the stock market at the expense of structural engineering. Robertson and Skilling would eventually have a falling out and the firm would, much later, cleave in two. Robertson possessed a deep creative brilliance of his own, and would demonstrate it in building after building during a long career. But his highly analytical style stood in sharp contrast to Skilling's. And Robertson, with his dark, penetrating eyes, snaggle-toothed smile, and somewhat evasive manner, would never remind anyone of a genial Irish bartender.

Robertson would ultimately belittle Skilling as the firm's "salesman," the man who "had the golden tongue," someone who played around with structural ideas but did not really understand the engineering complexities of the projects the firm had undertaken, including the World Trade Center. "He's a man of concepts, a 'grand conceptor,' if you like," Robertson would say. "The thing I don't admire is his lack of attention to detail and unwillingness to focus on his profession sometimes."

But for now, there were urgent questions on the structure of the twin towers to be answered. Robertson was more than clear when he went to Yamasaki with his description of the problem. "A billion dollars right down the tube," Robertson would later say when describing the threat that the project faced, in a reference to the constantly escalating cost of the trade center. "Gone," Robertson would add. "Wasted."

As explosive as the experimental findings would have been, Cermak had been ordered to keep quiet; no one had discovered what was going on in his miniature Manhattan. The only reporting to speak of had been done by a local paper, the Fort Collins *Coloradoan*, which gave the research the airbrush treatment that is so hallowed in American technical writing:

> Twentieth-century Gullivers, in the guise of engineering scientists, are working in the large wind tunnel of Colorado State University's Fluid Dynamics and Diffusion Laboratory. Where else can one step over the Empire State Building and the even taller gleaming white towers of the future World Trade Center of New York?

> To Dr. Jack Cermak, professor in charge of C.S.U.'s fluid mechanics program, and his aides . . . this feat is commonplace. They step carefully from Broadway to the East River and beyond to the Atlantic—not in seven-league boots, but in stocking feet, mandatory footgear in the tunnel.

The seemingly impenetrable wall of secrecy gave Robertson— bestriding the twin towers in his stocking feet and becoming ever more central to the later phases of their engineering design—time to figure out if there was a way to stave off what Cermak was seeing in his wind tunnel. Oddly enough, the political fights in New York also bought Robertson time by slowing down the project in the two years after Cermak first switched on his experiment in July 1964.

Robertson would start with one very big advantage, an advantage named Alan G. Davenport, a junior professor at the University of Western Ontario, located in the town of London, about one hundred miles northeast of Detroit across the Canadian border. Somehow Skilling and Robertson had stumbled upon this young scientist, one of the few people in the world with a chance of truly understanding what the experiments meant for the twin towers. At a time when even the rare facilities like Cermak's were being built to study the diffusion of smoke or radiation clouds or chemical weaponry or water vapor in the atmosphere, Davenport specialized in the study of how wind affects standing structures. The field was so new that Davenport did not even have his own wind tunnel. He had to collect data where he could find it.

Davenport, who looked rather dashing with his thin moustache and shock of dark hair, had studied at Cambridge and Bristol in England, and he possessed an almost magical ability to visualize the invisible antics of the wind and convert them to hard calculable mathematics. Within the insular world of engineering, word of his talents got around. Two years after he arrived in Ontario with his new Ph.D. in 1961, Davenport was back in England attending the first conference ever held on the study of structures with wind tunnels. Davenport's work was highlighted, and during a coffee break someone pulled him away to talk to some Americans he had never met before. The Americans, who obviously knew little about the subtleties of wind engineering, peppered him with question after question on his research. Then, without explanation, they left. He thought they might be building a bridge.

The phone rang in his London, Ontario, office in mid-January 1964. Skilling did most of the talking, though Robertson was also on the line "singing a duet," as Davenport would later recall it. And the ensuing scenes did play out almost like a familiar but still affecting opera. Could they count on Davenport to keep secret what they were about to reveal? Davenport promised that they could. How would he like, the Seattle duo coyly asked, to work on the design of two 110-story buildings? Davenport all but swooned. Skilling and Robertson immediately flew to London, taking out a suite of rooms in the best hotel in town—it was called the Hotel London—to discuss the possible shape of an elaborate experimental program. In the act's crowning scene, Skilling and Robertson asked if he was willing to pack up his entire family, leave his academic career temporarily behind, and move to Seattle in order to work on the project. Davenport replied that he was.

In literal terms, the meeting in London may have been the single most important historical moment in saving the project from the shortcomings of the structure that Tobin and Levy and Jaffe and the rest of the Port Authority were ardently defending in New York. Along with the data from the motion experiments in Eugene, Davenport's insights—he would ultimately design most of the experiments carried out by Cermak—would also have unforeseen but lifesaving implications almost four decades later.

Davenport was well aware that he would have to begin his scientific journey by groping in the dark.

Despite all the fear that wind forces on tall structures had inspired since the nineteenth century, he knew that not a single one had been tested under realistic wind conditions before construction. In some respects there was no need, since the earlier engineers had been content to build their structures to withstand stresses far greater than anything nature was likely to throw at them. "With regard to the exposed surfaces," wrote Gustave Eiffel of the wind pushing against his tower, "we have not hesitated in assuming, in spite of the apparent severity of the assumptions, that on the upper half of the tower all the lattice work is replaced by solid surfaces." Testing for the Empire State Building had been done in an aeronautical wind tunnel, with the kind of smooth nonturbulent flows that are assumed in checking out, say, stresses on an airplane wing. Although the atmosphere near the ground was not smooth, but in fact very choppy, the massy materials and powerful steel frame of that building had far more stiffness than the engineers even knew how to calculate. Nothing was going to push it around very much. Besides, people had put up plenty of similar skyscrapers in the past and they had withstood hurricanes.

None of those safeguards could protect the World Trade Center. Their wide tops would catch more wind than any skyscraper ever built, their structure was unlike anything that had been tried before on this scale, and their design would be "optimized"—put together with an absolute minimum of steel and concrete—rather than expensively "overbuilt." For all these reasons, Davenport knew he would have to take extraordinary steps to certify the design of the twin towers. He insisted that experiments be carried out at two separate wind tunnels, Cermak's in Fort Collins and the National Physical Laboratory in Teddington, England, so that he could be sure the findings were correct.

Davenport knew he was in for a long slog when the first, dispiriting results came back from Cermak's lab. Davenport's program produced at least four major reports on the experiments, in January, March, and July 1965, and June 1966. But out of the early disappointment came his first crucial insight: if they could not understand the mysterious atmospheric turbulence, it was unlikely that they could safely build the towers.

"This turbulent or 'boundary' layer has important consequences in the design of the towers of the World Trade Center," intoned the first of the reports, a full year after the public unveiling of the twin towers model in January 1964, whose structural design had not sufficiently taken the turbulence into account.

Cermak's experiments uncovered devilish contradictions within the turbulence. First, it actually seemed to break up some of the dangerous vortices that formed to the sides of each tower—vortices that gave the structure a rhythmic, side-to-side shove as they spun away, one after the other, like eddies around a blade of grass in a stream. But the turbulent gusts also created terrific new forces by buffeting the towers. The problem became even more complex when Cermak discovered that winds pushing directly against any of the eight tower faces caused much bigger oscillations than at any other angle. The wind's direction, speed, gustiness, and the strength of its eddies all came into play—how could a designer possibly take all those things into account and be sure some deadly combination of events would not take the towers down?

And aside from those scientific riddles, there was an even bigger practical problem. Using the experimental data, Davenport and Robertson discovered that a new structural factor, something that most engineers had never come close to understanding correctly, was influencing the sway of the models. That factor might be called, roughly speaking, the "creakiness" of a building. Imagine a giant finger reaching down from the sky and pushing the top of the Empire State Building sideways a foot or so, and then letting go. Engineers knew that the building would spring back and sway from side to side in about eight seconds. But the swaying would quickly stop, because all that brickwork and old concrete and tile and the masonry walls inside would creak and rub together like arthritic joints and put a brake on the motion. This creakiness, technically known as structural damping, helped protect the building against the devastating effects that even weak vortices could have with their regular push, push, push on the building like a father pushing his daughter on a swing. If there was one thing the sleek twin towers were not, it was creaky—a push from the giant finger, and one of those towers would spring back and forth again and again. The low structural damping was letting some of the wind tunnel models sway out of control, the engineers found.

The amount of missing creakiness was not small. At relatively high wind speeds, said the report on the British work, which confirmed all of the findings in Cermak's wind tunnel, "large values of structural damping are required to limit the amplitudes at the top of the tower blocks."

Robertson had gotten his first detailed lessons on the turbulence at the conference where he met Davenport. But he had something more important than a specialty in wind engineering: like Davenport, he spoke the language of advanced mathematics. Very quickly, theirs became the duet that mattered. They realized that they could deal with the turbulent winds statistically, by figuring out the most dangerous combinations of wind speeds, gusts, directions, and so on, that might occur in, say, five hundred years. In other words, all they had to do was use the data to determine how often the buildings would face very, very bad luck—and not, as Eiffel and his contemporaries had insisted, the worst possible luck. Once you knew what you were doing, it was just an invigorating little exercise in probability theory, like calculating the odds in poker of dealing fifteen royal flushes in a row.

But how were they going to make steel towers creaky?

One day Davenport walked into Robertson's office in Seattle with what turned out to be the answer. Airplanes sometimes used a layer of rubber between aluminum parts to damp out vibrations, Davenport remembered. Could they put something like that, he wondered, right inside the hollow pinstripe columns? It wouldn't creak, exactly, but it could damp out the oscillations.

"You know, if we could really get some damping into this structure, we wouldn't have to worry about wind tunnel tests and things," at least from that point on, Davenport said. "The damping by itself would be very helpful."

It was, for lack of a better term, artificial creakiness, a prosthetic version of something the old buildings had as a birthright. Whether Robertson had been thinking along the same lines or he just seized upon an idea that went straight to the heart of the problem, he quickly figured out how to make it work. Instead of trying to put something inside the columns—that would be too cumbersome—he would create the first shock absorbers ever fitted into a building. The geeky name that would stick was "viscoelastic dampers": sets of three flat metal pieces, about two feet long, held together like a double-decker sandwich with epoxy and a tough, rubbery glue called polyacrylic that was developed by 3M. The two outside plates would connect to an exterior column, and the middle plate would be fixed to the underside of a steel truss. When the building swayed in the wind, the plates would slide against one another and the polyacrylic and damp the motion a little—a shock absorber. Put ten thousand into each tower, or about a hundred per floor from the 7th to

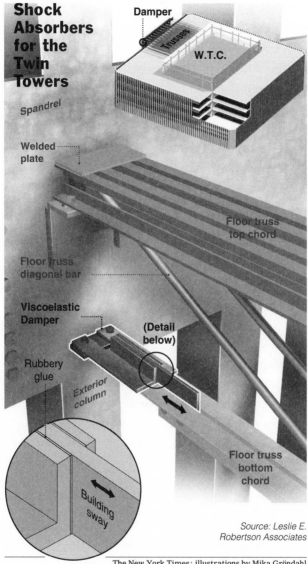

Shock Absorbers for the Twin Towers

Damper

Trusses

W.T.C.

Spandrel

Welded plate

Floor truss top chord

Floor truss diagonal bar

Viscoelastic Damper

(Detail below)

Rubbery glue

Exterior column

Floor truss bottom chord

Building sway

Source: Leslie E. Robertson Associates

The New York Times; illustrations by Mika Gröndahl

the 107th story, as Robertson planned to do, and they would become a very good shock absorber.

Even the dampers would not be enough. Robertson and John Skilling had to go to Yamasaki and tell him that all of the experimental data they had been collecting indicated that the towers would still sway too much unless three separate structural modifications were carried out. Two of them would have an enormous impact on the architectural design of the building, Robertson said, before explaining that he would have to widen Yamasaki's pinstripe columns slightly to make them stiffer. In part to ensure that the windows became no narrower than they already were, that meant widening the spacing between the columns slightly.

The increase in spacing was only an inch, so that each column would now be forty inches from its neighbor instead of three feet, three inches. But that tiny change meant that there would now be fifty-nine pinstripes per face instead of sixty-one, altering the look of the facade. The design was inherently stiffer for a given amount of steel, but that wasn't the main reason for the change. The time the big towers took to sway back and forth was too long. It was too easy for the side-to-side push of the vortices to take on the same rhythm, generating huge oscillations. The structural changes would help shorten the jiggle: eleven seconds back and forth, still slower than the Empire State Building but an improvement nonetheless.

There was more, Robertson said. Still another element of his solution was a huge support structure called a hat truss that would sit atop each building and tie its core to its exterior. Already under discussion as a brace to hold up a soaring TV antenna on the north tower, the hat truss could add robustness to the entire building from top to bottom, Robertson knew, with a few tweaks in the design. And finally, Robertson wanted to twist the orientation of the rectangular core—containing interior structural columns, fire stairwells, and elevators—in one of the towers. No longer true twins, the north tower's core would run east-west, and the south tower's north-south. The change would discourage the towers from dancing in unison.

Around Yamasaki's office, the three-foot, three-inch spacing, meaning nine-foot, nine-inch modules for Skilling's prefabricated, three-column panels, had taken on an almost talismanic significance. But whether because the new numbers had their own resonances—"Ten feet!" said Aaron Schreier, the project manager, when he multiplied out the new module spacing in his head—or simply because his friend Skilling had not been able to trick nature this time, Yamasaki relented.

At the conclusion of their June 1966 report, Davenport and Robertson could write down a triumphant little equation for the expected sway amplitude of the World Trade Center (WTC) compared to that of the Empire State Building (ES):

$$\frac{(\text{amplitude})_{\text{WTC}}}{(\text{amplitude})_{\text{ES}}} = 2.67$$

Because, in an 80-mile-an-hour wind, the Empire State Building swayed about 3.6 inches, the equation meant that the twin towers were calculated to sway 2.67 × 3.6, or about 9.6 inches. Given all the uncertainties and approximations of the analysis, that was remarkably close to the results from Cermak's experiments using the new tower design, which predicted about 14 inches. They decided that they could live with 14 inches in an 80-mile-an-hour wind.

In later years, little would be heard of Alan Davenport in World Trade Center lore, at least in New York City, as Les Robertson would loom ever larger in the public eye. Robertson would talk of having used an apartment near the Empire State Building to study the swirling wind flows around its tall shoulders while designing the twin towers; Robertson would take out a patent on the viscoelastic dampers. But none of that changed what had happened. The mathematical duet of Davenport and Robertson had transformed the towers from high-rise innovations to experiments-in-the-sky.

For a few satisfying moments, the engineers could truly say that they had saved the World Trade Center.

They were brief moments indeed.

■ ■ ■

In the life-size New York City, Austin Tobin had decided by mid-July 1966 that it was time to sling some mud. Whether emboldened by the engineering triumph that Lindsay knew nothing about, or just fed up with the stalemate, Tobin publicly accused Lindsay of lying to him on the trade center, asserting that the mayor had promised to let the construction go forward before breaking his word. Four years earlier, exactly the same tactic had worked with tired old Mayor Wagner, who had folded without a fight. But the occupants of City Hall were different now. They dismissed Tobin's accusation as a bargaining maneuver.

"Of course, if we were willing to give away Manhattan," Lindsay lobbed back at Tobin, "they could start digging up the city anytime."

Tobin did succeed in doing one thing—he enraged Lindsay's inner circle. "If we don't agree, nobody can make us agree," said the normally placid J. Lee Rankin, the mayor's chief counsel. Deputy Mayor Price, as usual, topped them all. From the New York waterfront to the regional railroads to the World Trade Center site, Tobin was carrying out "a rape of the city," Price charged, adding bitterly that "New York City must stop being the stepchild of the Port Authority."

The wind swirling through the Manhattan skyline was so much simpler.

With the political negotiations mired to the point of immobility, three things then happened almost at once. Someone came up with an immensely valuable new plum for the city, Rosaleen Skehan found the perfect third-party negotiator, and a kind of mishap that would, tragically, dog the trade center for much of its existence seemed to change everyone's mood overnight.

The timing of the events that closed the World Trade Center deal would always remain slightly murky. Sometime late on Thursday night, July 14, Tobin released to the press some of the detailed notes that Skehan had been taking on the meetings between the city and the Port Authority on the trade center. The notes, whether because they were to some degree slanted or because Lindsay had simply been ambushed with one of the oldest tricks in the political playbook, not only made the mayor seem untruthful but also ridiculous. In one intense hallway conversation at City Hall in late June, for example, the notes said, Lindsay gave a firm promise to issue the street permit if Tobin would only go back into a negotiating room and state his position on two crucial issues. They went inside, he stated his position—and Price tried to extract further concessions, which Tobin refused. And there was no permit.

"We expect you to keep that commitment," Tobin insisted in the next hallway confrontation. "Where is the permit?"

"You didn't give them anything," Lindsay said, to a chorus of complaints that he had double-crossed the Port Authority. According to the notes, Lindsay kept repeating, seemingly mindlessly: "You didn't give them anything. You didn't give them anything."

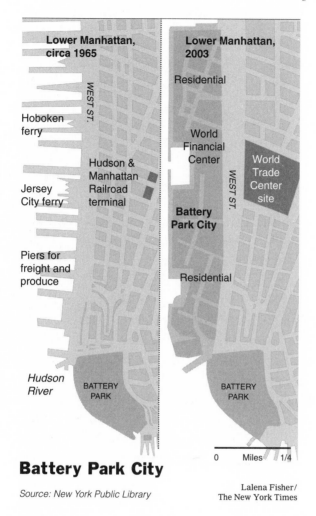

Lower Manhattan,
circa 1965

Lower Manhattan,
2003

Residential

Hoboken
ferry

WEST ST.

World
Financial
Center

World
Trade
Center
site

Hudson &
Manhattan
Railroad
terminal

Jersey
City ferry

WEST ST.

Battery
Park City

Piers for
freight and
produce

Residential

Hudson
River

BATTERY
PARK

BATTERY
PARK

0   Miles   1/4

Battery Park City

Source: New York Public Library

Lalena Fisher/
The New York Times

considerable difficulties," he said, "we groped our way to a mutually satis-factory agreement."

Less than forty-eight hours after the announcement, a pair of jack-hammers was rattling into the pavement at the intersection of Cortlandt and West Streets early on a Friday morning. Tobin was taking no chances with the telephone vaults, essentially locations where bundles of tele-phone cables punched through the walls of the Hudson Tubes before running beneath the river in the shelter of the tubes to New Jersey. Sub-merged sixty feet beneath the pavement, each big concrete vault—one for the tube that ran under Cortlandt Street and another for the tube under Fulton Street—had to be moved two hundred feet west so that it would be out of the trade center's enormous basement.

Then the monstrous equipment for gouging out the first elements of the basement clanged into place around the perimeter of the site. For the occasion, Tobin again declared that the project was destined to become "the United Nations of Commerce" and "the dynamo of the port's trade with the world." The construction of the World Trade Center, said Tobin, had begun in earnest.

And except for the few determined holdouts, Radio Row became more and more a ghost town, reverberating with the sound of walls collapsing and sledgehammers pounding and front-loaders dropping debris into dump trucks as the demolition accelerated. As the outcome of the battle became clear, Tom Dunn, the local television reporter who had covered the merchants from the beginning, stood beneath the crude wooden scaffolding that the Ajax Wrecking Company of Long Island City had put up around one doomed, hollow-eyed, and deathly silent building at 78 Dey Street. One hand clutching his big '60s-era microphone and the other a corner of his typewritten copy, which constantly threatened to flutter away in the stiff breeze coming in off the Hudson on a dreary, shadowless afternoon, Dunn said in his slightly tinny broadcaster's voice: "When the Port of New York Authority first announced the proposed construction of the World Trade Center, the brochure quoted from Walt Whitman: 'high growth of iron, slender, strong, light, splendidly uprising toward clear skies.'

"To the Port Authority, the construction of the World Trade Center might have meant growth," Dunn said, before adding that to many of the small businessmen he had met on the trade center site, "it meant disaster."

In truth, each of those merchants took the final act differently, and their fates varied widely.

Some left with their heads high. David MacInnes, a World War II marine whose Scottish family had opened its bar and grill on Cortlandt Street in 1872, hired a bagpiper in a kilt and proudly marched a parade of customers and employees down the street to his new location at noontime one day in May 1967. He took with him high hopes and his establishment's forty-five-year-old mahogany bar top, drenched with memories of his father, who like him had polished it to the sheen of a mirror. MacInnes cockily predicted that his clientele would follow him to his new location.

Within a few months, both his bar and his hopes for his business were gone. First, some Port Authority officials arrived, showed him the papers proving that they owned all his fixtures in the Cortlandt Street establishment, and carted off the mahogany bar top, which he never saw again. Within about a year his new bar and grill, which the Port Authority had placed in a temporary location on the eastern edge of the trade center site, folded; MacInnes started over and built a successful real estate business in Queens.

Some merchants, like David Flam, who moved his electronics shop from Cortlandt Street to 86 West Broadway, struggled on the edge of financial collapse because of lost business, but others prospered: Sy Syms, the clothier who had shouted anti–Port Authority slogans through a bullhorn, temporarily took over the floor space of abandoned shops next to his, creating the basis for what grew into a discount empire when he was finally forced to leave. Some, like Barry Ray, the delicatessen owner, seemed to disappear into the fabric of the city, their fortunes unknown after their brief moments of resistance.

And then there were the genuine disasters.

When the men from the Compass Van and Storage Co. pulled up and started taking the radios and phonographs and TVs off the shelves at 63 Cortlandt Street on Tuesday, May 2, 1967, Oscar and Rae Nadel both wept. Oscar looked across the street, where workers were already demolishing the buildings, and said, "I'm leaving a place I've loved for forty-seven years. I hate leaving it." He no longer sounded like the bantam rooster that had never known defeat. "Do you think it's easy for a little man like me at my age to go into hock for thirty-five or forty thousand dollars to open up a new place?" he said. "I've been driven out. They've said to me, 'Get the hell out of here' and I have to get out."

The Port Authority paid the moving expenses to his new location six blocks away, at 112 Fulton Street, which he named, with a last gesture of defiance, "Oscar's of Cortlandt Street." In part because of Price's negotiations, he received, the agency said, $16,853.30 for the unremovable fixtures in the two stores—an amount Oscar refused to confirm but still dismissed as "paltry." He ran ads with the new address ("OPEN ALL DAY SATURDAY," one of them said, in a hopeful reference to the big day on Radio Row) and gussied up the new storefront, but by February of the following year he had entered Chapter 11 bankruptcy proceedings and was struggling to pay off his new debts. "We'll be out of the Chapter 11 soon," Oscar assured Joe Fried of the *New York Times*. "You suffer the tortures of hell until your own ingenuity brings about a better situation." Oscar's situation, though, would only get worse. The strain of his failed crusade and the shock of the move had been showing for some time, and he suffered what his family described as a nervous breakdown, becoming largely homebound and unable to take care of his business. On May 11, 1969, an ad appeared in the classified section of the *Times*:

> PUBLIC AUCTION BY ORDER OF OSCAR'S RADIO SHOP, INC . . . ARTHUR ALBERT & CO. AUCTIONEERS . . . VERY LARGE BRANDED STOCK—72 TV'S—COLOR AND BLACK AND WHITE FROM 9" TO 23" IN PORTABLE, TABLE & CONSOLE MODELS BY ZENITH, RCA, SONY, PHILCO, ADMIRAL, EMERSON . . . **RADIOS—PHONOS— RECORDERS**—ALL SOLID STATE TABLE, CLOCK PORTABLE & TRANSISTOR RADIOS . . .

There would also be store fixtures and a half-ton 1967 Ford van for sale, the ad explained. By that time, Oscar was so unwell that his daughter, Leatrice, had to look after him while Rae arranged the auction on her own. Although he did some charity work for B'nai B'rith in his later years, he remained withdrawn and uncertain. In the long years before he died in 1992, those who had known the bantam rooster of Cortlandt Street would all describe him in about the same way. Oscar Nadel was a broken man.

■ ■ ■

Not everyone gave up fighting the World Trade Center so soon after the city made peace with the Port Authority.

Lawrence Wien, who kept his own schedule in all things, brought a variety of new court actions and marshaled the unlimited financial resources of his Committee for a Reasonable World Trade Center to produce a series of full-page newspaper ads attacking the project. The ads were excellently produced; Wien had hired Mortimer Matz, Nadel's publicist, when the work began to play out on Radio Row. Wien's final blast came on May 2, 1968, when he ran a nearly full-page ad showing an artist's rendition of a large commercial airliner, flying due south, a fraction of a second before it rammed the offices in the upper stories of the north tower, which stood directly in its path. The ad, titled "The Mountain

Comes to Manhattan," suggested the towers posed a danger for commercial aviation and pointed out that the north tower's proposed television mast, for example, would be some eight hundred feet taller than anything else in the immediate vicinity. "The total potential hazard is staggering," said the ad.

"Unfortunately," it continued, "we rarely recognize how serious these problems are until it's too late to do anything."

7

. . .

Pyramids on the Hudson

Five thousand years stand between the World Trade Center, now rising in lower Man-
hattan, and the Great Pyramid of Cheops at Giza in Egypt.
—Ed Wallace, "Our Most Towering Task," New York *Daily News*, August 3, 1969

The snowflakes came from the north, swirled around the big New York Telephone Company Building, blew across Vesey Street, and hit Arturo Ressi di Cervia in the face. He stamped his feet in the bitter cold of this day in February 1967. Ressi di Cervia, a husky, twenty-six-year-old Italian engineer with a ruddy face and an impressive handlebar moustache that he waxed each morning, was supervising the construction of the first of the underground concrete panels that would become the foundation walls for the World Trade Center. He stood above a trench of freezing mud three feet wide and twenty-two feet long that ran parallel to Vesey Street and was filled with a thick gray liquid slop called bentonite slurry. The slurry was supposed to keep the trench, which was seventy feet deep, from caving in before it was filled with concrete and then outfitted with the seventy-by-twenty-two-foot cage of steel reinforcing bars that already lay on the frigid ground nearby. It looked like a giant's bedsprings.

Out of this first scratch in the ground, the steel beams and columns of the twin towers would soon be rising above a city, and a world, that had never seen a structure so tall or one that held so much space. Simply the effort to manufacture the hundreds of thousands of pieces for the World Trade Center, before they were assembled in Lower Manhattan, would take years and involve dozens of factories across the country. This mammoth scale was beyond anything ever attempted in a high-rise project. It would be likened, at one time or another, to the Pyramids, the Panama Canal, the Brooklyn Bridge, the Apollo space program, and the effort to build an atomic bomb in World War II. More than 200,000 pieces of steel for the trade center were already being fabricated in more than a dozen cities around the country, from Seattle to Gainesville, Virginia. The trade center would call for 3,000 miles of electrical wiring, 425,000 cubic yards of concrete for the floors, 2.2 million square feet of aluminum cladding for the tower facades, seven thousand plumbing fixtures, 170 miles of connecting pipe, forty thousand doors, and 43,600 windows. There would be almost six acres of marble and a $1,547,800 tandem of automated window washers designed to crawl up and down the face of the towers.

Much of this fabric would be woven into the sky, raised a piece at a time to create monumental structures where there had been only space before. But the great building effort would not begin in the sky; instead, it would begin in the frozen mud around Ressi di Cervia's boots. The first major projects undertaken for the trade center would take place on, and soon beneath, the ground at the site itself and in the waters of the Hudson River. Those projects included building and excavating the giant foundation—which, after a promising start, quickly stalled as the excavation ran into unexpected difficulties—and the astonishing attempt to suspend the long-buried Hudson Tubes in the air as the dig went right past them and commuter trains continued to rumble inside. In another great project that would take place at the same time, the excavated soil from the foundation would be poured into the Hudson to create the newest piece of Manhattan real estate at Battery Park City.

In the backhanded way New Yorkers express their admiration, one writer could not resist calling this panorama "the biggest ditch in Manhattan."

The ditch started with the building of the foundation, which became known as "the bathtub" because its mission was to seal the basement against the Hudson River water that saturated the ground there. The bathtub wall would gradually stretch to some 3,294 feet, encircling about eleven acres on the westernmost part of the site. Of course, building a basement this gargantuan by simply digging a hole and then coating its inside with concrete walls, as if for the foundation of a suburban home, would be hopeless. So Ressi di Cervia—who ran the bathtub construction

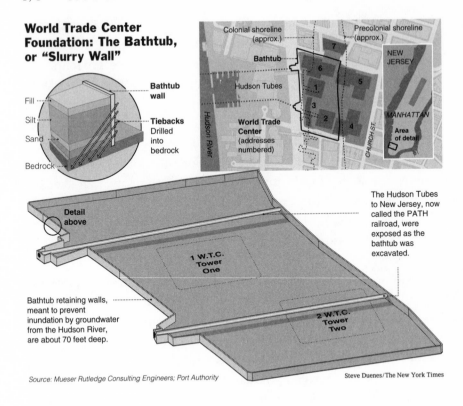

World Trade Center Foundation: The Bathtub, or "Slurry Wall"

Colonial shoreline (approx.)

Precolonial shoreline (approx.)

NEW JERSEY

Bathtub

Fill

Silt

Sand

Bedrock

Bathtub wall

Tiebacks Drilled into bedrock

Hudson Tubes

Hudson River

World Trade Center (addresses numbered)

MANHATTAN

CHURCH ST.

Area of detail

Detail above

The Hudson Tubes to New Jersey, now called the PATH railroad, were exposed as the bathtub was excavated.

1 W.T.C. Tower One

Bathtub retaining walls, meant to prevent inundation by groundwater from the Hudson River, are about 70 feet deep.

2 W.T.C. Tower Two

Source: Mueser Rutledge Consulting Engineers; Port Authority

Steve Duenes/The New York Times

job at the site for Icanda, the Italian-Canadian contractor hired by the Port Authority—and his workers set about to dig a huge trench around the site, twenty-two feet at a time. As they dug, they filled the trench with slurry and later squirted concrete in the bottom, forcing the slurry out. Only when the mostly invisible wall was finished would they begin excavating the basement itself.

As they carved out each section, workers first dug down as far as the Manhattan schist bedrock with sharp-toothed clamshell buckets dangling from what looked like the frame for a twenty-foot-high wigwam. The frames, made of four steel tubes painted light blue, ran on rails so that they could quickly slide from section to section. Once the workers had dug a twenty-two-foot section down to the bedrock and poured the slurry, a Port Authority engineer revved up a big gasoline engine that turned a hollow drill. He sent it down through the murk of the slurry to rip out a 2⅛-inch-wide core sample of the gray, banded schist, glittering with nuggets of mica and quartz, and bring it to the surface. The idea was to make sure the rock was solid enough to bear the wall. Then the workers positioned a steel-alloy blade of horrific size, three feet long and three feet wide, connected to hydraulics that would ram it into the bedrock. The blade, as designed, was to bury itself a full three feet into the stone with each chop. The point was to cut a notch that would create a watertight seal when the concrete hardened.

At least that was how the contractors and engineers had planned it. The digging and pouring soon began running seriously behind schedule. Ressi di Cervia and his company had already discovered that Lower Manhattan's geology was as refractory and complicated as its politics and people.

As late as the 1780s, the edge of the island had been at Greenwich Street, some seven hundred feet east of its position in 1966, and the land was loose and uncertain. The top twenty or thirty feet of the soil held ballast from the European ships that would jettison the stones before picking up cargo for the trip back. Below that were layers of Hudson River mud and a ruddy, quicksandlike substance called bull's liver, then hardpan clay, boulders, and crumbling, decomposed rock. The lightweight clamshell buckets did not want to bite into that mess, and the quartz nuggets in the schist gnashed at the fancy alloy blade and dulled its edge. To make matters worse, the schist also had a bizarre, springy structure. In short, the blade was bouncing instead of cutting. Icanda's Italian workers had taken to ridiculing their big *Adige* digging rigs—so named because they had first been used near the Adige River in Italy—as *adagio*, or slow. The job that had to be finished before anything else could proceed had bogged down almost before it began.

That delay threatened the entire project. The overall construction effort was so huge and multifaceted that when a planning engineer sat down and drew just the main construction tasks as a series of interconnected arrows, he had to use a roll of paper nearly ten feet long and three feet wide. According to the schedule on that roll of paper, the slurry wall had to be finished in about a year or little else could proceed. At the rate Icanda was progressing, the wall would take more than four years.

Ray Monti, the Port Authority's chief of construction for the trade center, knew that he could not let that happen. So he called in the one Port Authority employee he could think of who satisfied three conditions: he spoke Italian (the technology was largely Italian, and many of Icanda's workers had come straight from Italy for the job), he had actually seen a completed slurry wall, and he was a superb engineer. His name was George Tamaro, and Monti, who never hesitated to delegate authority to people he trusted, simply asked him to keep the entire World Trade Center project from lurching to a disastrous halt.

And almost from the moment Tamaro began tramping around the muddy site on April 1, 1967, the operation started to move. He was not the likeliest of taskmasters. Born in Weehawken, New Jersey, Tamaro, thirty years old, five feet, eight inches tall, and somewhat rotund, joked that he had learned Italian at the kitchen table so that he could eat. Both his parents had immigrated from towns in the regions of northern Italy. "I must speak Italian well," he would say. "You see how robust I am."

Working in tight coordination, Tamaro and Ressi di Cervia put the slurry wall operation at the World Trade Center site on a twenty-four-hour, six-day-a-week footing. They got rid of the much-touted blade and brought in a low-tech pulverizer used in coal mines, called a churn drill—in essence, an enormous battering ram with five heavy steel fins that intersected at a central point, forming a star pattern. The workers would simply drop the drill over and over on the schist, crumbling it to sand that they swept away with bursts of air. When the blade broke, welders were right there to repair it. For several weeks, Tamaro didn't tell anyone on the site that he spoke Italian, preferring to listen in on their side conversations during meetings, but word somehow got around. One day he was in a construction trailer looking at some drawings when a worker named Giosué Miotti walked in.

"Tamaro, ma tu capisci l'italiano!" Miotti said, to which an unruffled Tamaro replied in his Americanized Italian: *"Si, l'ho capito per trè settimani."*

The exchange ("So, Tamaro, you understand Italian!"—"Yes, I've understood it for three weeks") didn't do anything to hurt his reputation among the workers. And there was little doubt that Monti had picked the right engineer. In March, Icanda workers had completed three of the twenty-two-foot-wide sections, or panels, for the bathtub; on a single day in May after Tamaro arrived, they completed three. Tamaro and Arturo Ressi di Cervia sped through the 158 panels even as outrageous new subterranean barriers emerged. The slurry wall formed a giant parallelogram bounded by Vesey, West, Liberty, and Greenwich Streets, with two westward protuberances, called the north and south projections, where the Hudson Tubes entered the bathtub next to the river. Beneath panel

G44—the 45th of 46 panels along the soon-to-be-obliterated Greenwich Street, counting from north to south—the workers discovered an immense underground cave, next to a valley a hundred feet deep that had been carved out by a glacial stream eons ago. They had to pummel through the cave and hack their trench all the way to the bottom of the valley, and still they were never quite sure what the wall was resting on.

The strain of the job caused Tamaro to lose twenty-five pounds in the first month. The endless succession of crises, often cropping up in the watches of the night, assumed an almost predictable format. After working a fourteen-hour day, Tamaro would not hear the phone ring at 3 A.M., and his exasperated wife, Rosemary, who was expecting a baby, would have to hit him to wake him up. *"Arturo,"* Ressi di Cervia would announce himself as Tamaro stood in the hallway in his bedclothes holding the phone, *"grandi problemi."* Then Tamaro would make a series of calls to work out a fix and he would go back to bed. Sometimes a spectacular problem would turn up while he was there to see it. One day the Icanda workers were digging deep within a slurry-filled trench just across Vesey Street from the Telephone Company Building. All at once, the slurry disappeared, as if an invisible giant had sucked it out with a straw. After a few deeply puzzling moments, Tamaro saw three bellowing men sprint out of the Telephone Company Building onto the street. The slurry had rushed downhill to a deep subbasement of the building through an abandoned conduit for telephone lines that the Icanda workers had breached; the wooden plug at the end of the conduit had burst across the basement room like a cannon shot, followed by the murky, high-speed stream of slurry.

Things went well enough that Tamaro began gaining his weight back. But by about March 1968, when the wall had been completely poured, it looked like little more than a curiously narrow sidewalk encircling the site: the rest was still buried. Workers started excavating soil from the interior of the bathtub, and in a delicate bit of choreography inside "the biggest ditch in Manhattan," others started shoring up the wall so that the pressure of the water and soil around the outside did not simply tip it over into the hole. The plan was to insert cables through the wall, from the inside out, drilling long holes downward at a forty-five-degree angle for as much as 150 feet and then 35 feet further into the bedrock. Bundles of cables called tiebacks would be grouted into the bedrock for a permanent connection and then stressed with as much as 600,000 pounds of force using hydraulic jacks. The tiebacks—some 1,440 of them arranged in anywhere from four to six neat tiers at different places around the bathtub—would hold the wall up, acting as support lines on the biggest tent humanity had ever pitched.

No more than ten vertical feet of the wall could be exposed without tiebacks at any point in the excavation; otherwise it ran the risk of collapsing. In charge of the tieback operation, unsurprisingly, was another Italian speaker, named Gennaro Liguori, who had grown up in the Bronx and now worked as a superintendent for Slattery Construction. When a section of the wall had been exposed, Liguori's men would roll up to it with something that looked like an artillery piece on metal tracks, but was actually a huge drill called a Jumbo Air Track. What would have been the muzzle was a steel pipe with the shaft of the drill inside. As the drill bit led the way, a hydraulic hammer rammed the pipe into the soil and then attempted to socket it into the bedrock. There were countless buried surprises. When the bit struck old timbers, it would bounce. Other times, it would lodge in some obstacle and snap the shaft like a dry twig; the hole would have to be capped off and abandoned. Late one night, when a specially placed sentry with a two-way radio fell asleep near a locker room in the basement of the luckless Telephone Company Building, the Jumbo Air Track drilled through, the grout was poured, and the lockers were forever bound to the floor. But when all went well, the device was relentless, forcing air and water down the center of the drill shaft and burbling the "fines," or drill detritus, back up the pipe and out of the hole.

And as the excavation went deeper and deeper, the Port Authority had to deal with the twin, cast-iron, sixteen-foot, seven-inch-diameter Hudson Tubes, which ran straight through the bathtub and had never seen the light of day since they were completed in 1909.

Eighty thousand people a day rode the train through the tubes, getting on and off at the station beneath the Hudson terminal buildings just west of Church Street and outside the easternmost edge of the bathtub. The Port Authority was going to build a new train station for what was now called PATH, just inside the Greenwich Street slurry wall, tucked away at the very bottom of the bathtub. But until the new station was ready, the Port Authority—and especially Ray Monti—had decided that there would be no interruptions of the commuter service. The trains would run on time. And the only way to do that was to suspend the tubes in midair.

By early June 1968, 75 percent of the north tube was exposed, "appearing from the distance like a giant drain pipe," as Austin Tobin put it in his notes. About two feet of soil had been removed from the top of the south tube for three-quarters of its length. It was time to begin the World Trade Center's next great experiment, and Port Authority engineers knew that if it went even slightly awry—skewing or buckling the tracks, let alone collapsing the tubes—trains could derail, and at a minimum there would be a huge commuting snarl.

In preparation, crews had sunk heavy vertical elements called caissons every forty-two feet on either side of each tube, then ran stout steel supports along the caissons so that the cast-iron cylinders looked as if they were enclosed in cattle chutes. Now, slowly, gingerly, the workers started digging under the north tube, exposing no more than ten feet at a time before slipping crisscrossing steel straps underneath. They wedged chunks of wood between the straps, nicknamed belly bands, and the cast iron to form a cushion before jacking up the bands ever so carefully and fastening their ends to the horizontal steel supports. The workers went ten more feet. They added another set of belly bands. As more and more of the north tube hung in the air, Liguori thought the bands resembled a Speidel Twist-O-Flex watch band. A young Port Authority engineer named Charlie Maikish, who had been elevated from a job working in the muck that was being poured to form the Battery Park City landfill, and who now spent most of his time in the bathtub beneath the structure, saw a series of tremendous jock straps. "It's doubtful there's ever been anything like it," said Harry Druding, the tall, imposing, and occasionally volatile engineer who had started with the Port Authority in 1929 and was its chief field engineer on the site.

Disinterring the tubes called for some other extreme measures. One night on the graveyard shift, Maikish and Liguori went down into the north tube, where they had both been doing some work, with a construction crew and a set of "burning bars"—flammable metal bars that burn white-hot when oxygen is pumped through them. The mission was to cut a three-inch notch, or "key," all the way around the tube, to serve as an expansion joint so that exposure to warm air and sunlight would not cause the tube to buckle. They cut nearly all the way around and were just finishing up when there was a sudden deafening sound like an explosion. Some of the workers spooked and started running into the gloom of the tunnel.

When everyone had calmed down, Maikish realized that there had already been enough strain on the iron that the gap had snapped shut as soon as the crew cut it. Otherwise, nothing seemed damaged, so he simply left a note for Druding, who usually arrived at about 6 A.M. The note went something like: "Dear Mr. Druding, Last night cut through final piece of the key and the tube slammed shut. Here's my home phone number if you want any more information. Charlie."

Maikish got in his Volkswagen and drove to his apartment on West Eighty-fifth Street. He walked in the door around 6:30 and the phone rang. It was Druding.

"What do you mean, the tube slammed shut, you idiot?" Druding said, adding some graphic language natural to construction sites.

"Mr. Druding, that's what it did."

"Tubes don't just slam shut."

"Okay—it moved."

Maikish could see that this wasn't going to get him anywhere. "Mr. Druding," he said, "I'll be right back down."

"You bet your life you'll be right back down," Druding said. "I want to see you in my office in fifteen minutes."

Maikish got back into his Volkswagen.

They solved the problem by cutting a new gap, sliding wood chocks in as they went, and then replacing them with a big rubber gasket. But there was nothing to be too distressed about, given that Maikish's surveying measurements in the tubes showed that neither of them had moved more than a sixteenth of an inch during the entire epic procedure— something like nonelective intestinal surgery on a cosmic scale. Still, when curious onlookers gathered at the viewing gallery the Port Authority set up on the seventeenth floor of a building at Liberty and Greenwich Streets that wasn't due to be demolished for a while, the bathtub so dwarfed the tubes that passersby continually mistook them for sewer lines, just as Tobin had suggested would happen.

The dig went down, down. Old artifacts began turning up in droves, as if time in Lower Manhattan were making one last, frenzied plunge backward before giving way to the inevitability of the aluminum-faced towers. Workers dug up cannonballs, animal carcasses, a goat's horn, clay pipes, oyster shells, the muzzle of a cannon, a Portuguese fishing gaff, a century-old bedroom slipper, ancient bottles, and a time capsule from the cornerstone of the Washington Market containing some old newspapers—at least one of them with a front-page article lamenting the number of good jobs in Manhattan that were being taken by immigrant Italian workers—and the cards of some of the produce sellers at the market.

And they began to strike bedrock.

In July and August 1968, as the excavation reached as far down as sixty feet below the streets, the rock was not solid enough at first to serve as the base of a great skyscraper, so the crews began blasting with dynamite to go deeper. When the rock started to look better, workers chipped at it a little more with picks and chisels to form a nice even area, and they called Harry Druding over.

Druding held a four-foot piece of common steel reinforcing bar, known the world over as rebar. There was really no foolproof way to tell what Manhattan's tortured geologic history had put under that spot— whether the rock was hard and deep and continuous enough to support the slab of reinforced concrete upon which one of the dozens of steel columns at the base of the trade center was to rest. But a few specially skilled engineers like Druding had learned to strike the stone with a bar and, as the heavy equipment nearby stood silent, listen to the ring. A sound with a certain muffled overtone meant the rock could have faults, or be too soft, or have a gap underneath. A clear melodic ping meant the rock was solid.

Druding swung the rebar and listened, a first violinist searching for a perfect A amid the mighty walls of the excavation.

A Stradivarius couldn't have sounded prettier.

"Pour the concrete," Druding barked.

■ ■ ■

There wasn't much in Gainesville, Virginia, besides the Atlas plant. Strung out along Route 29 somewhere between Manassas and the Blue Ridge Mountains was a little shop called Phil's Market, a roadside motel, a bedraggled trailer park, a few scattered houses, a diner without a sign, known as Queenie's, a barbershop that no one with any sense visited, Sam's Junkyard, and not a single stoplight. Just about the only local lore to speak of had to do with ornery old Sam. It was said that he ate his breakfast cereal out of a hubcap.

Ah, but the plant was something different. Lined up along Route 29, just south of the point where the Southern Railroad tracks crossed the road at a shallow angle, were three green, corrugated-metal buildings seven hundred feet long, fifty feet high, and from sixty-five to eighty feet wide. Spurs curved away from the main tracks to let flatbed railcars carry gigantic pieces of steel in and out of the three buildings, called bays, and a cluttered work yard in back. Cranes tossed the steel around as if it were dry tinder, a swarm of workers pounded, cut, and welded their pieces before sending them to the next stage of assembly, and if you stood for more than a minute or two amid the deafening clatter, you would begin to taste the steel in the air—like a penny on the tongue but sweeter, and much, much harder to forget. Red letters two feet high on the bays proclaimed the identity of this raucous challenge to the serenity of the Virginia countryside: ATLAS MACHINE AND IRON WORKS.

The company had made its name in bridges. In fact, the reason the bays were that green hue at all was that someone had bought a little too much paint one year for a job in the District of Columbia, where pea green was the standard color for bridges. But the flatcars leaving the plant were carrying enormous columns, some of them four feet wide, forty feet long, and made of steel so thick that they weighed up to sixty tons apiece. That steel did not look like anything a bridge could use. Attached to some of the column sections were curvy crosspieces that looked a lot like ten-foot-long bow ties, each of which was stenciled with the company name in big red letters.

Atlas had won the contract to spin twelve thousand tons of raw steel into the massive lower columns of the twin towers that would reach—once the sections were spliced together end to end—nearly from the bedrock up to the fourth story above the street, where the columns would fork into triplets to produce Yamasaki's much lighter and more closely spaced pinstripes. The bow ties of adjacent columns would be welded together to hold the big columns in place.

As the time to lay steel at the World Trade Center drew near in the summer of 1968, scenes like the one in little Gainesville were playing out at more than a dozen plants around the country. Dreier Steel of Long Island City, New York, was making the tremendous steel feet called grillages that would support the big columns at the twin towers' base. Pittsburgh–Des Moines Steel was putting together the tridentlike forks, some of them fifty-five tons apiece, that would sit on the base columns and run to where the regular pinstripes began on the ninth floor. Pacific Car & Foundry Co. in Seattle was fabricating 5,828 panels—most of them ten feet wide and thirty-six feet high, consisting of three columns and three of the fifty-two-inch-deep spandrels connecting them—that would create the pinstripes when fastened together on the facade. Laclede Steel in St. Louis was fashioning thirty-two thousand floor trusses, and nearby Granite City Steel was providing the corrugated steel deck and the ductwork to be fitted atop them. Montague-Betts in Lynchburg, Virginia, Mosher Steel in Houston, Stanray Pacific in Los Angeles, and Levinson Steel in Pittsburgh all had a nice little piece of the job. It seemed that an entire nation had been mobilized to build the World Trade Center.

All the same, a casual observer might have been forgiven for concluding that of all the ways to fabricate 200,000 pieces for the biggest and most complicated jigsaw puzzle in the world—on an island so cramped that only a few of the pieces could be delivered at a time, using unionized shipping routes that could be shut down on a moment's notice—this was just about the most insane plan anyone could have devised.

In fact, the plan had been forced into existence by Austin Tobin's furious refusal to back down in the face of what he saw as extortionate bids by the industry's two giants, Bethlehem Steel and U.S. Steel.

Tobin thought he had a friendly understanding with the companies. In the summer of 1964, both companies had estimated that they could fabricate all the structural steel for the trade center at a cost of about $82 million, give or take. But when he opened the bids two years later, only a couple of weeks after making peace with Mayor Lindsay and the city, the companies not only came in some 50 percent higher than expected, but suspiciously close together: $118.1 million for Bethlehem, $122.2 for U.S. Steel.

To some, the numbers sounded like a death knell. And given the caustic political climate, Tobin and his advisers were probably correct in believing that a sudden escalation of that size could doom the project, especially since Lawrence Wien quickly learned of the problems and trumpeted them in full-page attack ads. "The figures are shocking," Wien wrote, cementing his position as Tobin's favorite gadfly.

So Tobin threw the bids out, knowing full well that no other companies in the world could give him all the steel he needed. Under pressures so terrific that perhaps only a great builder with Tobin's poise could have found room to maneuver, he had Les Robertson's office in New York divide the job into lots, each of which would now be bid separately. The remarkable dispatch with which the Port Authority moved is revealed in the chain of events following a meeting on Friday, October 21, 1966, that was attended by A. Carl Weber, a vice president and structural engineer at Laclede Steel in Saint Louis, which the agency had invited to bid on the floor trusses. Among those present at the meeting, which took place at Tishman Construction's 666 Fifth Avenue building in New York, were Mal Levy; Jim Endler, the West Pointer who served as project manager for Tishman; Wayne Brewer, one of Les Robertson's top engineers; and Robert W. Koch, vice president at Karl Koch Erecting, the Bronx-based company that would soon receive a $20 million contract to erect the World Trade Center's steel.

By the following Monday, Weber had sent detailed sketches of his proposed trusses to Endler (which he wrote as "Ender" in what would become a chronic misspelling) with a letter saying that "we feel sure we shall be able to develop a most efficient and economical prefabricated structural grid that will satisfy the dimensional limitations shown in your basic plans." On Friday of that same week, Weber received this dashed-off, typographically shaky telegram from a colleague who was monitoring the situation in New York:

HAVE JUST BEEN INFORMED BY MR JAMES R ENDER OF TISHMAN THAT BID DUE DATE ON WORLD TRADE CENTERHAS BEEN EXTENDED TO NOVEMBER 21 1966

L H VAUGHAN WHEELING CORRUGATING CO

Tobin's generous "extension" on what was still a speeded-up, skunkworks-style schedule would have made any entrepreneur, let alone a ponderous government agency, proud. And it was no ordinary truss that Tobin's engineers were angling to buy. Unlike the flimsy bar-joist trusses familiar from the roofs of warehouses and big-box stores, Weber's design featured webs of reinforcing bars that formed a square grid, rather than running in one direction only—meaning that whole floors in the trade center would become seamless, rigid, cross-connected units once all the truss panels were fastened into place. Another patented element had the zigzagging reinforcing bars rising above the sheet-metal floor decking at regular intervals, like the back of a serpent arching above the surface of the water. Weber, who was a clever speaker and a much sought-after toastmaster for social events around St. Louis, liked to refer to those elements as the "knuckles." He said they would make the trusses "an integral part of the structure of the building" when the concrete for the floors was poured onto the decking, enveloping the knuckles before hardening in place.

With those innovations, Weber had no trouble grabbing the attention of the Port Authority engineers. They knew that the trusses would not only be expected to hold up the floors but also to provide lateral support for the perimeter columns, keeping them from bending sideways and buckling. Those safety-minded structural features were just what the engineers were looking for. As a welcome bonus, cranes could hook onto the knuckles, simplifying the process of hoisting the floor panels into place during construction. It was obvious that under normal operating conditions this system would support the floors every bit as ably as standard, heavy girders and beams. And still it would let all the ductwork pass through without obstruction, saving much in overall cost. Capping a dizzying four months, a story in the February 1967 issue of *The Ladle* ("Published Monthly for Employees of Laclede Steel Company") ran under the chest-pounding headline "Tallest Buildings in World to Use Laclede Trusses."

In a nice bit of hometown boosterism, the story noted Minoru Yamasaki's role as architect of the trade center and included this line:

> Mr. Yamasaki will be remembered as the designer of the St. Louis Airport Terminal for which Laclede has furnished over 2,500 tons of high strength multi-rib reinforcing steel.

From Gainesville to Los Angeles, from Pittsburgh to Houston, the fabricators started gearing up to pump out steel. Tobin's revenge was qualified—he succeeded in bringing his contracts in for under $90 million, but many of the smaller companies simply went to Bethlehem and U.S. Steel to purchase the raw steel anyway. And as the time approached to deliver that steel and lay it in the ground, there were signs that a degree of haste verging on incredible in an effort of this size had crept into some aspects of the project: as late as January 1968, Robertson was still fiddling with his viscoelastic dampers, forcing serious design changes in the trusses, including 503 tons of additional fabrication and an add-on cost of $151,828.

For all those stomach-churning moments, however, perhaps the most spectacular feats of the countrywide effort were the ones that became routine. For example, no more than any four of the three-column panels being fabricated by Pacific Car & Foundry in Seattle, about four miles south of Skilling's office in an industrial zone, were identical. Although each had box-shaped columns and fifty-two-inch spandrels, they came in several grades of steel with various combinations of steel thickness for different parts, from three inches thick near the bottom of the towers to a quarter inch at the top. So Les Robertson's New York office, which was renting an early, room-sized mainframe computer called an IBM 1620—its disk drive alone was the size of a dishwasher—sent boxes of computer punch cards coded with design information to Pacific Car's structural steel division. The manager, Nicholas Soldano, would run a couple of them through his computers, get a printout with specs for one of the panels, and pass it along to his workers. They would run the steel through the assembly line and paint the panel a ruddy color, light and almost rougelike in its hue. Then, since each panel was designed for a specific place in the great jigsaw puzzle of the trade center, the workers would both etch and stencil it with a telltale code.

One panel, for instance, was marked: PONYA A-251-92-95. Decoded, that meant the panel would span three floors, from the ninety-second to the ninety-fifth, in the north tower, also called tower A. The faces of each building were numbered from 1 through 4, clockwise starting with the north, so the first digit of 251 meant that this one would go on the east face. Finally, there were a total of fifty-nine columns per side, and this was number 51. Because the numbers on the east face started on the northern edge and went south (once again in the clockwise sense), the designated column would end up about thirty feet from the tower's southeast corner. PONYA, of course, stood for Port of New York Authority.

This was the smooth, intuitive operation of high technology, circa 1968. And the workers at Pacific Car & Foundry had to do it only 5,828 times.

■ ■ ■

The first grillage was trucked like fresh-baked goods from Dreier Steel in Long Island City in the early morning of August 6, 1968, just before it was due to be set on a concrete pedestal resting on bedrock. It was the trade center's first piece of structural steel, and it did look a little like an over-grown wedding cake without the bride and groom on top. It weighed thirty-four tons, and its lowest level was fifteen feet long and eleven feet wide, consisting of nine immense girders fused together side by side. Above that was a smaller array of girders running at right angles to the first, above that a slab of solid steel that managed to look petite despite being six inches thick, and, above that, four brackets for connecting to the steel column that would stand atop the grillage. White stenciled lettering spelled out DREIER STEEL in four different places so that the cameras would be sure to pick it up.

The whole layer-cake structure stood seven feet high. Once the truck that was carrying it had driven slowly down a ramp just inside the east slurry wall, an operating engineer named Tommy Bracken used a towering red crane called a Manitowoc 4000, which maneuvered on steel treads and had a boom 150 feet high, to lift the grillage by inch-thick cables attached to its four corners. Led by their foreman, George Bachert, five sweating men in red hard hats emblazoned with the word KOCH—for Karl Koch Erecting, the local company that had won the contract to put up the steel—muscled the grillage into place once Bracken lowered it from the bed of the truck.

The ascent to the sky had finally begun.

It would not take place without a heavy dose of the gritty meticulousness that had characterized the job so far. Charlie Maikish, the young Port Authority engineer who was moving up the chain of command thanks to some of those same qualities, drew his latest stunningly unglamorous assignment when it came time to grout the big grillages into their spots above the bedrock. Sandwiched between the grillages and their concrete slabs were sets of machined metal blocks called shims that were there to ensure that the steel was perfectly level, lest a tiny irregularity at the bottom produce a grotesque misalignment 116 stories later, counting basement floors. Maikish first had to certify that the grillages were in fact level, and then monitor the temperature of the mudlike grout—a special concoction called EMBECO nonshrink grout—that workers pumped from portable mixers into the gaps opened up by the shims between the steel and the concrete slabs. If the grout warmed up too quickly in the summer heat, it would not set properly. Maikish stabbed at the grout with an instrument known in the trade as a "concrete

thermometer"—but which looked, in truth, a lot like a meat thermometer. When Maikish's temperature readings ran too high, he had the
men drop dainty ice shavings into the mixers. Nothing was going to spoil
his perfect grout.

As mundane as the task was, it was not without an element of danger.
The grillages were generally set in three- or four-foot pits that had been
chipped out of the bedrock, which often developed a slick, muddy surface that inspectors like Maikish were forced to crawl over. One day his
immediate superior, a heavyset man named Sal Marino, slipped and
plunged into a pit, breaking a leg and a hip before being hoisted out on a
stretcher. Maikish, with what was becoming his trademark carefulness,
took over as a senior inspector for a time.

There may have been no glamour in grout, but there was all the dazzle
that a red-blooded construction man could crave in putting up the steel.
Koch Erecting had won that contract amid bitter quarrels in the Koch
family over whether they had underbid the job and could even find cranes
powerful and fast enough to bring it in on schedule. In the early 1960s,
Koch had built the Robert Moses Causeway out to Fire Island, among many
other projects, but the company had never attempted anything remotely
like the twin towers. This was not a bridge to Fire Island. Still, the company had managed to become a major irritant for Bethlehem and U.S.
Steel, which had forged a quite comfortable coexistence and would
become the subjects of a federal antitrust inquiry as a result of their cheek-
by-jowl World Trade Center bids. Big Steel executives had taken to ridiculing the little firm as a "scrap dealer from the Bronx."

The pressures of such a large job quickly started to build after Koch
had been given the contract in 1967, but at the site, observers saw only an
epic construction project beginning its leap upward. And that was a stirring panorama indeed. The brightly painted, improbably tall Manitowoc
cranes lifted the columns for the north tower's core (the south tower had
not been started yet) high in the air and placed them atop the grillages.
Then another set of columns extended the core higher, the cross-bracing
was added, and finally the immense perimeter columns around the bottom, with ATLAS MACHINE AND IRON WORKS stenciled on each one, were set
on their base plates and connected together with the bow ties and an
array of gigantic angling beams.

"Ironworkers hoisted steel girders into place in the elevator core of the

North Tower Building," wrote Tobin in September 1968, sounding more pleased about the project than he had in years, after escorting a group of four hundred prospective tenants out on one of the two deceptively delicate-looking steel trestles that crews had built over the pit to help move equipment in and out. "Bulldozers chugged across the floor of the site, fifty feet down. To our right, crews were demolishing the remaining three floors of 50 Church Street. Five earth-laden trucks were ready to move across the trestle to the landfill area as soon as our guests had cleared out above." And in a stunt that Tobin simply could not get enough of, "a Port Authority helicopter hovered at 1,350 feet, the height of the Tower Buildings," he added.

Behind that bustling panorama, Koch came close to bankruptcy in December 1968 after grossly underestimating how difficult it was going to be to weld the giant lower columns of the twin towers. Realizing what the bankruptcy would mean for the project, the Port Authority bailed the company out. Without a hint of public acknowledgment, Tozzoli and his staff started advancing Koch money and crediting the company with innumerable "extras"—jobs like hauling steel a few hundred feet around the site that had not been specified in the contract—to help make it all work out. The extra that would remain vivid in manager Jack Daly's mind was hoisting portable latrines up to workers in the towers: around $500 a lift, depending on how you charged it. Koch was in the clear.

And the job started to move.

When the core reached to about street level, Koch mounted one looming crane on each of its four corners. Although from a distance the cranes looked something like the scariest praying mantises ever to wait for a passing beetle, they were named for a different part of the animal kingdom—called kangaroo cranes. In part, that was because they had been designed by a slightly mad genius of steel erection named Eric Favelle, who happened to be Australian, and in part because each crane sat on a base that was designed to jack itself up as the towers rose. Booms on the cranes occasionally crumpled, bolts anchoring them to their bases blew out like musket shots, and more than sixty of the hydraulic pumps that powered the cranes broke down and spilled their oily guts all over the job, but the steel went up. The pieces would generally travel by barge from the staging areas in New Jersey, get stacked on the Battery Park City landfill, and be trucked "under the hook"—within reach of a cable lowered by one of the kangaroo cranes—just when they were needed.

In each corner of the rising towers, swaggering across the highest completed floors and clambering on the skeletal columns projecting above them, were six-man "raising gangs" of ironworkers who put the steel, and every other worker on the site, firmly in their places. Of the five thousand construction workers who would eventually swarm over the towers and their surrounding buildings, the 540 ironworkers were the men on the flying trapeze for this special kind of circus—and the thirty or forty foremen, crane operators, and members of the raising gangs at the top were in effect the spinning, leaping, rhinestone-sleeved daredevils that all eyes followed, from the gawkers on West Street to the steady procession of photographers and reporters to Tobin's oft-helicoptered guests, typically hovering at that magical 1,350 feet.

Like trapeze artists, the ironworkers tended to run in families, clans, and regional networks. The Ringling Bros. and Barnum & Bailey Circus had the Wallendas of Old Bohemia; the World Trade Center had the Doyles of Newfoundland. Since at least the turn of the twentieth century, the fishing villages along the Newfoundland coast had been a prolific source of union ironworkers. The reasons were not hard to find: the old "guy derricks" that hoisted steel before the kangaroo cranes were almost exact copies of the equipment fishermen used to haul in their catch on the big boats, and the money was a lot better up on the steel. But the Doyles, from around Conception Bay, were something special.

Consider Jack Doyle, a twenty-five-year-old journeyman ironworker with a grin a mile wide and a powerful "Newfie" accent. Jack's foreman on the raising gang that clustered around the southwest kangaroo crane on the north tower, where he worked, was his older brother George. Their brother-in-law Dick Brady (married to their sister Geraldine) was foreman of the gang catty-corner from them on the northeast end. Their cousin Leo Doyle began the job as the overall superintendent of Tower A, the north tower. Their kid brother Norman was an ironworker on the same tower before he got homesick, went back to Canada, and much later became a Member of Parliament for Newfoundland. Their father, George Sr., also an ironworker in New York, had given Dick Brady his first job, getting coffee and running errands for ironworkers at a schoolhouse in Harlem. Another brother, Jim, never liked New York City but did some ironworking jobs around town anyway, and still another relative, Fred Doyle, would work for a time on 7 World Trade Center, the forty-seven-story skyscraper that would rise just north of Tower A. Jack Doyle would ultimately work on every one of the Port Authority's buildings on the site: 1, 2, 3, 4, 5, 6, and 7 World Trade Center.

There were, of course, plenty of Newfoundlanders on the site who were not part of the Doyle clan—like Willy Quinlan, also known as the Penguin, on the northwest crane of Tower A. And the ironworker culture as a whole was an ethnic mishmash of every conceivable group. Walter Beauvais, known as Chickenbone or Hambone, started the job as foreman on the southeast crane on Tower A and was one among dozens of Mohawk Indian ironworkers at the trade center. They came down from reservations in Canada like Kahnawake, where ironworking had been something like the official trade since around the turn of the century. One of the men in Chickenbone's gang, Peter Fontes, universally known as Hahdahn because that was the nickname he used when hailing coworkers in his Boston accent, had been born to Cape Verdean immigrants and learned about steel at the dinner table from his father, who worked at the plants in Youngstown and Canton, Ohio. George Bachert, the respected foreman who had set the first grillage and eventually took over for Leo Doyle on Tower A, almost seemed out of place. His father had been a sales manager at a distillery on Long Island.

"Setting the steel," as they called it, seemed to take on the flawless rhythm of a good circus act. Each raising gang had five or six ironworkers. A typical gang had a foreman, two connectors, a hooker-on, a tagline man, and a signalman. Stacks or "divisions" of steel would often be sitting, ready for placement, on the highest completed floor. From there, the hooker-on did what his name suggested, hooking the steel to the choker or sling or clip at the end of the crane cable. The crane, its operating engineer sitting above everyone else in the cab, "picked" the steel (ironworkers frequently omit the preposition "up," perhaps considering it superfluous) while the signalman, using hand gestures or a phone connection, told the operator how to guide it into place. The tagline man would help make the finer adjustments by tugging on a rope or some other line that was also latched to some purchase on the steel. Finally the connectors would "manhandle" the steel—that was the term of art—grabbing it with their gloved hands, lining up a few bolt holes, and fastening it loosely into place. You could almost hear the trumpet flourish and see the triumphant somersaults as the raising gang went on to the next piece.

Next came the only slightly less spotlighted gangs. The plumber-ups made sure the steel was perfectly straight, the bolting gang fastened it firmly in place, and the welders—if the engineers hadn't decided that the bolts were sufficient—followed behind. The prefabricated panels and floors of the trade center imposed a larger overall rhythm to the job. The cranes would jump three floors and would build up the core beneath them before turning to the three-column, three-story perimeter panels from Pacific Car & Foundry, which fit together in a sort of scalloped pattern so that there would never be a long line of connections (and a possible fault line) on a single floor. When enough of those were in, the cranes would latch on to Carl Weber's curious "knuckles" on the Laclede floor panels and raise them all the way from the ground before lowering them into place between the core and perimeter columns. A second and a third floor would be assembled, and the cranes, always racing to see who would be finished first, would jump another three floors and start over.

Following behind were legions of electricians, concrete pourers, plumbers, heating and ventilation specialists, and elevator contractors, as well as the people who emplaced the marble in the reception areas, finished the offices, and, presumably, hung the nondescript paintings and wheeled in the potted plants.

Still farther below, crews built what would become six basement levels inside the bathtub. Once those reinforced concrete floors and their support structures were completed, workers cut the tiebacks and capped off the holes in the slurry wall. There was no possibility of leaving the tiebacks there—the brackish Hudson River water would have rusted them away in no time. Now, only the internal floors themselves would support the wall, from the inside.

Up on the towers, the raising gangs could do two or three floors a week when everything was clicking, although their average pace was considerably slower. By April 1969 they had reached the ninth floor above the streets. By July, the twenty-fourth, as steel for the south tower had begun rising alongside. By the end of the year, the north tower's steel had reached the forty-fifth floor, and the structure was already out of proportion to everything around it, looking almost like a colossal toy box that some of the other Lower Manhattan skyscrapers could be put back into at night. At this point, everything about the job seemed outsized. The crane operators would avoid locking their booms in place at quitting time in case a dangerous crosswind kicked up overnight, and one evening, Doyle noticed, all four booms pointed uptown as he left work; when he returned the next morning, all four booms, like the biggest weather vanes on the biggest barn ever conceived, were pointing downtown. Ironworkers also began to notice that unlike any other job they had worked on, this one forced them to take a minute and get their landlegs after returning to the ground at the end of a day's work. The tower had begun to sway in the wind.

In the turbulent heights above Manhattan, where the view was ever more akin to the two-dimensional, maplike city seen from an airplane than from an ordinary building, there began to be other reminders that this was a structure like no other the ironworkers had seen. The lightweight, sail-like floor panels were horizontal as they came up from the ground, but one windy day the clips failed on two of the knuckles on one side and a big panel hung vertically. The wind hurled it against the exterior columns. The engineer tried to hoist it over the side anyway, but every time he pulled it away from the building, the wind, as if at the behest of some outraged god, bashed it against the steel again. The panel progressively disintegrated until the two intact knuckles with their wiggly truss bars dangled alone in the wind. Although Carl Weber had produced something that was a cut above an ordinary truss, the bare steel panels again revealed how intrinsically light and wispy they were during a tugboat strike as the north tower reached the fifty-first floor in February 1970. With steel running short, Tobin and Monti ordered their men to try hauling the panels over from the staging area in Carteret, New Jersey, using—no surprise—a freight helicopter called a Skycrane. But the harbor wind caught one thirty-five-foot panel and started dragging the helicopter down.

"I'm having trouble! I'm having trouble!" the pilot radioed, as Jack Daly and others listened at Koch headquarters on Liberty Street. "I can't control it—I'm cutting it loose," the pilot said, ditching the panel into the Kill van Kull, a busy shipping channel, to remain for eternity.

The Port Authority switched to trucks.

Of course, once the trusses were in place, the support system gained greater strength when the concrete for the floors was poured and it hardened around the knuckles. But as the building rose higher and higher, the steel in the vertical members also got thinner and thinner and the increasingly willowy structure swayed more and more noticeably in the wind; some ironworkers found the experience unnerving. Edward Iannielli, a veteran ironworker who in 1969 was plying his trade on an enormous structure at Kennedy Airport that happened to be its first Boeing 747 hangar, transferred to the trade center and was astonished when he saw the floor panels. "Can you believe they're building that big, gigantic building with bar-joist floors?" he said to a tough old foreman, who replied, "Keep your mouth shut and do your job." So Iannielli went to his younger brother, Don, a former marine who had some intellectual firepower, and who was a foreman on one of the surrounding trade center buildings. "That's an aerodynamic building," Don Iannielli said, "built to withstand all kinds of wind pressures just from its design." Ed, with a less refined appreciation, said, "It don't look right to me," and went back to work.

The towers grew, seemingly without end. Chickenbone, Walter Beauvais, was transferred off the job for riding to the top on a floor panel during an elevator operators strike, and when he was replaced by a despised foreman named Rotten John McKiever, Fontes, the Cape Verdean with the Boston accent, moved to George Doyle's raising gang on the southwest corner. Eventually Dick Brady, foreman in the northeast corner, found a better-paying job and his brother-in-law Jack Doyle took over his gang. The Doyle brothers raced each other to the sky, partly with the ambition of "topping out" the tower by being the first gang to set the highest piece of steel, and partly for the sheer full-throated youthful hell of it.

Down below, in the lower and much less rarefied reaches of Tower A, workers had started spraying the lightweight fireproofing onto the steel. Louie DiBono, the president of Mario & DiBono Plastering, which received the contract for the work in March 1969, was a 350-pound giant who could be by turns menacing and ingratiating. He once shook Mal Levy's hand and declined to let go before reminding him—a little joke, ha-ha-ha—that DiBono could crush it if he wanted to. In another scene that could have come out of a Mario Puzo novel, DiBono showed up in Levy's office with a handful of imported cigars and some nicely boxed pastries from Little Italy. He passed them around to all present before telling Levy that he had a handshake deal with Ray Monti for a $111,000 escalation in one of DiBono's contracts. This time Levy exploded with obscenities, refusing to honor the agreement. Although DiBono had a reputation as a solid contractor, he would also become known as a Gambino crime family member, and would finally be gunned down in one of the World Trade Center's own basement parking lots on orders from the crime boss John Gotti. "Louie DiBono," Gotti would be caught saying on a surveillance tape. "You know why he's dying? He's gonna die because he refused to come in when I called. He didn't do nothing else wrong."

The fireproofing job would be almost as complicated as DiBono's outside business interests. The Port Authority approved a fairly common fireproofing material manufactured by United States Mineral Products of Stanhope, New Jersey, under the trade name Cafco Blaze-Shield. The product contained about 20 percent asbestos, 65 percent "mineral wool"—essentially rock that was melted and spun into fibers—bound together with cementlike components called binders. But how thickly should the product be applied onto the steel? That question would normally be answered by the city's Buildings Department. Every type of steel component in ordinary buildings is tested in huge steel furnaces (by independent organizations like Underwriters Laboratories) with various thicknessess of fireproofing in place. From those tests, experts determine how thick the fireproofing must be to keep the steel from softening too much and potentially buckling in a large fire. But the Port Authority, as a quasi-independent government entity, was not subject to city laws, so it had no legal need to consult with the Buildings Department or to comply with its standard building code.

That still left the question of how thickly DiBono should apply the fireproofing to, say, the most vulnerable component of the twin towers, their floor trusses. In May 1963, Levy had written a letter instructing Port Authority engineers to comply with the New York City building code. There was a severe problem with that order: the new and innovative floor trusses had never been tested in any furnace. There was no technical information available to tell the engineers how thick the fireproofing should be in order to be sure that the trusses were safe. And Levy would never carry out those tests. Instead, in early 1969, before DiBono won the contract, the Port Authority began tinkering with its fireproofing requirements in a way that seemed to leave them arbitrary at best.

An architect at Emery Roth & Sons, the New York firm that was working with Yamasaki and had apparently helped draft fireproofing specs, complained about the change in a letter to the Port Authority on February 11,

1969. "We cannot be expected to accept responsibility for specifications which have been revised in such a manner; that which we originally stated clearly and simply, has become a meaningless document," the architect wrote.

On October 30, 1969, a mysterious letter from Levy's office, addressed to Louie DiBono, would settle the question of how thick the fireproofing on the bar joists—the main structural components of the floor trusses—should be. "All Tower beams, spandrels, and bar joists requiring spray-on fireproofing are to have a one-half-inch covering of Cafco," the letter said. "The above requirement must be adhered to in order to maintain the Class 1-A Fire Rating of the New York City Building Code."

In reality, the specification could have no known relation to the building code without the furnace tests that could determine its validity. A federal investigation would later determine that there was no technical basis for choosing one-half inch as the thickness of the fireproofing. Levy's office—almost certainly Levy himself—had simply picked a number. No one would ever be able to say whether the twin towers were safe in a fire.

The story became even more tortuous after DiBono started spraying the material on the steel, probably sometime late in 1969. At about the same time, scientific studies showing that exposure to asbestos was linked to cancer were being showered with publicity. In April 1970, a CBS crew showed up and used the rising north tower as the backdrop for a news report on the dangers of loose asbestos.

A ban seemed imminent, and a few days after the CBS report, with the north tower's steel at the sixty-ninth floor and interior fireproofing completed to the thirty-sixth floor, Tobin ordered an abrupt switch to a non–asbestos-containing material that U.S. Mineral had just developed, also under the brand name Cafco Blaze-Shield. It was essentially the earlier product without the asbestos, a formula that Tobin said "independent laboratory tests" had confirmed was just as good. Since there had been no tests of the trusses, it is unclear what Tobin was referring to. In any event, there were soon problems when wind-driven rains stripped the material from the steel, rust flaked off and took the fireproofing with it, and Louie DiBono's workers had to improvise dams and diverters to channel the water away. The workers then reapplied the fireproofing. That spring, someone at the agency snapped a picture of a worker actually applying the fireproofing. It showed a man wearing a respirator, a hard hat, and a white protective suit standing on the deck of one floor and spewing the material through an eight-foot-long nozzle toward the exposed truss of the floor above. Finely calibrated the process was not.

"Our new fire-proofing material has been pronounced 'acceptable' by New York City's Environmental Protection Administration," the pleased-sounding picture caption explained.

Above it all, the steel rose and rose over the city. And at 2:51 P.M. on October 19, 1970, a triplet of reddish steel columns dangled from a cable at the World Trade Center construction site.

In the afternoon sun, which threw the shadows of five ironworkers and a picket fence of lower columns across the steel deck of the 99th floor at a rakish angle, the white stenciled code on the panel of columns was clearly visible: PONYA A-342-100-103. Since the last two numbers indicated that the columns would go from the 100th floor to the 103rd, the top of the panel would rise to a height of 1,254 feet, or four feet above the nominal height of the Empire State Building without its antenna, meaning that this piece of steel made the north tower the tallest building in the world. The number 342 meant that the steel was on the south face of the tower—near the southwest corner, George Doyle's corner.

George had outraced his younger brother Jack to the highest piece of steel ever set, and he had an insurmountable lead on the way to setting the topmost steel and collecting the bragging rights of a lifetime. Peter Fontes, the sun in his face, wearing a canvas jacket and blue jeans rolled up at the ankles besides his gloves, boots, and red KOCH hard hat, waved the steel in and connected it with his partner while an obviously proud George Doyle kept an eye on them. When they were finished, first one or two of the men and finally the entire raising gang exuberantly started yelling James Cagney's last words as the psychotic gangster atop a giant gas tank at a chemical plant in *White Heat*, when instead of giving himself up to the lawmen surrounding him far below, he empties his pistol into the tank and is engulfed in a tremendous mushroom of flame: "Made it, Ma! Top of the world! Top of the world!" And they went back to work.

A few weeks later, the ceremonial highest piece of steel, the one that would lift the north tower to its final height of 1,368 feet, was brought to the site. It was an awkward-looking column with some flanges at the top that bore a distant resemblance to a tricorner hat. The kangaroo crane in George Doyle's corner readied to make its final jump and start setting the steel at the top.

The crane's hydraulic pump broke down.

The pumps had been a headache from the start, constantly belching to a stop and marring the operation of Eric Favelle's beautiful kangaroo cranes. When one of the pumps broke down, there was no fixing it at the site. It had to be replaced. Jack's team shot past his brother's and was chosen to top out the tower.

The day of the topping out, December 23, 1970, was not much different from any other working day for most of the construction crews. George Bachert put an American flag on the column before it was hoisted up from the ground, and by the time he got to the top, most of the ceremony was already over. It was foggy at the top, so the officials who crowded the floor—Tobin, Tozzoli, Levy, Monti, among others— couldn't see how high they were. And Jack Doyle knew his gang was no better than his brother's. The chips had just fallen his way.

But even years later, after his beloved older brother had passed away and Jack Doyle was no longer setting steel but putting in his last working days behind a desk, he could not recall rushing up those last half-dozen floors at the trade center without flashing his mile-wide grin, now with a few creases around the edges.

The south tower followed about seven months behind the north tower. Somehow, as the south tower rose, the site below became less secure, with a series of security breaches and thefts. Some of the breaches hardly seemed threatening. Having a few beers after quitting time, the ironworkers would goad besotted patrons at Volk's Restaurant, the Commuters Café, and other establishments that hadn't yet been demolished on the eastern edge of the site, into performing feats of daring on the steel. One night, a very drunk man climbed the south tower on a dare and painted, one big letter per perimeter column, EAT AT VOLKS, as Port Authority police gathered below with bullhorns and spotlights. Another night an equally soused man in a business suit fell over the edge of the slurry wall to the muddy bottom seventy feet below. Maikish phoned for an ambulance and rushed into the pit, fearing what he might see. When Maikish arrived, the man was partly submerged in mud but sitting up and looking around. "Are you okay? Are you conscious?" a confused

Maikish asked as the sirens wailed above. "I'm fine," the man said, before standing up, staggering up a ramp in his filthy suit, and going back to the bar at Volk's.

Other incidents were less amusing. The site became plagued with bomb threats, and just thirty minutes after one of them was phoned in, a huge explosion at the foot of the south tower blew out windows along Liberty Street and sent flames shooting a hundred feet into the air. Men scattered and some jumped from the steel. It turned out to be a coincidental accident: a truck had backed into some propane tanks. There were six injuries but no deaths—and in a lighter vein, press photos clearly showed the word "VOLKS" still painted on the steel above where the blast had occurred.

The site also started to change drastically in appearance as the south tower rose, the white marble plaza was being constructed, and Tobin inaugurated an art program that put, most visibly, a twenty-five-foot-high bronze sphere by the German artist Fritz Koenig within a fountain at the center of the plaza. Tobin and Tozzoli decided that the sphere, a stylized map of the earth, symbolized world peace through trade, although Koenig wasn't so sure.

But of all the happenings around the site as the construction neared its end, perhaps the most poignant was one that could easily have been missed amid the noise and motion and the two gargantuan structures that had risen from the Lower Manhattan soil. The address of the Commuters Café was 32 Cortlandt Street but it was actually tucked into the side of 30 Church Street, the south Hudson terminal building, the last major structure to be demolished because the old train station was still being used beneath it. It was run by three brothers named Tretter—Joe, John, and Herman—who had immigrated from the Burgenland region of Austria. The entrance to the café was on the left as you came into the terminal building from Cortlandt Street; on the ground floor there was a ninety-foot, S-shaped mahogany bar, and above there was a restaurant that could seat 220 patrons. Oscar Nadel had held his "Important Emergency Meetings" here, local merchants had packed the restaurant at lunchtime for the sauerbraten and wienerschnitzel, countless New Jersey commuters had taken a nip at the bar before catching their trains, and before the trade center was finished, Charlie Maikish was hosting Port Authority safety dinners upstairs. Maikish, whose family had arrived from the same region of Austria, would hand out certificates for crane safety and safety in excavation and so many accident-free days on the job.

The café had another occasional patron named Austin Tobin. He seemed to like the operation, the Tretters thought in their slightly officious, Austrian way.

"Mr. Tobin," Joe Tretter ventured to ask him on one of his visits, "is there any chances that we can go into the new building?"

Tobin was honest—he said it depended on whether all the services around the new underground PATH station were contracted to a single company or opened to a variety of businesses. Only in the latter case, he said, would the Tretters have much of a chance. But he introduced them to the right Port Authority official and, as it turned out, the space was rented to all kinds of merchants. The Commuters Café found a prime spot right at the top of the escalators going down to the PATH station. The day the new station opened up, the Tretters became the only merchants to move from Radio Row to the World Trade Center. They polished their new bar, arranged the chairs, and waited for the first train.

8

• ■ •

City in the Sky

When completed, these stolid, banal monoliths came to overshadow Lower Manhattan's
cluster of filigreed towers. . . . A visit to the top, however, is a must.

—*AIA Guide to New York City,* 1988

Irving R. Boody & Co., exporter of fatty acids from Denmark, menthol crystals from Brazil, and wool from New Zealand, was moving into Suite 1163 on the eleventh floor of the north tower on December 16, 1970, a Wednesday. As his employees unpacked boxes, strung Christmas lights, and hung pictures of sailing ships, Rick Boody, the company president, listened to the sweet chatter of the telex machines as they pounded out updates on his shipments around the world.

The north tower had not even been topped out, but far below, opening day for the World Trade Center had already arrived. Inside Suite 1163, the scene was picture perfect. Yet all it took was a glance out Boody's window to realize that the holiday postcard—duly recorded by the Port Authority public relations staff—was largely a charade. These World Trade Center pioneers had been assigned offices inside what was more like a ship in dry dock than a superliner ready for its maiden voyage.

The entranceway to what the Port Authority was calling the first office building of the twenty-first century was a long plywood tunnel reminiscent of a nineteenth-century cattle shoot. Just approaching the towers was hazardous. Not only were the cranes still outside swinging back and forth, lifting the enormous steel columns and floor assemblies up into the sky, but projectiles of plywood and ice flew downward and sideways from the open upper floors, forcing the closure of the local subway station entrance and nearly hitting Margaret Sliss, a secretary at Boody, as she showed up for work. Even construction workers occasionally had to scramble for cover like infantrymen in a bombing raid.

"Is this really the World Trade Center?" Sliss asked one of the workers as she emerged from the chute and entered the plywood-clad lobby of the tower on her first day. "There are walls upstairs, right?"

The odd opening day at the World Trade Center was largely a result of a desperate desire to move in at least some rent-paying tenants before the end of 1970. Still, Rick Boody had been excited about becoming one of the trade center pioneers. His family had a long and distinguished association with Lower Manhattan and the city at large. His great-grandfather David A. Boody was known as the "grand old man of Wall Street," having spent sixty-five years working on the stock exchange. Rick's father, Irving R. Boody, started the family firm in 1923, sagely anticipating the changes already percolating through the city's economy in the decades before World War II. Irving R. Boody & Co. did not harvest the raw materials and it did not own the ships that moved them or the factories that turned these commodities into durable goods. Instead, it was purely a financial services firm. When soap makers like Colgate-Palmolive and Procter & Gamble needed vegetable oil, Boody would negotiate with shippers he knew from England to China to find the exact product, price, and delivery date required.

With that kind of family history, Boody knew he had to be a part of a shining new office complex that would pull together importers and exporters, customs brokers, freight forwarders, and international banks, and offer special services like high-tech telecommunications and a computerized database of commodities. Yet on his first day, Boody had to wonder if the place would ever live up to its sales pitch. "Don't get hit by that hammer," he joked with his staff.

George Rossi, a Port Authority interior designer, had the difficult assignment of somehow making these first World Trade Center tenants feel at home. This meant comforting them when news broke, a week after Boody moved in, that the Fire Department had issued—then rescinded—an order to vacate the north tower, citing "deep concern" with "the moving of tenants into an uncompleted office." Rossi also had to explain why toilets in this ultramodern tower would freeze over (most of the building was not yet heated), passenger elevators did not work (the bugs in the lifts had not been straightened out yet), and the only food service available within a twenty-minute walk was a coffee stand on an unfinished floor upstairs nicknamed the Red Ball Express (the lobby and other details like restaurants would not be ready for another two years). True, there weren't all that many people to placate yet. Boody's entire firm took up 2,537 square feet, the equivalent of a modest-sized bookstore. Even accounting for the space already leased by the state and federal government, the Port Authority somehow had to find 4 million square feet of private tenants. That was twice the capacity of the Empire State Building.

The Port Authority had already spent tens of thousands of dollars on cocktail parties and dinners in cities around the United States and in Europe. The World Trade Mart, a resurrection of Winthrop Aldrich's 1946 plan, was the highlight of those sales pitches, since it was one of the many amenities that the agency promised would make the World Trade Center so much more than just another office building. "A buyer, for example," said the trade center's promotional material, "could view a massive automatic computer, fully assembled; a powerful bulldozer; a towering yacht; or any of the countless other pieces of equipment and merchandise that are routinely shipped via the New York–New Jersey Port. After inspecting the product, he could sit down in a modern, comfortable, and quiet office to discuss the purchase. Financial and shipping arrangements could be made in another part of the center."

It sounded good—well, actually, it sounded like promo copy written by bureaucrats who were not versed in the current realities of international trade. A primary target for the World Trade Center had been the "foreign departments" of major corporations, divisions that specialized in international trade. But corporations were already rejecting this approach; it made no sense to further isolate a corporate division that never should have existed in the first place. The answer was to make the entire corporation a multinational entity, not set up a separate foreign staff in a New York office building. So when Port Authority sales teams returned to New York, they had little but a stack of new travel and entertainment bills.

Sidney Nulman, a letter carrier from the Bronx, was told that someday fifty thousand people would work at this place. "They may need twenty or fifty postmen here," Nulman said, marveling, on his first day at the

World Trade Center. The Port Authority was prepared for such an onslaught, having even set up its own zip zode: 10048. On opening day, though, Nulman stood all alone on the north tower's squeaky-clean eleventh floor. No office workers were in sight. And in his hands he was holding the entire batch of mail for the World Trade Center. He paused and counted them up. Fifteen letters.

■ ■ ■

One morning late in 1972, the telephone rang in the community affairs office at the New York City Fire Department headquarters. On the line was someone from the Attorney General's Office, an agency that during the protracted fights in court had helped defend the Port Authority's right to bulldoze Radio Row. A lawyer in the Attorney General's Office had a slightly awkward question. Amy Herz Juviler, one of the top litigators in the Attorney General's Office, had a simple question: Was the World Trade Center a safe place to work?

Juviler was no easily ruffled soul. She had spent the last eight years taking on mobsters, labor unions, and civil liberties lawyers. Now she was calling the Fire Department on behalf of a couple of her colleagues. They were petrified. Governor Nelson A. Rockefeller wanted the two-hundred-lawyer staff to leave behind their offices at 80 Centre Street and help fill up the towers. The office agreed to do so, but even before they moved in, more than forty fires had been reported at the trade center. Most had been small affairs, but oftentimes the towers had acted like chimneys, as the smoke rose through ducts and shafts dozens of floors above the spot where the fire was taking place. Fire experts called the phenomenon the stack effect. Juviler was sure that there was nothing to worry about. No one would move so many people into a building without an excellent fire-protection plan, she assured her colleagues.

Still, she put the call into the Fire Department just to make sure. "You think you could perhaps send someone to talk to us, to let people know that the World Trade Center is a safe place to work?" she asked the fire officer. "I am sorry, ma'am, I just don't think I can help you," came the reply. "There is not much I can say about those towers you would want to hear." He surprised her by rapidly ticking off a list of weaknesses: the lightweight floors, the large open spaces across which a fire could quickly spread, the substandard fireproofing on the steel, and, worst of all, no automated sprinklers. "The bottom line is that it is not a place I would want to be in a fire," he told Juviler.

For once, the self-confident lawyer was not sure what to do with a piece of information.

She was not the only person outside the Fire Department who had heard the claims that the towers would be unsafe in a blaze. Cornelius J. Lynch, the head of Tozzoli's real estate team, had also heard them. It is true, he told the nervous types; the Port Authority is exempt from city building codes. But it had voluntarily built the trade center to an even higher standard than required by law. The buildings had three emergency escape stairwells per tower, not the required two, he said, along with other state-of-the-art safety features.

"We are the safest building in the whole world," Lynch said, realizing the claim was a bit bold. Just look at the coat hooks on bathroom stall doors, he and others pointed out. They were installed a tad lower than usual to prevent thieves from reaching over the top and grabbing coats or handbags. "We have in the premises our own major police presence," Lynch told prospective tenants. "If something happens in terms of crime, or a major emergency, there is a captain down there, a sergeant, and a bunch of lieutenants around the clock. We don't have rent-a-guard; we have policemen down there."

Like other people who were thinking of moving into the towers, Juviler heard these assurances. She remained uncertain about what to do. Governor Rockefeller had given the attorney general no choice but to move; that much was clear. So Juviler decided to do something unusual for such a garrulous lawyer. She decided to keep her mouth shut.

■ ■ ■

"Three things are to be looked to in a building," the newspaper ad said in a February 1971 pullout section on the World Trade Center, quoting Goethe in heavy, faux-Gothic type: "That it stand on the right spot; that it be securely founded; that it be successfully executed.

"Fiduciary Trust Company is looking forward to moving into new sky-high quarters in early 1973."

Since its founding during the Depression as a place for the risk-averse wealthy to sock away their savings, Fiduciary Trust had maintained its offices at the bluest of blue-chip addresses: 1 Wall Street. But as the 1970s dawned, a different kind of chief executive took over. Lawrence Hunting-ton, a six-foot-four graduate of Exeter and Harvard, was transforming this staid, carriage-trade bank into a high-flying global enterprise. He fig-ured it was only appropriate to find a new headquarters that also entailed a bit of excitement and risk: four floors near the top of the still unbuilt south tower of the World Trade Center.

Huntington knew the move was a gamble. But for a chief executive whose leisure activities included mountain climbing and competitive sail-ing, the idea of working so high up in the sky thrilled him. It created the perfect image for his company, whose assets grew during his tenure from $5 billion to more than $50 billion. The Port Authority was even more delighted. Fiduciary not only rented a giant piece of real estate space—for years it was the Port Authority's largest private tenant—but its presence there also raised eyebrows. Austin Tobin had adamantly reminded his staff that the agency must only approve leases for companies explicitly tied to world trade. That had meant the rejection, in the late 1960s, of an inquiry from the accounting firm Lybrand, Ross Bros. & Montgomery, which wanted to rent 300,000 square feet. "Let them go," Tobin told Lynch. "We will get someone else." Fiduciary seemed to represent a bending of this rule. Yes, it invested a fair share of its money overseas and it handled the pension funds for the United Nations staff. But it was not a foreign depart-ment of a company or bank, as the original guidelines required.

This qualification issue seemed meaningless to Huntington. What he wanted was an impressive piece of office space. And, starting with two acres of space on the ninety-fourth and ninety-fifth floors of the south tower—he had them connected by a glassed-in spiral staircase—that is just what he got. Even through Yamasaki's narrow windows, Huntington thought the views were superb. On the most routine day, he could sit at his desk and watch the land and sea mutate as the light from the sky turned from noontime intensity to dusk. In the summer, each approach-ing thunderstorm was a marvel, the angry gray clouds and sheets of rain moving ever so slowly across the horizon. In the winter, Huntington watched snow fall upward, carried by the wind. On some days he could see giant ice floes moving slowly down the Hudson. When a fog or low cloud cover had settled over New York, Huntington and his staff would be left there alone, towering over an infinite meadow of soft, gray cotton spread out below his desk. The only evidence that they were atop one of

David Rockefeller (*right*), the chairman of the Downtown–Lower Manhattan Association, and John D. Butt, the group's president, hold a sketch of the original World Trade Center proposal during a January 1960 press conference. As first conceived, the tallest building in the complex—which would have been constructed along the East River, not the Hudson—would have been about seventy stories. (J. P. Morgan Chase Archives)

Guy Tozzoli, the director of the World Trade department of the Port of New York Authority, in 1962. (Port Authority of New York and New Jersey)

Austin Tobin, the executive director of the Port of New York Authority, made building the World Trade Center a personal crusade. (Allyn Baum/*The New York Times*)

On Friday, July 13, 1962, merchants and clerks on Radio Row staged an anti–World Trade Center protest dripping with dark humor. Carrying a coffin bearing a mannequin that represented Mr. Small Businessman, they paraded past Oscar's Radio & TV, whose owner, Oscar Nadel, the leader of the Downtown West Businessmen's Association, also rode in the coffin that day. (Neal Boenzi/*The New York Times*)

Oscar Nadel (*seated*) and Lee Merin, one of his lawyers. Nadel and his legal team ultimately took their challenge to the World Trade Center to the United States Supreme Court, which declined to hear the case (Meyer Liebowitz/*The New York Times*)

Minoru Yamasaki in 1958, standing over his design for the Wayne State University education building in Detroit. Its elaborate decorative fa-cade drew such criticism that Yamasaki cut back on ornamentation for future projects, including the World Trade Center.
(United Press International, Inc.)

Alan Davenport, Minoru Yamasaki, Malcolm Levy, John Skilling, Jack Cermak, and Leslie Robertson (*left to right*) crouch inside Cermak's wind tunnel beside a model of Lower Manhattan containing the proposed twin towers, in Fort Collins, Colorado, in 1964.
(Colorado State University)

GRANT AIDS LATINS IN THE SOUTHWEST

Ford Fund Gives $2-Million to New Legal Defense Unit

By KATHLEEN TELTSCH

An organization has been created to provide legal safeguards against discrimination for the country's five million Mexican-Americans.

Establishment of the Mexican American Legal Defense and Educational Fund was announced here yesterday by the Ford Foundation, which provided an initial grant of $2.2-million for the undertaking.

Ceremonies also were held in San Antonio, Tex., where the new organization will make its headquarters.

McGeorge Bundy, president of the Ford Foundation, in announcing the grant, also underscored the community's needs.

Bundy Stresses Needs

"In terms of legal enforcement of their civil rights," he said, "American citizens of Mexican descent are now where the Negro community was a quarter-century ago. There are not nearly enough Mexican-American lawyers, and most of them have neither the income nor experience to do civil rights work."

Another element, he declared, is the hesitancy of the Mexican-American community in seeking recourse to the courts.

"Because the law has often been used against Mexican-Americans, as well as other minority groups, they are suspicious of legal processes," he said.

Although he did not offer illustrations, advocates of the new organization in seeking Ford assistance had alleged police brutality, illegal arrests and exclusion from juries.

Studies Cited

The appeal for Ford assistance was buttressed by studies made in the Southwest showing that Mexican-Americans were recruited for lower-paying jobs, were discriminated against in employment in Government and private industry, and were often denied equal pay.

One-third of all Mexican-American families in the area, according to the studies, had an annual income below $3,000, the generally accepted poverty line. Many are farm or migrant workers living in California; large numbers also are in Texas, New Mexico, Colorado and Arizona.

The studies showed that Mexican-Americans as a group were the most poorly educated in the Southwest, with a school dropout rate of 50 per cent.

School segregation persists, it was charged, and Mexican-American youngsters often wind up in classes for the retarded because language and cultural differences lead them to make a poor showing on aptitude tests that do not take these differences into account.

Lack of funds has kept lawyers from challenging segregation practices, it was said.

Patterned on NAACP Group

The establishment of the new legal defense fund was the outcome of discussions with community leaders and the NAACP Legal Defense and Educational Office for the Rights of the Indigent. Jack Greenberg serves as director-counsel of both organizations.

The Mexican-American Fund will be modeled on the NAACP fund, set up nine years ago to defend Negroes' civil rights. The Field Foundation also assisted the Mexican-American fund in formulating its request for outside help.

Part of the Ford grant will go for scholarships to permit 35 Mexican-Americans to attend law schools. A separate $430,000 grant will be made to the Fund for Public Education, a unit of the American Bar Association, to support legal education of students from the Negro, Indian and Mexican-American communities.

Judge Carlos C. Cadena, associate justice of the state Civil Appeals Court at San Antonio, was named to head the new organization.

EISENHOWER RESTS; PROGRESS IS NOTED

Special to The New York Times

MARCH AIR FORCE BASE, Calif., May 1—Former President Dwight D. Eisenhower, who suffered what is described as a mild heart attack on Monday, spent a comfortable day in the hospital on this base today.

Doctors said that all evidence than far indicated that General Eisenhower's heart attack was "not as severe" as his two previous ones. They said that a prognosis on the General's condition is very difficult to make at this time, but his progress has been "very encouraging."

The doctors explained that the most critical period for any patient with a heart attack was during the first three or four days.

General Eisenhower has seen no visitors other than his wife, who is living in a suite in the hospital. The General's son, John, has not come to this Air Force base, but he is being kept informed of the General's progress by telephone.

THE MOUNTAIN COMES TO MANHATTAN

We are a strange and mysterious people.

We build cars to cruise at 100 m.p.h., then try to make everybody keep them under 50.

We build airports that can handle gigantic jets but can't handle our luggage.

We undertake great projects with enthusiasm and never consider the consequences until we're choking on them.

Consider the case of the "Mountain"

New York's air traffic patterns are perilously overburdened. LIFE magazine reports this. So does THE NEW YORK TIMES. And the President of the Allied Pilots Assn., who speaks for 3500 commercial pilots, is "deeply concerned over the safety problems arising out of traffic congestion in this area."

"Safe navigation," he says, "includes not only planned flight patterns, but also provisions for unforeseen and uncontrolled diversions."

Yet the Port of New York Authority is trying to build a trade center which, according to this pilot, "adds an additional risk to air navigation."

Its two towers are scheduled to be 1350 feet high. But at that height they will so thoroughly foul up TV reception that the Port Authority has agreed to top them out with new TV broadcasting facilities. By the time antennas are added, the North Tower, according to one TV expert, will be close to 1700 feet high...800 feet taller than anything else in the immediate area!

This means, according to the Federal Aviation Administration, that air traffic patterns will have to change, landing approaches will have to be altered, minimum altitudes in the area will be affected. The total potential hazard is staggering. No wonder airline pilots feel the risk is unjustified.

Unfortunately, we rarely recognize how serious these problems are until it's too late to do anything.

But in this case, there's still time.

The problem can be solved by keeping the height of the Trade Center at 900 feet.

The one problem that hasn't been solved is how to convince the Executive Director of the Port Authority to scale down his dream so it will coincide with the public interest.

Governor Rockefeller, the man he calls "my boss," is the one man in a position to say "900 feet" and make it stick.

If you're concerned about TV reception and safe air travel, write to the Governor today. Before it's too late.

Governor Nelson A. Rockefeller
22 West 55th Street, NY 10019.

He's the only man who has the power to keep the "Mountain" from coming to Manhattan.

Committee for a Reasonable World Trade Center
450 Seventh Avenue, NY 10001
(212) Judson 2-3931

Lawrence A. Wien, *Chairman*   Robert Kopple, *Executive Director*

On May 2, 1968, Lawrence A. Wien, the owner of the Empire State Building, ran an ad in the *New York Times* predicting that a commercial airliner was likely to strike the World Trade Center. (*The New York Times*)

At Laclede Steel in St. Louis, A. Carl Weber (*right*) designed the stout but lightweight floor trusses for the World Trade Center. In the foreground, a prototype of his design, displayed at a Laclede plant in Illinois, shows the steel "knuckles" that let the trusses be easily hoisted into place and joined the concrete floors and the steel into a single structural unit. (Alton Steel)

n August 6, 1968, workers hoisted into place the st piece of structural steel for the World Trade nter: a thirty-four-ton grillage, or steel footing, r the columns of the north tower.
arl T. Gossett Jr./*The New York Times*)

The ends of cable tiebacks emerge like carrot tops from the portion of the bathtub wall along West Street in May 1969. A section of the suspended Hudson Tubes passing beneath the partially completed south tower is visible in the background. (Neal Boenzi/*The New York Times*)

The first section of the Battery Park City landfill, created using soil from the trade center excavation, is seen at right as the north tower begins to rise in May 1969. (Neal Boenzi/*The New York Times*)

The north tower reaches to approximately the forty-third floor in mid-November 1969.
(Edward Hausner/*The New York Times*)

Both towers were speeding toward the sky when this picture was taken on October 8, 1970.
(Patrick A. Burns/*The New York Times*)

Peter Fontes, an ironworker, signals to an unseen crane operator as a perimeter panel is lowered into place just before 3 P.M. on October 19, 1970. When the steel was fastened in its spot, the north tower became the world's tallest building at 1,254 feet, surpassing the Empire State Building by four feet.
(Bill Sauro/*The New York Times*)

On the first day of operation at the World Trade Center—December 16, 1970—it had only two tiny paying tenants: Irving R. Boody & Co., an importer and exporter of raw materials for consumer products, and Export-Import Services Inc., a freight forwarder and customhouse broker. (Neal Boenzi/*The New York Times*)

New York Governor Nelson A. Rockefeller, speaking at the April 1973 dedication ceremony for the World Trade Center, a celebration that occurred more than two years after the first tenants moved in. (Don Hogan Charles/*The New York Times*)

The World Trade Center as seen from Brooklyn in 1980, with the Brooklyn Bridge in the foreground.
(Barney Ingoglia)

The World Trade Center plaza, at five acres, was one of the largest public spaces downtown, but it never became the vibrant gathering place that Minoru Yamasaki had envisioned. The plaza was dominated by the twenty-five-foot-tall bronze sculpture by Fritz Koenig.
(Port Authority of New York and New Jersey)

In August 1974, after months of meticulous planning, Philippe Petit performed the most famous high wire act of all time by walking back and forth between the twin towers. (AP/Wide World Photos)

When George Willig, a toy designer and amateur mountaineer, clamped home-made climbing devices into steel tracks and then hoisted himself to the top of the south tower one morning in May 1977, he earned himself the nickname "the Human Fly," and cemented the role of the twin towers as the stuntman's greatest target. (Paul Hosefros/The New York Times)

As soon as Windows on the World opened on the 107th floor of the north tower, it was a hit. Guy Tozzoli had fought and won a battle to ensure that the restaurant's windows were wider than those elsewhere in the north tower, providing outstanding views.

(Jack Manning/ *The New York Times*)

Shortly after noon on February 26, 1993, a bomb packed into a rented van that had been parked on a ramp in the underground garage exploded, killing six people and injuring hundreds of others as they rushed to evacuate the smoke-filled towers. (Marilynn K. Yee/*The New York Times*)

With the north tower burning at its side, a fireball erupts from the south tower at 9:02 A.M. on September 11, 2001, when it was struck by United Airlines flight 175.

(Steve Ludlum/*The New York Times*)

Deputy Chief Charles R. Blaich, holding blueprints of the World Trade Center, arrived at the disaster zone less than an hour after the towers had fallen. He is standing among other fire-fighters in front of the crushed Marriott World Trade Center Hotel, in the southwest corner of the site. A surviving chunk of the south tower's facade looms behind the remains of the hotel. (AP/Wide World Photos)

Ground Zero

Main aerial photo taken on Sept. 23, 2001.

Tower facade fragment

3 W.F.C.

6 W.T.C.

Crater

Face of north tower (1 W.T.C.)

7 W.T.C.

U.S. Post Office

VESEY ST.

St. Paul's Chapel

6 W.T.C.

5 W.T.C.

3 W.F.C.

Millenium Hilton Hotel

Winter Garden

North Bridge

WEST ST.

1 W.T.C.

CHURCH ST.

Century 21

2 W.F.C.

3 W.T.C. Marriott Hotel

2 W.T.C.

4 W.T.C.

1 Liberty Plaza

South Bridge

St. Nicholas Greek Orthodox Church

LIBERTY ST.

Deutsche Bank building

South tower (2 W.T.C.) remaining facade

90 West St.

The New York Times; photographs by National Oceanic and Atmospheric Administration (main aerial); New York City Police Aviation Unit (North Bridge, 90 West St., Deutsche Bank); Ozier Muhammad/ The New York Times (south tower facade)

S. Shyam Sunder, an investigator at the National Institute of Standards and Technology, points to a photo showing a sagging floor truss system on the east face of the south tower, twelve minutes before its collapse. (Don Hogan Charles/*The New York Times*)

In February 2002, after crews had dug nearly to the bottom of the seventy-foot-deep basement at the World Trade Center, they uncovered PATH commuter rail cars that had been parked at the trade center station at the time of the attack. (Port Authority of New York and New Jersey)

From left: Engineers Ramon Gilsanz, Anthony W. Chuliver, David F. Sharp, and Dean Koutsoubis examine steel from the World Trade Center at a New Jersey scrap yard. (Fred R. Conrad/*The New York Times*)

David Rockefeller (*left*), who first proposed the World Trade Center; Les Robertson (*center*), a structural engineer who helped create the design that held them up; and Guy Tozzoli, the Port Authority official who supervised the development and startup, returned to the site in July 2002. Robertson is looking up at an unsupported floor that still had not been demolished at the site.
(Vincent LaForet)

the world's greatest concentrations of humanity came from the silvery spires of the Empire State and Chrysler Buildings and the suspension towers of the Verrazano-Narrows Bridge, glinting above the clouds. Huntington did what he could to share his love of towers, even putting a 1942 British artillery telescope on a pedestal in the Fiduciary lobby through which visitors could, on clear days, peer out beyond the New York Harbor into the deep blue world of the Atlantic Ocean.

But not everyone was sold. Irene Humphries, a file clerk, was at her desk one windy spring day, about six months after taking a job at Fiduciary. Feeling a bit nauseated, Humphries stood up and walked to the bathroom, hoping to gain her composure. Once there, she heard a creaking noise, as if from the hold of a ship that was being thrown around in a rough sea. The building was making noise! "Oh my God," she said. "It is Jacob Marley and he is coming in, with his chains." As she listened, something else became apparent. Water was sloshing back and forth in the toilets. The twin towers, as these early tenants learned, were so tall that when the wind in the New York Harbor started to blow, it whipped up whitecaps—and not just in the harbor. In spite of Les Robertson's shock absorbers, the towers still swayed quite enough to be noticeable—and enough to swish the water in the toilets around. Humphries was at first frightened by the sounds and what they meant. When she got home that night, she quizzed her husband, who was in the construction business. He assured her the towers were safe. Gradually, she trained herself to ignore the motion.

For others, it would not be so easy. Candice Tevere came into the World Trade Center to apply for a job at Fiduciary, but she never made it to the interview. As soon as she stepped into the cattle-car-size express elevators, she felt uneasy. The doors closed, and with fifty or so people standing around her, she could not lean against any wall. Then the elevator started to move. It was impossible to tell just how fast, but it felt to Tevere as if she were on a supersonic jet. As soon as she reached the seventy-eighth-floor sky lobby, Tevere said to herself, "That's it. This is nuts." She rode back down and then went home. Two days later, a staff member at Fiduciary called, urging her to give it another try. Tevere did go back. And she did take a job. But she could never step into one of those express elevators without a friend or colleague by her side. While the elevator was moving, she would keep her mind occupied by looking through her purse. She never left the building for lunch. The strategy worked fine until one Friday morning. As usual, she had a girlfriend by her side, ready for that uncomfortable ride into the sky. But then, midway up, the elevator just stopped. It sat there for one hour and fifty-five minutes. "How many people are in the elevator?" the security guards kept asking through the intercom. "Why, so that papers will know that twenty-two of us in here died on Friday the thirteenth?" one man yelled back. Tevere stayed calm until the firefighters arrived, took the side wall off the elevator, set up a plank, and then told everyone there to walk across the plank to the next elevator. "I am going over," Tevere said, convinced she would fall. "Just look at me, just walk to me," the firefighter replied. "Just don't look down."

It was not long before Huntington started to hear about his employees' fears. So, with his usual panache, he decided to show them how unconcerned he was. One day, as dozens of people on the ninety-fourth floor watched with puzzlement, Huntington turned toward the nearest window and started running across the floor. He finally turned his shoulder, pushed himself off the ground like a football player throwing a flying block, and slammed his side into the window glass. Thankfully, he bounced back.

· · ·

Huntington was no match for Steve McQueen.

In 1974 and 1975, events that seemed to step from movie screens into reality began turning the World Trade Center into a famously scary place to work. It began with *The Towering Inferno.* Late in 1974, advertisements for the movie, starring McQueen as a grimy-faced Fire Department battalion chief, starting running across the nation:

One minute you're attending a party atop the world's tallest skyscraper. The next, you're trapped with 294 other guests in the middle of a fiery hell . . . No way down. No way out.

The plot: a fire starts in a utility closet on the eighty-first floor of a 138-story skyscraper and then quickly spreads upward. The automated fire alarm fails and the security staff does not respond quickly to hints that something might be wrong. By the time firefighters arrive, hundreds of partygoers, including the mayor, the building's developer, the architect, and many other dignitaries, are trapped in an opulent penthouse ballroom. Shoddy fireproofing—duct holes did not have proper "fire-stopping" components—the lack of a working sprinkler system, and a blocked fire stair combine to doom many of the people in the tower. The building's developer repeatedly assures anyone who will listen that no fire could threaten his tower. "I don't believe you are familiar with the many modern safety systems we have designed into this building. We have got them all," William Holden, playing the developer, says.

But the message of the movie was clear: "If you had to cut costs," Paul Newman as the architect asks the developer, "why didn't you cut floors instead of corners?" Although the acting was mediocre, the special effects were nothing short of thrilling. Vincent Canby of the *New York Times* called it "this year's best end-of-the-world movie." Among the many truly awful scenes were burning victims tumbling from windows, an elevator filled with panicked partiers that caught fire and then fell, a helicopter crashing and exploding as it attempted a rooftop rescue.

In other words, it was a World Trade Center tenant's worst nightmare.

The New York City Fire Department loved the film so much so that Fire Commissioner John T. O'Hagan was there for the gala Times Square screening in December 1974, with six fire engines outside as his escort. McQueen ended the film by looking over at victims laid out in body bags and telling the architect, "One of these days, they are going to kill ten thousand in one of these fire traps. And I am going to keep eating smoke and bringing out bodies until somebody asks us how to build them." The firefighters cheered.

That was about the time that Oswald Adorno, a tall, somewhat chubby nineteen-year-old kid from the Bronx who held a nighttime job as a World Trade Center custodian—his unenviable assignment was washing the buildings' ceilings and walls—decided to become an arsonist.

Angry that he had too many floors to clean, Adorno started by setting a fire on the eleventh floor of the north tower, down the hall from Rick Boody's office. He lit it just before midnight on February 13, 1975, inside a closet filled with telephone switching equipment and filing cabinets filled with paper. Another custodian happened to pass by and hear a crackling sound as the fire burned. New York City Fire Department captain Harold Kull soon led his men into what could only be described as a towering inferno. As it happened, the room also held a large supply of alcohol-based duplicating fluid for mimeograph machines; feeding on all the combustibles in the room, the blaze was already out of control.

There was another reason the fire spread so quickly. For anyone who knew nothing of the long-standing problems with fireproofing at the trade center, this unexpected factor would be shocking: just as in the make-believe tower where Steve McQueen did the firefighting, the "fire-stopping" at the World Trade Center was missing. A foot-wide hole between the floors allowed hot gases to snake upward, setting fires all the way to the seventeenth floor, while burning embers dropped down the hole, igniting fires all the way to the ninth floor. Kull concentrated on the eleventh floor, which he said "was like fighting a blowtorch," so hot that all of his men got their necks and ears burned. A second and then a third alarm had to be called, ultimately drawing 132 firefighters to the north tower. It would be three hours before the last of the fire was out.

The damage would take weeks to repair—the southeast corner of the eleventh floor was little more than a charred shell—but the impact of the fire would be permanent. After assuring the New York City Fire Department that the fire-protection systems in the twin towers were first rate, the Port Authority now had to contend with clear evidence to the contrary. "Had the building been occupied, and given the stack action that exists in this 110-story building," Fire Commissioner O'Hagan later wrote, "the rescue problem would have been tremendous."

Adorno was not finished with his mischief. "More fires," a man said in an anonymous call to the Port Authority security desk, unless the maintenance workers received a promised raise. Adorno then waited three months. Over the night of Monday, May 19, 1975, he set seven fires, this time in the south tower, on the twenty-fifth, twenty-seventh, twenty-eighth, thirty-second, and thirty-sixth floors. He was arrested one day later, but the consequences were just beginning to play out. Spurred by the fires, a group of state employees, including experts in state and city fire codes, organized an impromptu inspection squad. Gennaro Fischetti, a workers' compensation judge who led the effort, was literally having nightmares about the trade center. The recurring dream involved his being trapped in a stairwell during a fire. During his waking hours, he sat in his courtroom at the trade center looking at the fifty to one hundred disabled people who filed in each day for workers' compensation cases. In case of a fire, "we couldn't possibly get enough employees to carry them," Fischetti said. "And if we just put them in the stairways, that would block them and panic would ensue."

The survey by Fischetti and his volunteers turned up thirty-eight violations, including exit doors that were locked or blocked by a steel gate, fire-stopping insulation that was still missing, and deficiencies in the fire alarm system that meant it could not be heard across most areas of the acre-size floors. State legislators had already started their own investigation. The next step was a press conference, held right in the World Trade Center plaza on May 23, 1975, just five months after the *Towering Inferno* premiere. There was "clear and potential danger to fifty-five thousand persons," declared State Senator Norman J. Levy. "The Port Authority's word 'safe' is not enough."

By this time, the Port Authority had no choice but to act. The agency would spend $14 million to install more walls and doors on open floors to prevent the spread of fires, improve the alarm and communications systems, add more smoke detectors, and train extra staff to help the handicapped in case of an emergency. Yet despite the continued insistence by Fire Commissioner O'Hagan that the single most important step would be to install fire sprinklers in the towers, the agency balked. The estimated $43 million it would cost to install the sprinklers was "a figure that at this time is not feasible," said William J. Ronan, the chairman of the Port Authority board and the man who had been Governor Nelson Rockefeller's chief of staff when the trade center was approved.

■ ■ ■

There was another PR problem at the World Trade Center, one so enormous that not even the masters in the art of media management at the Port Authority could make it disappear. The twin towers by 1974 were complete—the Program had been delivered. But even after so many government agencies subsidized the project by occupying nearly half of all the space in the World Trade Center complex, there was still acre after acre of empty real estate.

Like the Empire State Building, which opened just in time for the Depression, the Port Authority's timing could hardly have been worse. Here was a complex dedicated to world trade—with a ribbon-cutting in April 1973, just months before the OPEC oil embargo was about to send fuel prices soaring and the United States economy into a tailspin. New York City, meanwhile, was entering its most difficult era in modern times, as the local government, facing insolvency, slashed its police force, its fire department, even its trash collection crews. Citywide, there was an awesome 29 million square feet of empty office space, more than the combined total inventory of Los Angeles and Detroit.

The Port Authority was offering dirt-cheap rents in a desperate attempt to draw tenants to its empty floors. Even so, it was having trouble. The Port Authority's diligent legal division wasn't helping matters, often taking months to get approval on leases. And the far west side of Lower Manhattan was still considered an out-of-the-way address: Battery Park City was not much more than a weed-and-gravel-filled plot where pools of rainwater would freeze over in the winter.

"We are knocking our heads against the wall," Tom Donovan, then the director of leasing, told Guy Tozzoli. "We get prospects to come in and talk to us and then you never hear from them again."

Even the title "the world's tallest" had been lost, just as Yamasaki had foreseen. Predictably, a *New Yorker* cartoon captured the deflation of that event to perfection. "For once," said a disgruntled-looking man in a hard hat to a coworker as they stood atop the north tower during its construction, "let's start the day without you telling me there's a taller one going up in Chicago." The World Trade Center remained the tallest building in the world for only two and a half years. The Sears Tower took the crown a month after the Port Authority held its formal dedication ceremony.

Nothing seemed to go right for the Port Authority and its twin behemoths. Owners of a neighboring building filed a lawsuit claiming that the violent vortex of wind created as it twisted its way through the frequently empty World Trade Center plaza had caused hundreds of thousands of dollars of damage. Others blamed the twin towers for killing migrating birds. Still others called for the buildings to be condemned because they were dumping raw sewage into the Hudson.

The Port Authority was still intent on trying to prove it could live up to its word, charging ahead with its various promotional plans intended to distinguish the trade center from run-of-the-mill office buildings. The agency teamed up with the United Nations and the federal government and invested tens of thousands of dollars to organize an exhibit of goods manufactured in Third World countries, with the intention of kicking off the World Trade Mart, the showplace that Richard Sullivan's report had proposed back in 1961—a throwback modeled after the first World Trade Center at the 1939 World's Fair in New York. But when the ten-day trade bazaar came to a close, one finding was unmistakable: no one would ever again be willing to foot such an exorbitant bill. The World Trade Mart would never open. "I guess politics played a bigger role than did honest miscalculation," John Brunner, a Port Authority aide assigned to the project, wrote to his boss, since it was now obvious that this concept, from the start, had been hatched purely as a promotional tool. "And to think I used to think it was the other way around!"

Tobin, at least, was not there to watch his dream unravel. He would never even occupy the towers he had done so much to build. After a bitter struggle with New Jersey governor William T. Cahill over mass transit, in which Cahill wanted the Port Authority to build a sprawling new rail transit network and Tobin refused—citing the damage that the resulting deficits would have on the Port Authority's credit rating—Tobin left the agency in early 1972. He said little more than that "the time has come for the orderly transfer of executive responsibility to other hands." And it was over. Tobin did not even attend the ceremonial dedication of the World Trade Center the following year. "It was raining," Tobin said to explain his absence. He refused to comment further.

Tozzoli, nineteen years younger than Tobin, was far from ready to give up on the trade center. And as always, he had an optimistic spin. Across Lower Manhattan, he charged, a string of new office towers had been constructed by developers looking to cash in on the new business generated in the area by the trade center. And now, there was a glut. "I should be bitching at *you*," Tozzoli said, of the developers who had followed the Port Authority's lead.

Whatever the causes, the Port Authority board member came up with a name that would stick for the towers the agency had built on the Hudson: "a giant white elephant." Audits by the New York State comptroller found that by 1976, the trade center was operating at a $20-million-a-year deficit, even after taking into consideration the rent collected from the state government.

• • •

A wiry man in a striped shirt was climbing up the side of the south tower. It was May 26, 1977, and the climber, a 155-pound, twenty-seven-year-old toymaker from Queens named George H. Willig, was inching up the silvery, sheer facade of the tower, using royal-blue nylon ropes and special metal clamps he had built to fit into the tracks that guided window-washing equipment. A huge, buzzing crowd gathered on the streets and the plaza below after Willig, who was also a mountain climber, began his ascent at 6:30 A.M. For the next three and a half hours he gradually became "a tinier and tinier speck of mortal frailty," as one writer would put it. There was something enthralling about the little shadow up there.

"What's holding him up?" someone on the street asked when Willig reached about the seventieth floor.

"A lot of guts," a police officer replied.

Two officers, one of them an expert in talking people out of committing suicide, were lowered down the side of the building in a window-washing basket. When it came to Willig's level, he swung to one side and refused to get any nearer until he was sure the officers would not try to snatch him into the basket. The suicide expert, Dewitt C. Allen, then reached over and handed the climber a pad of paper and a pen. Willig scribbled something on it and handed it back.

"Best wishes to my co-ascender," the note said.

They started to talk, and Allen quickly determined that Willig was neither insane nor suicidal. "Every response he gave me was reasonable," Officer Allen would say. "The only thing unreasonable was the fact that he was on the outside of the building."

At about 10:05 A.M., Willig handed a knapsack he was wearing to Allen and let himself be hoisted to the very top of the tower by police, who arrested him. Willig could hear the crowd cheering more than thirteen hundred feet below.

He instantly became known as the Human Fly. Standing before reporters outside the station house where he was booked—Mayor Abe Beame would later accept a $1.10 fine from him, 1 cent a floor—Willig tried to explain what had possessed him: "It's a very appealing wall, so to speak. It looked unscalable—I thought I'd like to try it."

In so doing, he helped push along the fascinating but seemingly irrational process by which the cold, forbidding, and in many ways frightening towers were softened and humanized and finally loved by the ordinary citizens of New York City. His climb also recalled a much more chilling moment in the history of skyscrapers in the city. Willig's mother, the former Therese Fortier, had been an employee of the Catholic War Relief Services on the seventy-ninth floor of the Empire State Building when it was struck by the B-25 bomber in July 1945. During the subsequent fire,

Fortier had thrown out the window the ruby ring given to her by a man named George Willig. After she survived, she married Willig and they had a son whom they also named George, and who as a boy would read newspaper clippings of her travails—before becoming the Human Fly.

The humanizing of the towers had actually started a few years earlier when a lithe French juggler, magician, pickpocket, and aerialist named Philippe Petit decided that he was going to walk between the towers on a tightrope. Eight months of feverish planning in 1974 produced a custom-made, 26-foot-long, fifty-five-pound balancing pole, buffalo skin slippers, fake identification cards for a fictitious World Trade Center contractor who was supposedly installing a rooftop electrified fence, a five-foot crossbow to shoot a line across the towers, and enough galvanized steel cable to bridge the 131-foot gap. Shortly after 7:15 A.M. on August 7, 1974, having smuggled his equipment to the top of the north tower, Petit and his confederates shot a hemp line over to the other tower, dragged the steel cable across, and braced it with guy lines. Dressed all in black, and hesitating for a moment because of a brisk breeze, Petit walked across the void. Eight times.

Somewhere among the crowd below, Rick Boody paused to watch the act. "Now that man is crazy," Boody said. "Completely crackers."

Petit's explanation was about as opaque as the Human Fly's would be. "When I see two towers, I just want to put my wire across, *bon!*" Petit said. Likewise, he pointed out, "if I see three oranges, I have to juggle."

Guy Tozzoli was so excited that he gave Petit a lifetime complimentary pass to the World Trade Center observation deck. Petit was such a sensation that the only sentence he received was an order to perform a high-wire act over Belvedere Lake in Central Park as a Bavarian oom-pah band played below. This performance, too, was a smash. "The greatest event that has ever come to the City of New York," the parks administrator called it.

About a year later, a skydiver parachuted off the north tower, landing safely in the plaza. Then Willig pulled his stunt, and the World Trade Center had become an exhibitionist's magnet. Frolicking in the sky would do more to enhance the image of the World Trade Center than anything the Port Authority's PR staff could ever have orchestrated.

All of a sudden, the towers were not looking like mere aluminum boxes anymore. They had become supersized toys to go with New York's supersized ego. Like the Eiffel Tower—which at first had been condemned as a "gigantic black factory chimney, its barbarous mass overwhelming and humiliating all our monuments," and then was printed on the 200-franc bank note—something fundamental had changed.

The Port Authority did everything it could to play its part. It opened an observation deck in 1975 atop the south tower as schoolchildren waved colorful flags and a Dixieland band played. Within eleven months, it had 1 million visitors. "It's hard to be down when you are up," read the advertising campaign, an interesting slogan considering that not only the twin towers but also the city was on the edge of bankruptcy.

The purest piece of magic that the Port Authority actually delivered—the investment that perhaps more than anything else gave the trade center a certain verve and glitz—was that stupendous expression of opulence, the restaurant cum theme park, Windows on the World. Setting up a restaurant atop a skyscraper had been a favorite gesture in Lower Manhattan for decades, and both Cass Gilbert's 90 West Street, across from the trade center, and the now-demolished Hudson terminal buildings had penthouse eateries. Still, Windows on the World was in a league by itself. The Port Authority invested $10 million just for interior decorating and other preparatory work. Tozzoli brought in an old friend to create the Windows concept, the hot-tempered perfectionist Joe Baum, who eventually won a contract to set up twenty-two different food and drink outlets serving thirty thousand people a day at the World Trade Center. At the center of this gastronomical universe was Windows on the World, which opened its doors in April 1976.

As restaurant guests stepped out of the elevator—after a fifty-eight-second, thirteen-hundred-foot ride to the 107th floor—they entered a mirrored hallway decorated with giant pieces of semiprecious stones from around the world. The restaurant's main bar—a thirty-six-foot slab of white and black marble topped with teak—offered sixteen thousand bottles of wine, everything from an 1865 Rainwater Madeira to a 1947 Cheval Blanc. The main dining room had fabric-covered walls and lots of brass. And then there were the bathrooms: oyster-gray silk ceilings and sinks made of solid Norwegian rose marble. These trappings were so heavy the Port Authority had to add extra structural supports in the bathroom floors.

The Port Authority paid $3,500 each for a collection of chairs for the restaurant. Guy Tozzoli took some heat for these extravagances—until the reviews started coming in. "The Most Spectacular Restaurant in the World," screamed the headline on the cover of *New York* magazine. "Few additions to the local scene have been so outright an affirmation of confidence in New York City's future as Windows on the World, the stunning and lavish restaurant atop the north tower," wrote Mimi Sheraton in the *New York Times*. For World Trade Center tenants, or those considering a move there, this was finally an amenity that mattered. Almost as soon as it opened, Windows had a waiting list several months long; the restaurant attracted not only New Yorkers but also tourists from everywhere in the world.

Countless memories of special dinners atop the tower would be created at Windows on the World. Among the most spectacular came on July 13, 1977, when six hundred guests at the restaurant on a hot summer night watched as the nation's biggest city went entirely black. The twin towers, which went dark with the city, faded from the skyline, no longer anchoring Lower Manhattan's tip. The metropolis below melted away at the same moment. No electricity meant no elevators, no running water, no ventilation fans. The restaurant grew warm and filled up with the haze of smoke from cigarettes and candles. Guests took off jackets and loosened ties and refused to panic. The waiters kept pouring the wine and serving dinner. A freighter on the East River, tied up south of the Brooklyn Bridge, was the brightest object in sight. Fluid lines of red, on avenues going north, and white, on southbound avenues, also gleamed below. Amid all this good feeling, the Port Authority managed to make itself look foolish, announcing over the public address system three hours after the lights darkened: "We are experiencing a citywide blackout." There was laughter but no irritation. "We planned this night a long time ago," said Ivy Stevens, one of the diners at Windows that night. "But we never thought it would be so special."

Something inexplicable had happened. Despite their enormousness, their obstinate disregard for everything else that stood around them, regardless of the lingering questions about safety and the difficulty the Port Authority had encountered in trying to find tenants, the Word Trade Center had become an essential piece of the city's fabric. New York City, for all its toughness, is bound together by deeply personal moments, thoughts, affections, and discoveries that are as taut and delicate as the tightrope that Philippe Petit strode upon in the emptiness between the towers. The trade center, in that night of darkness, finally belonged.

• • •

There was no doubt about it; a bad winter storm was on the way. The sky was the color of slate. The temperature was just below freezing. The wind was blowing, steady and heavy, from the west. The air was already damp. Alexander Leslie did not seem to notice. Leslie, the longtime treasurer of the Port Authority, opened the door to the terrace at his East Seventy-second Street apartment that night in January 1978 and climbed the four-and-a half-foot railing. Then he jumped, falling eight stories to his death.

Leslie, sixty, had resigned from the Port Authority a few months before. He took early retirement a month after being suspended without pay after a review of his expense accounts turned up what the agency called irregularities. The details of the irregularities never became public. They involved theater tickets he had purchased with Port Authority money to see a show with his wife. Their value was listed as $193.35. While this was Leslie's only personal misdeed, it was only the beginning of the rot at the Port Authority.

Investigations by state auditors and a New York Times reporter had found that on Leslie's watch as treasurer, the Port Authority had been turned into a virtual junket machine. Staff at the agency, such as the public relations director, John Tillman, had made a habit of creating phantom dinner guests to explain away expensive meals. The Port Authority helicopter fleet had become a private ferry service, offering trips to grandchildren on birthdays or wives headed out on shopping sprees. Guy Tozzoli and Mal Levy both got caught up in the scandal. Tozzoli had often traveled around the globe with his wife, going to Paris four times, Tokyo four times, Hawaii three times, along with other trips to San Juan, Caracas, Marrakesh, Rome, Madrid, Marseille, São Paulo, Saint Tropez, Nice, and Moscow between 1972 and 1977. Levy had listed members of Yamasaki's staff as his dinner companions even when they were at home in the Midwest. Tozzoli was furious at the news reports, saying his travels were critical to his efforts to promote the trade center and the New York port while organizing an international group he called the World Trade Centers Association. "Never have I put a penny in my pocket," Tozzoli insisted. But Levy, Tillman, and Leslie either admitted to the allegations immediately or pleaded guilty after being formally charged with larceny.

With the World Trade Center hemorrhaging cash, and its overseers charged with, and in some cases convicted of, wrongdoing, it was now irrefutable: something very big had to change. All the way back in 1959, McKinsey & Co. had warned David Rockefeller that a World Trade Center could be a financial loser. Executives had told the consultant that foreign departments at major corporations were becoming obsolete. No one could continue to deny that McKinsey had been right. Now that the trade center had been built, the only workable solution was to abandon the long-ago commitment to accept only companies or corporate divisions involved with international trade.

Peter C. Goldmark Jr., the new executive director of the Port Authority, was willing to say it out loud. "There aren't that many freight forwarders in the entire western world to fill it up," he said. "It is time to open the floodgates." Goldmark was something of an unusual choice for the top spot at the Port Authority. He had no graduate degrees in finance or economics. He was not an engineer or a transportation expert. After getting his undergraduate degree from Harvard, he had spent two years teaching history at a school in Vermont. Besides history, what he did know was money and politics. He had been the New York State budget director during the city's fiscal crisis and, before that, an executive assistant to Mayor John V. Lindsay. Goldmark may also have inherited a few creative, risk-taking tendencies: he was the oldest child and namesake of the maverick inventor and physicist who had come up with the LP phonograph and the first commercially viable color television.

Goldmark's willingness to drop the old admission rules was largely a matter of endorsing conclusions that others had already reached. Tozzoli, with his trademark optimism, backed the change, although he saw it in different terms: financial services companies, he pronounced, were actually trading firms; they were just "exporting their expertise." No sooner had the Port Authority made the move than Goldmark caught a bit of a break: the economy began to improve. And with the relaxed rules, the trade center's finances turned around almost overnight.

In 1978 and 1979 alone, the list of new tenants included giant engineering firms like Ebasco Services and Heyward-Robinson; investment banks like Shearson Hayden Stone, and Dean Witter; and accounting firms like Deloitte Haskins & Sells. Companies including John Hancock Mutual Life

Insurance and the Cantor Fitzgerald Group soon followed. Few of these new tenants had anything to do with importing or exporting merchandise through the New York port. But they were taking entire floors or even blocks of floors. Ebasco, for example, ultimately occupied the eightieth through the ninety-third floors in the south tower, as well as the seventy-seventh and seventy-eighth floors, enough space for two thousand employees.

With the World Trade Center's arrival as a known and respected business address, it became an international draw for companies of every description. Back in the early 1970s, Cornelius Lynch, the trade center's real estate chief, had tried to convince the Bank of Tokyo to rent some space in the twin towers. The answer was a blunt no. "Your address is unknown," the Japanese executive told Lynch. "Wall Street and Broadway, those words mean something in Tokyo. The World Trade Center does not." Now the Bank of Tokyo was ready to sign on the dotted line, along with a long string of other Japanese banks, including Fuji Bank, Dai-Ichi Kangyo Bank, Yasuda Trust and Banking, Sumitomo Bank. By 1990, Japanese banks would be renting 10 percent of all the trade center office space. "Thank heavens for the Japanese!" exclaimed George Rossi, who eventually took over from Lynch as manager of trade center real estate.

The impact on the bottom line at the Port Authority was enormous: revenues from the World Trade Center went from $83 million in 1978 to $204 million in 1983. Space was in such demand, now, that even the state agencies moved out, abandoning their 2.2 million square feet of office space in the south tower, including the office where Amy Herz Juviler had worked.

McKinsey & Co.'s doubts had been right. So had Lawrence A. Wien and the city's real estate barons, who had predicted that the World Trade Center would never thrive as anything but a tremendous center for office rentals that accepted all comers. Those warnings, all so long ago, had been forgotten by now, of course. But Wien, who had finally walked away from the World Trade Center fight as if it never existed, must have shaken his head somewhere when, in the midst of the fiscal turnaround, another of his warnings nearly proved terribly prophetic. It happened on a cloudy night in February 1981, when the pilot of an Aerolineas Argentinas Boeing 707, approaching New York on his way to John F. Kennedy Airport, misunderstood the air traffic controller and descended to a dangerously low altitude. The plane, headed directly toward the north tower, was already two hundred feet below its television mast and still descending. It was less than ninety seconds from impact.

"Climb, climb immediately," the pilot was ordered by an alert air traffic controller named Donald Zimmerman, who was so shaken by the near collision that he went on traumatic-injury leave afterward.

History is swept away so quickly in New York by the next day's news, and the next, and the next, that none of the old debates had any influence on how the trade center was seen in the wake of the Boeing 707 incident. Instead, the flush finances and newfound cultural acceptance of the towers colored the way they were seen among city leaders.

"Once perceived as Nelson Rockefeller's folly," the trade center had become "one of our greatest assets," Mayor Edward I. Koch said in July 1985, when the Port Authority announced an $800 million, twenty-year lease with Dean Witter Financial Services, which took twenty-four floors.

There was one serious and largely ignored set of casualties in this boom. No one was there to hold a press conference or file a lawsuit on their behalf, but the importers and exporters, customs brokers and freight forwarders that the place had been built to nurture were now, effectively, being shown the door. With rentals now surging at the twin towers, from about $6 per square foot in 1975 to about $30 per square foot by the mid-1980s, most had no choice. "They priced us out of the market," said Patricia A. Farrell, president of Export-Import Services, which had moved in the same day as Irving R. Boody & Co., but left in 1985. Boody's company would soon follow, taking an office in Midtown.

The Port Authority saw no reason to mourn their departure. The words that Oscar Nadel had wielded, the words that had nearly stopped the World Trade Center—*public purpose*—would have sounded, by the 1980s, like something from a buried epoch sprinkled with fossils. The words certainly had little to do with the trade center now. Did it matter? The demand for space was so great that the two final pieces of Yamasaki's plan for the overall complex, the Vista International Hotel and the forty-seven-story skyscraper called 7 World Trade Center, were now rising. Only six years since Alexander Leslie's suicide, the turnaround was essentially complete. "The trade center's absolutely been a success, without question," Lynch said in 1984 during the groundbreaking for 7 World Trade Center, the last piece of the complex to be built. "It helped anchor Lower Manhattan. It brought foreign companies to New York. It's become a world symbol."

• • •

Peter Goldmark sat thinking one afternoon, his worn loafers up on his desk, in his World Trade Center office, the spacious executive suite on the southwest corner of the sixty-seventh floor that had been built for but never occupied by Austin Tobin. Somehow, Goldmark reflected, the world was changing. A new kind of terrorism was spreading around the globe like a rogue virus. Not only were United States military facilities being bombed, as in Beirut, but civilians were now becoming targets of attacks in Europe. A telephone call to one intelligence source raised more alarms. Roughly half of the bomb threats in the United States, he was told, occurred in New York. Goldmark considered what that meant for his agency. "We are operating some of the largest, most attractive, most symbolic facilities in the world," he said in 1984 to his staff. "Doesn't that mean they are vulnerable targets?"

Goldmark already had taken one big step to improve safety at the Port Authority's most important piece of real estate. He had set aside $45 million to install, at long last, sprinklers in the twin towers. But a sprinkler system, Goldmark knew, could combat only fire. In early 1984 Goldmark created an innocuously named division called the Office of Special Planning (OSP). He named Edward J. O'Sullivan, a Vietnam veteran and Naval Academy graduate, as its chief and gave him a simple order: travel anywhere in the world, talk to anyone, but within a year, become one of the nation's foremost terrorism experts. O'Sullivan, the son of an Upper East Side grocery store owner, had spent much of the last decade overseeing security at Kennedy Airport. He had also earned degrees in engineering and an M.B.A. But those were really only secondary achievements. During the Vietnam War, he was a marine corps captain whose job was to train South Vietnamese paratroopers in antiterrorism tactics and hunt down recruiters for the Vietcong.

O'Sullivan talked to the FBI, the Secret Service, the CIA, and the Israeli intelligence service. He traveled to Scotland Yard, to Paris, and to Italy, where intelligence squads had gained expertise combating, respectively, the Irish Republican Army, bombers of Jewish targets, and the Red Guard, an Italian terrorist group. And then he toured each of the Port Authority facilities to look at them again and again. He even brought in U.S. Special Forces to the trade center for a foot-by-foot tour. He was worried: every time he turned on CNN, he saw the World Trade Center in the images the station flashed during station breaks. The World Trade Center, he realized, had become one of the foremost symbols of American capitalism and power, making it the most spectacular single target, in his opinion, in the United States. "The listing of tenants is a veritable who's who of the international finance and trading community," his 1986 report said. "Government offices occupy a large portion."

When O'Sullivan looked at security at the trade center, he found one vulnerability after another. Explosive charges could be placed at key locations in the power system. Chemical or biological agents could be dropped into the coolant system. The Hudson River water intake could be blown up. Someone might even try to infiltrate the large and vulnerable subterranean realms of the World Trade Center site, he said. One threat in particular was troubling to him. There was no control at all over access to the underground, two-thousand-car parking garage. "A time bomb–laden vehicle could be driven into the WTC and parked in the public parking area," O'Sullivan wrote. "The driver could then exit via elevator into the WTC and proceed with his business unnoticed. At a predetermined time, the bomb could be exploded in the basement. The Assistant Deputy Director of the FBI thinks this is a very likely scenario for the WTC and has described it graphically in conversations with OSP staff." Many groups might try such an attack, the report continued, but "extremist Muslims pose an especially disturbing threat to the trade center. They are not deterred by typical security measures and they have little regard for inflicting large numbers of innocent casualties, as evidenced by their heinous attacks on American and French installations overseas."

Thankfully, there was one possible outcome that O'Sullivan all but ruled out. He consulted with one of the trade center's original structural engineers, Les Robertson, on whether the towers could collapse because of a bomb or a collision with a slow-moving airplane, at least. The message that O'Sullivan said he heard was that there was little likelihood of a collapse no matter how the building was attacked. "We have a Gibraltar," O'Sullivan said.

That the towers were not at risk of collapse was good news. But thousands could still be killed or injured in an attack or a plane crash, and the building must be better protected, O'Sullivan concluded. The list of recommendations was a long one. Eliminate all public parking at the trade center, or at least randomly inspect cars that enter. Disperse emergency operations centers so that a terrorist could not knock out all communications, fire systems, and security systems at once. Install better internal radio systems. Place battery-powered lighting in all the emergency stairwells. And given that any terrorist contemplating an attack was likely to visit repeatedly beforehand, set up more video cameras and security inspection points. These steps alone could deter an attack that otherwise could "have monumental effects on the city, or in certain instances on the entire country," the 1986 report said.

There was just one problem. By the time O'Sullivan had completed his report and submitted it to the Port Authority, Goldmark had resigned from the agency to take a new job. There were no major attacks to emphasize the need for an escalation in security, and only a few new measures were taken by the Port Authority: a security booth was set up at the entrance to the garage, and the Port Authority installed equipment to record license plates of entering vehicles. But the most critical recommendations in the report, from improving emergency lighting equipment in the stairwells to restricting access to the garage, were set aside. And after the hundredth anniversary of the Statue of Liberty had passed in 1986 without a major incident, the level of concern at the Port Authority dropped.

What the agency could not know was that not long after, a blind cleric in New Jersey, Sheikh Omar Abdel Rahman, a follower of his named Sayyid Nosair, and an explosives expert, Ramzi Ahmed Yousef, began to plot an attack. The goal, at least in Nosair's mind, was to do exactly what O'Sullivan had feared: strike at a symbol of American capitalism and culture. Nosair wrote his thoughts down quite explicitly in a notebook, handwritten in Arabic. The idea was not just to bomb the World Trade Center, but to knock it down. "Break and destroy the enemies of Allah," Nosair wrote. "And this by means of destroying [and] exploding the structure of their civilized pillars such as the touristic infrastructure which they are proud of and their high world buildings." Yousef, looking for a way to create huge numbers of casualties, then took the next step detailed in O'Sullivan's playbook. Four or five times he visited the World

Trade Center. He cased the concourse and the underground floors, including the garage.

■ ■ ■

Irene Humphries, the Fiduciary Trust administrative aide, was finishing up her leftover pasta in the company's ninety-sixth-floor cafeteria in the south tower. It was Friday, February 26, 1993. Humphries and her colleague Brenda Fogarty, who had been having a sandwich and ginger ale for lunch, cleared off the Formica table and were ready to leave well before the 1 P.M. rush. Without warning, what sounded like a thunderclap reverberated through the room. Humphries thought the twin towers must have blown some kind of giant fuse. "Must be the alternator again," she said vaguely. Whatever it was, the two were sure, it was nothing to worry about. They stood up and headed down Fiduciary's interior stairs toward their desks on the ninety-fourth floor.

In fact, a yellow Ford Econoline van, packed with the equivalent of fifteen hundred pounds of dynamite, had just exploded in the basement parking garage between the Vista Hotel and the north tower. Except for the sound, little of the concussion reached high in the towers.

By the time Humphries and Fogarty walked down the two floors, Lawrence Huntington, the chief executive, was already gathering his four hundred employees. The telephones in his office had backup power, so they still worked. But no one they could reach could tell him exactly what was going on. Although he didn't know it, the trade center's sprinkler system, internal communications, basement-level emergency command center, and five of eight electricity feeder lines were destroyed. What Huntington could see was that the stairwells were already filled with smoke and the elevators were not running. The lights were out. Huntington pulled his senior staff members aside and asked them to hold everyone in the office until they knew more. Irene Humphries started to walk around the ninety-fourth floor in circles, not really looking at anything, just pacing. Her march stopped only when someone yelled out and asked for help in stuffing Xerox paper under the doors to slow the infiltration of smoke. But no matter what they did, the smoke kept getting thicker.

Like a mountain climber reconsidering his latest trail, Huntington began to wonder if in keeping everyone there, he had given the wrong order. "What are we going to do?" Huntington asked Ben Fisher, another senior executive. "We are going to start losing people. They are going to start fainting."

The tenants were not the only ones in the dark. Port Authority officials—including Guy Tozzoli and Eugene Fasullo, the Port Authority's chief engineer—were learning firsthand about what else the Port Authority could have done to prepare for a possible terrorist attack. Fasullo, along with several of his colleagues, was headed out to lunch when the bomb went off. Now they were stuck in an elevator somewhere around the fifty-eighth floor. Pressing the emergency button simply elicited a recording that said, "Message has been heard; we will responding," over and over again, an entirely insufficient response given the cloud of ash and black smoke that had started to settle in the car. Frank Lombardi, a Port Authority engineer who was in the car, looked at another engineer with a glance that carried a clear meaning: this could be it. Then the lights went off. Tozzoli was in his seventy-seventh-floor office for a meeting with a group of Romanian businessmen when he heard the muffled roar. He too figured it was a transformer explosion, confidently telling his guests that they should sit and wait for the public address system to advise them what to do.

It took Tozzoli only about five minutes to change his mind. He asked his guests to get their coats and get ready to leave. The smoke was already so thick in the stairwell that the walk was extremely difficult. He made it down to the fifty-second floor when the lights went off. The stairwell was packed with hundreds of panicked office workers. People were choking, crying, calling out for help.

Not surprisingly, Tozzoli took control as best he could. Concerned that people were about to start stampeding in the pitch-black stairwell, he yelled out: "Make two lines, one against the railing, one against the wall. There are twenty steps to a floor, ten to a landing. Put your hand on the person in front of you and then follow them down. And pass these instructions up and down." At least in that stretch of the stairwell, people started counting and very slowly, they made their way down. It took another hour and fifty minutes to reach the bottom, a process that got much easier once they encountered a firefighter with a searchlight on the twentieth floor.

Fasullo and his fellow Port Authority engineers demonstrated a similar ingenuity. The engineers all knew that the elevator walls were not solid concrete—they were merely two layers of lightweight plasterboard. Fasullo took out his car keys. Another of the men pulled out a money clip. One woman had a nail file. They pulled open the interior elevator doors and went to work. Using small yellow lights from their beepers, the men worked two hours, taking turns. Their eyes and noses were running from all the smoke and dust. They were nauseated. Some tried putting handkerchiefs across their faces in hopes that it would make it easier to breathe. No one knew what would be on the other side of the wall. Perhaps it was a conference room, perhaps it was a steel safe. After breaking open a small hole, they kicked at the wall, knocked at it with their shoulders and feet, until finally they could hear tiles falling into what they would learn was the fifty-eighth-floor women's bathroom. Lombardi reached in and his hand came to rest on the plastic cover of a toilet seat. One by one they slid through the one-foot by two-foot hole into the bathroom.

The ordeal would last the longest at the top of the south tower. Some of the Fiduciary staff had ignored Huntington's advice and attempted to take the stairwell down. But nearly three hours later, they reappeared. Exhausted, terrified, their faces and clothing blackened with soot, they announced that the stairwells were impassable. By 4:30 P.M., as the smoke finally started to clear, Huntington told his employees that if they wanted, it seemed safe to go. In groups of twenty-five they headed down. Not everyone, though, could handle such a walk. Humphries was recovering from leukemia treatment. Another office worker was pregnant. In all, that left about twenty still on the ninety-fourth floor. It was not until about 8 P.M. that rescuers finally arrived, carrying axes and other equipment. They insisted that the remaining workers go to the stairs. Huntington refused, saying he would not be responsible for causing a miscarriage. So then the impossible happened. Humphries and the other physically impaired Fiduciary staffers found themselves on the World Trade Center roof. A police helicopter had been called and it had just landed. Fire officials would later call this an irresponsible stunt. The city, they said, did not have the proper equipment or training to do roof rescues. It didn't matter to Humphries, who clutched her coat tight, bent her head, and walked out to the chopper. In two minutes, sometime around 11 P.M., she was on the ground and then on her way to Penn Station in a police cruiser, its lights and sirens blaring.

▪ ▪ ▪

Larry Silverstein stood in the brilliant sunlight on the World Trade Center's plaza and lifted a giant ring of gold and silver keys high in the air with his right hand, as if he were clutching a championship belt. This Tuesday in July 2001 was a good day for Silverstein, a seventy-year-old New York City developer who for more than a decade had dreamed of owning the twin towers. Silverstein had agreed to pay the equivalent of $3.2 billion over the next ninety-nine years to lease the twin towers, and he was here with his jacket off in the blistering heat—the sunlight glinting off the white marble plaza, the aluminum cladding of the towers, and even Silverstein's forehead—to claim his prize. His big gold cuff links and shimmering tie complemented the two-foot-long keys perfectly as he, New York governor George E. Pataki, and a crowd of other officials grinned for the cameras.

It had been twenty-eight years since the governors of New York and New Jersey, the chairman of the Port Authority, and a crowd of television and newspaper reporters gathered near this same spot for the formal dedication of the World Trade Center. "Today," Governor Nelson A. Rockefeller declared then, "the World Trade Center is not only a magnificent structure functionally; it is a visually exciting extension of the most breathtaking skyline on earth. It's not too often that we see a dream come true. Today, we have."

Rockefeller's words rang hollow then. On this day in July 2001, the plaza was no more hospitable a place on a hot day than it had ever been, but something had changed. When acting New Jersey governor Donald DiFrancesco said that "the World Trade Center has an economic and emotional impact that is felt far beyond the complex's sixteen acres," it is unlikely that anyone was inclined to object. The World Trade Center had more than recovered from the 1993 bombing. It was one of the most valuable and respected pieces of real estate in the world.

In the years since the bombing, the Port Authority had given the World Trade Center a makeover. After replacing the damaged steel and concrete, the Port Authority completed a $700 million renovation, upgrading the electrical systems and elevators, replacing worn-out paving stones on the plaza, and rebuilding the mall and much of the hotel. Windows on the World was refurbished, and became one of the top-grossing restaurants in the nation when it reopened in 1996. The renovation included a long list of safety improvements, like the battery-operated emergency lights in the stairwells, luminescent paint in the stairwells, and a separate emergency command center in each building. Lombardi, the Port Authority engineer, discovered that the fireproofing on the floor trusses was far too thin—a legacy of Mal Levy's mysterious letter specifying that the thickness should be one-half inch when there had been no fire testing of the trusses to determine a safe thickness. Lombardi ordered that, as tenants moved out and new ones moved in, the thickness should be increased to one and a half inches, triple the amount that Levy had authorized. The pace of turnover meant that the job was expected to take more than a decade, but Lombardi got it started.

The other buildings around the site also got plenty of attention. Mayor Rudolph W. Giuliani had set up a high-tech, ostensibly flood-, hurricane-, bomb-, and poison gas–proof emergency operations command center at 7 World Trade Center, known as the Bunker. It had its own fuel and water supply, beds, showers to accommodate thirty people, and rooms filled with video monitors from where the mayor could supervise city police and fire responses.

Of the 10.4 million square feet controlled by the Port Authority, over 99 percent was occupied by July 2001, with rents hovering at about $45 a square foot. The tenant list now had almost nothing to do with the importing and exporting of goods—financial firms dominated—but the statistics did little to convey the air of invincibility and optimism that had settled over the World Trade Center. Lawrence Huntington of Fiduciary Trust was so proud of how his company and the trade center had performed that he started to use the bombing almost as a marketing tool. "If we can overcome this, nothing can stand in our way," he said. Sometimes the braggadocio became more macabre. Les Robertson, the structural engineer who started out in John Skilling's office before breaking away and creating his own firm in New York, asked that a fourteen-thousand-pound steel brace that had been knocked out by the bomb be delivered to his Connecticut weekend home. He set it up as a sculptural testament to the strength of the towers. As this bit of "found art" revealed, the bomb had gone off among the stout, massive lower pieces of the World Trade Center, the ones fabricated long ago at places like Atlas Machine and Iron Works. The lightweight steel of the upper floors had not been tested.

Yamasaki's twins were still austere, off-putting monoliths. After all these years, they remained a jarring sight. But the city, and the world, had embraced them. The twins had become one of New York City's most popular postcards. It was not just CNN that featured the towers. Almost every time movie and television directors needed an "establishment shot" of New York, it was to the twin towers they turned. From *Almost Famous* to *Coyote Ugly* to *Independence Day*, from *Sex in the City* to *The Sopranos*, these steel boxes, in all their severity and grandeur, had become a shorthand symbol for New York. The neighborhood where they stood was now a vibrant extension of Manhattan. Battery Park City had been transformed from a landfill into a teeming minimetropolis, with ten thousand residents, restaurants, shopping, a yacht club, a movie theater, and the copper-topped towers of the World Financial Center. Immediately to the north of the towers, TriBeCa emerged as a hot residential neighborhood, inspired, in part, by all of the new activity downtown. This was not necessarily the place Austin Tobin had in mind. But it would be hard to argue that the city had not benefited from the creation of the World Trade Center.

On this blazing July day, there was still plenty of irony to go around as Larry Silverstein held his oversize keys in the air on his day of triumph. "I believe that government is at its best when it focuses on its core mission," Governor Pataki said on the plaza. "Today, as we make history, we can say: mission accomplished. By sharpening the agency's focus on our airports, seaports, bridges, and tunnels, the Port Authority can improve services to all its customers and become a stronger economic engine for the entire region." The governor could have said that sometimes, history can be made only if history is forgotten. On this day, finally, officially, and completely, the reason the World Trade Center had been built was lost and forgotten. The twin towers were just enormous office buildings with sweeping views, and they did not pretend to be anything else.

Just a few hundred feet away from Silverstein and Pataki stood Reg Presley, Chris Britton, and other members of the aging British proto-punk rock band the Troggs. The Troggs had produced the primitive rock anthem "Wild Thing" a year before the World Trade Center construction began. Their songs were considered so scurrilous at the time that some radio stations would not play them. Presley sat down on one of the plaza chairs to have a good look at the towers. "My God, they are big," he said to himself. With that he got up and prepared for a 1 P.M. gig on the plaza.

The vertical city above him hummed with life. On the north tower's eighty-second floor, Marc Cutler, a transportation consultant from Boston, was looking for someone he knew. A crowd of seventy transportation planners from government and private industry sat in a windowless, rose-colored conference room, waiting for a presentation that would answer a riddle that had teased New York since the rise of the railroad: How can one of the most densely populated islands in the world be better linked to the mainland? The Manhattan port was dead, in part because this question had never been answered. Cutler and his aide, Alex Brown, were there to sketch out a multibillion-dollar solution. Yet Brown was nowhere to be seen. Cutler stood up before the assembled mass, and he decided to start on his own. "Truckers complain about circuitous routes on local streets and difficult turning maneuvers between terminal gates and roadways," he said. Then Brown, perspiring and flustered, walked in. He had been trapped in Yamasaki's imposing marble lobby, waiting at the security desk for a clearance check. Now the presentation could really begin.

It was nearly noon, and to William Meehan, sitting in his 104th-floor office in the north tower, that meant one thing: it was time to send out the midday market report. Stocks were already headed downward on this July morning, although trading so far had been slow. As the chief market analyst at Cantor Fitzgerald, Meehan was expected to pontificate about what might happen next. "While I'm very negative on tech in the near term, I suggest OPWV as a good trade on the long side after reporting and subsequent to Lehman's downgrade," he wrote, not stinting on the opaque acronyms. Even as Meehan sat tapping out his thoughts, Alan Greenspan was in Washington testifying before the U.S. Senate, repeating his warning that the economy might not have bottomed out yet.

At Windows on the World on the 107th floor, Peter Lucas, a guitar player for the Troggs, was trying not to black out with fear as he contemplated the view. His friend Dave Maggs, the Troggs's sound engineer, held him by his trousers from the back, so that Lucas could lean toward the glass and grab a good long look down. He saw the postage-stamp splotch of Central Park; he saw the other tower, where dozens of tiny people were on the observation deck. From another window, he saw the Statue of Liberty looking like a Barbie doll; and he saw the endless blue expanse of the Atlantic Ocean. Lucas, feeling as if his blood had turned to water, stood there petrified and in awe.

9

...

9/11: The Collapse

Field: Battalion 1 to Manhattan.
Dispatch: Battalion 1.
F: We just had a plane crash into upper floors of the World Trade Center. Transmit
a second alarm and start relocating companies into the area.
D: Ten-four, Battalion 1.
F: Battalion 1 is also sending the whole assignment on this box to that area, K.

—Message in FDNY dispatcher's log,
beginning at 8:46 A.M. and forty-three seconds on September 11, 2001

G uy Tozzoli guided his black Mercedes sedan past a jumble of swaybacked old warehouses and manicured condominium developments on the back streets of Hoboken, New Jersey, winding his way toward the Holland Tunnel. He drove under a rusty train bridge held up by riveted steel braces and past an old brick post office building with tiled parapets and a big watertower on top. Over the years Tozzoli had figured out how to cut to the front of the ten-block line of traffic at the tunnel, shaving a few minutes off the journey through New Jersey, beneath the Hudson River, and into Lower Manhattan from his home in North Bergen. Tozzoli, at seventy-nine, was still a restless fireplug of a man who firmly believed that there was a workaround for every problem, and his daily commute was no exception. This shortcut took him down Jersey Avenue, between two Port Authority buildings dedicated to uninspiring roadway materials like concrete and asphalt, and straight toward the Holland Tunnel plaza near the tollbooths.

On this particular September morning, Tozzoli, looking sharp in a blue business suit and red tie, was running a bit behind schedule. He had left at his usual 7 A.M., driven south down the New Jersey Turnpike, but as he was about to exit onto Route 3, a bus accident brought traffic to a standstill for forty-five minutes. Naturally Tozzoli had made good use of the time. His radio was off, the windows of his car were up, the air-conditioning was running, and he was all but oblivious to the cloudless seventy-degree morning outside. But his briefcase was open on the beige leather of the passenger seat as he punched numbers into a dial pad and spoke toward a microphone on his rearview mirror to business colleagues in Hong Kong, Paris, and New York. Once the traffic had cleared and he zigzagged his way to Jersey Avenue, Tozzoli realized that if he hustled, he could still be on time for a nine o'clock meeting at his seventy-seventh-floor office in the north tower, with its lovely views north toward the Empire State Building and the other Midtown skyscrapers.

Every morning, more than forty thousand people went to work in the trade center. These days, only one of them—Guy Tozzoli—could truly say that he had created it. Austin Tobin was gone. Mal Levy was gone, having died suddenly in 1980 after pleading guilty to padding his expense accounts. Ray Monti, the trade center's construction chief, had died just a few months before this crystalline morning. Once, before his fellow builders had passed on, Tozzoli had wanted to make an even bigger mark on the region where his agency's power was centered. He'd had plans, thrilling plans, for what he would do when he achieved his greatest aspiration and succeeded Tobin as executive director of the Port Authority. He had wanted to push a vast new arm of the Port Newark containership facility north along the New Jersey Meadowlands, move the Midtown bus terminal to New Jersey and connect it to Manhattan with the world's biggest people mover under the Hudson River, and shift the west side passenger piers to Brooklyn or Staten Island. But when Nelson Rockefeller, one of the two governors with the power to veto the appointment of an executive director, was told after Tobin's resignation that Tozzoli was a top candidate for the job, Rockefeller delivered the unkindest cut he could have mustered. Rockefeller claimed he had never heard of Guy Tozzoli.

In time, the pain over Rockefeller's veto gradually turned to joy. Without new responsibilities, Tozzoli was able to stay in the buildings he loved while immersing himself in the World Trade Centers Association, a multinational group separate from the agency, whose goal is spreading world peace through trade. He became the association's president, and the license plates on his Mercedes now read WTCA. He liked to trace his own dreams of peace to an afternoon in 1930 when he and a buddy went to see *All Quiet on the Western Front* at a theater in North Bergen. After Lew Ayres was shot by a sniper while reaching for a butterfly in the last scene, Tozzoli said, he started thinking an eight-year-old's thoughts about war and peace and asked himself if he would have the guts to do what the people in that war had done. He also liked to tell stories about the time when a deeply skeptical Tobin had asked if Tozzoli was smoking opium when he predicted that Russia and China would join the association—in time, they did—and how Nelson Mandela and the South African government had opened talks on ending apartheid in that country's World Trade Center, the only neutral ground that was handy.

And for Tozzoli, all of it revolved around the twin towers. For thirteen years he worked for the Port Authority on the sixty-third floor of the north tower. When he retired from the agency in 1987, he moved up to the seventy-seventh floor as president of the World Trade Centers Association, where his office was jammed with memorabilia, like shelf upon shelf of dolls from around the world that he had started collecting to help him answer his daughters' questions about foreign cultures he had seen. Tozzoli's favorite, which he had received as a gift from Mobutu Sese Seko, Zaire's dictator, in 1976, was a skeletal doll of a medicine man wearing a frightening mask. It was all part of reaching for his personal butterfly high above Manhattan.

In the four decades that had passed since he had first heard of the World Trade Center, Tozzoli had never been away from the plot of land on Manhattan's west side for more than a few weeks. And in all that time, one of the most beautiful moments of each morning was when he turned left off Jersey Avenue and got his first view of the towers across the Hudson.

But this time, as he made the turn, his eyes were confronted with an incomprehensible sight. Waves of thick, oily smoke were billowing from a gash in the north tower, just a few floors above his office.

The tower had been struck by a plane at 8:46.

Tozzoli was almost instantly stuck in a motionless mass of cars in the nine-lane toll plaza. To one side of the plaza were a few desultory trees next to the shopworn Holland Motor Lodge. A little farther away, in the direction of the towers, west and a little south, was a mall and a Sears auto store. Straight ahead in the plaza, due west, was a huge beige sign that said HOLLAND TUNNEL above the entrances. Tozzoli stepped out of his car and stood among dozens of stupefied commuters in business suits, all staring helplessly over the mall and the Sears store at the smoke and flames in the distance.

"It's going to take us a long time to fix that," Tozzoli said in his gravelly voice to someone in the clot of people around him. No one answered.

Then at 9:02 he heard the scream of a second plane gunning its engine past the Statue of Liberty and watched it bank toward the south tower. An orange billow of flame exploded from the point of impact. Chunks of steel, shards of fuselage and landing gear, and a blizzard of paper burst from the side of the tower. As chaos and panic erupted around him, Tozzoli walked up to the tollbooth near the entrance, identified himself, then got back in his car and worked his way into the stream of ambulances and squad cars entering the tunnel in the leftmost lane. He had guided people down the dark exit stairways in 1993, and he knew he had to do something this time, too.

The people in the tollbooth let him through. He drove through the tunnel among the flashing lights, and when he emerged on the Manhattan side in a black Mercedes among ambulances and fire trucks, a uniformed police officer stopped him. Tozzoli again flashed his credentials.

"Listen, I built that place," Tozzoli said, pointing toward the burning towers. "I've got to get down there to help."

The police officer's reply was curt.

"I don't care if you're the pope," he said. "This is for emergency vehicles. You turn this car around and you go that way. Because you can't help anybody."

The south tower would collapse at 9:59, the north tower at 10:28.

▪ ▪ ▪

Some days, the Lower Manhattan skyline appeared with such perfect clarity, the contours of the buildings so stark, that the view from the Hudson suggested abstract sculpture carved from the blues of the water and the sky rather than from a pounding, shouting, honking metropolis. Almost as if looking at one of Yamasaki's models, the eye rose from the Battery at the southern tip of the island, passed through the stone canyons of Wall Street, stepped up to David Rockefeller's slablike steel-and-glass

Chase Manhattan Bank Building, swung around the white terra-cotta parapets of the Woolworth Building, and skipped across the droll skullcaps of the World Financial Center, before settling at the obvious trail head in the sky: the twin towers.

Inside, the teeming city in the sky was operating just as designed. It was shortly after 8:30 on a day that, for the people working in those towers, was looking a lot like an ordinary Tuesday.

On the 104th floor of the north tower, Andrew Rosenblum, a stock trader at Cantor Fitzgerald, was in his spot at one of the long lines of desks and computers on the wide-open trading area along the windows on the north part of the floor. As in much of this very practical city, any architectural pretensions were lost amid the industrial-size Xerox machines and unwashed coffee cups and the general clutter generated by doing business at a relentless pace. There were a few glassed-in offices on the northwestern part of the floor and a nice cafeteria in the core, near the elevators, but elegant it was not. Jimmy Smith, one of the five traders in the group that Rosenblum led, jokingly called their space "the ghetto in the sky." They would be a little shorthanded today, since John Sanacore, Rosenblum's clerk, had undergone some unpleasant medical tests on Monday that had left him feeling too queasy to work this morning. Rosenblum had just gotten an unexpected phone call from his wife, Jill, from their home in Rockville Centre, on Long Island. "How come you're not at the gym?" he said. "Well, I'm taking off this cabinet door," she said, referring to a home repair project that a family friend, Barry Kornblum, was going to help with. "Barry's going to come by and pick it up," she said.

If Andrew Rosenblum looked west along the floor, he could see all the way down to the trading desks in the northwest corner, just outside one of the glassed-in offices, where Ian Schneider and his global finance group were beginning work. Schneider, an avid coach of boys' and girls' baseball, soccer, and basketball teams in his spare time, had been with Cantor for twenty-three years, and his group was among the tightest on the floor. In another open trading area along the windows of the south facade, Stephen Cherry, an equity stockbroker, had just gotten off the phone with his wife, Maryellen, thanking her for making a special dinner—orange roast chicken—the night before. The entire tower was waking up. On the ninety-eighth floor, Patricia Massari, a financial analyst at Marsh & McLennan, was on the phone with her husband, Louis—she had learned early that morning that she was pregnant with their first child. Farther down, at Carr Futures on the ninety-second floor, brokers had already had an unusual 8 A.M. meeting and were getting ready for a day of trading, and just one floor below them, at the American Bureau of Shipping, three naval architects—Steve McIntyre, Greg Shark, and George Sleigh—were already working at their computers in offices lined up along the windows of the building's north facade.

Still farther down in this vertical city, Frank Lombardi, the Port Authority's chief engineer, was in his office on the 72nd floor of the north tower, getting ready for a 9 o'clock meeting. And so the day began, all the way down, floor after floor of human, mercantile, financial, and technical activity. In the south tower, things were not all that different. Judy Wein, a senior vice president at Aon, an insurance brokerage and consulting firm, had arrived at work at 7:15, had a banana, her usual low-fat yogurt, and mint tea, and settled into her office on the northwest corner of the 103rd floor. Alayne Gentul, senior vice president for human resources at Fiduciary Trust, was attending the regular Tuesday morning staff meeting in a conference room on the 94th floor. At the same company four floors below, Gentul's colleague Edgar Emery, wearing a blue blazer with a black hound's-tooth check that he had bought with his wife, Elizabeth, on Sunday, was at work in his own corner office overlooking the Hudson River and the Statue of Liberty. Stanley Praimnath, a deeply religious employee at Fuji Bank, and one with a delightful sense of humor, had picked up a bagel at Cornucopia downstairs and was going through his usual banter around the coffee machine on the 81st floor. The exchanges always went something like this: "Stan, how are you doing?"—"I'm special, thank you."—"Why are you special?"—"I'm a child of God."—"I know, I know, Stan, you're special."

There were about fifty-eight thousand people like these in the trade center complex altogether—in the towers, the surrounding trade center buildings, the concourse, the PATH station, the subway stations, chatting or just catching some sun on the plaza.

Over on the 104th floor of the north tower, Andrew and Jill Rosenblum were still fretting about the cabinet door with the broken hinge. He was talking on the phone at his desk.

"Did you hear that?" he suddenly said.

"Did I hear what?" she said.

"It was a really loud bang."

"No," she said, "I didn't hear anything."

"Okay, I'll call you right back."

Andrew Rosenblum did not know that a plane had just struck the building ten floors below him.

The impact came at precisely 8:46:26 A.M.

■ ■ ■

The plane, a hijacked Boeing 767 with ninety-two people aboard, was moving at an estimated 470 miles an hour. At that speed, it covered the final two blocks to the north tower in 1.2 seconds.

Designated American Airlines Flight 11, the plane measured 156 feet, 1 inch from wingtip to wingtip and carried about ten thousand gallons of jet fuel.

It had left Logan International Airport in Boston at 7:59 A.M. and flown in a hairpinlike pattern over Massachusetts and New York before soaring down the Hudson River Valley toward the cultural, physical, financial, and symbolic focal point that the World Trade Center had come to be in Lower Manhattan. The plane was piloted, in some very tangible sense, by hatred. A cunning and malevolent hatred.

The plane banked and flashed in the sun, and in the instant before it rammed the upper reaches of the north tower, it bore an eerie, horrifyingly precise resemblance to the image in Lawrence Wien's newspaper ad thirty-three years before, down to the direction the plane flew and the location of the impact, even if the reality was far more terrifying than Wien had ever imagined. And worse: a second hijacked jet, United Airlines Flight 175, was soaring across New Jersey with sixty-five people on board, about twenty miles to the northwest.

The first plane hit the north face of the north tower almost head on, descending at an angle of about six degrees, its wings canted at about twenty-one degrees so that the left wingtip struck the ninety-fourth floor and the right, the ninety-eighth floor. The steel in the perimeter columns at that height was so thin, about one quarter inch, that the light aluminum of the plane's fuselage and wings simply entered the building almost without slowing down. Along with heavier parts like engines, the aluminum sliced as many as thirty-six of the fifty-nine columns on the north face like a machete hacking palm fronds. The soft exoskeleton and the vast interior volume of the tower allowed it effectively to ingest the Boeing jet whole, as if an elephant had disappeared through a wall.

The resistance was so slight that the plane did not even explode on that first impact. Still, once inside, the aluminum of the plane was hacked to pieces by the concrete slabs of the floors, which acted like great axes when struck from the side. The entire nose probably splayed open, horribly, like a log being split. As the fragmented plane began to slow, parts of the concrete floors themselves were pulverized to dust. Whole sections of the lightweight steel trusses holding them up were annihilated. The plane scooped up and obliterated computers, carpeting, furniture, cubicles, gypsum partitions. Hundreds of people were killed within moments, especially at Marsh & McLennan, whose offices stretched from the ninety-third to the hundredth floor. Nevertheless, most of the fragments from the plane probably stayed in a relatively confined path rather than exploding laterally: in the wide-open floors, there was little to cause a horizontal ricochet. And after all, this was a plane—not a bomb designed to scatter shrapnel. So, as seen from the side, the hail of debris probably formed a somewhat tapering cavity, like a worm burrowing into an apple. This compression meant that relatively few people were immediately hurt outside the central zone of impact, and—as incredible as it seems—many survived those first instants on the fringes of the impact area itself.

About two-tenths of a second after the plane first touched the facade, the mangled shards, along with the heavier and more damaging steel of the engines, barreled into the forest of crucial structural columns in the core of the buildings, where a tightly clustered triplet of escape stairwells along with elevator and mechanical shafts were located. Certain parts of the plane plunged straight through the building and out the other side. Part of a landing gear soared five blocks south and came to rest at the corner of West and Rector Streets. Life jackets and seats from the plane landed on top of the Deutsche Bank Building across Liberty Street from the trade center.

The plane's heavily loaded fuel tanks did their own structural damage when they pummeled steel members like battering rams. The tanks also ruptured, spilling thousands of gallons of fuel across floors, down elevator shafts and air ducts. Within a second or two of impact, a vast cloud of

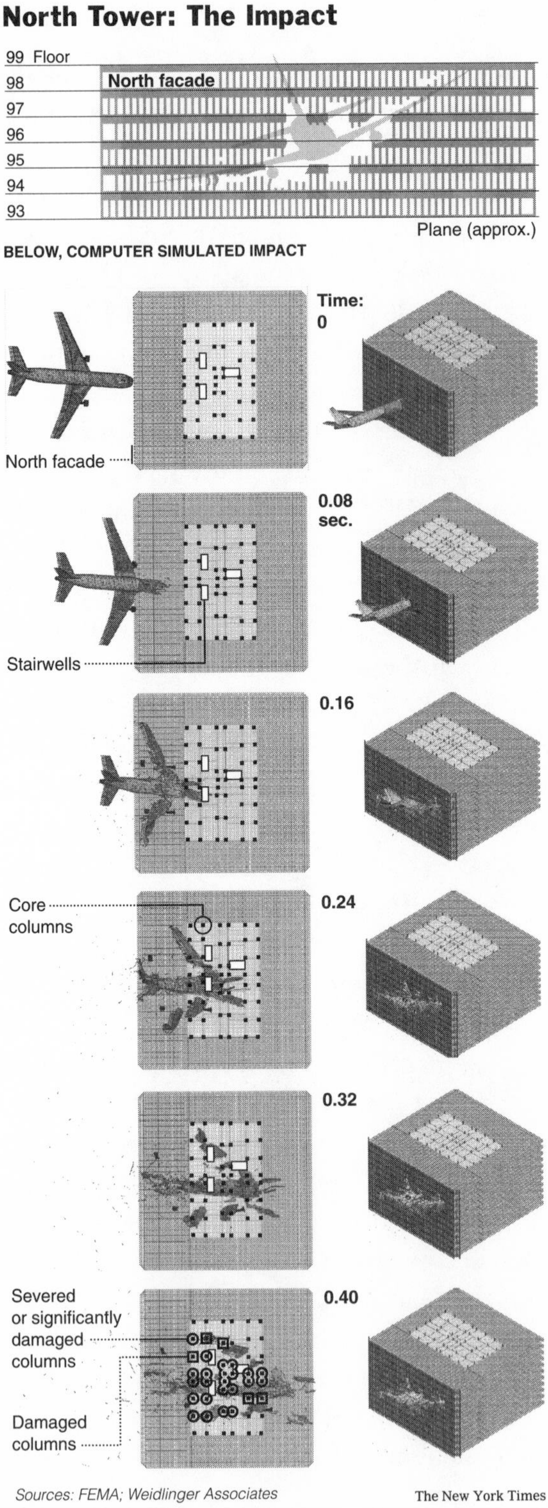

North Tower: The Impact

99	Floor
98	North facade
97	
96	
95	
94	
93	

Plane (approx.)

BELOW, COMPUTER SIMULATED IMPACT

Time: 0

North facade

0.08 sec.

Stairwells

0.16

Core columns

0.24

0.32

Severed or significantly damaged columns

0.40

Damaged columns

Sources: FEMA; Weidlinger Associates

The New York Times

dangerous vapor, containing as much as three thousand gallons of evaporated jet fuel, spread through the floors and created an invisible cloud stretching hundreds of feet around the wounded zone in the tower. The stench of fuel vapor instantly appeared as far down as the tower's lobby, probably billowing from the elevators. About two seconds after impact, a little smoke cloud emerged from a place quite distant from the impact: the rooms filled with heating and ventilation equipment on the 108th and 109th floors. The ducts and shafts connecting those rooms with the impact zone were evidently choked with fuel that had now caught fire somewhere deep in the building's core. And in the next instant, the vapor cloud ignited.

The orange balls of fire bloomed for two hundred feet around the building. Paper and other small debris from the offices burst from the windows, as if some sort of horrible piñata had cracked apart. Fire blasted from the elevator shafts almost one hundred stories below. Ken Summers, who worked for Empire Blue Cross and Blue Shield in the building, had seen a yellowish haze in the lobby, probably the fuel mist; now he saw a fireball coming toward him. It blew him through the lobby's revolving doors and severely burned him. The huge lobby windows were blown out. The great pools of jet fuel high in the tower began to burn and, like lighter fluid sprayed by an arsonist, spread fire across multiple floors. As smoke from the expired fireball rose and began drawing an endless dirty streak across the sky toward the southeast, fires raged on parts of five floors that were exposed by the terrible raking gash in the north facade.

The north tower had taken a flaming stab to its heart, absorbing perhaps 25 million pounds of force and widespread structural damage. The tower remained standing.

And just as John Skilling and Les Robertson and their engineers had predicted, the horizontal spandrel plates connecting the surviving perimeter columns above the gash acted like arches. Almost like a living being fighting to survive, the building used those arches to shift loads to undamaged columns. Calculations would later show the redistribution was so efficient that while intact columns just beyond the two ends of the gash were highly stressed, columns only ten feet farther away were forced to hold less than half the loads that would cause them to buckle. The support structure at the top of the building—the hat truss, whose main role was to hold up the 360-foot antenna—also helped spread the loads to intact columns, both in the building's core and in the perimeter.

As people on the lower floors began to flee, the fate of some of those in the impact zone was decided in an instant. Patricia Massari, the Marsh & McLennan employee on the ninety-eighth floor who had found out she was pregnant that morning, was pressing her husband, Louis, to study that day for some college classes he was taking. It was his day off work. "Oh my God," she said, and Louis heard what he thought was the sound of his wife falling from her chair before he lost the connection. It was the last time they would ever speak. Others, still alive, would be chased down by huge fires—the fires largely ignored by Port Authority engineers in their plane impact study—that quickly spread through the Marsh & McLennan offices. Visible fires began roaring through the ninety-sixth, ninety-seventh, and ninety-eighth floors, and they seemed especially intense on the east face of the building. Within a few minutes of the impact, people began falling from that face, often in tumbling, disjointed poses that suggested either semiconsciousness, paralyzing terror, physical injury, or all three. Some of the doomed fell directly onto the plaza; others first plunged through a temporary, tentlike bandshell set up for a performance, apparently a concert. People being herded through the lobby down to the concourse, where they were being evacuated from the site, were horrified to see body parts and flaming steel debris among the neat rows of folding chairs set up for the concert. Blood spattered what was left of the lobby windows.

For others wandering somewhere just out of the grasp of this merciless inferno, the ordeal lasted longer. A man in a dark shirt and light pants on the ninety-fourth floor walked right up to the opening that had been the north wall of his office and stood there, looking disoriented, shading his eyes from the bright morning light with his right arm. Janet Alonso, an analyst who worked near the southeast corner of the ninety-fifth floor, had time to call her husband, Robert, on her cell phone, tell him the office was filling with smoke, that they were evacuating, and that she loved him.

"I'm coming down to get you," Robert Alonso said.

■ ■ ■

Not a thing had budged in Steve McIntyre's office on the ninety-first floor, just three floors below the bottom of the impact zone. Not the slate paperweight shaped like a sailing ship. Not the family snapshots propped up on a bookcase. McIntyre, one of the three naval architects at the American Bureau of Shipping, found himself in front of a computer that was still on.

Then, seconds after the plane's belly had passed directly over his head, came the whiplash. A powerful shock wave quickly radiated up and down the flexible tower starting from the impact zone. The wave bounced from the top to the bottom of the tower, three or four seconds one way and then back, rocking the building like a huge boat in a storm.

"We got to get the hell out of here," yelled Greg Shark, who was bracing himself in the swaying while he stood outside McIntyre's office.

The area did not come away unscathed. The panels of the drop ceiling and gypsum board off the wall had collapsed onto George Sleigh, who had been sitting about thirty feet east of Shark and McIntyre, closer to where the plane's left wing had dipped before the collision. Sleigh, who was not seriously hurt, fell to his knees and proceeded to crawl from his cubicle. For some reason he glanced up from the rubble—and saw the exposed truss above him. This naval architect would recall that the bars of the truss looked dark and spindly, giving the appearance of bare steel rather than thick coatings of fireproofing.

Sleigh happened to be looking at one of the floors whose whitish, spray-on fireproofing had been upgraded to a thickness of an inch and a half on the orders of Frank Lombardi, the Port Authority chief engineer, after discovering the substandard insulation ordered by Mal Levy's office. (Lombardi himself was now feeling the tower's whiplash on the seventy-second floor.) The work had been completed on this floor in 1997, so the explanation was either that the fireproofing had been applied incorrectly, much of it had come loose in the years since then, the impact of the plane had knocked it off—and it is likely that the concussion jarred at least some of it loose—or Sleigh's clinical eye failed him in his hasty observation.

After the earsplitting *wham* of the impact and Shark's excited yelling, it was quiet enough that McIntyre heard Sleigh trying to extricate himself. McIntyre ran eastward to help, but the cubicle was so choked with rubble that he was forced to wait until Sleigh emerged under his own power. Sleigh regained enough of his presence of mind that after crawling out, he crawled right back in, rummaged around for ten seconds, and emerged with his address book.

Somehow, they were alive.

Shark grabbed a fire extinguisher in a file room and then he, McIntyre, Sleigh, and eight other employees, all uninjured, hustled out of the ABS reception area in the northwest corner and turned left toward the elevators and stairways in the tower's core.

Around a corner and on his left, McIntyre peered into a dim, shattered stairwell, billowing with smoke. It happened to be stairwell C, the most northwesterly of the three. He heard nothing but water cascading down the stairs, as if he had encountered a babbling brook on a mountain hike. The water almost certainly came from severed sprinkler pipes. Seeing and hearing no one else in the stinking gloom, he looked up.

The stairwell was blocked from above—not by fire or structural steel, but by huge pieces of the light gypsum drywall, often called Sheetrock, that had enclosed the stairwell to protect it. In huge hunks, the Sheetrock formed a great plug in the stairwell, sealing the passage from ninety-two, the floor above. Going down the stairs, it made a slightly less formidable obstruction, but still seemed impassable.

"This is no good," McIntyre said.

He could see down a smoking corridor that the northeastern stairwell, A, was blocked off by collapsed material, so he ran past some twisted, warped elevator doors and a small fire near a freight elevator, and peered down the third stairwell, B, which was the farthest south. Again he heard water, again it was plugged above, but it was darker and smokier than the first and seemed to be cluttered with more debris. So he went back to that first staircase, stairwell C. He stepped inside and immediately slipped down two flights of grimy, fallen gypsum, as if he had been on a big sliding board. Unhurt, he stood and noticed lights below. "This way!" he shouted. His colleagues followed and they began to descend toward the lights.

McIntyre could hardly have known it, but he had stood at a critical boundary. Above him, across nineteen floors, were 1,344 people, many of them alive, stunned, unhurt, calling for help. Not one would survive.

Below, across ninety floors, thousands of others were also alive, stunned, unhurt, calling for help. Nearly all of them lived.

For instance, in his seventy-second-floor office, Frank Lombardi at first thought there had been a big earthquake; then he saw the bottom edge of a fireball out of his window. He heard people screaming in an elevator,

The Stairwells in the North Tower

Impact 8:46 A.M. Collapse 10:28 A.M.

STAIRWELLS   STAIRS TO ROOF

B stairwell only goes up to the 107th floor.

106-107
Windows on the World
Heavy smoke fills the floors immediately. Stuart Lee, a vice president at Data Synapse, is trapped in an office in the northwest corner.

104
Cantor Fitzgerald
Smoke infiltrates the floor. Eventually, fire blocks the stairwells. Employees seek refuge in these offices, including about 50 in a conference room.

92
Carr Futures
"It's really bad here – the elevators are gone," Damian Meehan, a trader at Carr Futures, tells his brother in a telephone call.

91
American Bureau of Shipping
The impact causes little damage to the office. All staff members evacuate. Only two of the three stairwells are accessible, and only one of those, stairwell C, appears passable. Above this floor, no one will survive.

76
Stairwell C
Evacuees encounter a door in the transfer hallway that cannot be opened. They go back up a floor and switch to another stairwell before continuing down and out of the building.

NORTH FACADE

A
C
B

TRADING ROOM

106   OFFICES

104

98
97
96
95   ENTRY HOLE MADE BY PLANE
94

91

76
76
76

78
76
78
77
75
74
76

TRANSFER HALLWAY

All three stairwells are believed to be destroyed or made impassable.

Debris is seen blocking stairwells.

Doors to local elevators are twisted.

STAIRWELL TRANSFERS
The three stairwells in each tower do not run in continuous columns. The stairwells change shafts via transfer hallways on floors where mechanical equipment is in the way.

Sources: Interviews with survivors and people who had contact with victims; Leslie E. Robertson Associates; FEMA; Port Authority; N.Y. Fire Department dispatch records

Archie Tse/The New York Times

and the terror he felt in 1993 came back to him. With the nozzle from a fire hose and a staple gun, Lombardi worked to pry open the elevator doors. Then he hustled down an open stairway himself.

One floor above the American Bureau of Shipping, on the ninety-second floor, employees of Carr Futures were doing exactly what the ABS people had done: hunting for a way out.

They did not realize they were on the wrong side of the rubble.

On the ninety-second floor, Damian Meehan had dialed his brother Eugene, a firefighter in the Bronx. "It's really bad here—the elevators are gone," Damian told him. Eugene Meehan urged him to go to the office entrance and see if there was smoke there. He heard his brother put the phone down, then followed the sounds drifting into his ear. Yelling. Commotion, but not panic.

A few minutes later, Damian Meehan returned and reported that the front entrance was filled with smoke.

"Get to the stairs," Eugene advised him. "See where the smoke is coming from. Go the other way."

Then he heard his brother for the last time. Damian said something like "We've got to go" or "We're going."

Eugene Meehan was sure that he had heard "We."

• • •

By 8:57, eleven minutes after American Airlines Flight 11 had struck the north tower, a tremendous fire was sweeping across the 97th floor, particularly on the western face, where flames were leaping from some of the southernmost windows. Thick, steady plumes of smoke were also pouring from windows far above the fires, from the mechanical rooms on the 108th and 109th floors. Just below, at restaurants on the 106th and 107th floors, callers were already reporting desperate, stifling conditions. Among 171 employees, restaurant patrons, and people attending an information technology conference was Neil D. Levin, the Port Authority's executive director, who had gone to the 107th floor for breakfast at Wild Blue. People like Stuart Lee, a vice president with Data Synapse, had been setting up display booths at the conference, to be held at Windows on the World, on the 106th floor. The swiftly deteriorating conditions indicated that smoke and heat from the fires were finding quick pathways to the top through the building's maze of shafts and ductwork.

While all of that was happening, the disaster marched at an eerily deliberate pace just two floors below Windows.

The northwest conference room on the 104th floor held just one of many large knots of people in the five floors occupied by Cantor Fitzgerald. There, the smoke did not become overwhelming as quickly as at Windows. And the crash and fires were not as immediately devastating as they had been a few floors below, at Marsh & McLennan.

Andrew Rosenblum, the Cantor stock trader who had been talking to his wife, Jill, about the broken cabinet door, had retreated there with about fifty other employees to escape the increasing smoke on the trading floor. "Quick, put on the news," he said when he called Jill back on his cell phone. "Tell me what happened." As she listened, he shouted the information to the room. But there seemed to be a sense of composure in this corner of the 104th floor, a sense that there was still plenty of time to find a way out of their predicament. In fact, Andrew thought it would be a good idea to reassure the families of the people that fate had put in the room with him. Since he seemed to have the only working cell phone, he announced to the room: "Give me your home numbers," and started giving names.

"Tim Betterly," Rosenblum said, reeling off a phone number. "James Ladley." A number. "John Schwartz." Another number. "Please call their spouses, tell them we're in this conference room and we're fine," he said to his wife. She scribbled the names and numbers on a yellow legal pad in her kitchen, as the burning towers played on a thirteen-inch television in a cubbyhole near the sliding backdoor. She handed pieces of paper with the numbers to friends who had shown up. They went either to the leafy, fenced-in backyard, where the dog wandered among them, or to the front lawn, calling the families on cell phones.

Andrew Rosenblum's group had apparently crossed the trading floor to the west to be as far as possible from the smoke and flames in the building's core. That would have taken them toward the spot just outside the conference room where Ian Schneider usually sat at the head of a string of desks where he led a global finance group. Michael Wittenstein, John Casazza, and Michael DeRienzo were all in that area, and, like Schneider, were using land lines at their desks to take calls from concerned customers and loved ones, according to six people who spoke with them. "The building rocked like it never has before," said Schneider, who had been there for the 1993 bombing, in a phone call with his wife, Cheryl, after the collision. Schneider and, probably, some of those near him chose a different strategy from Rosenblum's group. A few minutes after Schneider talked to his wife, a fire department dispatcher logged this entry: AC MC SCHNEIDER STS ON 105 FLR THERE IS SMOKE W ALOT OF PERSONS INSIDE.

Translated, it meant that a "male caller" named Schneider stated that he was now on the 105th floor with many of his Cantor colleagues. Schneider had decided to go up, perhaps toward the roof, where a number of people were rescued with helicopters after the 1993 bombing. If he got that far, he found that the doors to the roof were locked. For a variety of reasons, the Port Authority had decided, with the agreement of the Fire Department, to discourage the use of helicopters in emergencies at the building. The helicopters that Austin Tobin could not seem to do without during the construction of the trade center would not be available. Ordinary building occupants were not briefed on the policy change after 1993 and there were no signs explaining that the doors were locked, although the Port Authority's emergency drills directed people down the stairs, not up. But there was an inferno in that direction, and in any case, all three exit stairs—encased in lightweight gypsum, consistent with the innovative structural philosophy of the building—had crumbled somewhere below the 104th floor.

In the equities trading area in the southern part of the 104th floor, looking toward the Statue of Liberty, there was a third group. Here, Marc Zeplin and Stephen Cherry, who had just thanked his wife for the dinner of orange roast chicken, pushed a button at their desk to activate the squawk box, a nationwide intercom to other Cantor Fitzgerald offices around the country. "Can anybody hear us?" Cherry asked. A trader in Chicago who was listening in managed to reach a firehouse near the trade center. "They know you're there," the trader told them. Elsewhere, probably in some offices along the west side of the floor, Richard Y. C. Lee, managing director of equities at Cantor, reached his wife, Karen, who had no idea anything had happened at the trade center.

"Hi!" he said brightly, perhaps trying not to worry her. "Can you do me a favor?"

"Okay," she said. "What?"

"Don't panic, but a plane just hit the building. There's smoke, and I need you to call nine-one-one or World Trade Center maintenance and give them my cell phone number," he said. "We need to know what to do. Should we break a window, or what?"

"Okay, I'll call someone," said Karen Lee, who began to hear only static and was unable to reestablish contact.

The drama at Cantor Fitzgerald, which had its offices on floors 101 and 103 through 105 and had 658 employees in the upper reaches of the tower that day, took place on a vast stage. The calls were not just coming from people with desks and offices on the 104th floor. Mike Pelletier, a commodities broker in a Cantor office on the 105th floor, reached his wife, Sophie, who had just videotaped a few minutes of their two-and-a-half-year-old daughter's first day at nursery school. "Soph, an airplane just went through the building," he said, adding, "I don't know what we're going to do." She said: "Oh my God, is there help?" His answer: "We don't know. We don't know. We can't tell." He was later in touch with a friend who told him that the airplane crash had been a terrorist attack. Pelletier swore and shouted the information to the people around him.

And the temperatures rose. The jet fuel probably burned itself out in most places in a few minutes, but it set broad swaths of the tower aflame before it did. Even after the jet fuel was largely gone, the fires, taken together, produced roughly as much heat as a large nuclear power plant. Air temperatures reached over fifteen hundred degrees in some places, depending on how well ventilated they were and how much in the way of files and furniture the fire had to burn. One perhaps unanswerable question was how much of the fireproofing insulation had been knocked away from the steel, as the material over George Sleigh's desk on the ninety-first floor may have been. At one thousand degrees, steel has softened enough to lose half its original strength. At twelve hundred degrees, it is down to one-quarter of its strength. And by sixteen hundred degrees, the steel will buckle under less than 10 percent of the load it could have withstood at room temperature. Without insulation, the thin steel trusses would take on almost exactly the temperature of the air and fire around them. Even with protection, they were vulnerable. Vertical members like core and perimeter columns were also getting hotter and weaker. No one inside the tower—and few outside it—knew that a physical clock was ticking, an apocalyptic moment was approaching.

In Rockville Centre, on the front lawn of the Rosenblums' two-story colonial house, surrounded by trees and crisp sunshine, friends like Debbie Cohen and Sara Mandinach dialed the numbers on the yellow pieces of paper they had been handed by Jill Rosenblum.

"Hello? You don't know me, but I was given your number by someone who is in the World Trade Center," Mrs. Cohen said. "About fifty of them are in a corner conference room, and they say they're okay right now."

. . .

Yes, Stanley Praimnath told the caller from Chicago at approximately 9:02, he was fine. He had actually evacuated from his office in the south tower all the way down to the lobby, but a security guard told him to go back. One of Praimnath's bosses even decided to poke a little fun at him, much as his colleagues would kid him at the coffee machine about the religious convictions he wore on his sleeve: "Stan the man, you're not scared to come in the elevator?" Before getting in, Praimnath couldn't help looking around and remarking that it was a good time to take a look at relocation. "You've got that right," said another Fuji Bank employee.

Now, Praimnath was again at his own desk at Fuji, against the south face of the south tower. "I'm fine," he repeated, reassuring his business colleague in Chicago.

Those were his final words before he spotted it.

A gray shape on the horizon. An airplane, flying past the Statue of Liberty. The body of the United Airlines jet grew larger until he could see a red stripe on the fuselage. It was at the level of his eyes and headed toward him.

Another plane.

"Lord, you take over!" he yelled before dropping under his metal desk.

As this plane shot past the Statue of Liberty and the Battery and Wall Street, traveling at about 560 miles an hour, or about 100 miles an hour faster than the first jet, its angling trajectory could easily have taken it right past the southeast corner of the south tower. But at the last instant its eastward wingtip canted up, and the plane banked to the west. At 9:02:54, the nose of the jetliner smashed directly into Praimnath's floor, about 130 feet east of where he cowered under his desk.

People a few floors away could distinguish a terrifying double outburst—bang, thump—which probably emanated first from the impact, then the fireball igniting. Once again the plane split apart and became a hail of white-hot shrapnel, but stayed on a remarkably confined path. The plane hacked through as many as thirty-two perimeter columns on the south face from the seventy-eighth to the eighty-fourth floors and damaged an undetermined number of core columns. A chunk of the fuselage, part of a landing gear, and one of the plane's Pratt & Whitney engines hurtled from the north side of the tower and landed below. Dozens of people were killed instantly, especially along the eastern side of the impact zone. A blast wave threw computers and desks through windows and ripped out bundles of arcing electrical cables. Then the south tower seemed to stoop, swinging gradually toward the Hudson River, ferociously testing the steel skeleton before snapping back. Analysis of a high-resolution video would later show that, almost as if it were a living thing writhing from a grievous wound, the tower shuddered, swayed, and convulsed for more than four minutes after the strike.

This plane came shrieking in on a slightly flatter trajectory than the first, descending at an angle of about three degrees, with its wingtips canted a little more steeply. But those were not the differences that would have the most devastating, life-and-death consequences. Because of its higher speed, this plane carried as much as 50 percent more kinetic energy than the first, potentially doing greater damage. The impact occurred at a lower point in the building—so, while the core columns were made of somewhat heavier, tougher steel, more of the building's weight bore down on whatever structural members were damaged. The hit was also more off-center, toward the eastern part of the face; and the plane was moving on a slightly eastward angle. In fact, the plane's momentum shoveled a great burning heap of computers, carpeting, furniture, and probably contents from the plane into the building's northeast corner. Violent flames soon began spitting from that spot. Then flames and smoke rapidly charged across the entire east face of the building on the eightieth and eighty-first floors, like searing arrows pointing to the conflagration in the northeast corner.

The building writhed and shook, but it did remain standing, just as the north tower had. Still, like a tired shopper walking home with an awkward, unbalanced bag of groceries, the asymmetry of the damage—more toward one side of the building—may have made it more difficult for the building to reapportion its loads as the steel heated and weakened in the fires.

In a measure of the fateful complexity of the disaster, there were also ways in which that off-center hit would save lives. Through most of both towers, the staircases were tightly clustered, and in the north tower, they were all immediately severed or blocked by the blast. Along the impact

South Tower: The Impact

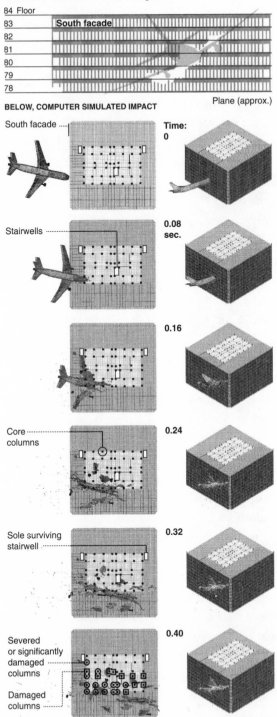

84 Floor
83 | **South facade**
82
81
80
79
78

BELOW, COMPUTER SIMULATED IMPACT

Plane (approx.)

South facade

Time: 0

Stairwells

0.08 sec.

0.16

Core columns

0.24

Sole surviving stairwell

0.32

Severed or significantly damaged columns

Damaged columns

0.40

Sources: FEMA; Weidlinger Associates

The New York Times

zone of the south tower, however, the stairs had to divert around heavy elevator machinery. So instead of running close to the building core, two of the stairways serving those floors were built closer to the perimeter. One of them, on the northwest side, called stairwell A, survived. The surviving stairway—the farthest one from the plane's hail of aluminum and steel—might also have been shielded by the machinery.

However the stairway survived, it made all the difference to Stanley Praimnath, who, huddled under his desk, could see a shiny aluminum piece of the plane lodged in the remains of his door.

There was also devastation and seemingly unreasonable survival three flights up from him in the office of Euro Brokers, on the eighty-fourth floor. Most of the company's trading floor there was annihilated. Yet even there, other people were alive: Robert Coll, Dave Vera, Ronald DiFrancesco, and Kevin York, among others. Within minutes, they headed toward the closest stairwell, led by Brian Clark, a fire warden on the eighty-fourth floor, who had his flashlight and whistle. They picked their way past door frames that had fallen out of the wall, concrete floor slabs that had buckled, light fixtures and speakers dangling down from above. At the center crossroads of the floor, Clark could have gone in any of three directions. For whatever reason, he turned left, toward stairwell A—the northwest corner.

A fine powder mixed with light smoke floated through the stairwell. As they approached the eighty-first floor, Clark would recall, they met a slim man and a heavyset woman. The woman spread her arms and wouldn't let them go by. "You can't go down," she screamed. "You got to go up. There is too much smoke and flame below."

This assessment changed everything. Hundreds of people apparently came to a similar conclusion—an estimated three hundred people at or above the impact zone survived the crash in the south tower, but only eighteen of them would find the open stairway—although the smoke and the debris in the stairwell proved less of an obstacle than the fear of it. This very stairwell was the sole route out of the building, running from the top to the bottom of the south tower. Anyone who found this stairwell early enough could have walked to freedom.

This plain opportunity hardly looked that way to the band of survivors who stood on the eighty-first-floor landing, moments after the plane crash. They argued the alternatives, with Clark shining his flashlight into his colleagues' faces, asking each, "Up or down?" The debate was interrupted by shouts on the eighty-first floor.

It was Stanley Praimnath.

"Help me! Help me!" Praimnath yelled. "I'm trapped. Don't leave me here!"

With no further discussion, the group in the stairs turned in different directions. As Clark would recall it, Coll, York, and Vera headed up the stairs, along with the heavyset woman, the slim man, and two others he knew from Euro Brokers but could not identify. York and Coll hooked arms to support the woman, doing the best they could to be Good Samaritans in a terrible moment of distress. One of them said: "Come on, you can do it. We're in this together."

They began to climb.

Clark and DiFrancesco headed toward the man yelling for help. Praimnath saw the flashlight beam and crawled toward it. Minutes earlier, this had been Fuji Bank's loan department, employee lounge, and computer room. Now he scrambled over toppled desks and across fallen ceiling tiles. Finally, he reached a damaged wall that separated him from the man with the flashlight. He was having a hard time breathing. "I'm here, I'm here, don't leave me," Praimnath said.

"Knock on the wall and I'll know where you are," a voice said.

Praimnath was pounding on it.

Finally, from both sides, they ripped at the wall. A nail penetrated Praimnath's hand. He knocked it out against a hard surface in the darkness. Finally, the two men could see each other, but were still separated.

"You must jump," Clark told Praimnath, whose hand and left leg were now bleeding. "There is no other choice."

As Praimnath hopped up, Clark helped boost him over the obstacle. They fell in a heap and then ran to the stairwell and headed down. The steps were strewn with shattered wallboard. They lifted some of the debris out of the way. Flames licked in through cracks in the stairwell walls. Water from severed pipes poured down, forming a treacherous slurry. They moved past the spot with the heavy smoke that the woman had warned Clark against. Perhaps the draft had shifted; perhaps the smoke had not been all that bad to begin with. In any case, the stairs were clear and would be clear as late as thirty minutes after the south tower was hit.

Meanwhile, DiFrancesco took a detour in search of air, climbing about

The Stairwells in the South Tower

Impact 9:02 A.M. Collapse 9:59 A.M.

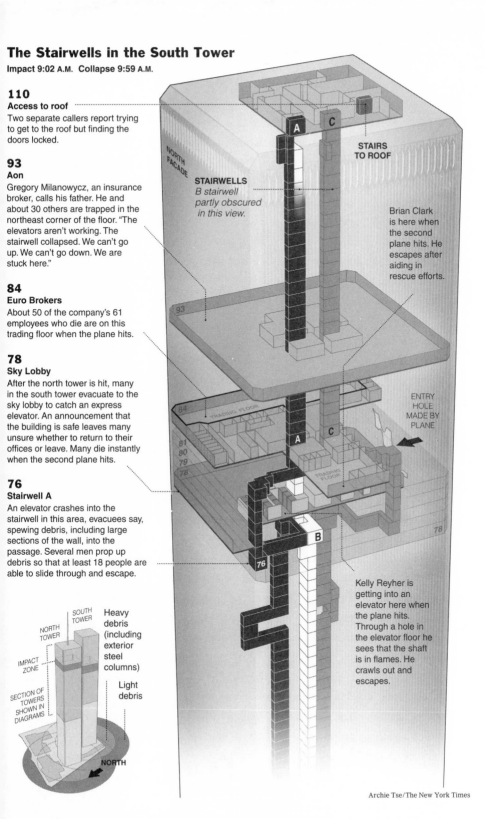

110
Access to roof
Two separate callers report trying to get to the roof but finding the doors locked.

93
Aon
Gregory Milanowycz, an insurance broker, calls his father. He and about 30 others are trapped in the northeast corner of the floor. "The elevators aren't working. The stairwell collapsed. We can't go up. We can't go down. We are stuck here."

84
Euro Brokers
About 50 of the company's 61 employees who die are on this trading floor when the plane hits.

78
Sky Lobby
After the north tower is hit, many in the south tower evacuate to the sky lobby to catch an express elevator. An announcement that the building is safe leaves many unsure whether to return to their offices or leave. Many die instantly when the second plane hits.

76
Stairwell A
An elevator crashes into the stairwell in this area, evacuees say, spewing debris, including large sections of the wall, into the passage. Several men prop up debris so that at least 18 people are able to slide through and escape.

STAIRS
TO ROOF

STAIRWELLS
B stairwell partly obscured in this view.

Brian Clark is here when the second plane hits. He escapes after aiding in rescue efforts.

ENTRY HOLE MADE BY PLANE

Kelly Reyher is getting into an elevator here when the plane hits. Through a hole in the elevator floor he sees that the shaft is in flames. He crawls out and escapes.

SOUTH TOWER
NORTH TOWER

IMPACT ZONE

SECTION OF TOWERS SHOWN IN DIAGRAMS

Heavy debris (including exterior steel columns)

Light debris

NORTH

Archie Tse/The New York Times

ten floors, where he found the first group to go upstairs. They could not leave the stairwell; the doors would not open. They were either jammed or locked. The heavyset woman was struggling so much to breathe that DiFrancesco gave her his backpack. He thought she might be able to breathe into it and filter some of the smoke and dust out of the air. Even that did not seem to help. DiFrancesco pushed upward to somewhere around the ninetieth floor, then turned around and found that the others, exhausted, in heavy smoke, were lying down on a landing in the stairwell. He lay down himself. People around him looked as if they were going to sleep. Then, he sat up, thinking: "I've got to see my wife and kids again."

He ran down the steps.

■ ■ ■

Mary Jos cannot say for sure how long she was lying there, unconscious, on the floor of the south tower's seventy-eighth-floor sky lobby, outside the express elevator. Perhaps a few minutes after the plane impact at 9:02, perhaps longer. She was covered with pieces of debris that could have been wallboard or tiles from the ceiling. Her first recollection of stirring is when she felt searing heat on her back and face. Maybe, she remembers thinking, she was on fire. Instinctively, she rolled over to smother the flames. She saw a blaze in the center of the room, and in the elevator shafts.

That was terrifying enough. Then, below the thick black smoke and through clouds of pulverized plaster, she gradually noticed something worse. The seventy-eighth-floor sky lobby, which minutes before had been bustling with office workers unsure whether to leave the building or go back to work, was now filled with motionless bodies.

The ceilings, the walls, the windows, the sky lobby information kiosk, even the marble that graced the elevator banks—everything was smashed as the second hijacked plane dipped its left wingtip into the seventy-eighth floor.

Witnesses had seen a brilliant light, felt a blast of hot air and then a shock wave that knocked over everything. Lying amid the deathly silence, burned and bleeding, Mary Jos had a single thought: her husband. "I am not going to die," she said to herself.

In the north tower, people's fates had been determined by where they happened to be in their morning routine when the plane struck—a coldly mechanical mix of location, the nature of the impact, and the peculiarities of the building's structure. But here in the south tower, human decisions made in the chaotic sixteen minutes between the attacks did much to shape the geography of life and death. Survivors would recall that the mood in the sky lobby was awkward and uncertain before the second plane hit. There was relief at announcements over the public-address system that staying in their building was safer than walking on the street; there was also fear that it really wasn't. In these critical moments, people milled about, trying to decide: Be at trading desks for the opening of the market, or grab a cup of coffee downstairs?

At Keefe, Bruyette & Woods, nearly the entire investment banking department left and survived. Nearly all the equities traders stayed and died. Among the veterans of the 1993 bombing at Fiduciary Trust, Candice Tevere and Irene Humphries lived; Ben Fisher died.

In the moments before the second impact, everyone in the 78th-floor sky lobby was poised between going up or down. Kelly Reyher, who worked on the 100th floor at Aon Corporation, stepped into a local elevator headed up. He wanted to get his Palm Pilot, figuring it might be a while before he could return to his office. Judy Wein, the executive and office early-bird at Aon, debated with her colleague Gigi Singer whether to go back and get their pocketbooks from their 103rd-floor offices. They stood with their boss at Aon, Howard Kestenbaum, a risk analyst whose former career as a physicist was not hard to guess: a makeshift pendulum hung from the ceiling of his office to let him watch how the tower was swaying in the wind. "Should we go back?" Wein said. Kestenbaum told them to forget it. He would give them carfare home. "Let's just go," he said.

There was even a bit of humor as some office workers talked nervously of the loved ones they were hurrying to rejoin.

"I have a horse and two cats," Karen Hagerty, thirty-four, joked as she was squeezed out of an elevator spot.

There was no sound of an approaching engine. Just a gigantic boom. The building seemed to lurch in one direction, throwing Wein to the ground, cracking three of her ribs and puncturing her right lung. Before she could right herself, the building snapped back the other way, lifting her up and tossing her toward an express elevator. The impact had apparently knocked the elevator doors open a bit, and as she fell toward them, helplessly, she could see flames billowing up and down the shaft and was sure that she was going to tumble in. But she came to rest on the debris-strewn floor.

What had been a busy lobby filled with somewhere between fifty and two hunderd people was now silent, dark, almost lifeless.

All around Judy Wein were people with horrific injuries, dead or close to it. She yelled out for her boss, Howard Kestenbaum. When she found him, she would recall, he was expressionless, motionless, silent. Karen Hagerty, who had joked about the cats at home, showed no signs of life when a colleague, Ed Nicholls, saw her. And Richard Gabrielle, another Aon colleague, was pinned to the ground, his legs apparently broken by marble facing from the sky lobby that had fallen on them.

Wein tried to move the stone. Gabrielle cried out from pain, she would later say, and told her to stop.

Gradually, those who could move, did. Wein found Vijayashanker Paramsothy and Singer, neither of whom had life-threatening injuries. Kelly Reyher, who had been on his way to get his Palm Pilot, found himself trapped in an elevator that had split at the seams, with what looked like firestorm raging in the shaft and choking black smoke surging around him. The fatalistic thought that flashed through his mind was this: "Now I know. I'm going to die in an elevator." But then he noticed that, on the other side of a tongue of flame, the elevator doors were still open about an inch. He reached through the flame, singeing his arm, and discovered that he could pull the doors apart farther. Then he used his briefcase to make a little bridge over the flaming breach in the floor and crawl out. The air was so hot in the lobby he couldn't stand up. He pulled his shirt over his face and crawled. Horribly, he had to crawl over bodies—shaking each, almost reflexively, to see if anyone was alive. He found Donna Spira, another Aon employee, on the floor fifty feet away from the elevator. She had been standing with five of her friends. All five were now dead. Spira's pocketbook and her cell phone had fallen on top of one of the bodies. "Please don't leave me, please don't leave me," she pleaded when she saw Reyher. Though her arm was fractured and her hair burned, Spira could still walk. Apparently the air had cooled somewhat, and they both stood up.

Amid the carnage, a mysterious man appeared at one point, his mouth and nose covered with a red handkerchief. He was looking for a fire extinguisher. Judy Wein would remember him pointing to a stair-case and making an announcement that saved lives: *Anyone who can walk, get up and walk now. Anyone who can perhaps help others, find someone who needs help and then head down.* And they did. In groups of two and three, the survivors strug-gled to the stairs. A few flights down, they propped up debris blocking their way, leaving a small passageway to slip through. One of those to pass through that gap, Ling Young—who worked for the New York State Department of Taxation and Finance—also survived the impact in the sky lobby. She, too, said she had been steered by the man in the red bandanna, hearing him call out: "This way to the stairs." He trailed her down the stairs. Young said she soon noticed that he was carrying a woman on his back. Once they reached clearer air, he put her down and went back up.

Others never left.

The people who escaped said Paramsothy, who had only been scraped, stayed behind. Young said that Sankara Velamuri and Diane Urban, col-leagues of Mary Jos from the State Department of Taxation and Finance, tried to help two more seriously injured friends, Dianne Gladstone and Yeshavant Tembe, both also state employees.

All five of these people would die.

Of the dozens of people waiting in the sky lobby when the second plane struck, twelve are known to have made it out alive.

▪ ▪ ▪

By 9:35, smoke from the spreading fires was pouring out of all the upper floors of the north tower, from at least the 94th floor to the 109th. In the pitiless lower reaches of that zone, smoke emerged from the raking gash torn out by the airplane and from long rows of windows burned through by the bright orange flames glittering behind them. At the very top, on the 108th and 109th floors, the tower expelled smoke from the flames in its belly through its ventilation ducts. In between, countless individual smoke holes puffed gray streamers into the sky, where they rose and coa-lesced with the great black streak moving away from the towers to the southeast. Those holes had been broken out by people. And those people could be seen, most of them more than a thousand feet off the ground, straining through the veils of smoke for a gasp of clear September air.

They were struggling in what had become an unforgiving place.

There were people piled four and five high in window after window, their upper bodies hanging out, especially on the north and west faces of the tower, where the wind swept the smoke away rather than collecting it. Two men, one of them shirtless, stood on the windowsills, stretching their bodies so far outside that they could peer around a big intervening column and see each other, an analysis of photographs and videos reveals. Two other people reached all the way around a column on the 106th floor, appearing to clasp hands just a few feet above a chalky streamer of smoke, like lofty angels in some Renaissance painting. On the 103rd floor, a man stared straight out a broken window toward the northwest, bracing himself against a window frame with one hand. He wrapped his other arm around a woman, seemingly to keep her from tumbling to the ground. One man ceaselessly spun a white towel, or perhaps a shirt, at the northwest corner of the tower on the 107th floor, as if to say: I am here, I am alive, I am in distress at the top of the world, please help me. Another man, wearing what appeared to be a dark shirt rolled up to his elbows, leaned so far out into space, his left hand pressed almost casually against a column for balance, that he seemed to be gauging the chances of climbing down the outside of the tower to the ground and safety.

Helicopters, circling ineffectually without ever landing on the building, passing again and again through the same space where the Port Authority had flown its guests to boast about the unmatched views the upper stories would afford, this day revealed where the desperate had assembled behind unbroken windows of the north tower. "About five floors from the top you have about fifty people with their faces pressed against the window trying to breathe," a police officer in a helicopter reported. And more and more people were falling from the building—perhaps overcome by smoke, perhaps caught in an agony of flames, perhaps having reached the point of irrevocably lost hope—often right past others who were still clinging to life. From the north face, 106th floor. From the west face, somewhere above the 101st floor. Once again from the north face, 106th floor. From the west face, 94th floor. From the north face, 100th floor. From the west face somewhere in the blinding smoke. From the west face, 96th or 97th floor. Two from the 93rd floor, north face, and four more in quick succession from somewhere on the same side of the building. Five more from the west face, one after the other. North face. North face. West. North. West. North. West. North. North. West.

The office of Cantor Fitzgerald, and just above it, Windows on the

World, would become the landmark for this doomed moment. Nearly nine hundred would die on floors 101 through 107.

But many still held on.

In the restaurant, at least seventy people crowded near office windows at the northwest corner of the 106th floor. Stuart Lee, the Data Synapse vice president who had been preparing an exhibit for the information technology conference, used his Blackberry handheld device to e-mail his office in Greenwich Village.

"Any idea which floor/side the plane crashed?" Lee asked in his e-mail.

His boss, Peter Lee, no relation, e-mailed back, "Where are you?"

"Don't know exactly," Stuart Lee wrote back. "We're more or less trapped in one of the offices on 106th floor. Window faces West. Everywhere else is smoked out. Any news from outside?"

His boss asked who else was there and assured Stuart Lee that someone had spoken with his wife and that she was bearing up well. "We have called the police and spoken directly with people there," his boss wrote. "There is a team heading to the hundred-sixth floor."

"Appreciate the update. Garth is a few feet away in this crowded office," Stuart Lee wrote back, referring to Garth Feeney, a coworker. "Currently an argument going on as whether we should break a window. Consensus is no for the time being."

Others had also found ways to protect themselves, however tenuously, from the increasingly desperate conditions. In the northwest conference room on the 104th floor, Andrew Rosenblum and fifty other people temporarily managed to ward off the smoke and heat by plugging vents with jackets. "We smashed the computers into the windows to get some air," Rosenblum reported by cell phone to Barry Kornblum, his friend and golf partner—and the person who had been scheduled to help with that broken hinge in Rockville Centre, now so long ago. "We're trapped," Rosenblum said. Fires had broken out between the conference room and the escape stairways, he said.

As someone in the conference room fanned fresh air through a broken window with a dark piece of cloth, it seemed clear that they had done as well as could be hoped, creating one of the few places on the entire upper facade of the tower where broken windows did not become chimneys of escaping smoke, videos of the disaster show.

Still, there was no hiding.

As people began falling from above the conference room, Rosenblum broke his preternatural calm. In the midst of speaking to his wife, Jill, he suddenly interjected, without elaboration, "Oh my God."

• • •

"Ed, be careful!" shouted Alayne Gentul, the director of human resources at Fiduciary Trust, as Edgar Emery slipped off the desk he had been standing on within the increasingly hot and smoky ninety-seventh floor of the south tower. Emery, one of her office colleagues, had been trying to use his blue blazer, the one with the hound's-tooth pattern that he and his wife had just picked up on Sunday, to seal a ventilation duct that was belching smoke—one sign, although they couldn't have known it, that the tower was dying from within. As Gentul spoke to her husband on the phone—he could overhear what was happening—Emery got back up and spread the coat over the vent.

But that was not the only vital system that was failing. Emery next swung a shoe at a sprinkler head, hoping to start the flow of water.

"The sprinklers aren't going on," Gentul said to her husband, Jack, who listened in his office at the New Jersey Institute of Technology in Newark. He had called in his own building's engineer to listen in and lend advice over the phone.

No one knew that between the impact of the plane and the violent rocking of the tower, the water pipes had probably been cut. And even if some survived, the building could not handle such a large fire, since there would not be enough water pressure to power dozens of sprinklers across multiple floors, fire experts would later conclude.

As Gentul and Emery slowly discovered that their building was edging toward failure, their movements also showed how different conditions here were, in some ways, from those in the north tower. To evacuate Fiduciary employees who worked on the ninety-seventh floor, Emery and Gentul had climbed seven floors from their own offices. There were thirty-seven floors to absorb the rising smoke and heat in the south tower—from the seventy-fourth floor up—compared to just nineteen in the north tower, counting from the fateful demarcation line just above the ninety-first floor. And because of the oblique hit in the south tower, little fuel poured directly into the shaft's ductwork in the building's core. So, although conditions soon did become dire throughout the south tower, many people had relative freedom of movement for a time, and few if any broke windows or fell from the tower.

Many of those people saw and described a structure in its final throes, as floors began to buckle, heat rose, and the building's defense systems failed.

This final odyssey had begun for Edgar Emery as it did for many who were in their offices in the south tower when the first plane hit at 8:46. The fireball from the north tower billowed across the entire western facade of the south tower, filling the rows of narrow windows with an orange glow, as Emery worked in his office near the southwest corner. Anne Foodim, like Emery a member of the human resources department and who was working nearby, felt the intense heat on her face as she looked toward the windows.

Emery, a marathon runner who was known for steadiness in a crisis, emerged, the lapels on his blue blazer flapping as he waved people out. "Come on, let's go," he said, escorting five employees into a stairwell, including Foodim, who had just completed a round of chemotherapy and was still not feeling strong. They walked down twelve floors, reaching the seventy-eighth floor and the express elevator, with Emery giving encouragement. "If you can finish chemo," Emery told an exhausted Foodim, "then you can get down those steps." When they finally reached a packed elevator on the seventy-eighth floor, Emery made sure everyone got aboard. He squeezed Foodim's shoulder and let the door close in front of him. Then he headed back up, joining Alayne Gentul, the director of human resources. Like Emery, Gentul had herded a group out before the second plane hit. Together, they went to evacuate six people on the ninety-seventh floor who had been working on a computer backup operation, Alayne Gentul told her husband.

Soon after Emery and Gentul learned firsthand of the building's failing vital signs, their situation began to deteriorate. Emery was hunting for a stairwell on the increasingly smoky ninety-seventh floor when he reached his wife, Elizabeth, by cell phone. The last thing Mrs. Emery heard before she lost the connection was Alayne Gentul screaming from somewhere very near Ed Emery, "Where's the stairs? Where's the stairs?"

Another phone call was under way nearby. Edmund McNally, director of technology for Fiduciary, called his wife, Liz, as the floor began buckling. McNally hastily recited his life insurance policies and employee bonus programs. He told her that she meant the world to him and that he loved her, and asked that she tell their daughters how much he loved them. They exchanged what Mrs. McNally thought were their last good-byes. Then her phone rang again. Her husband sheepishly reported that he had booked them on a trip to Rome for her fortieth birthday. "Liz, you have to cancel that,'" he said.

At 9:47, a photographer outside the buildings trained his camera on the ravaged east face of the south tower, where fires now raged across at least five different floors above the impact zone, causing thick smoke to creep up this leeward face of the tower like some horrible legion of black-clad invaders scaling a wall. In the northeast corner of the eightieth floor, where office furniture had been shoved by the plane, the fire burned so hot that a stream of molten metal began to pour over the side onto the plaza like a flaming waterfall. The apparent source of this waterfall was molten aluminum from the jet's wings and fuselage, which had also piled up in that corner. But the photographer's high-resolution camera picked out a different fantastical detail in the carnage: the floor truss supporting the eighty-third floor sagging deeply, like a clothesline overloaded with wet clothing.

If the lightweight steel of the truss had now become hot enough to soften, it would be expected to sag in just such a way. The critical danger was that the trusses did not just hold up floors: they also provided lateral support to the perimeter columns, preventing them from buckling. And the situation was worsening. The first photographs showed the truss sagging to the top of the eighty-second-floor windows; soon it had sunk down to near the bottom of the windows.

Whether the heat was doing similar damage throughout the building, or the sagging truss above impact was now pulling inward like a belt that is notched too tight, distorting the entire structure, other people were reporting buckling floors and ceilings.

In the northeast corner of the ninety-third floor, twenty-five-year-old Gregory Milanowycz, an insurance broker for Aon, had urged others to leave—some of them survived—but went back himself, after hearing the announcement that the building was safe. "Why did I listen to them—I shouldn't have," he moaned after his father, Joseph Milanowycz, called him. Now he was trapped. He asked his father to ask the Fire Department what he and thirty other people should do. His father said he passed word from a dispatcher to his son that they should stay low, and that firefighters were working their way up. Then, he says, he heard his son calling out to the others: "They are coming! My dad's on the phone with them. They are coming. Everyone's got to get to the ground."

But conditions kept worsening, and no one came. The air became almost unbreathable as he spoke with Marcia De Leon, who had been handed the phone by his father while he called the Fire Department.

"This is not good," Gregory Milanowycz said. "This does not look good, Marcia. It really, really doesn't look good."

"Please, please, let me talk," she said.

"Marcia. The ceiling is caving. The ceiling is caving."

They were cut off as she tried to reply. It was 9:56.

Three minutes later, a strange line of dust began to blow out of the east face of the tower around the eightieth floor, as if multiple trusses had fallen and were spilling their ash-laden floors onto the streets. And whether as a direct result of the fallen trusses or through some other mystery of structural failure deep within the building, a single column on the east face of the south tower—about thirty feet north of the south-east corner—seems to have been the first to go. As other columns snapped, one by one, the entire top of the building tipped in that direction and, like a tree leaning toward the notch sawed by a lumberjack, began to fall. The force of the upper stories coming down then crushed the entire tower, ripping it apart as it fell.

When the top of the tower hit the ground, it was moving at an estimated 120 miles an hour.

■ ■ ■

Steve McIntyre could not breathe. He could not see his hands; everything was black. He thought that he was dead. A moment before, he had been helping a woman named Ruth, who had hurt her ankle, walk through the trade center concourse one level beneath the plaza. At some point during his halting, confusing descent after discovering the open stairwell outside his office on the ninety-first floor of the north tower, he had been paired with Ruth by a police officer who was making sure that injured people could evacuate the building. When McIntyre and his charge had finally descended to the bottom of the tower and he looked out the smashed lobby windows, he could see not only the lower facade of the intact south tower but also bits of flaming debris raining down onto the plaza. A cordon of emergency workers, saying, "Move fast, keep moving," waved him down a bank of escalators, which were not working, and onto the concourse between a Banana Republic and a recently emptied Store of Knowledge. He clutched Ruth's purse in one hand and supported her as she limped over broken glass and standing water in her bare feet. "We're fine," McIntyre reassured her again and again. They walked east amid the other fleeing people, turned left between a Gap and the great bank of escalators leading down to the PATH station, then turned right at the spot where Sbarro, Godiva chocolates, and Fine and Shapiro clustered in the northeast corner of the concourse. They turned right again at a Nine West shoe store. The escalator leading up to the street was in front of them. "Ruth, we're fine," McIntyre said once more.

At that instant there was a tremendous rumble, and a wind that felt like a hurricane picked him up off the floor. Everything went black as the south tower, only four hundred feet southwest of the shoe store, collapsed and forced air that was fouled with pulverized concrete and plaster and glass through the concourse and the other basement floors like a giant bellows. When McIntyre landed, his mouth and nose were so clogged that he was suffocating. He knew that his glasses had been blown off his face; he could feel his hands but could see nothing. Something made him spit. His mouth partially cleared, he took a gulp of air. He was not dead—but he still could not see anything. He heard screams and shouts around him in the pitch darkness. Finally he saw the round gleam of a light. "Come to me, come to the light," someone yelled. McIntyre stumbled in that direction, encountered a firefighter, and grabbed his utility belt. Other people were now reaching for the belt or for someone else who had hold of it. The opaqueness of the air lessened to a gray-black, and the clot of people snaked about, seemingly randomly, running into a glass storefront at one point. McIntyre saw sunglasses on display behind the window. The firefighter and another rescue worker began quarreling about which direction to go. Suddenly McIntyre felt a plume of cooler air and he could see again. Somehow, he was not twenty feet from where he had been standing when he heard the rumbling sound, but Ruth was nowhere to be seen.

He ran up the escalator. Out in the murky light, he could see that his forearms were bristling with tiny glass shards. He kept running, toward a street, and realized he was still clutching Ruth's purse. He dropped it in horror. "Where's a hospital?" he yelled at someone, who answered, "That way, that way." He found an ambulance attended by medics with shock on their faces. One of the medics poured a bottle of saline solution over his head. McIntyre knew from the sting that he was hurt.

■ ■ ■

At 10:19, a line of smoke suddenly appeared nearly all the way across the north face of the north tower at the ninety-second floor, as if something inside—perhaps floor trusses again, perhaps something else—had given way and spread fire from the burning floors above. About the same time, new fires broke out on parts of the ninety-third, ninety-fifth, and ninety-sixth floors, suggesting that whatever breakdowns had occurred inside were spreading like a fatal malady to other parts of the structure.

Jill Rosenblum's phone in Rockville Centre rang at 10:23. "Hello?" she said, but heard only silence. "Hello? Hello? Hello?" After about three minutes of talking into the emptiness, she hit star-69, the code for identifying a caller's number.

It was her husband's cell phone.

When the north tower began its collapse at 10:28, sheets of fire spewed from the impact zone as if expelled by a colossal explosion. Some videos of the collapse seem to show that its television antenna began to drop a fraction of a second before the rest of the building. That could mean that something in the steel core gave way first, pulling down the rest of the building with it.

For a few unreal moments after the north tower had plummeted to the ground, a giant spearlike fragment of the facade remained standing, as if defiantly, still looming above the lesser skyscrapers around it. Then the last shard of the tower fell, leaving behind only its arched, cathedral-like base and a narrow trail of smoke to trace its path to the ground.

■ ■ ■

As the twin towers burned that morning, a shaken Guy Tozzoli—after narrowly missing a high-speed collision in one of several attempts to race to the towers—drove home at the speed of a funeral cortège, his phone off, listening to the radio. The policeman had been right. Tozzoli, for the first time in his life, couldn't help anybody at the World Trade Center.

And as the structures weakened and collapsed, someone else watched with thoughts that would have been hard to discern. David Rockefeller stood at the window of his fifty-sixth-floor office in Rockefeller Center, looking south at the smoke billowing over the business district he had done so much to create. He could see the Empire State Building, the old rival to the towers, in the foreground, a little to the east. When Rockefeller was a child, his family lived just a few streets north of where his office is now, and his mother commissioned a painting of the view from his bedroom window. The painting, which still hangs a few feet from where Rockefeller watched as the weakened steel lost its grip, depicts the 1930s New York skyline to the south, a jumble of lower buildings dominated by the Empire State Building to the east. On the west side of the city, there is only the great swath of sky running the length of the island.

There was so much smoke and dust, he did not realize at first that the towers had fallen. When the smoke thinned, he saw again the swath of empty sky in the west, much as it once appeared from his bedroom window. But now even the sky had been invested with a horrible meaning. Lives had been lost. History had been undone.

10

...

Ruins

tillness. No movement, and few sounds. There was only the crack-ling of the fires, the rustle of office paper in the breeze, the distant whine of car alarms, all punctuated by the ominously sporadic voices on the emergency radios. A deputy fire chief named Charles R. Blaich hurried through the thick gray dust and the paper in Battery Park, the towers of the World Financial Center rising between him and what had been the World Trade Center until less than an hour before. He had rushed here from his home on Staten Island with little besides his father's battered white fire hat, which he had grabbed from his basement, and a few men carrying axes, picks, and crowbars. Blaich, who was on medical leave, had watched the south tower fall from the Staten Island Ferry, then worked his way here on foot. The fires gave the air a piercing sour-ness; dust still fell from the sky. He could see no one but his men in this desolate place, which had been sheltered from the hail of steel by the financial center. There were no firefighters, no cops, none of the thou-sands of people who would be out in the sun on a morning like this one.

Finally he ran into a dazed, dust-caked man wearing a surgical mask who was wandering near some abandoned ambulances. The man turned out to be a Fire Department doctor, a lung specialist Blaich happened to know. The medic exchanged a few confused words and walked on. The only other sign of a living thing was the chirping of birds. Blaich did not understand where the birds could be.

He went east, toward the trade center site, passing under a walking bridge that linked two of the World Financial Center towers. The passageway, which opened onto Liberty Street at the southwest corner of the site, framed what Blaich saw, as if he were walking into a horrifying picture. What he should have seen was the shiny, twenty-two-story Marriott World Trade Center Hotel at the corner of Liberty and West Streets, flanked by the south tower. Instead, the hotel was no more than a mangled stump about seventy feet high. A few of the misshapen windows on the lower floors were still visible, rimmed by dirty, jagged fringes of glass. Piled on top of it all like a wild shock of hair was the ruddy steel from the towers that had fallen and crushed the hotel. Rising behind it was the gaunt-looking remnant of the south tower's facade, a swatch of the column-and-spandrel checkerboard perhaps two hundred feet high, with an L-shaped hole blown straight through the southwest corner at about half that height. It took Blaich some time to realize he was looking at all that remained of the tower. Smoke drifted across his field of view, past the empty space where the center of the tower should have been, and through the blown-out windows of the facade. The south tower had not just collapsed. It had apparently disappeared.

In the silence, the stump of the Marriott and the fragment of the south tower facade were about the only things he could see that made any sense at all. West and Liberty Streets had disappeared beneath chaotic mounds of steel and aluminum debris. A few hundred feet north of him, a triplet of hundred-foot-high sections of the facade had dived down from somewhere in the upper reaches of the towers and stuck into the ground like spears, remaining there at crazy angles. And right next to where he was standing, he saw abandoned, dust-fouled Fire Department vehicles, their doors thrown open. The whimsical logo on the side of the department's Rescue 2 emergency rig—RES2CUE, with the oversized 2—was there, just above the height of his father's hat. Like some of the other emergency vehicles around him, it looked a little like a sandwich truck with the equipment boxes in its side opened up. Behind Rescue 2 was a pumper with its headlights flashing. But where were the firefighters? Where were the injured people who should be running about or calling for help? And the question that kept coming back to him: Where were the towers? He had arrived at a five-alarm fire in a complex containing fifty thousand people to find himself alone.

Blaich looked at the little axes and picks his men had brought along and knew they were going to be useless here. He had a bad feeling about where all the people had gone.

But that same morning, hopes were stoked all over the site when the emergency radios crackled to life. "Mayday, Mayday, Mayday!" crackled the faint voice. It was Captain John A. Jonas, a firefighter who had rushed into the north tower along with the rest of his crew from Ladder Company 6 on Canal Street in Chinatown. He was trapped with five other members of his company, an exhausted woman named Josephine Harris they had stopped to help, and nine other firefighters and Port Authority employees. "We are coming for you, brother," came the reply from Battalion Chief William Blaich, Charles's brother, who was also at the site. "We're coming for you." Working the radio, Jonas grew testy when he tried to explain how to locate his position in stairwell B of the north tower—enter the glass doors in the lobby, turn right, look for the first stairwell on the left—and someone asked him where the north tower was. Jonas and his colleagues had no idea what had happened to the building until, three hours after they were trapped, a ray of light shone into the stairwell.

"Guys, I see sunshine," Jonas said. "There is nothing over our heads."

The sixteen people were eventually pulled out alive. With estimates of the number of people in the buildings at collapse ranging as high as twenty thousand, the message for the Blaich brothers and the other rescue workers at the site was blindingly clear: there must be others, many others, still alive inside the debris pile. The rescuers scattered over the pile, peering, shouting, listening.

■ ■ ■

A white police van rolled along West Street, approaching the northern edge of the site, which had rapidly been cordoned off by people in uniforms of every description. Fires had been burning out of control in 4,

5, and 6 World Trade Center—the low buildings in the plaza that remained partly standing in the three corners of the site not occupied by the Marriott Hotel—and in at least two adjacent high-rises that had survived the morning of September 11. Those high-rises were 7 World Trade Center, the forty-seven-story building on the north side of Vesey Street where Mayor Giuliani had put his emergency command bunker, and the vintage twenty-two-story building at 90 West Street, just south of where Blaich and his crew had begun combing the rubble near the abandoned rescue vehicles. Now, in the middle of the afternoon, firefighters thought that these five buildings were in imminent danger of collapsing, just as the twin towers had, and they were barring access to the site there.

The van stopped near the corner of West and Chambers Streets, the place a few blocks north of the site that was already turning into a kind of scrum where people with official credentials were allowed to pass and others were turned away. Some of the people inside the van got out. They included Richard Tomasetti, cochairman of Thornton-Tomasetti Engineers, a New York–based firm that had designed some of the world's most prominent skyscrapers, and Jim Abadie, a civil engineer and senior executive at Bovis Lend Lease, one of the biggest construction management companies in the world. Tomasetti, a Brooklyn native who lived in Greenwich Village and had worked in the construction business since high school, couldn't help being jarred by the sight of the young national guardsmen patrolling his city with their camouflage suits and automatic rifles.

The city, working through an obscure agency called the Department of Design and Construction, had quickly called in these engineers to develop some comprehension of the vast and sinister structure that had just formed in the spot that had already been named ground zero. If anything, that structure was likely to be more complicated—and certainly more mysterious—than the towers that had fallen. No one knew what was supporting the big open areas called voids that searchers were finding inside the rubble as they looked for survivors. No one knew where the intense, acrid fires burning deep underground might destabilize the pile and cause further collapse. No one really knew why a few massive structures, like the looming chunks of facade around the bottoms of the twin towers, were still standing rather than tipping over and falling like rotten trees in a storm.

Before lives could be saved and debris unearthed at ground zero, a partnership would have to be formed that was, in its own way, as ambitious as the army of engineers and officials and architects and laborers who three decades ago had put the towers up. The firefighters and police officers could scamper along the edges of the debris field, searching the few voids that were accessible. They could even climb toward the center of the pile, which shifted unpredictably as the debris settled. But before they could get any kind of fresh rescue equipment close to the site, before they could lift large beams that might be covering underground pockets with survivors, before they could really begin cleaning up the site at all, they were going to have to place their faith in the group of men who had arrived in the police van. They would have to figure out how the steel was all put together now.

By the time Tomasetti, Abadie, and the others arranged for official escorts so that they all could start inspecting the site, 7 World Trade Center had suffered a fiery collapse at 5:21 P.M. An event that in isolation would have shocked the entire city—the crumbling of a forty-seven-story skyscraper—was almost lost in the chaos of the day's events. The landscape that the engineers found at the site went a long way toward explaining how September 11 could swallow up an isolated disaster of that magnitude. Ground zero would not become completely familiar to the engineers after a single inspection, but it would slowly sear itself into their minds as a terrible, smoking, alien world with its own set of dangers and habitable zones and strange physical laws.

The first walking tour through this valley of death began in the northwest corner of the site, where the charred, smoking hulk of 6 World Trade Center, the Custom House, loomed above them, now with nothing there to dwarf it by comparison, as the north tower had. From West Street, it looked as if monstrous bites had been taken out of the top of 6 World Trade Center on its western and northern sides. The reality was even worse: the north tower had spilled some of its steel guts straight through the middle of the building, tearing out a two-hundred-foot oblong crater from the roof all the way down to the basement levels. The building was a precarious shell and, even more alarming, a huge section of the north tower's facade had tipped forward and was now resting against the south side of the hollowed-out structure like the side of a gigantic lean-to. The north tower, like the south, had mostly vanished, leaving behind a mound of debris no higher than about 150 feet above the street. A few heavy, rectangular pillars of steel—probably core columns—protruded out of the mound at wild angles.

Tomasetti stared. He knew he was there, watching his feet as he tried to climb through the debris in the streets without hurting himself. Even so, he could not believe it. He had the weird feeling of observing himself during a preposterous dream. "This didn't really happen," Tomasetti kept saying to himself. "This didn't really happen."

His eyes went to the slumping remains of what had been called the north walking bridge. Tomasetti's firm had designed it—an enclosed pathway above West Street from the World Financial Center to the northwest corner of the trade center. Port Authority engineers had kidded him for making the structural steel members of the bridge so massive. Now it was lying there in a wavy line, the panes of its big square windows all blown out, the entire structure tilted northward like a boat that was about to capsize. The nose of a red-and-white fire truck marked LADDER 3 had been crushed when the bridge fell. An ambulance, its rear door open, looked almost as if it could back up and drive away—except that it, too, had been half-crushed and was moored inextricably amid the debris. Tomasetti and the other engineers walked south, behind the World Financial Center—West Street was impassable, partly because of the fallen bridge—and emerged where Blaich was working at the smashed hotel. Tomasetti was overtaken by the feeling of unreality again. What he saw reminded some perverse part of himself of vacations in the Alps, when he knew that the postcards he sent back would never convey the stunning three-dimensionality of it all. And the heavy veil of dust and smoke in the air nearly erased the rest of the city from his view. Whichever way he looked, an impossible topography of destruction engulfed his senses.

Elsewhere at ground zero, it got only stranger. When the columns in the southeastern corner of the south tower had given way in the impact zone and started the collapse, the top thirty floors of the tower had tilted in that direction as they fell. Parts of the upper floors had fallen directly onto 4 World Trade Center, smashing most of its southern half into the netherworld below the plaza. A huge sheet of the south tower's perimeter remained stuck in the ground there, with upside-down markings indicating that it had fallen from the seventy-seventh floor, just below where the plane had hit. What looked like the top few floors of one corner of 4 World Trade Center had either been sheared off or driven down from above, and now it sat there next to Church Street, slumping sideways like a poorly molded pudding. The northern half of 4 World Trade Center still stood, exposing its charred contents where the building had been chopped in half by the falling debris.

Everywhere, there were isolated exhibits of the supernatural forces involved in this collapse: a car crushed into a three-by-four-foot clump of steel; a steel plate, weighing perhaps fifteen tons, twisted like a Christmas ribbon; a thirty-five-ton box beam bent over like a hairpin. And there were hints that could help explain the mystery of the towers' fate: columns whose fireproofing had been knocked away; connections between columns that were repeatedly torn. One thing that was hardly ever seen was the floor trusses. On the standing columns, only the little angle irons where the bar joists of the trusses had been fastened were visible. Seldom did even a fragment of the floor supports remain in place; they had disappeared, presumably in the compressed debris that had fallen straight down into the basement levels directly beneath each tower. Most of the perimeter columns that had been flung outward in the collapse—and had not only crushed parts of the trade center's plaza buildings but also littered the surrounding streets and the plaza—were similarly unconnected to anything resembling a floor truss.

For now, cataloguing those clues was well down the list of priorities at ground zero. First came looking for survivors and human remains. Only then could crews begin thinking of cleaning up the site and starting on the recovery of a deeply wounded city.

■ ■ ■

"United States Marines. If you can hear us, yell or tap."

It was 8 P.M. and the center of the smoking debris pile, where Sergeant David Karnes and another marine were walking and shouting, was deserted. Karnes, a marine reservist who worked as an accountant at Deloitte & Touche, had left his office in Connecticut in midmorning, picked up his marine corps fatigues, and headed for the site. To help him pass through checkpoints, he had quickly had his hair trimmed into a marine buzz cut and lowered the top on his Porsche so that he would be easily identified. Now, he was picking his way near the spot where the Koenig globe had been in the center of Yamasaki's plaza.

Karnes thought he heard a voice. He told whoever it might be to yell louder, then listened again.

"Over here," the voice said.

It was Will Jimeno, a Port Authority police officer who was pinned where the concourse had been, one level below the plaza, with concrete across his chest and leg and a cinder block on one foot. He was buried along with Sergeant John McLoughlin; they were the only survivors of a party of five Port Authority officers who had been helping tenants evacuate. Karnes decided to avoid the overwhelmed circuits in Manhattan by calling his sister in Pittsburgh, who got word to the New York Police and Fire Departments. Soon, two officers from the Police Department's Emergency Services Unit (ESU) and a paramedic in a blue sweatshirt named Chuck Sereika crawled into the hole and began helping the survivors. It was hard to pass tools back and forth into the hole, so someone grabbed a $20 pair of handcuffs that Jimeno had bought seven years before and used them to dig. Heavier equipment was eventually used as well, from above. There was a great sense of urgency; everyone thought that what remained of 4 World Trade Center, still burning wildly, would collapse as 7 World Trade Center had. The structure hung on, and Jimeno, tied in a basket, was lifted out by 11 P.M., an intravenous tube that Sereika had put in place dangling from his arm. Hundreds of police officers, firefighters, and ESUs who had gathered passed him hand to hand across the rubble. McLoughlin would not be pulled free until dawn, after a fresh team of rescuers had arrived to take over the job.

▪ ▪ ▪

Derek Trelstad listened to the wheeze of his double-snouted respirator. Between breaths, he could hear the drone of diesel engines, the *beep-beep-beep* of heavy equipment backing up, and the strangely muffled crash of steel dropping onto flatbed trucks just outside the building he found himself in. Somewhere, there was an incessant dripping from the abandoned fire hoses snaking up the dark stairwell that he and two other structural engineers from Richard Tomasetti's office were trying to climb. It was the afternoon of Thursday, September 13. This building he was in, the twenty-three-story skyscraper at 90 West Street, had burned out of control for more than a day and a half.

Ninety West Street stood just across the street from where Charles

Blaich was toiling with a team of firefighters to search the still-standing lower floors of the Marriott Hotel for any possible survivors. Blaich and the other fire chiefs had tried to put out the fire at 90 West Street. But without a decent supply of water, or a way to get trucks up close, they could do little for most of the past two days but spray at 90 West from the ground outside or a building next door. The fires had started when forty-ton javelins of steel falling from the World Trade Center towers ripped out heavy girders inside 90 West and smashed sections of the foot-thick terra-cotta on the building's north facade like so much window glass. Saint Nicholas Greek Orthodox Church, which had huddled just between 90 West and the south tower, was gone in the same rain of steel, smashed flat as if it had never existed. If Blaich looked up from his work, he could still see a twisted-up, three-story section of reddish perimeter columns leaning against the older building's fire-blackened stone facade.

Trelstad and the other engineers now wearily ventured into 90 West for what might almost be seen as a suicide mission: to see whether the building was close to collapse. The building, Trelstad knew, was almost a century old. Now it had the feel of a huge and terribly grim haunted house, with the hallways and offices filled with a black haze of dust and smoke. That day, at the request of the city, Tomasetti had scattered engineers throughout the damaged buildings around the site to find out how dangerous they were.

If any of them fell without warning, the structures would not only kill anyone inside but also cause catastrophe among the crews swarming around the perimeter of ground zero. The work of the rescue crews was repeatedly interrupted as panic spread with rumors that another building would collapse, and everyone would evacuate the site until it was declared safe again. In some ways, the surrounding structures were more frightening than the debris pile, because although many had been heavily damaged, they still stood many stories above the site—and the crews. To the east, on Church Street, windows were blown out of the grime-caked, steel-and-glass high-rise at 1 Liberty Plaza, and the repetitive, horizontal structural elements encircling the facade at every floor looked cockeyed to some observers, as if this fifty-four-story building were slumping. Nearby, the big letters above the Millenium Hilton Hotel's blasted ground-floor entrance on Church Street now read: HE MI   LENIUM H   TON.

On the northern edge of the site, the collapse of 7 World Trade Center caused grievous damage to at least two other huge structures: it blew out a hole nearly eight stories high in one side of the old New York Telephone Company Building, now called the Verizon Building, and sheared off most of one corner of a fifteen-story building with a layer-cake design owned by the City University of New York.

And if all of that evidence of damage around the smoking core of ground zero were not enough, the collapse of the north tower had hurled a pair of steel columns with unimaginable force westward toward Battery Park City, where they had lodged in the southeast corner of the twentieth floor of the American Express Building. Next door to 90 West Street was the boxlike Deutsche Bank Building, where falling steel from the south tower had torn a ghastly twenty-four-story gash down the front, and some of the steel—red-tinted panels of the perimeter columns from the World Trade Center—hung like gigantic daggers from the damaged area.

So Tomasetti's engineers went into all of these buildings. Flashlights in hand, Trelstad and his partners climbed over debris choking the narrow, claustrophobic lobby and searched for a stairwell at 90 West Street. Two people had died in the building, and body parts had been hurled from the south tower onto some scaffolding that had stood around the outside of the building, including a hand with a woman's wedding ring still on a finger and the fingernails painted a bright red. When Trelstad and his companions found the stairwell, they shined their flashlights up into the darkness and tried not to think about what had happened here.

From the start of the survey, there were reassuring signs. The building, shaped like an irregular U with a small courtyard in the back, had a heavy, riveted, traditional steel-cage structure, each column separated from the next by no more than sixteen feet. Deep steel girders supported the floors, which were made not of a thin layer of concrete but of foot-thick terra-cotta blocks, much like the heat-insulating lining of a blast furnace. Four to six inches of tile fireproofing surrounded the columns. Trelstad knew that the architect Cass Gilbert had put up the building with its graceful Gothic facade sometime before 1910, just before his more famous Woolworth Building. Gilbert hadn't skimped on fire protection. Although the modern drop ceilings had been annihilated by the fires and the blasts from the firefighters' hoses, Trelstad could see the wires that had held the ceiling tiles still hanging down from the sooty terra-cotta blocks of the floor above him. The blocks seemed intact.

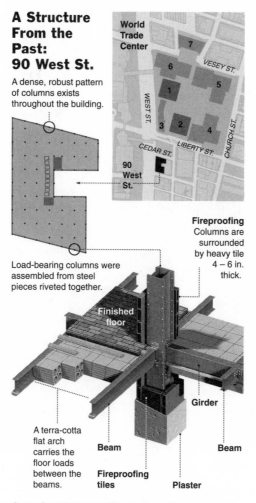

A Structure From the Past: 90 West St.

A dense, robust pattern of columns exists throughout the building.

World Trade Center

VESEY ST.

WEST ST.

CEDAR ST.

LIBERTY ST.

CHURCH ST.

90 West St.

Load-bearing columns were assembled from steel pieces riveted together.

Fireproofing Columns are surrounded by heavy tile 4 – 6 in. thick.

Finished floor

Girder

A terra-cotta flat arch carries the floor loads between the beams.

Beam

Fireproofing tiles

Beam

Plaster

Source: Derek Trelstad, LZA/Thornton-Tomasetti

The New York Times; illustration by Mika Gröndahl

The signs of ultra-intense heat—the kind that had not only brought down 7 World Trade Center but also collapsed portions of 5 World Trade Center, both more modern structures with lighter steel and spray-on fireproofing rather than tile and terra-cotta—were everywhere at 90 West Street. A mangled heating duct ran from ceiling to floor in a hallucinatory cascade of heat-deformed sheet metal. Another lay on the floor, folded over as neatly as a pillowcase. An elevator door was pitted and had been warped into a shape like a tortilla chip. On the third floor, the finishes on the walls and the fabric of the cubicles had vanished, as if incinerated by an atomic flash, leaving behind only skeletal metal supports and hollow electrical outlets.

Still, there were other curious indications that the fires, as violent as they were, had been contained. In contrast to the wide-open, column-free spaces of the newer buildings, the floors of this one were rife with interior walls and partitions. Those barriers, Trelstad observed, largely stopped the spread of the fires from the north side of the building, where they had started, to the south side. A plastic EXIT sign above a door in the south half of the fourth floor had gotten so hot that it now hung down in clear molten strands, with red streaks where the letters had been. Yet the office itself, though filthy, was unburned and intact.

In inspecting the structural integrity of the building, Trelstad and his colleagues confirmed that on the north facade a whole series of steel spandrels, or crossbeams between windows, had been torn out by the same flaming debris that had set the fires, creating at least one horrible slice from the eleventh floor down to the third floor. But even there, the thick stone of the facade and the heavy steel had helped to ward off the blow, and the structural damage had not spread far into the building. And try as they might, the engineers could find few places where the fireproofing had allowed the inferno to weaken or buckle the steel and do any structural damage on its own.

The engineers were beginning to realize that the landmark they were exploring—so old that its top floor, the twenty-third, had once held a restaurant that billed itself as the highest in the city—had battled the fires and the seemingly apocalyptic hail of steel debris and won. Like the Empire State Building, 90 West was built to last.

Even as Trelstad was coming to the conclusion that 90 West was safe, another group of Tomasetti's engineers was exploring 1 Liberty Plaza, the fifty-four-story skyscraper on Church Street. This tower had not caught fire, and other than broken windows, there was no obvious sign on the exterior that it had been struck by large falling steel objects. But nerves remained taut around the building, and the engineers were searching everywhere inside it for potential structural problems. Gary Mancini and another engineer from the inspection squad were taking a rest on the third or fourth floor after having climbed all the way to the top and worked their way down. Two more engineers were still inspecting areas above them. As he sat there, Mancini heard footsteps below, the sound of people racing up the stairwell. In a moment, two very agitated emergency workers in blue windbreakers appeared below him.

"This building is unstable," one of them said, gasping for breath. In the flurry of explanation that followed, Mancini most clearly heard the words "in danger of collapsing immediately."

Mancini felt a sudden rush of adrenaline.

"Is there anyone else in the building?" one of the rescue workers asked.

"Yeah," Mancini said. "There's two other people above us."

His heart pounding wildly, Mancini ran up several flights, found his colleagues, and returned to the people in the blue windbreakers. "Just run," he heard, and everyone did, tearing down the stairwell. Part of his mind—the faint, overwhelmed rational part—was profoundly confused. They had turned up no obvious structural damage in this building. There seemed to be mainly light debris and blown-out windows. But he ran. And he ran.

When Mancini burst out of the lobby of 1 Liberty Plaza, he saw a group of city officials standing out on Church Street and looking up at the building with deep concern. Around the site, workers and rescue crews had already scattered. As he ran toward the officials, his cell phone rang. It was his wife, Patrice, so he answered.

"Where are you?" she said immediately.

"I'm on Church Street right now," said Mancini, who had been deliberately vague about his job at ground zero to keep his family from worrying too much. But she had reached him while he was high in the building, and he had mentioned his location then.

"Are you still in that building 1 Liberty?" his wife asked. "The TV just reported that the building has collapsed."

"I'm standing literally fifty feet from the building," he said.

"Get out of that area!" she pleaded.

"I was in the building," he said, his rational powers returning after his panicked flight. "There's nothing wrong with that building. Believe me, it's as safe as can be."

He asked the group of city officials what the problem was. "See the top, how it's leaning out," one of them said, pointing up at 1 Liberty Plaza. "We think it's unstable." Mancini knew immediately that the building's repetitive horizontal stripes—which created the weird optical illusion that some were spaced farther apart than others, conveying a wavy appearance—were the cause. Straining not to be too condescending, he told them that they had raised a false alarm. The officials had concluded that one of the most stable and least damaged buildings on the site was about to collapse.

Everyone returned to the site.

Trelstad had been forced to make a panicky evacuation of 90 West Street at the same time Mancini was rushing down the stairwell at 1 Liberty Plaza. But it would turn out that none of the major buildings around the site that had not already collapsed was in serious danger of falling. Most of them, like 90 West, were older and "overbuilt" by modern standards, with an ability to withstand loads or fires or both that were, in some ways, far in excess of their younger cousins. By the time all the confusion at the site was sorted out, it was too late for Trelstad and his colleagues to accomplish much more within the fire-blackened interior of the building on that day. The next morning, a small fire broke out on one of the floors again, the flames licking above the walls of the cubicles in a dark corner of the building. Trelstad walked outside, onto the pile, and found a deputy fire chief who sent a team of firefighters to put out the blaze.

■ ■ ■

"If you try to interfere, I will have you taken out of here in handcuffs," shouted John Norman, the Fire Department battalion chief who was leading the search-and-rescue effort.

At the moment, working to the north of Charles Blaich, the usually soft-spoken Norman was trying to clear Tomasetti's massive walking bridge from West Street. Only then could crews roll in with the waiting armada of heavy equipment needed to clear huge steel beams away from the debris pile so that rescuers could search inaccessible spots around the site. Faced with that crucial task, Norman had lost patience with the thousands of rescuers who were alternately standing around—most of them with little to do at the moment—and pressing forward to search for victims under the bridge itself. As the smashed fire trucks and ambulances under the bridge suggested, firefighters and others had sought shelter beneath the bridge before it had collapsed. Norman—who had assumed his present job after his boss was killed—asked politely at first, telling everyone not involved in cutting up the bridge to stand back and wait for the job to be completed; then he vented his frustration at one group of rescue personnel who repeatedly ignored orders to stay clear. In the end, he had to post a firefighter and a cop to stand guard.

There was another reason for Norman's dark mood: the task of clearing the bridge had not been going well. "Get us through that bridge," Fire Commissioner Thomas Von Essen had told Norman on September 11. The obstruction, Norman promised the Fire Department chiefs, would be gone in eighteen hours. A giant backhoe with scissorslike attachments was called in to slice up the bridge, but it succeeded in doing little but scrape the structure. The ironworkers on the job were forced to call in high-temperature "burning bars"—metal-and-oxygen-fed flames that burned at temperatures of up to ten thousand degrees, like the devices Charlie Maikish, the Port Authority engineer, had used to cut through the Hudson Tubes, only a few feet from the same spot, during the trade center's construction. But the job dragged on for days.

Finally, on Sunday, September 16, the burning bars had cleared the bridge and West Street was opened for heavy equipment traffic. By then every void in the debris pile that was accessible by foot, even in places so hot that they melted the rubber on the firefighters' boots, had been checked for survivors. Now the cranes could be brought in to remove heavy pieces and open up the remaining voids. "If there's anybody alive, those staircases are where they're going to be," Norman kept telling Bob Stewart, a consultant working as the supervisor of on-site construction labor for AMEC, one of the four big construction companies that had divided the site into sectors to make the job more manageable. Stairwell B in the north tower had yielded those sixteen survivors. There must be more, Norman thought. There had to be.

The big equipment was ready. From a construction site in Maryland, police had escorted a caravan of more than twenty-five trucks that carried 950,000 pounds of pieces to be assembled into a single crane known as the Liebherr LR 1550. From a nuclear power plant in Ohio, fifty trucks carted in a 2-million-pound crane, the Manitowoc 21000, one of only seven in the world, with a base the size of a basketball court. The Manitowoc 21000 could, in a single lift, pick up a thousand tons.

As soon as the pedestrian bridge had been cleared, Stewart was ready to move the cranes up close to the edge of the site. The idea was to lift large steel columns that might be blocking the escape routes for people who had been trapped underground for nearly a week. Already, any survivors might have died from lack of food or water. The only hope now was to press ahead, and the closer the crane was to the site, the more weight it could lift.

But when the heavy equipment started moving more freely around the site, Stewart and the other workers discovered that the job was going to be far more complicated than they had imagined. One day in the first week, a huge crane began rolling toward the pile around the corner of Liberty and West Streets.

"Stop!" shouted a bulldog-stocky man with some old Port Authority security passes dangling around his neck. "You can't do that!"

It was George Tamaro, who had overseen construction of the underground bathtub wall with Arturo Ressi di Cervia in 1967 and 1968. Tamaro, who had been called in by Richard Tomasetti after the walking tour on September 11, realized that the crews were not just ignorant about the existence of the underground bathtub wall, which could collapse under the weight of the equipment; many did not know there was a giant, six-story basement underneath them at all. "This deck can't carry the load," Tamaro explained. "You're liable to lose the crane."

The bathtub wall, made of concrete strengthened with the cages of steel reinforcing bars, still ran for a distance of 3,294 feet around the site, averaging about 70 feet in height from the bedrock to the level of the Lower Manhattan streets. Even after the attacks, the wall seemed to be doing its job: sealing the vast basement from an inundation of groundwater fed by the Hudson River. But when it was first built, the wall had been secured with hundreds of steel cables—the tiebacks—that had been drilled down through the soft soil and then grouted into thirty-five feet's worth of bedrock. These cables had been cut once the basement floors of the twin towers were in place; the basement walls were then deemed robust enough to keep the bathtub in place without the tiebacks. Besides, the steel would have corroded anyway in the brackish tidal water that permeated the soil. No one, of course, had ever imagined that the towers and much of their basement substructure would cease to exist. Now, the wall was being supported by whatever basement floors remained intact and by the compressed debris itself. A wrong move could cause the wall to cave in. If the bathtub barrier was breached, it could create a rushing conduit of water into the basement of the site and possibly through the underground PATH network as far north as Thirty-fourth Street.

The Cranes at Ground Zero

Ground zero was divided into quadrants, each assigned to a cleanup contractor. Cranes were set up very close to the bathtub.

Construction companies' zones

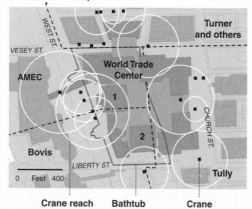

Crane reach   Bathtub   Crane

New York City Office of Emergency Management

Sources: LZA/Thornton-Tomasetti; Liebherr Nenzing Crane Co.; Caterpillar Inc.; the contractors

Sarah Slobin/The New York Times

Stewart made it clear that he had no patience with what he regarded as theoretical advice from clipboard-carrying engineers. He was a proud and stubborn man whose family had its own rich history. His grandmother, Elinore Pruitt Stewart, had been one of the most famous women on the western frontier. Born in poverty and orphaned at age eighteen, she moved to the wilds of Wyoming with her two-year-old daughter and recounted her adventures in *Letters of a Woman Homesteader*. Her son, Stewart's father, had left behind the Wyoming farmland to pursue a career in construction, helping build such mammoth projects as the

Grand Coulee Dam and the Pentagon. Bob Stewart himself had already spent thirty-five years building skyscrapers in New York City before he arrived at ground zero.

Excessive caution and delay, Stewart decided, simply were not options worth considering. The Liebherr LR 1550 had just arrived from Maryland and his crews immediately began to assemble its dozens of pieces. If the crane had to sit on top of the bathtub wall, he thought, so be it.

But in short order, Tomasetti and two of his engineers, Gary Panariello and John Abruzzo, came up with a brilliant engineering solution that would let the crane hover directly over the debris pile without compromising the underground wall. They decided to do what sounded like the impossible: balance half of the crane's 950,000 pounds directly on top of the bathtub wall, which could sustain the weight as long as it did not tip an inch one way or the other. To support the second half of the weight, the engineers proposed constructing a makeshift bridge that could hold up the back end of the crane, with the weight resting on the ground a safe distance from the bathtub wall. The bridge would also stabilize the crane and make sure the wall received only forces that went straight down. Stewart suggested they speed up the process by building this bridge out of the steel columns that littered the site.

Even though the bridge was in part his contraption, Panariello remained uneasy. Though the bridge would speed the recovery effort, this was not the way an engineer liked to work. There was no testing. No time for second thoughts. And the lives of the crane operator, the firefighters, and other contractors working nearby would be at risk along with the integrity of the bathtub wall. As Stewart's crane slowly crawled up the makeshift bridge and onto the top of the slurry wall, Panariello felt he had no choice but to stand right there on top of the recycled steel pieces—core columns from the north tower—that were now holding this giant up. "If it flips," he said, "I'm going with it."

With Panariello standing there in a bit of a grandstand play, the bridge held.

A second flash of brilliance by Tomasetti's partners allowed the crews on the east side of the site to bring a crane onto the World Trade Center plaza itself. A thirty-four-foot-long and fourteen-foot-tall black granite sculpture by Masayuki Nagare was scarred but still intact on the plaza, between the remains of 4 and 5 World Trade Center. "That sculpture weighs as much as the crane does," Panariello said. "There's got to be something underneath." And sure enough, the World Trade Center plans showed that the plaza in this spot had extra steel supports. The jackhammers were out there before the end of the first week, smashing the sculpture to bits so its pedestal could hold up another crane.

Norman appreciated this ingenuity. A little more than a week and a half after the attacks, the first of the big cranes were in place. They hoisted ironworkers and firefighters in "man baskets" so they could reach otherwise inaccessible spots, and pulled steel away from spots where maps said the stairwells should be. But time was running out. Back at Fire Department headquarters, one of the officers had done some research to find out the longest period that anyone trapped underground had ever survived. In Italy, Norman was told, a group of infants at a nursery were found alive fourteen or fifteen days after an earthquake.

Norman knew the truth. It was already too late. Only a few days after the attack, he had gone up on top of the pile. When he paused to look around, he had noticed something dripping over the plastic faceplate of his helmet. Condensation, he figured. But as it dripped down he noticed it was not water at all. It was a thick black sticky substance, almost like nicotine. Whatever the substance was, it was coming up from deep below, where he knew the atmosphere had been too poisoned for anyone to live long, even after surviving the collapse.

The cranes confirmed his fears. In just over two weeks after the attack, more than four thousand body parts had been collected from ground zero. But in total, only twenty-one people had been found alive, sixteen of them from that one surviving stairwell. The last rescue had come just twenty-six hours after the collapse, when Genelle Guzman, a Port Authority employee who had worked on the sixty-fourth floor of the north tower, was found.

The time had come. Norman and Frank P. Cruthers, the World Trade Center incident commander, met in an old firehouse not far from the site seventeen days after the attack. "We've done everything physically possible," Norman said. "And everything points to the fact that there is not one chance left that there's anybody still alive." The word would be given to Mayor Giuliani that evening. The rescue operation was over. The recovery operation would start.

• • •

George Tamaro had helped avert catastrophe by keeping the big cranes from collapsing the bathtub wall. But he had not come close to solving a much more fundamental problem: If the wall was now being held up by compressed debris and partly smashed floors in the World Trade Center basement, then how could the construction crews clean up the site without bringing down the wall?

Although Tamaro had been elected to the National Academy of Engineering and had worked on structural foundations from Berlin to Washington, D.C., to the World Financial Center, little had changed about the urgency and resourcefulness of his style since the 1960s. He decided that only an elaborate program to observe, map, and document the conditions underground—beneath the smoking debris itself—could form the basis for a plan to preserve the bathtub wall and let the cleanup go forward without creating any new disasters. And the bathtub was not the only reason for mapping those subterranean realms. If firefighters and construction crews did not know where dangerous voids and unstable areas existed, they could plunge right through and be killed, but if they had photos and drawings of the underground world, the information could help their work. That kind of information, in fact, was becoming more and more crucial as the recovery wore on. The World Trade Center cleanup had turned into the biggest game of pickup sticks ever played. Pull a shaft of steel out of one place in the pile and it could cause another to shift, precipitating an avalanche. Pick away at debris that appeared solid but actually had a void lurking beneath, and men and equipment could suddenly plunge inside. The only way to know which sticks to pick up first was to start mapping the pile from below.

Someone was going to have to go down there.

Such a thing was possible. The World Trade Center's basement levels had not been completely annihilated. It was a dark region where obliterated shops and concourses and trains and car-strewn parking lots lay side by side with zones that seemed untouched, save for a little dust on the pay phones.

Two weeks after the attack, a man who might have been a giant stalking forbidden realms of the dead was picking his way around the jagged northern edge of the two hundred-foot-wide crater in the middle of 6 World Trade Center. He was Pablo V. Lopez, a six-foot-four, three-hundred-pound engineer who worked at Tamaro's firm, Mueser Rutledge. Lopez and his colleague Andrew Pontecorvo had been chosen to serve as Tamaro's eyes and ears underground. Lopez and Pontecorvo were three levels below what had been the trade center's plaza, but light filtered in through the ragged tapestry of steel beams and pipes and ductwork and crooked concrete slabs dangling from intact floors at the edges of the crater. The area he was walking in, a level the engineers called B2, had been a parking garage; around the lip of the crater, half-burned cars teetered at crazy angles, like fishing boats caught in some horrible whirlpool at sea.

Lopez and Pontecorvo first walked east, along a kind of ledge between the crater and the north slurry wall parallel to Vesey Street, then followed the rim of the crater around to the south. Now they were walking directly toward what had been the north tower. After a few minutes, their flashlights illuminated a solid, rocklike mass where the basement levels of the tower had been. At first, as the flashlights played over the rocky surface behind the columns, the mind simply could not interpret what the eyes saw: the recognizable traces of twenty floors, very much like geologic strata revealed by a road cut, compressed into a ten-foot vertical span. In one place, the steel decks of half a dozen floors protruded like tattered wallpaper, so close together that they were almost touching where they were bent downward at the edge. Nothing between the decks was recognizable except as a rocky, rusty mishmash. In a few places what might have been carbonized, compressed stacks of paper stuck out edgewise like graphite deposits. They could not be removed.

Lopez and Pontecorvo had found where the vanished floors had gone. They had not just fallen straight down. The forces had been so great and the floors so light that they had simply folded up like deflated balloons.

But even that was not what Dennis O'Connor, an Emergency Services Unit cop, had brought them there to see. The immense columns, at least two feet across, made of steel plate four inches thick, had suffered what looked like a compound fracture: the upper sections looked as if they had been kicked, with incalculable fury, about a foot south of the sections they were resting on.

"Wow, man," said Lopez. "Look at the size of those sections. Can you imagine the force?"

These were the mighty columns that had rolled out of Atlas Machine & Iron Works on flatbed cars. It did not escape either Lopez or Pontecorvo that

Mapping the World Trade Center's Damaged Basement

The maps below represent engineer surveys of the World Trade Center basement levels through Nov. 27, 2001.

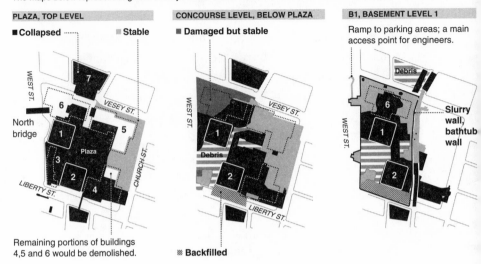

PLAZA, TOP LEVEL

■ Collapsed ······· ▨ Stable

North bridge

Remaining portions of buildings 4,5 and 6 would be demolished.

CONCOURSE LEVEL, BELOW PLAZA

■ Damaged but stable

▨ Backfilled

B1, BASEMENT LEVEL 1

Ramp to parking areas; a main access point for engineers.

Slurry wall, bathtub wall

Source: Mueser Rutledge Consulting Engineers

the broken columns, resting so precariously on their edges, not only rose up through the rest of the basement but also supported as much as one hundred feet of the north tower's facade that was leaning—at an angle very much like the one in front of them—against the mangled remnants of 6 World Trade Center.

Lopez and Pontecorvo started piecing together a three-dimensional map of what had once been so mundane and familiar—the World Trade Center's basement—and now had become a steaming, treacherous, alien place beneath the rubble. Often during their "penetrations," one of them would set up in some spot with a map of what the area had been before 9/11, and the other would walk into the darkness with a flashlight, counting structural columns to pinpoint the location and shouting descriptions of what he observed. The most generic notations were "collapsed," "stable," and the like, but the men made dozens of specific observations on localized danger spots: "roof penetrations observed," "local beam damage," "structure intact," "stair filled with debris." Pontecorvo noted a weird and worrisome crack, much like a seismic fault line, running along the B3 level's concrete floor for about seventy feet from the north slurry wall to the 6 World Trade Center crater.

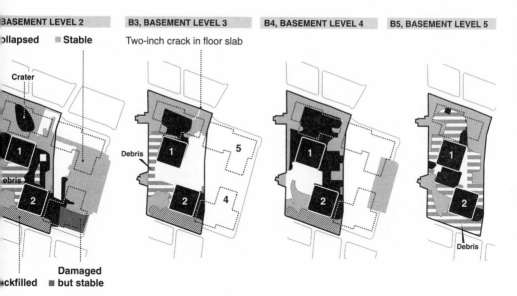

The New York Times

The engineers went back to the concourse where Steve McIntyre had been lifted in the air after the collapse of the south tower and charted the boundary between zones of destruction and survival. To the west of that line—Ben & Jerry's, Radio Shack, The Gap, Bath & Body Works, Banana Republic, Golden Nugget, Crabtree & Evelyn—everything was collapsed. To its east—Sbarro, Nine West, Warner Bros., Casual Corner, The Body Shop, Sunglass Hut, Borders Books—nearly everything was intact.

Lopez and Pontecorvo also mapped a rubble-filled canyon along the edge of Liberty Street, just inside the bathtub wall. The top of the south tower had tipped southeastward to begin its collapse, and some of its heavier core columns had blasted out this canyon on the south side of this tower, where most of the concrete floors below the street level had collapsed. The result was a giant underground void along Liberty where the bathtub wall had no support at all. This was the finding that was most worrisome to Tamaro.

Deeper in the basement, the topography was both more horrifying and more complex. On Sunday, September 30, Lopez and Pontecorvo went all the way to the bottom, walking down a set of concrete stairs inside the "north projection," the westward pucker of the slurry wall where the northern PATH tube entered the bathtub. At the bottom, on the basement level designated B6, the engineers and their police escorts found the train tracks that ran in a wide loop around the inner edge of the wall, to the PATH station on the eastern boundary of the bathtub, and then the other tube at the south projection. They walked along the tracks, splashing through murky standing water. The water got deeper the farther east they went, so they took to walking on the cover above the third rail. Moving in separate teams, Lopez and Pontecorvo climbed onto a steel platform that they encountered, saw deep water ahead, and waited for their escorts, including O'Connor, to set up the gear they had brought along for this penetration.

The police escorts, wearing chest-high waders, inflated gray rubber rafts with their emergency air tanks, then got in the water and physically pushed the rafts along after the engineers had gotten in. They continued until the train station came in range of their flashlights.

An empty PATH train was sitting at the station, as if it had just pulled in. The police escorts pushed the rafts up to the concrete platform next to the train and everyone got out. With the presence of the abandoned train, Lopez felt his apprehensions rise, wondering what he might see there. But spray-painted markings on the train indicated that the area had already been searched by a team called Florida Task Force No. 1 and that no bodies had been found. He relaxed. The platform was in good shape, with all the advertisements and signs still in place. "See what's NEW in local NEWS," one ad said. A prosaic sign inside one of the cars, which contained no personal effects whatever, said: CONDUCTOR OPERATOR POSITION PLEASE STAND CLEAR.

Lopez walked south along the platform, toward where the south tower had risen directly above the tracks. He passed four intact train cars. Then he reached a spot where half a train car emerged from the nothingness between the tracks and a collapsed slab of ceiling, angling downward among the sodden chaos of fallen steel and smashed walls. On their map, he and Pontecorvo wrote, "Floor slabs above collapsed, no access," and the more alarming "Daylight observed" and turned back. They walked past signs of interrupted normality and a hasty evacuation. A few feet from the collapsed slab, an unopened eight-ounce can of Arizona Iced Tea sat upright on a bench at the center of the platform. Nearby, covered in a film of fine white dust, lay two newspapers dated September 11 that looked as if they had just been set down by commuters. The *Daily News*

carried a front-page headline for a crime story: "COPS BAG PANTHER."
A copy of the *New York Times* was open to the op-ed page. In the upper-right-hand corner was a column by Thomas L. Friedman. It was eerily titled "Walls."

Lopez and Pontecorvo decided to climb the debris-strewn escalator and inspect the floor above. Metal strips that had fallen from somewhere on the ceiling made a tremendous clatter as they forced their way up. At the top was the semicircle of turnstiles that the train riders passed through every day. The engineers played their flashlights across the floor.

They were standing in front of the Commuters Café. It looked dusty but completely intact. A few feet to one side, the floor ended abruptly, as if something lurking in the pitch blackness had bitten it off, but the liquor bottles still sat in neat rows on the shelves and glasses still hung upside down from a rack over the bar. A couple of half-finished drinks and ashtrays with cigarette butts in them sat next to chairs that were turned just so, as if invisible patrons—call them ghosts—were still laughing and talking and paying their tabs before rushing off to catch trains in the darkness.

■ ■ ■

Not everyone at ground zero was so wrapped up in the mysteries lurking beneath the debris piles. Nine days after the attacks, Rusty Griffin sat on an overturned five-gallon bucket near the curb along West Street. With a pair of binoculars, he ran his eyes over the standing piece of the south tower's facade, the piece that Charles Blaich had tried so hard to figure out in the momentary silence of September 11. By now, this piece of the facade, wrapped around the southwest corner, had become famous, the most recognized symbol of the attacks. As macabre as the setting was, the austere Gothic arches that Yamasaki had put at the base, now freed from the overpowering tower that had risen above them, were finally conveying breathtaking emotion and capturing the attention of the world. But Rusty Griffin was not here in New York to admire the tenacity of this 240-foot-tall remnant of Yamasaki's dream. His job was to destroy what was left of it, in a way that was fast, safe, and cheap. The name of his family's North Carolina–based company was D. H. Griffin Wrecking.

Griffin had never before set foot in Manhattan. But he and his cousin,

David Griffin Jr., were here to offer their services. "I'm a demolition guy," Dave explained to some ironworkers he met after sneaking onto the site without an invitation shortly after the disaster. They had come at the right time. "Getting it down to grade" is what the engineers and contractors called the next set of tasks at the site: a demolition job. The bulk of what once was the World Trade Center now was compressed into the six underground levels. But before the crews could start to dig down into this hellish place, the contractors would have to take down these few pieces of the twin towers that had not collapsed on their own, and clear what was still standing of the Marriott and the three other plaza buildings. Many of these upright shards of buildings were so precarious that work could not even proceed anywhere near them. As Griffin watched the towering piece of facade, the wind made it shudder back and forth. If it toppled, it would crush anything below. The critical question was how best to bring these pieces down in a controlled fashion so the journey into the pit could begin.

The tool of choice for the Griffins was explosive charges. The charges could be placed at critical columns and topple any structure in seconds. Abadie liked that approach at first: it would have accelerated the job. Given the calamity that had occurred at the trade center, though, city officials ruled this option out. So Rusty turned his attention to the facade. He had no degree in structural engineering. But he had an instinct for finding a structure's weak points. With his binoculars, he had picked out the exact spots along the top where bolts connecting the three-column panels together had popped out. By nightfall, Rusty and Dave had come up with a startlingly simple method of getting the unstable parts of the facade down: yank them. The plan was to get three backhoes and three long cables; after strapping them up to the facade at the spots where Rusty had identified weak points, they would work the backhoes like a tractor pull, swinging the steel back and forth until it snapped. "You get a building moving and it's gone," Dave said.

To Bob Stewart, working in the AMEC sector to the north, where huge pieces of the other tower's facade were still standing, the Griffin plan was not only simple, it was stupid. Stewart thought the steel in the lower part of the towers was far too thick to be yanked over. "It will never work," Stewart declared. The approach he wanted to take would never have occurred to a low-budget demolition crew. Stewart wanted to build a new steel bridge right over the debris pile, so that a crane could just drive right out and grab the standing pieces of the north tower, one giant chunk at a time. To be sure, Stewart faced a much more daunting demolition task than the Griffins did. Although the northeast corner of his tower stood there, mirroring the Griffins'—and creating what sometimes looked like an eerie conversation on mortality across the devastated site—that was not all Stewart had to deal with. The fractured steel columns that Lopez and Pontecorvo had seen in the basement were the same ones that had fallen forward from the north face of the tower and now rested against 6 World Trade Center. Just one of these ninety-five-foot-tall sections weighed more than one hundred tons, each section looking like a giant, three-pronged tuning fork. And there were eighteen of them, meaning that all together, about two thousand tons' worth of steel had to be removed, without destabilizing the building they were leaning against.

Choosing between the two demolition strategies fell to the Department of Design and Construction, the city agency overseeing the cleanup. Michael J. Burton, the deputy commissioner, looked over both of the plans. Burton, who had become the effective czar for the cleanup job, had made it clear that he cared very little about engineering subtleties like the question of why the towers first stood, then collapsed on September 11. "We know why they fell," he said. "Because they flew two planes into the towers." But he was deeply immersed in the details of hauling steel out of the debris pile. Burton decided there were so many unknowns involved in bringing down the facades that he would let both men try out their idea. Stewart would move forward with his plans at the north tower, and the Griffins with theirs at the south.

The Griffins got started first. Hundreds of recovery workers and contractors were cleared from a large swath of the World Trade Center site shortly after 5 P.M. on Tuesday, September 25. Rusty had already gone up in a basket to mark the spot where the cables should be strapped. The stepwise connections that John Skilling and Les Robertson had chosen for the column panels—so that there would not be a long line of connections at any one floor—gave the facade that much more resiliency. The cables would have to go at varying heights, at a carefully calculated angle determined by the spots where one of the bolts had failed or the steel was now misaligned or rotated. With a can of orange fluorescent spray paint, he and an ironworker scrawled USA at the location where Rusty had decided the top cable must go.

Three giant backhoes, with attachments on them that looked like pinchers, were standing with their engines idling, ready to make the pull. The trick would be to somehow make these 150,000-pound machines pull in unison. Rusty stood alongside one of the backhoes, while Dave stepped back farther, with a radio, to survey the whole scene. Hundreds of people lined up two blocks away on Broadway to witness the act. Then the cousins from North Carolina began to sweat. Bob Stewart, it turned out, knew what he was talking about. First, the grappler operators could not get the rhythm right. One of them—always the same one—was constantly pulling just as the other two were letting the cable swing back, like someone in a chorus line whose kick was always a beat late. After half an hour of frustration, Rusty told the operator to stand down. They would try it with two, not three.

With the engines on the grapplers whining as they yanked with all their might, the steel began to swing back and forth, groaning with the strain. Then, suddenly, the upper section of the standing piece of the south tower twisted one last time and gave way. A seven-story chunk had snapped free, landing on Liberty Street with an enormous, earthshaking thud. Although it would be weeks before the remaining sections would be entirely cut down, the facade's reign as a dark symbol of the attacks was nearing an end. The slow pace of the takedown, including numerous near catastrophes like steel plummeting unexpectedly or broken cables whipping with lethal force through the air, was proof enough for some of their critics that the Griffins were just sweet-talking out-of-towners who had landed an assignment they never deserved. "Go back down south and go tear down your little three-story buildings," Pia Hofmann, one of the few union women working at the site as a heavy equipment operator, told Dave Griffin. He chuckled, perhaps thinking that Hofmann was not being serious.

It was not long after the first successful pull-down that Dave Griffin had earned himself a new nickname. Some would still mockingly call him Jethro. For others who had seen his work, he would be known as "Demo Dave."

Stewart's plan did not go quite so well. Even as his shiny steel bridge was being assembled in early October, some of the workers, including Dave Griffin, grew skeptical, dubbing it "Stewart's Bridge to Nowhere." Engineers like Gary Panariello were worried from the start about building a crane bridge right into the middle of the disaster zone. The fires were still burning across ground zero, and on certain days, as the trade center ruins melted and shifted, the piles almost seemed to swell like a slow-moving wave in the Dead Sea. Hesitation turned into alarm only two days after Stewart had moved the crane out far enough on his bridge to start the demolition work, as a twenty-foot-long chunk of what served as the cap of the bathtub wall, near where the crane bridge entered the site, broke off and fell into the pit. After dirt was poured into the pit at this spot to ensure the entire bathtub wall did not crumble, the concrete slabs that had once been part of 6 World Trade Center's basement—and now were critical to maintaining the integrity of Stewart's bridge—also collapsed. Stewart scrambled to find a way to reinforce his ramp, but the entire operation in his sector was slowed down by the debacle. "The integrity of the ramp support columns is questionable," two engineers wrote in their daily field report on November 3. "Contractor is aware and has stopped work."

Mike Burton had no trouble with contractors who liked to think big. At the Department of Design and Construction, Burton, a marathon runner in his off-hours, managed a staff of thirteen hundred engineers, architects, and other personnel who together managed more than one thousand different city projects. His marathon man's approach to the World Trade Center job was to set daily, weekly, and monthly goals, this time marking the progress in tons of debris removed instead of minutes per mile. Nobody was allowed to miss the mark. Stewart tried to meet Burton's standard and save his bridge by coming up with one new idea after another, including rerigging one of his giant cranes on West Street so he could reach all the way from there into 6 World Trade Center to help finish the demolition job.

But before Stewart could finish explaining his new plan at the daily conference among the contractors, firefighters, and city construction officials, Lou Mendes, Burton's top aide for field operations, stood up and interrupted. "Why do you think you are going to get it done this time?" Mendes yelled. "What are you going to do different? You have been saying this every meeting—you are going to get this done, you are going to get this done. But you don't get anything done." Stewart tried to respond, telling Mendes to sit tight, pay the bills, and watch the progress. "You don't know what you are talking about," Stewart told Mendes. "Don't you fucking patronize me, Bob," Mendes yelled back.

Bob Stewart was still fighting, still stubbornly convinced that he was right. But he had lost his odd little battle, and the demolition would go on without him. Gradually, Stewart stopped attending the contractor meetings. "I got thirty other jobs that I can be working on," he announced. One day Stewart disappeared from the site.

▪ ▪ ▪

October 1, 2001, was a day of icy winds and rain. Battalion Chief Tom Richardson climbed into a hole near the base of the south tower facade that the Griffins had been pulling down. He went in with a couple of iron-workers and firefighters and returned with a simple message. "It's doable," Richardson concluded. "It is just going to take awhile." What he meant was that the body of firefighter Neil J. Leavy could now be extricated. Leavy, stationed with Engine 217 in Bedford-Stuyvesant, had arrived with his unit at the World Trade Center at 9:40 A.M. on September 11, and headed into the south tower. He made radio contact and said he was headed for the stairs to search for those in need of rescue. The tower collapsed nineteen minutes later.

As the monumental effort to remove steel from the site geared up, Leavy's body had become another of the ghosts that the World Trade Center just could not put to rest. Only five days after the attack, his father, John, got the call that his son's body had been recovered. Funeral arrangements were made; an obituary was published in the *Staten Island Advance*; flowers were ordered. But when it came time to pick up the remains, John Leavy was told that there had been a delay. Then he learned the truth: his son's body was impaled on a piece of rebar and pinned by giant columns about thirty feet below the level of the street, in a spot that was difficult and dangerous to reach. A week passed. Then a second week. When John Leavy saw on television that heavy equipment had started yanking on the facade of the south tower, he called the Fire Department and asked why his son was not out. A Fire Department aide made Leavy an offer: he would send a car for him the following Monday so that he could go to ground zero, look in the hole, and see his son.

John Leavy now lost his composure. "I will go down there myself tomorrow and I will get him out!" he screamed. "I am going to dig him out myself and no one is going to stop me!" Richardson, who heard about the father's outburst, told John Norman, who was leading the search-and-rescue effort for the Fire Department, that many firefighters were ready to volunteer for the mission of taking Neil Leavy's body out of the hole. And Norman knew that the situation was about to get much worse. As the work on the facade proceeded, there were plans to pour dirt in and fill in the hole. The young firefighter's body could be buried until at least the spring. So Richardson went down himself to determine whether the body could be removed. It could, if the steel columns were cut and lifted in just the right way. The ultimate solution involved tying cable around the columns and then pulling at them with a grappler from the street above. It would take more than one such pull before Neil Leavy's body could be wrested free.

Here was the recovery of a single firefighter, of the 343 killed, a single victim among the universe of 2,792. On the same day that Neil Leavy's remains were collected, the bodies of 15 other firefighters were recovered from ground zero, along with those of about two dozen civilians. The commanding fire officer marked each firefighter's removal by calling out: "Company! Attention!" Many of these were found not far from Neil Leavy, in a stairwell that had been buried between the ruins of the south tower and the Marriott hotel.

■ ■ ■

A week later, about an hour before dawn on October 8, a drilling supervisor named Ron Smalley walked onto Liberty Street, at the southern edge of the World Trade Center site, to check on the progress that his five-man crew had made overnight. Illuminated by a bank of hot-burning stadium lights, the men had been hard at work, hunched over an eighty-thousand-pound truck-mounted drill. The giant drill was designed to bore foot-wide holes for wells that would suck water from the ground outside the slurry wall to relieve some of the pressure on the damaged underground structures of the trade center. The drill added a high-pitched hissing to the cacophony of grinding and beeping that emanated from the machines and crews working at ground zero in defiance of the night. For no particular reason, Smalley paused and looked down at the mud underneath his work boots.

His eyes were drawn to an inch-wide fissure in the mud along Liberty Street, just south of where the towers once stood. When he bent down to look at it more closely, he could not see to the bottom of the crack. He then turned and looked east and west along Liberty Street, taking in a sight that made his stomach muscles instantly tighten up. The cut in the earth stretched for perhaps 100 or even 150 feet. And on the north side of the crack, the side closest to the debris piles, the earth seemed to have dropped slightly. Steel roadway plates, laid down to make a hard surface for trucks and heavy equipment to drive across, had been lying flat on the mud when he left; now one side was suspended slightly in the air, like a seesaw. An earthquake of sorts had taken place overnight. The bathtub wall was in danger. "We have got to stop what we are doing and get out," Smalley yelled to his men.

The drill crew had been trained not to leave their $1 million machine behind. The only way they could quickly pull out of the hole they had been driving and take their equipment away was to break the steel shaft of the drill and let it drop. The foreman threw the engine into reverse, locking the shaft in place in the ground. The machine whined and rattled as the crew tried to use its force to snap the steel and extract the drill. "Don't worry about getting the shaft out," yelled Billy Klingler, a field superintendent. "Just let it go. Let's get the hell out of here."

George Tamaro, who had become a sort of patron saint of the slurry wall, got word of Smalley's discovery the moment he arrived at his Midtown office that morning. The canyon that the south tower had torn out along Liberty Street had made this part of the wall Tamaro's biggest focus of concern since the day of the attack. Now, Tamaro immediately hurried down to the site to see the crack that Smalley had found. Smalley and his crew had already decided to go ahead with the plan and start pumping groundwater out of the holes his big drill had been punching in the earth. That would ease the problem right away, since two-thirds of the inward pressure on the bathtub came not from the soil outside the wall but the groundwater itself. "We have got to get some of these pumps going now," Klingler said, even as Smalley's crew was moving the drilling equipment off Liberty Street. "We need some type of pressure relief." Klingler spent the next sixteen hours frantically hooking up hoses and pumps. The impact was immediate: the groundwater level along Liberty Street dropped that same day to seventeen feet below the surface, down from the typical five feet. This was progress, but it was far from enough. The movement was too slow to see with the naked eye, but as the hours passed, the effect was obvious: a crack that had started as a hairline in some places and an inch in others was now a gash six inches wide in some spots and four inches in others. The disaster script was still playing out, in slow motion. Ground zero was caving in from below.

Tamaro knew that just sucking the water out of the ground was not going to save the bathtub wall. He decided that the only sure way to shore it up was backfilling, piling up enormous loads of dirt inside the wall to hold it in place. And so the dirt started to move. Dump trucks were soon pulling up to the site and dropping their loads at a rate of about one every five minutes. From the east, bulldozers simply pushed the heaps of dirt into the pit. Along Liberty Street, two giant conveyor belts were brought in so the crews could drop the dirt just inside the bathtub wall without having to place earthmoving equipment anywhere near the unstable structure. Around the clock, the dirt kept coming. But each day, after lurching forward, the wall moved farther, until the gap had stretched to almost a foot.

Tomasetti got so worried that he told his staff to stop going near the spot. Firefighters too were getting worked up. "We got guys down there, digging with hand tools trying to recover somebody," Battalion Chief Tom Richardson said, perhaps thinking about the episode involving Neil Leavy in the same part of the site. "Now what are you doing? You are piling in dirt. You are talking about burying people." The questions only escalated when a sudden burst of dust and noise shot out across the site. The weight of the dirt had collapsed some of the few remaining slabs holding the wall in place at Liberty Street.

Tamaro insisted that he knew what it would take to stabilize the wall he had built. He couldn't prove it to the last decimal place—the water-logged soil of Lower Manhattan contained too many imponderables, a complexity of forces that perhaps only someone who had dug into this ground and squeezed it in his hands could understand. Tamaro asked the city to stay with his plan. Despite conflicting advice from other engineers, Burton's gut told him to trust Tamaro. Twelve days after the wall started moving—it was leaning over fourteen inches but still had not cracked a leak—the movement all but stopped.

A disaster had been averted. But the real labor had not even really started. The goal was to clear out the pit, not fill it with dirt. Again, Tamaro and the city's engineers reached into the past, into the plans that had guided the construction of the towers themselves. The slurry wall had to be shored up. There had to be a way of supporting the wall that would allow the debris and compromised structures in the trade center's basement to be cleared away without causing a new calamity. Steel cables—tiebacks—like the ones that had been drilled into the earth three decades ago would have to be installed once more. The city, Tamaro calculated, would have to install nearly one thousand new tiebacks, emplaced at the same downward angle as before, down through the soil and into the bedrock. Four or five rows of these new tiebacks would be needed to support the entire seventy-foot-deep wall. The cleanup would become a choreographed affair, just like the construction, and the tiebacks would be installed as the debris came out, one row at a time. The drilling began on Liberty Street, near the stabilized but still precarious wall. A crowd gathered to watch the first tieback go in on October 18; the drill crew worked within a twenty-foot-wide foxhole that had been dug in the emergency backfill. Just as when the bathtub wall went in the first time, the angled tieback drill looked like a little artillery piece on treads.

"Keep coming straight ahead, Eddie, keep coming," Danny Mirt, the superintendent of the Nicholson Construction Company, yelled out to Eddie Gibbs, his best driller, as he inched ahead with the machine. Gibbs listened carefully to the hum of his drill and the pace of its rotations as it entered the wall for clues of what it was encountering—dirt, an abandoned pipe, or even an old ship anchor. Hit something dense and Gibbs knew he would have to slow the drill down, or ease up on the downward pressure. Everything went smoothly for once; he struck the Manhattan schist that same day. Over the next few days, the eighteen-strand steel cable they lowered eighty feet into the earth and another thirty feet into the bedrock was grouted into place. And by October 24, a hydraulic jack was used to pull at the cable with more than three hundred tons' worth of tension, a force greater than the earth leaning against the wall could ever create. The force was so great, in fact, that it moved the slouching wall two inches, nudging it back into shape. But Gibbs, the drill operator, could not relax. There were months of labor ahead and a thousand tiebacks to go.

■ ■ ■

A Sunday drive outside West Bend, Wisconsin, is still a glorious excursion through rolling woodlands of poplar and ash and oak and maple. It was from this quiet landscape that Gordon Haberman, his wife, Kathleen, and other members of their family would travel six times to Manhattan while the bleak and chilling work at ground zero progressed. They came to walk the city streets wearing T-shirts printed with the image of Andrea, their twenty-five-year-old daughter, as they posted missing-person fliers at bus stops, on newspaper boxes, and around streetlight poles. They came to turn over samples of DNA, collected with swabs they had to swish around their mouths. They came with Andrea's fiancé in hopes of bringing her favorite flowers to ground zero; they had to rely on a dump-truck driver to deliver the bouquet of purple irises when the family was barred from the site. They came to meet with other families who had lost loved ones from the ninety-second floor of the north tower. They came again and again to stand for hours looking from a viewing area into ground zero, as the hundreds of workers dug down into the pit. On each visit they struggled, with little success, to figure out just how and why a young woman who seemed to have everything in life could, on one fine, late summer day, simply vanish from the earth.

This was what they knew: Andrea had arrived in New York City late on the night of September 10, flying in from Chicago on the first business trip of her young career at Carr Futures, the Chicago-based trading firm where she worked. She had spent the night in a hotel a block south of the World Trade Center and arrived at the company's New York office in the north tower by 8 A.M., a good forty-five minutes early. Her boss from Chicago was supposed to meet her there before a morning meeting, but he was stuck in traffic. There was enough time before the meeting to call her fiancé. She was on the phone with an office colleague in Chicago when the first plane struck.

It was the rest of the story that Gordon and Kathleen Haberman lacked. Why, if she was below where the plane had struck, did she not get out, when so many others had escaped the north tower? Why, after the remains of so many other Carr Futures employees had been identified, had no trace of their daughter been found? And would they ever find any of her remains so that they could at least bring her home and have a real funeral? The answer to their first question was a chilling one—Andrea had been just above the fateful line of demarcation that Steve McIntyre had seen in the stairwells when he looked upward from the ninety-first floor. No one had survived from above that point. But the family still had not despaired of finding answers to their other questions. "Please, please, help us find Andrea," Gordon Haberman begged Charlie Vitchers on one afternoon in April 2002, after the Habermans had worked their way into ground zero in search of the man in charge of the cleanup. Seven months had passed since the attack, and still they were desperately searching for any news, anything at all, about their daughter. "We have nothing," Gordon Haberman said.

The couple showed Vitchers a photograph of Andrea on the day of her engagement to Al Kolodzik, whom she had met in a gazebo on a small college campus near Green Bay, Wisconsin. Standing beneath the oak, maple, and hickory trees in her parents' backyard, the sun illuminating her oval face, Andrea seemed so at ease. The gentle smile; her long, dirty-blonde hair; her left hand conspicuously on Al's broad shoulder, showing off the sparkling gold and marquis diamond engagement ring. Vitchers was almost speechless. He felt powerless, angry. He thought of his own children—he had six, including a daughter, Maureen, nearly Andrea's age. He went into his office and came out with a heavy iron cross one of the ironworkers had cut from a column of World Trade Center steel. Then he made a solemn vow. "We will find your daughter," Vitchers told the couple. "Be patient. We will find Andrea. Don't give up hope." With that, the Habermans thanked Vitchers, and, unsure what to do next, they simply walked off the site. They soon found a spot on a curb outside of St. Paul's Church, a few blocks from the site. Holding the cross that Vitchers had given him, Gordon Haberman sat down on the curb, next to his wife and his sister. And then the tears flowed.

■ ■ ■

Thirty years earlier, Willy Quinlan had ridden the north tower into the sky. He had been an ironworker, a connector, in the raising gang that worked beneath the kangaroo crane in the northwest corner of the tower. Like George and Jack Doyle, the brothers who had run the raising gangs on either side of him and who raced each other for the right to top out the tower, Quinlan was from Newfoundland, having come to New York at fifteen and started on the World Trade Center at nineteen. In the decades since, Quinlan had gone on to build so many skyscrapers that he had lost count. None would deliver such an intense sense of pride as the World Trade Center. None would evoke such an irresistible urge to say, as he passed within sight of the towers, "You know, I built that." Now, though, he was at ground zero to clear out its remains. Two of the iron-workers who would be there with him for most of the cleanup had their own connections to the trade center as it rose heavenward: Danny Doyle, part of the extended Doyle clan, who had worked on 7 World Trade Center, and John Kirby, who as a twelve-year-old had visited the towers when they were going up, collecting tidbits about them from his father, a foreman on a trade center welding gang.

As George Tamaro's tiebacks began supporting the wall that girded the site, the city would increasingly rely on ironworkers like Quinlan, Kirby, and Doyle to take the cleanup deeper and deeper into the pit. From a distance, it looked as if the grappler operators dominated the site, maneuvering their giant machines as they tore up the rubble. But it was the ironworkers who knew best where to make the cuts that kept the pile from shifting as a piece of steel was lifted away; they had the torches and the burning bars that let the debris be picked apart by the snorting heavy equipment; they understood the forces at play without even thinking about them. Quinlan could still remember the weights and markings on the steel he had set at the trade center, and now he could not believe he was back here pulling it away from a mangled pile. All those days fighting the wind, putting the steel in place, he thought. It just couldn't be.

Doyle had an even more miserable reintroduction to the familiar site. Called out to the pile by a firefighter, Doyle walked right into the middle of a horror show: an elevator car that had to be cut open so that the bodies of office workers could be pulled out; a steel bar that had to be sheared off so a decapitated woman, her fingernails painted pink, could be removed. "Welcome to hell," he said. "This is ugly, ugly."

In one of the strange meetings with history that this piece of Manhattan seemed to foster, Quinlan ended up working right back in the area of the north tower. By reading the markings on the steel, he kept an eye out for the floors he knew he had put up. This was where his knowledge of the towers could really help. Even without construction plans, Quinlan could estimate, within a ton or two, the weight of just about any column there. He knew how the dimensions of the steel had changed as the tower grew upward, with the thickest pieces near the base, where the most strength was needed. It was an eye that countless times would help him figure out what could be lifted by that steel undertaker called a grappler and what could not, a determination that told him how and where the steel needed to be cut. These were not the only insights his experience offered up. Quinlan and the other ironworkers were busy, in their own minds at least, piecing together what had happened to these mammoth towers.

With their burning bars as their guides—easy to spot at the site because they sent an acrid yellow cloud of smoke drifting through the air—the ironworkers would be the first to get a close look at the city that had been buried here. The grappler operators would dig a pit around a heavy core column, and then the ironworkers would climb into the hole and burn the column on three sides, weakening the steel so the grappler could knock it over and yank it out. After all the core columns had been removed on one level, the cycle would begin again; the descent would continue.

As these men went down into the pit, they encountered unfathomable sights. Ironworkers who had spent decades putting up steel-and-glass towers were asked to work their magic atop a pile of debris that warmed them even in the winter by what resembled a mine fire. At night, the steel they had cut would glow bright orange in the dark as it was pulled out of the pile.

One day, Doyle was carving away at the steel of a yet another column when he noticed something he could not at first understand. It was a distinct mound of debris set into the pile, about six feet high, with strands of wire and pieces of rebar sticking out. It looked like layers of sediment that had turned into rock and been lifted up on some mountainside. From one to ten he counted the layers, before it began to dawn on him just what he was looking at. "Jesus Christ," he yelled out. "Look at this. It just can't be." Here were ten stories of the south tower, compacted into an area of about six feet. "My God," said Kirby, who walked up to see what Doyle was yelling about. "My God. What these people went through. I just cannot imagine it."

They had found the same sort of formation that Lopez and Pontecorvo had discovered in the basement—an answer, as bizarre as it seemed, to the question of where the towers went when they collapsed. This was what was left of the heart of the towers. That idea was reinforced by what they did not find. For months, these men worked atop piles that contained the equivalent of 220 floors' worth of first-class office space. Yet Doyle, Quinlan, and Kirby almost never saw a desk, chair, telephone, or file cabinet. There were strands of telephone wire. On a few occasions, there were bits of broken computer keyboards or small pieces of broken glass. They also found a few piles of paper and photographs. But the tens of thousands of everyday objects that filled these giant skyscrapers were missing. Again and again these men found themselves posing the same question Charles Blaich had posed the moment he had arrived at the scene on September 11. "Where the hell did everything go?" Doyle said.

Quinlan had come to his own conclusions about what had brought the twin towers down. It was a design feature that had bothered him since the days he had worked on the towers, and to Quinlan it explained just how it was possible that so many floor trusses could be compacted into the space of five or six feet. "The core of the building was very solid," he said. "The perimeter of the building was very solid. But everything going from the center of the building to the perimeter was only a bar joist holding up a floor truss, which had no real strength to it." It was not a scientific assessment—after all, the trusses had worked just fine until the fires weakened them, along with all the other elements of the towers— but it came from somewhere deep in the bones of a man who had spent a lifetime with steel. "The floors had collapsed, and when they collapsed, they pulled the outside in and the core down," Quinlan said. "That is what I saw out there."

Every time a grappler pulled down another layer of debris, clearing out the pulverized material so that the ironworkers could burn through another collection of core columns, there was a good chance they might unearth evidence of the people who had worked here. In certain spots, the way the victims were found served almost as a diary of their deaths. In February, about sixty feet below street level, the grapplers were moving through an area with large chunks of spotted gray-and-white floor tile. There was no mistaking it: this was the lobby of the north tower, even though it had settled five flights underground. The work came to a stop when a spot of blue surfaced amid this mess of crumpled floor tile. The standard excavation began. It took thirteen and a half hours before the hand tools were put away. The blue fabric had been the uniform of one police officer, the body still in it. Next to this officer, the remains of four other Port Authority police officers were found, as well as one other victim: an obese woman, still strapped into a rescue chair that the officers were apparently using to try to get her out, when the tower came down. Each time a body emerged, flags were draped over the remains, workers took off their hardhats, and the remains were escorted from the site.

Not everyone recovered at ground zero received such deferential treatment. That cold fact bothered some of the construction workers, like Pia Hofmann. Hofmann, a onetime housewife and part-time dress designer who learned how to operate heavy machinery after a divorce, had spent months watching the firefighters "bag and tag" the remains of office workers, while any firefighter or police officer they found would get a formal honor guard.

One afternoon, Hofmann decided to change that. She had been sitting on top of her seventy-five-thousand-pound grappler when the distinctive odor of ground zero started to drift through the air. Somewhere nearby, there was a body, perhaps many. Hofmann stepped down from her rig to take a break, allowing the firefighters to dig by hand in the spot where she had been working. Shortly after she returned, the recovery crews found what they had been looking for: the upper half of a body of a victim. It seemed obvious to the firefighters that this was a female office worker. Hofmann knew what that meant. "Oh, that's great. It means I can be back to work in no time," Hofmann said sarcastically. "All you guys will do is shove the body in a black bag and get it out of here."

The firefighters were not sure what to make of Hofmann. But she was only warming up.

"Listen, I want the priest here. I want an honor guard," she said. "I want the American flag. I want the same thing that you're doing to your people. Because these people demand the same respect."

And so it happened. A priest was called. A flag found. Hofmann and other operators, along with several ironworkers and other laborers, lined up in two rows. They took their hardhats off and placed them over their hearts. They stood tall as a flag was draped over the body bag, and then the remains of an office worker, whom Hofmann had never met and whose name she would never know, were carried out.

Charlie Vitchers, the scruffy general superintendent of the cleanup who worked for Bovis and knew how to bridge the conflicting cultures of the engineers, firefighters, and contractors, decided to favor the call for equal treatment of civilians. Vitchers, who had developed a logistics plan with Jim Abadie that the entire operation had been following since the cleanup went "below grade," was more than ready to accommodate these pauses, even if it meant getting criticized by the Department of Design and Construction for failing to move as many loads out of the pit as demanded. His clashes with the agency infuriated Vitchers. "This job is going to take as long as it takes. And anybody that doesn't like that answer, then you tell me what the answer should be," Vitchers would say. "When you hit a recovery, the work stops. I mean we have windows that break in a grappler and it takes an hour to repair—I never heard anyone complain about that. The only complaint I get is when we shut the job site for recoveries." Vitchers's willingness to stand up for the recovery work, which the firefighters regarded as a sacred trust, earned him plenty of respect. Despite the friction, Michael Burton insisted he had no objection to letting the firefighters do their job. "The intention was always to allow them to do it in a dignified way," he said.

The long hours, endless weeks, and month after month of labor wore down many of these workers. The tension between the firefighters and the Giuliani administration over the pressure to speed the cleanup boiled over at times in vicious confrontations. The city kept pushing to cut back the number of firefighters on the pile—citing safety concerns—and the firefighters kept pointing to the human remains that slipped through their dragnet and were being found at Fresh Kills, the Staten Island dump where much of the lighter debris was being shipped. The world outside the pit seemed so trivial, so irrelevant, so make-believe compared to the harsh truths of the pit. Ironworkers and firefighters found themselves getting angry over the smallest things. On one day off, Doyle was trying to set up some outdoor furniture at his place at the New Jersey shore, and he had trouble getting a bolt into the proper hole. The next moment, he was kicking it, cursing, yelling, hitting the bolt in his hand. His wife looked out of the house and said: "What the hell is going on out there?" Doyle snapped back: "Shut up." Only when he returned to the pit that Monday did he realize what had happened. Every single one of the men he talked to had had a meaningless dustup with their wives.

■ ■ ■

The black vinyl logbook at the Office of the Chief Medical Examiner in New York City contained page after page after page of handwritten entries. "Metacarpal fragment, 2 inches," read one line. "2-inch rib fragment," said another. "4-inch scapula fragment," it continued, followed by "right arm, hand, bones," then "proximal ulna fragment." Next to most of these descriptions, in addition to a record number, was a simple abbreviation: "Unkn," written in on the line where the victim's name should have appeared.

By the end of April 2002, the medical examiner's office had made nearly twenty thousand entries in the two separate World Trade Center logbooks—the first one had run out of space. On the face of it, that made no sense: no more than twenty-eight hundred people had died there on September 11. Yet the numbers did not lie. Spelled out here was one of the most gruesome truths about the aftermath of the attack. The forces unleashed in the collapse and the fires that burned for weeks in the pit had not only pulverized and charred all of the office equipment, computers, and furniture, as Quinlan and Doyle had found. Those pitiless conditions had done the same to the victims in the towers. A certain number of them had simply been vaporized or rendered into dust. Others had burned so completely they were what the medical examiner's staff now called cremains. What remained of many of the others had been broken up into so many small bits that individual victims, although they had still not been identified, often had been assigned dozens of different case numbers—sometimes more than a hundred—and stored in a line of refrigerated trucks.

Numbers like these transformed the seemingly simple task of identifying the dead into one of the most elaborate forensic investigations in history. In charge of that investigation was the city's chief medical examiner, Charles S. Hirsch, a meticulous, reed-thin man who wore suspenders over perfectly pressed shirts, smoked a pipe, and never seemed to lose his imperturbable calm. The odds he faced—and faced down—every day in his work were enormous. It had been only sixteen years since DNA was pioneered as a forensic tool and just five years since it had been first used to identify all victims of a commercial plane crash, after TWA Flight 800 crashed off Long Island in July 1996. Now this identification tool would be put to its most stringent test. Only 733 of the victims of the attack could be identified through dental records, fingerprints, X rays, engravings on rings, or tattoos. Fewer than 50 of those could be identified by viewing a body or a photograph of one. DNA would have to be used for the rest.

Working with the police in the weeks after the attack, the medical examiner's staff collected more than ten thousand different samples from toothbrushes, combs, razors, and swabs given by mothers, fathers, and siblings for genetic analysis. These samples contained DNA that could be used to make a match—or rule one out—with a fragment of human remains collected from the rubble.

The city then hired a network of some of the most advanced DNA laboratories in the United States to help analyze the remains, to try to isolate a unique DNA profile for each sample. The job of coordinating all this testing went to Robert Shaler, a biochemist on Hirsch's staff whose career, up to now, had been sheltered from almost any contact with the families of victims whose deaths he had spent decades analyzing. The investigation for the September 11 attacks would change that, as Shaler got to know some of the husbands and wives, mothers and fathers of the victims, and what had been a science experiment became a personal obsession to help these grieving families. His part of the labor, and it was a critical part, was to make the judgment on whether the data on his screen, the numbers crunched by specially designed computer software, was evidence enough to make positive (or at least extremely likely) identifications.

"Can I make matches, can I make matches?" Shaler would mutter as he sat in front of his computer terminal for hours at a time. As April turned to May, Shaler and his staff would discover that seven case numbers listed as "Unkn" in the black logbook—16,568, 16,728, 16,729, 16,780, 16,971, 16,998, and 17,048—all belonged to a young woman from West Bend named Andrea Haberman. Charlie Vitchers could never, on his own, have lived up to the vow he made to Gordon and Kathleen Haberman that "we will find your daughter," but his crews had collected those precious fragments, and the scientists did the rest.

On May 15, a Wisconsin police officer knocked on the Habermans' door in West Bend and delivered the news. Back in New York there were seven tiny fragments of Andrea. Nothing was even recognizable. But in some inexplicable way, it was enough. Her parents could take something home, back to the rolling hills where their daughter had grown up. The family would also be given Andrea's purse, which was found at ground zero intact, containing her wallet and the cell phone that her father had dialed constantly for weeks after September 11.

The family returned to New York after they got the news. Gordon Haberman's sister went down to the pit on Andrea's birthday and laid a bouquet of purple irises at the spot where the family had been told Andrea's remains had been found. The family also looked up Charlie Vitchers and others he worked with, taking them out to dinner, and again to lunch. Vitchers brought along his daughter, Maureen. Gordon Haberman was not sure what the proper words were to thank everyone. His daughter was still gone. There was nothing to celebrate, except perhaps his faith in humanity—in the kind of profound decency represented by people like Vitchers—that on September 11 had suffered a grave blow. "We've been exposed to the worst," Gordon Haberman finally told Vitchers. "But we've met the best."

■ ■ ■

The city and the nation marked the end of the recovery effort with a formal ceremony at ground zero on Thursday, May 30, 2002, after Danny Doyle, Willy Quinlan, and several other ironworkers helped remove the last steel column from the site. A long silence was observed at 10:29 A.M., about the time the north tower collapsed on September 11. But any sense of finality was elusive. The remains of about a dozen victims were discovered around the site—some in the gutters and drainpipes on the roof of 90 West Street— about a week after the ceremony. Then, a delay by Deutsche Bank in letting firefighters search its battered high-rise at 130 Liberty Street also stirred anger. Finally, though, the company gave them permission to enter, and it was on this day, Monday, June 24, that the job would be truly complete.

"Our work is done here," said Battalion Chief Ronald W. Werner as he carefully edged his finger under a collection of photographs that had been taped to the wall of a firehouse across Liberty Street from the World Trade Center site. The tiny firehouse, a three-story brick building that was a relic of another era, was known as 10-10, for the ladder and the engine companies that were stationed inside, and it was here that the passage of time, and the sad success of the brutal labor at ground zero, was tracked with a yellow fluorescent marker. Each time a firefighter or a city or Port Authority police officer was identified amid the ruins, the chiefs would highlight the name underneath the row upon row of head shots of the deceased men that had been posted on the firehouse wall. Only five names had been colored in during the last month, bringing the total to 227, or about half of the total number of rescue personnel who died.

Chief Werner's voice echoed through a nearly empty room, one that had already been cleared of most of the maps, telephones, computers, desks, and chairs used by the Fire Department since September to orchestrate the recovery of remains. Other than his voice, the only noise in this room was the whirring of an air conditioner, the buzz of the ceiling lights, the clacking from the computer keyboard where one of the final daily reports for department superiors was being typed. "We wished we could have found all the people that died," the chief said. "But we've done the best we could. All we need is the dust brooms to sweep the place. And we are out."

As the end of the line approached and the shovels scraped bedrock, many of the workers at ground zero expressed the odd sensation of not wanting to let go—an awkward apprehension that the battlefield community of the pit was breaking up. There was also the growing recognition that there were fewer and fewer places where human remains might be found, meaning less and less chance of drawing the fluorescent marker across one more name. "You've got a great number of people that you want to find, and you've got a certain amount of dirt that's left," said firefighter Keith J. Dillon. "And there's a gap. That gap is going to be a sorrowful one. But we can't make more dirt."

Unlike the declared end of the recovery a month before, this moment on June 24 drew almost no notice. The television satellite trucks had long since pulled out. The city had opened up Liberty Street on the southern edge of the pit, generating a near-endless wave of camera-toting tourists. Liberty Street, insulated for so long from anything not involving the deadly serious tasks of the recovery, instantly became the informal gathering place for anyone who wanted to peer into the pit—now framed, starkly, by the sheer, seventy-foot walls of the bathtub—and ruminate on what had happened here.

For Charlie Vitchers and his crews, the last day started as all others had. At 8 A.M., the firefighters, contractors, city officials, and all the other ground zero managers gathered to review the status of the logistics plan. Everyone knew there was a special significance to this day, that near sunset the family that had labored together night and day through three seasons would be breaking up. The task now was to make sure that the last possible piece of human remains had been collected from this site. The four firefighters who remained donned their respirators and protective suits and entered the shrouded, abandoned crypt that was the Deutsche Bank Building, the only building in or around ground zero that had still not been thoroughly searched. Their charge was to search out any bit of rubble or other unidentifiable debris, which Vitchers's crew would then place into plastic bags, seal up with duct tape, load into the freight elevator, and put on a truck for shipment to Fresh Kills. By late in the day, the floors had been swept clean.

Captain Michael Banker, one of the four firefighters, knew he had one final task to perform. The 10-10 firehouse had a single window ledge where a pile of crumbled debris was resting. He knew it was there. He knew it had to be cleared. So Banker climbed up onto the scaffolding, and with a knife he pushed the rubble into a bucket. In a moment, it was over. As he came down from the ladder, he stepped into the wave of tourists who had no idea this was still a recovery site.

When 5:30 came, it was time for the final joint meeting, again called to order by Vitchers. "We made it," he announced to the thirty-two men and women who had gathered around plywood tables. There was talk of a Department of Design and Construction punch list, for the final duties remaining at the site, like some of the last bathtub tiebacks that still needed to be installed along Vesey Street. But with the business wrapped up, everyone paused. "It is the last load," Vitchers said in the still room. One at a time, they went around the room, some in fire helmets, others in hard hats, saying a few words. "Months ago, when we were rescue workers, you were construction workers," said Battalion Chief Stephen Rasweiler, who also had been there since the start. "There is nobody here in this room now who is not a recovery worker. Bar none, you all came through. We all will be eternally grateful for your effort." More than a few of the people in the room were sobbing. They paused for a moment of silence. Then Ron Vega, a construction manager from the city, stood up, took off his hard hat, and in his deep, husky voice sang the Irish folk song "Danny Boy."

Oh Danny boy, the pipes, the pipes are calling
From glen to glen, and down the mountain side
The summer's gone, and all the flowers are dying
'Tis you, 'tis you must go and I must bide.

On the southwest corner of the pit, they gathered one final time. Vitchers leaned against a chain-link fence, with a flag folded into a square and signed by the workers. At first, he was not sure where to drape it on the big steel box filled with the debris bags, which were to be searched at Fresh Kills for any possible human remains. "Where do we want it?" he asked a crowd of sunburned, unshaven men. They tied the flag down, their signatures visible. Then Anthony Pasquale, the truck driver, drove off.

■ ■ ■

Epilogue

The grappler was moving closer.

The steel bones of the World Trade Center were piled at this Jersey City scrap yard in jagged, rusting heaps forty and fifty feet high. Rising out of the oily mud, the mangled, oversized trade center debris gave the scrap yard a prehistoric, almost apocalyptic aura, even as the Statue of Liberty and the Lower Manhattan skyline shimmered across the water, seemingly close enough to touch. The grappler seized and tossed ten-ton fistfuls of steel like reeds, the hinged apex of its great arm appearing and disappearing above nearby piles of steel. For all the strangeness of the scene, it was being played out at numerous scrap yards and landfills and loading docks around the rim of the Port of New York, as the remains of the trade center—often delivered from Manhattan by barge—were rapidly being sorted and cut into pieces and piled into waiting freighters. Those freighters were transporting the scrap to recycling plants around the world, where the steel would be melted down and turned into new I-beams, car parts, and appliances.

Dashing amid the piles of steel at this scrap yard, with nervous glances now and then toward the snorting grappler, was a small troupe of people in hard hats and rugged clothes who were not quite grimy enough to mark them as everyday workers in this place. Ramon Gilsanz, stopping to peer closely at the steel pieces he was clambering over, wore baggy blue jeans and a pale blue windbreaker emblazoned with the logo of the American Society of Civil Engineers. David Sharp took notes on a clipboard and sported a rust-brown hard hat with a circular brim, in the style of a safari hat. Anamaria Bonilla, wearing a tan down vest, rolled over almost on her back in the mud and slid her head into a small gap under a ruddy steel column mottled with patches of whitish scum—the remains of the trade center's fireproofing.

With the sleeve of her sweatshirt, Bonilla furiously rubbed at a rusty spot on the surface of the steel—a fragment of one of John Skilling's thirty-six-foot-long, three-column perimeter panels—in order to expose some obscured markings.

"One-oh-one," she said.

"The hundred-and-first floor," Sharp confirmed after squeezing into the gap himself.

They had found the codes put on almost thirty-five years before at Pacific Car & Foundry in Seattle.

These engineers and a few of their colleagues, scrambling like mountain goats over the steel to avoid the big rigs, were there on that Tuesday in January 2002 to collect physical data: pieces of steel from the zones where the planes hit. The data were an essential part of the evidence being gathered for the sole federal inquiry that was in place to understand exactly how and why the towers fell. Nevertheless, their work involved a rather crude ritual. Inexplicably, the engineers had been given no official powers to keep pieces of the steel from heading to the recyclers. There was also little financing for the effort, so the steel collection was being done almost entirely on a volunteer basis, with the engineers sometimes being forced to take vacation days to make up for their absences from work. Because the engineers had no authority to stop the grapplers, they would climb debris piles when they found a piece they coveted, spraying the word SAVE on the steel with orange fluorescent paint. At other times they would watch pieces being lifted off the barges, and approach, paint can in hand, when the steel came back to earth. The grapplers were supposed to set the marked pieces aside.

Fortunately for their work, the engineers knew that the thinnest steel had been used at the top of the buildings, where the planes had hit and the collapses began. In the perimeter-column panels, for instance, spandrel plates three-eighths of an inch thick or less were used only above about the eightieth floor. That striking thinness, which gave the plates the look of dirty aluminum foil next to the heavier debris, helped the sharpest-eyed engineers spot crucial pieces from fifty yards away. Bonilla, who had spent years on rooftops working as a carpenter before she became an engineer, was one of the most aggressive spotters, bounding onto the steel piles before others had even climbed out of a rusty Chevrolet truck that drove them around the scrap yard.

Bonilla's find on that Tuesday had run from the 98th to the 101st floors of one of the towers—no one was sure which yet. A few days before, Sharp had found a twenty-one-foot-long fragment of another important perimeter panel: a spandrel plate wrapped around a column, spotted with rust, reddish paint, gray mud from the scrap yard, burn marks, and a few traces of the fireproofing. Enough of the Pacific Car markings remained to determine that it came from Tower A, the north tower, between the 92nd and 95th floors, about thirty feet from the southeast corner, on the east face of the building. John McKiever's raising gang would have put it into place. The plane had struck the building at just this level.

Scanning the scrap yard for other clues, the eyes could not help drifting to the debris that looked out of place, even among the lightest of the other steel remains. Like a wildly tangled ball of yarn, a clot of crazily bent, meandering steel bars and pieces of angle iron stuck from the side of one of the piles. At first glance, it seemed impossible that these crumpled little bars had ever had a structural function comparable to that of the other steel in the pile. In fact, though, these pieces had all but defined the gloriously lightweight structural concept of the twin towers and had been among their most important components.

The floor trusses.

There was nothing remaining of the concrete, and little of the steel decking, that had formed the surfaces of the floors themselves. And only a few of the trusses seemed to have survived the collapse and fires and then made it to the scrap yard at all. In one place, a bundle of truss bars wandered up the side of a steel pile like a little mountain road. In another, the bars wound into and out of lighter compacted debris, like roots on the side of a cliff. The tangled, yarnlike clot of truss bars was close enough to the ground to touch and marvel at. It sat there suggestively. Had these little bars given way, somewhere deep in the inferno, and brought the whole structure down?

The engineers did not know. And they were aware that the seemingly obvious solution is not always the correct one. They scoured the piles. The point of their investigation was to assess the performance of the twin towers on September 11. In the face of the horrific attacks, did the way the towers were built save lives or cost them?

What the engineers knew was that for a span of time that lasted thousands of heartbeats and spared thousands of lives, the twin towers had withstood the crashes of the Boeing 767 jetliners and the flames stoked by their fuel. Eventually, those flames softened the steel structures, and each tower collapsed in a terrifying structural avalanche whose aftermath was now spread out in this scrap yard and others.

The investigation aimed to determine exactly why the towers first stood, then suddenly fell. That information would, for those who chose to weigh it, help answer a less technical but equally searing question: Do the innovative but peculiar structures deserve praise or blame after September 11?

• • •

Any attempt to answer those questions has to start with the assessments that the Port Authority and its engineers carried out before the buildings ever went up. For it is clear that the people who built the twin towers did try to research their likely risks and vulnerabilities. The World Trade Center was grandiose not only in its scale but also in the technical ambition and brilliance of the people who designed it, column by column and bolt by bolt. Changes in the design of the great structures flowed from the extensive scientific and technical effort that the Port Authority set in motion to study the risks and their potential consequences. Some of those changes probably saved lives on September 11 for reasons the builders of the trade center never anticipated.

Before the World Trade Center was even built, the barrage of innovative tests carried out by its designers had taken on the quality of a modest epic all by themselves. To begin with, no tall building had ever been shrunk down into a scale model and subjected to the kind of turbulent winds that actually blow above the rooftops of a physically complicated metropolis like New York. John Skilling and Les Robertson, the engineers the Port Authority hired to carry out the structural design, commissioned the studies, which revealed that their original design had serious shortcomings. The engineers, especially Robertson, then went through the difficult process of redesigning the structural skeleton of the towers, making them better able to withstand the lateral forces of the wind—and probably the lateral force of a jet slamming into the structure. In general, the redesign created a building whose parts were tied more tightly together and better able to handle an unforeseen calamity.

Because there was no way to keep the lightweight towers from swaying to some degree in the wind, the Port Authority and its engineers also carried out the first studies ever on the tolerance of human beings to movements of the office space in which they are working. The odd—but scientifically pathbreaking—experiments in the optometrist's office in Eugene, Oregon, showed that people were extraordinarily sensitive to that motion, so Robertson and Alan Davenport, the wind expert, came up with the idea of placing thousands of little shock absorbers, called viscoelastic dampers, in the towers to reduce their sway even further. No one has (publicly at least) shown calculations assessing what effect the damper had on September 11, but it's a good bet that they had a positive influence. Had the towers swayed more wildly after the jet impacts, probably more sections of the stairwells would have been torn up, more escape doors jammed, and more water pipes snapped. By suppressing that sway to some extent, the dampers may have let people escape who would not have made it out otherwise. The Eugene experiments may have saved lives. They certainly led to a better overall design for the towers.

At the time they were carried out, the value of those technical studies was, unfortunately, diminished by the absolute secrecy surrounding them: there could be no open, democratic debate about the wisdom of the project when few people knew that the grand structures, at least as originally conceived, could not have been built without disastrous results. New York City, in effect, did not know what it was getting into.

The trade center's innovations did not stop with the wind tunnel and the motion simulator, and not all of them remained secret. Perhaps the most remarkable was the effort to study what would happen if a jet airliner struck one of the towers: no study of the kind had ever been done before in the history of tall buildings. It was, of course, a clear possibility that a plane could hit the twin towers one day, whether deliberately or otherwise. Only two decades before Yamasaki unveiled his design, planes had blundered into the tallest building in Midtown (the Empire State Building) and the tallest building downtown (40 Wall Street). In 1968 Lawrence Wien published an advertisement featuring a doctored photograph of a jetliner hitting the north tower. And indeed, an Argentine commercial airliner came within ninety seconds of accidentally striking the north tower in 1981.

But knowing that the peril was real did not diminish the accomplishment of figuring out *before the towers had even been built* what would happen if a jetliner crashed into them. The studies examined planes traveling at different speeds, and the most ho-hum of conclusions was that gale-force winds blew more powerfully against the towers than anything a jet could easily muster. The force of impact would probably not shear off the towers, the studies found. Much more remarkably, the Port Authority's engineers discovered that even the giant hole punched into a tower by the collision of a plane would not bring it down. The structure of the towers, so unusual with their tightly spaced perimeter columns and the hat truss at the top, would redistribute loads from damaged elements to undamaged ones, forming spontaneous Vierendeel trusses that created archlike support over the gashes to keep the buildings standing. It must have sounded like wild theorizing to conventional engineers, accustomed to stolid, heavy, traditional structures. But it was not just theorizing: on September 11 the columns of the twin towers really did shift loads around the dark, smoking holes punched by the planes, forming the arches and keeping the building standing. Otherwise the towers would have crumbled in a heartbeat.

The accuracy of this study meant an enormous amount in terms of the death toll on September 11. Miraculously, all but about a hundred of the civilians who were at least two floors below impact had enough time to get out of the towers before they collapsed. If the towers had collapsed immediately or the evacuation had been less successful, the death toll on September 11 could have reached ten thousand or more.

▪ ▪ ▪

The Port Authority's calculations were right—up to a point. Unfortunately, the agency's foresight ended when the fires began.

The Port Authority had received ample warning that tremendous fires could break out in the towers. That is what had happened when the plane that struck the Empire State Building spilled its fuel and ignited. At least one of the Port Authority studies of a plane hitting the twin towers considered this possibility. There were additional warnings once the buildings opened. In 1975, for instance, the fire set by Oswald Adorno led to isolated buckling of parts of the bar-joist trusses in the north tower. But the sophistication reflected in the structural design of the towers would not be matched in the quality of their fire resistance.

Part of the reason probably had to do with the moment in high-rise history when the twin towers were born. Older skyscrapers, with their heavy structural skeletons and thick masonry fireproofing, had not been designed using refined mathematical calculations. Those structures were more like Gothic cathedrals, the outcome of much practical experience, including the observation that certain kinds of poorly designed high-rises—Hyde's Equitable Building, for instance—had collapsed in fires. By the time the twin towers were being designed, engineers had developed much greater sophistication in their ability to calculate mathematically how their structures would stand up to the forces of gravity and, to some extent, wind. But quantitative fire science was still in its infancy, so when the Port Authority commissioned a radically different kind of structure, one for which the old base of experience meant little, there were few tools available to figure out how this new beast would behave in a large fire. The problem was compounded for the trade center, since the old asbestos-based spray-on fireproofing, which had proved its mettle in actual fires, was banned as construction began. That forced the Port Authority into a hasty switch to an untried alternative.

Although a building's architects, and not its structural engineers, are responsible for choosing the fireproofing, in practice many architects are qualified to do little more than pick a fireproofing plan out of a catalogue. But there was no catalogue that covered the innovative structure of the twin towers. And a hard fact of high-rise projects is that even structural engineers often display a striking lack of inquisitiveness when it comes to the basic physics of fire. Thin steel, like that of the floor trusses, will generally heat up more quickly than heavy traditional steel beams—even when the two systems are capable of carrying similar loads. Structural engineers often wave their hands and say there is really no difference as long as the fireproofing is thicker on the lighter members. Even discounting the distressing oversimplification at work here, the question remains: How thick should the fireproofing be? The only way to answer that question would have been to test the components in special furnaces, the same type of testing that is required by all city fire codes for the components built into high-rises as well as other buildings.

Instead, that crucial issue was neglected by the Port Authority. Malcolm Levy, chief of the planning division in the agency's World Trade Department, and the man who ultimately called the shots in the twin towers' design, exploited a legal loophole: because the Port Authority is a bistate agency, it is exempt from city fire codes. So Levy simply skipped the fire tests that would have told him how much fireproofing was required by at least one critical component—the floor trusses themselves—to ensure that they could withstand the heat of a large fire.

If Levy had performed the tests, he would have discovered one of two things. He might have learned exactly how thick the fireproofing needed to be to render the buildings safe, at least in the kind of fires envisioned by city codes. Then he could have ordered that just such a thickness be applied to the structure. Or he might have discovered that the trusses—and possibly some of the other lightweight components of the buildings—could not be safely fireproofed under any conditions. This second possibility could well have arisen because thin steel naturally heats up faster, and spray-on fireproofing often has trouble sticking indefinitely to the tight corners and sharp bends of those small elements.

If Levy had discovered that the innovative structure of the twin towers could not be safely fireproofed, he would have had to order a redesign of the entire project. He decided not to take that risk. Instead, a mysterious letter from his office in 1969 declared—with no apparent technical justification whatever—that the trusses would be coated with a half-inch of fireproofing. Three decades later, a Port Authority engineer with a deeper concern for the towers' occupants discovered the problem and ordered that the originally specified thickness be tripled. That upgrade had been partially completed on September 11. In the north tower, the upgrade had been carried out on all the floors struck by the jetliner; by contrast, in the south tower all but one of the impact floors had not been upgraded. Whether the upgrades made any difference is still uncertain, since some engineers believe that large amounts of fireproofing—whatever its thickness—was probably knocked off by the impact of the planes. In any case, the Port Authority never actually performed the fire tests, even after learning of the problems.

As incredible as it sounds, the Port Authority had built what were then the tallest buildings in the world without knowing how their components would hold up in a fire. Moreover, the components it neglected to test were just the ones most likely to endanger the occupants in the buildings, the components physically most prone to problems in a large fire. The agency made sure that the risk of fire—the same risk that John Skilling was worried about—was never part of the public discussion of a plane crashing into the towers. The engineering studies had shown that the towers would stand; there was nothing to worry about. That was the public message put out by the Port Authority.

On September 11, the hijacked Boeing 767s were not much different in size or weight from the Boeing 707s that the Port Authority had assumed in its studies of a collision with the towers. That fact may account for how uncannily correct those studies were when the towers stood in the minutes after the impacts. And even with Levy's neglect of the potentially devastating effects of a fire, the ultimate outcome on that day might still have been a smaller loss of life if the occupants of the upper floors could have walked down to safety. There were, after all, 102 precious minutes between the impact of the first plane and the fall of the last tower standing. But almost none of the people on those upper floors could get down because the planes' impact also cut off five of the six emergency stairwells in the two towers, trapping people in their upper reaches. Partly because the stairwells were encased only in lightweight gypsum board, the extensive crumbling of the escape routes trapped even some people who were well below where the planes actually struck, like Andrea Haberman of West Bend, Wisconsin, attending a business meeting on the ninety-second floor. If the Port Authority had thoroughly considered the scenario of a plane hitting the building, it is probable that the stairwells would have been constructed of materials, like reinforced concrete, with a better chance of withstanding flying aluminum parts and remaining intact. (Clearly few structures, no matter how sturdy, could withstand a direct hit from a heavy steel component like one of the planes' engines.) When the towers fell, all of these people in the upper reaches—or at least those who had not already been killed by the smoke or the flames—died.

The collapse of the towers also left a crater rimmed by a zone of devastation in Lower Manhattan and an enormous psychic wound that remains raw for Americans and for people in many other nations around the world. The collapse of the towers crystallized the terror of September 11, and not just for those who fled the filthy clouds that billowed down city streets or watched the tragedy unfold from across the Hudson or the East River. The fall of the towers has been permanently imprinted in the minds of everyone who saw the terrible images of that day. As an outraged America reacted to the attacks, the power of those images, combined with the count of the dead, was a prime argument for war.

Two Theories of Collapse

THEORY: SAGGING FLOORS As the floors weaken, they tug at their connections, which tear away from the core and exterior columns.

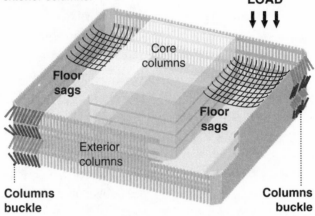

Having lost their lateral support and already softened by the fire, the exterior columns buckle catastrophically.

THEORY: CORE COLLAPSE The damaged core columns heat up, weaken and ultimately fail.

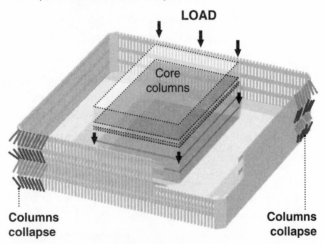

The core plummets a split second before the exterior columns buckle and collapse.

Sources: Dr. Eduardo Kausel, M.I.T.; Dr. Tomasz Wierzbicki, M.I.T. (sagging floors); Weidlinger Associates (core collapse)

The New York Times; illustrations by Mika Gröndahl

The Port Authority could never have foreseen the wider implications of the potential failure of its buildings. What should have been obvious to the agency is that its longstanding lack of concern for fire displayed a serious disregard for the safety of the thousands of people who came to work in its grand buildings every day. That same neglect, while suggestive and deeply troubling, is by no means a technical proof that the light steel components of the towers gave them an Achilles' heel in a fire, leading to their collapse. It certainly does not prove that the trusses, after softening and sagging in the heat of the fires, were the first structural element to fail, as one theory has it. Engineers have pointed out that city building codes, for example, would not have required the World Trade Center to be constructed to a standard so stringent that it could withstand the impact of a commercial jetliner and remain standing. A standard office fire would never be that intense or instantly widespread. Nevertheless, if the Port Authority had met the codes, it is highly likely that the towers would have been better prepared for such a cataclysmic event. And of course the agency repeatedly said that the towers could withstand such an impact.

The uncertainty on these issues has created deep divisions among those best qualified to unravel what happened on September 11. Some engineers, in fact, believe that the damage caused by the planes was so severe that the towers were left barely standing after the impacts—like trees sawed nearly through, ready to fall at the slightest provocation. According to this theory, the towers had no special vulnerability to a fire at all; they were doomed to fall under almost any circumstances as soon as the Boeing 767s plunged into their structural hearts. Only a thorough investigation, of course, could determine which of those views—if either—was right.

■ ■ ■

Within days of the attacks, the American Society of Civil Engineers (ASCE) began organizing an assessment of why the towers collapsed, to be led by W. Gene Corley, a Chicago structural engineer. Corley had led the investigation of the truck bombing and collapse of the Alfred P. Murrah Federal Building in Oklahoma City in 1995. He and his team discovered that most of the 168 people who died there had been killed by the building's collapse, not by the bomb itself. Corley also found that subtle structural modifications, like those required in the seismic building codes in California, could have staved off collapse and prevented as much as 85 percent of the damage, and presumably the deaths, in Oklahoma City.

There was just one thing nobody bothered to tell Corley when he accepted the ASCE's invitation to lead the World Trade Center investigation. Although his work in Oklahoma City had relied in part on data from the rubble of the building, officials at the Department of Design and Construction, including Michael Burton, had decided to ship virtually all the trade center steel to scrap yards, where it would be cut up, shipped away, and melted down for reuse before it was inspected. That decision eliminated the question of where to store the roughly 200,000 tons of steel from the twin towers alone. Burton cleared the decision with Richard Tomasetti of Thornton-Tomasetti Engineers. Months later, Tomasetti would say that had he known the direction that investigations into the disaster would take, he would have adopted a different stance. But the decision to quickly melt down the trade center steel had been made.

There was a second, and even more serious, problem with the investigation. Although the ASCE was providing much of the expertise, the investigation was financed and given its authority by the Federal Emergency Management Agency (FEMA), with which Corley's team had a shaky relationship from the start. For months after September 11, the investigators—twenty-six of the nation's most respected engineers—were unable to persuade FEMA to obtain basic data like detailed blueprints of the buildings that collapsed. Bureaucratic restrictions often kept the engineers from interviewing witnesses to the disaster, making forensic inspections at ground zero, or getting crucial information like recorded distress calls from people trapped in the buildings. For reasons that would remain known only to FEMA, the agency refused to let the team appeal to the public for photographs and videos of the towers that could help with the investigation.

"This is almost the Dream Team of engineers in the country working on this, and our hands are tied," said one angry team member just before Christmas 2001. He spoke anonymously, since members had been threatened with dismissal for speaking with the press. "FEMA is controlling everything," he said. "It sounds funny, but just give us the money and let us do it, and get the politics out of it."

The money was not forthcoming either. FEMA had little background in investigating a structural failure like the collapse of the towers. By late

December, FEMA had spent roughly $100,000 on the worst building disaster in recorded history. Months later, when the unsatisfying outcome of this effort persuaded Congress that a new investigation was necessary, $16 million would be authorized for the task.

Airplane crashes, where fatalities are in the hundreds, routinely receive detailed investigations by the National Transportation Safety Board. When the *Titanic* sank in April 1912, the U.S. Senate immediately summoned the 705 survivors for eighteen days of intensive hearings on the causes of the disaster. After all, more than fifteen hundred people had died; lessons had to be drawn from the incident to prevent a recurrence. But in the case of the World Trade Center, where nearly three thousand people died, the investigation began as an afterthought. A federal agency with little interest in investigations was in charge, and the main cache of physical evidence was being sent away to be melted so that it could be gotten out of the way.

For a time, the publicly undeclared decision to recycle the steel, and the absence of any real authority granted to Corley's team—which included Ramon Gilsanz and many of the others who struggled to collect steel at the scrap yards—brought clear elements of farce into the investigation. On September 19 a member of the team was getting ready for bed at the Tribeca Grand Hotel, a few blocks north of the trade center site, when he noticed a flatbed truck, loaded with steel, parked outside— waiting, as it turned out, to take it to barges at a Manhattan dock. Hungering for a close-up look at the steel, the engineer got dressed and went downstairs to take notes and photos. For three nights he continued his work as a kind of irregular militia of the forensic investigation, cataloguing thirty or forty of the beams and columns.

A few days later, on September 28, the *New York Times* learned that the city was recycling the steel. When the *Times* contacted Kenneth R. Holden, commissioner of the Department of Design and Construction, he said that no one from the investigative team had asked him to keep or inspect the steel. The ASCE, it turned out, had faxed a request, but to the wrong fax machine. Late that afternoon, after reporters shuttled the correct fax number to the ASCE, Holden said that a request had finally reached him. "I just got handed a letter literally sixty seconds ago," he said at 5:40 P.M. The recycling continued, although the city agreed to let investigators inspect the steel.

The decision to go on with the recycling program fueled outrage among the victims' families. On December 14, nearly three months after the program had been disclosed, Sally Regenhard was standing in a drizzle outside City Hall protesting the recycling decision. Her son, Christian, a firefighter, had died in the towers' collapse. "We're here today to call for a stop to the destruction of evidence, composed mainly of steel," she said. The city ignored the calls to stop the recycling, pointing out that it was now letting investigators into the scrap yards. The controversy did not go away. Regenhard was soon joined by the families of nonuniformed victims of the tragedy. She gained an articulate ally in Monica Gabrielle, whose husband, Richard, was last seen in the seventy-eighth-floor sky lobby of the south tower, pinned down by the slabs of fallen marble, his legs gravely injured, crying out in pain. Regenhard framed the situation this way: "My son should have been able to save her husband."

It was probably too much to expect federal and city agencies with little or no forensic expertise to spearhead what would have been one of the most complex structural investigations ever. FEMA and the Department of Design and Construction had engineers—but they were largely "build it and clean it up" engineers, not "solve the mystery" engineers. It would have been like asking a weightlifter to analyze the physics at work in each clean-and-jerk. After embarrassing articles appeared in the press, FEMA did hunt down some of the drawings and increase the financial support somewhat. Corley pushed ahead, and the report by his investigative team, released publicly in April 2002, contained important details about what had happened on September 11. It pointed out that, amid the many systems like water sprinklers and fireproofing that were disabled on September 11, improvements in the lighting system in the stairwells made after 1993 meant that people below the impact zones were able to move relatively quickly down the stairwells to safety. The report confirmed that 7 World Trade Center had housed as much as forty-two thousand gallons of diesel fuel to run emergency generators for Mayor Rudolph Giuliani's emergency command center, offices for the Secret Service, and other tenants. It was possible—but not proven—that the burning diesel fuel had been a primary cause of 7 World Trade Center's collapse.

Not surprisingly given the barriers the investigators had faced, the report ended with many unresolved questions. "The fire-performance of steel trusses with spray-applied fire protection," the report concluded, "is not well understood, but is likely critical to the building collapse." *Not well understood*: the investigators were not able to decide among the competing theories of why the towers fell, among the possible answers to the question of what had happened here.

Sherwood Boehlert, an affable upstate New York Republican who as chairman of the House Science Committee was known for his inquisitive mind and his maverick ways, was far from satisfied. Following up on the calls by Sally Regenhard and Monica Gabrielle, he shepherded through Congress a bill that would allow the federal government, through the National Institute of Standards and Technology—an agency in the Commerce Department—to investigate building catastrophes much as the National Transportation Safety Board dissects any major plane crash. The legislation, when it was signed into law in October 2002 as the National Construction Safety Team Act, applied not just to the World Trade Center but to any future building disasters; when a hundred people died after a fire broke out in a Rhode Island nightclub in Februrary 2003, the agency quickly used its new authority to begin an investigation.

With enhanced federal powers, like the ability to subpoena evidence, and a great deal more money, a new investigation began immediately. Still, the confusion and lost time at the start of the original effort means that much evidence is gone forever. The new investigation is still in progress, with its report due in 2004.

■ ■ ■

The builders of skyscrapers, those conspicuously ambitious strivers who have been reaching upward at least since Elisha Otis perfected his emergency brake for elevators, have not waited to incorporate some of the obvious lessons of 9/11 into their buildings. At a new skyscraper in Times Square, steel plates, more than an inch thick, have been added to strengthen the link between two crucial structural beams, a reinforcement that was not part of the original pre–9/11 blueprints for this building. At two other skyscrapers in Midtown—a thirty-five-story office high-rise at 300 Madison Avenue and the enormous twin-towered AOL Time Warner Building at Columbus Circle—workers have installed, respectively, thick, steel-reinforced concrete and masonry walls where original plans had called for lightweight gypsum, and a state-of-the-art communications system to allow firefighters, rescue workers, and building tenants to complete calls even during emergencies.

All of those revisions have been voluntary but, at least in New York City, officials have been studying the possibility of sweeping changes to the city building code as a result of 9/11. Under consideration have been a ban on bar-joist trusses in high-rises, a requirement that stairwells be sturdily encased, and regular inspections of fireproofing. City codes have never taken into account the possibility of terrorist attacks or demanded that structures be able to stand up to deliberate explosions, airplane impacts, or the fuel-fed fires like those that broke out after the collisions on September 11. For that reason, it is still unclear whether the towers would have stood up even if they had complied with city building codes. It is highly improbable that officials will demand that buildings be absolutely safe in the event of a 9/11–style attack—that would require a structure on the order of a nuclear containment vessel. A more likely goal is the creation of standards that would prevent the catastrophic collapse of a building in the event of, say, a car-bomb explosion, or would ensure that stairwells remain passable even when several floors are engulfed in fire. Still, city officials will be hard-pressed to push through politically difficult—and potentially expensive—changes until investigators come up with solid lessons from the collapse of the twin towers.

▪ ▪ ▪

As the nation waits for these lessons, the latest fight about the future of ground zero has been joined. From the moment that question returned to the public realm, all the old spirits seemed to fly up out of the Lower Manhattan bedrock and assume new shapes in a battle that echoed everything that had already taken place on this profoundly contentious spot.

A public competition in 2002 and 2003 chose a design by the architect Daniel Libeskind, but his artistic vision for the site was ridiculed by Larry Silverstein, the holder of the long-term lease to the site, who contended that the design would not allow for enough open, column-free real estate to make the project profitable. Silverstein, whose expected insurance reimbursement for damage in the attacks made him a multibillion-dollar force in the rebuilding drama, then succeeded in installing his own choice, David Childs, as the lead architect for the office buildings at the site, pushing Libeskind into a consulting role. Governor George E. Pataki has feuded with Mayor Michael R. Bloomberg over the issue of whether the city or the Port Authority will control the site in the future. And community groups and city planners have pushed for the restoration of the street grid that the Port Authority had fought the city so bitterly to erase forty years before.

Many of the families of 9/11 victims want the footprints of the original towers to remain free of any development whatever, all the way down to the bedrock, a stand that has brought them in conflict with the Port Authority, which in 2002 began rebuilding the PATH station and its tracks at the bottom of the bathtub.

Engineering debates have also returned to the World Trade Center site. George Tamaro was concerned about his slurry wall, which had not been designed to be exposed to the elements, as it would be in the Libeskind architectural plan. He feared that the three-foot-thick wall, the only part of the trade center to survive the attacks, was too delicate to go on public display, like a piece of ancient artwork that had not yet been properly restored. And he had the engineering calculations to prove it. Tamaro came up with requirements on bracing and coating the wall that he insisted be met before he would agree to leave part of it exposed.

"I have become the conscience of the slurry wall," Tamaro said.

In many ways, the September 11 attacks turned back the clock for the part of the city most freighted with history. The destruction of the PATH station brought large-scale ferry traffic back to the Hudson River for the first time in decades as commuters struggled to maintain the rhythms of their working lives. An area that was becoming one of the city's most inviting places to live as well as work now had a dark crater blown through the middle of it. Even with financial help, small businesses that depended on foot traffic from the trade center suffered economically, just as the shops on Radio Row had when ridership on the Hudson Tubes declined. Instead of remaining in Lower Manhattan, many of the firms that lost their offices in the trade center fled to Midtown or New Jersey. Residents of Battery Park City and local merchants have questioned whether a sunken, and presumably somber, memorial like the one proposed by Libeskind would impede the easy circulation of people through the area. Guy Tozzoli even reappeared at one point in the debate, having drawn up plans for a giant underground convention center that would occupy much of the bathtub.

More than anything else, these battles revolved around conflicting visions of the future of Lower Manhattan, just as they did when David Rockefeller set out to remake the area in the 1950s.

· · ·

The round, barren hills at the Fresh Kills landfill in Staten Island were swollen with more than fifty years of the city's garbage. The city had stopped hauling its trash to Fresh Kills early in 2001, but began using it again as a ready destination for the wreckage being shipped from ground zero. In late September 2001, an armada of mechanical grapplers, steel cutters, front loaders, and trucks were working near a large compound of dark green tents at the landfill. There, investigators—crime investigators, not the structural kind—had put together a sort of assembly line to sift the conical piles of light metal. Debris ran down a humped conveyor belt where some of the dirt was sifted out. In another place, dozens of people in clean white jumpsuits raked small piles of debris like otherworldly gardeners.

Slightly lower on the hill, steel from the trade center was piled thirty feet high in a series of stacks that wandered along the slope like an immense barrow. Nearby, carefully stacked, were hundreds of vehicles that had been smashed in the collapse. Perhaps because they instantly evoked the dead, these smashed passenger cars, police cruisers, ambulances, and fire trucks created their own aura of silence and awe on the dusty hill. The torn metal on the front of one fire truck split a small decal of the American flag into three pieces. A black New York Police Department squad car lay stacked on a blue one. A partly crushed car with a silvery paint job advertised ORION MECHANICAL SYSTEMS INC. on its door.

The power of these haunted things would also help explain why the remains of the World Trade Center—its wrecked steel and ductwork and piping and shiny aluminum cladding—would never be dealt with quite rationally. The immeasurable importance of those remains, the preciousness of the messages they carried from the inferno on September 11, could not be confronted squarely without facing the howls of the dead in every buckled strut or beam that had once sheltered humanity. It was far simpler to deny that importance and send the metal off to be cut up and melted for new car bumpers or bridge supports—something like plowing up a shadowy and disturbing old graveyard and planting it over with a fresh crop of corn.

Fresh Kills was one of several landfills and scrap yards that were collecting the great piles of steel. From those places, the World Trade Center, which had once been assembled with so much care and hope and effort, was cut up and sent away on the seas that still nurtured the Port of New York, the great harbor that Austin Tobin had believed his buildings would do so much to replace. The effort was as monumental as the original construction had been. At another New Jersey scrap yard with a crisp view of the broken Manhattan skyline, a seemingly endless, temple-pounding boom rose in a crescendo and echoed as mound after mound of trade center steel was dumped into the belly of a waiting freighter. Named the *Firmeza*, it would carry the steel to recycling plants around the world.

Near the docks, men with crackling blue cutting torches sliced up more of the steel so that it could be loaded into a twenty-foot-long scoop that rested beside the freighter. But it was only up on the ship itself, at the edge of the great maw of one of the ship's bays, that the essential dignity and awesomeness of the structure, the World Trade Center, could once again be seen.

A big green crane raised the overloaded scoop and swung it over the ship's bay with such fluid grace that the steel seemed to be soaring one last time, propelled into the sky with great skill and determination—firmness, *Firmeza*—above a land filled with admiring, angry, and wondering eyes. The scoop tilted. A cascade of steel fell deep into the ship's bay, struck bottom with an overwhelming crash, and caused the entire vessel to quake for long seconds. A stray piece of concrete bounced, came to rest. Fine dust rose from the belly of the ship and slipped away on a breeze.

SOURCES AND NOTES

■ ■ ■

Abbreviations

BW   *Business Week*
CFAH   Center for American History at the University of Texas, Austin
DLMA   Downtown–Lower Manhattan Association
DR   David Rockefeller
ENR   *Engineering News-Record*
HT   *New York Herald Tribune*＊
NR   Nelson Rockefeller
NYT   *The New York Times*
PA   The Port of New York Authority
WSJ   *Wall Street Journal*
WTC   World Trade Center
WZ   William Zeckendorf
Yama   Minoru Yamasaki

PROLOGUE

Sources

Books and Articles

Gillespie, *Twin Towers*; Doig, *Empire on the Hudson*; Clayton Knowles, "New Fight Begun on Trade Center," *NYT*, Feb. 14, 1964; Thomas W. Ennis, "Critics Impugned on Trade Center," *NYT*, Feb. 15, 1964; "PA Scores Enemies of Big Trade Center," *World-Telegram*, Feb. 14, 1964, CFAH; William McFadden, "Realty Men Battle Big Trade Center," *Journal-American*, Feb. 14, 1964, CFAH.

Authors' Interviews

Matthew Quesada; Peter Rinaldi; George Tamaro; Gennaro Liguori.

Notes

page
1   *Site visit:* Glanz visited the site escorted by PA officials Peter Rinaldi and Greg Trevor on June 10, 2003, and rode in the cherry picker with Quesada.
The sentiments on the effective presence of the vanished trade center should not be attributed to Quesada.

＊All articles from the *Herald Tribune* newspaper morgue are courtesy Center for American History at the University of Texas, Austin. This includes not only *HT* articles but also those from the *World-Telegram* and the *Journal-American*.

1 *Condition of the wall:* Tamaro interview.
3 *Constructing the wall:* Liguori interview.
5 *Shouldered their way:* Gillespie, *Twin Towers*, explored this idea extensively.
6 *Opponents warn of crash:* Knowles, *NYT*, Feb. 14, 1964; Ennis, *NYT*, Feb. 15, 1964; *World-Telegram*, Feb. 14, 1964; McFadden, *Journal-American*, Feb. 14, 1964, *Journal-American*, Feb. 16, 1964.

CHAPTER 1: DAVID'S TURN

Sources

Books, Articles, and Pamphlets

Rockefeller, *Memoirs*; Rockefeller, *Creative Management in Banking*; Collier and Horowitz, *The Rockefellers: An American Dynasty*; Chernow, *Titan: The Life of John D. Rockefeller*; Zeckendorf, *The Autobiography of William Zeckendorf*; Wilson, *The Chase: The Chase Manhattan Bank, N.A., 1945–1985*; Pacelle, *Empire: A Tale of Obsession, Betrayal, and the Battle for the American Icon*; Harr and Johnson, *The Rockefeller Century*; Joe Alex Morris, *Those Rockefeller Brothers: An Informal Biography of Five Extraordinary Young Men*; Mujica, *History of the Skyscraper*; Wermiel, *The Fireproof Building: Technology and Public Safety in the Nineteenth-Century American City*; Hart, Henn, and Sontag, *Multi-Storey Buildings in Steel*; Allen, *New York, New York: A History of the World's Most Exhilarating and Challenging City*; Willensky and White, *AIA Guide to New York City*; Caro, *The Power Broker: Robert Moses and the Fall of New York*; Karwatka, *Technology's Past*; Landau and Condit, *Rise of the New York Skyscraper: 1865–1913*; Doig, *Empire on the Hudson*.

Vartanig G. Vartan, "Zeckendorf Struggle to Save His Real-Estate Empire Has Been Long and Arduous," *NYT*, May 19, 1965; Michael Sterne, "William Zeckendorf, Real Estate Developer, 71, Dies," *NYT*, Oct. 2, 1976; E. J. Kahn Jr., "Profiles: Resources and Responsibilities-2," *New Yorker*, Jan. 16, 1965; E. J. Kahn Jr., "Profiles: Resources and Responsibilities-1," *New Yorker*, Jan. 9, 1965; "Wreckers Attack Morningside Site," *NYT*, Jan. 12, 1954; C. G. Poore, "Greatest Skyscraper Rises on a Clockwork Schedule," *NYT*, July 27, 1930; "Tallest Tower Built in Less Than a Year," *NYT*, May 2, 1931; "Empire State Tower, Tallest in World, Is Opened by Hoover," *NYT*, May 2, 1931; "Dewey Picks Board for Trade Center," *NYT*, July 7, 1946; Charles B. Crisman, "Plans Are Tabled for Trade Center," *NYT*, Nov. 10, 1946; Roger Cohen, "Casting Giant Shadows: The Politics of Building the World Trade Center," *Portfolio*, winter 1990–1991, vol. 3, no. 1; "A New Downtown Manhattan," *NYT*, editorial, Oct. 15, 1958.

"Relocation: Critical Phase of Redevelopment; The Experience of Morningside Gardens, New York City," pamphlet printed by Morningside Heights Inc., October 1957, in the Morningside Area Alliance Records, Columbia University Archives-Columbiana Library; Charles R. Otis, "Inventor; Originator of Otis Safety Elevator Business; 1811–1861," Elisha Graves Otis biography published 1911 by Otis Co., Otis Elevator Co. Archives, Record Group 8; "Machinery at the Crystal Palace," *New-York Daily Tribune*, May 30, 1854, Otis Elevator Co. Archives; "Otis' Improved Elevator," *Scientific American*, Nov. 25, 1854, p. 85, Otis Elevator Co. Archives; Donald Dale Jackson, "Elevating Thoughts from Elisha Otis and Fellow Uplifters," *Smithsonian*, November 1989, vol. 20, no. 8, p. 2184, courtesy National Inventors Hall of Fame; Glenn Collins,

"New Body for a Seaport's Soul; At Maritime Museum's Remade Home, Old Walls Talk," *NYT*, July 3, 2003.

Authors' Interviews

Christopher Schuberth; David Rockefeller; Warren T. Lindquist; William Zucker; Francis L. Kellogg.

Documents

Lower Manhattan Recommended Land Use Redevelopment Areas, Traffic Improvements, Oct. 14, 1958, report by Downtown–Lower Manhattan Association; McKinsey & Co., *Proposed Study of a World Trade and Finance Center, Downtown–Lower Manhattan Association*, May 25, 1959; Rockefeller Archive Center; Progress Report by David Rockefeller, copy of his speech at the Bankers Club, Oct. 8, 1959; *A Proposal for the Port of New York Downtown–Lower Manhattan Association*, Jan. 27, 1960, signed by DR and John D. Butt, by the Downtown–Lower Manhattan Association.

Oral History

John J. McCloy, July 19, 1978, JP Morgan Chase Archives; DR, Oct. 23, 1980, Chase oral history project at JP Morgan Chase Archives.

Notes

page

7 *DR's commute:* DR, *Memoirs*, pp. 127, 162; Collier and Horowitz, p. 310.

7 *Discussion between WZ to DR:* DR tells this story in an Oct. 23, 1980, oral history interview, and in his autobiography, *Memoirs* (p. 162); it is also told in Wilson's *The Chase*, an official biography of the bank by its retired senior vice president and chief economist. WZ has his own version of it in his own autobiography.

8 *WZ at work:* Zeckendorf, p. 98, and photo in insert following p. 152; Vartan, *NYT*, May 19, 1965; Sterne, *NYT*, Oct. 2, 1976.

8 *"alive at 18 percent":* Vartan, *NYT*, May 19, 1965.

8 *Rockefeller family money:* The Rockefeller family had among the largest set of holdings at Chase.

9 *Chase's real estate:* Chase did not end up owning 40 Wall Street, even though it had merged with Bank of Manhattan. Rockefeller, *Creative Management in Banking*, p. 25, cites nine thousand employees downtown.

9 *Chase's corporate brethren:* Seagram Building, 1954–1958 at 375 Park Avenue; Lever House, 1950–1952 at 390 Park Avenue; Colgate-Palmolive Building at 300 Park Avenue at East Forty-ninth Street, NW corner to East Fiftieth Street, completed in 1955.

9 *"You know, the big fellow":* from McCloy's 1978 oral history. He was specifically discussing WZ's role in creating the new Chase tower.

10 *"grapefruit out of lemons":* Sterne, *NYT*, Oct. 2, 1976.

10 *Moving uptown:* In his oral history interview, McCloy said Sheperd came back to him "after our plans came out," presumably meaning Chase's preliminary plans to stay downtown.

10 *"Sentiment should never be":* DR, *Memoirs*, p. 161.

10 *DR and McCloy bucking the trend:* "Downtown was the hearthstone of the city,"

McCloy said in his interview in the oral history project at JP Morgan Chase Archives. McCloy suggested that from his perspective, even before WZ came up with this solution, he had in effect decided Chase would somehow find a way to stay downtown. "The decision, as I look back on it, was largely mine, for better or for worse," he said in the Aug. 20, 1962, oral history interview, although he repeatedly mentioned Rockefeller's involvement.

10 *New York Stock Exchange:* Wilson, p. 104.

10 *Stockholders' interests:* Chase's assets were valued at $7.5 billion in 1955, according to Wilson.

11 *Stop the sale:* New Yorker, Jan. 9, 1965; Wilson.

11 *WZ's proposal:* DR, Memoirs, p. 163; Zeckendorf, p. 265.

12 *DR's view:* Pacelle, p. 32; DR's mother, Abby Aldrich Rockefeller, commissioned a painting of the view from this window that the authors were shown in DR's fifty-sixth-floor office in Rockefeller Center on June 17, 2002. The painter was Stefan Hirsch. Peter J. Johnson, a Rockefeller biographer, provided the following information by e-mail on July 23, 2002: "The title of the painting is 'Midtown Range.' It was painted in 1931. The view was to the south from David Rockefeller's fifth floor bedroom at his parents' home at Number 10 West 54th Street. . . . It is a cityscape with the spires of St. Patrick's Cathedral in the near distance and the Chrysler Building and Empire State Buildings (both recently completed) in the distance. The painting was commissioned by Mrs. Rockefeller and purchased from the Downtown Gallery." The view is also described in DR's *Memoirs*, p. 51.

13 *John D. Rockefeller Sr.:* Chernow, in *Titan*, p. 430, says this. (Collier and Horowitz give a higher figure of 95 percent—p. 29.) The $2,000 investment in 1859 comes from a biography of John D. Rockefeller Sr. in the Rockefeller Archive Center.

13 *"cheap and good":* Chernow, p. 256.

13 *"Our great money makers":* Wealth against Commonwealth, 1894, by Henry Demarest Lloyd, quoted in Collier and Horowitz, p. 43.

13 *Stewardship:* New Yorker, Jan. 16, 1965: "All the Rockefellers have heard the word 'stewardship' so often that it makes them squirm; John, who, as the oldest brother, is the chief steward of his generation, cannot utter the word without a wry smile."

13 *Rockefeller brothers:* Morris, pp. 86, 103, chapter 8.

14 *Beetles:* Rockefeller's beetle collecting would last much of his life. Ultimately, he would have at least forty thousand different bugs, making it one of the nation's most important private collections. He would even hire an aide to help him maintain it. And Rockefeller carried small glass bottles, with a stockpile of cotton and formaldehyde, to collect specimens as he traveled around the world.

14 *DR's blandness:* See, for example, "Born to Be Mild," by David Brooks, NYT Book Review, Oct. 20, 2002.

14 *DR's Ph.D.:* DR's remarks about why, in part, he got a Ph.D., were made during a talk at George Washington University in Washington, on Nov. 1, 2002. That same month, on PBS Newshour, DR himself said that he was somewhat lonely as a kid. "I think I was a bit isolated. . . . I probably did not have the kind of youth that the average American boy has growing up in New York City" (Nov. 29, 2002). DR also cited William Lyon Mackenzie King, a close friend of John D. Rockefeller Jr. and the former prime minister of Canada, as an influence in his decision to get a doctorate.

14 *"the kind of face"*: New Yorker, Jan. 9, 1965.

15 *"There is a moral stigma"*: Dissertation is quoted in *New Yorker* profile of DR, Jan. 16, 1965.

15 *DR studies in northern Africa*: DR, Memoirs, pp. 115, 119, and telephone interview with Warren T. Lindquist, who worked with DR in Paris, at the military attaché office.

15 *Aldrich's question*: From 1980 interview with DR, by Chase oral history project, p. 4.

15 *DR at Chase*: DR, Memoirs, p.127; Collier and Horowitz, p. 430.

15 *Leaflet*: Columbia University Archives.

16 *Morningside Heights*: For general references on this section, see: "Wreckers Attack Morningside Site," *NYT*, Jan. 12, 1954; Charles Grutzner, "City's 'Acropolis' Combating Slums," *NYT*, May 21, 1957; "3-Year Slum Plan Relocates 5,935," *NYT*, Oct. 21, 1957; Wayne Philips, "Slums Engulfing Columbia Section," *NYT*, June 9, 1958; "Morningside Group Expands Activities," *NYT*, Jan. 28, 1952; "Morningside Area Asks More Schools," *NYT*, May 20, 1948; "Morningside Area Depicted in Study," *NYT*, April 14, 1949; "Communities Stressed; David Rockefeller Calls for an Attention to Needs," *NYT*, Oct. 5, 1950; Lee E. Cooper, "Housing Families of Middle Income," *NYT*, Jan. 2, 1954; "Expert to Battle Crime Is Hired by Morningside Heights Group," *NYT*, Jan. 25, 1954.

16 *Morningside Heights Inc.*: "Relocation: Critical Phase of Redevelopment; The Experience of Morningside Gardens, New York City," October 1957 pamphlet, Columbia University Archives.

17 *"unguided urban evolution"*: "Outline of Talk to the Men's Class by Mr. David Rockefeller," Riverside Church, Oct. 5, 1948, Columbia University Archives.

17 *Relocating tenants*: Caro, p. 495 and chapter 41. Orton would blow the whistle on false relocation statistics put out by Robert Moses in his Title I slum-clearance projects.

17 *"The Present Crisis"*: Memorandum from Lawrence M. Orton to DR, Jan. 1, 1953, Subject: The Present Crisis, courtesy Columbia University Archives.

18 *"71 deteriorating"*: "Relocation: Critical Phase of Redevelopment; The Experience of Morningside Gardens, New York City," October 1957 pamphlet, Columbia University Archives.

19 *Morningside residents*: The number would soar to some thirty-five hundred families displaced when Moses tacked the General Grant Houses public housing project onto the north side of the Morningside Heights project. See "Wreckers Attack Morningside Site," *NYT*, Jan. 12, 1954.

19 *"If we accept the co-op"*: Many of these details come from a November 1951 memo written by Bernard Weinberg to Lawrence M. Orton, executive director of Morningside Heights Inc., Columbia University Archives. Weinberg had attended the meetings and gave a firsthand account of them.

19 *Handbill*: Pamphlets and handbills in the Columbia University Archives.

19 *"Communist inspired"*: November 1951 memo by Bernard Weinberg to Lawrence M. Orton, in the Columbia University Archives. Weinberg notes that at one meeting, a question from the floor dealt with "what to say to those who claimed that the Save Our Homes Committee was Communist inspired"; "Estimate Board Ejects Two in Housing Row," *New York World-Telegram*, May 8, 1952, Columbia University Archives.

20 *Demolition day:* NYT covered the groundbreaking in Jan. 12, 1954, story, "Wreckers Attack Morningside Site."

20 *"As you realize":* Letter from Robert Moses to DR, Sept. 27, 1955, in the JP Morgan Chase Archives.

20 *Moses liked big construction:* "Hardly ever": as Michael Shapiro demonstrated in *The Last Good Season: Brooklyn, the Dodgers and Their Final Pennant Race Together,* Moses did occasionally oppose a construction project that didn't serve his interests, as when Walter O'Malley, the owner of the Brooklyn Dodgers, wanted to build a new field for his team.

20 *Moses wanted DR's support:* Moses also wanted DR's support for a housing project at Battery Park, a tougher sell. "Dear David," read a letter Moses sent to DR on Oct. 20, 1955, as the Chase approvals for its headquarters were pending. "We should like to move ahead with the arrangement for the proposed Title I Battery Park project if we can be assured that you and Chase and related interests will undertake to provide the sponsorship for this project." A letter from DR to Moses on Oct. 26, 1955, made clear that DR would get behind this project as well. Letters in the JP Morgan Chase Archives.

21 *Stabilizing the financial district:* Zeckendorf, chapter 19. According to Peter J. Johnson, a Rockefeller historian: "The meeting with Robert Moses occurred on October 31, 1955, and was held in the Executive Dining Room of Chase's headquarters at 18 Pine Street. David and Walter Severinghaus of Skidmore, Owings & Merrill lunched with Moses and his associate, George Spargo. That was when the request was made to close Cedar Street."

21 *"future in Lower Manhattan":* Interview by Lipton and Glanz with DR, June 17, 2002, at 30 Rockefeller Plaza, in which he recalled this meeting with Moses.

21 *"they are simply letterhead":* Dec. 10, 1955, letter from Moses to Rockefeller, on his personal stationery, listing his home address, courtesy JP Morgan Chase Archives.

21 *Members of Downtown–Lower Manhattan Association:* The names included Robert Lehman of Lehman Brothers, Henry S. Morgan of Morgan, Stanley & Co, Peter Grace Jr. of W. R. Grace & Co., Ralph T. Reed of American Express Co., and Henry C. Alexander of Morgan Guaranty Trust Co. of New York, each enormous powers of their time.

22 *"Spectacular":* McCloy, oral history interview, July 19, 1978, p. 17, courtesy JP Morgan Chase Archives.

22 *Bank building dimensions:* The bank vault is in the fifth subbasement floor, 350 feet long and 100 feet wide, with 8-foot ceilings. From a Chase fact sheet issued at the time the building was proposed. Chase claim that it was tallest since the RCA Building in 1933, in documents at JP Morgan Chase Archives.

22 *Otis and the elevator:* Mujica, chapter 1; Otis, "Inventor"; *New-York Daily Tribune,* May 30, 1854; *Scientific American,* Nov. 25, 1854, p. 85; *Smithsonian,* November 1989; Karwatka.

23 *Hyde:* Hyde's story, of how he started Equitable, is told in a book published by the company, Equitable Life Assurance Society of the United States, in 1901: *Henry Baldwin Hyde: A Biographical Sketch.* See also Landau and Condit.

24 *Stairway rendered pointless:* See also Landau and Condit, p. 71.

24 *Building with iron:* Wermiel, chapter 5, and private communications with Sara E. Wermiel.

24 *John Noble Stearns:* Mujica, chapter 2. Stearns is identified only as the owner here.
25 *"Is there someway":* Bradford Lee Gilbert letter, written to the *NYT* and published on Aug. 19, 1899, in which he discussed the origin of the Tower Building.
25 *Plaque:* NYT, May 21, 1905.
25 *The starting gun:* See Domosh, chapter 3, for a detailed inventory of the surge in skyscraper construction in Manhattan after 1890.
26 *Ad for the Singer Building:* Advertisement in the *NYT* on April 14, 1907, a year before it opened. The building was ultimately demolished in 1968.
26 *Cass Gilbert:* Gilbert was one of the first architects to incorporate the Gothic form into skyscrapers, something that would become a major feature in so many tall buildings, including the World Trade Center.
27 *The new Grand Central Terminal: In Pursuit of Gotham: Culture and Commerce in New York,* by William R. Taylor (Oxford University Press, New York, 1992), among many other books, details the features of the new Grand Central Terminal, as do articles that appeared in the *NYT* at the time. The 56-story Chanin Building, the 53-story Lincoln Building, and the 35-story Daily News Building were all erected on Forty-second Street around 1929. The 33-story Graybar Building went up on Lexington Avenue, the 35-story New York Central Building rose a block over on Park Avenue, and the 42-story Lefcourt Building was built on Madison.
27 *Chrysler Building spire:* Allen, p. 265; Willensky and White, p. 253.
28 *Empire State Building construction:* Caro, see p. 293 on Smith's role with the building; Poore, *NYT,* July 27, 1930; *NYT,* May 2, 1931.
28 *Perisphere dimensions:* Paul Goldberger, "World's Fair of '39 Revisited," *NYT,* June 20, 1980.
29 *Historical role of New York in World Trade:* NYT, July 3, 2003.
31 *Idea for WTC comes and goes:* NYT, July 7, 1946; *NYT,* Nov. 10, 1946; *Portfolio,* winter 1990–1991, vol. 3, no. 1.
31 *Aldrich meets Hitler:* Aldrich, concerned in part about the fate of the bank's millions invested in Germany, met with Hitler to encourage him to cool his confrontational ways. The banker was startled, after being escorted into Hitler's mountain chalet, to see the German leader step forward, raise his arm, and say "Heil, Hitler." See Johnson's *Winthrop W. Aldrich, Lawyer, Banker, Diplomat* for meeting with Peron (p. 324) and with Hitler (p. 163).
31 *DR meets dictators:* Even DR's own daughter, Peggy, seemed skeptical, saying that her father "always tried to justify support for dictatorships via the notion that the economic growth which stability brought to these countries made the average person there better off" (Collier and Horowitz, p. 539).
32 *DLMA Report: Lower Manhattan Recommended Land Use Redevelopment Areas, Traffic Improvements,* Oct. 14, 1958, by DLMA.
32 *NYT coverage:* DR and his staff at the DLMA had a very carefully thought-out plan for how to try to get positive coverage in the *NYT,* which included meetings with editors and letters to Arthur Ochs Sulzberger, the publisher, when something was ignored, or printed that he did not like. "In accordance with your own suggestion," DR wrote in one letter to Sulzberger on March 12, 1964, regarding the WTC project, "I am calling these things to your attention, in the interest of full and impartial discussion of the news about this great project which you agree is so vitally important for New York and the bi-State port area."

Copies of DR's letter, as well as a December 1963 letter where DR complains to Sulzberger and then another in which Sulzberger defends the paper's coverage, are maintained at the Rockefeller Archive Center; *NYT*, Oct. 15, 1958.

34 *"You better stand there":* Interview with Zucker, December 2002. Lindquist separately said he discussed the McKinsey report with DR and decided together that the project should go ahead anyway.

34 *The meeting went on as scheduled:* Staff at McKinsey & Co. said that they could not address the accuracy of the story about Clee, as he is deceased and the partner who worked with him at the time on the report, John S. Crowley, was not able to be interviewed.

34 *"discontinue further study":* McKinsey & Co. preliminary study of World Trade and Finance Center, discussed at Aug. 11, 1959, meeting of executive committee of DLMA.

34 *design for riverside complex:* Sept. 8, 1959, special meeting of the executive committee, 3:30 P.M., at 24 Pine Street, copy of the minutes. Also interview with Lindquist: "There was no need to do a lot of fooling around," Lindquist said. "Unless we moved on it, it would die."

35 *"I firmly believe":* Progress Report by David Rockefeller, copy of his speech at the Bankers Club, Oct. 8, 1959.

37 *"on the brink of a boom":* A Proposal for the DLMA, Jan. 27, 1960, signed by Rockefeller and John D. Butt.

CHAPTER 2: GAMBIT

Sources

Books and Articles

Doig, *Empire on the Hudson: Entrepreneurial Vision and Political Power at the Port of New York Authority;* Doig and Hargrove, *Leadership and Innovation;* Kutz, *Rockefeller Power;* David Rockefeller, *Memoirs;* Ruchelman, *The World Trade Center: Politics and Policies of Skyscraper Development;* Danielson and Doig, *New York: The Politics of Urban Regional Development;* Eric Darton, *Divided We Stand;* Gillespie, *Twin Towers;* Caro, *The Power Broker: Robert Moses and the Fall of New York.*

Charles Grutzner, "A World Center of Trade Mapped Off Wall Street," *NYT,* Jan. 27, 1960; "Idlewild's Defender," *NYT,* July 14, 1959; Richard Oliver, "I Call on Austin Tobin," *New York Newsday,* March 29, 1969; Frank J. Prial, "Austin J. Tobin, Executive Director of Port Authority for 30 Years, Dies," *NYT,* Feb. 28, 1978; "Clarence Tobin, 79, Ex-Court Reporter," *NYT,* March 9, 1957; Guy Savino, "PA Stormy, But Honest," *Newark Evening News,* February 1952; Victor Wilson, "Port Authority's Tobin Guilty of Contempt," *HT,* June 16, 1961; Joseph C. Ingraham, "Tobin Convicted of Balking House Study of Port Body," *NYT,* June 16, 1961; Bruce Rosen, "Austin Tobin, Shaper of PA, Dies," *Record* (Bergen and Passaic Counties, N.J.), Feb. 9, 1978; Roger Harris, "Austin J. Tobin: P.A. Pioneer Dies of Cancer in N.Y. at 74," Newark Star-Ledger, Feb. 9, 1978; George Cable Wright, "Tobin Fears End of Port Authority," *NYT,* April 8, 1954; Theodore W. Kheel, "How the Port Authority Is Strangling New York," *New York,* 1968; "The Port Authority Battles Its Critics," *BW,* April 3, 1971; "The Port Authority Hearings," *NYT,* Dec. 6, 1960; "What a Political Invention Did for N.Y.," *BW,* July 14, 1956, p. 74; Walter Hamshar, "Port Unit Duels with Celler," *HT,* Nov. 30, 1960; "Erie Plans to End Food Delivery Here; Arranges to Quit Manhattan

Piers and Carry Only to Jersey Terminals," *NYT*, Feb. 14, 1923; "Aid to Fruit Men Promised by City," *NYT*, Nov. 17, 1948; "New Weehawken Banana Terminal Set to Handle 8,000 Stems an Hour," *NYT*, Aug. 16, 1952; "Railways to Join at Produce Piers," *NYT*, May, 1, 1955; "City's Waterfront Held 'Savage Jungle,'" *NYT*, Feb. 11, 1953; Guy Savino, "Big Trade Center Endorsed by PA," *Newark Sunday News*, March 12, 1961; "Trade Center Plans Outlined," *Journal American*, Oct. 26, 1960; "Who'll Run Trade Center?" *Daily News*, Oct. 27, 1960; Charles Grutzner, "$250 Million Trade Center Here Wins Backing of Port Authority," *NYT*, Oct. 26, 1960; Roger Cohen, "Casting Giant Shadows: The Politics of Building the World Trade Center," *Portfolio*, winter 1990–1991, vol. 3, no. 1; Milton Honig, "Jersey Official Backs H&M Sale," *NYT*, Jan. 27, 1961; George Cable Wright, "Rail Plan Drawn by Port Agency," *NYT*, March 21, 1961; "Rockefeller Signs Bi-State Package," *NYT*, April 9, 1961; "Port Agency Bill Fought in Jersey," *NYT*, May 24, 1961; "Hughes Okays Trade Center & Tubes Deal," *HT*, Dec. 28, 1961; 1961 Annual Report, PA; Bernard Stengren, "Port Agency Gets a Record Budget," *NYT*, Jan. 17, 1964; Charles G. Bennett, "Wagner Demands Tubes-Bill Delay," *NYT*, Feb. 16, 1962; "Mayor Says Tubes Bill Makes City 'Outsider,'" *HT*, Feb. 16, 1962; "Trade Center to Be Surveyed," *NYT*, Feb. 12, 1966.

Authors' Interviews

Patrick Falvey; Richard Sullivan, Jack Brendlen; Lloyd Schwalb; Lou Gambaccini, Austin Tobin Jr.; Mortimer Matz; Leatrice Yelman; Meryl Yelman; Richard Leone; Edward Kresky; William Ronan; John Dragonette; Guy Tozzoli; Farley Tobin; Joseph Solomon; Joseph Lesser; Robert Price.

Documents

"A World Trade Center in the Port of New York," Port of New York Authority, March 10, 1961, courtesy Richard Sullivan; "The Hudson & Manhattan World Trade Center Project," PA, Jan. 29, 1962; Maynard Trimble Robison, "Rebuilding Lower Manhattan," City University of New York Ph.D. dissertation, 1976 (Xerox University Microfilms, Ann Arbor, Mich.); Tobin, Weekly Report to the Commissioners for the week ending March 20, 1961, courtesy Angus Kress Gillespie; 1961 Annual Report, PA.

Notes

page

38   *PA headquarters:* Doig, chapter 9; Glanz was given a tour of the building by its current owners and shown, among other things, a core sample taken from one of the floors.

38   *Tobin gathering:* Falvey interview. The meeting must have taken place by Feb. 11, 1960, when the study was publicly announced. *NYT*, Feb. 12, 1960; Doig and Hargrove, p. 125; Jameson Doig, private communication, Nov. 25, 2002, based on his interviews with Roger Gilman; Sullivan interview; Robison, "Rebuilding Lower Manhattan," City University of New York Ph.D. dissertation; Lindquist interview; Ronan interview. Some of the ideas in this chapter were explored in Gillespie, chapter 1; and throughout Doig, Doig and Hargrove, and Danielson and Doig.

39   *Headline:* Grutzner, *NYT*, Jan. 27, 1960. The cited line was a subhead.

39   *"What's a World Trade Center?":* Sullivan interview.

40   *"promotion of the port":* Falvey interview.

41 *Outmaneuvered:* Doig, chapter 11 and epilogue.

41 *Tobin's Suite 1503 description:* Brendlen interview.

41 *William Mortimer Tobin and Clarence Tobin:* Tobin Jr. interview; Prial, *NYT*, Feb. 28, 1978; *NYT*, March 9, 1957; Doig and Hargrove, p. 97.

42 *Salutatory address:* Courtesy Holy Cross College Archive, Worcester, Mass.

42 *Yearbook entry:* Courtesy Farley Tobin and Jameson Doig.

42 *Tobin's rise:* Obituaries courtesy Farley Tobin: *Daily Journal; Asbury Park Press; Herald-News*, Passaic, N.J.; *Jersey Journal; Staten Island Advance; New York Post; Journal of Commerce; Newsday; New York Daily News; Thursday Dispatch*, Union City, N.J.; *Daily Bond Buyer; Record* (Bergen and Passaic Counties, N.J.); all Feb. 9, 1978. See also editorial, "Austin J. Tobin," Newark *Star-Ledger*, Feb. 13, 1978.

42 *Tobin description:* Savino, *Newark Evening News*, Feb. 1952; *NYT*, July 14, 1959; Matz, Kresky, and Yelman interviews.

43 *Creation of PA:* Portions of the general history of the Port Authority here rely on Doig. See also *BW*, July 14, 1956; "A Chronology of The Port of New York Authority: 1921–1967," produced by Port Authority public relations department, undated; Michael Aronson, "The Port Authority: Austin Tobin," *New York* Daily News, Oct. 25, 1999; Michael Tomasky, "The Story Behind the Towers," *New York Review of Books*, March 14, 2002; Michael Tomasky, "The World Trade Center: Before, During, & After," *New York Review of Books*, March 28, 2002; Darton; Gillespie.

43 *"ruinous competition:"* Wright, *NYT*, April 8, 1954.

44 *"Above all else":* Kheel, *New York*, 1968.

44 *Profitability: BW*, April 3, 1971, p. 48; Honig, *NYT*, Jan. 27, 1961; Senate Resolution No. 7, Supplementary Statement of Austin J. Tobin on Commuter Rail Transportation, Trenton, N.J., Sept. 27, 1960; Address by Austin J. Tobin before the Regional Plan Association, 15th Regional Plan Conference, Hotel Roosevelt, New York City, Oct. 5, 1960; Wright, *NYT*, April 8, 1954.

44 *PA statistics: NYT*, Dec. 6, 1960; *BW*, July 14, 1956, p. 74; Hamshar, *HT*, Nov. 30, 1960.

44 *Cartoon:* Specific details from an undated cartoon in the *Elizabeth Daily Journal*, courtesy Farley Tobin.

44 *Salary:* "I have read that in the press, where my salary has been published many times," was all Tobin would say when he was once asked about it under oath. Hearings before Subcommittee No. 5 of the Committee on the Judiciary, House of Representatives, 86th Congress, Nov. 28, 29, 30, Dec. 1 and 2, 1960, Serial No. 24 (U.S. Government Printing Office, Washington, 1961), p. 26.

45 *Revision of Lazarus poem:* Schwalb interview; *Newsweek*, from morgue files of Center for American History, University of Texas at Austin.

45 *Holland Tunnel statistics:* Details come from *NYT* coverage in 1927 of the events.

46 *Erie Railroad rail car floats: NYT*, Feb. 14, 1923.

47 *"If you think":* Ibid.

47 *"relieve the railroad":* Ibid.

46 *Lighterage barge service:* "Free Lighterage Upheld by I.C.C.; Port Called a Unit," *NYT*, Aug. 3, 1934. This decision came after a decade of debate about requests by the railroads to either discontinue the lighterage service—Erie and Pennsylvania railroads both threatened to stop delivering certain goods by barge to Manhattan—or later to impose a charge for the service.

47 *Why PA was created:* The entire issue of the reasons for creating the PA and the

freight tunnel itself is examined extensively in Doig. PA offered a plan shortly after it was created so that the island of Manhattan would be "connected with New Jersey by bridge or tunnel or both and freight destined to and from Manhattan to be carried underground, so far as practicable, by such system." In a way, the plan suggested what was the "most expeditious, economical and practical transportation of freight, especially meat, produce, milk and other commodities comprising the daily needs of the people." See Doig, p. 438.

48 *"The freight rates":* McCormack made these remarks in "The Decline of the Port of New York, a Report to the Mayor," which he wrote in 1952 to Mayor Vincent Impellitteri, but his remarks were recalling his reaction to the imposition of the fee, back in 1948.

48 *"Horse and buggy facilities":* Grant's comments made in two stories in the *NYT,* Oct. 11, 1949, and Dec. 11, 1949.

49 *"Drastic action or finis":* McCormack made these remarks in "The Decline of the Port of New York, a Report to the Mayor."

49 *McCormack's small empire:* Page 3535 of NY State Crime Commission transcript of hearing on Jan. 29, 1953, where McCormack testified.

50 *McCormack at corruption hearings:* New York State Crime Commission, report, five volumes, complete transcript of the 1952–1953 hearings. These hearings—and the stories that surfaced during them—helped inspire the 1954 film *On the Waterfront.* McCormack was cited by Budd Schulberg as one of the inspirations in a Jan. 6, 1980, *NYT Magazine* article, "The Inside Story of 'Waterfront' "; Ryan's State Crime Commission testimony, Jan. 30, 1953.

51 *"savage jungle":* "City's Waterfront Held 'Savage Jungle,'" *NYT,* Feb. 11, 1953.

51 *"leader in commerce":* William Longgood, "Port Authority Executive Has Poet's View of Job," *Sunday World-Telegram,* Feb. 1952, courtesy Farley Tobin.

52 *Sullivan's report:* "A World Trade Center in the Port of New York," PA, March 10, 1961, courtesy Richard Sullivan.

54 *Estimated cost:* Savino, *Newark Sunday News,* March 12, 1961.

54 *Tobin flogging the project:* "I am privileged to have this opportunity to talk to you today about an exciting project," Tobin told the Society of Foreign Consuls in New York as early as May 4, 1960, before describing a WTC with 5 to 6 million square feet of floor space and lots of parking.

54 *PA study: Journal American,* Oct. 26, 1960; *Daily News,* Oct. 27, 1960; Grutzner, *NYT,* Oct. 26, 1960.

55 *NR as builder:* DR, p. 191; DR, Kresky, and Tobin Jr. interviews.

55 *PA history:* References on the political history include Cohen, *Portfolio,* p. 14, as well as a more extended version of the article provided by Cohen to the authors; Ruchelman; and numerous interviews, including those with Gambaccini, Kresky, and Sullivan.

55 *Tube operations:* "The Hudson & Manhattan World Trade Center Project," PA, Jan. 29, 1962; Robison, "Rebuilding Lower Manhattan," City University of New York Ph.D. dissertation, p. 71.

56 *NR bundles projects:* Wright, *NYT,* March 21, 1961; *NYT,* April 9, 1961.

56 *Not for the PA:* Tobin, Weekly Report to the Commissioners for the week ending Mar. 20, 1961, courtesy Angus Kress Gillespie.

56 *Stalemate: NYT,* May 24, 1961; Sullivan interview; Cohen, *Portfolio.*

57 *New site idea:* The idea for the west side site may have originated earlier in the PA. John Dragonette, a former PA official, said in an interview that soon after the east side site had been announced, he told Roger Gilman, "Whoever picked this site couldn't have picked a worse location." Then, according to Dragonette, he prepared a dated drawing for an alternative on the west side, including much of Radio Row. According to Jameson Doig [private communication], Schachter recalled in an interview that he first had the idea to combine the projects on the west side.

But in a letter to one of the authors (J.G.) dated Aug. 25, 2003, Dragonette said he hoped "to clarify for you the reasons that I am so adamant in my belief that I was the first person to find the exact West Side site of the WTC and to bring this information to the appropriate person, i.e., Mr. Austin J. Tobin, Executive Director of the Port Authority, including some of his top staff. . . . This information, in the form of two (2) maps on tracing paper and an article on Building Activity Downtown from the New York Times data 1/18/61 were delivered within days to Mr. Tobin. . .

"From the time in the late 1960's that I first heard that the Lower East Side of Manhattan was the most suitable site for the development of a WTC and that among its attributes was its excellent transportation access, which I knew to be incorrect, I questioned the selection of this east side site. The reply was 'that it has to be here.' Not satisfied with this reply, I independently prepared a rudimentary study map showing the East Side Site, the West Side Site, the existing subway lines and their service areas, the location of new office buildings built between the years 1955 and 1960 and the location of buildings with major alterations in this downtown area.

"Almost immediately it became apparent that the place to look for this was on the West Side, not the East Side. There was on the West Side unsurpassed rapid transit facilities, mostly very old, low and underutilized buildings, virtually no buildings of architectural or historical importance and only a handful of residents, mostly in furnished rooms."

Dragonette also provided the text of an "Award of Distinguished Service Medal to John Dragonette," approved by the Port Authority board on Feb. 12, 1987. The text says that he "sat down and independently came up with a site, which later became the site for the World Trade Center."

In an interview, Sullivan said he did not recall the earlier proposal but could not rule out having seen it.

57 *Sullivan, Gilman, and Tobin discuss:* Richard Sullivan interview; Cohen, *Portfolio*, p. 19. Cohen's piece is largely based on PA memos and documents that have since been destroyed in the collapse of the north trade tower, where the authority's main library occupied the sixty-seventh floor.

58 *"face toward New Jersey":* HT, Dec. 28, 1961.

58 *DR's endorsement:* "Those words have to be eaten now," *NYT* editorialized on Jan. 25, 1962.

58 *Jaffe's memo:* "The Hudson & Manhattan World Trade Center Project," PA, Jan. 29, 1961. The cover letter by Jaffe said simply, "The attached memorandum . . . was delivered to members of the New Jersey legislature today," probably indicating that the copies in the *NYT* morgue were among those sent to members of the press.

59 *Staff member:* Lou Gambaccini.

59 *Combined cost:* 1961 PA annual report.

59 *"immediate medicine":* HT, Dec. 28, 1961.

59 *"very strong displeasure":* Cohen, *Portfolio,* p. 22.

59 *Wagner hardly consulted:* Bennett, *NYT,* Feb. 16, 1962; *HT,* Feb. 16, 1962; Tobin's Weekly Report to the Commissioners, Feb. 19, 1962, courtesy Angus Kress Gillespie.

60 *10 million square feet:* Tozzoli interview. According to Tozzoli, Tobin pushed the number up to the absolute maximum amount of floor space that typical building codes would allow for the sixteen-acre "footprint" of the site.

60 *First phase secret:* "We weren't about to tell people what we were going to do," Tozzoli said in an interview. The reason, he said, was that the PA did not want to stimulate any further criticism on the cost of the complex. In dozens of articles on the WTC in *NYT* in 1962 and 1963—analyzing cost, politics, physical design, legal fights, and other topics—the authors have not found one that mentioned that the expected amount of rentable space would be 10 million square feet or greater or that the project would create the world's largest office complex. The conclusion is based on the *NYT* morgue file and ProQuest searches. First mention of 10 million or 11 million total square feet in the context of the west side trade center is after the January 1964 unveiling of the twin towers.

61 *Revenue as motive:* Danielson and Doig, chapter 10, serves as a general reference and backdrop for the beginning of this chapter; Stengren, *NYT,* Jan. 17, 1964.

61 *Pressure to spend:* The later push by Ronan, New Jersey governor William T. Cahill, and others for the PA to spend its surpluses on mass transit ultimately led to Tobin's embittered resignation. The issues of Tobin's resignation and the pressure on Tobin to spend surpluses on mass transit are dealt with in Doig, pp. 376–79 and pp. 388–90; Doig and Hargrove, chapter 4; Caro, p. 924; and *BW,* Apr. 3, 1971.

61 *Old drunk:* Schwalb interview.

CHAPTER 3: STREET FIGHTERS

Sources

Books and Articles

Jacobs, *The Death and Life of Great American Cities;* Ernst, *Too Big;* Talese, *The Bridge;* Doig, *Empire on the Hudson;* Caro, *The Power Broker: Robert Moses and the Fall of New York;* Derrick, *Tunneling to the Future: The Story of the Great Subway Expansion That Saved New York;* Cudahy, *Over and Back: The History of Ferryboats in New York Harbor;* Comprehensive Planning Office, PA, *Metropolitan Transportation—1980;* Darton, *Divided We Stand.*

"A World Trade Center out of Bankrupt Tube?" *HT,* Dec. 23, 1961; Richard P. Hunt, "Port Unit Offers Compromise Plan on Trade Center," *NYT,* Dec. 23, 1961; Guy Savino, "Putting Democracy to Work—at $200,000," *Newark Evening News,* February 1963; Douglas Martin, "Sam Osman, 88, Founder of Job Lot Trading," *NYT,* Feb. 18, 2000; Alfred Clark, "Injunction Asked on Trade Center," *NYT,* June 27, 1962; Martin Arnold, "Merchants Score Downtown Plan," *NYT,* April 20, 1962; Guy Savino, "Score for Little Merchants: 231-Word Sentence Upsets Trade-Tube Package," *Newark Evening News,* February 1963; "Trade Center Fought," *NYT,* April 21, 1962; "Attack on Business

Laid to Port Body," *NYT*, May 11, 1962; "Marchers Protest Crosstown Road," *NYT*, Aug. 10, 1962; "Action Likely on Crosstown Road," *NYT*, Nov. 21, 1962; "40,000 Celebrate New Tubes' Opening," *NYT*, July 20, 1909; David Pirmann and Mark S. Feinman, "The 9th Avenue Elevated: A Brief History," www.nycsubway.org/irt/irt-els/9th-ave-el.html; Tom Barrett, "Business Men's Rally Hits at Trade Center," *HT*, May 11, 1962; "Court Denies Writ to Delay Trade Center," *HT*, July 19, 1962; "PA to Take H&M Tube Terminals," *HT*, July 27, 1962; John Sibley, "Port Authority Takes Over H&M," *NYT*, July 27, 1962; John Sibley, "Legal Doubt Cast on Trade Center," *NYT*, Nov. 6, 1962; "Justice Peter A. Quinn, 14 Years on State Supreme Court, Dead," *NYT*, Dec. 24, 1974; Edith Evans Asbury, "Small Business Men Assail Center: Downtown Merchants Parade to Protest World Trade Center," *NYT*, July 14, 1962; "A Challenge for the Port Authority," *HT*, July 14, 1962; Tom Barrett, "PA Offers Downtown-Merchants Concessions," *HT*, Aug. 9, 1962; "Trade Center Plan to Relocate Stores Called 'Good Sign,' " *NYT*, Aug. 11, 1962; Walter Hamshar, "Creators for a World-Within," *HT*, Sept. 21, 1962; "City Held in Violation of Charter on Land Sale," *NYT*, July 22, 1965; Paul Crowell, "World Trade Center Here Upheld by Appeals Court," *NYT*, April 5, 1963.

Authors' Interviews

Ronald Nadel; Meryl Yelman; Leatrice Yelman; Mortimer Matz; Sy Syms; Guy Tozzoli; Lloyd Schwalb; Ed Schneck; Francis Yonker; George Shea; Patrick Falvey; Richard Sullivan; Joseph Lesser; Anne Schwartz; Donald Elliott; Robert Dichiara; Herman Tretter; David and Virginia MacInnes; Bill Schneck.

Documents

Tobin's Weekly Report to the Commissioners, courtesy Angus Kress Gillespie; Oscar Nadel, "President's Message," typeset brochure published in 1962; "Chronological Sequence of Port Authority Efforts to Assist WTC Site Store Tenants," undated memo from PA files, courtesy Roger Cohen; Mortimer Matz, "It Could Happen to You: A Weekly Newsletter for Members of the Downtown West Businessmen's Association," July 25, 1962, courtesy David MacInnes; Joseph Lesser, "Great Legal Cases Which Have Shaped the Port Authority," *Port Authority Review*, 1969, vol. 7, no. 2, courtesy Tony Carroll.

Notes

page

62 *"Shaping up in New York City":* WCBS Radio Editorial No. 182 by Sam J. Slate, CBS radio vice president and general manager of WCBS. Broadcast date was Oct. 4, 1962, at 8:15 A.M. and 8:15 P.M. Courtesy David MacInnes.

62 *Oscar Nadel and Radio Row:* Nadel and Yelman interviews. Darton discusses Oscar Nadel in chapters 5 and 6.

62 *Luncheonette owner:* We have not been able to determine the owner's name. It was apparently called the Alkor Luncheonette and was located at 73 Cortlandt Street.

63 *PA announcement:* *HT*, Dec. 23, 1961; *NYT*, Dec. 23, 1961.

63 *"Buster, once the legislation:"* *Newark Evening News*, 1963.

64 *Handbill:* Courtesy David MacInnes.

64 *Northern boundary:* There was a good reason for that strangely shaped northern boundary, one that could not help but goad the small businesses in the H&M

buildings and on Radio Row and along the waterfront on West Street when the facts became apparent. As Austin Tobin confirmed in a memo on the trade center bill, enterprises other than those small businesses had been quietly assured that they would be left untouched: "We never entertained any idea of acquiring the Telephone Company property or the Federal Building at 90 Church Street between West Broadway and Church Street. With the concurrence of the offices of the two Governors, therefore, an amendment was prepared under which the northern boundary of the area is spelled out in detail, thus eliminating the blocks occupied by both major structures." Weekly Report to the Commissioners, Feb. 13, 1962.

67 *"the uses of sidewalks":* Jacobs, chapter 3.

67 *Nadel's principles:* Note also that Nadel seems to have adapted some of Jacobs's language. Nadel repeatedly refers to the "World Trade Center hoax," using the phrase at least once in the title of a pamphlet. Compare to Jacobs, "the economic rationale of current city rebuilding is a hoax."

67 *Kallimanis, Syms, and Osman:* Matz and Syms interviews; Martin, *NYT*, Feb. 18, 2000.

67 *Nadel's estimates:* Clark, *NYT*, June 27, 1962.

67 *City Planning Commission's numbers:* The planning commission said that only businesses dealing in the following products contributed to its roster of employees: electronics; hardware, appliance, department store; clothing; specialty foods; florists; pets; food services; barbering and locksmith; drugs and candy; parking. There is no mention of the government, shipping, and financial agencies that filled the 668,673 net rentable square feet at 30 Church Street and the 782,520 net rentable square feet at 50 Church Street, both twenty-story structures. See Paul T. O'Keefe, "Appraisal of 30 and 50 Church Street," submitted as part of the lawsuits over the Port Authority's taking possession of the buildings.

67 *Others not counted:* In addition, neither Nadel's accounting of his area's employment nor the planning commission's counted the Hudson shoreline's contribution to the forty thousand jobs the longshoremen's union, which quickly joined the fight, said the New York port created for them (letter by William P. Lynch, international vice president of Manhattan, International Longshoremen's Association, AFL-CIO, Local 791, Feb. 11, 1964, courtesy David MacInnes).

67 *PA says numbers too high:* Tobin's Weekly Report, April 16, 1962.

67 *Condemned area:* Arnold, *NYT*, April 20, 1962. The fluidity of the actual boundaries of the plot to be condemned probably also reflected how uncertain the PA was about the scale of the project, its architecture, and its engineering at this point.

68 *Kallimanis on money:* Savino, *Newark Evening News,* 1963.

68 *"We intend to fight":* Arnold, *NYT*, April 20, 1962.

68 *Nadel opens first shop:* Savino, *Newark Evening News,* 1963.

68 *Nadel like Ralph Kramden:* Several tapes of the meetings have been kindly provided to us by Leatrice Yelman and Meryl Yelman.

69 *Sales on Radio Row:* "Frontier News: Voice of Upper & Lower Manhattan," Dec. 21, 1965. Courtesy David MacInnes.

69 *Nadel's manifesto:* "Why Small Business Men Are Fighting the World Trade Center Hoax." Pamphlet courtesy David MacInnes.

70 *entire bill would become invalid:* Savino, *Newark Evening News,* February 1963. The heart of the provision reads: ". . . so long as the act or remainder of the act shall

nonetheless permit the effectuation, as a unified project, of the Hudson tubes, Hudson tubes extensions and the World Trade Center."

70 *Nadel hires Ernst:* Schwalb interview; *NYT,* April 21, 1962.

70 *Nadel talking about luck:* Matz interview; tape recordings of rallies courtesy Leatrice Yelman and Meryl Yelman.

70 *Academy Hall meeting: NYT,* May 11, 1962.

70 *Handbills:* Courtesy David MacInnes. It specifies Thursday, May 10th, 6:30 P.M., as the start of the meeting.

70 *Tobin's response:* Weekly Report to the Commissioners, April 16, 1962.

71 *"private purpose":* Courtesy David MacInnes.

71 *Goldstein's brief:* Sidney Goldstein, "Memorandum in Opposition to Motion for Injunction Pendente Lite against Officers of the Port of New York Authority in Their Personal Capacities," Courtesy Sandwich Shop, Inc., et al., Plaintiffs, against The Port of New York Authority, et al., defendants, brief filed with the Supreme Court of the State of New York, County of New York, July 10, 1962.

71 *ten-foot architectural model:* Sullivan, Tozzoli, and Schwalb interviews.

72 *Moving residents:* Talese, chapter 2; Doig, pp. 331–35; Caro.

73 *Nadel as bantam rooster:* This image was first suggested to us by Mortimer Matz.

73 *Nadel biographical details:* Many of these details rely on Yelman and Ronald Nadel interviews.

74 *Nadel's savings:* Savino, *Newark Evening News,* 1963.

74 *1924 photo:* Ed Schneck, "H. L. Schneck—A Legend of Cortlandt Street," *Antique Radio Classified,* July 1990, p. 6; Ed Schneck interview.

74 *Radio Row:* Robert Hertzbert, "Radio a la Cortlandt Street!" *Radio-Craft,* Sept. 1932. Courtesy Joe Richman.

74 *Sounds of Radio Row:* Some of this material comes from a 1929 Movietone newsreel, including outtakes, courtesy Joe Richman; Yonker interview.

75 *The radio merchants:* The history of the World Trade Center site can be traced back to the Dutch. The first recorded owner, around 1630, was Jan Jansen Damen, a farmer and church warden who earned the animosity of other Dutch colonists when he submitted a fraudulent petition to the local Dutch governor urging him to retaliate against the Indians, inspiring the massacre of 120 Indians. Oloff Stevensen Van Cortlandt, an affluent brewer, and Dirck Jansen Dey, a farmer, ultimately took control of Damen's land. The northern edge of the future trade center site was known through the years as the Old Company's Bouwerie, the Duke's Farm, the King's Farm, and the Queen's Farm. Trinity Church, under the leadership of its first rector, William Vesey, ultimately took control of this property, after 1698. The streets within the site—including Church, Vesey, Dey, and Cortlandt, obviously named after these men and the church—showed up on city maps by 1760. Washington and West Streets were laid out in the decades to come, as the shoreline was extended into the river, widening Manhattan. For more history, see I. N. Phelps, *Stokes's Iconography of Manhattan Island 1498–1909.*

75 *Hudson Tubes:* The first run actually went from the Hudson terminal buildings to Jersey City. *NYT,* July 20, 1909; Derrick; "Metropolitan Transportation—1980," Comprehensive Planning Office, PA, 1963.

76 *"Hi, I'm Oscar":* Ronald Nadel interview.

76 *Ferry and Hudson Tubes:* "Metropolitan Transportation—1980," Comprehensive Planning Office, PA, 1963; Cudahy.

77 *Commuters:* Syms interview; Syms stated that as much as 98 percent of his customer base came from New Jersey commuters.

77 *Nadel's claim about Cortlandt Street:* Oscar Nadel, "President's Message," typeset brochure published in 1962; Morris Ernst picked up the idea and expanded on it in his brief for the *Courtesy* court of appeals case that was decided on April 4, 1963.

77 *Nadel vs. PA:* "Chronological Sequence," PA memo. The latest date cited in the memo is May 25, 1965, and it was likely written soon after.

78 *"It is clear":* Barrett, *HT,* May 11, 1962.

78 *"Overall discussion":* "Chronological Sequence," PA memo. The meeting with Mr. Buff, of 69 Dey Street, on May 7, 1962. The business is identified as "Buff & Buff Manufacturing" in *Frontier News: Voice of Upper & Lower Manhattan,* Dec. 21, 1965. This memo calls it by the slightly more formidable-sounding "Buff Industries."

78 *Nadel and Tobin meeting:* "Chronological Sequence," PA memo. The memo gives the names but does not specifically say where the meeting took place. Ronald Nadel recalls his uncle Oscar returning from the meeting and saying that he had turned down an offer to relocate in the trade center.

78 *Nadel doesn't let others talk much:* Tozzoli interview.

79 *Tobin's conviction:* The authors have obtained hundreds of memos by Tobin. Never does he express more than wonderment that opponents of the trade center imagine they might have scored a significant or really substantive point against the trade center project. His direst warnings tend to focus on what he regards as lost revenue as the project is delayed by the challenges mounted against it. Initially, at least, Tobin was sure that some of the demolition for the WTC could start by the middle of 1962 and that the construction could be nearing completion by 1967. See Cohen, "Casting Giant Shadows," p. 22; "A World Trade Center in the Port of New York," PA, March 10, 1961, p. 29.

79 *First court decisions: HT,* July 19, 1962; *HT,* July 27, 1962; Sibley, *NYT,* July 27, 1962.

79 *Court refuses part of Tobin's argument:* Justice Thomas C. Chimera of the State Supreme Court in Manhattan denied Morris Ernst's request for an injunction to stop the condemnation. But the only immediate effect was to allow the PA to take over the H&M terminal buildings—the first phase of the demolition plan, and the part Chimera said he could be certain was within "the scope of the power of the Port of New York Authority."

79 *Different reactions to court decisions:* Matz, "It Could Happen to You," July 25, 1962, courtesy David MacInnes; Sibley, *NYT,* Nov. 6, 1962.

80 *"might be declared invalid":* In his ruling, Quinn had bent over backward to stress that whether or not the trade center, and its claims to be a new vehicle for saving the port and generating international commerce, was a legitimate "public purpose" would have to wait for the constitutional test on appeal. Greenbaum, Wolff & Ernst, Jurisdictional Statement in the Supreme Court of the United States, October term, 1963, no. 399. Courtesy *Sandwich Shop v. Port of New York Authority,* Appendix D; Sibley, *NYT,* Nov. 6, 1962.

80 *Nadel's emergency meeting:* Meeting was held on Nov. 7, 1962. Tape recordings courtesy of Leatrice Yelman and Meryl Yelman.

80 *First formal hotdog-eating contest:* In this case, their boast seems to be true. (George Shea interview.)
81 *Rosey's protest:* Matz interview; Asbury, *NYT*, July 14, 1962; *HT*, July 14, 1962.
82 *Tobin concedes then explodes:* Barrett, *HT*, Aug. 9, 1962; *NYT*, Aug. 11, 1962; Tobin's Weekly Report to the Commissioners, Aug. 22, 1962.
82 *Constitutionality case:* Hamshar, "Creators for a World-Within," *HT*, Sept. 21, 1962.
82 *"PATH decals":* Tobin's Weekly Report to the Commissioners, Sept. 10, 1962, courtesy Angus Kress Gillespie.
82 *Ernst's speech:* The tape is dated 11/27/62; courtesy Leatrice Yelman and Meryl
83 Yelman.
83 *Envelope with court decision opened:* Falvey interview.
84 *Rabin's decision:* *NYT*, July 22, 1965.
85 *Case reaches Court of Appeals:* Joseph Lesser, "Great Legal Cases Which Have Shaped the Port Authority," *Port Authority Review* 1969, vol. 7, no. 2, courtesy Tony Carroll. Lesser's article refers to Feb. 28, 1963, as a "Friday afternoon" when in fact it was a Thursday. In an interview, Lesser clarified the error; *Courtesy Sandwich Shop v. Port of New York Authority*, Court of Appeals of New York, 12 N.Y. 2d 379, 1963 LEXIS 1263, Feb. 28, 1963 argued; April 4, 1963 decided.
86 *Goldberg's performance:* Lesser interview.
86 *Court of Appeals decision:* Crowell, *NYT*, April 5, 1963.
86 *Tobin's and Nadel's flyers:* Courtesy David MacInnes.

Chapter 4: SURPRISE, SERENITY, DELIGHT

Sources

Books and Articles

Yamasaki, *A Life in Architecture*; Lambert, *Mies in America*; Jacobus, *Twentieth-Century Architecture: The Middle Years, 1940–1965*; Ruttenbaum, *Mansions in the Clouds: The Skyscraper Palazzi of Emery Roth*; Heyer, *Architects on Architecture*; Wright, *Frank Lloyd Wright: A Testament*.

Jane Schermerhorn, "The Yamasakis," *Detroit News Magazine*, Sept. 7, 1969; "American Architect Yamasaki," *Architectural Forum*, August 1958; "Mrs. Yamasaki . . . a Modern Design," *Detroit Free Press*, Sept. 20, 1959; *Time*, Jan. 18, 1963; notes on an interview with Yamasaki by a *Newsweek* reporter, Jan. 22, 1964, CFAH; Bernard Stengren, "Biggest Buildings in World to Rise at Trade Center," *NYT*, Jan. 19, 1964; Richard Henry, "New Trade Center Towers to Be Taller Than Empire State," *Daily News*, Jan. 19, 1964; Ada Louise Huxtable, "Biggest Buildings Herald New Era," *NYT*, Jan. 26, 1964; "Going Up—World's Two Tallest Buildings," *NYT*, Jan. 19, 1964; W. A. Lee, "Tall Witness to WTC's Fall Has New Perspective," *American Banker*, Sept. 21, 2001.

Authors' Interviews

Aaron Schreier; Jerry Karn; Kip Serota; Jim Herman; Richard Knight; Harold Tsuchiya; Gunars Gruzdins; Henry Guthard; Grant Hildebrand; Daniel Bartush; Don Hisaka; George Anselevicius; Gunnar Birkerts; John Haro; Balthazar Korab; Guy Tozzoli; Calvin Kort; Carl K. Panero; John Brunner; John R. Dragonette; Herman Roberts; Herb Tessler; Thomas J. Kearney; Joseph H. Solomon; Jim White.

Documents

WTC Evaluation of Architectural Firms, Books 1 and 2, PA, internal document produced to review the firms that applied for the job.

Oral History, Speeches, Interviews, Correspondence, and Essays by Yamasaki

"Oral History Interview with Minoru Yamasaki," Smithsonian Archives of American Art, August 1959, by Virginia Harriman; Lecture, Detroit Institute of Arts, Aug. 13, 1959, Smithsonian Archives of American Art; "A Conversation with Yamasaki," *Architectural Forum*, July 1959; "A Humanist Architecture for America and Its Relation to the Traditional Architecture of Japan," the Marley Lecture, Nov. 15, 1960, reprinted in *RIBA Journal*, January 1961; "Toward an Architecture for Enjoyment," *Architectural Record*, August 1955; "Minoru Yamasaki, a Retrospective," remarks at testimonial dinner, Nov. 16, 1974, Meadow Brook Art Gallery, Rochester, Michigan, on file at New York Public Library; "The Challenge of Industrial Architecture," speech, November 1952, at University of Michigan, published in April 1953 *Journal of the AIA*; "An Interview with Minoru Yamasaki," conducted by Emily Genauer, transcript of interview broadcast on WNDT television, 1967, maintained in CFAH; "Interview, Minoru Yamasaki," by John Peter, transcript of recorded interview, 1960, on file, Library of Congress; letters written by Yamasaki to David Rockefeller, Ada Louise Huxtable, and the DLMA, on file at the Rockefeller Archives and from personal records of John Brunner.

Notes

page

88 *World's Fair:* Description of the Seattle World's Fair comes from reproductions of original promotional material from the 1962 event (Apr. 21 to Oct. 21).

88 *Tozzoli at the fair:* Tozzoli interview.

89 *Largest office complex:* Pentagon facts: The building provides a gross floor area of 6,636,360 square feet. There are 3,705,793 square feet for offices, concessions, and storage. At 12 million square feet of net office space, the WTC was three times as large.

90 *Yama's early years:* Yamasaki, pp. 9, 13–17.

90 *Yama's parents: Time*, Jan. 18, 1963, cover story about Yamasaki says that his father arrived in the United States in 1908. Yamasaki in his autobiography says that his mother arrived separately and that the two were introduced by a "go-between." Yamasaki, p. 9.

91 *Yama, outstanding student:* Yamasaki says that in his senior year in high school, he was the only student citywide in Seattle to get a perfect grade on an annual mathematics exam. Yamasaki, p. 10.

91 *Yama's outburst:* The outburst cost him a summer bonus, but the plant was so desperate for labor, he was not fired, or at least that was Yama's explanation in his autobiography.

91 *One afternoon:* Yamasaki's autobiography, p. 16.

92 *Yamasaki and his wife: Detroit News Magazine*, Sept. 7, 1969; Yamasaki, p. 20.

92 *Yamasaki's family life: Architectural Forum*, August 1958.

92 *"We don't really know": Detroit Free Press*, Sept. 20, 1959.

93 *"Yama, if he is": Architectural Forum*, August 1958.

93 *Lafayette Park and Mies:* Details on this event are collected from a photograph of the ceremony, a *Detroit News* article of Oct. 17, 1958, and Yamasaki's recollections in his autobiography.

94 *Yamasaki drunk:* John Haro recalled this in an interview. Others told stories about Yamasaki taking the staff out to long lunches and having so many drinks with his meal that he would be drunk in the middle of the day.

94 *"Well, I'm an architect":* Yamasaki tells this story in "The Challenge of Industrial Architecture," a November 1952 speech at University of Michigan, Ann Arbor, which was reprinted in the *Journal of the AIA* in April 1953, pp. 160–166.

94 *860–880 Lake Shore Drive:* Description from Lambert, p. 354.

94 *Buildings angled:* The similarities with the WTC design are obvious—Yamasaki himself cited this particular work by Mies as an inspiration. But one real difference, other than of course the height, is that Mies had one building facing the lake with its broad side, and the other facing the lake with its narrow side. So they were almost perpendicular, instead of parallel, as the WTC was.

95 *In the early 1950s:* The St. Louis Housing Authority demolished the first three buildings at Pruitt-Igoe in 1972, then a year later declared the complex unsalvageable and destroyed the entire thing. See Alexander von Hoffman, "Why They Built Pruitt-Igoe," in John F. Bauman, Roger Biles, Kristin M. Szylvian, eds., *From Tenements to the Taylor Homes: In Search of an Urban Housing Policy in Twentieth-Century America* (University Park: Pennsylvania State University Press, 2000).

95 *Katsura Palace:* Yamasaki wrote or submitted to interviews for a series of articles for architectural journals after his return from these trips in which he described his reaction to what had seen. They include "Toward an Architecture for Enjoyment," *Architectural Record,* August 1955, pp. 147, 148, and August 1958; and "Oral History Interview with Minoru Yamasaki," Smithsonian Archives of American Art, August 1959, by Virginia Harriman.

95 *"Something was missing":* *Architectural Forum,* August 1958, pp. 84–85, 166–168.

96 *Tozzoli biographic details:* Tozzoli interview.

99 *"Even a single error":* Recollection of Henry Guthard, associate of Yamasaki, about his comment in meeting of partners and associates after the letter arrived, in the late spring 1962.

99 *"the letter is correct":* Both Sullivan interview and one with Yama by the *Detroit Free Press,* April 2, 1967.

99 *Yama's new firm:* Yama's application for the WTC job, dated June 29, 1962, p. 2.

100 *"We hope that":* Detroit Institute of Arts talk, 1959; also extensive discussion of this in 1959 Smithsonian oral history interview.

100 *"twittering aviary":* *Time,* Jan. 18, 1963.

100 *"prissy":* Jacobus, p. 208.

100 *"mere artistic caprice":* *Time,* Jan. 18, 1963.

100 *Yama's new lifestyle:* Divorce proceedings filed against Yamasaki by his wife, covered in Detroit papers, Jan. 28, 1961, "Wife Asks Divorce from Yamasaki," and June 13, 1961, "Yamasaki and Wife Divorced." The stories also say that in court papers, Yamasaki ordered his wife to leave their house after she complained about his parents and a cousin living with them; *Detroit News,* Sept. 7, 1969, article about Yamasaki and his wife, Teri, after they got remarried in 1969; Korab interview.

101 *Yama's application process: WTC Evaluation of Architectural Firms*, Books 1 and 2, courtesy John Brunner.

102 *Rothscapes:* Ruttenbaum, pp. 203–204.

102 *Hiring a Japanese architect:* Tozzoli interview.

102 *Yama's office and phone number:* Telephone number is on his application for the job street names come from a map; view and the building described by Schreier.

103 *"a quite blighted section":* Yamasaki, p. 112.

103 *Yama petrified: Newsweek*, notes, Jan. 22, 1964.

103 *Yama at Empire State Building:* Schreier interview; Yamasaki, p. 113.

104 *Mal Levy:* During the 1950s, Levy and Tozzoli got to know each other, building warehouses on the New Jersey and New York waterfront, "where the main objective was to build it cheap," said Panero, who later worked with Levy and Tozzoli on the WTC project. "Mal Levy was very good at this. He would count light bulbs and the next building was sure to have fewer light bulbs than the previous one." From letter by Panero, which he provided to the *NYT*.

105 *"I know it is enormous":* Words recalled by Schreier.

105 *Triplet of towers:* Reproductions of the models were provided by Henry Guthard, a member of Yamasaki's staff. Yamasaki wrote in his autobiography (p. 115) that his staff prepared about a hundred different schemes. At about scheme 40, he said, they felt pretty much as though they had the right composition, but they continued to do more. Several of the staff members in his office, including Kip Serota and Karn, said the additional models were done to convince the Port Authority that they had not just arbitrarily arrived at the twin towers scheme. "Atrocious looking little schemes that had no thought in them," is how Karn described them.

106 *Yama's comments on models:* Heyer; recollections of architects who were in the room, including Karn and Richard Knight.

106 *Levy challenges Yama:* Words recalled by Karn, who was there. Guy Tozzoli, in an interview forty years later, said he does not dispute that Levy may have criticized Yama's initial designs, believing that they were not bold enough. But Tozzoli, who was not present for this discussion, has for many years claimed he was the first to tell Yama that the towers must be the world's tallest.

106 *"A whole bunch of little buildings":* Tozzoli interview.

106 *"too strong or brutal":* The Marley Lecture, given at the Royal Institute of British Architecture on Nov. 15, 1960. It was republished in *Art in America*, vol. 50, no. 4, 1962, and previously in *RIBA Journal*, January 1961.

107 *"grandest project ever":* Karn's recollection of Yama's remarks.

107 *Sketch:* Karn and Serota both say they recall such a sketch. Yamasaki directly referred to Mies's composition in explaining his choice of the twin towers: "New York is a single tower skyline. Obviously two (towers) would be more significant. . . . Twin towers are not new. Mies van der Rohe used them in Chicago—860 Lakeshore Drive. They're used in Brasilia," he said in the Jan. 22, 1964, interview with *Newsweek*.

108 *Record wouldn't stand:* Yamasaki repeatedly made this point about the 110-story design in interviews and letters.

108 *"looks like a fat lady":* Serota interview.

108 *"cash flow":* Sullivan interview.

108 *"You guys are crazy":* Panero's recollection of Roth's repeated remarks.
108 *"the tallest buildings in the world":* Tozzoli's recollection of conversation with Yamasaki. In a prior interview with Angus Kress Gillespie on Nov. 15, 1994 [Gillespie, private communication], Tozzoli recalled the same exchange with slightly different wording. See also Gillespie, pp. 47–48.
109 *"That thing is big":* Karn interview.
109 *Herman remarks:* Herman interview.
109 *Yama on the narrow windows:* April 10, 1973, letter about WTC design to Ada Louise Huxtable of the *NYT; Architectural Forum,* July 1959.
110 *Window mockup:* Tsuchiya and Serota interviews; "The purpose of buildings is to have comfortable working areas and not to be observatories where one stares out of the window at the view all day long," Yamasaki later wrote in his autobiography, p. 117.
110 *Topping the buildings:* Karn and Serota interviews.
110 *Early models' flowery design:* Interviews with Serota, Karn, and Gruzdins, all architects on Yama's staff. Jim Herman also provided a reproduction of several of these alternatives.
111 *"You shouldn't put veils":* Time, Jan. 18, 1963.
111 *"something we should celebrate":* Serota interview.
111 *Yamasaki told others:* Interview with Henry Guthard, a partner at Yama's firm at the time and a longtime friend of the architect. He argues that Yama very consciously and intentionally moved the design in this direction based on a revision in recent years that had occurred in his esthetic, as well as a concern that applied decoration on towers this big would look foolish. Guthard believes it is incorrect to see the simplification of the design—which he agreed occurred—as an indication of weakness by Yamasaki. "Yama never considered elimination of applied ornamentation because he was timid or afraid of it," Guthard wrote in a personal correspondence. "It was simply not the way to go in confirmation of his studied opinion as the chief designer." Yama himself would write about the final design: "In nature, most trees and plants have only sufficient material for their particular structures. The heft of the redwood and the Douglas Fir is only because of their great heights," in a June 3, 1966, letter to Ada Louise Huxtable, *NYT* architecture critic.
111 *Carol's visit:* This story comes from Serota and Schreier. Serota said that in a conversation with Carol, she said she did not remember this event.
112 *Artsy details left to Yama:* Panero and Tozzoli interviews.
113 *Kort enamored of Wright:* Kort interview.
113 *"elevator transit":* Wright.
113 *Headlines:* Stengren, *NYT,* Jan. 19, 1964; McCullam, "Trade Center to Be Colossus," *Sun World-Telegram,* Jan. 19, 1964; Henry, *Daily News,* Jan. 19, 1964; Huxtable, *NYT,* Jan. 26, 1964; *HT,* Jan. 19, 1964; picture headline on *HT,* Jan. 19, 1964.
113 *"become a living representation":* "Statement by Minoru Yamasaki of Minoru Yamasaki and Associates," Jan. 18, 1964, courtesy Richard Sullivan.
113 *Jaffe's press release:* The date on the press release on Lee Jaffe's PA letterhead is Monday, Jan. 20, 1964, indicating that the unveiling had been moved up after the materials were prepared.
114 *Plaza:* Serota described in an interview the design and the reason it was rejected.

114 *"I don't like it"*: Several people recall this scene, including Schreier and Panero. Panero's account, which was based on Tessler telling the story to him, includes the suggestion that Yamasaki whispered, "You Hitler," after Levy's actions. But others there said they did not hear it. Tessler, who was there, does not remember the event.

114 *Tozzoli holds his ground*: Tozzoli interview. Among the other intense battles Yamasaki had with Tozzoli was one over the antenna installed on the north tower. Yamasaki was so angry about the antenna—and the damage it did to the symmetry of the twins—that he tried to go over the head of the PA staff, writing letters to the commissioners of the PA and to DR and NR, whom he begged to intercede. "With the Trade Center towers as its central motif, the skyline is a more exciting composition, and for years will symbolize the importance of world trade to the Port of New York. The antenna will throw the silhouette of downtown Manhattan out of balance. Everything possible should be done to stop this monstrous antenna from being erected. To impose this terrible intrusion would seriously mar what may already be a symbol of the great man-made landscape of Manhattan," Yama wrote in a Feb. 1, 1977, letter to the Rockefeller brothers; the antenna was not installed until several years after the towers opened.

114 *Mal Levy was sent*: Henry Guthard was present in the hotel room when this exchange occurred.

115 *"When you look at the wall"*: Tsuchiya interview.

115 *Lobby*: Yamasaki personally traveled with Tozzoli to Stockholm, Sweden, and Venice to look at some of the finest glass crystal in the world. Madame Venini of Venice beat out Orrefors of Sweden. And the reward was great: an order for nearly one hundred chandeliers, each with 315 pieces of custom-made glass, would total approximately $1 million, an estimate that comes from Tozzoli and Dragonette.

115 *"spending so much time"*: Schreier interview.

116 *Yama has seizures*: Interview with Guthard, who was with Yama. He cannot remember what city they were in.

116 *"so that the house"*: Detroit News Magazine, Sept. 7, 1969.

116 *"as the joke went"*: The joke is attributed to the architecture critic Paul Goldberger. See *American Banker*, Sept. 21, 2001.

116 *Critics*: Nation, Feb. 28, 1966; *Architectural Forum*, April 1966; *Harper's Magazine*, May 1966; Mumford from *The Myth of the Machine*, 1970. Yamasaki was so disappointed with Ada Louise Huxtable's reviews of the trade center in the *NYT*—she called his style "General Motors Gothic"—that he wrote her a seven-page letter in April 1973 trying to defend his design. Huxtable had previously been a big fan of Yama's work, and in a letter he wrote to her in 1966, he told Huxtable that she was "the only knowledgeable architecture critic who does not approach a subject on the basis of his bias." Now he wrote to her again, obviously distressed. "Normally I pay little attention to criticisms written about our buildings; sometimes they are fair, sometimes they are prejudiced and sometimes they lack an understanding of our designs." In the letter, he defends the narrow width of the windows, the design of the lobby, the size of the plaza and he boasts about the technological innovations, such as the use of structural columns on the exterior and the high-speed and high-capacity elevators. He concludes: "I am happy

I was able to design very large buildings which have the scale relationship to man so necessary to him; they are intended to give him a soaring and inspiring feeling, imparting pride and a sense of nobility in his environment. They are set back five hundred feet from Church Street; their changing qualities as one approaches the plaza are, to me, greatly inspiring. So many tall buildings say nothing at all when you are next to them; or their great beams and columns are gloomy and fearsome from directly below, as they sit so solidly and so closely to the sidewalk and street. Finally, these advances in building technology allow us to economically compete with lower buildings, giving opportunity to open up our urban centers with spaces, be they green or paved, which are so important to life in the heart of our cities. I hope you take this letter in the spirit in which it is intended; I have no malice because of the article."

117 *"nicer to her"*: Detroit News Magazine, Sept. 7, 1969.

117 *"He's an architect"*: Tozzoli interview. Yamasaki died in 1986.

CHAPTER 5: STEEL BALLOONS

Sources

Books and Articles

Weingarten, *The Sky Is Falling*; *Henry Baldwin Hyde: A Biographical Sketch*; Ali, *Art of the Skyscraper*; O'Hagan, *High Rise/Fire and Life Safety*; Stein and Greider, *Triangle Fire*; Talese, *The Bridge*; Dwyer, *Two Seconds under the World*; Gillespie, *Twin Towers*; Landau and Condit, *Rise of the New York Skyscraper*.

Clayton Knowles, "New Fight Begun on Trade Center," *NYT*, Feb. 14, 1964; Thomas W. Ennis, "Critics Impugned on Trade Center," *NYT*, Feb. 15, 1964; "PA Scores Enemies of Big Trade Center," *World-Telegram*, Feb. 14, 1964; William McFadden, "Realty Men Battle Big Trade Center," *Journal-American*, Feb. 14, 1964; "Empire State Building Jealous? Trade Center Says 'Yes,'" *Sun Journal-American,* Feb. 16, 1964; "110-Story Twin Towers for World Trade Center," *HT*, Jan. 19, 1964; "Empire State Building's 33-Year-Old Record to Be Topped: Twin Towers to Go 110 Stories," *ENR,* Jan. 23, 1964; Clayton Knowles, "All Major Builders Are Said to Oppose Trade Center Plan," *NYT*, March 9, 1964; "Realty Men Oppose Trade Center Plans," *NYT*, Feb. 26, 1964; R. W. Apple Jr., "Real Estate Men Fight Port Agency," *NYT*, April 1, 1964; "Free Enterprise Titan Tackling Port Authority," *HT*, March 1, 1964; "Prospects Fade for Syndicates," *NYT*, Nov. 17, 1963; "Tall—but True—Tales Run in Her Family," *NYT*, Sept. 27, 1977; James Barron, "Flaming Horror on the 79th Floor," *NYT*, July 28, 1995; Thomas W. Ennis, "100 Specialists Oversee Sale of Empire State," *NYT*, Dec. 28, 1961; Thomas W. Ennis, "Empire State Sold; Price Is $65 Million," *NYT*, Aug. 23, 1961; "Empire State Building: A Realty Legend in Its Time," *Real Estate Forum*, December 1965; Owen Moritz, "The Romance of Property: Harry Helmsley," *Daily News*, Nov. 23, 1999; "Empire State Building: One of the Greatest Architectural and Building Achievements of the 20th Century," *Real Estate Forum*, Nov. 14, 1971; Don Ross, "Free Enterprise Titan Tackling Port Authority," *HT*, March 1, 1964; "World's Highest Towers Planned in CSU Wind Unit," *Fort Collins Coloradoan*, Sept. 13, 1964; Eric Nalder, "Seattle's Man of Steel—John Skilling," *Seattle Times*, Jan. 5, 1986; "Engineer Skilling Dies at Age 76," *ENR*, March 6, 1998; Leslie E. Robertson, "Reflections on the World Trade Center," *The Bridge* (National Academy of Engineering), spring 2002; Doug

Morris, "An Interview with John Skilling," *Arcade*, April/May 1988; "Structures Can Be Beautiful," *ENR*, April 2, 1964; "Is a Revamped Steelworkers' Design One Solution to City's Sign Pollution?" *Pittsburgh Post-Gazette*, March 12, 2002; "A Look at the New Record," *ENR*, Jan. 30, 1964; "Miss Rosaleen Skehan Bride of Austin Tobin," *NYT*, June 30, 1967; Edward Marshall, "A Skyscraper Disaster That Will Stagger Humanity," *NYT*, June 16, 1912; Will Hilliard, "Steelworker Recalls Building Center," *St. John's Telegram*, Sept. 17, 2001; Eric Nalder, "Twin Towers Engineered to Withstand Jet Collision," *Seattle Times*, Feb. 27, 1993; "PA Scores Enemies of Big Trade Center," *World Telegram*, Feb. 14, 1964.

Documents

Via Port of New York, special issue on the WTC, PA, January 1964; Fire Underwriters report; "Memorandum for the Deputy Chief of Air Staff: Preliminary Report Concerning B-25 Army Airplane Crash at New York City," July 30, 1945, courtesy National Archives and Records Administration; Worthington, Skilling, Helle & Jackson Wind Report, June 1966; "Salient points with regard to the structural design of The World Trade Center towers," typed copy with Mal Levy's initials appended, dated Feb. 3, 1964, courtesy John Dragonette; Jaffe's Feb. 14 memo to the *NYT* with attached telegram, courtesy Anthony Robins; "The World Trade Center: An Innovation in Steel Construction," PA, August 1968; Letter from Lawrence A. Wien to New Jersey governor Richard J. Hughes, Sept. 10, 1964, courtesy Douglas Durst; "World Trade Center Performance Study: Data Collection, Preliminary Observations, and Recommendations," Federal Emergency Management Agency, FEMA 403/May 2002; Paul R. Eskildsen, "Oregon Research Institute Vision Center Report on the Four Factor Experiment in Horizontal Acceleration Thresholds," Oregon Research Institute, September 1965, revised June 2002; material submitted for John Skilling's successful 1993/1994 nomination as an honorary member of the American Institute of Architects, courtesy Ann Yoder.

Authors' Interviews

Jon Magnusson; William Bain; Alvin Silverman; Art Barkshire; William Ward; William Ronan; John Dragonette; Melvin Larson; Leslie Robertson; Alan Davenport; Mortimer Matz; Paul Hoffman; Paul Eskildsen; Jack Cermak; James White; Mir M. Ali.

Notes

page

118 *"Regardless of any regulations"*: The report, by the Bureau of Fire Prevention and Water Supply of the New York Board of Fire Underwriters, is courtesy of the George F. Mand Library, Fire Dept. of the City of New York; the report is based in part on interviews with FDNY members.

118 *Skilling's presentation*: Robertson recalled that the presentation focused on the general themes of high-rises, pinstripe columns, and other favorite Yamasaki motifs. Robertson confirmed that Skilling went alone to New York. According to John Dragonette, the PA's contracts with the Yamasaki firm and the Skilling firm were executed on the same day: Sept. 12, 1962. But because Robertson and the rest of the office were already intensively involved in design work that would be reflected in the later structure of the twin towers, the basic outlines of

Skilling's concept at that point would also have included the open floors and wind-resisting tube exterior; Robertson, Magnusson, Ward, and Barkshire interviews. Robertson said the firm may have prepared graphics that Skilling chose not to use.

119 *Skilling biographical details:* Nalder, *Seattle Times,* Jan. 5, 1986.

119 *PA group in conference room:* Dragonette interview; *ENR,* March 6, 1998. Leslie Robertson specifically recalled learning that Mal Levy had been present. As to the precise timing of Skilling's interview, it must have taken place after Yamasaki (who insisted that Skilling be interviewed) received his invitation to compete for the architectural design contract in late spring of 1962 and before the contracts were executed on September 12 of that same year. Therefore late summer of 1962 is the most likely time.

120 *"You don't need to":* Larson interview. Jack Christiansen led the structural design work itself for the thin concrete arches. See Robertson, *The Bridge,* spring 2002.

120 *Architects adored Skilling:* Morris, *Arcade,* April/May 1988; Nalder, *Seattle Times,* Jan. 5, 1986.

120 *Load-bearing pinstripes:* Yamasaki, with his engineering interests, also favored making his decorative motifs structural elements.

121 *Chaos eliminated:* Dragonette interview.

121 *PA praised tube design:* Via *Port of New York,* PA, January 1964.

121 *Skilling's 1957 Pittsburgh building:* Arcade, April/May 1988; material submitted for John Skilling's successful 1993/1994 nomination as an honorary member of the American Institute of Architects; *ENR,* April 2, 1964. According to Professor Mir M. Ali, the technical term for the structure used in this building is an "exterior space truss," basically the same type of structure used in the Eiffel Tower or in modern transmission-line towers. Fazlur Khan is credited with having come up with the first true tube design for the Dewitt-Chestnut building in Chicago in 1961. Engineers at the Skilling firm apparently discovered the concept independently in 1962 as they were working out the structure of the twin towers. See also Ali, *Art of the Skyscraper.*

123 *IBM Building in Seattle:* Larson and Bain interviews.

124 *"castellated beam" method:* Bain, Ward, and Barkshire interviews.

124 *WTC weight statistics:* Worthington, Skilling, Helle & Jackson wind report, June 1966; *ENR,* Jan. 30, 1964.

124 *"we're more conservative":* *ENR,* April 2, 1964.

125 *NR discusses oddity of design:* Ronan interview.

125 *Skehan appalled:* Dragonette interview. Skehan disliked the towers and knew as soon as they were unveiled that the design would spark major controversy [Jameson Doig, private communication].

126 *Hyde's Equitable Building:* Hyde's story of how he started Equitable is told in a biography published by the company, Equitable Life Assurance Society of the United States, in 1901. See also Landau and Condit.

126 *Fire at the Equitable Building:* O'Hagan, p. 2. O'Hagan was a retired New York fire commissioner at the time he wrote the book; photographs of this scene were reproduced in the *NYT* on Jan. 11, 1912.

126 *Triangle Shirtwaist fire:* Stein and Greider.

126 *"The Titanic was unsinkable":* Marshall, *NYT,* June 16, 1912.

126 *Empire State Building plane crash:* For the history of the July 28, 1945, plane crash, see the extensive coverage by the *NYT* on July 29, which remains the most authoritative source and stands as a testament to deadline journalism at its finest; the Fire Underwriters report, July 30, 1945; Weingarten's *The Sky Is Falling.* Weingarten obtained a copy of the then-classified final army report on the incident for his book; that copy has since been lost, and the authors have been unable to identify any military, governmental, or private organization now in possession of the final report. See also Klemesrud, *NYT*, Sept. 27, 1977; Barron, *NYT*, July 28, 1995.

127– *Fortier, O'Connor, and Fountain in the crash:* Weingarten, pp. 214–15.
28

128 *Alvin Silverman:* Silverman interview.

129 *Real estate syndication: HT*, March 1, 1964; *NYT*, Nov. 17, 1963.

129 *Most complex transaction in real estate history:* Ennis, *NYT*, Dec. 28, 1961; Ennis, *NYT*, Aug. 23, 1961; *Real Estate Forum*, December 1965; Moritz, *Daily News*, Nov. 23, 1999; *Real Estate Forum*, Nov. 14, 1971.

130 *Purchase of the Empire State Building:* The partnership that made the purchase was led by Lawrence Wien and Peter L. Malkin. Harry Helmsley was the broker on the purchase.

131 *PA white paper:* "Salient points with regard to the structural design of The World Trade Center towers," typed copy with Mal Levy's initials appended, dated Feb. 3, 1964, courtesy John Dragonette. Leslie Robertson, who led a later study of an airplane striking the WTC, says that he does not recall the 600-mph study's being done at the Skilling firm.

132 *Airplane study:* Nalder, *Seattle Times*, Feb. 27, 1993; Jaffe's Feb. 14 memo to the *NYT* with attached telegram, courtesy Anthony Robins. See also the Feb. 14–16 stories in the New York papers, referenced below, on the safety allegations. The study may be implicit in some of the technical information on building damage presented in *ENR*, April 2, 1964; note, for example, the following statements and accompanying discussion: "A design procedure that will be used for structural framing of the 1,350-ft-high twin towers of the World Trade Center of New York City gives the exterior columns tremendous reserve strength. Live loads on these columns can be increased more than 2,000% before failure occurs. . . . Thus, the World Trade Center towers will have an inherent capacity to resist unforeseen calamities."

132 *Sleuthing out calculations:* "The World Trade Center: An Innovation in Steel Construction," *PA*, August 1968; *World-Telegram*, Feb. 14, 1964. The situation is, of course, more complicated than just looking at the force. Engineers speak of the "overturning moment," or the amount of *bending load* needed to tip a building over. Like a hand on a lever, a given lateral force on a building exerts a greater bending load the farther it is from the base of the building. In addition, a collision force would be much more impulsive in nature than a wind gust, generating wave motion up and down the building. So the calculation in the text should be considered an extremely rough estimate only. Still, it is just the kind of rough estimate that engineers make in such cases.

133 *Cutting the columns: ENR*, April 2, 1964. According to the calculations, the cut could be made as low as the first story and the statement would still hold.

133 *Wien's window:* Ross, *HT*, March 1, 1964.

134 *Wien and Helmsley's accusation:* For this episode, see: Knowles, *NYT*, Feb. 14, 1964; Ennis,

NYT, Feb. 15, 1964; *World-Telegram*, Feb. 14, 1964, CFAH; McFadden, *Journal-American*, Feb. 14, 1964, CFAH; *Journal-American*, Feb. 16, 1964, CFAH. See also Jaffe's Feb. 14 memo to the *NYT* with attached telegram from Richard Roth of Emery Roth & Sons. The telegram, also dated Feb. 14, is addressed to "MR. JOHN B. OAKES, EDITOR OF EDITORIAL PAGE, THE NEW YORK TIMES." Both the memo and the telegram are courtesy Anthony Robins. Attached note from Robins states: "My guess is this was a retrospective reaction to the incident of an airplane slamming into the Empire State Building. I came across the telegram in the PA's WTC archives, and made a copy, back in 1987 when researching my book."

134 *Real estate barons:* Knowles, *NYT*, March 9, 1964; *NYT*, Feb. 26, 1964; Apple Jr., *NYT*, April 1, 1964.

134 *Wien's structural criticisms:* According to Mortimer Matz, Carl Morse, the prolific construction man who had built, among dozens of other structures, the Pan Am Building, probably informed some of Wien's structural conclusions. Morse was an early ally of the Committee for a Reasonable World Trade Center.

134– *Sixty-one columns:* Later, after Leslie Robertson's redesign, the number would drop
35 to fifty-nine per face.

135 *"unsafe in an explosion":* McFadden, *Journal-American*, Feb. 14, 1964.

137 *"unconquerable Frankenstein":* Letter from Lawrence A. Wien to New Jersey governor Richard J. Hughes, Sept. 10, 1964. Courtesy Douglas Durst.

138 *"Our analysis indicated":* Nalder, *Seattle Times*, Feb. 27, 1993.

138 *Plane impact study:* Robertson, for example, in his testimony during the trial for the 1993 bombing of the WTC: "It was designed for a sabotage operation, that is the towers were designed for the circumstance where through some unknown circumstance that part of the building would be destroyed, and it was designed to stand in the face of a reasonable sabotage effort. The towers were designed for the impact by a 707 aircraft. That was the largest jet aircraft in the air at the time fully fuel laden out of JFK striking the building at any location." Robertson is apparently referring to the 1960s, when the towers were designed. Yet his description was only technically correct. The first order for the much larger Boeing 747 was placed in April 1966, and the plane went into service in January 1970, long before the towers were even completed. A Boeing 747 can weigh more than 800,000 pounds on takeoff. We would like to thank Robert Mackey for pointing these facts out to us. The Boeing Web site, www.boeing.com, has the dates in a brief history of the 747. FEMA 403/May 2002, pp. 1–17; Glanz, *NYT*, Sept. 12, 2001; Robertson and O'Sullivan interviews. Alan Davenport recalled that work on the study was probably done shortly after Robertson moved to New York around August 1964.

139 *Not taken into account:* "With the 707, to the best of my knowledge, the fuel load was not considered in the design. Indeed, I don't know how it could have been considered," Robertson said in the *Nova* documentary "Why the Towers Fell," which first aired on April 2, 2002.

139 *Woman at optometrist's:* This section is largely based on Hoffman, Eskildsen, and Robertson interviews and Eskildsen's "Oregon Research Institute Vision Center Report on the Four Factor Experiment in Horizontal Acceleration Thresholds." All details aside from subjects' names (which were not recorded in the August 1965 study) are based directly on the interviews, report, and several contemporary photographs that are courtesy Leslie Robertson.

140 *Swaying structures:* Worthington, Skilling, Helle & Jackson Wind Report, June 1966. Hoffman first did a literature search and found that human sensitivity to horizontal motion of this kind had never been studied scientifically.

142 *A forty-year secret:* Hoffman contacted one of us (J.G.) by e-mail after 9/11 and put us in contact with Eskildsen, who discovered a mimeographed copy of the report somewhere deep in his garage.

CHAPTER 6: ENDGAME

Sources

Books and Articles

Cannato, *The Ungovernable City: John Lindsay and His Struggle to Save New York*; Beedle, ed., *Second Century of the Skyscraper*; Dwyer, *Two Seconds under the World*; Gillespie, *Twin Towers*; Doig, *Empire on the Hudson*; Robbins, *The World Trade Center*.

Terence Smith, "City-Port Authority Talks on Trade Center Enter Crucial Stage," *NYT*, June 7, 1966; William Longgood, "The Fugitives from Progress," *World-Telegram & Sun*, Feb. 10, 1966; Charles G. Bennett, "Delay Is Sought on Trade Center," *NYT*, Feb. 9, 1966; George Carpozi Jr., "Trade Center Foes Notified on Eviction," *New York Post*, Feb. 9, 1966; "PA Director Fails to Stem Probe of World Trade Center," *World-Telegram & Sun*, Feb. 15, 1966, CFAH; Charles G. Bennett, "Way Opened for Council to Hold Hearings on Big Trade Center," *NYT*, Feb. 16, 1966; Anthony Prisendorf, "Corso Sees Month Delay on Trade Center Hearing," *World-Telegram & Sun*, Feb. 18, 1966; "Hearing Is Held on Trade Center," *NYT*, May 3, 1966; J. B. Holloway, "The Questions Are Out in the Open," *Villager*, May 5, 1966; Terence Smith, "Critics of World Trade Center Voice Their Protests at Hearing," *NYT*, May 14, 1966; Laurence G. O'Donnell, "Skyscraper Controversy," *WSJ*, March 5, 1966; "WCBS Restates Opposition to World Trade Center Scheme Proposed for Lower Manhattan," WCBS editorial no. 375, aired June 13 and 14, 1966; Ada Louise Huxtable, "Who's Afraid of the Big, Bad Buildings?" *NYT*, May 29, 1966; "Grasp All, Lose All," *Daily Bond Buyer*, June 13, 1966, courtesy Angus Kress Gillespie; Terence Smith, "Tobin Charges City Seeks $3-Billion to Clear Center," *NYT*, June 8, 1966; "It Smells Like Blackmail," *Daily News*, June 9, 1966, and accompanying cartoon, courtesy Angus Gillespie; "World's Highest Towers Planned in CSU Wind Unit," Fort Collins *Coloradoan*, Sept. 13, 1964; "Dampers Blunt the Wind's Force on Tall Buildings," *Architectural Record*, September 1971; Lester S. Feld, "Superstructure for 1,350-ft World Trade Center," *Civil Engineering*, June 1971; Robert E. Rapp, "The World Trade Center: An Architectural and Engineering Milestone," *Contemporary Steel Design*, 1964; "How Columns Will Be Designed for 110-Story Buildings," *ENR*, April 2, 1964; Terence Smith, "Lindsay Assails Charge by Tobin," *NYT*, July 16, 1966; Terence Smith, "A Trade Center Row," *NYT*, July 24, 1966; "Price Assails Port Authority for New Plan to Aid Jersey," *NYT*, July 19, 1966; Terence Smith, "City and Port Authority Mired in Deadlock on Trade Center," *NYT*, July 15, 1966; "Mrs. Austin Tobin Is Dead of Burns," *NYT*, July 17, 1966; "Government Leaders Attend Funeral of Mrs. Austin Tobin," *NYT*, July 20, 1966; Steven V. Roberts, "Governor Urges 'City' at Battery," *NYT*, May 13, 1966; "The Battle Round by Round," *ENR*, April 13, 1967; "New York Gets $90 Million Worth of Land for Nothing," *ENR*, April 18, 1968; Terence Smith, "City Ends Fight with Port Body on Trade Center," *NYT*, Aug. 4, 1966; "The

Shotgun Victory," Newark *Star-Ledger*, Aug. 5, 1966, courtesy Robert Price; "Jackhammers Bite Pavement to Start Trade Center Job," *NYT*, Aug. 6, 1966; "Miss Rosaleen Skehan Bride of Austin Tobin," *NYT*, June 30, 1967; John G. Rogers, "World Trade Center—Demolition Is Begun," *HT*, March 25, 1966; "Start Razing for Center," *Journal-American*, March 25, 1966, CFAH; Erwin Savelson, "Trade Center Site Razing under Way," *World-Telegram*, March 25, 1966, CFAH; Judson Hand, "Sole Scottish Tavern Moving into 'Limbo,'" *World Journal Tribune*, May 4, 1967, courtesy David MacInnes; Joseph P. Fried, "Demise of Radio Row Is Still Causing Static," *NYT*, Feb. 18, 1968; Don Ross, "'Octopus' Evicting Cortlandt St. Foe of Port Authority," *HT*, May 3, 1967; James Glanz, "Towers Believed to Be Safe Proved Vulnerable to an Intense Jet Fuel Fire, Experts Say," *NYT*, Sept. 12, 2001; John Crosby, "Small Guys Finish Last," *HT*, May 2, 1962; *Frontier News*, Dec. 21, 1965; Gerard Patterson, "Radio Row Fading from the Scene," *World-Telegram & Sun*, Jan. 10, 1966.

Authors' Interviews

Robert Price; Donald Elliott; Lloyd Schwalb; Patrick Falvey; Jack Cermak; Alan Davenport; Leslie Robertson; Aaron Schreier; Guy Tozzoli; Charles Urstadt; David MacInnes; Virginia MacInnes; Sy Syms; Leatrice Yelman; Mortimer Matz; Edward J. O'Sullivan; John Brunner; Roger Cohen; Peter J. Johnson; Terence Smith.

Documents

"The World Trade Center: Wind Program Interim Report, Supplement #1," Worthington, Skilling, Helle & Jackson, Jan. 15, 1965; "The World Trade Center: Wind Program Interim Report, Supplement #2," Worthington, Skilling, Helle & Jackson, March 15, 1965; "An Investigation of the Aerodynamic Stability of a Model of the Proposed Tower Blocks for the World Trade Center, New York," R. E. Whitbread and C. Scruton, National Physical Laboratory Aerodynamics Division (NPL Aero Report 1156), U.K., July 1965; "Part I, Final Chapter, WSHJ Wind Report," June 1966; P. Mahmoodi, L. E. Robertson, M. Yontar, C. Moy, L. Feld, "Performance of Viscoelastic Dampers in World Trade Center Towers," undated 3M technical report, courtesy Leslie Robertson; D. B. Caldwell, "Vibration Damping in World Trade Center Using Viscoelastic Material," 3M technical report, Jan. 26, 1972, courtesy Leslie Robertson; Leslie E. Robertson, "Limitations on Swaying Motion of Tall Buildings Imposed by Human Response Factors," undated technical report, courtesy Leslie Robertson; "World Trade Center in the Port of New York," PA, September 1966; "Via Port of New York: Greatest West Side Story Begins," PA, September 1966; "World Trade Center Performance Study: Data Collection, Preliminary Observations, and Recommendations," Federal Emergency Management Agency, FEMA 403/May 2002.

Notes

page
145 *Price and Lindsay:* Cannato; Price, Smith, and Elliott interviews.
146 *PA deal in lieu of taxes:* Smith, *NYT*, June 7, 1966.
146 *Lindsay tries to halt PA:* Longgood, *World-Telegram & Sun*, Feb. 10, 1966; Bennett, *NYT*, Feb. 9, 1966.
147 *Evicting Radio Row:* Carpozi Jr., *New York Post*, Feb. 9, 1966; *World-Telegram & Sun*, Jan. 10, 1966; in Nadel recording of the May 13, 1966, hearing at City Hall, Price

attacks Skehan on the issue. Recording courtesy Leatrice Yelman and Meryl Yelman.

147 *Lindsay's allies announce plans: World-Telegram & Sun,* Feb. 15, 1966; Bennett, *NYT,* Feb. 16, 1966; Prisendorf, *World-Telegram & Sun,* Feb. 18, 1966.

147 *Price insults Tobin:* Schwalb interview.

148 *Price sees decrepit streets:* Longgood, *World-Telegram & Sun,* Feb. 10, 1966. Longgood probably made his reporting trip within days of Price's drive through the area. The descriptive details (aside from the rats) are taken from Longgood's contemporaneous observations, not Price's recollections.

149 *Price Committee:* This and the following series of meetings, phone conversations, and exchanges of letters among the PA, state officials, and the city were recorded in great detail in a series of confidential memoranda retained in PA files until they were destroyed on Sept. 11, 2001. Skehan kept detailed notes on the meetings and Tobin filed copies of all letters along with lengthy descriptions (most of them dictated by him) of meetings, conversations, and his impressions of them. Copies of some of those memoranda were made by Roger Cohen, a PA official, for a political history of the trade center that he prepared before Sept. 11. Cohen has kindly provided this material to us, and it informs much of this section of the book. For convenience, we will refer to these in subsequent reference as "Cohen memos."

149 *Price vs. Tobin:* Price interview; Cohen memos.

151 *Tobin and Falvey at City Council meeting:* Falvey interview.

151 *Tobin's forty-four-page speech:* "The World Trade Center," Statement Submitted to City Council of the City of New York by Austin Tobin, Executive Director on behalf of the PA, City Hall, May 2, 1966. The *NYT* reported that Tobin read the "40-page statement," a tally that did not include the summation and conclusions. The speech is courtesy Farley Tobin.

152 *Charges hurled at Tobin: NYT,* May 3, 1966; Holloway, *Villager,* May 5, 1966; Smith, *NYT,* May 14, 1966.

152 *Ray and Price argument:* Crosby, *HT,* May 2, 1962; *Frontier News,* Dec. 21, 1965; Oscar Nadel's tape recording of the hearing is courtesy Leatrice Yelman and Meryl Yelman.

153 *Wien's structural criticisms:* See also O'Donnell, *WSJ,* March 5, 1966: "Finally, in their efforts to block construction of the towers, critics are raising the explosive issue of safety. The architects of the twin skyscrapers admittedly have employed a design concept never before used in a building anywhere near as tall as 110 stories. So critics are asking many 'what if' questions, which they quickly point out won't have to be answered because the building plans—due to the Port Authority's special status—are exempt from scrutiny by New York City building officials."

153 *"he really said that":* The part of this Weekly Report in our possession is dated—apparently in the hand of Angus Kress Gillespie, who copied it from the PA library in the north tower—May 2, 1966. Therefore the report would have been describing Wien's appearance at the earlier City Council meeting. The report is courtesy Gillespie.

153 *Media critics:* WCBS editorial no. 375, June 13 and 14, 1966, courtesy David MacInnes; Huxtable, *NYT,* May 29, 1966; *Daily Bond Buyer,* June 13, 1966.

154 *Shaughnessy assigned to leak letter:* Price interview.

154 *Tobin's frenzy:* Smith, *NYT,* June 8, 1966.

154 *"Shaughnessy shouldn't have leaked":* Cohen memos. These words appear in quotation marks in Tobin's contemporaneous notes, although he indicates the words may be approximate.

154 *"Cough up!" cartoon: Daily News,* June 9, 1966.

155 *Wind tunnel:* Much of this material derives from interviews with Cermak, technical papers he has written over the years, and a visit to the Fort Collins wind tunnel, which is little changed from the 1960s. According to the wind tunnel's schedule for 1964, experimental work on the twin towers model began at 8:00 A.M. sharp on July 1, 1964, and ran continuously until 5:00 P.M. that day.

155– *Tunnel description:* Fort Collins *Coloradoan,* Sept. 13, 1964; Cermak also filmed the
57 experience and retains the footage; one of us (J.G.) was shown some of the film in Fort Collins.

157 *Tacoma Narrows Bridge:* Talese.

157 *Negative damping:* Cermak and Davenport interviews.

159 *Robertson criticizes Skilling:* Robertson interviews. See also Robertson, *The Bridge,* Spring 2002. Robertson credits Skilling with developing the relationship with Yamasaki, but implies that Skilling was little more than the pitchman in "our interview with the PA"—an interview at which Robertson was not present, although he did help Skilling prepare for it. Nalder, *Seattle Times,* Jan. 5, 1986. Robertson is blunt when responding to criticisms from the Skilling family (John Skilling died in 1998) and former members of the Skilling firm that Robertson has allowed himself to be portrayed as the lead designer of the World Trade Center in the rush of publicity after Sept. 11, 2001. In an Aug. 31, 2003, e-mail response to questions on this book posed by one of the authors (J.G.), Robertson wrote, referring to John B. Skilling by his initials: "You mentioned that the folks in Seattle feel that JBS has been left out over the 11 September disaster. In my mind, the 11 September buck stops with me . . . not with JBS or with others in the partnership. I've taken the heat and do not seek the publicity. Should anyone in Seattle want to deal with the widows and the bereaving [sic] children, they are more than welcome to take over that responsibility. The events of 11 September are not roads to fame or to fortune . . . they are roads to grief and to despair. The thought that anyone is hogging the limelight can come only from persons who don't understand the enormity of the responsibility of the structural engineer in designing these enormous projects." Robertson also said he had never been disappointed by the apparent neglect of his contributions to the trade center project in press coverage in the 1960s. "You see, such things are not important to me," Robertson wrote. "Everyone who really mattered knew of that which I did, that which others did and so on. To the best of my knowledge there was no friction between John and me over such matters. My problems with JBS were never over such issues."

159 *"Wasted":* Robertson interview.

160 *"Twentieth-century Gullivers":* Fort Collins *Coloradoan,* Sept. 13, 1964.

160 *Davenport biographical details:* Contemporaneous photo courtesy Jack Cermak; Davenport interview.

161 *Davenport's phone call:* Davenport: "The contact that was perhaps most memorable was being a junior professor at a university and getting a call one morning say-

ing would I please help with the design of a 110-story building. And I practically fell off my chair, as you can imagine." The conversation did proceed under a confidentiality agreement, he said.

162 *"replaced by solid surfaces":* From a talk presented by Eiffel to the Société des Ingenieurs in 1885; cited in Beedle, p. 705 (in a paper by Davenport).

162 *Reports on experiments:* See Worthington, Skilling, Helle & Jackson; and Whitbread and Scruton reports.

164 *Davenport has the answer:* This is Davenport's recollection of the meeting. Robertson also recalled the meeting and was able to confirm most of the details.

164 *Viscoelastic dampers: Architectural Record,* September 1971; Mahmoodi, Robertson, Yontar, Moy, Feld, undated 3M technical report; Caldwell, 3M technical report, Jan. 26, 1972; Feld, *Civil Engineering,* June 1971. Robertson, in one of his papers, says the dampers spanned the tenth to the hundredth floors.

166 *Robertson explains about the pinstripes:* Robertson interviews.

166 *Pinstripes:* The final number of pinstripes can be simply counted from pictures— for example, from p. 33 of James Glanz and Eric Lipton, "Towering Ambition," *NYT Magazine,* Sept. 8, 2002. For the earlier design, see Rapp, *Contemporary Steel Design,* 1964. See figure of detailed floor framing plan with the three-foot, three-inch column spacing. The same framing plan is printed in *ENR,* April 2, 1964.

166 *Elements of solution:* Robertson, "Limitations on Swaying Motion of Tall Buildings Imposed by Human Response Factors," undated technical report; Schreier, Robertson, and Davenport interviews.

166 *"dancing in unison":* This is Davenport's description of the underlying physics.

167 *Amplitude equation:* For clarity, it is actually the inverse of their printed equation.

167 *14-inch sway:* See Feld, *Civil Engineering,* June 1971: "The design criterion was a 140-mph (100-year) hurricane wind. This is equivalent to a static wind load of 55 psf for the upper 100 ft and 45 psf over the remaining portion of the tower. . . . Design criterion adopted is 10 milli G's at the top occupied floor, not to exceed a frequency rate of 12 times a year. The building has a period of vibration of approximately 10 seconds and a $2\frac{1}{2}$ percent damping ratio. To achieve this level of comfort, the amplitude of static plus dynamic deflection was limited to a maximum of $\frac{3}{8}$ in. per story with 140-mph winds, in part by use of the damping units discussed earlier." In other words, the engineers expected the building to sway between five and six feet in the 140-mile-per-hour winds.

167 *Robertson studying wind flow:* Robertson interviews with the authors and Jim Dwyer. See Dwyer, *Two Seconds under the World.*

167 *Tobin slings mud:* Smith, *NYT,* July 16, 1966.

168 *"give away Manhattan":* Smith, *NYT,* July 16, 1966. See also Gillespie, p. 51.

168 *Lindsay's inner circle enraged:* Smith, *NYT,* July 24, 1966; *NYT,* July 19, 1966.

168 *Tobin releases notes:* Smith, *NYT,* July 16, 1966. Smith calls the material "a series of letters disclosed late Thursday night." In Tobin's Weekly Report of July 18, he says that "it became advisable" to release the material "last Thursday afternoon," but does not specify when the material was released. The combative tone of the report, a day before the funeral of Mrs. Tobin, is one of the puzzles of the episode. Report courtesy Angus Kress Gillespie.

169 *"kidnapper on the other end":* Cohen memos.
169 *Geraldine Tobin dies:* NYT, July 17, 1966; NYT, July 20, 1966.
169 *Skehan and Price agree on Shapiro:* The day-by-day train of events is described in Tobin's Weekly Report to the Commissioners for the week ending Aug. 8, 1966; report courtesy Angus Kress Gillespie.
169 *Tozzoli's deal sweetener:* Tozzoli and Urstadt interviews; Roberts, NYT, May 13, 1966; Tobin's Weekly Report to the Commissioners for the week ending Aug. 8, 1966: "The feature of using material excavated from the World Trade Center site to create new land off the Manhattan shore was the brainchild of Guy Tozzoli. He presented the idea months ago as something constructive and economically feasible from our standpoint and which might be sufficiently attractive to the new City administration to help break the impasse." For his part, Price leans toward Shapiro as the originator of the idea; ENR, Apr. 13, 1967; first announced as 28 acres, the number was later revised downward to 23.5. The value of the land was originally given as $30 million; later a number of estimates were used, ranging up to at least $90 million.
170 *Price's calculations:* Cohen memos.
170 *"The shotgun tactics":* Newark *Star-Ledger*, Aug. 5, 1966.
171 *"jackhammers":* NYT, Aug. 6, 1966.
172 *"United Nations of Commerce":* "Via Port of New York: Greatest West Side Story Begins," PA, September 1966. Tobin also soon began a personal renewal; in June 1966, he and Rosaleen Skehan were married.
172 *"it meant disaster":* The broadcast, a videotape recording of which is courtesy Joe Richman, was made on Channel 2, WCBS-TV, Mar. 24, 1966, the day the first demolitions began. See also Rogers, HT, March 25, 1966; *Journal-American*, Mar. 25, 1966, CFAH; Savelson, *World-Telegram*, Mar. 25, 1966.
172 *David MacInnes:* Hand, *World Journal Tribune*, May 4, 1967; David MacInnes and Virginia MacInnes interviews. Their restaurant and bar carried an earlier spelling of the family name: McInnes, without the *a*.
173 *Flam and Syms:* Fried, NYT, Feb. 18, 1968; Syms interview.
173–*Nadel forced out:* Ross, HT, May 3, 1967; ad in NYT, June 2, 1967; Leatrice Yelman
74 interview.
174–*Wien's newspaper ads:* Matz interview and electronic images of the plane ad in the
75 NYT of May 2, 1968.

CHAPTER 7: PYRAMIDS ON THE HUDSON

Sources
Books and Articles
Koch, *Men of Steel: The Story of the Family That Built the World Trade Center.*

Louis Effrat, "Weather Fails to Chill Fervor of 14,058 Yonkers Trot Fans," NYT, Feb. 14, 1967; McCandlish Phillips, "Giant 'Bathtub' Will Hold 110-Story Towers," NYT, Dec. 30, 1966; "Big Steel Cage Goes Underground," ENR, June 1, 1967; "Work on Trade Center Is Moving into Higher Gear," NYT, July 6, 1967; "Artifacts Are Dug Up at Trade Center Site," NYT, June 10, 1968; "Problems Plague Construction of New York World Trade Center," ENR, April 13, 1967; "Construction's Man of the

Year: World Trade Center's Ray Monti," *ENR*, Feb. 11, 1971; Martin S. Kapp, "Slurry-Trench Construction for Basement Walls of World Trade Center," *Civil Engineering—ASCE*, April 1969; Edith Iglauer, "The Biggest Foundation," *New Yorker*, Nov. 4, 1972; George J. Tamaro, "World Trade Center 'Bathtub': From Genesis to Armageddon," *The Bridge*, publication of the National Academy of Engineers, Spring 2002; Michael T. Kaufman, "Trade Center Is Doing Everything Big," *NYT*, June 6, 1969; "Marble, Plumbing Contracts Announced," *World Trade Center Newsletter*, October 1968; "Additional Construction Contracts Announced," *World Trade Center Newsletter*, August 1971; Monti, "A Tall Order," *Portfolio*, winter 1990–1991; William E. Burrows, "World Trade Center's Construction Chief Wrestles to Keep Huge Project on Target," *WSJ*, Aug. 20, 1969; "New Machine to Wash Trade Center Windows," *NYT*, Sept. 22, 1968; Maurice Carroll, "A Section of the Hudson Tubes Is Turned into Elevated Tunnel," *NYT*, Dec. 30, 1968; Dennis Overbye, "Engineers Tackle Havoc Underground," *NYT*, Sept. 18, 2001; Jane Stuart, "Shovels Dig and History Comes Alive," Bergen County *Record*, April 12, 1968; Jerry Landauer, "New York Port Agency's $30 Million Saving on Steel Work Prompts Antitrust Inquiry," *WSJ*, July 16, 1969; David K. Shipler, "Trade Center Started as Men of Iron Install Steel," *NYT*, Aug. 7, 1968; "The Port of New York Authority and the World Trade Center: More Facts You Should Know . . . More Questions That Should Be Answered," *NYT*, Oct. 3, 1966; "A. Carl Weber, 85; Noted Structural Engineer and Civic Leader," *St. Louis Post-Dispatch*, Nov. 29, 1994; Robert W. Duffy, "Twin Towers That Withstood Bomb Couldn't Withstand Jetliner Attacks," *St. Louis Post-Dispatch*, Sept. 12, 2001; Charlene Prost, "Area Man's Joist Design Stood Up," *St. Louis Post-Dispatch*, March 5, 1993; Dan Coughlin, "World's Tallest Towers to Carry Seattle Label," *Seattle Post-Intelligencer*, Jan. 24, 1967; Richard E. Taylor, "Computers and the Design of the World Trade Center," *Journal of the Structural Division*, Proceedings of the American Society of Civil Engineers, December 1966; James Glanz and Eric Lipton, "A Search for Clues in Towers' Collapse: Engineers Volunteer to Examine Steel Debris Taken to Scrapyards," *NYT*, Feb. 2, 2002; James Glanz and Michael Moss, "Since the Beginning, Questions Dogged the Trade Center's Fireproofing," *NYT*, Dec. 14, 2001; James Glanz with Michael Moss, "Faulty Fireproofing Is Reviewed as Factor in Trade Center Collapse," *NYT*; Arnold H. Lubash, "Jury Hears Gotti Tape: 'He's Gonna Die,'" *NYT*, Feb. 21, 1992; Arnold H. Lubash, "Gotti Summation Relies on Tapes and Testimony," *NYT*, March 3, 1992; James Glanz and Andrew C. Revkin, "Did the Ban on Asbestos Lead to Loss of Life?" *NYT*, Sept. 18, 2001; James Glanz, "Towers Untested for Major Fire, Inquiry Suggests," *NYT*, May 8, 2003; "City to Stop Spraying Asbestos; Material Was Linked to Cancer," *NYT*, June 16, 1970; "Trade Center 'Topped Out' with Steel Column 1,370 Feet above Street," *NYT*, Dec. 24, 1970; Lawrence Van Gelder, "Propane Blasts Hit Trade Center," *NYT*, March 17, 1970; "World Trade Center Hit by Fire, Explosion; Origin Isn't Confirmed," *WSJ*, March 17, 1970; Pat R. Gilbert, "The Price of Lost Art; PA Nears Settlement for Pieces Destroyed on 9/11," Bergen County *Record*, April 28, 2003; Glenn Collins, "Notes on a Revolutionary Dinosaur," *NYT Magazine*, Aug. 6, 1972.

Authors' Interviews

Vincent Miller; Arturo Ressi di Cervia; George Tamaro; Charles Maikish; Charles Smith; Gennaro Liguori; Guy Tozzoli; Werner Quasebarth; William Quasebarth;

Richard Geyer; Thelma Elder; Donald Winter; Julian Saunders; Sid Combs; James White; Nicholas Soldano; Jack Daly; James Endler; Richard Brady; Jack Doyle; Fred Doyle; George Bachert; Peter Fontes; Walter Beauvais; Edward Iannielli; Saul Wenegrat; Herman Tretter; John Dragonette; Frank Lombardi; Eugene Fasullo; Abe Levine; Robert Walsh; James Verhalen; Roger G. Morse; Richard Taylor.

Documents

Austin J. Tobin, "The World Trade Center Moves Ahead," PA publicity materials, spring 1968; "Progress Report on the Federal Building and Fire Safety Investigation of the World Trade Center Disaster," National Institute of Standards and Technology, NIST Special Publication 1000–3, May 2003; "World Trade Center Performance Study: Data Collection, Preliminary Observations, and Recommendations," FEMA 403, May 2002; "Facts on the World Trade Center in the Port of New York–New Jersey," PA, April 1973; Austin Tobin's Weekly Report to the Commissioners, courtesy Angus Kress Gillespie. The pages of the report in our possession for 1968 are undated except for the following line: "This report covers World Trade Center construction activity through Wednesday, June 13."

Notes

page

176 *"Five thousand years":* The citation gives the first line of the piece. The second line is as follows: "Five millenniums were to pass before man, on the threshold of A.D. 2000, would build a structure comparable in size and conception with the stone pile a pharaoh built to encase his tomb in the year 3000 B.C."

176 *At Washington and Vesey Streets:* Miller, Ressi di Cervia interviews. Miller recalls that it was probably the day Lincoln's birthday was celebrated that year, Monday, Feb. 13, 1967, which would normally have been a day off for him. There were snow flurries with temperatures in the teens that day. See Effrat, *NYT,* Feb. 14, 1967.

176 *Ressi di Cervia:* Ressi di Cervia interview; Phillips, *NYT,* Dec. 30, 1966.

176 *Trench and foundation walls:* Test panels had already been constructed around the Hudson Tubes at West Street; *ENR,* June 1, 1967; *NYT,* July 6, 1967.

177 *Fabrication in more than a dozen cities:* Kaufman, *NYT,* June 6, 1969.

177 *Materials statistics:* Tobin, PA publicity materials, spring 1968; *World Trade Center Newsletter,* October 1968 and August 1971; "Facts on the World Trade Center in the Port of New York–New Jersey," PA, April 1973; Monti, *Portfolio,* winter 1990–1991; Burrows, *WSJ,* Aug. 20, 1969; *NYT,* Sept. 22, 1968; Collins, *NYT Magazine,* Aug. 6, 1972.

177 *"biggest ditch in Manhattan:"* *NYT,* June 10, 1968.

178 *PA engineer:* Much of this work was led by Vincent Miller.

179 *Steel-alloy blade:* *ENR,* Apr. 13, 1967.

179 *Lower Manhattan's geology:* Kapp, *Civil Engineering—ASCE,* April 1969; Phillips, *NYT,* Dec. 30, 1966; the ballast is discussed in *ENR,* April 13, 1967: "Oddly enough, the most troublesome obstruction is the easiest to remove. It is the 10 to 15-ft thick layer of small ballast stones dumped over the side of sailing ships when the river covered what is now the job site. The stones are no problem for the bucket, but those adjacent to the trench area continue to roll into the cut, causing tremen-

dous overbreaks. In one section the overbreak was 85%, according to Arturo Ressi d. Cervia [*sic*], Icanda's field engineer." Tamaro, Ressi di Cervia interviews; Iglauer, *New Yorker*, Nov. 4, 1972; Tamaro, *The Bridge*, spring 2002.

179 *Engineer draws construction tasks:* Charles Smith, the first engineer Monti hired; Smith interview.

180 *Slurry wall progression:* Tamaro interview: "for example, in the month of March [1967] I think they were able to do three panels. On May 30, we did three panels in one day. We were doing a panel a day, and the job finally started to move, which was critical. And it just went like hell from there, until April of the next year when the last panels were going and the job was demobilized." There were—and are—158 panels, so 3 panels a month translates to about four years and five months. Tamaro's best estimate is that Monti encountered Brunner on the site in March 1967. The exact timing is uncertain, but it must have been before Apr. 1, 1967, when Tamaro joined the project. Monti told the story often, according to Tamaro.

181 *Cave and valley:* The valley curves southward after entering the perimeter of the bathtub, and exits around panel L4 (counting from east to west on Liberty Street). Tamaro says he now believes the cave structure also continues and probably exists under panel L5. Tamaro: "In L5, we think now that we have the same cave down there, because we're now drilling the piling for the new liner walls, and we've punched through the shelf." The stream would have been a tributary to the Hudson, which was at a much lower elevation in prehistoric times.

182 *Tiebacks and the Jumbo Air Track:* Liguori interview.

182 *Suspending the tubes:* Carroll, *NYT*, Dec. 30, 1968; Smith interview.

183 *"giant drain pipe":* Tobin's Weekly Report to the Commissioners, June 1968.

183 *Caissons:* Kapp, *Civil Engineering—ASCE*, April 1969.

183 *Bands as Speidel Twist-O-Flex and jock straps:* Liguori and Maikish interviews.

183 *"It's doubtful":* Carroll, *NYT*, Dec. 30, 1968.

184 *"the tube slammed shut":* The details are largely from interviews with Maikish; Liguori confirmed many of those details (aside from the direct conversation with Druding), and others recalled the incident in more general terms.

184 *Artifacts dug up:* Overbye, *NYT*, Sept. 18, 2001; Iglauer, *New Yorker*, Nov. 4, 1972; *NYT*, June 10, 1968; Stuart, Bergen County *Record*, Apr. 12, 1968; Tozzoli and Tamaro interviews.

185 *Druding strikes the stone:* Maikish interview.

186 *Atlas Machine:* Depictions of the Atlas Machine plant are based largely on interviews with Werner and William Quasebarth, Geyer, Elder, Winter, Saunders, and Combs.

186 *Steel contracts:* Landauer, *WSJ*, July 16, 1969; Shipler, *NYT*, Aug. 7, 1968. For detailed references to the steel contracts, see "The Steel Goes Up: World Trade Center Construction Shifts into High Gear," *Via Port of New York*, PA, October 1968; "Nine New Trade Center Contracts Announced," The World Trade Center in the Port of New York, PA, March 1967; "Trade Center Contracts Let," *ENR*, Feb. 2, 1967; "All Systems Go!" *Via Port of New York*, PA, October 1967; "Contracts of $74,079,000 Awarded for Building New York Trade Center," *WSJ*, Jan. 24, 1967; "Contracts Totaling $74,079,000 Awarded for the Trade Center,"

NYT, Jan. 24, 1967; "Tallest Buildings in World to Use Laclede Trusses," *Ladle* (published monthly for employees of Laclede Steel Company), February 1967, vol. 7, no. 1; www.cee.vt.edu/alumni/ alumnidetails.asp?AlumniID=11; White interview.

187 *Bethlehem and U.S. Steel:* Landauer, *WSJ*, July 16, 1969; *NYT*, July 18, 1969.

187 *Escalation could take down the project:* See, for example, John Tishman's remarks to the New-York Historical Society, March 13, 2002: "This almost sabotaged the whole project, because there was so much concern about these buildings being too large or too dominant in the real estate market that the port was really almost ready to abandon." The reference is clearly to Wien and the Committee for a Reasonable World Trade Center. See also interview with Tozzoli: "Well, put yourself in my place. The foundations are under way. I knew that this was the first major contract other than the foundation contract. And everybody in the business was watching. The PA had never done anything like this before. If these numbers come out wrong, the project is a dead duck. A dead duck meaning you either stop it or, worse than that, the PA will have wasted billions of dollars."

187 *"The figures are shocking":* *NYT*, Oct. 3, 1966.

187 *Tobin throws the bids out:* Weekly Report to the Commissioners for the Week Ending Aug. 29, 1966, courtesy Angus Kress Gillespie.

188 *Division into lots:* White interview. See also Les Robertson's remarks to the New-York Historical Society, March 13, 2002. In those remarks, Robertson said that the initial division included eleven lots. The origin of the idea to divide the job into lots is a subject of some dispute, and the idea is claimed by several people. Whatever the origin, it seems unlikely that Tobin would have thrown out the bids before having in hand the plan to break the job up and open it to bidding by a number of smaller companies.

188 *Meeting at Tishman's headquarters:* Notes and papers from the archives of Laclede Steel, which is no longer in business, are thanks to the kind help of former Laclede employees, including Larry Hutchison, David Neptune, and David McGee; all the papers referred to are original documents. *St. Louis Post-Dispatch*, Nov. 29, 1994; Duffy, *St. Louis Post-Dispatch*, Sept. 12, 2001; Prost, *St. Louis Post-Dispatch*, March 5, 1993; Koch, p. 135; *ENR*, Feb. 2, 1967; attendees were deduced from the business cards stapled to Weber's notes on the meeting.

188 *"HAVE JUST BEEN INFORMED":* The misspelling of Endler's name and the running together of the two words are *sic*.

189 *Last-minute changes:* The letter from A. Carl Weber to Mal Levy describing the necessary changes is dated Jan. 31, 1968. It indicates that Weber and another Laclede engineer were to meet with Levy in his office at 11 A.M., Tuesday, Feb. 6, to discuss the problems. The last-minute changes, Weber wrote Levy, involved "additional fabrication on practically all joist ends," increasing the amount of steel by "some 503 tons which are indicated by the engineer as necessary to revise the damping units originally considered in the contract."

190 *Seattle panels:* Soldano interview; Coughlin, *Seattle Post-Intelligencer*, Jan. 24, 1967.

190 *Mainframe computer:* Taylor, *Journal of the Structural Division*, December 1966; Richard Taylor and Soldano interviews.

190 *PONYA A-251-92-95:* Glanz and Lipton, *NYT*, Feb. 2, 2002.

191 *The ascent begins:* People whose interviews have informed this section include the following: Daly, Endler, Brady, Jack Doyle, Maikish, Fred Doyle, Bachert, Fontes, Beauvais, Iannielli, Wenegrat, Tretter, Dragonette, Lombardi, Fasullo, Levine, Ray Monti (taped interview courtesy Angus Kress Gillespie), Smith, Walsh, and White. Specifically on setting the grillage, see *Via Port of New York*, PA, October 1968; Tobin's Weekly Report to the Commissioners, 1968, otherwise undated but probably for the week ending Aug. 13, 1968; *World Trade Center Newsletter*, PA, October 1968; Shipler, *NYT*, Aug. 7, 1968; *NYT* morgue photo from Aug. 6, 1968, with this caption: "this morning a 34-ton steel grillage (15 feet long, 11 feet wide and 7 feet high) was lowered into concrete footing 70 feet below street level at the World Trade Center near Greenwich Street amd [*sic*] Fulton St. It will be the first of 28 to be used to support the 1,350 foot high North Tower building."

191 *Maikish grouts the grillages:* Maikish interview.

191 *Koch family quarrels:* Koch; Daly interview.

192 *Antitrust inquiry:* Landauer, *WSJ*, July 16, 1969; *NYT*, July 18, 1969. No charges were brought in the case.

193 *Construction scene:* Tobin's Weekly Report to the Commissioners, 1968, probably for the week ending Sept. 17, 1968. In interviews with the authors, Endler and Werner Quasebarth indicated that they were actually flown to that spot by PA helicopters to see the view and appreciate the height.

193 *Kangaroo cranes broke down:* Daly, Jack Doyle interviews.

194 *Workers on the site:* Burrows, *WSJ*, Aug. 20, 1969; Daly and Bachert interviews.

196—*Booms and floor panels:* Jack Doyle interview.

 97

197 *Skycrane incident:* Daly interview.

198 *Iannielli astonished:* Iannielli interview.

198 *Beauvais fired:* Beauvais interview. According to Beauvais, he was transferred to Kennedy Airport but returned to the trade center later as a planker. Beauvais said in an interview that he had been caught riding up twice, first on a floor panel and then on a headache ball.

199 *Fireproofing:* Parts of the following section on fireproofing are based on NIST Special Publication 1000—3, May 2003, p. 73.

198—*DiBono:* Dragonette interview and dated documents described by Dragonette.

 99 The contract, according to Dragonette, was WTC 116.00, dated May 2, 1972, and the relevant PA memo on the escalation was dated March 29, 1972; Glanz and Moss, *NYT*, Dec. 14, 2001; Lubash, *NYT*, Feb. 21, 1992; Lubash, *NYT*, March 3, 1992.

199 *Cafco Blaze-Shield:* Verhalen and Morse interviews; Glanz and Revkin, *NYT*, Sept. 18, 2001.

200 *"We cannot be expected":* For the relevant letters, see NIST Special Publication 1000—3, May 2003.

200 *Asbestos:* Tobin's Weekly Report to the Commissioners, April 20, 1970. Tobin wrote that the CBS report "pointed out that the Trade Center is the only construction project in the City in which tarpaulins are being used on the exterior of the building to prevent the spread of the asbestos." Mayor Lindsay did order an early ban on the use of asbestos on June 15, 1970. See *NYT*, June 16, 1970.

200 *Switch to nonasbestos fireproofing:* Tobin's Weekly Report to the Commissioners, April

30, 1970. In the same report, Tobin wrote that "exterior steel beams," presumably meaning columns, "had been sprayed up to the 18th floor." Roger Morse, who inspected the buildings as part of a later series of asbestos lawsuits, confirmed in interviews that the interior fireproofing originally contained asbestos only to the thirty-sixth floor. In interviews, Guy Tozzoli said he recalled that the asbestos spraying stopped at the thirty-ninth floor. The thirty-ninth floor is also the one cited by FEMA 403, May 2002, pp. 2–12, as the spot where asbestos spraying stopped. Guy Tozzoli has said that comparative tests of the two types were made—how well each stuck to steel, for example.

200 *Fireproofing stripped and reapplied:* Maikish interview. Maikish observed the problems with water washing away fireproofing but said they were found and corrected; Tobin's Weekly Report to the Commissioners, June 22, 1970. The photo, from Austin Tobin's Weekly Reports, is courtesy Angus Kress Gillespie.

201 *Record height: NYT* morgue photo dated Oct. 19, 1970. Peter Fontes's name is misspelled as "Ponte" in the morgue photo caption. The error did not find its way into the printed photos or the brief story on the event, "World Trade Center Becomes World's Highest Building—by 4 Feet," *NYT,* Oct. 20, 1970; *NYT,* Dec. 24, 1970.

202 EAT AT VOLKS: Maikish and Daly interviews.

203 *Explosion:* Van Gelder, *NYT,* Mar. 17, 1970; *NYT,* Mar. 17, 1970; Daly interview; Associated Press photo in *NYT* morgue, dated Mar. 16, 1970.

203 *Koenig sphere:* Wenegrat interview; Gilbert, Bergen County *Record,* Apr. 28, 2003.

203–*Commuters Café:* Tretter and Maikish interviews.
04

CHAPTER 8: CITY IN THE SKY

Sources

Books and Articles

Goldman, *The Empire State Building Book*; O'Hagan, *High Rise/Fire and Life Safety*; Ruchelman, *The World Trade Center, Politics and Policies of Skyscraper Development*; Petit, *To Reach the Clouds: My Highwire Walk between the Twin Towers*; Dwyer, *Two Seconds under the World*; Gillespie, *Twin Towers*; Doig, *Empire on the Hudson.*

Vincent Lee and Owen Moritz, "Corrected Fire Hazards Keep Trade Center Open," New York *Daily News,* Dec. 24, 1970; "Trade Center 'Topped Out' with Steel Column 1,370 Feet above the Street," *NYT,* Dec. 24, 1970; Joseph C. Ingraham, "Group Going Abroad for Port Authority in Trade Center Bid," *NYT,* May 5, 1964; Owen Moritz, "Trade Center Opens on a Many-Storied Day," *Daily News,* Dec. 17, 1970; "6 City Fire Engines at a Premiere," *NYT,* Dec. 19, 1974; Joseph B. Treaster, "Suspect, 19, Is Charged with Trade Center Fires," *NYT,* May 21, 1975; "Arson Threatened at Trade Center," *NYT,* Feb. 20, 1975; "7 Suspicious Fires Hit Trade Center," *NYT,* May 20, 1975; Edward C. Burks, "Trade Center to Improve Precautions against Fire," *NYT,* Jan 16, 1976; "World Trade Center Becomes World's Highest Building—by 4 Feet," *NYT,* Oct. 20, 1970; Glenn Collins, "Notes on a Revolutionary Dinosaur," *NYT Magazine,* Aug. 6, 1972; "The Port Authority Battles Its Critics," *BW,* April 3, 1971, courtesy Farley Tobin; Linda Charlton, "Tobin Leaving Port Body after

30 Years as Chief," *NYT*, Dec. 13, 1971; "Tobin, Citing the Rain, Passes Up Dedication," *NYT*, April 5, 1973; Frank J. Prial, "Port Authority Has Fallen on Hard Times," *NYT*, Nov. 10, 1974; Mary Breasted, "Toymaker Hailed by Crowds but Sued by City," *NYT*, May 27, 1977; Edith Evans Asbury, "Toymaker, 27, 'Never Scared' on the Way Up," *NYT*, May 27, 1977; Judy Klemesrud, "Tall—but True—Tales Run in Her Family," *NYT*, Sept. 27, 1977; Murray Schumach, " 'Fly' Pays $1.10, a Cent a Floor; City Drops Suit," *NYT*, May 28, 1977; Grace Lichtenstein, "Stuntman, Eluding Guards, Walks a Tightrope between Trade Center Towers," *NYT*, Aug. 8, 1974; "Just Because They Were There," *NYT*, Aug. 11, 1974; "Aerialist a Hit in Central Park," *NYT*, Aug. 30, 1974; Lee Dembart, "Queens Skydiver Leaps Safely from Roof of the Trade Center," *NYT*, July 23, 1975; "World Trade Center Honors New Jersey Woman as Millionth Visitor," *NYT*, Nov. 5, 1976; Philip H. Dougherty, "Trade Center to Promote at Top," *NYT*, Dec. 9, 1975; Deirdre Carmody, "A City unto Itself: Shops, Restaurants and People," *NYT*, May 28, 1984; William Grimes, "Windows That Rose So Close to the Sun," *NYT*, Sept. 19, 2001; "Publicity over Chairs Helps Fill Restaurant," *NYT*, Dec. 3, 1975; Mimi Sheraton, "The Two Faces of Windows on World," *NYT*, Jan. 28, 1977; "New Outlook at Windows on the World," *NYT*, July 15, 1977; Alan S. Oser, "Japanese Help Fill Trade Center," *NYT*, May 16, 1990; Richard Witkin, "Radio Warning Keeps Jetliner from Hitting Mast on Trade Center," *NYT*, Feb. 26, 1981; "Jet Crew to Be Asked about 'Near Miss,' " *NYT*, Feb. 27, 1981; John T. McQuiston, "Air Controller in 'Near Miss' Is Still Feeling Shock," *NYT*, March 1, 1981; Isabel Wilkerson, "Dean Witter Agrees to Lease 24 Floors of the Trade Center," *NYT*, July 9, 1985; Susan Girardo, "Letting the Twins," *Portfolio*, winter 1990–1991, vol. 3, no. 1; Joseph Berger, "Work Set on Last Trade Center Unit," *NYT*, Oct. 1, 1984.

Authors' Interviews

Rick Boody; Margaret Sliss; Amy Herz Juviler; Lawrence Huntington; Irene Humphries; Candice Tevere; George Zuckerman; Shirley Adelson Siegel; Gennaro Fischetti; Margaret Jourdan; William G. Schoenmuller; Guido Zehnder; Harold G. Brauner; Roland Hummel Jr.; John Keenan; Louis Jerome; Bertram French; Matthew J. Statcom; Peter C. Goldmark Jr.; George Rossi; Tom Donovan; Cornelius Lynch; Thomas J. Kearney; John Brunner; Jack Zwick; George Daddi; Tom Donovan; Guy Tozzoli; Edward O'Sullivan; Eugene Dockter; Raymond W. Gimmer; John Dunn; Edwin Jennings; Dave Corcoran; Harold Kull; George Willig; Larry Silverstein; Marc Cutler; Alex Brown; Frederic S. Berman; Reg Presley; Chris Britton; Jeanette Way; Peter Lucas.

Documents

"High Rise Fire Safety," a May 1975 report by New York State Standing Committee on Labor, at the New York State Legislative Library; "Analysis of World Trade Center Occupancy and Rentals," report by Office of the State Comptroller, Feb. 6, 1981; "Options for the Disposition of the World Trade Center, Report to the States of New Jersey and New York and the Port Authority of NY and NJ," Bear Stearns, June 1984, from the NYS Legislative Library; "The Future of the World Trade Center, a Report to Gov. Hugh L. Carey," April 1981, Rockefeller Archives; "The World Trade Center Bombing: Report and Analysis," United States Fire Administration, no date; "The World Trade Center Bombing: A Tragic Wake Up Call," Senate Committee on Investigations, Taxation, and Government Operations, August 1993; "The Stenographic Record before the New York State Senate Standing Committee on Investigations, Taxation, and Government Operations," March 1993; transcript, *USA v. Omar Ahmad Ali Abdel Rahman et al.*, U.S. District Court, Southern District of New York, 2/27/1995; transcript, *US v. Ramzi Ahmed Yousef and Eyad Ismoil*, U.S. District Court, Southern District of New York, Oct. 22, 1997; letter from Roger H. Gilman to Warren T. Lindquist, Oct. 6, 1970, regarding tenants at WTC, at Rockefeller Archive; *World Trade Center Newsletter*, May 1971, December 1971, April 1973, June 1973; The Port Authority of New York and New Jersey Annual Report, 1970–76, on file at Rutgers University Library.

Notes

page

205 *Irving R. Boody & Co.:* The company had nearly completed its move the day before, on December 15, 1970, and employees were making final arrangements. The full name of the company is Irving R. Boody & Co. Inc.; interviews with Boody and Sliss. See Gillespie, p. 114; Emanuel Perlmutter, "Tenants Settle in Trade Center," *NYT*, Dec. 17, 1970.

205 *Falling ice:* Sliss interview; *NYT* morgue photo, Dec. 15, 1970. "As Ice Fell from World Trade Center" shows a construction worker dodging falling ice and a police officer closing the subway entrance at Cortlandt Street.

206 *Odd opening day:* Rossi interview.

206 *Boody family history:* David A. Boody served as mayor of Brooklyn before it merged with New York City; history from Irving R. Boody & Co.; Boody interview.

206 *Rossi deals with first tenants:* Rossi interview; Lee and Moritz, *Daily News*, Dec. 24, 1970; *NYT*, Dec. 24, 1970. In total, on this opening day, the occupied space at the WTC was 5,040 square feet as one other tiny firm had moved in, Export-Import Services Inc., on the tenth floor, renting 2,503 square feet, in addition to Boody's 2,537-square-foot office. Numbers included in a Dec. 15, 1970, PA press release.

207 *Empire State Building:* 2.158 million square feet of rentable space at Empire State Building: Goldman, *The Empire State Building Book*, p. 92. That 4 million was set aside for private tenants meeting occupancy requirements, detailed in Jan. 20, 1964, "Information for Brokers" sheet included in announcement of project (Rockefeller Archive Center).

207 *PA expenditures:* Interviews with Donovan and Lynch, who organized and went on the trips; Ingraham, *NYT*, May 5, 1964.

207 *"A buyer, for example":* PA brochure; Lynch interview.

207 *Letter carrier:* Moritz, *Daily News*, Dec. 17, 1970; Nulman is featured in a photograph, standing alone as he delivered mail.

208 *Forty fires:* By 1972, there had been forty-one fires since the first tenant moved in, according to a May 1975 report by New York State Standing Committee on Labor. Part of this chatter was a surge in general unease about working high up in the sky. Prior to 1970, it had been decades since there was a catastrophic office fire in New York City. But then in August of that year, just as the WTC was preparing to open its doors, there was a devastating blaze at the brand-new skyscraper on South Street known as 1 New York Plaza. Then, in early December, there was another major office tower blaze, this one in Midtown, at 919 Third

Avenue. Between these two fires, five people were killed and eighty-eight injured.

208 *Juviler speaks with fire officer:* Juviler interview.
209 *"we have policemen":* Lynch interview.
209 *"Three things" ad:* Appeared in *NYT.*
210 *Huntington's Fiduciary Trust:* Huntington interview; figures from Fiduciary and Huntington.
210 *Tobin rejects leases:* Tobin said in a speech to the New York City Chapter of Financial Executives Institute, Feb. 23, 1967, about leases that were already being signed: "These eligibility requirements are strictly enforced. We have rejected many firms which wanted space in the trade center. In several cases, we have rejected firms desiring to rent several hundreds of thousands of square feet of trade center space because the firms did not meet our eligibility requirement." Lynch interview; interview with an agent at Cushman & Wakefield, which was representing Lybrand, Ross Bros. & Montgomery. The PA, in 1981, also claimed that it turned down AT&T and General Motors, which wanted to lease space (letter by Patrick Falvey, Jan. 11, 1981, to NYS Comptroller).
210 *Fiduciary bends the rules:* The PA defended its decision by saying that the company "specializes in investment management and plays a unique role in this field in that it is one of the largest managers of foreign-owned assets in the country and probably the largest of any bank in New York," Roger H. Gilman, the director of the PA's Planning and Development Department, wrote in a 1970 letter.
211 *British artillery telescope:* Huntington interview.
211 *"It is Jacob Marley":* Humphries interview.
211 *Tevere uneasy:* Tevere interview.
212 *Huntington hits the window:* Huntington interview.
213 *"We have got them all":* All quotes come from the film itself.
213 *Arsonist:* PA records; Treaster, *NYT,* May 21, 1975.
213 *WTC blaze:* Kull interview; report by the New York Board of Fire Underwriters, which describes the fire and the damage in detail, as does O'Hagan, pp. 37–47.
214 *"given the stack action":* O'Hagan, p. 47.
214 *Adorno lights more fires:* Treaster, *NYT,* May 21, 1975; *NYT,* Feb. 20, 1975; *NYT,* May 20, 1975; Dockter interview.
214– Fischetti's and legislators' investigations: Fischetti interview; May 1975 report by New
15 York State Standing Committee on Labor. Fischetti is cited in this report.
215 *"not feasible":* Burks, *NYT,* Jan. 16, 1976.
215 *Empty real estate:* Report by Office of the State Comptroller, Feb. 6, 1981, shows that in 1975 the WTC was renting out 2.2 million square feet to the Custom House and the PA, among other agencies, and another 2.3 million square feet to the state of New York. That compared to a total 2 million square feet occupied by commercial tenants. The analysis showed that about 60 percent of the total available space was rented. Ultimately, the government occupancy would peak in 1978, when the total space occupied by the government was 4.7 million square feet, according to this study.
215 *Bad timing:* Mark Thornton, an economist at the Ludwig von Mises Institute in Auburn, Alabama, noted in a paper, "Skyscrapers and Business Cycles," that historically the construction of "world's tallest" buildings has tended to coin-

cide with major downturns in the economy, citing not only the WTC and the Empire State Building but the Singer Building and Metropolitan Life Building, which coincided with the Panic of 1907, and the Petronas Towers in Kuala Lumpur, which was completed in 1997, around the time of the East Asian financial crisis.

216 *Citywide empty office space:* Cushman & Wakefield data.

216 *"We get prospects":* Donovan interview.

216 *Tallest building:* NYT, Oct. 20, 1970, said it reached this point on Oct. 19. The Sears Tower was topped out on May, 3, 1973, taking the title.

216 *Lawsuit:* Filed by the owners of 22 Cortlandt in March 1977. They claimed that the wind coming from the towers would reach 60 miles per hour (Ruchelman, p. 119). The bird problem was admitted by the PA, which finally, in November 2000, agreed to dim the lights on the roof of 1 WTC at night, citing "500 dead and injured birds outside the World Trade Center," counted in just a two-month period; the sewage discharge, which ultimately was stopped, was cited in Collins, *NYT Magazine*, Aug. 6, 1972.

216 *PA charges ahead with promotion:* Boody interview.

216 *World Trade Mart:* This center, although it never opened, was called several names, including International Products Mart and International Trade Mart. It was highlighted in a WTC newsletter of May 1971, which said the goal was to have three hundred different American and foreign companies signed up as sponsors who would display goods at the center; Brunner interview.

217 *"politics played a bigger role":* Oct. 1, 1973, letter from John Brunner, a PA aide assigned to try to get the World Trade Mart going, to John McAvey, a PA budget official.

217 *Tobin resigns:* Charlton, *NYT*, Dec. 13, 1971; he said at the time that his resignation would take effect on March 31, 1972; *NYT*, Apr. 5, 1973.

217 *Ages:* Tobin born 1903, Tozzoli born 1922.

217 *"bitching at you":* Tozzoli interview.

217 *White elephant:* Prial, *NYT*, Nov. 10, 1974; report by Office of the State Comptroller, Feb. 6, 1981, p. 6. Between 1972 and 1979, this analysis showed that the WTC, after accounting for debt service costs, lost a total of $125.7 million.

217 *Man climbs a tower:* Willig interview; Breasted, *NYT*, May 27, 1977. The theme of humanizing the twin towers was explored in Gillespie, chapter 4.

219 *Tightrope walker:* Lichtenstein, *NYT*, Aug. 8, 1974; *NYT*, Aug. 11, 1974; *NYT*, Aug. 30, 1974; Petit; Boody interview.

219 *Skydiver:* Dembart, *NYT*, July 23, 1975.

220 *Eiffel Tower:* Feb. 14, 1887, "Protest against the Tower of Monsieur Eiffel," published in *Le Temps*, as excerpted in an official history of the Eiffel Tower, http://www.toureiffel.fr/teiffel/uk/documentation/dossiers/page/debats.html.

220 *PA promotes towers:* NYT, Nov. 5, 1976; Dougherty, Dec. 9, 1975, *NYT*, cites the slogan.

220 *Windows on the World:* Feeding thirty thousand a day comes from Carmody, *NYT*, May 28, 1984; fifty-eight-second elevator ride comes from Grimes, *NYT*, Sept. 19, 2001; the wines come from a PA brochure put out at the time the Windows on the World opened, as does description of the bathrooms and other areas, which are shown in photographs included in this brochure, in the Rockefeller

Archives; *NYT*, Dec. 3, 1975; headline in *New York* magazine is cited by Grimes; Sheraton, *NYT*, Jan. 28, 1977; *NYT*, July 15, 1977.

222 *Leslie's "irregularities":* Brunner interview; he said he was told at the time that apparently Leslie intended to go out with PA clients, but after the clients canceled, took a friend or members of his family instead.

223 *Larceny:* Levy was indicted on grand larceny charges. But he pleaded guilty in April 1979 to two counts of offering a false instrument for filing and petty larceny and official misconduct, the *NYT* reported on Sept. 20, 1980, in the obituary about Levy's death in August 1980. He had been fined $1,000 and had reimbursed the PA twice the amount for the overcharges, which had totaled only about $1,500; Tillman pleaded guilty to petit larceny and other charges and was fined $1,000; Leslie was not charged, but he admitted he had improperly billed the PA for an expense account item and repaid the agency. He was suspended without pay in September 1978 and then resigned in October 1978, according to *NYT* stories.

223 *"There aren't that many":* Goldmark interview.

224 *"Thank heavens":* Rossi interview; Oser, *NYT*, May 16, 1990.

224–*Boeing 707 near miss:* Witkin, *NYT*, Feb. 26, 1981; *NYT*, Feb. 27, 1981; McQuiston,
  25 *NYT*, March 1, 1981; transcript of air traffic controller conversation with pilot was published Feb. 27, 1981, by UPI.

225 *Dean Witter lease:* Interviews with French, real estate agent at Cushman & Wakefield who negotiated the deal; Wilkerson, *NYT*, July 9, 1985. This was considered the biggest lease in the trade center's history.

225 *Rentals surge:* Change in rent comes from Girardo, *Portfolio*, winter 1990–1991, vol. 3, no. 1; Farrell interview; Boody's firm left in about 1995. He is not sure of exact year.

226 *"a world symbol":* Lynch interview and Berger, *NYT*, Oct 1, 1984.

226 *"vulnerable targets":* Goldmark interview.

228 *level of concern at PA dropped in 1986:* Tozzoli interview.

228 *"Break and destroy the enemies":* Transcript of testimony on Feb. 27, 1995, trial of Omar Ahmad Ali Abdel Rahman, as well as El Sayyid Nosair and nine other defendants. The prosecutor read translated excerpts from Nosair's journal in court.

228–*Yousef cased the building:* Oct. 22, 1997, transcript of trial against Ramzi Ahmed
  29 Yousef and Eyad Ismoil in United States District Court. Yousef, after his arrest, told an FBI agent that his intention in the 1993 bombing was clear. "One tower fall into the other tower," Yousef explained. "It would cause around 250,000 casualties." He even had a rationale for the attack. "During World War II, the Americans dropped the atomic bombs on Hiroshima and Nagasaki killing 250,000 civilians," Yousef explained. Take down the World Trade Center, he said, and "Americans would realize if they suffered those types of casualties that they were at war." From the Oct. 22, 1997, transcript of the trial in United States District Court, quoting Agent Brian Parr, who spoke with Yousef as the two flew back to the United States after Yousef was arrested in Pakistan.

229 *1993 bombing:* Humphries, Fogarty, Huntington, and tenant interviews; details of damage come from sworn testimony by PA executive director Stanley Brezenoff, p. 71 of transcript, Mar. 22, 1993, New York State Senate Standing Committee on Investigations, in the New York State Legislative Library.

229 *Yellow Ford Econoline:* Robert Kirkpatrick, a locksmith, William Macko, a maintenance worker, Monica Smith, a secretary, and Steven Knapp, a maintenance su-

pervisor, all Port Authority employees, who were in a basement office, were killed in the attack, as well as Wilfredo Mercado, a World Trade Center restaurant worker, and John DiGiovanni, a dental equipment salesman, who had been in the trade center parking lot.

230 *"start losing people":* Fisher was killed in the Sept. 11 attack. Source of conversation is Huntington.

230 *Escape:* Fasullo's account of the escape in a transcript of sworn testimony, as well as Tozzoli's sworn testimony to the New York State Senate Committee, March 1993; Tozzoli and Huntington interviews.

232 *Silverstein gets keys:* NYT morgue photo of Larry Silverstein, George Pataki, and Donald DiFrancesco by Jeff Zelevansky, taken July 24, 2001.

232 *"visually exciting extension":* Copy of Rockefeller's remarks, with handwritten last-minute changes, on file at the Rockefeller Archive Center.

232 *"economic and emotional impact":* Quoted in a PA press release, July 24, 2001.

233 *"nothing can stand in our way":* Thomas J. Lueck, "For Twin Towers, It Is Back to Work," NYT, March 30, 1993. Huntington also said in interview that the company's uninterrupted service to clients became a point that it made to demonstrate its stability.

233 *Upper floors not yet tested:* Dwyer, p. 374.

234 *Symbol of New York:* Zap2it.com, an Internet site about television and film, studied WTC use in TV and film, September 2002. It compiled a list of sixty-five films and television shows in which the WTC appeared, but said these were just a sampling of the hundreds if not thousands of appearances.

235 *"negative on tech":* Copy of e-mail written by Meehan on this date, provided by Cantor Fitzgerald. Meehan was killed during the September 11 attack. Floor for Meehan provided by Steve Montano, editor of *Cantor Morning News*, for which Meehan wrote.

235 *Troggs:* Interviews with three Troggs band members.

235 *Lucas at Windows:* Lucas interview.

CHAPTER 9: 9/11: THE COLLAPSE

Sources

Books and Articles

Portraits: 9/11/01, The Collected "Portraits of Grief" from the New York Times.

Jim Dwyer, Eric Lipton, Kevin Flynn, James Glanz, and Ford Fessenden, "Fighting to Live as the Towers Died," NYT, May 26, 2002; James Glanz and Eric Lipton, "In Data Trove, a Graphic Look at Towers' Fall," NYT, Oct. 29, 2002; James Glanz and Eric Lipton, "Towering Ambition," NYT Magazine, Sept. 8, 2002; Frank J. Prial, "Governor Limits Port Unit Choice," NYT, April 18, 1972; Ralph Blumenthal, "Ronan's Planned Trip Criticized by Levitt," NYT, June 16, 1977; Ralph Blumenthal, "Ronan Resigns the Chairmanship of Port Unit; Sagner Is Named," NYT, June 18, 1977; Ralph Blumenthal, "An Unannounced Port Authority Aide Accompanied Ronan and Others on Paid Round-the-World Air Tour," NYT, July 9, 1977; Ralph Blumenthal, "More Free Travels by Port Aides Found," NYT, July 14, 1977; "Port Unit Is Scored by Landes for 'Blatant Waste' in 'Junketeering,'" NYT, July 19, 1977; Ralph Blumenthal, "Port Aide Defends

World Trips as Honest and Beneficial to Area," *NYT*, July 23, 1977; Ralph Blumenthal, "Port Authority Extended Contract for Guards Despite Critical Report," *NYT*, Oct. 4, 1977; Ralph Blumenthal, "Levitt Says Expense-Account Cheats Bilked Port Agency of $1 Million," *NYT*, Oct. 21, 1977; Iver Peterson, "Let There Be Peace, and Trade," *NYT*, June 21, 1998; "Five Who Survived," *Newsweek*, Sept. 9, 2002; "Skiing Fireman, a Do-It-All Mother, a Stockbroker Who Sang Country," *NYT*, Dec. 17, 2001; Jane Fritsch, "Amid the Ruins, Some Hope, but Little Sign of Survivors," *NYT*, Sept. 16, 2001; Vivian S. Toy, "Trade Center Burn Victim's Long Road," *NYT*, Oct. 14, 2001; Dennis Cauchon, "For Many on Sept. 11, Survival Was No Accident," *USA Today*, Dec. 19, 2001; Michael Daly, "Second-by-Second Terror Revealed in Calls to 911," New York *Daily News Online*, Sept. 30, 2001; Eric Lipton and James Glanz, "DNA Science Pushed to the Limit in Identifying the Dead of Sept. 11," *NYT*, April 22, 2002; James Glanz, "Towers Untested for Major Fire, Inquiry Suggests," *NYT*, May 8, 2003; Eric Lipton and James Glanz, "First Tower to Fall Was Hit at Higher Speed, Study Finds," *NYT*, Feb. 23, 2002; Dennis Cauchon and Martha T. Moore, "Machinery Saved People in WTC," *USA Today*, May 17, 2002; James Glanz and Eric Lipton, "Towers Fell as Intense Fire Beat Defenses, Report Says," *NYT*, March 29, 2002.

Authors' Interviews

Guy Tozzoli; John Sanacore; John Gaudioso; Jill Rosenblum; Maryellen Cherry; Louis Massari Jr.; Steve McIntyre; Greg Shark; George Sleigh; Frank Lombardi; Judy Wein; Jack Gentul; Anne Foodim; Mona Dunn; Stephanie Koskuba; Stanley Praimnath; Francis Calton; Sara Mandinach; Debbie Cohen; Karen Lee; Sophie Pelletier; Yogesh Jaluria; Brian Clark; Ronald DiFrancesco; Mary Jos; David Kestenbaum; Ed Nicholls; Kelly Reyher; Donna Spira; Joseph Milanowycz; Marcia De Leon; Eduardo Kausel.

Documents

"World Trade Center Performance Study," Federal Emergency Management Agency, FEMA 403, May 2002; "World Trade Center Structural Engineering Investigation," Hart-Weidlinger, expert report for Silverstein insurance lawsuit, Aug. 1, 2002; "Progress Report on the Federal Building and Fire Safety Investigation of the World Trade Center Disaster," NIST Special Publication 1000–3, May 2003.

Notes

page
236 *Log entry:* Courtesy Jim Dwyer.
236—*Chapter note:* Large extracts of this chapter first appeared in another version in
72 Dwyer, Lipton, Flynn, Glanz, and Fessenden, *NYT*, May 26, 2002; interviews with more than one hundred people who communicated with individuals in the upper floors of the towers during the disaster, as well as other interviews with people who escaped the towers; the extensive "Portraits of Grief" profiles in *NYT*, profiles of those who died on Sept. 11; corporate biographies of the lost; numerous videos collected by the authors and incorporated into a continuous pictorial time line by Steve Duenes and Archie Tse of the *NYT*; and analysis of the progression of fires and structural failures by several groups of experts, including the American Society of Civil Engineers, the Federal Emergency Management Agency (FEMA

403, May 2002), the National Institute of Standards and Technology (NIST Special Publication 1000–3, May 2003), and experts called in the Silverstein court cases (see Glanz and Lipton, *NYT*, Oct. 29, 2002). Alain Delaquérière and Tom Torok of the *NYT* compiled large amounts of information for the May 26, 2002, story and we are grateful for the use of this information. We are also most grateful to our coauthors in that piece, Dwyer, Flynn, and Fessenden, for their permission to make use here of some information they collected. Portions of this chapter first appeared, in another form, in the May 26, 2002, piece and in Glanz and Lipton, *NYT Magazine*, Sept. 8, 2002. We would also like to thank Joe Sexton and the many other *NYT* editors who helped shape the original "102 Minutes" article and ensure that it found its way into the newspaper.

236–*Tozzoli's morning:* Details in these passages come from interviews with Tozzoli and
37   firsthand examination of the route by the authors.

237   *NR never heard of Tozzoli:* Prial, *NYT*, April 18, 1972.

237   *NR's veto:* It is unclear if NR ever formally vetoed Tozzoli or simply killed his appointment by making it clear that he opposed it. Tozzoli's last years at the agency were also marred by accusations of junketeering. He responded to the charges and remained with the PA for a decade after they were made. See Blumenthal, *NYT*, June 14, 1977; Blumenthal, *NYT*, June 16, 1977; Blumenthal, *NYT*, June 18, 1977; Blumenthal, *NYT*, July 9, 1977; Blumenthal, *NYT*, July 14, 1977; *NYT*, July 19, 1977; Blumenthal, *NYT*, July 23, 1977; Blumenthal, *NYT*, Oct. 4, 1977; Blumenthal, *NYT*, Oct. 21, 1977.

238   *Tozzoli on war and peace:* Peterson, *NYT*, June 21, 1998.

240   *Rosenblum on 104th floor:* Sanacore; Gaudioso, and Rosenblum interviews; interview with former member of Rosenblum's group.

240   *Ian Schneider: Portraits of Grief,* p. 451. Many of the portraits have been collected in *Portaits: 9/11/01, The Collected "Portraits of Grief" from the New York Times.* For simplicity, we will cite this reference whenever possible, rather than the original newspaper profiles.

240   *Stephen Cherry:* *NYT*, Dec. 17, 2001; Cherry interview.

240   *Patricia Massari:* Massari Jr. interview; *Portraits of Grief.*

241   *Carr Futures:* Iliana McGinnis interview, courtesy Jim Dwyer.

241   *American Bureau of Shipping:* Steve McIntyre, Greg Shark, and George Sleigh interviews.

241   *Frank Lombardi:* Lombardi interview.

241   *Judy Wein:* Wein interview.

241   *Edgar Emery:* Jack Gentul, Anne Foodim, Mona Dunn, and Stephanie Koskuba interviews.

241   *"I'm a child of God":* Praimnath interview.

241   *Fifty-eight thousand people:* This is a PA estimate, given in the FEMA report on the WTC.

241   *Andrew and Jill Rosenblum on the phone:* Jill Rosenblum interview. She had called him at his desk. All his later calls were from his cell phone, according to Mrs. Rosenblum's description of cell phone records she obtained from Verizon.

242   *470 miles an hour:* FEMA 403, May 2002; see also Lipton and Glanz, *NYT*, Feb. 23, 2002. We have used the FEMA figures, which are consistent with the earlier *NYT* report.

242   *First plane's impact:* Some of these details come from the computer simulations in

the Weidlinger structural report and Silverstein documents. Experts have generally said that the computer simulations of the initial impact are the most solid element of the Weidlinger work for the case.

243 *Many survived those first instants:* This fact is proved not just by phone calls from those floors (and survivors from the impact floors in the south tower) but by observations of people apparently jumping from the windows in those areas as the fire became intolerable, minutes after impact.

243 *Jet fuel fire:* Many of the details on the development of the fire come from the FEMA WTC report and the expert reports by ArupFire and Hughes Associates compiled for the Silverstein court case.

245 *Ken Summers:* Toy, *NYT*, Oct. 14, 2001; Hughes Associates expert report for the Silverstein court case, Appendix D.

245 *Load redistribution:* Weidlinger expert report; Silverstein case. The calculations in the FEMA report lead to similar conclusions.

246 *Patricia Massari:* Louis Massari interview.

246 *Rows of folding chairs:* Shark interview.

246 *Man at the opening:* Roberto Rabane photo reprinted in Weidlinger expert report and in the FEMA report.

246 *Janet Alonso:* Robert Alonso interview; *Portraits of Grief* and reporter's notes. According to Mr. Alonso, the call came at 9:07 A.M.

247 *American Bureau of Shipping:* Episodes were described by Shark, Sleigh, McIntyre, and Calton. A number of ABS employees also compared recollections to ensure that the account would be as accurate as possible. See also Cauchon, *USA Today*, Dec. 19, 2001, and as described in the FEMA report.

247 *Frank Lombardi:* Lombardi interview.

250 *Damian Meehan:* The account is courtesy Jim Dwyer, who interviewed Eugene Meehan.

250 *Fires on 106th through 109th floors:* *NYT* video time line, courtesy Archie Tse and Steve Duenes; north tower transcripts at www.nytimes.com/wtc.

250 *Neil D. Levin:* Dwyer, Lipton, Flynn, Glanz, and Fessenden, *NYT*, May 26, 2003.

251 *Cell phone call from Rosenblum:* Jill Rosenblum, Mandinach, and Cohen interviews.

251 *Ian Schneider at the head of desks:* Gaudioso interview.

252 *Dispatcher log:* Courtesy Jim Dwyer. See also Daly, New York *Daily News Online*, Sept. 30, 2001. According to the log, the call came in at 9:03:12 A.M.

252 *"They know you're there":* Interview with former Cantor Fitzgerald trader.

252 *Richard Y. C. Lee:* Karen Lee interview.

253 *658 Cantor Fitzgerald employees:* Lipton and Glanz, *NYT*, April 22, 2002.

253 *Mike Pelletier:* Sophie Pelletier interview.

253 *Steel softens:* Jaluria interview.

254 *Praimnath's experience:* The details on the south tower are based on interviews with Praimnath. See www.nytimes.com/wtc, south tower transcripts. The "Stan the man" line later turned up in *Newsweek*, Sept. 9, 2002.

254 *Speed of second jet:* NIST Special Publication 1000–3, May 2003.

254 *Second plane's impact:* Clark interview; Weidlinger Associates expert report; Silverstein court case; FEMA report.

255 *Tower shuddered for four minutes:* Glanz, *NYT*, May 8, 2003; NIST Special Publication 1000–3, May 2003, p. 36.

255 *More kinetic energy:* Lipton and Glanz, *NYT*, Feb. 23, 2002.

255 *Fires in south tower:* ArupFire expert report; Silverstein case.

257 *North tower survivors:* According to the best estimates by reporters at the *NYT*, some eight hundred people were trapped, still alive, above or just below the impact zone in the north tower after the impact there. An estimated three hundred people at or above the impact zone survived the crash, but only eighteen of them were able to find the open stairway, make their way past the gypsum debris, and escape (Dwyer, Lipton, Flynn, Glanz, and Fessenden, *NYT*, May 26, 2002).

257 *Stairwell and elevator machinery:* Cauchon and Moore, *USA Today*, May 17, 2002.

257 *Euro Brokers:* DiFrancesco and Clark interviews.

260 *Seventy-eighth-floor sky lobby:* Mary Jos inteview.

261 *Howard Kestenbaum's pendulum:* David Kestenbaum interview.

261 *Decisions at the elevators:* Wein and Nicholls interviews.

262 *Reyher and Spira at elevators:* Reyher and Spira interviews.

263– *People at the windows:* These observations are based on an extensive archive of private
64 videos compiled by the authors and numerous photographs of the disaster maintained on databases at *NYT*. Some of the images have been published; others have not. Helicopter dispatch record courtesy Jim Dwyer. The list is by no means exhaustive. It is compiled from the video spreadsheet created by Steve Duenes and Archie Tse. The time span covered from the words "From the north face, 106th floor" to the final "West" of the paragraph is approximately 9:48 A.M. to 10:26 A.M.

265 *Stuart Lee's e-mail:* The e-mail transcript is courtesy Lynn Udbjorg.

266 *Edgar Emery's blazer:* Jack Gentul interview.

266 *Jack Gentul calls engineer:* The engineer's name was John Griscavage. Gentul also spoke to Mike Kirk, police chief at the New Jersey Institute of Technology.

267 *Foodim felt the heat:* Foodim interview.

267 *Emery and Gentul evacuate people:* Koskuba and Dunn interviews.

268 *Sagging floor truss:* NIST Special Publication 1000–3, May 2003; Glanz and Lipton, *NYT*, March 29, 2002.

269 *Buckling at 9:56:* This was the last moment of Gregory Milanowycz's phone call; Joseph Milanowycz and De Leon interviews.

269 *South tower collapses:* These details are clear in video records collected by the authors. Thanks to "Here is New York" for extensive help in collecting the videos; Kausel interview.

269 *McIntyre and Ruth:* McIntyre interview. His recollections and a map of the concourse in the LZA Technology expert report for the Silverstein court case are the main sources for this section. McIntyre would never encounter Ruth again or learn who she was. According to the *NYT* database of WTC victims, no one whose first name was Ruth and who worked in the north tower died on 9/11.

271 *North tower collapses:* NIST Special Publication 1000–3, May 2003.

271 *Rosenblum's last call:* According to Mrs. Rosenblum, Verizon records for the cell phone show that her husband's cell phone made an outgoing call at 10:23 A.M., lasting for one minute.

CHAPTER 10: RUINS

Sources

Books and Articles

A Nation Challenged: A Visual History of 9/11 and Its Aftermath; *Here Is New York: A Democracy of Photographs*; *New York September 11 by Magnum Photographers*; *The September 11 Photo Project*; *Above Hallowed Ground: A Photographic Record of September 11, 2001, by Photographers of the New York City Police Department*; Friedman, *After 9-11: An Engineer's Work at the World Trade Center*; Campbell, *Learning from Construction Failures: Applied Forensic Engineering*; *Portraits: 9/11/01, The Collected "Portraits of Grief" from the New York Times*.

Jim Dwyer, "Beneath the Rubble, the Only Tool Was a Pair of Cuffs," *NYT*, Oct. 30, 2001; Jim Dwyer, "Medic, Out of the Rubble, Finds an Identity Restored," *NYT*, Nov. 6, 2001; Jim Fitzgerald, "Last Survivor Pulled from WTC Rubble Is Released from Hospital," *Associated Press*, Jan. 18, 2002; John Lehmann and Andy Geller, *New York Post*, Sept. 15, 2001; Charles Laurence, "The Drunk Who Found Redemption in the Ruins," *Sunday Telegraph* (London), Nov. 11, 2001; Rebecca Liss, "An Unlikely Hero," *Slate Magazine*, Sept. 10, 2002; James Glanz and Eric Lipton, "Rescuing the Buildings beyond Ground Zero," *NYT*, Feb. 12, 2002; James Glanz, "Wounded Buildings Offer Survival Lessons," *NYT*, Dec. 4, 2001; David W. Dunlap, "From the Rubble, Icons of Disaster and Faith," *NYT*, Dec. 25, 2001; David W. Dunlap, "Hulking Neighbor Buries a Church," *NYT*, Sept. 17, 2001; James Glanz, "Below Rubble, a Tour of a Still-Burning Hell," *NYT*, Nov. 15, 2001; James Glanz and Eric Lipton, "In Data Trove, a Graphic Look at Towers' Fall," *NYT*, Oct. 29, 2002; James Glanz and Eric Lipton, "Expert Report Disputes U.S. on Collapse," *NYT*, Oct. 22, 2002; James Glanz and Eric Lipton, "Vast Detail on Towers' Collapse May Be Sealed in Court Filings," *NYT*, Oct. 9, 2002; Dennis Cauchon and Martha T. Moore, "Miracles Emerge from Debris," *USA Today*, Sept. 6, 2002; Jim Dwyer, "Searchers Find Remains of 50 People, Officials Say," *NYT*, Oct. 2, 2001; Eric Lipton, "For 5 Officers, Apparent Last Heroic Act," *NYT*, Feb. 11, 2002; Kirsten Scharnberg, "Crane Operator Finds Self among Trade Center's Lost," *Chicago Tribune*, Sept. 2, 2002; Eric Lipton and James Glanz, "Last 4 Firefighters Leave Ground Zero: 'Our Work Is Done,'" *NYT*, June 25, 2002; Eric Lipton and James Glanz, "Victims' Remains Found near Ground Zero," *NYT*, June 8, 2002; Dennis Cauchon, "For Many on Sept. 11, Survival Was No Accident," *USA Today*, Dec. 19, 2001; Dennis Cauchon, "Four Survived by Ignoring Words of Advice," *USA Today*, Dec. 19, 2001; Martha T. Moore and Dennis Cauchon, "Delay Meant Death on 9/11," *USA Today*, Sept. 3, 2002.

Authors' Interviews

Charles Blaich; Richard Tomasetti; John Norman; Charlie Vitchers; Derek Trelstad; Gary Mancini; Donald Friedman; Jim Abadie; Bob Stewart; Jack Swan; Gary Panariello; Frank Cruthers; Pablo Lopez; Andrew Pontecorvo; George Tamaro; Rusty Griffin; Michael J. Burton; Tom Richardson; Mark Leavy; Robert Shaler; Ron Smalley; Billy Klingler; Danny Mirt; Eddie Gibbs; Paul Martin; Chris Hynes; Steve Holcomb; Renee Holcomb; John Kirby; Willy Quinlan; Danny Doyle; Pia Hofmann; John Ryan; Gordon Haberman; Charles Hirsch; Ellen Borakove; David Sharp; Robert Kelman.

Documents

"Damage/Debris Assessment Report," LZA Technology/Thornton-Tomasetti Group, Aug. 1, 2002, expert report prepared for the Silverstein insurance lawsuit; *The First 24 Hours*, an Isis documentary film produced by Etienne Sauret and David Carrara (www.thefirst24hours.com); "World Trade Center Performance Study," Federal Emergency Management Agency, FEMA 403, May 2002; CBS News Transcripts, *The Early Show*, Oct. 18, 2001; World Trade Center Collapse Field Report, Oct. 23, 2001.

Notes

page

273 *Blaich rushes downtown:* Blaich interview.

273 *Chapter note:* Portions of the description in this chapter rely on visual resources including the following: *NYT* digital photo archives; *LZA Technology*, Aug. 1, 2002; *A Nation Challenged: A Visual History of 9/11 and Its Aftermath*, *NYT*; *Here Is New York: A Democracy of Photographs*; *New York September 11 by Magnum Photographers*; *The September 11 Photo Project*; *Above Hallowed Ground: A Photographic Record of September 11, 2001, by Photographers of the New York City Police Department*; *The First 24 Hours*.

274 *Marriott World Trade Center Hotel:* Photo courtesy Charles Blaich and lidar height data courtesy EarthData Holdings Inc., Hagerstown, Md., and Washington, D.C.

274 *Rescue 2 emergency van:* The spot was filmed that day. See *The First 24 Hours*, an Isis documentary film; Blaich, in an interview, also recalled the presence of the Rescue 2 vehicle and the pumper.

275 *"Mayday, Mayday, Mayday!":* Blaich heard these calls, also on Sept. 28, 2001, *Dateline NBC* broadcast excerpts of radio transmissions on Sept. 11, after the towers collapsed, that included these words. Nick Visconti, a Fire Department commander at the time of the attack, also describes the effort to rescue these trapped firefighters, in a first-person account, published in *Fire Engineering* magazine, Sept. 2002. Fourteen of the survivors from this stairwell were in a group very close to Jonas; two more survivors had been somewhat higher in the stairwell.

275 *"We're coming for you":* The *Dateline NBC* transcript of radio transmissions has this comment, identifying the speaker as Battalion Chief Blaich.

277 *Mound of debris:* According to EarthData lidar maps.

278 *"This didn't really happen":* Tomasetti interview.

278 *Upside-down markings:* Friedman, p. 70.

280 *Karnes and Jimeno:* The principal sources for this section are: Dwyer, *NYT*, Oct. 30, 2001; Dwyer, *NYT*, Nov. 6, 2001; and conversations with Dwyer. See also: Fitzgerald, *Associated Press*, Jan. 18, 2002; CBS News Transcripts, *The Early Show*, Oct. 18, 2001; Lehmann and Geller, *New York Post*, Sept. 15, 2001; Laurence, *Sunday Telegraph* (London), Nov. 11, 2001; Liss, *Slate Magazine*, Sept. 10, 2002.

280 *90 West Street:* Glanz and Lipton, *NYT*, Feb. 12, 2002; Glanz, *NYT*, Dec. 4, 2001; Trelstad, Friedman, and Mancini interviews. Blaich said that they never were able to fight the fire from inside the building. They used one fire truck to fight it from the ground and also used the water supply from a hotel next door to 90 West to shoot at the burning building. For the most part, the fire just burned out itself. As Tomasetti's engineers ventured into 90 West Street and the Deutsche Bank Building, dozens of other engineers from the Structural Engi-

neers Association of New York were studying numerous other surrounding buildings on a voluntary basis.

281 *St. Nicholas:* Dunlap, *NYT*, Dec. 25, 2001; Dunlap, *NYT*, Sept. 17, 2001.

281 *Engineers venture into 90 West:* The other two structural engineers were Donald Friedman, who led the team, and David Wolfson.

281 *Buildings surrounding ground zero:* Some of these details come from firsthand notes taken by Glanz during a visit by him and Lipton to ground zero on Sept. 19, 2001. The hotel spells its name with a single *n*.

281–7 *WTC collapse:* FEMA 403, May 2002.
 82

282 *Woman's hand:* Vitchers interview.

282 *Gilbert and 90 West:* The actual date, which Trelstad recalls learning after Sept. 13, 2001, is 1907.

284 *Tour of 90 West:* Some of the visual details were recorded during a tour of the building by Glanz and Lipton on Jan. 29, 2002. The floors remained choked with debris from the fires, although paths had been cleared in some areas and the early stages of the cleanup had begun.

286 *Norman tries to clear bridge:* Norman interview; Norman did not officially assume the post of chief of the Fire Department's special operations unit until several days after the attack, but he was already handling duties as the coordinator of the rescue mission before that.

287 *West Street opened:* Thornton-Tomasetti logbook: "southbound lane of West Street is now linked with Bovis sector," 4 P.M. to midnight shift, Sept. 16.

287 *Boots:* Abadie said in an interview that firefighters' boots were melting.

287 *"If there's anybody alive":* Norman and Stewart interviews.

287 *Manitowoc 21000:* Interview with Swan, vice president of operations of All Erection and Crane Rental Co. of Cleveland, which supplied these cranes.

289 *Stewart vs. engineers:* "The 800 ton crane is parked and is not anticipated to be moved tonight. Weidlinger to notify TT if 800 ton crane is moved," says an engineering log dated Sept. 21. "We have strongly advised AMEC personnel that the crane should not move forward," said the handwritten notes of one engineer watching Stewart work on Sept. 16. After referring to Stewart by name, the notes add: "He plans to disregard our warnings." Engineering log maintained by Thornton-Tomasetti, from Sept. 16.

290 *Stabilizing the crane:* Tomasetti, Panariello, and Stewart interviews.

290 *A second flash of brilliance:* The two partners of Tomasetti who came up with the idea for the place to locate the plaza crane were Dan Cuoco and Tom Scarangello.

291 *Smashing the sculpture:* "Tasks requiring attention," read the Thornton-Tomasetti logbook on Sept. 16, which described the new plan to demolish the sculpture with jackhammers and a backhoe to create a second new crane base. "Getting the cranes working. They are currently doing very little: See attached sketch."

291 *Infants survived earthquake:* Norman did not know the source of this information. It was passed on to him from Fire Department headquarters.

291 *Twenty-one people found:* This count was most completely documented in Cauchon and Moore, *USA Today*, Sept. 6, 2002. Of the twenty-one pulled out alive, one victim died subsequently from injuries, according to this report.

291 *"We've done everything":* Norman and Cruthers interviews.

292 *Underground exploration:* Material in this section is derived from interviews with Lopez, Pontecorvo, and Tamaro; notes taken by Glanz during an extensive tour of most of the same underground areas on Nov. 14, 2001 (Glanz, *NYT*, Nov. 15, 2001). We have also had access to a large number of photographs taken by the Mueser Rutledge engineers, as well as many other photographs, diagrams, maps, and written observations compiled by lawyers and engineers retained for Larry Silverstein in his insurance lawsuit involving payments for his losses in the attacks. On information compiled for the lawsuit, see Glanz and Lipton, *NYT*, Oct. 29, 2002; Glanz and Lipton, *NYT*, Oct. 22, 2002; Glanz and Lipton, *NYT*, Oct. 9, 2002. Mueser Rutledge has also kindly made available to us its detailed maps of the subterranean damage, as well as other diagrams of the underground structure and conditions.

294 *Observation maps:* Mueser Rutledge kindly provided us with full-size copies of the maps that Lopez, Pontecorvo, and their colleagues prepared.

295 *Layout of stores:* Taken from maps prepared by LZA Technology for the Silverstein court case.

295 *Bathtub along Liberty Street:* Photograph provided by Mueser Rutledge; one theory by a Mueser Rutledge engineer was that the air pressure of the collapsing tower was so intense it lifted up the floors from the bottom and they collapsed as they fell back. The upper floor was stronger and so this was not blown out.

296 *Rafts:* This is Pontecorvo's recollection. Lopez thought the police escorts had perhaps pulled the rafts from the front, using ropes.

296 *Signs in station:* Some of these details are from Glanz's notes on observations from the same spot.

296 *Iced tea can:* Allan Morrison made this observation as Glanz took notes on the platform. More precisely, the can's label said it contained 7.7 ounces.

297 *Griffin downtown:* Interview with Rusty Griffin; also copies of his field notes from that day.

297 *240-foot-tall remnant:* Twenty-three-story figure is provided by Jim Abadie of Bovis. Griffin's field survey notes show that it was 240 feet high and that there were parts of seventeen of the "Gothic trees" standing that had to be removed.

298 *Explosive charges:* Abadie interview.

298 *"It will never work":* Griffin recalling what Stewart said; also Stewart interview.

298 *Griffin and bolts that had popped out:* According to Les Robertson, some of the lower connections were also welded.

299 *Ninety-five-foot-tall sections:* Rusty Griffin's calculations, showing that each fork weighs about 112 tons. The pieces, which were leaning over at a nineteen-degree angle onto 6 WCT, reached up to a point a bit less than ninety-five feet off the ground, at the spot where they came to rest on the old United States Custom House. Data all from Griffin sketch, dated Oct. 30, 2001.

299 *"We know why they fell":* Burton interview.

300 *"Go back down south":* Hofmann interview.

300 *"Stewart's Bridge to Nowhere":* Panariello, Griffin, and Abadie interviews. World Trade Center Collapse Field Report, Oct. 23, 2001, details the collapses in these two locations. "TT recommended that the area be roped off and cleared and that no load be applied to the WTC 6 crane ramp. In the morning, the structure

below WTC 6 should be evaluated and compared with previous observations to determine the extent of the collapse." World Trade Center Collapse Field Report, Nov. 3, 2001.

301 *DDC details:* Burton interview.

301 *"The night shift":* Comments by Stewart and others at this meeting are recalled by Griffin, who was there.

302 *Neil J. Leavy:* This section is based on interviews with Norman and Richardson, who both worked on this recovery, as well as John Leavy, father of Neil Leavy, and with Dr. Shaler from the Medical Examiner's Office. See *Portraits of Grief*, p. 276. Kati Cornell Smith, "Firefighter Neil J. Leavy, 34, Was Helping with Rescue," *Staten Island Advance*, Sept. 18, 2001. Story says "his body was pulled out of the rubble on Sunday night."

303 *The same day the remains were collected:* Dwyer, *NYT*, Oct. 2, 2001. Medical examiner's records show that on Oct. 1 and Oct. 2, 398 body parts were recovered, compared to 111 in the prior two days.

303 *Fissure:* Smalley, Tamaro, and Klingler interviews.

304 *Relieving groundwater pressure:* Joel L. Volterra of Mueser Rutledge provided data on how the groundwater level dropped that same day. He also had data that showed movement of the Liberty Street wall, on a daily basis, for the weeks following the formation of the crack.

305 *"We got guys down there":* Richardson interview.

305 *Collapse of remaining slabs:* Volterra, who was monitoring the wall movement, and Pablo Lopez, both of Mueser Rutledge, described how the wall collapsed while the fill was being put in.

305 *Tamaro's plan works:* Tamaro and Burton interviews; data from Volterra.

306 *Tiebacks:* Mirt, Gibbs, Martin, and Hines interviews.

306 *West Bend, Wisconsin:* Steve and Renee Holcomb interviews.

307 *Habermans at ground zero:* This section is based on interviews with Gordon Haberman, Vitchers, Shaler, and Hirsch, as well as Borakove, spokeswoman for the medical examiner's office.

308 *Andrea Haberman: Portraits of Grief*, p. 202.

308 *Ironworkers:* This section is based on interviews with Kirby, Quinlan, Doyle, Vitchers, and Hofmann.

309 *Officers and woman recovered:* Lipton, *NYT*, Feb. 11, 2002; Ryan interview.

312 *Treatment of civilians:* Hofmann and Vitchers interviews; see Kirsten Scharnberg, "Crane Operator Finds Self among Trade Center's Lost," *Chicago Tribune*, Sept. 2, 2002.

315 *Seven package numbers:* Data from medical examiner's office. The first piece of Haberman's remains were logged in at the medical examiner's office on March 15. Two more fragments were found and logged in on March 16; others on March 17, March 19, and March 20. The seventh was found and logged in around March 20.

316 *"Our work is done":* Lipton and Glanz, *NYT*, June 25, 2002; Lipton and Glanz, *NYT*, June 8, 2002.

EPILOGUE

Sources

Articles

James Glanz and Eric Lipton, "A Search for Clues in Towers' Collapse," *NYT*, Feb. 2, 2002; James Glanz, "Towers Untested for Major Fire, Inquiry Suggests," *NYT*, May 8, 2003; Stephen Hegarty, "Engineer: Impact Showed World Trade Center's Strength," *St. Petersburg Times*, Sept. 14, 2001; Chris Casteel, "Report Claims Design of Federal Building Increased Death Toll," *Daily Oklahoman*, Nov. 15, 1996; "Progressive Collapse Felled Murrah Building, Report Says," *ENR*, Nov. 25, 1996; "Design Lessons Lie In Disasters," *ENR*, Oct. 20, 1997; "Prepared Testimony of Dr. W. Gene Corley, P.E., S.E., on Behalf of the American Society of Civil Engineers before the House Committee on Transportation & Infrastructure, Public Buildings and Economic Subcommittee on Security in Federal Buildings," *Federal News Service*, June 4, 1998; Delroy Alexander, "Questions on Tower Construction; Could Buildings Have Been Saved?" *Chicago Tribune*, Sept. 15, 2001; James Glanz and Eric Lipton, "Experts Urging Broader Inquiry in Towers' Fall," *NYT*, Dec. 25, 2001; Jim Dwyer, "An Unimaginable Calamity, Still Largely Unexamined," *NYT*, Sept. 11, 2002; Kenneth Chang, "Scarred Steel Holds Clues, and Remedies," *NYT*, Oct. 2, 2001; James Glanz and Kenneth Chang, "Engineers Seek to Test Steel Before It Is Melted for Reuse," *NYT*, Sept. 29, 2001; James Glanz, "Demand Rises for Widening Investigation into Collapse," *NYT*, Dec. 15, 2001; James Glanz, "Report on Towers' Collapse Ends Mostly in Questions," *NYT*, May 1, 2002; James Glanz and Eric Lipton, "U.S. Agency to Take Over Investigation into Collapse," *NYT*, Jan. 17, 2002; Eric Lipton, "Widows Seek Wider Inquiry into Trade Center Collapse," *NYT*, Mar. 4, 2002; Eric Lipton, "Mismanagement Muddled Collapse Inquiry, House Panel Says," *NYT*, Mar. 7, 2002; Eric Lipton, "Government Orders Inquiry into Trade Center Collapse," *NYT*, Mar. 23, 2002; James Glanz, "Wider Inquiry into Towers Is Proposed," *NYT*, May 2, 2002; James Glanz, "U.S. Announces New, Tougher Look into Why the Towers Collapsed," *NYT*, Aug. 22, 2002; Eric Lipton and James Glanz, "9/11 Prompts New Caution in Design of U.S. Skyscrapers," *NYT*, Sept. 9, 2002; Edward Wyatt, "Plan Approved to Reshape 7 World Trade Block," *NYT*, Apr. 19, 2002; Edward Wyatt, "Transit Hub and 'Freedom Park' Part of Blueprint for Rebuilding," *NYT*, Apr. 10, 2002; Edward Wyatt, "Even Critics Say Some Designs for Downtown Aren't So Bad," *NYT*, July 23, 2002; Edward Wyatt, "Selection of Consultant in Rebuilding Is Questioned," *NYT*, May 21, 2002; Edward Wyatt, "Support Builds for One Plan for Center Site," *NYT*, Feb. 20, 2003; Edward Wyatt, "Panel Supports 2 Tall Towers at Disaster Site," *NYT*, Feb. 26, 2003; Edward Wyatt, "Design Chosen for Rebuilding at Ground Zero," *NYT*, Feb. 27, 2003; Edward Wyatt, "Practical Issues for Ground Zero," *NYT*, Feb. 28, 2003; Charles V. Bagli, "Vision for Lower Manhattan Is Still in Flux," *NYT*, Feb. 28, 2003; Edward Wyatt, "Designs Pour In to Competition for Memorial at Ground Zero," *NYT*, July 1, 2003; David W. Dunlap, "A Through Street Restored, Looking Thinner," *NYT*, July 10, 2003; John Holusha, "7 World Trade Center; Building Being Restored Using Part of Old Foundation," *NYT*, July 13, 2003; Edward Wyatt, "Architect and Developer Clash over Plans for Trade Center Site," *NYT*, July 15, 2003; Edward Wyatt, "Officials Reach an Agreement on Rebuilding Downtown Site," *NYT*, July 16, 2003; Edward Wyatt, "Compromise to Build On," *NYT*, July 17, 2003; Charles V. Bagli and Edward Wyatt, "At Helm of Trade Center Site, as He Always Planned to Be," *NYT*, July 21, 2003; Edward

Wyatt, "Planned Tower Is Likely to Stay at Northwestern Corner of Site," *NYT*, July 22, 2003; Charles V. Bagli, "9/11 Payment Issues Are Argued in Appeal," *NYT*, July 23, 2003; Charles V. Bagli, "Transit Links Called Vital to a Revival of Downtown," *NYT*, Sept. 19, 2002; Edward Wyatt, "Relatives Say Plans Infringe on Twin Towers' Footprints," *NYT*, July 9, 2003; Edward Wyatt, "New Design for Concourse Will Avoid Site of Towers," *NYT*, Sept. 1, 2002; Glenn Collins, "A Wall Once Unseen, Now Revered; At Ground Zero, a Symbol of Survival Is Mended for Posterity," *NYT*, June 23, 2003; James Glanz, "Fresh Kills Journal; Mountains of Twisted Steel, Evoking the Dead," *NYT*, Oct. 1, 2001; Eric Lipton and James Glanz, "From the Rubble, Artifacts of Anguish," *NYT*, Jan. 27, 2002; Tamer El-Ghobashy and Greg Gittrich, "WTC Steel's Being Put to Work Again," *Daily News*, Jan. 17, 2002; Greg Gittrich, "Metals Dealer Reselling World Trade Center Steel in $30 Medallions," *Daily News*, Jan. 30, 2002; Greg Gittrich, "A Tragedy Is Recycled," *Daily News*, Jan. 30, 2002; "Medallions Made with Trade Center Steel Anger Some Victims' Relatives," *Associated Press*, Jan. 30, 2002; Tamer El-Ghobashy and Greg Gittrich, "Mourners Say Selling World Trade Steel for Scrap a Disgrace," *Daily News*, Jan. 18, 2002; James Glanz and Eric Lipton, "Towers Fell as Intense Fire Beat Defenses, Report Says," *NYT*, Mar. 29, 2002; Paul von Zielbauer, "Band Lawyer Says Nightclub Wanted Pyrotechnics," *NYT*, Feb. 28, 2003; Lydia Polgreen, "Death Toll from Fire at Rhode Island Club Rises to 100," *NYT*, May 6, 2003.

Authors' Interviews

David Sharp; Richard Tomasetti; Ramon Gilsanz.

Documents

"World Trade Center Building Performance Study: Data Collection, Preliminary Observations, and Recommendations," Federal Emergency Management Agency, FEMA 403, May 2002; "Commerce's NIST Details Federal Investigation of World Trade Center Collapse," press release, National Institute of Standards and Technology, Aug. 21, 2002 (www.nist.gov/public_affairs/releases/n02-14.htm).

Notes

page

319 *Scrap yard:* Hugo Neu Schnitzer East scrap yard in Jersey City details come from notes taken by the authors during a visit on Jan. 30, 2002. See also Glanz and Lipton, *NYT*, Feb. 2, 2002.

320 *Volunteer steel collection:* The effort was organized by the Structural Engineers Association of New York.

321 *Trusses:* What little remained of trusses may have been preferentially shipped to Fresh Kills with the lighter debris, like aluminum ductwork and cladding.

323 *Jet airliner study:* The military and nuclear industry had performed such studies previously.

324 *Civilian survivors below impact:* The primary exception was the ninety-second and ninety-third floors of the north tower, where, apparently, damage to the stairwells prevented occupants from escaping. Otherwise, most of the civilians below impact survived. Firefighters and other rescue personnel who were on the floors below impact make up the majority of the casualities in these areas.

324 *Possible death toll:* An estimated twelve thousand people were in the twin towers at the time of the first impact. Because those in the south tower had time to

leave before the second plane hit, it is impossible to know how many people would have been killed if both towers had collapsed at the instant they were hit. But clearly it would have been many times more than the final death toll.

326 *Fireproofing:* Frank Lombardi, the engineer who found the problem, apparently thought he was only doubling the specified thickness, since his measurements of actual fireproofing on the trusses suggested that they had three-quarter-inch fireproofing; Glanz, *NYT,* May 8, 2003.

329 *Oklahoma City bombing:* W. Gene Corley, "Lessons Learned from the Oklahoma City Bombing," Campbell, chapter 14. See also Casteel, *Daily Oklahoman,* Nov. 15, 1996; *ENR,* Nov. 25, 1996; *ENR,* Oct. 20, 1997; *Federal News Service,* June 4, 1998; Alexander, *Chicago Tribune,* Sept. 15, 2001. At the time the Murrah Federal Building was built in 1976, local codes did not require the seismic design details.

330 *Decision to ship steel out:* Tomasetti interview. Tomasetti referred largely to the later federal investigation by the National Institute of Standards and Technology. But he conceded that the FEMA/ASCE investigation also attempted to gather steel for forensic purposes.

330 *Troubles with FEMA:* Glanz and Lipton, *NYT,* Dec. 25, 2001.

331 *$16 million authorized:* Glanz, *NYT,* May 2, 2002; press release, NIST, Aug. 21, 2002.

331 *Titanic hearings:* Dwyer, *NYT,* Sept. 11, 2002.

331 *Investigator in nightclothes:* Chang, *NYT,* Oct. 2, 2001. The team member was Abolhassan Astaneh-Asl, a structural engineering professor at the University of California, Berkeley. He later left the team.

331 *City was recycling steel:* Glanz and Chang, *NYT,* Sept. 29, 2001.

331 *Holden gets the letter:* Some of these details are courtesy Kenneth Chang, who kindly provided notes and recollections from brief interviews with James Rossberg and Ed DePaula.

332 *Outrage among victims' families:* El-Ghobashy and Gittrich, *Daily News,* Jan. 17, 2002; Gittrich, *Daily News,* Jan. 30, 2002; Gittrich, *Daily News,* Jan. 30, 2002; *Associated Press,* Jan. 30, 2002; El-Ghobashy and Gittrich, *Daily News,* Jan. 18, 2002.

332 *Sally Regenhard:* Glanz, *NYT,* Dec. 15, 2001; Glanz's notes on May 1, 2002, hearing by the House Science Committee, Washington, D.C. Regenhard's remarks were made at a press conference before the hearing.

332 *Corley's report:* Glanz and Lipton, *NYT,* Mar. 29, 2002; Glanz, *NYT,* May 1, 2002.

332—*"fire-performance of steel trusses":* FEMA 403, May 2002, pp. 2–39.

33

333 *Building catastrophe bill:* Glanz and Lipton, *NYT,* Jan. 17, 2002; Lipton, *NYT,* Mar. 4, 2002; Lipton, *NYT,* Mar. 7, 2002; Lipton, *NYT,* Mar. 23, 2002; Glanz, *NYT,* May 2, 2002; Glanz, *NYT,* Aug. 22, 2002.

333 *Rhode Island nightclub fire:* Von Zielbauer, *NYT,* Feb. 28, 2003; Polgreen, *NYT,* May 6, 2003.

333 *New investigation begins:* NIST had begun an investigation without the full powers of the Safety Team Act in August 2002.

333 *Skyscraper in Times Square:* Lipton and Glanz, *NYT,* Sept. 9, 2002.

334—*New battle over downtown:* Wyatt, *NYT,* Apr. 19, 2002; Wyatt, *NYT,* Apr. 10, 2002; 35 Wyatt, *NYT,* July 23, 2002; Wyatt, *NYT,* May 21, 2002; Wyatt, *NYT,* Feb. 20, 2003; Wyatt, *NYT,* Feb. 26, 2003; Wyatt, *NYT,* Feb. 27, 2003; Wyatt, *NYT,* Feb. 28, 2003; Bagli, *NYT,* Feb. 28, 2003; Wyatt, *NYT,* July 1, 2003; Dunlap, *NYT,* July 10,

2003; Holusha, *NYT*, July 13, 2003; Wyatt, *NYT*, July 15, 2003; Wyatt, *NYT*, July 16, 2003; Wyatt, *NYT*, July 17, 2003; Bagli and Wyatt, *NYT*, July 21, 2003; Wyatt, *NYT*, July 22, 2003; Bagli, *NYT*, July 23, 2003; Bagli, *NYT*, Sept. 19, 2002; Wyatt, *NYT*, July 9, 2003; Wyatt, *NYT*, Sept. 1, 2002.

335 *Engineering debates:* Collins, *NYT*, June 23, 2003.
336 *Fresh Kills:* Glanz's trip to Fresh Kills was made with Robert Kelman of Hugo Neu Schnitzer East on Sept. 29, 2001. See Glanz, *NYT*, Oct. 1, 2001.
337 *The Firmeza:* Glanz notes on visit with Lipton to Metal Management Northeast in Port Newark, N.J., Jan. 23, 2002. See also Lipton and Glanz, *NYT*, Jan. 27, 2002.

BIBLIOGRAPHY AND INTERVIEWS
■ ■ ■

BOOKS

Above Hallowed Ground: A Photographic Record of September 11, 2001, by Photographers of the New York City Police Department. New York: Viking Studio, 2002.

Adams, Arthur G. *The Hudson through the Years*. New York: Fordham University Press, 1996.

Albion, Robert Greenhalgh. *The Rise of New York Port, 1815–1860*. New York: Scribner, 1970.

Ali, Mir M. *Art of the Skyscraper: The Genius of Fazlur Khan*. New York: Rizzoli, 2001.

Allen, Oliver E. *New York, New York: A History of the World's Most Exhilarating and Challenging City*. New York: Atheneum, 1990.

Augustyn, Robert T., and Paul E. Cohen. *Manhattan in Maps, 1527–1995*. New York: Rizzoli, 1997.

Beedle, Lynn S., ed. *Second Century of the Skyscraper*. New York: Van Nostrand Reinhold, 1988.

Bernstein, Richard. *Out of the Blue*. New York: Times Books, Henry Holt and Co., 2002.

Bone, Kevin, ed. *The New York Waterfront: Evolution and Building Culture of the Port and Harbor*. New York: The Monacelli Press, 1997.

Brannigan, Francis L. *Building Construction for the Fire Service*, 3rd ed. Quincy, Mass.: National Fire Protection Association, 2001.

Burrows, Edwin G., and Mike Wallace. *Gotham: A History of New York City to 1898*. New York: Oxford University Press, 1999.

Campbell, Peter. *Learning from Construction Failures: Applied Forensic Engineering*. New York: John Wiley & Sons, 2001.

Cannato, Vincent J. *The Ungovernable City: John Lindsay and His Struggle to Save New York*. New York: Basic Books, 2002.

Cantwell, Anne-Marie, and Diana diZerega Wall. *Unearthing Gotham*. New Haven: Yale University Press, 2001.

Caro, Robert A. *The Power Broker: Robert Moses and the Fall of New York*. New York: Vintage Books, 1975.

Chernow, Ron. *Titan: The Life of John D. Rockefeller, Sr.* New York: Random House, 1998.

Collier, Peter, and David Horowitz. *The Rockefellers: An American Dynasty*. New York: Holt, Rinehart and Winston, 1976.

Comprehensive Planning Office. *Metropolitan Transportation—1980*. New York: Port of New York Authority, 1963.

Condon, Thomas J. *New York Beginnings: The Commercial Origins of New Netherland*. New York: New York University Press, 1968.

Cudahy, Bruce J. *Over and Back: The History of Ferryboats in New York Harbor*. New York: Fordham University Press, 1990.

Danielson, Michael N., and Jameson W. Doig. *New York: The Politics of Urban Regional Development.* Berkeley: University of California Press, 1982.

Darton, Eric. *Divided We Stand: A Biography of New York's World Trade Center.* New York: Basic Books, 1999.

Derrick, Peter. *Tunneling to the Future: The Story of the Great Subway Expansion That Saved New York.* New York: New York University Press, 2001.

Doig, Jameson W. *Empire on the Hudson: Entrepreneurial Vision and Political Power at the Port of New York Authority.* New York: Columbia University Press, 2001.

Doig, Jameson W., and Erwin C. Hargrove. *Leadership and Innovation.* Baltimore: Johns Hopkins University Press, 1990.

Dolkart, Andrew S. *Guide to New York City Landmarks,* 2nd ed. New York: John Wiley & Sons, 1998.

Domosh, Mona. *Invented Cities: The Creation of Landscape in Nineteenth-Century New York and Boston.* New Haven: Yale University Press, 1996.

Dunn, Vincent. *Collapse of Burning Buildings.* Saddle Brook, N.J.: Fire Engineering, 1988.

————. *Command and Control of Fires and Emergencies.* Saddle Brook, N.J.: Fire Engineering, 1999.

Dwyer, Jim, with David Kocieniewski, Dierdre Murphy, and Peg Tyre. *Two Seconds under the World: Terror Comes to America—The Conspiracy behind the World Trade Center Bombing.* New York: Crown Publishers, 1994.

Ellis, Edward Robb. *The Epic of New York City.* New York: Kodansha International, 1966.

Equitable Life Assurance Society of the United States in 1901. *Henry Baldwin Hyde: A Biographical Sketch.* New York: De Vinne Press, 1902.

Ernst, Morris L. *Too Big.* Boston: Little, Brown and Company, 1940.

Feld, Jacob, and Kenneth L. Carper. *Construction Failure.* New York: John Wiley & Sons, 1997.

Feldschuh, Michael, ed. *The September 11 Photo Project.* New York: Regan Books, 2002.

Friedman, Donald. *After 9-11: An Engineer's Work at the World Trade Center.* Philadelphia: Xlibris Corporation, 2002.

George, Alice Rose, Gilles Peress, Michael Shulan, and Charles Taub, eds. *Here Is New York: A Democracy of Photographs.* New York: Scalo, 2002.

Gilchrist, D. T. *The Growth of the Seaport Cities.* Charlottesville: The University Press of Virginia, 1967.

Gillespie, Angus Kress. *Twin Towers: The Life of New York City's World Trade Center.* New Brunswick, N.J.: Rutgers University Press, 1999.

Goldman, Jonathan. *The Empire State Building.* New York: St. Martin's Press, 1980.

Harr, John Ensor, and Peter J. Johnson. *The Rockefeller Century.* New York: Charles Scribner's Sons, 1988.

Hart, F., W. Henn, and H. Sontag. *Multi-Storey Buildings in Steel.* London: Granada Publishing, 1978.

Hawkes, Nigel. *Structures: The Way Things Are Built.* New York: Macmillan, 1993.

Heyer, Paul. *Architects on Architecture.* New York: Van Nostrand Reinhold, 1993.

Huxtable, Ada Louise. *Architecture Anyone?* New York: Random House, 1986.

————. *The Tall Building Reconsidered: The Search for a Skyscraper Style.* New York: Pantheon Books, 1984.

————. *Will They Ever Finish Bruckner Boulevard?* Berkeley: University of California Press, 1989.

Isachsen, Y. W., E. Landing, J. M. Lauber, L. V. Rickard, and W. B. Rogers, eds. *Geology of New York: A Simplified Account*. Albany: The State Education Department, 1991.

Jacobs, Jane. *The Death and Life of Great American Cities*. New York: Random House, 1961.

Jacobus, John. *Twentieth-Century Architecture; The Middle Years, 1940–65*. New York: Frederick A. Praeger, 1966.

James, Theodore, Jr. *The Empire State Building*. New York: Harper & Row, 1975.

Johnson, Arthur M. *Winthrop W. Aldrich, Lawyer, Banker, Diplomat*. Boston: Harvard University, 1968.

Karwatka, Dennis. *Technology's Past: America's Industrial Revolution and the People Who Delivered the Goods*. Ann Arbor: Prakken Publications, 1996.

Koch, Karl, III, and Richard Firstman. *Men of Steel: The Story of the Family That Built the World Trade Center*. New York: Crown, 2002.

Kutz, Myer. *Rockefeller Power*. New York: Simon & Schuster, 1974.

Lambert, Phyllis. *Mies in America*. New York: Harry N. Abrams, 2003.

Landau, Sarah Bradford, and Carl W. Condit. *Rise of the New York Skyscraper, 1865–1913*. New Haven: Yale University Press, 1996.

Lee, Nancy, Lonnie Schlein, and Mitchel Levitas. *A Nation Challenged: A Visual History of 9/11 and Its Aftermath*. New York: Callaway, 2002.

Levy, Matthys. *Why Buildings Fall Down: How Structures Fail*, 2nd ed. New York: Norton, 2002.

Manchester, William. *A Rockefeller Family Portrait*. Boston: Little, Brown and Company, 1959.

McAllister, Therese, ed. *World Trade Center Performance Study: Data Collection, Preliminary Observations, and Recommendations*, FEMA 403. New York: Federal Emergency Management Agency, May 2002.

Merguerian, Charles, and John E. Sanders. *Geology of Manhattan and the Bronx*. New York: The New York Academy of Sciences, 1991.

Morris, Joe Alex. *Those Rockefeller Brothers: An Informal Biography of Five Extraordinary Young Men*. New York: Harper, 1953.

Mujica, Francisco. *History of the Skyscraper*. New York: Da Capo Press, 1929.

Nash, Eric P. *Manhattan Skyscrapers*. New York: Princeton Architectural Press, 1999.

National Institute of Standards and Technology. *May 2003 Progress Report on the Federal Building and Fire Safety Investigation of the World Trade Center Disaster*, NIST Special Publication 1000–3. Washington, D.C.: U.S. Government Printing Office, 2003.

New York September 11 by Magnum Photographers. New York: powerHouse Books, 2001.

O'Hagan, John T. *High Rise/Fire and Life Safety*. Saddle Brook, N.J.: Fire Engineering, 1977.

Pacelle, Mitchell. *Empire: A Tale of Obsession, Betrayal, and the Battle for the American Icon*. New York: John Wiley & Sons, 2001.

Petit, Philippe. *To Reach the Clouds: My Highwire Walk between the Twin Towers*. New York: North Point Press, 2002.

Petroski, Henry. *Design Paradigms: Case Histories of Error and Judgment in Engineering*. Cambridge, UK: Cambridge University Press, 1994.

Plunz, Richard. *A History of Housing in New York City*. New York: Columbia University Press, 1990.

Portraits: 9/11/01, The Collected "Portraits of Grief" from the New York Times. New York: Times Books, Henry Holt and Co., 2002.

Rink, Oliver A. *Holland on the Hudson: An Economic and Social History of Dutch New York.* Ithaca, N.Y.: Cornell University Press, 1986.

Robins, Anthony. *The World Trade Center.* Englewood, Fla.: Pineapple Press, 1987.

Rockefeller, David. *Creative Management in Banking.* New York: McGraw-Hill Book Company, 1964.

————. *Memoirs.* New York: Random House, 2002.

Ruchelman, Leonard I. *The World Trade Center: Politics and Policies of Skyscraper Development.* Syracuse, N.Y.: Syracuse University Press, 1977.

Ruttenbaum, Steven. *Mansions in the Clouds: The Skyscraper Palazzi of Emery Roth.* New York: Balsam Press, 1986.

Sabbach, Karl. *Skyscraper: The Making of a Building.* New York: Penguin Books, 1989.

Saliga, Pauline A. *The Sky's the Limit: A Century of Chicago Skyscrapers.* New York: Rizzoli, 1990.

Schuberth, Christopher J. *The Geology of New York City and Environs.* Garden City, N.Y.: The Natural History Press, 1968.

Severance, John B. *Skyscrapers: How America Grew Up.* New York: Holiday House, 2000.

Shapiro, Michael. *The Last Good Season: Brooklyn, the Dodgers and Their Final Pennant Race Together.* New York: Doubleday, 2003.

Sheperd, Roger, ed. *Skyscraper: The Search for an American Style.* New York: McGraw-Hill, 2003.

Stein, Leon, and William Greider. *Triangle Fire.* Ithaca, N.Y.: Cornell University Press, 2001.

Stokes, I. N. Phelps. *The Iconography of Manhattan Island, 1498–1909.* 6 vols. New York: Robert H. Dodd, 1915–28.

Talese, Gay. *The Bridge.* New York: Harper & Row, 1964.

Tauranac, John. *The Empire State Building: The Making of a Landmark.* New York: Scribner, 1995.

Taylor, William R. *In Pursuit of Gotham: Culture and Commerce in New York.* New York: Oxford University Press, 1992.

Teaford, Jon C. *The Rough Road to Renaissance: Urban Revitalization in America, 1940–1985.* Baltimore: Johns Hopkins University Press, 1990.

Van Diver, Bradford B. *Roadside Geology of New York.* Missoula, Mont.: Mountain Press Publishing Company, 1985.

Weingarten, Arthur. *The Sky Is Falling.* New York: Grosset & Dunlap, 1977.

Wermiel, Sara E. *The Fireproof Building: Technology and Public Safety in the Nineteenth-Century American City.* Baltimore: Johns Hopkins University Press, 2000.

Willensky, Elliot, and Norval White. *AIA Guide to New York City*, 3rd ed. New York: Harcourt Brace Jovanovich, 1988.

Wilson, John Donald. *The Chase: The Chase Manhattan Bank, N.A., 1945–1985.* Boston: Harvard Business School Press, 1986.

Wright, Frank Lloyd. *Frank Lloyd Wright: A Testament.* New York: Horizon Press, 1957.

Yamasaki, Minoru. *A Life in Architecture.* New York: Weatherhill, 1979.

Zeckendorf, William. *The Autobiography of William Zeckendorf.* Chicago: Plaza Press, 1987.

ARTICLES BY THE AUTHORS

Glanz and Lipton have written nearly two hundred articles on the World Trade Center since September 11. A partial list of those articles follows:

Glanz, "Towers Believed to Be Safe Proved Vulnerable to an Intense Jet Fuel Fire, Experts Say," *NYT*, Sept. 12, 2001; Glanz, "Terrorists Were Well Trained, but Not Necessarily in Flying," *NYT*, Sept. 13, 2001; Lipton and Richard Pérez-Peña, "Still Reeling from Losses, New York Looks for Makeshift Solutions," *NYT*, Sept. 13, 2001; Johnson, Kirk, and Lipton, "First Inspections Show Most Buildings Are Structurally Sound," *NYT*, Sept. 14, 2001; Glanz and Andrew C. Revkin, "Haunting Question: Did the Ban on Asbestos Lead to Loss of Life?" *NYT*, Sept. 18, 2001; Lipton, "Returning to the Office on the First Monday Since the City Changed," *NYT*, Sept. 18, 2001; Lipton and Glanz, "Engineers Say Buildings near Trade Center Held Up Well," *NYT*, Sept. 20, 2001; Lipton and Charles V. Bagli, "Conflicting Visions of How to Rebuild Lower Manhattan," *NYT*, Sept. 21, 2001; Lipton, "Officials Say Number of Those Still Missing May Be Overstated," *NYT*, Sept. 22, 2001; Lipton, "Many Buildings Stood Fast on Shaky Ground," *NYT*, Sept. 23, 2001; Glanz and Lipton, "The Excavation: Planning, Precision and Pain," *NYT*, Sept. 27, 2001; Glanz and Kenneth Chang, "Engineers Seek to Test Steel Before It Is Melted for Reuse," *NYT*, Sept. 29, 2001; Glanz, "Fresh Kills Journal; Mountains of Twisted Steel, Evoking the Dead," *NYT*, Oct. 1, 2001; Lipton, "Red Tape Cut and Rivers Dredged to Carry Debris by Water," *NYT*, Oct. 2, 2001; Lipton and Raymond Hernandez, "Vastness of Request Is Greeted by Doubts," *NYT*, Oct. 4, 2001; Lipton, "Taking Account of the Dead, Feeling Weight of History," *NYT*, Oct. 6, 2001; Glanz, "From Torn Steel, Cold Data of Salvage," *NYT*, Oct. 9, 2001; Lipton and Glanz, "Slowed by Site's Fragility, the Heavy Lifting Has Only Begun," *NYT*, Oct. 13, 2001; Lipton, "Slowly, More Roadways Reopening in Manhattan," *NYT*, Oct. 13, 2001; Lipton, "Numbers Vary in Tallies of the Victims," *NYT*, Oct. 25, 2001; Lipton and Kirk Johnson, "Safety Becomes Prime Concern at Ground Zero," *NYT*, Nov. 8, 2001; Glanz and Randy Kennedy, "Past Lessons Guide Transit Planning for Attack," *NYT*, Nov. 9, 2001; Glanz, "In Collapsing Towers, a Cascade of Failures," *NYT*, Nov. 11, 2001; Lipton and Adam Nagourney, "Grim Giuliani Presides over Another Tragic Scene, This Time in Queens," *NYT*, Nov. 13, 2001; Glanz, "From 70's Relic, a Possible PATH Station," *NYT*, Nov. 13, 2001; Glanz, "Below Rubble, a Tour of a Still-Burning Hell," *NYT*, Nov. 15, 2001; Glanz and Lipton, "Workers Shore Up Wall Keeping Hudson's Waters Out," *NYT*, Nov. 16, 2001; Lipton, "Facing Criticism, the City Again Adds Firefighters to the Search," *NYT*, Nov. 16, 2001; Lipton and Andrew C. Revkin, "With Water and Sweat, Fighting the Most Stubborn Fire," *NYT*, Nov. 19, 2001; Lipton, "Safer Working Conditions," *NYT*, Nov. 21, 2001; Lipton, "Toll from Attack at Trade Center Is Down Sharply," *NYT*, Nov. 21, 2001; Glanz, "Engineers Have a Culprit in the Strange Collapse of 7 World Trade Center: Diesel Fuel," *NYT*, Nov. 29, 2001; Lipton, "A New Count of the Dead, but Little Sense of Relief," *NYT*, Dec. 2, 2001; Lipton, "Draining a Hazardous Coolant Takes Caution, and a Long Hose," *NYT*, Dec. 4, 2001; Glanz, "Wounded Buildings Offer Survival Lessons," *NYT*, Dec. 4, 2001; Glanz, "Ground-Penetrating Radar to Aid in Cleanup," *NYT*, Dec. 5, 2001; Lipton, "In the Ongoing Search for Bodies, Hope Is Derived from the Horror," *NYT*, Dec. 7, 2001; Lipton, "Warm Place in a Cold Season," *NYT*, Dec. 11, 2001; Glanz, "FBI Studies Terrorists' Engineering Expertise," *NYT*, Dec. 12, 2001; Glanz with Michael Moss, "Faulty Fireproofing Is Reviewed as Factor in Trade Center Collapse," *NYT*, Dec. 13, 2001; Glanz and Michael Moss, "Since the Beginning, Questions Dogged the Trade Center's Fireproofing," *NYT*, Dec. 14, 2001; Glanz, "Demand Rises for Widening Investigation into Collapse," *NYT*, Dec. 15, 2001; Glanz and Lipton, "City Had Been Warned of Fuel Tank at 7 World Trade Center," *NYT*, Dec. 20, 2001; Glanz and Lipton, "Experts Urging Broader Inquiry in Towers' Fall," *NYT*, Dec. 25, 2001; Lipton, "At Ground Zero, New Manager, New Machines, New Focus," *NYT*, Jan. 3, 2002; Lipton and Michael Cooper, "City Faces Challenge to Close Widest Budget Gap since 70's," *NYT*, Jan. 4, 2002; Lipton, "Cleanup's Pace Outstrips Plans for Attack Site," *NYT*, Jan. 7, 2002; Lipton and Glanz, "In the Pit, Dark Relics and Last Obstacles," *NYT*, Jan. 13, 2002; Glanz and Lipton, "U.S. Agency to Take Over Investigation into Collapse," *NYT*, Jan. 17, 2002; Lipton and Glanz, "9/11 Inspires Call to Review Response Plan for Crises," *NYT*, Jan. 23, 2002; Lipton and Glanz, "From the Rubble, Artifacts of Anguish," *NYT*, Jan. 27, 2002; Glanz and Lipton, "A Search for Clues in Towers' Collapse; Engineers Volunteer to Examine Steel Debris Taken to Scrapyards," *NYT*, Feb. 2, 2002; Lipton, "New Retaining Wall Considered for Ground Zero," *NYT*, Feb. 8, 2002; Lipton, "For 5 Officers, Apparent Last Heroic Act," *NYT*, Feb. 11, 2002; Glanz and Lipton, "Rescuing the Buildings beyond Ground Zero," *NYT*, Feb. 12, 2002; Lipton and Glanz, "First Tower to Fall Was Hit at Higher Speed, Study Finds," *NYT*, Feb. 23, 2002; Glanz and Lipton, "Burning Diesel Is Cited in Fall of 3rd Tower," *NYT*, March 2, 2002; Lipton, "Widows Seek Wider Inquiry into Trade Center Collapse," *NYT*, March 4, 2002; Lipton and Glanz, "New Rules Proposed to Help High-Rises Withstand Attacks," *NYT*, March 6, 2002; Lipton, "Mismanagement Muddled Collapse Inquiry, House Panel Says," *NYT*, March 7, 2002; Glanz with Andrew C. Revkin, "Some See Panic as Main Effect of Dirty Bombs," *NYT*, March 7, 2002; Glanz and Lipton, "After Sections of Basement Collapse, Work at a Part of the Trade Center Site Is Halted," *NYT*, March 12, 2002; Lipton and Glanz, "Remains of 11 Firefighters Are Found at Trade Center," *NYT*, March 13, 2002; Glanz, "No Tower Can Withstand Attack as Jets Get Bigger, Expert Says," *NYT*, March 14, 2002; Lipton and Glanz, "In Last Piles of Rubble, Fresh Pangs of Loss," *NYT*, March 17, 2002; Glanz and Lipton, "A Rush to Fix Ground Zero's Damaged Dike," *NYT*, March 21, 2002; Lipton, "Government Orders Inquiry into Trade Center Collapse," *NYT*, March 23, 2002; Glanz, "Report Sees Lower Towers That Can Empty Faster," *NYT*, March 28, 2002; Glanz and Lipton, "Towers Fell as Intense Fire Beat Defenses, Report Says," *NYT*, March 29, 2002; Lipton and Glanz, "Tower Disaster Echoes Lessons of Earlier Fires," *NYT*, April 2, 2002; Lipton and Glanz, "Towers' Collapse Raises New Doubts about Fire Tests," *NYT*, April 8, 2002; Lipton, "Injuries Few among Crews at Towers Site," *NYT*, April 12, 2002; Lipton, "In Cold Numbers, a Census of the Sept. 11 Victims," *NYT*, April 19, 2002; Lipton and Glanz, "DNA Science Pushed to the Limit in Identifying the Dead of Sept. 11," *NYT*, April 22, 2002; Glanz, "Report on Towers' Collapse Ends Mostly in Questions," *NYT*, May 1, 2002; Glanz, "Wider Inquiry into Towers Is Proposed," *NYT*, May 2, 2002; Glanz, "A Physicist Considers the Cosmos, through the Prism of 9/11," *NYT*, May 21, 2002; Dwyer, Jim, Eric Lipton, Kevin Flynn, James Glanz, and Ford Fessenden, "102 Minutes: Last Words at the Trade Center; Fighting to Live as the Towers Died," *NYT*, May 26, 2002; Glanz, "The Haunting Final Words: 'It Doesn't Look Good, Babe,'" *NYT*, June 2, 2002; Lipton, "The Nation; A Silent Salute Punctuated by Doubts and Goodbyes," *NYT*, June 2, 2002; Lipton and Glanz, "Victims' Remains Found near Ground Zero," *NYT*, June 8, 2002; Lipton, "City and Bank Agree on Plan to Sift through 9/11 Debris," *NYT*, June 15, 2002; Lipton and Glanz, "Last 4 Firefighters Leave Ground Zero: 'Our Work Is Done'," *NYT*, June 25,

2002; Lipton, "In a Jittery Downtown, Fears Rise as Power Fails," *NYT*, July 21, 2002; Lipton and Glanz, "Sweeping Changes Pushed for Code on City High-Rises," *NYT*, Aug. 2, 2002; Lipton, "Many Voices, but One Call to Change Building Codes," *NYT*, Aug. 14, 2002; Glanz and Lipton, "A Midtown Skyscraper Quietly Adds Armor," *NYT*, Aug. 15, 2002; Glanz, "U.S. Announces New, Tougher Look into Why the Towers Collapsed," *NYT*, Aug. 22, 2002; Lipton, "Struggle to Tally All 9/11 Dead Anniversary," *NYT*, Sept. 1, 2002; Glanz and Lipton, "The Height of Ambition," *NYT*, Sept. 8, 2002; Lipton and Glanz, "9/11 Prompts New Caution in Design of U.S. Skyscrapers," *NYT*, Sept. 9, 2002; Lipton, "Death Toll Is Near 3,000, but Some Uncertainty over the Count Remains," *NYT*, Sept. 11, 2002; Glanz, "Con Ed and Insurers Sue Port Authority over 7 World Trade," *NYT*, Sept. 11, 2002; Lipton, "All Names Read, Even if Some May Be Alive," *NYT*, Sept. 12, 2002; Lipton, "Giuliani Says City Was Prepared on 9/11," *NYT*, Sept. 29, 2002; Glanz and Lipton, "Vast Detail on Towers' Collapse May Be Sealed in Court Filings," *NYT*, Sept. 30, 2002; Glanz, "Silverstein Sending Tower Data to U.S. Agency," *NYT*, Oct. 1, 2002; Glanz, "Living Large; Atomic Weight: We Gain, but What Loses?" *NYT*, Oct. 13, 2002; Glanz and Lipton, "Expert Report Disputes U.S. on Collapse," *NYT*, Oct. 22, 2002; Glanz, "Comparing 2 Sets of Twin Towers; Malaysian Buildings Offered as Model," *NYT*, Oct. 23, 2002; Lipton, "Wealthy Few Use Loopholes in Law to Give Pataki Campaign Big Sums," *NYT*, Oct. 25, 2002; Glanz and Lipton, "In Data Trove, a Graphic Look at Towers' Fall," *NYT*, Oct. 29, 2002; Lipton, "Sept. 11 Death Toll Declines as 2 People Are Found Alive," *NYT*, Nov. 3, 2002; Glanz, "Lessons Drawn from Attack on Pentagon May Stay Secret," *NYT*, Nov. 5, 2002; Glanz, "Towers Untested for Major Fire, Inquiry Suggests," *NYT*, May 8, 2003; Lipton, "At Firefighter's Funeral, Mayor Says 9/11 Memorial Should Identify Rescuers," *NYT*, June 8, 2003.

SELECTED AUTHORS' INTERVIEWS

Jim Abadie, a civil engineer and senior vice president, Bovis Lend Lease, project executive at ground zero.

Ali M. Mir, professor of architectural structures, University of Illinois at Urbana-Champaign.

George Anselevicius, an architect and one of Yamasaki's first employees.

Paul Ashlin, Bovis Lend Lease, supervised Charlie Vitchers at ground zero.

George Bachert, first foreman on WTC.

William Bain, NBBJ architect.

William Baker, structural engineer, Skidmore, Owings & Merrill.

Art Barkshire, partner at Worthington, Skilling, Helle & Jackson.

Daniel Bartush, a photographer who took pictures of Yamasaki's models.

Walter Beauvais, ironworker who worked as a foreman on WTC construction.

Gunnar Birkerts, chief designer for Yamasaki at the time he rose in fame; designed McGregor Memorial Community Conference Center.

Charles Blaich, deputy fire chief and logistics commander of cleanup project.

Ken Blum, Berkel & Co. Contractors, did tiebacks in areas not handled by Nicholson Construction.

John J. Bonomo, public affairs, Verizon.

Rick Boody, president of Irving R. Boody & Co.

Ellen Borakove, spokeswoman for chief medical examiner's office.

Richard Brady, ironworker at ground zero.

Jack Brendlen, mailroom worker at PA headquarters.

John Brunner, PA aide during trade center project.

Michael Burton, executive deputy commissioner, Department of Design and Construction, which supervised ground zero cleanup.

Francis Calton, employee at American Bureau of Shipping in the north tower.

Jack Cermak, professor of fluid mechanics and wind engineering at Colorado State University; worked on wind testing of WTC.

Maryellen Cherry, wife of Stephen Cherry, an equity stockbroker at Cantor Fitzgerald in the north tower.

Brian Clark, executive vice president at Euro Brokers.

Debbie Cohen, friend of the Rosenblums (Andrew Rosenblum died in the trade center).

Sid Combs, draftsman at Atlas Machine and Iron Works.

Frank Cruthers, Fire Department incident commander at ground zero.

Jack Daly, manager for Karl Koch Engineering on WTC construction.

Alan Davenport, professor at the University of Western Ontario specializing in wind engineering; worked on WTC.

Marcia De Leon, friend of Gregory Milanowycz, an insurance broker at Aon in the south tower.

Ronald DiFrancesco, employee at Euro Brokers in the south tower.

Danny Doyle, ironworker at ground zero; member of extended Doyle family.

Fred Doyle, ironworker on construction of 7 WTC; father of Danny Doyle; member of extended Doyle family.

Jack Doyle, ironworker on WTC; member of extended Doyle family.

John Dragonette, PA official who once worked for Mal Levy.

Mona Dunn, receptionist, Fiduciary Trust, south tower.

Thelma Elder, buyer at Atlas Machine and Iron Works.

Donald H. Elliott, official, Mayor Lindsay administration.

James Endler, project manager for Tishman during WTC construction.

Paul Eskildsen, optometrist and research assistant at the Oregon Research Institute.

Patrick Falvey, legal and legislative aide to Austin Tobin.

Patricia Farrell, president of Export-Import Services, Inc., one of the two tenants to move into the WTC on the first day.

Eugene Fasullo, engineer of PA during WTC construction.

Brenda Fogarty, Fiduciary Trust employee.

Peter Fontes, ironworker on WTC construction.

Anne Foodim, vice president of human resources at Fiduciary Trust.

Donald Friedman, a structural engineer who worked at LZA Technology and inspected buildings around ground zero.

Lou Gambaccini, headed PATH system for PA.

John Gaudioso, trader at Cantor Fitzgerald in the north tower.

Jack Gentul, husband of Alayne Gentul, director of human resources at Fiduciary Trust.

Richard Geyer, draftsman at Atlas Machine and Iron Works.

Eddie Gibbs, drill operator, Nicholson Construction, tieback installer at ground zero.

Peter Goldmark, created the Office of Special Planning at PA.

Robert Gray, master mechanic, Bovis Lend Lease, supervised heavy equipment operators at ground zero.

Donna Griffin, wife of Dave Griffin, who traveled to New York City with her husband for the demolition job.

Rusty Griffin, D. H. Griffin Wrecking Co., ground zero contractor.

Gunars Gruzdins, architect on Yamasaki's staff.

Henry Guthard, engineer and partner at Yamasaki's firm.

Gordon Haberman, father of victim Andrea Haberman.

George Harlow, curator, Department of Earth and Planetary Sciences, American Museum of Natural History.

John Haro, architect on Yamasaki's staff.

Jim Herman, architect on Yamasaki's staff.

Charles Hirsch, chief medical examiner, New York City.

Don Hisaka, architect in Yamasaki's office.

Paul Hoffman, director of the Oregon Research Institute.

Pia Hofmann, grappler operator at ground zero.

Renee Holcomb, resident of West Bend, Wisconsin.

Steve Holcomb, resident of West Bend, Wisconsin.

Sidney Horenstein, coordinator of environmental programs at the American Museum of Natural History.

Irene Humphries, file clerk at Fiduciary Trust.

Lawrence Huntington, Fiduciary Trust chairman.

Larry Hutchison, employee of Laclede Steel.

Chris Hynes, project manager of Nicholson Construction at ground zero.

Edward Iannielli, ironworker at ground zero.

Jakob Isbrandtsen, president of Isbrandtsen Co., a steamship line on the New York City waterfront.

Yogesh Jaluria, professor of mechanical and aerospace engineering at Rutgers.

Peter J. Johnson, Rockefeller historian.

Mary Jos, employee at the New York State Department of Taxation and Finance in the south tower.

Amy Herz Juviler, litigator in the Attorney General's Office.

Jerry Karn, architect on Yamasaki's staff.

James Kaufman, Mueser Rutledge senior associate.

Eduardo Kausel, MIT engineer who studied collapse of towers.

Thomas J. Kearney, Port Authority aide who worked on World Trade Center promotional activities such as Interfile and the World Trade Institute.

Larry Keating, ironworker at ground zero.

John Keenan, lawyer who worked in the state offices at the World Trade Center.

Francis L. Kellogg, member of DLMA board of directors.

Robert Kelman, senior vice president and general manager of Hugo Neu Schnitzer East scrap yard.

Ed King, Mazzocchi Wrecking, which worked with D. H. Griffin on demolition at ground zero.

John Kirby, general foreman for ironworkers at Koch Engineering, at ground zero.

Billy Klingler, site supervisor for Moretrench America, which installed dewatering wells at ground zero.

Richard Knight, architect on Yamasaki's staff.

Balthazar Korab, photographer for Yamasaki.

Calvin Kort, consultant to PA on the elevator design.

Stephanie Koskuba, vice president of human resources at Fiduciary Trust in the south tower.

Dean Koutsoubis, engineer who was part of the steel recovery team.

Edward Kresky, aide to Governor Nelson Rockefeller.

Melvin Larson, NBBJ architect, technical chief for firm on IBM Seattle Building.

John Leavy, father of Neil J. Leavy, firefighter.

Karen Lee, wife of Richard Y. C. Lee, managing director of equities at Cantor Fitzgerald in the south tower.

Dick Leone, PA chairman.

Joseph Lesser, represented the PA in legal fight.

Abe Levine, a manager for Tischman on WTC construction.

Gennaro Liguori, engineer who worked on WTC slurry wall for Slattery Construction.

Warren T. Lindquist, aide to David Rockefeller and Downtown–Lower Manhattan Association.

Frank Lombardi, PA chief engineer.

Pablo Lopez, Mueser Rutledge engineer, at ground zero.

Peter Lucas, guitar player for the Troggs.

Cornelius J. Lynch, real estate chief of WTC.

David MacInnes, owned a restaurant on Cortlandt Street, Radio Row.

Jon Magnusson, chairman of Magnusson Klemencic Associates, the current incarnation of Skilling's firm.

Charles Maikish, engineer, later World Trade Department director at PA.

Sara Mandinach, friend of the Rosenblums (Andrew Rosenblum died in the north tower).

Paul Martin, project engineer of Nicholson Construction, which installed the tiebacks at ground zero.

Louis Massari Jr., husband of Patricia Massari, a financial analyst at Marsh & McLennan in the north tower.

Thomas R. Mathes, vice president of Aegon USA Realty Advisors, owner of 90 West.

Bill Matre, Koch, worked at ground zero.

Mortimer Matz, did PR for Radio Row merchants and for Lawrence Wien.

Steve McIntyre, naval architect at American Bureau of Shipping in the north tower.

Charles Merguerian, professor at Duke Geological Laboratory.

Jack Mesagno, assistant vice president of Bovis Lend Lease, project manager at ground zero.

Joseph Milanowycz, father of Gregory Milanowycz, an insurance broker at Aon in the south tower.

Vincent Miller, PA engineer who worked on WTC slurry wall.

Danny Mirt, general superintendent at Nicholson Construction, tieback installer at ground zero.

Roger Morse, consultant who inspected fireproofing in WTC as part of a lawsuit, claimed to have found widespread missing patches of fireproofing.

Ronald Nadel, Oscar Nadel's nephew.

Ed Nicholls, Aon employee.

John Norman, director of FDNY Special Operations Command unit, which handles rescue operations.

Edward J. O'Sullivan, PA supervisor who specialized in security issues.

Gary Panariello, senior associate at Thornton-Tomasetti Engineers.

Carl K. Panero, PA architect.

Sophie Pelletier, wife of Mike Pelletier, a commodities broker at Cantor Fitzgerald in the north tower.

Dave B. Peraza, vice president of Thornton-Tomasetti.

Andrew Pontecorvo, Mueser Rutledge engineer, at ground zero.

Stanley Praimnath, loan officer at Fuji Bank in the south tower.

Robert Price, deputy mayor for Lindsay, negotiated WTC deal with PA.

Werner Quasebarth, president of Atlas Machine and Iron Works.

William Quasebarth, plant engineer at Atlas Machine and Iron Works.

Willy Quinlan, ironworker on construction and cleanup of WTC.

Arturo Ressi di Cervia, with George Tamaro, led the building of the WTC's underground bathtub wall, working for a PA contractor, Icanda.

Kelly Reyher, Aon employee in the south tower.

Tom Richardson, FDNY battalion chief, search-and-rescue operation supervisor at ground zero.

Herman Roberts, supervisor of tenant coordination for WTC.

Leslie Robertson, engineer at Skilling's firm; now at Leslie E. Robertson Associates.

David Rockefeller, banker who led group that first proposed the WTC.

William Ronan, former chief of staff to Governor Nelson Rockefeller; former PA chairman.

Jill Rosenblum, wife of Andrew Rosenblum, a stock trader at Cantor Fitzgerald in the north tower.

George Rossi, tenant representative and then leasing director at WTC.

John Ryan, PA police, supervisor at ground zero.

Robert St. Germain, engineer at Skilling firm in Seattle and New York.

John Sanacore, Andrew Rosenblum's clerk at Cantor Fitzgerald in the north tower.

Julian Saunders, employee at Atlas Machine and Iron Works.

Thomas Z. Scarangello, managing principal at Thornton-Tomasetti.

Bill Schneck, son of Harry L. Schneck, Radio Row storeowner.

Ed Schneck, son of Harry L. Schneck, Radio Row storeowner.

Aaron Schreier, project director on Minoru Yamasaki's staff.

Christopher Schuberth, author of *The Geology of New York City.*

Lloyd Schwalb.

Kip Serota, architect on Yamasaki's staff.

Robert Shaler, chief of forensic biology, Office of Chief Medical Examiner.

Greg Shark, naval architect at American Bureau of Shipping in the north tower.

David Sharp, structural engineer, member of steel collection team for the Structural Engineers Association of New York.

George Shea, publicist who worked with Mortimer Matz and Max Rosey.

Alvin Silverman, chief counsel on Wien's purchase of the Empire State Building.

George Sleigh, naval architect at American Bureau of Shipping.

Margaret Sliss, secretary at Irving R. Boody & Co.

Ron Smalley, foreman at Moretrench American Corporation, which drilled dewatering wells at ground zero.

Charles Smith, the first engineer Ray hired during WTC construction.

Nicholas Soldano, in charge of WTC steel fabrication job at Pacific Car & Foundry in Seattle.

Joseph Solomon, architect who worked on WTC at Emery Roth & Sons.

Donna Spira, Aon employee.

Peter Stanford, president emeritus of the National Maritime Historical Society, as well as founding president of South Street Seaport, on history of the waterfront.

Bob Stewart, consultant to AMEC, a ground zero contractor.

Richard Sullivan, deputy director of World Trade Department, PA, during WTC planning and construction.

Sy Syms, owned a clothing store on Radio Row.

George Tamaro, Mueser Rutledge engineer, built the WTC's underground bathtub wall.

Richard Taylor, computer specialist in Skilling firm's New York office.

Herb Tessler, PA aide who worked on elevator design, among other matters.

Candice Tevere, Fiduciary Trust employee.

Austin Tobin Jr., son of Austin J. Tobin, executive director of PA.

Farley Tobin, granddaughter of Austin Tobin.

Richard Tomasetti, managing principal of Thornton-Tomasetti Engineers.

Guy Tozzoli, World Trade Department director at PA.

Derek Trelstad, Thornton-Tomasetti engineer who assessed some of the buildings at ground zero.

Herman Tretter, owner of Commuters' Café.

Harold Tsuchiya, architect on Yamasaki's staff.

Charles Urstadt, former director of Battery Park City Authority.

Charlie Vitchers, superintendent, Bovis Lend Lease, at ground zero.

Joel Volterra, engineer at Mueser Rutledge.

Robert Walsh, ironworker on WTC construction.

William Ward, partner at Worthington, Skilling, Helle & Jackson.

Jeanette Way, travel agent who was at Windows on the World during a fire there in April 1980.

James Webster, geologist at the American Museum of Natural History.

Judy Wein, a senior vice president at Aon in the south tower.

Arthur Weingarten, author of *The Sky Is Falling.*

Saul Wenegrat, led WTC art program.

James White, engineer assigned to Yamasaki's office from Worthington, Skilling, Helle & Jackson; later worked at the Skilling firm's New York office.

Donald Winter, employee at Atlas Machine and Iron Works.

Leatrice Yelman, Oscar Nadel's daughter.

Meryl Yelman, Oscar Nadel's granddaughter.

Francis Yonker, Radio Row storeowner.

William Zucker, aide to David Rockefeller and Downtown–Lower Manhattan Association.

ACKNOWLEDGMENTS

• • •

This book is a reconstruction of the World Trade Center's past. As such, it relied not only on hundreds of books and articles and newspaper clippings but also on documents, recollections, and advice from many quarters. We would first like to thank the New York Times for supporting this project; we would also like to thank all of our colleagues in the newsroom, too many to name individually, who did so much to help us understand and define the overall story as we have covered it since September 11, 2001. On the metropolitan desk, Joe Sexton edited much of our coverage and relentlessly pressed us to explore each important reporting trail, to check and recheck every issue of fact, and finally to tell the tale in the most compelling way possible. Jonathan Landman and his crack team of editors on the metro desk supported our work every step of the way, including putting one of us (E.L.) on the World Trade Center assignment from the first day. On the science desk, numerous colleagues provided help and expertise at crucial moments, and Laura Chang gave one of us (J.G.) the assignment of understanding the structure of the twin towers on September 11 before either of them had fallen. Cornelia Dean, the science editor during our coverage of the story, provided advice, encouragement, and much gracious collegiality during a difficult collaborative project. Adam Moss, Paul Tough, and Katherine Bouton edited and helped us shape an earlier version of some of this history that appeared in the New York Times Magazine. From the start, Howell Raines and Gerald Boyd encouraged our lines of reporting and provided every resource we requested.

Our book could not have been written without Susan Chira, our editor at the Times, who provided an irreplaceable mix of encouragement and literary wisdom over many months. At Times Books and Holt, John Sterling, Paul Golob, and David Sobel gave what amounted to a master class on narrative nonfiction while guiding a difficult and complicated project through to completion. Steve Duenes, Archie Tse, Mika Gröndahl, and the rest of the crew in the graphics department functioned as our structural conscience and provided critical explanatory graphics for the newspaper and for our book. Fred Conrad accompanied us on our trips to ground zero to shoot his stellar photos. The photos and graphics were assembled through the dedicated work of Robin Dennis at Times Books. Alex Halperin and Lauren Wolfe, students in the Columbia University Graduate School of Journalism, volunteered their labor to do important research for this book. Wolfe also helped check facts and assemble citations. At the Times, Tomi Murata was an invaluable factotum as we grappled with deadline after deadline on the book.

We would especially like to thank the reporters and researchers we worked with on "102 Minutes: Last Words at the Trade Center," which appeared in the Times on May 26, 2002, parts of which—along with our magazine article—form the core of chapter 9 of this book. Jim Dwyer was the lead writer on "102 Minutes," and some of the haunting grace of his prose is still to be found in our chapter. Kevin Flynn not only reported portions of that article but directed us to crucial new historical sources for this book. Ford Fessenden, Alain Delaquérière, and Tom Torok also contributed importantly to "102 Minutes." We would also like to acknowledge our collaborators and colleagues on other significant articles on the World Trade Center: Dennis Overbye, Kenneth Chang, Michael Moss, Andrew C. Revkin, and Kirk Johnson.

In many ways, our work is a direct outgrowth of the writers who came before us in their own examinations of the World Trade Center. Angus Kress Gillespie (*Twin Towers: The Life of New York City's World Trade Center*) first explored the strange disconnect between the highbrow disdain and popular affection for the towers and uncovered some of the most fascinating morsels of history surrounding their creation. Jameson Doig (*Empire on the Hudson: Entrepreneurial Vision and Political Power at the Port of New York Authority*) has written the definitive word on the history of the Port Authority and the politics of the regional development of this part of the nation. Anthony Robins (*The World Trade Center*) wrote the first serious history of the buildings. Eric Darton (*Divided We Stand*) examined the sociopolitical backdrop to the creation of the World Trade Center. Gillespie, Doig, and Robins have, in addition, either provided us with, or led us to, original documents on the trade center—in many cases, documents that now exist nowhere else because of the destruction of the Port Authority library in the north tower. We have tried to convey our indebtedness to these authors in our chapter notes, but if any particular idea or reporting trail has gone unacknowledged there, we would like to express more general thanks here.

Many engineering firms and individual engineers generously gave their time in helping us to understand an array of complicated technical issues. We offer apologies for mentioning only a few of those sources, which have been so important for our work, by name: W. Gene Corley (Construction Technologies Laboratories), who led the initial investigation of the towers' collapse; William Baker (Skidmore, Owings & Merrill), Ramon Gilsanz (Gilsanz Murray Steficek), and Jon Magnusson (Magnusson Klemencic Associates), members of the investigation team; Richard L. Tomasetti and his staff at Thornton-Tomasetti Engineers; George Tamaro and his colleagues at Mueser Rutledge Consulting Engineers; Leslie E. Robertson and William Faschan at Leslie E. Robertson Associates; the American Society of Civil Engineers, especially Norida Torriente and Jane Howell; the Structural Engineers Association of New York; the Department of Design and Construction in New York City; and the Port Authority of New York and New Jersey, in particular Frank Lombardi, Peter Rinaldi, Greg Trevor, and Allen Morrison.

Among the many other people who provided important documents and other original information from various epochs of the World Trade Center's history are Peter Malkin; Brian Logan and Debbie Simerlink of EarthData; Ann Yoder; John Brunner; Leatrice and Meryl Yelman; Farley Tobin; Richard Sullivan; John Dragonette; David MacInnes; Roger Cohen; Larry Hutchison; and Peter J. Johnson. A number of people kindly consented to read portions of our manuscript and comment on it, including Aaron Schreier, Jerry Karn, Henry Guthard, Guy Tozzoli, Peter Collier, Jameson Doig, Angus Kress Gillespie, George Tamaro, Richard Tomasetti, Gary Panariello, Pablo Lopez, Andrew Pontecorvo, Alan Davenport,

Jack Cermak, Charles Maikish, Glenn Collins, Dan Barry, and Edward Wyatt. The authors are, of course, responsible for the final product.

We have received help from many sources in compiling images for the book. We are especially grateful to Phyllis Collazo and Marilyn Cervino at the *Times*; Cavan Farrell at the *Times Magazine*; Gregory Trevor at the Port Authority of New York and New Jersey; Henry Guthard, at Yamasaki Associates; and Jack Cermak, at Cermak Peterlea Peterson and Colorado State University.

Chris Campbell, Amy R. Rowland, Dan McComas, and Sherry Lynne Zipp of the Recording Room, and Elizabeth F. Molina, the manager of telecommunications, were exceptionally generous in transcribing so many interviews. Carolyn Wilder in News Research at the *Times* also provided help during the preparation of news stories that were in part the basis of the book. Nancy Palley, a consultant at J. P. Morgan-Chase Archives; Marilyn H. Pettit, director of the University Archives and Columbiana Library; Shelley Lavey, library director of the *Detroit Free Press*; Norman J. Brouwer at the South Street Seaport Museum; and Robert J. Battaly and Darwin H. Stapleton at the Rockefeller Archive Center were all critical in helping us find archival material.

Finally, we would like to thank those who endured the most throughout this project and whose encouragement and support never flagged, Nancy (J.G.) and Farhana (E.L.). Yes, it's really finished.

INDEX

. . .

Page numbers in *italics* refer to illustrations.

Abadie, Jim, 276, 277, 298, 312
Abruzzo, John, 290
Adorno, Oswald, 213-14, 324
AIA Guide to New York City, 205
Aiman, Lieutenant Allen, 127
Airports, 41
    Port Authority control, 41, 43, 45, 149,
        170
Aldrich, Winthrop W., 15, 28-31, 33, 34,
    207
Allen, Dewitt C., 218
Alonso, Janet, 246
AMEC, 287, *289*
American Airlines Flight 11, North Tower
    hit by, 242-54
American Bureau of Shipping, 241, 247,
    249, 250
American capitalism, WTC as symbol of,
    227, 228
American Express, 21
American Express Building, 282
American Society of Civil Engineers
    (ASCE), WTC collapse study by, 329-
    31
American Stock Exchange, 21
Aon Corporation, 241, *259,* 261-62, 268
Architectural design, 5-6, 9, 22, 66, 88
    117
    choice of architect, 97-102
    decorative elements, 110-12, *112,* 120
    facades, 109-12, *112,* 120
    by Libeskind, 334, 335
    lobbies, 115

models, 108-9, 110, 111, 113-14
"The Program," 104-8, 112
tops, 110, 111
twin tower plan, 107-10, 116-17
west side site, 66, 82
windows, 114-15
by Yamasaki, 98-112, *112,* 113-17, 119,
    134, 138, 143-44, 159, 166, 189, 210,
    297, 323
Architectural Forum, 116
Argentina, 29, 31
Asbestos, 199-201
Asia, 29-30, 31
Associated Press, 81
AT&T, 21
Atlas Machine and Iron Works, 185-86,
    192, 233, 293
Attorney General's Office, 208

Bachert, George, 195, 202
Banker, Captain Michael, 318
Bank of Tokyo, 224
Barclay Street, 66
Barker, Elizabeth, 19-20
Basement, 196, 288
    September 11 attacks, 288, 292-95, *294-
    95,* 296-97, 303-6
Bathtub. *See* Foundation
Battery Park City, 169-71, *171,* 177, 216,
    234, 239, 273, 282, 335
    landfill, 170, 177, 183, 193
Baum, Joe, 220
Bay Ridge, Brooklyn, 72

Beame, Abe, 218
Beauvais, Walter, 195, 198
Bedrock, 178-82, 185, 191, 288, 334
Bethlehem Steel, 187, 189, 192
Blackout (1977), 221
Blaich, Charles R., 273-76, 278, 280-81, 286,
  297, 311
Blaich, William, 275
Bloomberg, Michael R., 335
Board of Education, 19
Boehlert, Sherwood, 333
Bolting gangs, 196
Bomb threats, 203
Bonds, public authority, 43-44, 47, 52,
  56
Bonilla, Anamaria, 319-21
Boody, David A., 206
Boody, Irving R., 206
Boody, Rick, 205-7, 219
Boody (Irving R.) & Co., 205-7, 225
Boston, 46, 242
Bovis Lend Lease, 276, *289,* 312
Bracken, Tommy, 191
Brady, Dick, 194
Brazil, 29, 31
Breitel, Justice Charles D., 85
Brewer, Wayne, 188
Bridges. *See* Tunnels and bridges
Britton, Chris, 234
Broadway, 23, 25, 26
Bronx, 20
Brooklyn, 72
Buff, Mr., 78
Buildings Department, 199
Building Trades Council, 151
Bull's liver, 179
Bunker, 233, 332
Bunshaft, Gordon, 98, 100
Burke, Judge Adrian P., 86
Burton, Michael J., 299, 301, 305, 313,
  330
Bus terminals, 72, 78, 149
Butt, John D., 35

Cafco Blaze-Shield, 199, 200
Cahill, William T., 217
Canal Street, 48, 275

Cantor Fitzgerald Group, 224, 235, 240
  September 11 attacks, *249,* 251-53, 264-
    65
Carr Futures, 241, *249,* 250, 307
Casazza, John, 251
CBS, 81, 200
Cedar Street, 11, 12, 20, 23
Centre Street, 208
Cermak, Jack, 155-67
Chambers Street, 169, 276
Chase Manhattan Bank, 7, 8-11, 15, 29-30,
  44
  downtown headquarters project, 8-12,
    20-22, 32-37, 98, 100, 156
Chase Manhattan Bank Building, 240
Chemical Bank, 21
Cherry, Stephen, 240, 252
Chicago, 24, 25, 93, 94, 216, 307
Childs, David, 334
China, 30, 31
Christiansen, Jack, 120
Chrysler, Walter, 27
Chrysler Building, 8, 12, 107, 110, 211
  construction, 27
Church Street, 56, 66, 74, 193, 279, 281, 284,
  285
Churn drill, 180
CIA, 226
Cities Services Co., 21
Citizens Union of the City of New York,
  19
City Council, 151-52, 159
City Hall, 25, 149, 150
City Planning Commission, 67
City University of New York, 282
Clark, Brian, 257-58, 259
Clee, Gilbert H., 34
Climbers and parachuters, 217-20
CNN, 227, 234
Colgate-Palmolive, 9
Coll, Robert, 257, 258
Collapse, WTC:
  North Tower, 239, 271, 282, 322
  South Tower, 239, 269, 270, 278-79, 295,
    302, 322
  theories of, *328,* 329-33
Columbia University, 16, 18

Columns. *See* Core columns; Perimeter
  columns
Commerce:
  international, 28-31, 33, 35-36, 40, 53,
    69-70, 85-86, 134, 207, 209, 215-17,
    223-27, 233, 237-38
  waterborne, 46-53
Committee for a Reasonable Trade
  Center, 134-37, 150, 174
Communism, 19, 31
Community protest, 18-20, 72-73
  Radio Row, 62-87, 102, 146-54, 170, 172-
    75
Commuters Café, 80, 202, 203-4
  move to WTC, 204
  September 11 attacks, 297
Computers, 190
Concrete, 177, 185, 191, 196, 288
Condemnation, 38, *65*, 66-87
  money, 68, 72, 151, 170, 173
  Radio Row protests, 62-87, 102, 146-48,
    160, 172-75
Congress, U.S., 331, 333
Construction, 4-6, 9, 121, 149, 176-204,
    205-7
  basement, 196
  beginning of, 171-72
  bids and contracts, 186-89, 192, 198
  bomb threats, 203
  concrete, 177, 185, 191, 196
  delivery of steel pieces, 187, 193, 197
  end of, 202-4, 205
  erection of steel pieces, 191-204
  excavation, 177-85
  fabrication of steel pieces, 176-77, 185-
    90
  façades, 177, 186-87
  fireproofing, 198-201
  floors, 177, 187-89, 195-98
  grillages, 186, 190-92
  PATH and, 177, *178*, 180, 182-84
  perimeter columns, 186-87, 189
  raising gangs, 193-98, 201, 308
  schedule, 179, 188
  slurry wall, 176-78, *178*, 179-85
  steel, 5, 24-28, 118-44, 159-67, 176, 185-
    204

  street permits, 146-54, 168
  tieback operation, 181-82, 196
  trusses, 187-89, 197-98
  See also specific materials
Coolidge, Calvin, 45
Core columns, 120-21, *122*, 166
  collapse theory, *328*
  September 11 attacks, *244*, 246, 254, *256*,
    271, 293-94, 310-11, *328*
Corley, W. Gene, 329-30, 332
Cortlandt Street, 62, 66, 67, 68, 73-77, 171-
    74
*Courtesy Sandwich Shop v. Port of New York
  Authority*, 38, 71, 77-80
Cranes, 191-98, 202, 205
  ground zero operation, 287-88, *289*,
    290-92
Creakiness, 163-67
Critics, architecture, 5, 100, 102, 116-17,
    153
Cross-Bronx Expressway, 72
Crystal Palace Exhibition (1854), 22-23
Cuba, 29-31
Customs House, 277
Cutler, Mark, 235

Dai-Ichi Kangyo Bank, 224
Daily Bond Trader, 153
Data Synapse, 250, 265
Davenport, Alan G., 160-67, 323
Dean Witter Financial Services, 223, 225
Deloitte & Touche, 279
Deloitte Haskins & Sells, 223
Department of Design and Construction,
    299, 301, 318, 330, 331, 332
Depression, 28, 76, 209
DeRienzo, Michael, 251
DeSalvio, Louis, 152
Detroit, 93, 98, 99, 104, 216
Deutsche Bank Building, 243, 282, 316, 317
Dewey, Thomas E., 30, 55
Dey Street, 66, 74, 172
DiBono, Louie, 198-200
DiFrancesco, Donald, 232
DiFrancesco, Ronald, 257-58, 260
Dillon, Keith J., 317
DNA samples, 307, 314-15

Donovan, Tom, 216
Doors, 177, 215
Downtown. *See* Lower Manhattan
Downtown-Lower Manhattan
    Association (DLMA), 21, 32-37, 39, 60
Downtown West Businessmen's
    Association, 63, 66, 77, 78
Doyle, Danny, 309-13, 316
Doyle, Fred, 194
Doyle, George, 194, 198, 201, 202, 308
Doyle, Jack, 194-95, 198, 201, 202, 308
Doyle, Leo, 194, 195
Dragonette, John R., 104
Dreier Steel, 186, 190-91
Drill crew, 303-6
Druding, Harry, 183, 184, 185
Dunn, Tom, 172

East River, 54, 327
Ebasco Services, 223, 224
Eiffel, Gustave, 162, 164
Eiffel Tower, 162, 220
Electrical wiring, 177, 196
Elevated trains, 75, 76, 77
Elevators, 22, 24, 112-13, 166, 196, 211-12
    1993 bombing, 229-31
    safety brake, 22-23, 333
    September 11 attacks, 245, 259, 260, 262,
        267, 309
Elizabeth, New Jersey, 51, 70
Emery, Edgar, 241, 266, 267
Empire Blue Cross and Blue Shield, 245
Empire State Building, 12, 103, 107, 124,
        133, 134, 140, 211, 237, 323
    construction of, 27-28, 284
    plane collision (1945), 118, 126-31, 133,
        135, 218-19, 324
    sale of, 130-31
    sway, 140, 141, 162, 163, 166, 167
    WTC rivalry, 135-38, 167, 207, 272
Endler, Jim, 188
Engineering. *See* Structural engineering
Engineering News-Record, 121
Environmental Protection
    Administration, 201
Equitable Life Assurance, 23
Equitable Life Building, 23-24, 126, 325

Equitable Trust Co., 29
Erie Railroad, 46, 47, 49
Ernst, Morris, 70-71, 77-78, 82-83, 87
Eskildsen, Paul, 139-40, 142-44
Euro Brokers, 257, 258, *259*
Europe, 29, 31, 49, 95
Excavation, 177-85
Exhibitionists, 217-20
Export-Import Services, 225

Facades, 109-12, *112*
    construction, 177, 186-87
    plane impact study, 133
    September 11 attacks, 243, *244, 256,* 271,
        274, 276, 277, 294, 298-300
    structural engineering, 120-21, *122, 123,*
        166
Falvey, Patrick, 40, 83-84, 151
Farrell, Patricia A., 225
Fasullo, Eugene, 230-31
Favelle, Erick, 193, 202
FBI, 226, 227
Federal Emergency Management Agency
    (FEMA), role in September 11
    cleanup, 330-32
Federal Housing Act (1949), 18
Feeney, Garth, 265
Ferries, 46, 75, 76, *171*
    post-September 11, 335
Fiduciary Trust Company, 209-12, 229-30,
    231, 233, 241, 261, 266-68
Fire, 125-26
    alarm system, 215
    Empire State Building, 128-30
    Equitable Building, 126
    1993 WTC bombing, 230-31
    plane impact study, 131-39
    September 11 attacks, 238-72, 275-76,
        281, 284, 286, 300-301, 311, 314, 321-
        26, 333
    stack effect, 208
    Triangle Shirtwaist Company, 126
    WTC (1975), 213-15, 324
    WTC safety issues, 199-201, 208-9, 12-15,
        226, 233, 247, 324-29
    See also Fireproofing
Fire Island, 192

Fireproofing, 130, 138-39, 333-34
asbestos, 199-201
inadequacies, 134, 138-39, 199-201, 208,
214, 233, 247, 253, 324-26
masonry, 134, 138, 283
90 West Street, *283*
September 11 attacks, 247, 253, 279
upgraded, 233, 247, 326
WTC construction, 198-201
WTC investigation, 321, 324-26, 333, 334
First National City Bank, 21
Fisher, Ben, 230, 261
5 World Trade Center, 195
September 11 attacks, 276, 283
Flam, David, 173
Flatiron Building, 26
Floors, 120, *122,* 325
collapse theories, *328,* 329-33
construction, 177, 187-89, 195-98
fireproofing, 199-201, 233
September 11 attacks, 245-47, 253, 267-
69, 271, 278-79, 293, 295-97, 310-11,
321-22, 324, *328,* 329
structural engineering, 120, *122,* 124,
187
WTC investigation, 321-22, 324-26, *328,*
329
See also Trusses
Fogarty, Brenda, 229-30
Fontes, Peter, 195, 198, 201
Foodim, Anne, 267
Forensics, 314-15, 331
Fortier, Therese, 127-28, 218-19
40 Wall Street, 9, 27, 156, 323
plane collision (1946), 135
Foundation ("the bathtub"), 1-4, 335
construction, 176-78, *178,* 179-85
excavation, 177-85
September 11 attacks and cleanup, 288-
97, 303-6, 317
Fountain, Joe, 128
4 World Trade Center, 195
September 11 attacks, 275, 278-79, 280
Fox Movietone News, 81
Fresh Kills landfill, ground zero debris
taken to, 313, 317, 318, 336-37
Fuji Bank, 224, 241, 254, 258

Fulton, Robert, 76
Fulton Fish Market, 35
Fulton Street, 66, 74, 76, 172

Gabrielle, Monica, 332, 333
Gabrielle, Richard, 262, 332
Gambino crime family, 199
Geller, Stanley, 152
Gentul, Alayne, 241, 266, 267
Geology, 178-81
George Washington Bridge, 40-41, 43, 70
Germany, 30, 31
Gibbs, Eddie, 306
Gilbert, Bradford Lee, 25
Gilbert, Cass, 26-27, 220, 282
Gilman, Roger, 39, 57
Gilsanz, Ramon, 319, 331
Giuliani, Rudolph W., 233
September 11 attacks, 276, 291, 313, 332
tension between firefighters and, 313
Gladstone, Dianne, 263
Goldberg, Daniel B., 86
Goldmark, Peter C., Jr., 223, 226, 228
Goldstein, Sidney, 71, 77-78, 83-84
Gotti, John, 199
Grand Central Terminal, 9, 27, 126
Granite City Steel, 187
Grant, George M., 49
Grappler operators, 300, 309-13, 319-21
Gravity, 119, 134, 143, 325
Great Britain, 33
Greece, 29, 31
Greenspan, Alan, 235
Greenwich Street, 63, 66, 74, 75, 152
slurry wall, 179-82, 184
Griffin, David, Jr., 298, 300
Griffin, Rusty, 297-300
Griffin (D.H.) Wrecking, 297
Grillages, 186, 190-92
Ground zero:
bathtub wall, 292-97, 303-6, 317
cranes, 287-88, *289,* 290-92
demolition, 297-313
drill crew, 303-6
end of recovery effort, 316-18
future of, 334-36
grappler operators, 300, 309-13

Ground zero (*cont'd*)
  identification of dead, 307, 313-16
  investigation, 319-37
  quadrants, *289*
  rescue and recovery operations, 273-
    318
  See also Rescue and recovery operations;
    September 11 terrorist attacks;
    specific buildings and streets
Grout, 191-92
Guzman, Genelle, 291

Haberman, Andrea, 307-8, 315-16, 327
Haberman, Gordon, 307-8, 315-16
Haberman, Kathleen, 307-8, 315
Hagerty, Karen, 261, 262
Harlem, 15-20
Harper's, 116
Harris, Josephine, 275
Harrison, Wallace, 97-98
Hat truss, 166, 245-46
Hayden, Stone, 223
Helicopters, 53, 55, 222, 252, 264
Helmsley, Harry, 130, 134, 135
Herman, Jim, 105, 109
Heyward-Robinson, 223
Hildebrand, Grant, 105
Hirsch, Charles S., 314-15
Hoboken, 46, 236
Hoffman, Paul, 141-42
Hofmann, Pia, 300, 312
Holland Tunnel, 20, 43, 46-47, 236,
    238-39
  opening of, 45, 46
Home Insurance Building (Chicago), 24
Hong Kong, 31
Hudson & Manhattan Railroad, 55-61,
    75-77
  -WTC bill, 55-61, 69-70, 71, 82-85
Hudson River, 3, 5, 12, 16, 46, 70, 75-76,
    106, 156, 237, 288, 327, 335
  Battery Park City, 169-71, *171*
  lighterage system, 46-49
  raw sewage dumped in, 216
Hudson Terminal buildings, 76, 77, 80, 82,
    103, 203, 220
Hudson Tubes, 75-77, 84, 171, 177, 335

WTC excavation and, 177, *178,* 180, 182-
    84, 287
  See also PATH
Hughes, Richard, 57-59, 66, 71
Human Fly, 217-19
Humphries, Irene, 211, 229-30, 231, 261
Huntington, Lawrence, 210-12, 229-31, 233
Hurricanes, 162
Huxtable, Ada Louise, 116, 145, 153
Hyde, Henry Baldwin, 23-24, 126, 325
Hylan, John F., 47

Iannielli, Don, 198
Iannielli, Edward, 198
IBM Building (Seattle), 123
Icanda, 178-82
Idlewild Airport, 45, 97
International Longshoremen's Union, 50
International trade, 29-31, 33, 35-36, 40, 53,
    69-70, 85-86, 134, 207, 209, 215-17,
    223-27, 233, 237-38
International Trade Mart, 207, 216-17
Interstate Commerce Commission, 47
Investigation, WTC, 315, 319-33, 336
  collapse theories, *328,* 329-33
  engineering studies, 319-30, 333-34
  FEMA involvement, 330-31
  fireproofing, 321, 324-26, 333, 334
  floor trusses, 321-22, 324-26, *328,* 329
  forensic, 314-15, 331
  steel, 319-24
Iron construction, 24

Jacobs, Jane, 66-67, 72-73, 152
Jacobus, John M., 100
Jaffe, Lee, 64, 68, 113, 121, 135, 137, 153, 161
Japan, 92, 95-96, 129, 224
  banks, 224
Jaros Baum Bolles, 112-13
Jenney, William Le Baron, 24
Jersey City, 46, 55, 75
Jimeno, Will, 280
Job Lot Trading, 67
John Hancock Mutual Life Insurance Co.,
    223-24
Jonas, Captain John A., 275
Jos, Mary, 260, 263

Jumbo Air Track, 182
Juviler, Amy Herz, 208-9, 224

Kallimanis, George, 63, 67, 68, 81
Kangaroo cranes, 193, 202
Karn, Jerry, 105, 107, 109, 110, 111
Karnes, Sergeant David, 279-80
Keefe, Bruyette & Woods, 261
Kennedy, John F., 108
Kennedy Airport, 45, 198, 224, 226
Kennedy Center, Washington, D.C., 97
Kestenbaum, Howard, 261, 262
Kill van Kull, 197
Kirby, Jack, 309, 310
Kirk, Grayson L., 18
Klingler, Billy, 304
Koch, Edward I., 152, 225
Koch, Robert W., 188
Koch Erecting, 188, 191-98
Koenig, Fritz, 203
Koenig globe, 203, 279
Kort, Calvin, 112-13
Kull, Harold, 213, 214

Laclede Steel, 187, 188, 189, 196
La Guardia, Fiorello H., 15
LaGuardia Airport, 129
Latin America, 29, 31
Lazarus, Emma, 45
Leavy, Mark, 302-3
Leavy, Neil J., 302-3
Le Corbusier, 22, 94-95, 96
Lee, Richard Y.C., 252-53
Lee, Stuart, 249, 250, 265
Leslie, Alexander, 222-23, 225
Lever Brothers, 9
Levin, Neil D., 250
Levinson Steel, 187
Levy, Leonard, 78
Levy, Malcolm P., 101, 104-8, 112-15, 117,
    123, 125, 131-37, 143, 153, 161, 188,
    198, 202, 222, 233, 237, 247, 325-26
Levy, Norman J., 215
Liberty Street, 66, 148, 180, 188, 203, 243,
    274, 295, 300, 303-5, 316, 317
Libeskind, Daniel, 334, 335
Liebherr 1550 crane, 287, 290

Lighterage system, 46-50
Liguori, Gennaro, 182, 183
Lincoln Tunnel, 41, 155
Lindquist, Warren T., 34, 35
Lindsay, John V., 145-46, 223
    WTC deal, 145-54, 167-70
Logan International Airport, 242
Lombardi, Frank, 230, 231, 233, 241, 247,
    248-50
Lopez, Pablo V., 292-97, 310
Los Angeles, 216
Lower East Side, 73
Lower Manhattan, 9-10, 33, 216, 236
    future of, 334-36
    geology, 178-81
    history of, 10, 45, 179
    psychic wound of September 11, 327
    skyline, 239-40, 272
    waterfront, 45-52
    See also specific buildings and streets
Lower Manhattan Expressway, 20, 32, 72-
    73
Lucas, Peter, 235
Ludwig, Alfred, 126
Lybrand Ross Bros. & Montgomery, 210
Lynch, Cornelius J., 209, 224, 225

MacInnes, David, 172-73
Madison Avenue, 27
Maggs, Dave, 235
Maikish, Charlie, 183-84, 191-92, 202-4, 287
Mail delivery, 207-8
Mancini, Gary, 284-86
Manhattanville, 16-18
Manitowoc cranes, 191, 192, 287
Marble, 196
Marriott World Trade Center Hotel, 274,
    276, 281, 298
Marsh & McLennan, 240, 243, 246, 251
Masonry, 24, 26, 134, 140, 283, 284
    fireproofing, 134, 138, 283
Massari, Patricia, 240-41, 246
Mass transit, 2, 51, 75-77, 241
    Hudson Tubes, 75-77, 84, 171, 177
    Port Authority operations, 55-61, 149,
    217
    See also PATH; Subways

Matz, Mortimer, 71, 80-81
McAvey, John B., 104
McCloy, John J., 9, 10, 11, 22
McCormack, William J., 48, 49-51
McIntyre, Steve, 241, 246-48, 269-71, 295, 307
McKiever, Rotten John, 198, 321
McKinsey report, 33-35, 37, 54, 223, 224
McLoughlin, Sergeant John, 280
McNally, Edmund, 267-68
Media, 68, 97, 130, 232
    twin tower imagery in, 234
    on WTC construction, 176, 200
    on WTC proposal, 37, 68-69, 81-84, 114, 145, 168-69, 172, 174
    on Yamasaki, 100, 114
    See also specific media
Medical Examiner's office, 313-14
Meehan, Damian, 249, 250
Meehan, Eugene, 250
Meehan, William, 235
Mendes, Lou, 301
Merns, George, 67
Meyner, Robert, 55, 58
Michigan Consolidated Gas Building (Detroit), 98, 99-100, 101, 109
Middle East, 29, 31
Midtown, 9, 10, 21, 27, 33, 72, 237, 333, 335
Mies van der Rohe, Ludwig, 22, 93-95, 96, 102, 107
Milanowycz, Gregory, 259, 268-69
Millenium Hilton Hotel, 281
Mirt, Danny, 306
Montague-Betts, 187
Monti, Ray, 179-80, 182, 197, 198, 202, 237
Morgan, Stanley & Co., 21
Morningside Heights, 15-20, 21, 32, 33, 72
Morningside Heights Inc., 16-19
Moses, Robert, 12, 18-20, 32, 42-43, 44, 72, 86, 89, 97
    role in WTC creation, 12, 20, 39
Moses (Robert) Causeway, 192
Mosher Steel, 187
Motion. *See* Sway; Wind
Mueser Rutledge, 293
Mumford, Lewis, 116

Murrah Federal Building bombing (1995), 329-30
Museum of Modern Art, 12
Mutual Life Insurance Building, 10-12

Nadel, Oscar, 62-64, 66, 73-74, 76, 113, 137, 203, 225
    Radio Row protests, 66-87, 102, 146, 173-74
Nagare sculpture, 290-91
Nation, The, 116
National Construction Safety Team Act (2002), 333
National Institute of Standards and Technology, 333
NBC-TV, 130
Negative damping, 157
Newark *Star-Ledger,* 170
Newark Sunday News, 84
New Jersey, 35, 40, 46, 228, 232, 236, 242, 335
    commerce, 46-53
    economy, 40, 67
    Port Authority vs., 55-60, 64
    transportation system, 55-61, 75-77, 171
New Jersey Meadowlands, 237
Newsweek, 100
New York City, 9
    blackout (1977), 221
    Dutch settlement, 10, 29, 45, 49, 179
    economy, 29, 40, 46-49, 59, 206, 215-16, 223
    Lindsay administration, 145-54, 167-70
    Port Authority vs., 43-44, 52, 72, 168-69
    skyline, 239-40, 272
    transportation network, 45-47
    Wagner administration, 59-60
    waterfront history, 45-52
    See also Lower Manhattan; Midtown; Port of New York; *specific buildings and streets;* Wall Street; World Trade Center
New York *Daily News,* 154, 176, 296-97
New Yorker, The, 14, 216
New York Fire Department, 125-26, 129, 134, 208, 213-14, 216, 236, 252
    Giuliani administration and, 313

Ladder Company 6, 275
search-and-rescue effort, 302-3, 311-12
September 11 attacks and cleanup, 236,
  268, 273-81, 286-87, 291, 292, 302-3,
  311-13, 316-18, 332
New York magazine, 221
New York Police Department, 280
  Emergency Services Unit (ESU), 280
  September 11 attacks and cleanup, 280,
    296, 311-13, 314, 316, 336
New York Post, 82
New York State Court of Appeals, 85-87
New York State Department of Taxation
  and Finance, 263
New York State Supreme Court, 79-80, 85
New York Stock Exchange, 10, 21, 35
New York Telephone Company Building
  (later Verizon Building), 156, 176,
  181, 282
New York Times, 19, 26, 30, 32, 37, 68, 73, 75,
  80, 84, 97, 100, 130, 145, 153, 174, 213,
  221, 297, 331
New York World's Fair (1939), 28, 30, 33,
  41, 216
New York World's Fair (1964), 88-90, 97
Nicholls, Ed, 262
90 West Street, 220, 276
  September 11 attacks, 280-83, *283*, 284,
    286, 316
Ninth Avenue El, 75, 77
Norman, Captain John, 286-87, 291, 303
North Tower, *122*, 238
  Boeing 707 incident (1981), 224-25, 323
  collapse, 239, 271, 282, 322
  construction, 190, 191-202
  impact, 242-43, *244*, 247, 324
  1975 fire, 213-14, 324
  1993 bombing, 228-31
  opening day, 205-8
  rescue and recovery operations, 273-318
  September 11 attacks, 238-43, *244*,
    245-48, *249*, 250-54, 260-61, 263-66
  stairwells, *249*
  structural engineering, *122*, 166
  sway, 166, 323
  tenants and leases, 205-35
  TV antenna, 166, 175, 271

North walking bridge, 278, 286-88, 301
Nosair, Sayyid, 228
Nulman, Sidney, 207-8

O'Connor, A. G., 169
O'Connor, Dennis, 293, 296
O'Connor, Kay, 127-28
Office of Special Planning, 226
Office space, 5, 61, 102, 104, 134, 205-25, 310
  early glut of, 205-17
  growing popularity of, 219-25
  See also Tenants
O'Hagan, John T., 213, 214
Oklahoma City bombing (1995), 329-30
1 Liberty Plaza, and September 11 attacks,
  281, 284-86
OPEC oil embargo, 215
Organized crime, 198-99
Orton, Lawrence M., 17
Oscar's Radio Shop, 62, 73, 74, 76, 81
  closing of, 173-74
Osman, Sam, 67
O'Sullivan, Edward J., 226-29
Otis, Elisha Graves, 22-23, 333

Pacific Car & Foundry Co., 187, 190, 196,
  320, 321
Panama, 29, 31, 32
Pan Am building, 104
Panariello, Gary, 290, 291, 300
Panero, Carl K., 104
Paramsothy, Vijayashanker, 262, 263
Parking garage, 66, 67, 105, 227, 228, 293
Pataki, George E., 232, 234, 334-35
PATH (Port Authority Trans-Hudson
  railway), 59, 61, 75, 82, 85, 86-87, 204,
  241
  September 11 attacks, 270, 288, 295-97,
    335
  WTC excavation, 177, *178*, 180, 182-84,
    287
Pei, I. M., 8, 100
Pelletier, Mike, 253
Pentagon, 60
Perimeter columns, 120-21, *122*, 135,
  186-87, 189
  collapse theory, *328*

Perimeter columns (*cont'd*)
    construction, 186-87, 189
    September 11 attacks, 245-46, 254, 268,
        278, 279, 281, 282, 320, 324, *328*
Petit, Philippe, 219
Philadelphia, 46
Pine Street, 10-11
Pittsburgh, 123
Pittsburgh-Des Moines Steel, 186-87
Plane collisions, 131-39, 174-75, 227
    Boeing 707 incident (1981), 224-25, 323
    Empire State Building (1945), 118,
        126-31, 133, 135, 218-19, 324
    40 Wall Street (1946), 135
    impact study, 131-39
    predictions of, 174-75, 222, 242
    September 11 attacks, 1-6, 236-72
Plaza, 203, 232, 246, 279, 290, 293
Plumbing fixtures, 177, 193, 196, 206
Politics, 5, 9, 64, 145
    Lindsay administration, 145-54, 167-70
    Port Authority vs. New Jersey, 55-60, 64
    Port Authority vs. New York City, 43-
        44, 52, 72, 168-69
    Wagner administration, 59-60, 146, 153
    waterfront corruption and, 50-52
Pontecorvo, Andrew, 293-97, 310
Port Authority of New York and New
        Jersey, 35, 38, 42-52, 278, 335
    bonds, 43-44, 47, 52, 56
    corruption scandal, 222-23
    creation of, 47-52
    exemption from city building codes,
        199, 209, 325-26, 334
    Lindsay administration and, 145-54
    mass transit operations, 55-61, 149, 217
    motion study, 139-44, 154-67, 323
    vs. New Jersey, 55-60, 64
    vs. New York City, 43-44, 52, 72, 168-69
    1993 WTC bombing, 228-31
    post-1993 bombing WTC renovation,
        232-33
    public relations, 43-45, 71, 80, 113-14,
        121-23, 205-8, 215, 219-20, 222
    vs. Radio Row merchants, 62-87, 102,
        146-54, 170, 172-75
    revenues, 61
    role in WTC creation, 39-45, 52-61,
        68-73, 77-117, 118-44, 145-54, 161,
        167-72, 176-204, 324-27
    secrecy of, 57-60, 64, 66, 141, 160, 323,
        326
    security and terrorism issues, 226-31,
        233
    September 11 attacks and cleanup,
        236-72, 280, 316, 322-29
    Sullivan study, 40, 52-58
    Tobin reign, 39-45, 51-61, 68-73, 77,
        96-97
    WTC construction, 176-204, 326-27
    WTC tenants and leases, 205-25, 233
Port Compact, 43
Port Newark, 51, 237
Port of New York, 38, 45-52, 86, 319
    commerce, 46-53
    corruption and decay, 50-52
    history of, 45-52
    lighterage system, 46-50
    "unloading charge," 48
    WTC proposal, 52-61
Praimnath, Stanley, 241, 254, 257, 258
Prefabricated column panels, 121, *122,*
    123-24, 166
Presley, Reg, 234
Pressman, Gabe, 130
Price, Robert, 145-54, 168, 170
Price Committee, 149
Produce market, 46-49, 57
Public relations, Port Authority, 43-45, 71,
    80, 113-14, 121-23, 205-8, 215, 219-20,
    222

Queens, 28, 63
Quesada, Matthew, 1-4
Quinlan, Willy, 195, 308-11, 316
Quinn, Justice Peter A., 79-80

Rabin, Justice Samuel, 84-85
Radio, 68, 74-75
Radio Row, 57, 62-63, *65,* 74, 335
    "Black Friday," 81-82
    condemnation money, 68, 72, 151, 170,
        173
    merchants move to WTC, 204

protests, 62-87, 102, 146-54, 170, 172-75
  streets, 65
  WTC construction and aftermath,
    172-75
Rahman, Sheikh Omar Abdel, 228
Railroads, 46
  H&M, 55-60, 75-77
  Hudson Tubes, 75-77, 177-84
  lighterage system, 46-49
Raising gangs, 193-98, 201, 308
Rankin, J. Lee, 168
Rasweiler, Chief Stephen, 318
Ray, Barry, 152, 173
Real estate developers, 5, 7-8, 24, 60, 64,
    113, 129, 133-37, 224, 232, 334. *See also*
    specific real estate and developers
Rebar, 185
Recovery operations. *See* Rescue and
    recovery operations
Rector Street, 243
Recycling operations, 319-21, 330-33,
    336-37
Red handkerchief, man with, 262-63
Regenhard, Christian, 332
Regenhard, Sally, 332, 333
Rescue and recovery operations, 273-318
  basement, 292-95, *294-95*, 296-97
  bathtub wall, 288-97, 303-6, 317
  body parts, 282, 291, 309, 311-12, 313-16
  cranes, 287-88, *289*, 290-92
  culture clashes and equal treatment of
    recoveries, 312-13
  demolition work, 297-313
  drill crew, 303-6
  dust and smoke, 278
  end of recovery effort, 316-18
  end of rescue operation, 291
  engineers and, 276-306
  fires, 275-76, 281, 284, 286, 300-301, 314
  of firefighters' and police officers'
    remains, 302-3, 311-12, 316
  first day, 275-80
  grappler operators, 300, 309-13
  identification of dead, 307, 313-16
  90 West Street, 280-83, *283*, 284, 286, 316
  of office workers' remains, 311-13
  1 Liberty Plaza, 281, 284-86

  pedestrian bridge, 278, 286-88, 301
  start of recovery operation, 291-92
  survivors, 276-80, 288, 291
  tieback operation, 306, 209
Ressi de Cervia, Arturo, 176-81, 288
Reuther, Walter P., 93
Reyher, Kelly, 259, 261, 262
Rhode Island nightclub fire (2003), 333
Richardson, Chief Tom, 302-3, 305
Riverside Church, 12, 16
Roberts, Herman M., 101
Robertson, Leslie E., 138-39, 159-67, 188-90,
    211, 227, 233, 299, 322-23
Rockefeller, Abby Aldrich, 12, 28-29
Rockefeller, David, 7-37, 42, 44, 239, 336
  background of, 12-15
  Chase career, 7-11, 20-22, 31-37
  Morningside Heights project, 15-20, 21,
    32, 33, 72
  role in WTC creation, 9-12, 15-22,
    32-37, 39, 53-55, 58-61, 86, 223, 272
  September 11 attacks, 272
Rockefeller, John D., Jr., 12-13, 28-29
Rockefeller, John D., Sr., 13
Rockefeller, John D. III, 14
Rockefeller, Laurance S., 14
Rockefeller, Nelson A., 14, 15, 55, 56, 59,
    65, 71, 98, 125, 169, 208, 209, 215, 225,
    232, 237
Rockefeller, Winthrop, 14, 15
Rockefeller Center, 8, 12, 98, 108, 272
Rockefeller family, 12-14, 16, 29, 52
Ronan, William, 125, 215
Roosevelt, Franklin D., 14, 27-28
Rosenblum, Andrew, 240-42, 251, 252, 253,
    265-66, 271
Rosey, Max, 80-81
Rossi, George, 206-7, 224
Roth, Julian, 108
Roth, Richard, 135-37
Roth (Emery) & Sons, 102, 108, 135-38

Saint Nicholas Greek Orthodox Church,
    281
Sanacore, John, 240
Save Our Homes, 19-20, 72
Schacter, Sidney, 56-58

Schneck, Harry L., 74
Schneider, Ian, 240, 251-52
Schreier, Aaron, 104, 105, 115-16, 166
Scully, Vincent J., Jr., 100
Seagram's, 9
Sears Tower (Chicago), 216
Seattle, 88, 90, 99, 119, 121-24, 187, 190
Security, 226-31, 233
September 11 terrorist attacks, 1-6,
    236-72
  aftermath, 1-6, 273-318, 334-36
  body parts, 246, 282, 291, 309, 311-12,
    313-16
  casualties, 5, 243, 246, 248, *249,* 255, *259,*
    261-66, 272, 282, 303, 311-16, 324
  collapse theories, *328,* 329-33
  falling people, 246, 264-66, 267, 327
  fuel tank damage, 243-45, 253, 266
  identification of dead, 313-16
  investigation, 315, 319-33, 336
  lessons of, 333, 36
  North Tower collapse, 239, 271, 282,
    322
  North Tower hit, 238-43, *244,* 245-48,
    249, 250-54, 260-61, 263-66
  psychic wound of, 327
  rescue and recovery operations,
    273-318
  roof doors locked, 252, 259
  South Tower collapse, 239, 269, 270,
    278-79, 295, 302, 322
  South Tower hit, 239, 254-55, *256,*
    257-63, 266-70
  survivors, 6, 248, *249,* 257, *259,* 261-63,
    276-80, 288, 291, 331
  victim's families, 332
  See also Ground zero; Rescue and
    recovery operations
Sereika, Chuck, 280
Serota, Kip, 108, 110, 111
7 World Trade Center, 194-95, 225-26, 309
  Bunker, 233, 276, 332
  collapse, 277, 280, 281-82, 283, 332
  September 11 attacks, 276, 277, 280, 283,
    332
Shaler, Robert, 315
Shanghai, 30

Shapiro, George, 169, 170
Shark, Greg, 241, 247-48
Sharp, David, 319-320
Shaughnessy, Donald, 150, 154, 170
Shearson, 223
Sheperd, Howard, 10
Sidewalks, 67
Silverman, Private First Class Alvin,
    128-30
Silverstein, Larry, 232, 234, 334
Singer, Gigi, 261, 262
Singer Building, 8, 26
6 World Trade Center, 195
  September 11 attacks, 276, 277, 292, 294,
    299, 301
Skehan, Rosaleen, 83-84, 125-26, 132, 134,
    147, 149, 168, 169
Skidmore, Owings and Merrill, 22, 34
Skilling, John, 118-19, 190, 233, 299, 322
  role in WTC creation, 120-25, 132,
    137-39, 141-43, 159-67, 245, 322, 326
Skyline, 239-40, 272
Skyscrapers, modern, 24-28
Sleigh, George, 241, 247-48, 253
Slum clearance, 18-20, 57, 72-73, 86
  Radio Row protests, 62-87, 102, 146-48,
    170, 175-85
Slurry wall, 176, 335
  construction, 176-78, *178,* 179-84
  September 11 attacks and cleanup,
    288-97, 303-6, 317
  streets, 180-81
  See also Foundation
Smalley, Ron, 303-4
Smith, Alfred E., 27-28
Smith, Jimmy, 240
Snyder, H. C., 47
Soldano, Nicholas, 190
South Street Seaport, 58
South Tower:
  climbers, 217-19
  collapse, 239, 269, 270, 278-79, 295, 302,
    322
  construction, 196, 202-3
  impact, 254-55, *256,* 261-62, 268, 324
  1975 fires, 214
  1993 bombing, 228-31

rescue and recovery operations,
    273-318
September 11 attacks, 239, 254-55, *256,*
    257-63, 266-70
stairwells, *259*
structural engineering, 166
sway, 166, 323
tenants and leases, 209-35
Soviet Union, 31
Spandrels, 120, *122,* 187, 190, 200, 245
Spira, Donna, 262
Sprinklers, 226, 229
early lack of, 208-9, 215
September 11 attacks, 248, 266
Stairwells, 166, 327
emergency escape, 209, 228, 233
emergency lighting, 228, 233, 332
fires, 214, 230
1993 bombing, 229-31
North Tower, *249*
September 11 attacks, 243, *244,* 248, *249,*
    252, 255, *256,* 257-58, *259,* 267, 291,
    323, 327, 332, 334
South Tower, *259*
sway, 158, 166
Stanray Pacific, 187
Staten Island, 47, 273, 313, 336
Statue of Liberty, 45, 235, 252, 254
hundredth anniversary, 228
Stearns, John Noble, 24-25
Steel, 5
bids and contracts, 186-89, 192
ceremonial highest piece, 201-2
construction, 5, 24-28, 118-44, 159-67,
    176, 185-204
delivery, 187, 193, 197
erection, 191-204
fireproofing, 199-201, 208, 214, 233, 247,
    253
grillages, 186, 190-92
prefabrication, 121, *122,* 123-24, 166,
    176-77, 185-90
raising gangs, 193-98, 201
recycling operation, 319-21, 330, 331-33,
    336-37
September 11 attacks, 242-71, 277-82,
    286-88, 292-302, 306, 309-13, 316

Skilling tube design, 120-25, 132, 137-39,
    159-67, 245
WTC investigation, 319-24, 334
Stewart, Bob, 287-90, 298-302
Stone, Edward Durrell, 97
Street permits, 146-54, 168
Streets. *See specific streets*
Structural damping, 163-67
Structural engineering, 5-6, 9, 118-44,
    154-67, 189
choice of engineer, 118-23
creakiness, 163-67
facades, 120-21, *122,* 123, 166, 186-87
fireproofing, 134, 138-39, 198-201
floors, 120, *122,* 124, 187, 325
interior core columns, 120-21, *122,* 166
lessons of September 11, 333-34
motion study, 139-44, 154-67, 323
negative damping, 157
perimeter columns, 120-21, *122,* 135,
    186-87
plane impact study, 131-39
prefabricated column panels, 121, *122,*
    123-24, 166, 185-90
September 11 attacks, 276-306, 319-30,
    335
Skilling tube design, 120-25, 132, 137-39,
    159-67, 245
spandrels, 120, *122,* 187
steel, 24-28, 118-44, 159-67, 176, 185-204
structures, *122*
trusses, *122,* 124, *165,* 187-89, 325
viscoelastic dampers, 164-65, *165,* 166,
    167, 189, 211, 323
wind forces, 119, 123, 133, 134, 139-44,
    154-67, 197, 211, 216, 322-23
WTC investigation, 319-30, 33-34
Subways, 2, 61, 76, 77, 241
Sullivan, Richard, 39, 40, 52, 66, 99, 101, 104
WTC study, 40, 52-58, 216
Sumitomo Bank, 224
Summers, Ken, 245
Sunday Journal-American, 137
Supreme Court, U.S., 87
Sway, 139-44, 154-67, 197, 211, 325
creakiness and, 163-67
motion study, 139-44, 154-67, 323

Sway (*cont'd*)
    September 11 attacks, 255
    shock absorbers, 164-65, *165,* 166, 167,
        323
    wind turbulence and twin towers,
        154-58, *158,* 159-67, 211, 216, 322-23
Syms, Sy, 67, 80, 173

Tacoma Building (Chicago), 25
Tacoma Narrows Bridge, 157, 159
Tamaro, George, 180-81, 288, 292, 293,
        304-6, 335
Taxes, 59, 146
    Port Authority exemption, 146, 149
Telephone vaults, 171-72
Television, 68, 130, 172
    twin tower imagery, 234
    WTC antenna, 166, 175, 271
Tembe, Yeshavant, 263
Tenants, 205-35
    early lack of, 205-8, 215-17
    international trade interests, 207, 209,
        215-17, 223-27, 233
    1993 bombing, 228-31
    post-1993 bombing, 232-35
    safety fears, 208-15, 233
    security and terrorism issues, 226-33
    See also specific tenants
Terrorism, 226-31, 334
    1993 WTC bombing, 228-31
    September 11 attacks, 1-6, 236-72
Tessler, Herbert A., 104
Tevere, Candice, 211-12, 261
Thornton-Tomasetti Engineers, 276, 278,
        330
3 World Trade Center, 195
Tiebacks, *178,* 181-82, 196, 288
    ground zero operation, 306, 309
Tillman, John, 222
Time, 100
Title 1 housing, 18, 39
Tobin, Austin J., 38-39, 237, 337
    background of, 41-43
    Port Authority reign, 39-45, 51-61,
        68-73, 77, 96-97
    role in WTC creation, 39-45, 52-61,
        68-73, 77-101, 114, 134, 147-54, 161,

167-72, 183, 187-89, 193, 197, 200,
    202-4, 210-17, 226, 234, 252
Tobin, Clarence, 41
Tobin, Geraldine, 42, 169
Tomasetti, Richard, 276-79, 280, 282, 284,
    286, 288, 290, 305, 330
Tourism, 5, 221, 318
Tower Building, 25
Towering Inferno, The (movie), 212-13, 214,
    215
Tozzoli, Guy, 78-79, 335
    corruption scandal, 222-23
    1993 WTC bombing, 230
    role in WTC creation, 78-79, 88-90,
        96-108, 112-17, 169-70, 193, 202, 216,
        217, 221, 237-38
    September 11 attacks, 236-39, 271
Trelstad, Derek, 280, 281, 282, 284, 286
Tretter, Herman, 203, 204
Tretter, Joe, 203, 204
Tretter, John, 203, 204
Triangle Shirtwaist fire, 126
TriBeCa, 234
Triborough Bridge and Tunnel Authority,
    43
Trinity Church, 23
Troggs, 234, 235
Trusses, *122,* 325
    bar-joist, *122,* 124, 188, 200, 279, 311, 334
    construction, 187-89, 197-98
    fireproofing, 199-201, 233
    hat, 166, 245-46
    September 11 attacks, 245-47, 253,
        267-69, 271, 279, 310-11, 321-22, 324,
        328, 329, 334
    structural engineering, *122,* 124, *165,*
        187-89
    WTC investigation, 321-22, 324-26, *328,*
        329
Tsuchiya, Harold, 110, 114, 115
Tunnels and bridges, 39, 40-41
    Port Authority control, 40-41, 43-44
    tolls, 44, 47

United Airlines Flight 175, South Tower
    hit by, 242, 254-63
United Nations, 8, 39, 53, 97, 98, 217

U.S. Marines, 279-80
U.S. Steel, 187, 189, 192
Unloading charge, 48
Urban, Diane, 263
Urban League of Greater New York, 19

Van Dusen, Henry P., 18
Vega, Ron, 318
Velamuri, Sankara, 263
Vera, Dave, 257, 258
Verrazano-Narrows Bridge, 41, 72, 211
Vesey Street, 48, 66, 67, 148, 176, 180, 181,
    276, 293
Vierendeel arch, 133
Vietnam War, 226
Viscoelastic dampers, 164-65, *165,* 166, 167,
    189, 211, 323
Vista International Hotel, 225, 229
Vitchers, Charlie, 308, 312-13, 315-18
Von Essen, Thomas, 287

Wagner, Robert F., 59-60, 146, 148, 153, 1
    67
Wallace, Ed, 176
Wall Street, 9, 25, 67, 103, 239
Washington Building (Seattle), 123-24
Washington Market, 48, 57, 64, 148, 185
Washington Street, 66, 148
Waterfront, 45-52
    commerce, 46-50
    corruption, 50-51
    See also Port of New York
Weber, A, Carl, 188-89, 196, 197
Weehawken, 46, 49
Wein, Judy, 241, 261-62, 263
Welders, 196
Werner, Chief Ronald W., 316
West Broadway, 66, 173
West Street, 26, 48, 148, 180, 243, 274
    September 11 attacks, 274-78, 280-81,
    286-87
Whiplash, 247
Whitman, Walt, 123, 172
Wien, Lawrence A., 129-31, 133-37, 141,
    150, 152-53, 174-75, 187, 224, 242, 323
Willig, George H., 217-19
Wilson, Woodrow, 41

Wind, 119, 123, 132, 133, 134, 139-44,
    154-67, 197, 211, 325
    creakiness and, 163-67
    motion study, 139-44, 154-67, 323
    shock absorbers, 164-65, *165,* 166, 167,
    323
    turbulence and twin towers, 154-58,
    158, 159-67, 211, 216, 322-23
    See also Sway
Windows, 177, 210, 212
Windows on the World, 114, 220-21, 235
    renovation, 232
    September 11 attacks, *249,* 250, 251,
    264-65
Window washers, 177
Wittenstein, Michael, 251
Woolworth, Frank W., 26-27
Woolworth Building, 26-27, 105, 110, 156,
    240, 282
World Financial Center, 240, 274
World-Telegram & Sun, 137
World Trade Center, 1-6, 9
    admission rules abandoned, 223-26, 233
    architecture critics on, 5, 116-17, 153
    architectural design, 88-117, 166
    businesses condemned by, 38, *65,* 66-87,
    102, 146-54, 170, 172-75
    climbers and parachuters, 217-20
    collapse theories, *328,* 329-33
    constitutionality case, 82-87
    construction, 4-6, 176-204, 205-7
    costs, 54, 66, 104, 108, 159, 170, 187
    court decisions, 77-80, 82-87
    deficit (1970s), 217, 222-23
    early lack of tenants, 205-8, 215-17
    east side proposal 32-35, *36,* 37, 52-55,
    57, 58, 66
    Empire State Building rivalry, 135-38,
    167, 207, 272
    final deal, 168-71
    fire safety issues, 199-201, 208-9, 212-15,
    226, 233, 247, 324-29
    fiscal turnaround, 223-26
    footprints, 66, 335
    genesis of, 38-61
    growing popularity of, 219-26, 233-35
    -H&M bill, 55-61, 69-70, 71, 82-85

World Trade Center (*cont'd*)
  international trade interests, 33-37, 40,
    53, 69-70, 85-86, 134, 207, 209, 215-17,
    223-27, 233, 237-38
  landfill for Battery Park City, 170, 177,
    183, 193
  lessons of September 11, 333-34
  Lindsay administration and, 145-54,
    167-70
  maps, *36*
  McKinsey report, 33-35, 37, 54, 223, 224
  1975 fires, 213-15
  1993 bombing, 228-31, 252
  observation deck, 219, 220
  office space, 5, 61, 102, 104, 134, 205-25,
    310
  opening day, 205-8
  parking garage, 66, 67, 105, 227, 228, 293
  plane impact study, 131-39
  Port Authority role in, *see* Port
    Authority of New York and New
    Jersey
  post-September 11 cleanup operations,
    273-318
  post-September 11 investigation, 315,
    319-333, 336
  Radio Row protests, 62-87, 102, 146-54,
    170, 172-75
  recycling operation, 319-21, 330, 331-33,
    336-37
  renovation (1990s), 232-33
  revenues, 224-25
  risk of collapse, 227-28
  security and terrorism issues, 226-31,
    233
  September 11 attacks, 1-6, 236-72
  size, 4-5, 60, 64-66, 90, 101, 104-9, 112,
    113, 196, 201, 207, 216, 323
  street changes and traffic control,
    59-60, 66, 170, 335
  structural engineering, 118-44, 156-67,
    189, 322-29
  Sullivan study, 40, 52-58, 216
  sway, 139-44, 154-67, 197, 211, 216,
    322-23
  as symbol of American capitalism, 227,
    228

  tenants and leases, 205-35
  underground mall, 114
  views, 210-11, 235
  Wagner administration and, 59-60, 146,
    148, 153, 167
  west side plan, 57-61, 63-87, 97
  Windows on the World, 220-21
  See also Architectural design;
    Construction; Ground zero; North
    Tower; Office space; Rescue and
    recovery operations; September 11
    terrorist attacks; South Tower;
    specific parts; Steel; Structural
    engineering; Tenants
World Trade Centers Association, 237-38
World Trade Corporation, 30, 32
World Trade Department, 98, 104
World Trade Mart, 207, 216-17
World War I, 29, 49
World War II, 15, 30, 31, 49, 86, 128, 177
Worthington, Skilling, Helle & Jackson,
  120, 131
Wright, Frank Lloyd, 113

Yamasaki, Minoru, 82, 88, 89-117, 216, 222,
  239
  background of, 90-93
  critics of, 100, 104, 106, 111, 114-17
  engineers and, 119-20, 165-66
  Federal Science Pavilion (Seattle), 88,
    99, 100, 119
  McGregor Building, 98-100
  sway problem, 159, 165-66
  WTC design, 98-112, *112,* 113-17, 119,
    134, 138, 143-4, 159, 166, 189, 210, 297,
    323
Yamasaki, Teri, 92, 100, 116, 117
Yasuda Trust and Banking, 224
York, Kevin, 257, 258
Young, Ling, 263
Yousef, Ramzi Ahmed, 228

Zeckendorf, William, 7-8, 20
  role in WTC creation, 9-12, 20-21, 34
Zeplin, Marc, 252
Zimmerman, Donald, 225
Zucker, William, 34

ABOUT THE AUTHORS

⋅ ⋅ ⋅

JAMES GLANZ is a science reporter for the *New York Times* and has a doctorate in physics from Princeton University, where he did his research at the Plasma Physics Laboratory. In 1991, he joined the staff of the magazine *R&D*, moving to *Science* magazine in 1995 and the *Times* four years later. His first book, *Saving Our Soil: Solutions for Sustaining Earth's Vital Resource*, drew upon both his technical background and his childhood in Iowa. On the morning of September 11, 2001, before either of the twin towers had fallen, he was given the assignment of understanding and reporting on their structure. He has been covering this story ever since.

ERIC LIPTON has worked at the *New York Times* since 1999, where he was assigned to cover Mayor Rudolph W. Giuliani. After September 11, 2001, he was reassigned to write about the attack on the World Trade Center and its aftermath. He previously worked at the *Washington Post*, the *Hartford Courant*, and the *Valley News*, a small New Hampshire daily. In 1992, he won a Pulitzer Prize in explanatory journalism for a series of articles he cowrote about the flawed mirror in the Hubble Space Telescope. A native of Philadelphia and a graduate of the University of Vermont, Lipton lives in Manhattan.